THE
QUEEN

MATTHEW DENNISON is the author of
nine critically acclaimed works of non-fiction,
including *Behind the Mask: The Life of Vita Sackville-
West*, a Book of the Year in *The Times*, *Spectator*,
Independent and *Observer*. His most recent
book is the much-praised *Eternal Boy:
The Life of Kenneth Grahame*.

THE
QUEEN

MATTHEW DENNISON

An Apollo Book

First published in the UK in 2021 by Head of Zeus Ltd
This paperback edition first published in 2022 by Head of Zeus Ltd

9 7 5 3 2 4 6 8

A CIP catalogue record for this book is available from the British Library.

ISBN [PB] 9781788545921
ISBN [E] 9781788545907

Typeset by Ben Cracknell Studios

Cover images credits:
Front © National Portrait Gallery, London
Back © John Hedgecoe / TopFoto
Front flap © Marcus Adams, Camera Press London
Back flap © Lichfield Studios Limited, Getty Images

Inside cover images sourced from Alamy Stock Photo

Printed and bound in Great Britain by
CPI Group (UK) Ltd, Croydon CR0 4YY

Head of Zeus Ltd
5–8 Hardwick Street
London EC1R 4RG
WWW.HEADOFZEUS.COM

For my mother, with love

CONTENTS

'Well, she's it, really, isn't she, I mean,
she's the Realm...'

'I have always so behaved myself that under God I
have placed my chiefest strength and safeguard in
the loyal hearts and good will of my subjects.'

Elizabeth I

'The heaven for height, and the earth for depth,
and the heart of kings is unsearchable.'

Proverbs 23.5

INTRODUCTION

CONSIDER FOR YOURSELF if what follows is a fairy tale.

Here is a baby girl, tiny, with cowlicks of pale hair.

Here is the prince, her father: sensitive in appearance, though emotionally undemonstrative; orthodox in his tastes for shooting, hunting and tennis; a nervous man who stammers, afraid of his parents, impeccably dressed. Her mother is a smiling, dimple-cheeked woman, indelibly patrician. Her tiny feet are the delight of female journalists, like the columnist in the *Sunderland Daily Echo and Shipping Gazette* who, in June 1934, informs her readers that few women can compete with her 'for daintiness of feet and ankles'.[1] To one another father and mother are Bertie and Elizabeth, to the world at large a royal duke and duchess, and admired. Sugary reverence is the keynote of their record in broadsheets, illustrated papers and the fledgling medium of the cinema newsreel. It will remain so.

In the background a king and queen, the baby's paternal grandparents. They are everything a king and queen ought to be in 1926: earnest, unfashionable, imperturbably convinced of royalty's mission; dutiful, modest and intellectually unremarkable; concerned by the barbarism of the age and overstretched tentacles of British might that wind about the globe; preoccupied less constructively with minutiae of dress, and the horrors of jazz music and nail polish. Castles and palaces are home to them, as they shall be to Bertie and Elizabeth and their newborn daughter. Millions on millions acclaim them, for this king is also an emperor, global sovereign over men and women of myriad faiths and ethnicities – as his granddaughter shall be, though she will inherit only tatters of Empire and a hope for the future.

In time, in the best storyteller's tradition, the baby will acquire through marriage a sable-haired aunt, who is vilified and banished: the equivalent of a wicked stepmother whose shadow darkens her childhood and changes the course of her life. Later, she herself will marry a handsome prince from across the seas. His name, Philip, means 'lover of horses', her other passion, and their marriage, that lasts into its eighth decade, will support her into her mid-nineties. She will ride in a golden coach; diamonds will sparkle in her hair; hospitals, sports centres, a luxury liner, Parisian flower market, chocolate mints and a pale-flowered rhododendron, and global initiatives targeting leadership, blindness and forestry conservation will bear her name. Her sons and grandsons will marry beautiful women. And, late in life, the Vatican will bestow upon her a medieval-sounding epithet, 'the last Christian monarch', that smudges the boundaries between the sacred and the secular to raise her above the epoch-changing squabbles of statesmen.[2] Books will be written about her, films and plays. In a television drama called *The Crown*, a writer who dismisses her as 'a countryside woman of limited intelligence', occupying a 'theme park' of 'grown men with spurs and breastplates', will fictionalize her reign, muddying fact with distortion.[3] From infancy she will occupy public and private worlds. In her lifetime her fame will eclipse that of Augustus, Napoleon, even Hitler; her image will imprint coins, stamps and, apparently, the nation's dreams. Her legacy will be less bloody than those of history's 'great' men, less ambitious, without vainglory.

The fairy godmother at her cradle grants her long life, earthly riches, an equable disposition, stamina, humility and love;

she bestows conservative instincts. With age comes wisdom and moral authority. In lesser measure the baby inherits her mother's steel, her father's temper, caution and stubbornness, both parents' deep religious convictions.

※

The baby born by Caesarean section in the early hours of 21 April 1926, after a day of rain, is baptised five weeks later in the private chapel of Buckingham Palace, Elizabeth Alexandra Mary. She is Princess Elizabeth of York. She will become, as she swears at the meeting of her Accession Council on 8 February 1952, Elizabeth the Second by the Grace of God of Great Britain, Ireland and the British Dominions beyond the Seas Queen, Defender of the Faith. Her names are those of her mother, great-grandmother and grandmother, a family inheritance as well as her first (unknowing) encounter with that philosophy of continuity so dear to royalty. George V and Queen Mary are her grandparents. The name of the wicked aunt is Wallis, wrong on so many counts.

If a fairy tale requires a prophecy, in the late spring of 1926 sections of the media unite in their clairvoyance. The silent Pathé news bulletin that records her birth is filmed in black and white. Its promise is simple but startling: 'Queen of Hearts To-day, She may one day be Queen of England'. The *Daily Sketch* informs its readers 'a possible Queen of England was born yesterday'.

And so, as we have seen, it comes to pass – despite the baby's sex, her father's status as a king's second son and the good health of the uncle who ought to displace both father and daughter: Edward, Prince of Wales, so briefly and dramatically Edward VIII. The National Anthem's prayer for her protection is granted: hers becomes the nation's longest reign. Into a third millennium she perpetuates a model of monarchy traceable to her great-great-grandmother, Queen Victoria.

Let us agree at the outset that Elizabeth II's life story is not a fairy tale. Stripped of the bombast of former centuries, royal rhetoric in Elizabeth's lifetime has celebrated the idea of a reigning family of ordinary people in extraordinary positions. This is the Elizabeth II who, in 1982, told housewives in Sheffield that she, too, found it difficult to keep her floors clean; who, in 1990, requested designer John Anderson to shorten the neckline of a coat, given her diminutive stature; who, at a low point in royal fortunes, asked for clemency from press and public, and, in 2000, told viewers of her Christmas broadcast that 'the framework in which I try to lead my life' is one available to many millions: Christ's teachings. 'We do not want the Queen to be one of us,' wrote the women's editor of the *Reading Evening Post* in February 1991, 'but we do want her to be with us.'[4] For seven decades, despite media intrusiveness on a scale unprecedented in royal history, she has balanced this requirement of accessibility with distance, the white-gloved hand extended in greeting.

At the time of the thirtieth anniversary of her accession, the *Daily Mirror* pointed out that Elizabeth had 'lived a life of great privilege, but has never known the privilege of privacy which most of us enjoy'.[5] She has suggested she must be seen to be believed: unlike the widowed Queen Victoria, she has always been more than a diligent deskworker, concealed from view behind the scenes. Acclaimed in 1953 as 'the focal point of loyalty, justice, mercy, integrity', she has consistently worked to retain, and merit, this role as she understands it, aware that her status is inherited, respect and affection earned; and she rates highly her position as fountain of honour, symbolically rewarding integrity in others through the honours system at palace investitures.[6] The authors of *The Queen Elizabeth Coronation Book* described her as 'a combination of master and servant to [her] peoples'; her priority has been her servantship. Famously, at the age of twenty-one she dedicated herself to the service of a nation and its 'imperial family'. 'It was an incredible thing,' reflected her cousin Margaret Rhodes in 2015, 'to envisage a whole life ahead of you, where your own choices are not followed, where you know what you are going to be doing every day of the week for months ahead and where spontaneity goes out of the window.'

After seven decades, it is possible to see the considerable changes the monarchy has undergone on Elizabeth's watch. She is a cautious innovator, who regards her unique inheritance with respect. Nothing in her upbringing or the training she received from her father challenged her innate conservatism: indeed, so strong was the expectation among her first advisers, politicians, the press and many of the public that she perpetuate her father and grandfather's models of kingship that real opportunities for innovation were few, even had she so inclined. One result was that, from quite early in her reign, she was disparaged as old-fashioned. Over time, this judgement shifted. For many years, Elizabeth's fidelity to timeless (or old-fashioned) values has made her a figure of reassurance in our national life, a still point in the vortex of change, and more progressive views than hers have wilted in the face of her straightforward homilies that, for example, 'matters of the spirit are more important and more lasting than simple material development'.[7] She has outlived national habits of deference and ignored the culture of celebrity, evanescent and meretricious. She has maintained the crown's eminence and, like all her successful predecessors, humanized her own sovereignty just enough: when, in April 1960, twenty-two-year-old Mary Smith of Plumstead wrote to Elizabeth to request her intervention in revoking her husband's sentence for murder, she did so 'as one mother to another'.[8] She has not faltered in good behaviour, her deep religious faith or an unyielding sense of duty inherited from her parents and grandparents, and shared, until his death, by her husband, with the result that, as television commentary claimed at the time of her silver wedding anniversary, she is for many 'a non-governing monarch as powerful in her spiritual influence and example as any absolute tyrant of the past'.

Constitutional proprieties do not favour adventurous, fanciful monarchs. Overwhelmingly Elizabeth has accepted the constraints of her position. Her political neutrality is rigorous, and her subjects are content that her role as head of state occupy fewer of her public energies than that of head of the nation. She is not, however, wholly a passive figure. Presumably with her agreement, her closest advisors have been active in defending the crown's surviving powers. These include the convention known as Queen's consent that requires ministers to give notice of legislation likely to affect either the crown's private interests or the royal prerogative, ahead of parliamentary debate. 'I must protest most strongly at not being consulted at an earlier stage, in accordance with the rules which are clearly laid down', wrote her private secretary on one occasion when prior consultation had not been granted.[9] In her private life, her granddaughter Princess Beatrice of York has testified to her 'overwhelming curiosity': 'every day she's curious to learn something new, to do something new'; favoured royal architect Hugh Casson noted 'her very definite views', in his case on everything from door handles to lampshades.[10] Elizabeth's approach to her guardianship of the Commonwealth, for example, has been of her own devising. Her affection for and abiding interest in this global agglomeration of former imperial territories, inspired by her belief that 'the most important contact between nations is usually contact between peoples', has been key to its survival and its growth from nine to fifty-four nations. Fifteen of these independent territories retain Elizabeth as their queen. Alone among the world's monarchs, her prominence is global.

In 1972, Thames Television told viewers, 'In a line stretching back over a thousand years, no monarch has been more loved and no monarch more esteemed.' It is a statement to provoke unease among modern audiences. It is also, for many, many of Elizabeth II's subjects, true.

CHAPTER I

'A direct descendant in the male line of our family'

THE HOUSE IN WHICH Elizabeth II was born, like many building blocks of her childhood world, has not survived. 17 Bruton Street stood part way along an otherwise unremarkable thoroughfare connecting Bond Street with Berkeley Square (quieter and more exclusive then than now). It had been the home of her kindly, conventional, family-minded, unambitious, aristocratic maternal grandparents, the 14th Earl and Countess of Strathmore and Kinghorne, since 1920. Its newsworthiness predated her birth. Three years earlier, on a similarly grey April day, her mother, then Lady Elizabeth Bowes-Lyon, had emerged from the tall grey house along a strip of coloured drugget to marry her moderately handsome and mostly unassuming prince, Albert Frederick Arthur George, Duke of York, Earl of Inverness and Baron Killarney. Dark-painted railings onto the street held the curious at bay, holland blinds screened tall windows. It was less splendid than the family's previous London house at

20 St James's Square, but it was imposing enough: five storeys high, its lofty pilasters crowned by Corinthian columns, typical of the Mayfair establishments of landed families, like the unfashionable Strathmores, who lived chiefly on their estates in the country and, in 1926, retained ownership of a disproportionate percentage of the nation's wealth.

Inside, a room had been prepared for the baby's birth. In 1926, members of the royal family did not give birth in hospital. Royalty visited hospitals for the benefit of others: to open and inaugurate, to applaud fundraising initiatives in a pre-National Health Service Britain in which voluntary contributions built wards, bought beds, blankets and bandages and saved lives. Royal mothers gave birth at home; this occasion was no exception. Until the late discovery of the baby's breech position that necessitated intervention by surgeon Sir Henry Simson, the pregnancy had proceeded calmly. In late autumn, the duke had informed his parents. The duchess had confirmed the appointment of a monthly nurse, Anne Beevers, on 8 January. By mid-April she had acknowledged receipt of baby clothes and quantities of the finest linen, commissions overseen by an attentive Queen Mary. Much was the work of nimble-fingered but financially distressed gentlewomen, the workforce of the Royal School of Needlework, of which the duchess was patron. Other garments were worked by the duchess herself, by her mother, by Queen Mary, homely details let slip to the press. With the nursery ready, a decision taken the preceding weekend by the King's physician Sir Bertrand Dawson may have come as a relief: Dawson had asked the King's permission to bring on labour early. In a letter written on 12 April, the duchess had complained of boredom, her vexation at 'just sitting here waiting now'.[1] Three days later, she sought fleeting distraction in Archie de Bear's *RSVP*, a revue at the Vaudeville Theatre. Dragonfly-like, she skimmed across life's surface.

Then as now the birth of a royal baby prompted spikes

of happiness in the national cardiogram: congratulatory telegrams from provincial mayors, colonial governors, the 'Ruling Princes of India'.[2] The bulletin released by Simson and obstetrician Walter Jagger, consultant at the Samaritan Hospital for Women, that 'Her Royal Highness the Duchess of York was safely delivered of a Princess at 2.40am this morning', and an announcement the following morning that 'both had an excellent night; their progress in every way is normal and satisfactory', offered newspaper readers a distraction and editors a catalyst for syrupy outpourings. To the majority of George V's subjects the first-born child of the Duke and Duchess of York meant no more than this. The King had four sons. He had two grandsons, following the births, in 1923 and 1924, of George and Gerald Lascelles, sons of his only daughter, Mary, Princess Royal. The monarchy did not lack heirs.

For Bertie and Elizabeth – 'such a sweet little couple and so fond of one another'[3] – their daughter's birth represented a high-water mark in a marriage already happy. With rising impatience they had endured their three years of married childlessness. The previous August, Bertie had written to his eldest brother, the Prince of Wales, known in the family as David, 'I still long for one thing, which you can guess.'[4] Elizabeth's feelings matched her husband's. Bertie was highly strung. His nervousness and lightning flashes of temper, called his 'gnashes', rippled the calm surface of their marriage; Elizabeth described him gently as 'a very nervy person'.[5] He suspected the rumours of his infertility, attributed to childhood mumps; he inferred pressure from within the royal family, like the response of his aunt, Princess Alice, Countess of Athlone: 'I am thrilled over your news of Elizabeth's hopes; thank God.'[6] But his shiftlessness on the evening of 20 April, his restless, 'very worried & anxious' pacing about his parents-in-law's house, was of no ordinary prompting, a reflection of more than simple devotion to his wife. As he wrote afterwards to his mother, his conviction had always been that 'a child [would] make our happiness complete'.[7] He would find that it did.

Did the constitutional position of their baby, who automatically found herself third in line to the throne, concern the expectant parents, as that drab April evening gave way to colourless night and reporters shuffling in the cold wrapped grateful hands around the cups of coffee sent out to them in Bruton Street? Almost certainly not. Nor would any but those of ultramontane snobbery dwell on this baby's mixed heritage: the first legitimate baby born to the commoner wife of a king's son in three centuries. In the aftermath of the First World War, George V's subjects had applauded Bertie's choice of a home-grown bride rather than a foreign princess, as Prime Minister David Lloyd George had assured the King they would.[8] To the couple themselves the Archbishop of York had described 'a nation happy in your joy'; the press celebrated 'an alliance that appealed to the hearts and sympathies of every rank and class at home and beyond the seas'.[9] Their marriage, according to the royal family's favourite commentator, Dermot Morrah, 'marked the [royals'] emancipation... from a tradition of political and dynastic alliances, which to many people had always been distasteful, and in the circumstances of the modern world had become manifestly out of date'.[10] Instead the press made much of Scottish Elizabeth's lofty descent from Robert the Bruce. In April 1926, it was enough that any baby of the Yorks stood in the direct line of succession. She was not born in a palace, her father was not the King's first heir, but custom demanded the attendance at her birth of a member of the government. In 1688, prompted by spite, religious bigotry or opportunism, the future Queen Anne had chosen to believe rumours that the baby born to her father, James II, and his Catholic second wife, Mary of Modena, was not their own child but a healthy substitute smuggled into the birthing chamber in a warming pan. Ever since, the presence of a government minister at royal births had deterred skullduggery. Bertie was not alone in his nightwatch in the tall house in Bruton Street; he was joined by Sir William Joynson-Hicks, the Conservative home secretary. Unlike Bertie, an exhausted Joynson-Hicks jibbed at this out-of-hours imposition. By 20 April, a long-running dispute over rates of pay and working hours between miners and mine-owners threatened industrial action on an unprecedented scale. The Yorks' baby was born into a capital on the brink of the General Strike, in an atmosphere the right-wing press branded revolutionary: 'an odd... unnatural atmosphere', according to Virginia Woolf, 'great activity but no normal life'.[11] Joynson-Hicks needed all his energy for struggles more pressing – and less easily resolved – than the Duchess of York's confinement.

Like everyone else present, from the duchess down, he did his duty. While the city still slept, he informed the lord mayor of the glad tidings, a courtesy demanded by tradition. Separately messengers had conveyed the news to Windsor Castle; a telegram was despatched to the Prince of Wales at Biarritz. Queen Mary's reaction was of 'such... relief & joy' when, at 4 a.m., she and the King were woken to learn that 'darling Elizabeth had got a daughter'.[12] These were Bertie's own feelings, as shortly he wrote to his mother; they were 'darling Elizabeth's', too. Afterwards they were those of the crowd of onlookers that the *Morning Post* reported throughout the previous day 'outside the big grey facade of 17 Bruton Street... oblivious of the showers of rain, waiting'.[13] 'The weather', wrote novelist Arnold Bennett, 'ha[d] been evil for a week.'[14] Even at so joyful a juncture, the letter Bertie wrote to Queen Mary reveals his anxiety, shared by all of George V's children, over the approval of his sternly undemonstrative parents. 'I do hope that you & Papa are as delighted as we are, to have a granddaughter, or would you sooner have had another grandson.'[15] On this occasion the parents shared the son's delight. They visited son, daughter-in-law and new baby at Bruton Street on the afternoon of the baby's birth. Their absence during labour itself was a blessing. During the Princess Royal's first confinement in 1923, an anxious George V had 'paced up and down, regaling [those present] with tales of the wives of his friends who had died in childbirth'.[16] In her diary Queen Mary described her first granddaughter as 'a little darling with a lovely complexion & pretty fair hair'.[17] But two days passed before she wrote to Bertie of her pride in the baby, whom she labelled conventionally 'too sweet & pretty'.[18]

The new parents may well have settled their choice of names before the baby's birth, given Elizabeth's desire for a daughter and the recent death, in December 1925, of Bertie's much-loved grandmother, Queen Alexandra. Their wishes aligned with a sentiment voiced in the *Spectator* on 24 April that 'it will be very agreeable to the nation if the child is given a characteristically English name'.[19] The matter of the baby's names required the sanction of the King rather than public endorsement. Nevertheless it was only after an interval of six days that Bertie appealed to his father. His tone was cautiously insistent: 'I hope you will approve of these names... We are so anxious for her first name to be Elizabeth.'[20] The King approved. Characteristically he informed the Queen of his agreement before he replied to his son. It is unclear whether either agreed with Bertie's romantic suggestion that 'Elizabeth of York sounds so nice, too' the King noted without objection the absence from the trio of names of Victoria, on which the dynasty's long-lived matriarch had insisted for all her daughters, granddaughters and even great-granddaughters. Evidently all concerned were unaware of Queen Victoria's view of Elizabeth as one of 'the ugliest "housemaids" names I ever knew'.[21] Newspapers noted 'the initials of the new Princess are those of her mother, E A M, the name of the Duchess being Elizabeth Angela Marguerite'; they noted that three names were fewer than usual for royal babies, who typically received 'a redundancy of Christian names'; and one provincial hack congratulated himself on his hunch, on 22 April, that 'the choice of Elizabeth could hardly be improved'.[22] The baby's names were registered officially the following month. Mr W. R. C. Walker, the district registrar, called at Bruton Street, where the duke received him in the library, assisted by his secretary. Only a minority of papers commented on the Yorks' choice 'reviving in the Royal Family a name famous in the history of Britain's Queens'.[23] Comparisons of this sort came later.

∾

A letter written by her lady-in-waiting at Queen Mary's instruction indicates the light in which the King and Queen regarded their newest grandchild. It reports the royal couple as 'very much pleased with the baby and they think her very pretty'. Firmly it discounts for her the future pre-eminence the press had been so quick to confer. 'The sex mercifully in this case does not matter,' states the letter, and the decided tone suggests the Queen's own voice.[24] Did not matter because, despite earlier confiding to Bertie her joy in 'look[ing] forward to a direct descendant in the male line of our family', the dynastically minded Queen Mary recognized that, as the daughter of a younger son, the baby princess was virtually certain to be supplanted by a child of the still-unmarried Prince of Wales, or a son born subsequently to her parents (the Duchess of York was only twenty-five). Happily for their peace of mind, neither the Queen nor her husband was privy to the contents of a letter the Prince of Wales wrote to his friend Piers Legh: 'I'd have voted *for a boy myself*!! but they all seem very pleased.'[25] Nor could either yet countenance a suspicion already growing among the prince's inner circle that he 'would not raise his finger to save his future sceptre. In fact many of his intimate friends think he would be only too happy to renounce it.'[26]

Queen Mary's emphatic 'mercifully' suggests her relief at the likelihood of the baby escaping the burden of a throne. The little princess inherited fewer Victorian certainties than her immediate royal forebears. The constitutional crisis of the outset of George V's reign, when the House of Commons successfully challenged the House of Lords over budgetary measures, a symbolic defeat of the old order by democratic forces; the cataclysm of the First World War, which unseated kings across Europe, including the horror of revolution in Russia and the murder of the King's Romanov cousins; and the imminent unleashing of the power of organized labour in the form of the General Strike all indicated ideological shifts to challenge monarchy. Bluff, brusque, boring but (mostly) benign, George had done his best to shore up the crown's stability. In 1917, he had changed the royal family's name from Saxe-Coburg and Gotha to Windsor and abolished German titles held by British royalties, among them his wife's brothers. Deliberately he had attempted to bridge the gulf between crown and people, and the newspapers' view that '[his] is no Royal house of mere pomp and circumstance; they are at one with their people' was widely shared.[27] 'He will be remembered as Britain's greatest King and the World's Perfect Gentleman,' a schoolboy wrote in an essay after his death.[28] Despite his quarterdeck manner, his horror of change and a dislike of lawlessness amounting to incomprehension, his attitude throughout the General Strike was even-handed and carefully moderate. With some success, he urged conciliation on his ministers, his aim, in his own words, 'the hopefulness of a united people'.[29] That the post-war world inspired unease in the stamp-collecting, game-shooting king-emperor his wife fully understood. Neither dared take for granted, as wrote one of George's cousins, Prince Christopher of Greece, that 'in England... you find this personal love of the Sovereign and his family, a sentiment that passes even fidelity; a perfect understanding... Monarchy can never die out in England, whatever its fate in other countries. It is too deeply ingrained in the hearts of the people.'[30] With good reason, neither grandparent wished the shackles of sovereignty for the baby in Bruton Street.

~~~

The baby princess was born under the roof of her Strathmore grandparents. The pattern of the sporting year and his responsibilities as landowner and lord lieutenant shaped the existence of cricket-loving, luxuriantly mustachioed Claude Strathmore. His fixed habits and straightforward tastes are revealed by his choice, every day he was at home, of plum pudding for lunch. In essentials his life mirrored that of his royal counterpart, George V, described by the King's eldest son as 'a masterclass in the art of well-ordered, unostentatious, elegant living'; stewed plums with semolina were the royal couple's favourite pudding.[31] Music, gardening, needlework, local charities, her large family and chows unimaginatively named Brownie, a brown dog, and Blackie, a black dog, occupied the days of Cecilia, Lady Strathmore. Husband's and wife's were the preoccupations of a generation and a class. Their world was one of privilege; neither cherished ambitions outside their immediate sphere. The strength of character of their youngest daughter, Elizabeth, the ninth of their ten children, in an unsympathetic assessment 'not much better than the kind of person one met at a country house',[32] and the grateful thraldom of her husband Bertie would ensure that their unremarkable Edwardian mores left their imprint on the little princess: a focus on family and the blustery outdoorsiness of country life – dogs, ponies, picnics; a disregard for abstract speculation or high culture; benign paternalism and an attachment to the status quo; a kind of thrifty splendour, moving between large houses in Hertfordshire, London and Angus. As a preparation for leadership in the second half of the twentieth century and beyond, it would prove a curious prescription.

Initially, events confirmed the baby's royal status. The crowd that gathered in Bruton Street on 20 April knew that they awaited no ordinary birth. Over the course of the day their ranks eddied and replenished. Early the following morning, according to the *Morning Post*, the appearance of 'a neat, efficient nurse' rewarded their dank vigil. From an upstairs window she 'looked down into the street. The upturned faces must all have asked a question, for it was with a nod and the most reassuring smile that the owner of the uniform withdrew.'[33] Some bystanders lingered to cheer the Princess Royal, the baby's first royal visitor, who took crimson carnations to her sister-in-law, and the afternoon visit of the King and Queen. Others bought the illustrated papers that, after an interval, reproduced a first photograph of the duchess and her daughter. In this ethereal but romantically patrician image, commissioned by Bertie from the 'Photographic Laureate of Children's Photographers' Richard Speaight, the tiny baby lies against a lacy pillow amid gauzy, embroidered layers; enraptured, her mother wears snowy white and swan's down and three long necklaces of pearls. The photograph reproduced almost exactly a pose Speaight had chosen three years earlier photographing the princess's cousin, the Hon. George Lascelles, with his mother, the Princess Royal. The later image is more diaphanous, more theatrical, more remote; it lacks the homeliness of Speaight's Lascelles pictures. At a time when postcard writing was a national pastime, with up to a billion postcards sent annually, J. Beagles & Company issued as postcards two pictures from the sitting. Even in her cradle, the baby born to dynastic obscurity was available for public consumption.

In the majority of cases, it was affection for the duchess, with what one contemporary biographer called her 'happy blend of delicate dignity and radiant friendliness',[34] that prompted fascination with her child. 'The popularity of the Duchess has led the nation to take an abiding interest in her personal and domestic life,' wrote the *Yorkshire Post*;[35] later the *Graphic* explained 'the glamour of [the baby's] important position as fourth lady in the land' as 'strengthened by reflections from the spell cast over the public by her beautiful mother'.[36] Against the backdrop of the General Strike, which began on 3 May but overshadowed troubled days beforehand, the Yorks' baby, and the comings and goings of royals and nurses in Bruton Street, provided harmless diversions. In London, incendiarists attacked the *Times* offices. The capital's public transport effectively ceased, taxis struggling to replace buses and, across the city, vehicles 'packed together like a jigsaw puzzle, unable to move forward more than a few feet at a time'.[37] An unnerving silence gripped the streets, 'more like a Sunday with the shops open, but with no one shopping'.[38] Buckingham Palace sentries wore khaki and forage caps in place of scarlet coats and bearskins; their appearance suggested a siege mentality. To transport to Wales copies of an anti-strike news sheet the Prince of Wales lent his car and his chauffeur. 'The pulse-beat of British power, which had throbbed across the centuries into the farthest corners of the earth, all but died away,' the prince remembered, a statement of Establishment alarmism that was not shared by all George V's family.[39] Yet this 'revolutionary move', unique in scale, which the *Daily Mail* had warned aimed at 'destroying the government and subverting the rights and liberties of the people', did neither and ended after nine mostly peaceful days. Many found an antidote to its climate of uncertainty and fear on the Strathmores' doorstep. They were intent on a glimpse of the tiny princess in her nurse's arms or, even better, taken for an outing, 'carried, a white wisp... carefully and decorously around the quiet precincts of Berkeley Square, where the carpet of grass showed an amazing green, and the buds were beginning to throw a lace-work, like a veil, over the sooty bark of the branches'.[40] 'There are always a few people waiting to see her,'

Bertie told his mother's lady-in-waiting, Mabell, Countess of Airlie, when, on 14 May, ahead of the baby's christening, she delivered a bottle of water from the River Jordan, sent specially from the Holy Land, her second visit to the new princess. Of her first she recalled in her memoirs many years later, 'I little thought that I was paying homage to the future Queen of England, for in those days there was every expectation that the Prince of Wales would marry within the next year or two.'[41] Her point of view was shared – surely influenced – by her royal employer, indeed by all the baby's family except the Prince of Wales himself: glamorous, self-indulgent, his good sense addled by adulation, at odds with the constraints of his birthright and, according to his father's private secretary, 'bored with state functions and all the "outward and visible" signs of monarchy'.[42]

To that section of the public that cared about such things, the princess's chance or otherwise of inheriting her grandfather's throne scarcely registered. Perhaps, as the *Daily Graphic* cautioned, they had no mind to 'burden the bright hour of [the baby's] arrival with speculation of its Royal destiny'.[43] Day after day the crowds massed – so many people on one occasion that baby and nurse departed for their daily walk by a rear door. Photographs record the multitude that crowded the gates and railings of Buckingham Palace's forecourt on 29 May for the baby's christening in the palace's private chapel. They were women and children mostly, the men among them wearing coats against the late-spring chill, and they stood, many deep, every one hatted. Some climbed the railings for a better viewpoint. When the gates opened and the duke and duchess's car emerged for the short return journey to a christening tea in Bruton Street, they surged forward good-naturedly through the loose police cordon. Had they looked up, an enterprising ceramics manufacturer claimed, they would have seen two magpies. 'This luckiest of omens inspired the design of tableware for the Royal Nursery, which was graciously accepted by the Duchess of York and delighted Her Majesty the Queen,' ran advertising copy for Paragon's 'Two for Joy' magpie-patterned bone china, released the following year.[44]

The christening itself had been conducted by the Archbishop of York, Cosmo Gordon Lang, a friend of Bertie and Elizabeth and afterwards their staunch supporter through the abdication crisis that none yet anticipated. Instructed 'not to attempt anything elaborate in the way of decoration', court florist Edward Goodyear had 'contented himself by placing upon the altar a coronet of beautiful white lilies, other white blooms with just the suspicion of a pink tinge, and sprigs of white heather "for luck"'.[45] All four of the baby's grandparents were godparents. So were Bertie's sister, Mary, Princess Royal, and Elizabeth's eldest surviving sister, Mary, Lady Elphinstone. The baby shared a godparent with her father: her seventy-seven-year-old great-great-uncle Arthur, Duke of Connaught, favourite and last-surviving son of Queen Victoria. Otherwise, the roster of her sponsors was less illustrious than Bertie's, second son of a king-in-waiting, which had included Queen Victoria herself and her eldest daughter, the Empress Frederick of Germany.

Like her father, her grandfather and her great-grandfather, the five-week-old princess wore the Honiton lace and satin christening gown commissioned by Queen Victoria. Also in its fourth generation of royal service was the silver-gilt 'lily font' designed by Prince Albert, in which she was baptised according to the rites of the Church of England, of which her grandfather was supreme governor. At a symbolic level she was baptised into a family and a way of life. Both were bound by unwritten regulations concerning rank, opportunity and behaviour. It was a legacy mostly traceable to her great-great-grandmother Queen Victoria, whose credo, communicated with vehemence to her browbeaten family, included an insistence on royalty's uniqueness: 'our position, which is so totally different from other people's'.[46] Too young to protest otherwise, baby Elizabeth cried lustily throughout. The formal christening photographs are lugubrious. The only smiling face is Queen Mary's, in a photograph of baby and grandmother alone. On this occasion, the Queen wore a large diamond and baroque pearl brooch she had inherited from her own grandmother, Princess Augusta, Duchess of Cambridge, the historic jewel a link across five royal generations. Again, the photograph became a postcard. Its caption, 'HM Queen Mary with Grand-daughter HRH Princess Elizabeth Alexandra Mary', was a reminder that the baby's claim to public attention derived from her proximity to the throne. Only the elaborate christening cake, decorated with sugar cupids holding wreaths of flowers, made concessions to childhood. On its topmost tier was 'a sugar cradle adorned with a crown and the initials of the baby'.[47] The cradle contained a tiny doll much like the princess herself.

And she received a second christening cake, given to her by 'the poor children of Battersea'. In her letter of thanks to the gift's organizers, the duchess promised to tell her daughter about both cake and donors 'when she is old enough to understand'.[48]

࿐

In *The Story of Princess Elizabeth*, published when its subject was four and a half, the Duchess of York's former governess Beryl Poignand, writing under the pseudonym 'Anne Ring', claimed of her christening, 'Even on the day when the important question of her names was decided she remained tranquil.'[49] It was quite untrue, despite Poignand/Ring's account having 'the sanction of her Parents'. 'Of course poor baby cried,' Queen Mary noted, and Mrs Beevers, cosily acclaimed by the Duchess of York as 'our dear Nannie B',[50] liberally dosed the crying baby with dill water as soon as the service was over.

In the month since the baby's birth, Anne Beevers had

imposed tranquil efficiency in the Bruton Street nursery, situated, with its view across the rooftops of neighbouring Grafton Street, immediately above the duchess's bedroom. Her methods were old-fashioned – even the sexagenarian Mabell Airlie considered them so:[51] probable grounds for the *Times*'s approving description of the nursery's furnishing and arrangements as 'typically English'.[52] The Duchess did not complain. She rewarded Mrs Beevers on her departure with a gold watch and appointed in her place her own former nanny, the equally old-fashioned, forbiddingly middle-aged Clara Knight, called 'Alah' (to rhyme with 'gala'). In turn, Nannie B sent presents of knitted bootees in several colours to her most illustrious ex-charge.

Inevitably, contemporary accounts of the princess's nursery life, emerging within days of her birth, sounded a uniformly saccharine note; photographs would support their refrain that she was a baby of sunny disposition, contented and smiling, and, shortly, 'a curiously vivid little figure, full of life and character'.[53] Nannie B's old-fashioned ways were not at variance with the household in Bruton Street run along the late-nineteenth-century lines that had characterized the first years of her grandmothers' marriages. The nursery's principal feature was its cot. Like Elizabeth's christening service, it resembled those of Queen Victoria's babies; it resembled her cousin's cots, though without the earl's coronet that crowned the Lascelles boys' cradle. It compared poorly with the damask-swagged and tasselled affair in which her uncle David was photographed in 1894, or 'the cradle for the Prince of the Blood' designed by architect Edwin Lutyens for the night nursery of Queen Mary's Doll's House only a handful of years previously. To today's reader, Anne Ring's description – 'neither ostentatious nor elaborate, but soft as down and white as a snowdrift' – sounds conflicting notes of understatement and hyperbole: evidently the writer required the royal nursery to be simultaneously remarkable and ordinary.[54] So did any number of contemporary readers, their views of monarchy shaped by late-Victorian hagiography, their social outlook shifting in the democratic winds of the post-war world. The boat-shaped, canopied cot sported layer on layer of ruched white hangings, like frilly Victorian petticoats in a Hollywood extravaganza. Whether or not, as Ring claimed, the baby who occupied this snowdrift had 'the whitest skin in the world', she was pretty. Even Queen Mary said so. She grew quickly into a pretty, curly-haired infant. As much as her royal status and her symbolic embodiment of 'continuity and of hope in the future', it was her prettiness that perpetuated the baby's news value: eulogized in print, in the pixelated photographs of newspapers and postcards.[55] Interest in her Lascelles cousins had waned. (Public curiosity at the time of Gerald Lascelles's christening in 1924 was so great 'that it was decided to keep the actual day and hour [of the service] a secret'.[56]) Lacking royal titles and little boys of unremarkable appearance who frequently irritated their grandfather the King, they could not rival their younger princess-cousin.

❧

Princess Elizabeth, the *Spectator* reminded readers, 'was born in a house in a London street... cars and buses and taxis – all that makes up the swift and shifting life of London – [sped] ceaselessly past [her] windows day and night.'[57] For the writer in question, this was 'the comfort of an English home', a claim that implied domestic superiority, reassuring at such a pass in the nation's affairs. Yet it was not her own home. By the time of Anne Beevers's departure from Bruton Street, the Yorks' homelessness threatened to overshadow their baby's first summer.

Homelessness is not associated with kings' sons. It was a dilemma neither Bertie nor Elizabeth had resolved by the time of Elizabeth's confinement. Strictly they had a house and, to boot, a large one: White Lodge in Richmond Park. It had been Queen Mary's childhood home and her idea that her first married son make it his own. Weekend crowds of sightseers, high levels of discomfort including antiquated plumbing and a single downstairs loo, wiring that was unpredictable and unsafe, costly staffing requirements and a lengthy journey into and out of central London made husband and wife determined to live elsewhere. To her mother-in-law, in October 1925, Elizabeth's excuse was the fogs and loneliness of Richmond Park with the onset of autumn; she commended Mayfair's 'convenience'. Tactfully and astutely, she had postponed any suggestion of leaving White Lodge until news of her pregnancy had opportunity to act as bromide.[58] Unaccustomed to overruling of their plans, neither Queen Mary nor her husband had responded constructively. In the short term, the Strathmores' generosity provided an answer of sorts. With both Elizabeth's parents retaining use of rooms in Bruton Street, it was not an arrangement of any permanence nor conducive to feelings of settledness.

The solution presented itself in the form of a house on Piccadilly. In one direction it overlooked Green Park, with longer views of Buckingham Palace, in the other the trees and broad expanses of Hyde Park and Rotten Row, where riding schools plied a sedate trade. Described in a contemporary account as 'incongruously modest among the palatial buildings of Piccadilly, a home among hotels, clubs and shops', by modern standards 145 Piccadilly was colossal.[59] Agents particulars compiled in 1921 labelled it an 'important mansion' and directed the would-be taker to 'spacious and well-lighted accommodation' that included inner and outer halls, 'a secondary staircase with electric passenger lift, drawing room, dining room, ballroom, study, library, about twenty-five bedrooms, conservatory etc'. The garden 'consist[ed] of a lawn... and some long geranium beds'.[60] It was large enough for a nurse to push a perambulator and, later, a child to ride her tricycle; it was enclosed by railings that would afford the curious ringside seats for the baby's time outdoors and through which, at least once, a family of ducklings escaped from the Park.[61] Bertie seems to have quailed at the rent and the expense of essential repairs. The nursery required a fire escape; none of the White Lodge curtains fitted. Queen Mary offered to meet the cost of one room's decoration but cautioned against any direct approach to the King for loans of furniture or artworks. The elder Elizabeth made up her mind quickly. Confident of her husband's acquiescence in this as in most things, she embarked on her plans.

Despite the disparaging view of the Yorks' wedding presents expressed by Herbert Asquith, son of former Liberal prime minister H. H. Asquith – 'not a thing did I see that I would have cared to have or give'[62] – the couple had been fortunate in receiving on marriage the princely equivalent of a starter pack: in addition to what Asquith dismissed as 'every kind of gilt and silver ware',[63] a blue lacquer coffer on a gilded stand and, for Bertie, a handsome mahogany clothes press from a list of noblemen headed by the dukes of Devonshire and Sutherland; a Chippendale grandfather clock; and, from Lord and Lady Weir, a lavishly gilded crimson lacquer chest. A seventeenth-century Chinese jewel casket on a Queen Anne stand was a gift from Lord and Lady Waring; elaborately carved and gilded, Elizabeth's bed had been painted by Florentine artist Riccardo Meacci with Renaissance-style angels and the coats of arms of bride and groom. In anticipation of their second move, Lady Strathmore now added a card table and, for her letter-writing daughter, a bureau. The King and Queen found surplus chandeliers at Balmoral and Osborne House.

Yet it was not to be a summer of homemaking and the simple pleasures of motherhood. Clouds massed. Partly at his own suggestion, Bertie was chosen to open parliament buildings early in 1927 in Australia's new capital of Canberra. Elizabeth would accompany him; baby Elizabeth would remain at home, the pattern of royal tours. In 1901, the King and Queen had left behind four children, the youngest, like baby Elizabeth, less than a year old, for a tour lasting eight months. The prospect horrified Elizabeth. Queen Mary's suggestion that the baby spend three of the six months with her royal grandparents bore the weight of a command. In early August, Bertie, Elizabeth and baby Elizabeth left London for the Strathmores' Scottish castle of Glamis; Elizabeth parried her mother-in-law's summons to Balmoral. Unwilling to shorten the precious interlude and unable to alter, or even query, government plans for herself and her husband, it was her sole means of safeguarding time with her baby. At Glamis she retreated into the familiar routine of the ancient house that Cecilia Strathmore had imbued with an atmosphere of almost magical happiness. 'In a long low rambling wing... its oak boards beaming under their patina of fresh beeswax, and its diamond panes winking with delight', her baby occupied the same nursery in which she had once slept, attended by the same nurse, and spent her mornings outdoors, asleep in her pram, among the dahlia beds of the Dutch Garden.[64] With a degree of bad grace, to sympathetic (and unsympathetic) listeners Elizabeth bemoaned the New Year's 'horrible trip'.[65] She steeped herself in schemes for 145 Piccadilly, '[giving] minute attention to every detail of... decoration, carpets, furniture and general arrangement'.[66] She chose pale colours throughout and placed the Warings' Chinese jewel casket adjacent to the fireplace in the first-floor drawing room. Had Bertie's pockets run deep enough, she would have supplemented wedding presents with further purchases of eighteenth-century furniture for the light, lofty rooms. She copied the chintzy classicism perfected in the Edwardian country houses of her youth, recalling, as she would in all her interiors, that gilded patrician interlude before the devastation of the First World War. The house would be fitted up during the Yorks' overseas absence. Photographs taken on completion record rooms splendid by modern standards and, save in a certain sparseness, interchangeable with the capital's surviving aristocratic townhouses, several of which outstripped it for magnificence (Brook House, for example, the Park Lane home of Bertie's ambitious cousin Lord Louis Mountbatten, had a dining room able to seat a hundred and a quartet of Van Dyck portraits). The baby princess's first home closely resembled those of the tiny elite circle in which she would be raised. Its aesthetic rooted her socially and culturally, and every room she afterwards inhabited, even Hugh Casson's workaday interiors for the royal yacht *Britannia* that aimed 'to give the impression of a country house at sea', conformed more or less to this inherited pattern.[67]

Despite Elizabeth's misery at imminent parting from her baby, the end of the summer and early autumn were punctuated by visits to friends. On each occasion Elizabeth left her daughter behind at Glamis with Lady Strathmore. It was simply the way of the world and Elizabeth's instincts were conventional.

❧

On the eve of departure, mother, father and seven-month-old baby visited the Children's Studio in Dover Street for a sitting with photographer Marcus Adams. Their choice of Adams over Speaight on this occasion may have been intended as a statement of independence. In a long career Speaight had photographed both Bertie and Elizabeth as children, Bertie's mother and his siblings, numerous crowned heads of Europe and, repeatedly, the infant sons of his sister, Mary. Adams, by contrast, in the six years since the opening of his Mayfair studio, had achieved a modest following among the Yorks' aristocratic contemporaries. He represented a safe innovation, sharing his premises, with their distinctive, child-friendly, yellow- and blue-painted reception hall, with fellow photograper Bertram Park, for whom Elizabeth had sat the year before her engagement; Park's clients included the British-born Queen of Spain, a cousin of the King's. On 2 December, Adams photographed the baby with each of her parents and on her own. Squirrel-cheeked, with a fluffy cap of hair like down, she wore a white dress with a sash and large bows on each shoulder. This was the 'dainty, fairy-like style of dress' preferred by the duchess and commended by women journalists like 'Yvonne' of the *Aberdeen Press & Journal*.[68] Two of Adams's pictures, in a folding leather frame, accompanied Bertie and Elizabeth on their voyage. Two more were released as postcards.

For Elizabeth, separation proved every bit as challenging as she had anticipated. 'Feel very miserable at leaving the baby,' she wrote, and to modern ears, mistakenly, 'the baby' suggests detachment. 'Went up & played with her & she was so sweet. Luckily she doesn't realise anything.'[69] Weeks later, baby Elizabeth returned to Adams's studio, the first of four visits without her parents. This sitting produced a tactful photograph in which little Elizabeth gazes at pictures of her mother and father, to whom it was promptly despatched. By then, staying with the Strathmores at St Paul's Walden Bury, in Hertfordshire, she had become 'an ardent and very swift crawler'.[70] In Lady Strathmore's drawing room, she amused herself 'pulling handfuls of fluff out of the thick coats' of her grandmother's chows, 'vigorously unwinding her grandmother's balls of wool or scattering her patience cards all over the carpet; or, best of all, if someone was kind enough to hold her up... banging with all the tiny might of her doubled fists on both the high and the low notes of the piano'.[71]

Afterwards, she moved into Buckingham Palace for an extended visit to the King and Queen. The Duchess of York had written to Queen Mary that she missed her daughter 'quite terribly and the five weeks that we have been away seem like five months'.[72] The mother's loss proved the grandmother's gain. A new photograph taken by Adams in March corroborates Anne Ring's assessment that 'Queen Mary was enchanted to have her granddaughter with her, settled in... airy rooms in the north wing'.[73] As at the baby's christening, the picture shows a smiling Elizabeth on her grandmother's knee. It was published on the front cover of the *Tatler* on 13 April. 'Her Majesty', the magazine noted, 'is devoted to her little granddaughter, who, it will be observed, has the same bright smile as her mother.'[74] A copy of the same photograph would make its way into Princess Elizabeth's night nursery at 145 Piccadilly. The Queen's devotion revealed itself in her particular attentiveness to the little princess's needs. Ahead of the court's removal to Windsor Castle for Easter, she 'personally supervised' the arrangement of Elizabeth's apartments in the Victoria Tower, including ensuring that the nursery was 'always gay with many flowers from the royal gardens'.[75]

Alongside each consignment of pictures by Adams, Alah dutifully enclosed updates on the baby's progress. A note on 8 March was written in the third person as if from Elizabeth herself: 'If Mummy looks into my wide open mouth with a little magnifying glass, she will see my two teeth.'[76] Two more teeth appeared over the next three weeks. Elizabeth learned to say 'By-ee'; she was struggling to raise herself upright on Alah's knee. Queen Mary's letters to her daughter-in-law aimed at conveying the liveliness a black-and-white photograph missed. She described Elizabeth's interest in the King's African grey parrot: 'she was delighted with the parrot Charlotte this morning at breakfast & watched the bird eating pips with an air of absorption'.[77] To Bertie, in early April, reporting a shared car journey with the baby, she noted an interest that would last lifelong: 'your adorable child... was awfully good, giving shrieks of delight at each dog she saw'.[78]

The palace nursery had been redecorated for George and Gerald Lascelles; according to the *Westminster Gazette*, it contained 'toy treasures that formerly amused the Prince of Wales'.[79] Save for breakfast or teatime visits to her grandparents and outings to Hyde Park in a carriage of the Royal Mews, it was here that the baby spent her days. With a degree of affectionate unbending that surprised his second son, the King remarked happily on her enjoyment of her drives, bonneted and accompanied by Alah and, sometimes, as on her first birthday, the Lascelles boys and Alexander Ramsay, seven years older than Elizabeth, a grandson of her godfather, the Duke of Connaught, and afterwards inspiration for the naming of her canary 'Sandy'. 'From her first appearance in public, the affection felt by the nation for the Princess Elizabeth was apparent,' wrote the publishers of a commemorative album of Wills cigarette cards in 1937. Popular affection was manifest that London spring, when the tiny princess, temporarily orphaned like the heroine of a fairy tale, drove royally under the budding, sooty branches of the plane trees. It was Alah, not the baby, who noticed it — in the knots of smiling onlookers who waved at the passing carriage. With practice, and at Alah's prompting, Elizabeth learned to return their greetings; she did not understand their significance. Nor was she aware of her mother's unhappiness, a world away. To the King the duchess wrote simply, 'I have missed her all day and every day.'[80] The princess again appeared on postcards issued by Beagles & Co. One showed her in a carriage in the park. The same photograph was reproduced in the *Sketch*. The princess, the paper told readers, 'is the most discussed and most important of little ladies, and is constantly to be seen driving in the Park, where her appearance rouses great interest'.[81] A postcard issued later in the year depicted first attempts by the passenger-princess to acknowledge bystanders. Beagles captioned it 'The Princess Waving to Admirers'.

No one ever pretended that Elizabeth was an ordinary

baby: not the onlookers in Hyde Park, not the purchasers or recipients of postcards, not the crowds who greeted her parents in Jamaica, Fiji, New Zealand and Australia with three tonnes of presents for the unseen child. While the King and Queen provided carriages and a parrot at home, her parents amassed from wellwishers, civic and corporate bodies across the antipodes a collection of so many 'toys, ornaments, knick-knacks and gewgaws of every imaginable kind... several dolls far larger than the Princess herself, and a whole battalion of giant Teddy bears' that the ship's hold in which they were stowed required a guard of its own.[82] This was the dominions' tribute to the princess they hailed as 'Betty'. Australians' affectionate nickname, never used by 'Betty's' family, reflected the fictionalization of the child whose public life began at birth, and made clear to her parents the scale of popular interest in the baby they missed desperately. 'It is extraordinary how her arrival is so popular out here,' wrote Bertie to his mother. 'Wherever we go cheers are given for her as well & the children write to us about her.'[83]

'Betty' herself was too young to identify this dual existence, public and private, or to recognize wellwishers' bounty or be spoiled by it. At any rate, spoiling was strongly discouraged. Alah's regime imposed a one-at-a-time rule for toys: indeed, Alah's attachment to strict rules was central to her child-rearing. Elizabeth's nursery world would be conspicuously orderly, a habit the child retained into adulthood, and less luxurious than that of a number of children of wealthy parents. It lacked, however, any spartan element, which was alien to her comfort-loving mother. Its apparent straightforwardness by aristocratic standards – journalists praised the unaffectedness and common sense of the royal nursery, its simple food, the duchess's decision to dress Elizabeth in short rather than full-length smocked white cambric frocks – went some way to balancing unusually high levels of public interest.

The Yorks' return in June was marked by the *Illustrated London News* with a full-page photograph of a sturdily smiling Princess Elizabeth under the banner 'The Home "Magnet" of the Duke and Duchess of York'. 'As our photograph shows,' ran the caption, 'she is a charming child.'[84] Dressed as always in white, crossed bare feet emerging from rows of frills, her tousled hair a backlit halo, lips parted in a smile, and wearing round her neck the string of coral beads her mother had worn as a child, the baby presented readers with an image of generic irresistibility. She had been reunited with her parents in the company of all four of her grandparents and members of the Royal Household in the Grand Hall at Buckingham Palace, and only the duchess's spontaneity had imbued this courtly set piece, stage-managed by Queen Mary, with conventional intimacy. Afterwards there had been a balcony appearance, Queen Mary shading mother and baby under her parasol, and another the following day, at the Yorks' new home, 145 Piccadilly. There an oriental carpet draped the balcony balustrade; mother, father and child offered themselves, a secular Holy Family, to waving crowds who raised their hats high in the air. Their public welcome was rapturous; the length of their absence sharpened its intensity. 'Much of the affectionate enthusiasm shown on the return of the royal travellers was doubtless due to sympathetic rejoicing with them on this happy end to [their] separation,' asserted the *Illustrated London News*.[85] This focus on royalty's human dimension, at this stage positive, was to be the dominant note in the relationship between crown and country throughout the baby's life. It was shaped in the first instance by the duchess's commoner birth that enabled the Yorks to present themselves as an idealized version of an 'ordinary' family, centred on 'the universal recognition that their marriage had been a love match';[86] by the Duke of York's limits as a public performer, thanks to his nervous stammer, which encouraged a compensatory celebration of his domestic virtues; and by the Yorks' distance from the throne that exempted journalists from the awestruck tone with which they treated the King and Queen and, in lesser measure, the Prince of Wales. Even the *Times* appeared moved by the straightforward joy of a mother reunited with her child: 'Twice the Duchess, her face radiant with smiles, brought the Princess forward.'[87] After a parting of almost half her baby's life, the duchess's anxiety revealed itself in a letter to Nannie B. Elizabeth, she wrote, 'was nice to me at once, which was a great relief'.[88]

Three days after their return, duke, duchess and fourteen-month-old princess sat again for Marcus Adams. How much her parents had missed her is clear in a photograph of Elizabeth on her own, standing beside a damask-covered stool. In an indigo-printed envelope, postcard-makers Raphael Tuck & Sons issued 'six charming studies from portraits by Marcus Adams' of mother and daughter.[89] The two Elizabeths appeared on the front cover of the *Tatler* at the end of July. A caption stated that the photograph by Adams that the magazine reproduced was 'a quite exclusive portrait of two of the most popular ladies in the land, one of whom might some day be Queen of England'.[90] It was not an outcome that anyone realistically anticipated. Through frequent repetition it played its part in shaping public perceptions of the baby and maintaining her prominence.

In 145 Piccadilly, into which Queen Mary and Lady Strathmore had moved Elizabeth and her nursery staff, the family of three settled on the Yorks' return. To minister to them were a butler, Mr Ainslie, noted for his 'beautiful manners',[91] Mrs Evans the housekeeper and a cook, Mrs Macdonald. An under-butler, two footmen, three housemaids, three kitchen maids, a nightwatchman, a steward's room boy, an odd-job man and a chauffeur provided further help. There was a dresser for the duchess, the duke's valet and their comptroller, Captain Basil Brooke. A boy scout operated the telephones; a clock-winder visited weekly. A young woman from the Black Isle,

Margaret MacDonald, a railwayman's daughter whom Princess Elizabeth learned to call 'Bobo', joined the staff as nursery maid and remained in attendance on her tiny charge for seven decades. Proof that the duchess's manners matched the beauty of Mr Ainslie's, she troubled herself to learn everyone's names. On rarer occasions, she apparently troubled herself 'to visit the still room to revive her Scotch skill in the making of scones and cakes'.[92]

Into the large rooms newly painted went the wedding presents disparaged by Herbert Asquith, removed from White Lodge. To these were added a selection of the presents for Princess 'Betty' that Bertie and Elizabeth had brought back from their tour. Homes were found elsewhere for the two kangaroos, 'two singing canaries and twenty squawking macaws'; only a parrot called Jimmie was installed in the Picadilly mansion. Charities and children's hospitals benefited from the enormous haul.[93] For Elizabeth's day nursery Queen Mary added a present of her own: a picture by Margaret Tarrant, popular illustrator of children's scenes. Tarrant worked chiefly for the Medici Society, which supplied artistic reproductions to nurseries across Britain. Her pictures shaped the aesthetics of a generation; Medici Society prints after Old Masters provided cradle-side exposure to the best-known works of western art. One of the princess's contemporaries remembered the nursery passage of her family's Scottish castle 'lined with brightly coloured Medici prints of Old Masters and coffee-coloured pre-Raphaelite ones'.[94]

Elizabeth's top-floor domain consisted of day and night nurseries, a nursery kitchen and pantry, and bedrooms for Alah and, in time, a governess. Each was furnished simply. All opened off a cherry-carpeted circular landing, lit by a large skylight in the form of a dome. Here, with views down into the stairwell of comings and goings below, was 'plenty of room to push a perambulator, run a race with yourself, or pretend to be a train'.[95] At the front of the house, overlooking Piccadilly and the mounted policeman on the pavement, the day nursery resembled a modest, miniature version of her parents' sitting rooms: armchairs and a two-seater sofa loose-covered in striped chintz; matching curtains with frilled pelmets; a quantity of polished dark wood and, above the open fireplace, eighteenth-century-style wall lights flanking a mirror. Vases of flowers and leather-framed photographs of Bertie and Elizabeth stood on tables and on the chimneypiece. Only her rocking horse and a clothes horse for drying tiny nightdresses spoke explicitly of babyhood. From the outset, the baby princess was being prepared to inhabit her parents' world, with no apparent anticipation of change.

It was an impulse that played a key role in her childhood. The same year, 'with the personal approval of Her Royal Highness', Lady Cynthia Asquith produced a biography of the duchess; she described mother and daughter as 'this enchanting pair of smiling Elizabeths'.[96] An Establishment figure – daughter-in-law of a former prime minister, secretary to the author J. M. Barrie and, like the Duchess of York, the daughter of a Scottish nobleman – Lady Cynthia identified as the reader's long-term hope that 'the daughter may grow to resemble her mother'.[97] No more. It was a conventional and conventionally circumscribed aspiration, and typical of the time; it must have seemed appropriate for an infant for whom only intemperate journalists anticipated glittering prizes. As a child and beyond, Elizabeth would repeatedly experience pressures of this sort: an expectation that she conform to the mould of a royal parent or grandparent, which in due course shaped her approach to monarchy. In this instance half of a 'pair of smiling Elizabeths', and for the foreseeable future the junior partner, she was denied independent identity. Only later did the requirement to resemble her mother constrain her. It originated in a widespread belief that the future would demand no more of her than the modest programme of engagements currently carried out by the duchess, as well as in her father's willing uxoriousness, which transformed the duchess into a paragon.

Over time, the younger Elizabeth's presence inside 145 Piccadilly was felt more strongly – in toys that found their way into the drawing room, with its painted and gilded panelling and Brussels tapestry, or Tommy, the pony on wheels, stabled behind a coromandel screen in the morning room; in her portrait by Edmond Brock hung above the fireplace in her mother's ground-floor sitting room; in a little voice described as crystalline; in the sounds of running feet, audible even from her third-floor sanctuary, and occasional missiles (teddy bears or dolls) dropped from above onto visitors' heads. In the summer of 1927, it was her parents' house. The photographs on a sofa table in the drawing room were of her grandparents and the duke and duchess's golden labradors; the most prominent portrait was of her mother, by Russian artist Savely Sorine, painted the year of the Yorks' marriage and displayed on an easel. Elizabeth's nursery world and the grown-up realm of her parents were physically distinct, albeit the Yorks' affectionate and informal parenting style blurred boundaries between the two (whenever possible both parents shared nursery tea and bathtime). Despite partings, like the Australian tour of 1927, Elizabeth would never experience the everyday emotional severance that characterized the nursery upbringing of many of her contemporaries. None of those in a position to influence her childhood ever anticipated that she would or should. A domestic martinet incapable of expressing affection for his wife and children except in his letters, even the King was concerned for the Yorks' happiness. He wrote to his son on Bertie and Elizabeth's reunion with their baby, 'I trust yr sweet little baby begins to know her parents now & likes them.'[98]

That summer, when the duchess's decidedly light programme of public engagements left her free to concentrate on her husband and her child, Bertie and Elizabeth again departed London for Scotland. In Scotland baby Elizabeth learned to walk. She inspired in her adoring mother a feeling the elder Elizabeth called 'swelled headed[ness]';[99] she continued to enchant her royal grandparents. To Bertie, the King described her as 'more delightful than ever'.[100] His 'pleasure in his little granddaughter was touching', wrote Mabell Airlie; 'Lilibet always came first [of his grandchildren] in his affections.'[101] She in turn loved the gruff old man. The following Christmas, she responded excitedly to carol singers. 'Glad tidings of great joy I bring to you and all mankind,' they sang, and Elizabeth shouted, 'I know who Old Man Kind is!'; she called him 'Grandpa England'.[102] At a fête in the grounds of Balmoral in the summer of 1927, the informal royal procession was led by Princess Elizabeth, pushed in her pram by Alah, followed by her grandparents and her parents. Elizabeth's place of honour in the royal affections would persist. So, too, the habit of Scottish summers, common to royals and Strathmores, the baby's incarceration in a world of her elders and her frequent display to doting crowds.

In the autumn, the infant princess received an unorthodox visitor. Ahead of a charity ball, at which society women were to donate for auction dolls dressed in miniature versions of their own clothes, a toymaker arrived at 145 Piccadilly. As guests of honour at the ball, the Yorks had agreed to present a doll modelled on their daughter. For the lifesize 'Princess Elizabeth' doll 'the maker had been allowed to view his model in her nursery, so as to get the right shade of her hair and eyes'.[103] More conventional portraiture was the marble bas-relief of Elizabeth and her mother completed ahead of her second birthday by sculptor Arthur Walker. This unlovely piece failed to please the King, who 'saw a photograph of the plaque in a newspaper, and in conversation raised the question whether the work did justice to Baby Elizabeth.'[104] Only the duchess's intervention, following an interview between Walker and Royal Academy president Sir Frank Dicksee, prevented the plaque's removal to Buckingham Palace for closer royal inspection.

~∞~

Enchanting photographs of the two-year-old princess emerged from a sitting with Marcus Adams in July 1928. Once again, inspiration lay in the past. In 1857, Queen Victoria had commissioned from a Florentine photographer Leonida Caldesi a study of Elizabeth's godfather Prince Arthur as one of the putti in Raphael's Sistine Madonna. Adams revisited the same conceit. Caldesi's picture of a naked Arthur has a stark, solemn, vulnerable quality. By contrast, Adams's marshmallow-soft images of the plump-cheeked, plump-armed, frilly-frocked Elizabeth, her hair a mop of pale curls, a smile revealing full rows of teeth, suggest the impish vitality that journalists delighted in attributing to her. Of course, images were made public. One postcard was entitled 'A Royal Smile. HRH Princess Elizabeth'. The *Illustrated London News* chose a photograph from the same sitting of Elizabeth standing on a carpet of leaves for its cover on 27 October. As its caption, it borrowed a tag from Cynthia Asquith's biography of the duchess: 'The "Golden-Crested 'Little Friend of all the World'"'. To its readers, the paper pointed out that the princess had 'left behind the days of toddling babyhood'.[105]

Yet she remained uncertain on her feet. At Glamis in August, the duchess introduced her daughter to an upholsterer who had worked at the castle for many years. 'The upholsterer had the honour to be presented to her little Royal Highness, [who]... clasped his huge hand and showed no intention of letting it go.'[106] In September, Elizabeth, the duchess and Alah joined the King and Queen at Balmoral. Photographs in Queen Mary's private albums show the white-frocked toddler watching from the banks of Loch Muick as the King helps drag a large fishing net from the water; Alah stands close by, and Queen Mary bends down as if to steady the princess from behind. In photographs taken in front of the castle, Elizabeth's attention is divided between Charlotte the parrot and Snip, a Cairn terrier given to the King by the Princess Royal. Despite the monarch's attachment to a cigarette in a long holder, King and Queen take it in turns to hover over the diminutive figure. When Cynthia Asquith visited 145 Piccadilly in the autumn, she encountered a determined and talkative toddler. 'I remember,' she wrote later, 'that on this occasion she was still at the stage of having to plant each foot in turn on the same step all the way down the stairs, swaying in her gait.'[107] Childish chatter accompanied her faltering progress: at two and a half Elizabeth had begun to talk about herself in the third person. Asquith noted traits that would endure: her independence, 'a radiant smile', a talent for mimicry, 'lightning powers of observation [for]... anything out of place: an unfastened hook, a lace untied, an obtrusive safety-pin'.[108] She also noted a self-coined nickname, a child's corruption of Elizabeth: 'Lilibet'. This, not Betty, was the name by which her family would know her.

The child described as 'bright as an atom of radium' was present at a reception the Yorks gave for Australian cricketers at 145 Piccadilly;[109] in pristine white silk, she attended the King's Christmas party for workers on the Sandringham estate. 'Baby was too sweet & threw crackers & joined in the fun,' Queen Mary recorded, after the toddler threw at her fellow guests crackers handed to her by her mother.[110] To Bertie, in the aftermath of this Christmas visit, Queen Mary wrote with a grandmother's fondness that would never falter, 'I don't think you & Elizabeth realise what a great joy your child is to us & how we love having her with us now & again in the house, she is so sweet & natural & so amusing.'[111] With no conscious effort, the baby had made devoted admirers of the royal couple who, a generation earlier, had failed so spectacularly as parents. Their view was that of Winston Churchill, who, encountering Elizabeth that year at Balmoral, concluded that she was 'a character' and noted prophetically, 'She has an air of authority and reflectiveness astonishing in an infant.'[112] The result was a closeness to the King and Queen that exposed little Elizabeth from earliest infancy to the formalities of the court, its intricacies of ceremony, etiquette, hierarchy and loyalty; its culture of deference bordering on reverence; its hive-like structure centred on the queen bee figure of the sovereign, in line with George V's view that his 'people wanted him to keep up the state of a King'.[113] Before her second birthday she had already learned to curtsey. Her growing up was twofold: as child and as princess. Only later did she realize it. For the meantime she moved apparently easily between nursery and royal drawing room.

Elizabeth was not present at the Armistice Day ceremony at the Cenotaph on 11 November, at which the King caught what, ten days later, he called a 'feverish cold' and his doctor described as 'mischief in the lung': a streptococcal chest infection that developed into septicaemia, bronchial spasms, blood poisoning and a toxic, pus-filled abscess behind the diaphragm.[114] For weeks George V's life hovered in the balance. Sandringham remained empty that Christmas. The King's subjects prayed for his recovery in churches kept open specially. In London, Bertie and his younger siblings rallied to their mother's side. To her eldest sister, the Duchess of York described the anxiety as 'very wearing to mind & body'.[115]

Elizabeth's time would come during the King's lengthy convalescence. On 9 February 1929, the King left London for Craigweil House on the Sussex coast outside Bognor, loaned to him by Sir Arthur du Cros. At the same time, the Queen made a request of the Duke and Duchess of York that reveals the extent of the royal couple's attachment to their only granddaughter: an invitation to Princess Elizabeth to join them, to cheer the King's recovery. It was Bertie who replied to his mother: both Elizabeths were battling chest infections. Not until the second week of March did the princess make the journey to the seaside – impatiently, according to her mother's description of her 'looking forward wildly to digging in the sand'.[116] Ahead of her arrival, Queen Mary purchased at Burgess's Bazaar in Waterloo Square 'sand moulds' in the shape of bananas, pineapples, oranges and apples. 'I am told', a columnist of the *Sheffield Daily Telegraph* wrote winsomely, 'that soon after Princess Elizabeth arrived at Bognor, she said to the King, "Come and dig with me, Grandpapa. I'll lend you a spade."'[117] Wearing a cardigan against the March chill, Elizabeth spent breezy half-hours on the sand and shingle, accompanied by Alah and her nursery maid; 'much to the King's pleasure', she walked alongside him in his wheelchair on Craigweil's sheltered northwest terrace;[118] when cold winds confined the monarch indoors, he 'spent the morning in his bedroom and had another long chat with his granddaughter'.[119] Her conversation, claimed the *Sunday Dispatch*, contained 'the most amusing and original comments on people and events'.[120] At other times, the princess's 'great joy' was 'to be with the Queen, for whom she has a very tender affection'.[121] Postcard issues inevitably recorded the visit: the princess with her grandparents in Craigweil's garden, the princess alone making sandcastles. The latter was entitled 'Our little Princess', a tag that suggests a nation's affection and pride. While she was away, her nursery was redecorated. 'She will return to a suite with cream woodwork, soft blue walls, rose carpets, and chairs covered with pink and blue chintz. A grandfather clock has been introduced so that the little Princess can learn to tell the time,' enthused a writer at pains to make clear that, in the princess's surroundings, comfort and instruction combined.[122] After her seaside demonstration of her tonic qualities, reported in newspapers the length and breadth of her grandfather's kingdom, Elizabeth would return to London with prominence and prestige enhanced.

❧

At the time of Elizabeth's birth, a gossip-columnist called 'Mariegold' had prophesied 'plenty of adulation in store for the fourth lady in the land as soon as she is old enough to receive it'.[123] The full extent of this adulation, which began in the cradle and revealed itself months later in three tonnes of presents from New Zealanders and Australians, seems first to have troubled her parents in the spring of 1929. While Elizabeth remained at Windsor Castle with her grandparents, the Duke and Duchess were carrying out engagements in Edinburgh. The Scots' reception was particularly enthusiastic, the absence of 'our dear Princess Elizabeth' noted with regret. 'It almost frightens me that the people should love her so much,' the duchess wrote to Queen Mary. 'I suppose that it is a good thing, and I hope that she will be worthy of it, poor little darling!'[124] The idea that the public might take at face value Cynthia Asquith's description of Elizabeth as the 'Little Friend of All the World' caused her mother belated disquiet. At intervals it would continue to do so.

The extent of the duchess's anxiety on this occasion is not clear. Her own childhood outside the royal fold provided a benchmark for measuring the clamour of Elizabeth's upbringing. Press accounts exaggerated, like the American columnist who claimed 'the child spends her life in the limelight... A great crowd cheers whenever she appears. When she goes out with her nurse, guards and other soldiers stand at attention. She lifts up her little hand, which means they may relax.'[125] In the lush distortions were partial truths. Newspapers described 145 Piccadilly as 'the women's Mecca': 'All through the Season, indeed, nearly all the year round – her admirers wait outside the Duke of York's house in the hope of seeing her go in or out.'[126] The duchess's letter to her mother-in-law identified perennial challenges of royal life: the parent's powerlessness to lessen public fascination with her child; a requirement that the child merit the 'love' so indiscriminately lavished upon her by strangers. For her part, inevitably, the Queen had no answers.

It was a period in which aristocrats remained the celebrities of the day and members of the royal family the ultimate cynosure. Although the Yorks were less prominent than the Prince of Wales and, according to interwar biographer Hector Bolitho, 'still able to guard their domestic life from the splendour and fuss associated with high station',[127] as the King's only granddaughter and his first 'royal' grandchild, Elizabeth occupied from birth a unique position. Nothing in her life was too trivial for publication: her appearance, surrounds or nursery routine; antics labelled 'dainty' or 'rogueish'; party frocks in 'sapphire blue', 'primrose yellow or delicious flower-like pink';[128] her car sickness, taste for toffee, enjoyment of splashing in puddles; her 'shining', 'twinkling', 'bubbling', 'sunny', 'vital', 'engaging', 'quicksilver' personality. All was reported with treacly obsessiveness in a format that balanced celebration of her liveliness with an insistence on goodness (or its contemporary near-synonym 'sweetness'); and Elizabeth was four when her first biographer suggested that 'after a while, Princess Elizabeth will be aware that the eyes of all the other children are upon her, that they are looking to her with love and admiration – as to an Example'.[129] 'Because our likenesses seldom appeared in the Press, we were not often recognised on the street,' stated Elizabeth's uncle, the Prince of Wales, of the previous generation of royal children.[130] Postcards, cinema newsreels and, above all, photographs in newspapers and magazines lessened Elizabeth's chances of anonymity; commentary like Ring's imposed on her an expectation of exemplary behaviour, even as a four-year-old. The duke and duchess made what may have seemed a pragmatic compromise in collaborating with writers like Cynthia Asquith and Beryl Poignand ('Anne Ring'), whom the duchess had known since childhood; both submitted their manuscripts for royal approval. The outcome was a higher level of accuracy within the cloying bilge and, of course, a spur to the curiosity they sought to slake.

Contemporaries, however, judged successful the Yorks' efforts to bring up a child worthy of public adoration and unspoiled by attention. 'If Princess Elizabeth were old enough to have her head turned by the absolute adulation of a whole nation it would have happened long ago,' the *Tatler* commented on her sixth birthday.[131] 'The British are wise, and British Royalty... is particularly wise,' was the conclusion reached by one American. He argued that the modesty of George V and Queen Mary, their personal lack of arrogance, meant that 'Princess Elizabeth is safer from spoiling than the average rich American son or daughter'.[132] British readers would have seconded this flattering view. That the princess invited such approbation testified to the emotional anchor the Yorks were seen to provide for their daughter and Alah's stern common sense. For the moment, her innate sunniness enabled Elizabeth to take as they came the extraordinary trappings of her childhood world. The verdict of *Time* magazine, in 1929, that 'she does not know that she is but three removes from the Throne', was correct and, in the short term, remained so.[133] In 1932, a visitor to the Royal Academy described her portrait by Edmond Brock, painted when she was five, as 'quite devoid of self-consciousness'.[134]

Public interest – waving onlookers in Hyde Park, worshippers at 'the women's Mecca', the nosey parkers who pressed their faces between the railings of Hamilton Gardens behind 145 Piccadilly, to watch the princess at play – was simply a fact of her life. On at least one occasion, newspapers suggest, she demonstrated that, as a young child, acceptance was second nature to her. In February 1930, Elizabeth was playing with a friend, Lady Mairi Vane-Tempest-Stewart. Nearly five years separated Elizabeth and the older Lady Mairi, a daughter of the 7th Marquess of Londonderry. An acquaintanceship between their parents and the proximity of their gardens supplied grounds for the girls' friendship: the gardens of palatial Londonderry House on Park Lane were visible from 145 Piccadilly. 'Princess Elizabeth takes a friendly interest in the people who watch her playing in the garden,' reported the *Lancashire Evening Post*. 'The other day she adopted the attitude of one who had a pleasant surprise for them. She ran away and came back leading Lady Mary [sic] by the hand and brought her proudly to the railings. "This is Mary," she said. So then they all knew one another.'[135] On the surface an insignificant vignette, possibly fabricated, it encapsulated the openness of character and instinctive courtesy on which, accurately, writers insisted for the princess-exemplar.

∽✦∽

By 1930, the press had a new story about the golden-haired princess whose buoyant spirits had aided her grandfather's recovery: Elizabeth was growing up. Outside fairy tales, even princesses cannot halt time. For Elizabeth, an only child surrounded by adults, the process began by emulation. 'She always loved pretending to be grown up,' Cynthia Asquith wrote. '[She] used often to play at going into a small cupboard and holding, through an imaginary telephone, long conversations in tones that were a quaint blend of all the grown-up voices and intonations familiar to her. She also loved impersonating her mother at the dressing table, and liked to engage some super to act the lady's maid and hand her hair-pins, powder puff, et cetera.'[136] She enjoyed raids on Lady Cynthia's handbag, removing lozenges, loose change;

'spectacles were popped on to the tiny nose... the mirror ogled, and face powder dexterously applied'.[137] Marcus Adams photographed her on her mother's knee. The two Elizabeths wear similar floral prints, and one of the duchess's pearl necklaces encircles both their necks, binding them together. In May, the *Yorkshire Post* reported an anecdote about Elizabeth's love of the telephone. The paper's concern was not the story's improbability, but its evidence of ladylike politesse, key attribute for a princess. 'Princess Elizabeth is already showing charming independence,' it announced, and the shift from roguishness to independence indicated her abandonment of early childhood. 'When the news reached her that the Hon. Mrs David Bowes-Lyon (her mother's sister-in-law) had just had a baby, she went to the telephone and herself rang up to send congratulations.'[138] Most of all, it was the summer trip to Scotland that offered four-year-old Elizabeth opportunities for demonstrations of maturity. For the first time, on arrival at Glamis station, the princess made the short journey from the platform to the station exit, across the railway bridge, holding her mother's hand. 'The trip across the bridge was by way of an adventure for Princess Elizabeth, who has always hitherto been carried across the bridge by Stationmaster Buchan,' reported the *Forfar Herald*.[139] The paper underlined its point: 'on this occasion she was treated as quite a grown-up Princess, and successfully negotiated the steps herself, aided only by the clasp of her mother's hand.' Not content with scaling railway bridges, the following day Elizabeth navigated the business of purchase and payment in a local bookshop. It was an incident ideally suited to the press's new narrative. 'Princess Elizabeth yesterday demonstrated in decided fashion that she is no longer the baby princess when she visited Forfar on a shopping visit with her grandmother the Countess of Strathmore.' The report emphasized the princess's good nature and financial good sense; it drew attention to her knowledge and love of nature. After 'smiling sweetly', she asked to be shown books about animals. 'She examined numerous books with an expert eye, and several were rejected with the remark, "I have seen that already." At length one met with her approval but the Princess's Scottish blood, perhaps, made her cautious and before deciding on a purchase she asked the price.'[140]

The little princess's passion for dogs and ponies, her sorties with her grandmother into Forfar to buy books or, at Peter Reid's Rock Shop in Castle Street, chocolate or sweets, as well as a certain vigilance over pocket money, were characteristics to bring her closer to her grandfather's subjects, and more than a press invention. At the British Industries Fair at Olympia, in February 1931, her mother chose for Elizabeth an inexpensive present of 'a little toy Aberdeen terrier, with a Stewart tartan bow'; she also bought her a child-size blackboard and an easel of a sort popular in nurseries nationwide.[141] But in so many ways Elizabeth's was far from an ordinary childhood. On 22 May 1929, she sent a cheerful note to her mother in Edinburgh, written for her by Alah: 'Do come here [Windsor Castle] and see the soldiers and the band I am very well and very busy.'[142] Among photographs in Queen Mary's albums, taken that month, are pictures of Elizabeth in the castle quadrangle. In one, a tiny figure, with neither nurse nor grandparent close by, salutes the commanding officer of a company of Guards. The soldiers and their band are her grandfather's, her ringside position privileged, but the salute must have been a daunting requirement for a toddler. At Windsor on her fourth birthday again there were soldiers, again a salute for the princess; there were crowds of onlookers and her Lascelles cousins for company. Spectators noted a new way of dressing her hair, the 'little curls all over her head... transformed into large shining golden waves'.[143] The day's events began at half past ten, when soldiers appeared for the changing of the guard. 'Simultaneously the Princess came out into the Grand

Quadrangle with her small boy cousins, now Lord Lascelles and the Hon Gerald Lascelles. After the ceremony she went over to the pipers and admired them, then she returned to her place, and as the Guards marched back to the barracks, very gravely she stood to attention to take the officer's salute.'[144] Next the birthday princess had to acknowledge the 'hundreds of laughing and cheering people who were thronging the Norman Gate and St George's Gate'. She walked towards them and waved; she blew kisses. Only then was she wheeled away in her perambulator. 'Princess Elizabeth... is never allowed to take part in public ceremonies,' the duchess's lady-in-waiting, Lady Helen Grahame, had replied to an invitation in July 1929.[145] In the infant Elizabeth's life, the line between public and private would prove infinitely permeable, and few 'private' ceremonies could have been as public as Elizabeth's annual birthday parade of Guardsmen, with its attendant crowds clustering the castle gates.

Among fourth birthday presents from her father to his 'adorable Lilibet' were another two pearls to thread onto the thin platinum chain he had given her on her first birthday.[146] Like much in her childhood, the tradition of a daughter of the royal family receiving two pearls each birthday was traceable to Queen Victoria; precedent rooted the recipient among descendants of the great queen. The little Elizabeth who played at pretending to be her mother, coiffed, powdered and jewelled, attended by an imaginary lady's maid, wore her necklace proudly. Dutifully she played with the building blocks given to her by Queen Mary: they were made from fifty different woods garnered from across the Empire. Three months after her first riding lesson, in the private riding school in Buckingham Palace Mews, neither present could rival the King's offering that year. This was Elizabeth's first pony, a Shetland called Peggy, about nine hands and 'full of latent mischief'.[147] Peggy and her rider inspired a new exhibit at Madame Tussaud's, unveiled in the summer: a bare-headed Elizabeth astride a dark pony and attended by a groom. 'This, set on a stand to itself, drew the biggest crowds,' the *Daily Mirror* reported. '"Isn't she sweet" was the general criticism in many dialects.'[148]

～～～

In the summer of 1930 there were pressing reasons for this new narrative of pony-loving maturity imposed on Elizabeth. For several months the Duchess of York had played no part in the public life of the royal family. Pregnancy explained her withdrawal. Elizabeth's period as an only child was drawing to a close. A new maturity and the impulse to coddle and tend implicit in her love for dogs and ponies were appropriate characteristics for an elder sister. At stake was her status as the highest-ranking of the King's grandchildren, his heir in the second generation. 'Should the new arrival be a boy he will stand third in the direct succession to the throne, ranking after the Prince of Wales and the Duke of York,' explained the *Western Gazette* on 8 August 1930.[149] It was, as the *Gazette* stated, the 'position at present occupied by Princess Elizabeth'.

CHAPTER II

'Two folded roses, hush'd and still,
Buds of a royal spring'

❧❧❧

THE BABY, OF COURSE, was a girl. Nameless for three weeks, after George V vetoed the Yorks' suggestion of 'Ann Margaret', she was born after a lengthy delay at Glamis Castle on 21 August 1930. Newspapermen imagined the aftermath: 'The Duchess, with a happy smile on her face, listened to the heavy rain beating on the mullioned windows of the ancient Royal castle, and flashes of summer lightning lit up the sky.'[1] A purpose underpinned this whimsy: to ward off any suggestion of parental disappointment in the birth of a second daughter. It was not quite true.

Certainly the duchess had suspected her unborn baby of being another girl. To Queen Mary she wrote on 21 July, 'I... only hope that our new daughter (?) will not delay <u>too</u> long.'[2] A letter from the duke to his wife suggests both had hoped for a son: 'I would have liked a boy & you would too I know.' He contented himself that the new baby was a playmate for

Elizabeth.[3] Queen Mary, arch dynast, faltered in her response. As in all things she was guided by the King's reaction, his delighted view that one could play longer with girls than boys. The duke's conclusion that 'we still have plenty of time, we are still young' may have been intended to lessen his wife's self-reproach; alternatively it points to the couple's tentative awareness of the possibility that responsibility for the next royal generation lay with them. At thirty-six the Prince of Wales appeared no closer to marriage; his newest mistress, Thelma, Viscountess Furness, was married to her second husband. Neither Bertie nor Elizabeth had forgotten a conversation with the King during his convalescence the previous year, in which his father had told Bertie, 'You'll see, your brother will never become King.' 'We both looked at each other and thought "nonsense",' Elizabeth remembered afterwards.[4] Nonsense or not, for the present it was their own children who peopled the line of succession. The public was satisfied that it should be so. Following the birth of the baby, who, on 30 October, was christened Margaret Rose, the *Morning Post* stated unequivocally, 'Let us say that the people of this Realm are happy in the birth of a second daughter to the Duchess of York. Thus the succession to the throne, already amply secure, is strengthened.'[5]

For Princess Elizabeth, the birth of her sister brought changes within the nursery and beyond. Monthly nurse Nannie B returned to the Yorks, again to be replaced on her departure by Alah, with Elizabeth's care now chiefly Bobo MacDonald's responsibility. On the washstand in the night nursery at 145 Piccadilly appeared a second flower-patterned ewer and basin for washing: like the belongings of the three bears in the story of Goldilocks, baby Margaret's was appropriately smaller than Elizabeth's. Equally significantly, Margaret's arrival encouraged predictions about Elizabeth's future that had first been voiced at her own birth. 'By [Margaret's] birth,' ran one, 'the chances are increased that some day, in the natural sequence of events, another Queen will wear the British Crown.'[6] With the continuing absence of a male heir, a technicality in the laws of succession provided a diversion. 'The question arises... as to whether the law gives a sister precedence over another sister or whether they become co-heirs. It has been generally assumed that of the two sisters the elder would be heir as in the case of two brothers, but this assumption is one that might be challenged.'[7] George V requested clarification; to his pleasure, precedence was granted to Princess Elizabeth. To those who took note of such things, the Yorks' difficulty in conceiving – their three-year wait for Elizabeth, the four-year interval before Margaret's birth – cast doubts on the probability of a third pregnancy and a son to displace Elizabeth.

From the outset, Elizabeth delighted in her sister. Queen Mary described her as 'enchanted' by the four-days-old Margaret; 'even though not allowed to wash the baby', she watched her in her bath.[8] Elizabeth, ran claims, had a new game called 'copying baby': 'it consists of solemnly imitating on a favourite doll all Nurse Beever's ministrations to the younger Princess'.[9]

Elizabeth was ready for companionship. An anecdote recorded by Cynthia Asquith, of a curly-haired boy invited to Windsor Castle to play, demonstrated her enjoyment of the company of other children. 'Attracted by his irrepressible fuzz of curls, she instantly took off her gloves to – what she called – "feel his hair". This personal inspection having successfully broken any ice... she then led him up to Mr Baldwin [the prime minister]... and said, "Quite nice, isn't he?"'[10] Baby Margaret provoked a similar response. 'That wonderful child Elizabeth is very excited,' wrote a guest at Glamis. '[She] thought first of all that it was a wonderful Dolly & then discovered that it was alive. She then took each of the three doctors by the hand & said "I want to introduce you to my baby sister."'[11] As when she introduced Mairi Vane-Tempest-Stewart to watching crowds in

Hamilton Gardens, the princess's instinctive, if formal, courtesy guided her behaviour. At the end of the first week of September, the duke took Elizabeth with him to Balmoral, leaving behind at Glamis the duchess and their baby. At Elizabeth's dictation he sent a letter to his wife that ended with a page of pencil kisses: half 'For Mummy', half 'For our new baby'.[12] The letter itself did not refer to Margaret: instead Elizabeth related the excitement of feeding biscuits to the King's terrier Snip at teatime. In a second letter, two days later, Elizabeth wrote that she was looking forward to her coming return to 'my Mummy & my baby', but it was the duchess that she admitted she had 'been missing... very much indeed'.[13]

Her parents pre-empted jealousy of the new arrival by providing Elizabeth with a series of diversions. At Glamis they organized a children's garden party, with Elizabeth as hostess, twenty guests, balloons and hide-and-seek; it was Elizabeth's idea that the afternoon culminated in a visit to the nursery to see Margaret. The following week, Elizabeth played hostess to a children's house party. The duchess's nephews and nieces loomed large among her guests, including her sister Rose's children Mary and Granville Leveson-Gower, and daughters of her brother Jock, who had died of pneumonia at the young age of forty-three earlier in the year. Hide-and-seek was again on the programme, 'and all manners of out-of-the-way hiding places have been found in the long stone corridors and the sombre rooms'.[14] A week later, more playmates arrived at the castle: Andrew and Jean Elphinstone, children of Elizabeth's godmother Mary, another of the duchess's sisters.

A circle of friends dominated by her aristocratic Strathmore cousins represented narrow social exposure for the little princess. Until her position as heiress to the throne was confirmed, this was the world in which her parents anticipated her spending her life, with little expectation of contact outside this gilded coterie. With its possibility of rough and tumble and cheerful informality, it provided a counterweight of sorts to Elizabeth's royal experiences. Already Elizabeth was aware of another world outside the castle's gates. On walks with Alah in the village, she had asked to stop to watch children in the school playground.[15] Alah humoured her; the princess looked on. For the most part, it was she herself who was the object of attention. Even in distant Forfar, watchers jostled. While Elizabeth chose books in Mr Shepherd's bookshop, 'a large crowd of townspeople and children... gathered round the car, clamouring for a glimpse of the girl Princess, and when she emerged from the bookseller's with her grandmother, they followed her along the street to the confectioners'.[16] Status and celebrity transformed little Elizabeth into a spectacle to be glimpsed and followed; 'clamouring' has a predatory ring. Even at the age of four, 'normal' social contact was impossible.

In the short term her promotion to elder sister status did not overwhelm entirely her high spirits or her 'roguish' mischief. She was discovered, on a wet afternoon that September, in her father's dressing room. To hand was an empty brilliantine bottle. 'Her golden curls were dripping and on top of the dressing table sat four dolls and a Teddy Bear similarly treated.'[17] New photographs of Elizabeth taken by Marcus Adams on 22 January 1931, her first sitting in over a year, suggest no lessening of her puckishness. Toothily she grins. She is bright-eyed, dressed as always for the camera in a frou frou of pale frills.[18]

∼✸∼

Elizabeth's next visit to the Children's Studio took place only a fortnight later, on 2 February. On this occasion, she was photographed with her mother and baby Margaret. It was an unremarkable image that suggests Adams's struggle to evolve a composition with any of the magic of his earlier 'Raphael' pictures, a challenge he would not fully resolve for several years. With moderate success, he photographed all four Yorks early in the summer. One of the pictures from that sitting, of the duchess with her daughters, was released as a postcard.

Happiness in their daughters and as parents drew the Yorks to Marcus Adams with such frequency. Resulting images undoubtedly contributed to the public's view of them as an ideal family. Traditional trappings of royal portraiture were set aside in favour of photographs that celebrated the affection the couple felt for one another and their children. In part it was a choice that reflected their reluctance to consider themselves potential sovereigns, despite the King's prediction during his convalescence. 'It always irritates me, this assumption that the Prince of Wales will not marry – he is quite young and it is rude to him in a way too,' the duchess wrote to her lady-in-waiting.[19] She was also determined to recreate for her daughters the uncomplicated happiness of her own childhood, including loving ties between parents and children and the bonds of feeling of the Bowes-Lyon siblings. In a memo she entitled 'Hints to Bertie in case of anything happening to me', written at some point after Margaret's birth, all three of her 'hints' aimed at maximizing affection and 'delightful trust' between children and parents.[20] 'Please give [Lilibet] the enclosed from Margaret Rose – she held the pencil for the kisses specially for Lilibet. Will you give it to her & tell her this?' the duchess wrote to her husband, when Margaret was three weeks old.[21] From the outset her aim was her daughters' closeness.

On the surface the unemphatic plushness of Adams's pictures - the duchess's pearl necklaces, the princesses' frothy frocks – lay within the grasp of many wealthier middle-class British families. In the early 1930s, the Yorks' espousal of polished ordinariness made sense, given their remoteness from the throne and, measured against those of the King or the Prince of Wales, the modesty of their means. In troubling economic circumstances, following the stock market crash of 1929, the impulse was tactful and shrewd (and perfectly safe, since few contemporaries were ever likely to treat them as ordinary); caricaturist Osbert Lancaster identified at this period 'a nasty feeling about the upper classes' among those less fortunate.[22] Such understatement was in line with the couple's requirement that Elizabeth give up abandoned and surplus toys to children's charities. On 27 February 1931, the *Rugby Advertiser* carried ticket information for a children's dance and party in aid of Hamilton (Children's) Home in the town. 'One outstanding feature of this party will be the sale of HRH Princess Elizabeth's toys, by Lord Cromwell,' the paper announced.[23] If an approving public noticed that the Yorks' 'ordinariness', courtesy of Marcus Adams, was rather closer to perfection – never a hair out of place, no glimpse of fatigue or frayed tempers – few protested. For the foreseeable future, the joint purpose of duke, duchess and their two princesses was to embody make-believe.

Alah was responsible for Elizabeth's early education. For two hours each morning the nursery was transformed into a schoolroom; using picture books, letter blocks and beaded strings, Elizabeth was taught to read and spell and count. A workman-like approach was encouraged. Elizabeth wore a morning uniform of 'printed cotton overall dresses with capacious pockets and pearl buttons down the front'; 'silk "affairs" in flower designs' were saved for afternoons, for outings, for tea with her parents.[24] 'Apt and interested', on the cusp of her fifth birthday she learned quickly.[25] Tidbits offered to family friends quashed any suggestion of excessive enjoyment of her lessons; intellectualism inspired widespread mistrust, not least among her family. Instead, Elizabeth's diligence was attributed to a nascent sense of duty, an explanation that, variously applied, would become a cornerstone of her public image and afterwards defined her approach to sovereignty. 'When sums become a little tedious, or the spelling lesson seems a little long, Mrs Knight... has only to remind her that no real Princess could grow up without knowing how to count and spell, and the Royal pupil immediately becomes attentive.'[26] Her lessons formed a new daily routine. Claims that this was maintained whatever the Yorks' whereabouts served as further evidence, despite her own lack of formal education, of the duchess's sensible parenting, her understanding that 'a Princess who, later on, will have to take her share in public life, must have a training from childhood'.[27] Again, it was not quite true.

Alongside lessons in reading, writing and maths were French lessons. As proof of the up-to-dateness of the royal nursery, a set of gramophone records provided Elizabeth's instruction. Her progress was described as 'rapid'. Soon, it was claimed, she was able to spell 'chat' and 'jardin' as freely as she did 'cat' and 'garden'. She performed these feats for her grandparents. Tactfully overlooking the King's own limits as a linguist, newspapers pronounced him 'especially pleased to hear her repeating her latest Linguaphone lesson from the gramophone'.[28] There were piano lessons: Elizabeth's teacher was Mabel Lander, whose other pupils included the Russian concert pianist Prince George Chavchavadze. The first lesson consisted largely of 'screwing the music stool up and down'.[29] Published accounts preferred to focus on evidence of Elizabeth's aptitude, and in time princess and pianist became friends, Elizabeth referring to Miss Lander as 'Goosey'. When she was six, Elizabeth fared less well with a miniature set of bagpipes.

At the same time, Elizabeth was trained in tidiness and thrift. Bobo MacDonald encouraged her to save ribbons and wrapping paper, smoothed and carefully folded into a box. Alah concentrated on Elizabeth's toys and her clothes. She arranged the little girl's big mahogany wardrobe so that frocks hung

alongside their corresponding coats and hats, with matching
shoes placed immediately below. 'To impress on her the need
for tidiness, Princess Elizabeth has to assist her nurse to put
her clothes away every time they are changed.'[30] In this, too,
Alah found Elizabeth a willing, even zealous pupil. Later, her
governess Marion Crawford labelled her 'a very neat child',
who 'would hop out of bed several times a night to get her
shoes quite straight, her clothes arranged just so'.[31] Among
her favourite toys were horses on wheels, of which the two
princesses eventually acquired more than thirty. Every night,
these were 'stabled' on the nursery landing, placed with absolute
precision, as tidy as the shoes beneath the night nursery chair,
tack gleaming, coats smoothed.

The latest stage in Elizabeth's 'training', Alah's lessons
formed only one element of her days. Her life continued to
include features and events that marked Elizabeth out from
the most privileged of her peers. Many were the result of time
spent with her royal grandparents: Christmas at Sandringham
in Norfolk, Easter at Windsor, summer visits to Balmoral,
where Elizabeth 'rejoice[d] in the freedom [given] to her
exuberant spirits' and respite from her goldfish bowl world with
its curious onlookers.[32] At Christmas 1931, she shared dancing
lessons, or 'hops', with her mother and Queen Mary in the
Sandringham ballroom; all three learned to polka. Afterwards,
as she lay in her bed, according to an authorized account,
'she heard the stirring strains of the bagpipes, for the King's
Scotch piper always came into the dining room at the end of
dinner in full Highland dress and walked with swinging kilts
round and round the table playing his wild music.'[33] In June,
when the Queen took Elizabeth to the Royal Tournament at
Olympia, they were escorted by uniformed officials, their visit
commemorated in a full-page *Country Life* frontispiece. That
autumn, the two princesses received their own mention in the
Court Circular, the formal record of the royal family's activity.

Then, as now, it did not fall to many children's lots that their comings and goings were reported as matters of note in *The Times*. Still the duchess's friend Anne Ring asserted in October 1932 that Elizabeth knew 'nothing at all of that other side of her life, that aspect of herself as a Royal Princess'.[34] In the face of unrelenting public attention, the claim was untenable. Unlikely, too, following her parents' present to her of her own stationery, blue paper stamped with an 'E' below a coronet, and a little bag, like a reticule, also decorated with a coroneted monogram.[35]

Beyond the confines of home and family life, the little princess had another existence. This was her life as a figment of the collective imagination, a 'sunny-haired figure of charm, a nation's idol': the public's 'Princess Elizabeth'.[36] Attitudes towards this golden child lay outside her control and mostly, at this stage, her ken. This 'Princess Elizabeth' was an imaginary creation, invented and reinvented by gushing journalists and Marcus Adams, a metaphor for infant perfection, an opiate, and her name was bandied in connection with wide-ranging enterprises: charitable, commercial, patriotic. The Artificial Silk Exhibition at the Victoria & Albert Museum in February 1932 included a commercial display by Edmund Halstead Ltd of 'Princess Elizabeth' taffetas: a design of 'a moss rose spray in pastel shades for children's and lingerie wear in 100 per cent artificial silk'.[37] The following month, at the Queen's Hospital for Children at Bethnal Green, the Duchess of York opened a new ward of twenty-six cots for children under the age of five, the Princess Elizabeth Ward. The same week the naming of a new-found territory in the Antarctic was formalized. Sir Douglas Mawson, leader of the expedition that discovered it, called it Princess Elizabeth Land. On the other side of the globe, the princess made her first appearance on a postage stamp. The six cent stamp issued in Newfoundland, in Canada, a territory of her grandfather's far-flung Empire, featured an image of Elizabeth based on a photograph taken by Adams in November

1929. It was framed by drawings of an English rose and the Scottish thistle. Unsought by the child-princess, such tributes augmented her prominence. Implicitly they contributed to the expectation that she be exemplary.

This ongoing blurring of her public and private worlds was made clear during Elizabeth's parents' visit to Cardiff in March 1932. On behalf of their daughter the duke and duchess took formal receipt of a remarkable present. Y Bwthyn Bach to Gwellt ('the little cottage with the straw roof') was a child-size, thatched and white-stuccoed play house, a sixth birthday present to the princess from the people of Wales. To her parents Cardiff's lord mayor explained, 'The inception of the idea of this gift house is to be found partly in a desire to express in a concrete manner the loving loyalty and affection which the people of the Principality feel for the little Princess. In no less a degree it was felt that the house should in the fullest manner represent and further the arts and industries of the Welsh nation and give them the impetus which they needed and deserved.'[38] Elizabeth's present was in equal measure a commercial undertaking: its makers gambled on the alchemy of royal association.

With four rooms, a small hall and landing, 'well heated and lit, equipped with bells, telephone and every modern device for cooking and housekeeping', Y Bwthyn Bach was the perfect plaything.[39] It included an electric fire, a grandfather clock and, in the bathroom, a heated towel rail. Above a chimneypiece hung a portrait of the duchess by Margaret Lindsay Williams, who had previously painted Queen Alexandra and the Prince of Wales. Crested and monogrammed linen covered the half-tester bed, there was scented soap beside the basin, and the design of the curtains' blue chintz had been shrunk to the scale of the diamond-pane windows. In the kitchen cupboards the china was of buttercup yellow; the bookcases housed Beatrix Potter's tales, including one in Welsh. Everything worked, from the ticking clock to the wireless set; the house had its own fire insurance policy and miniature deed of gift. Y Bwthyn Bach was a costly and extravagant present for a child whose world included as a matter of course every material blessing; on the dressing table were engraved silver brushes. At a moment of considerable economic hardship in Wales's mining and industrial communities, it was a shop window for a workforce struggling to survive and its makers took pains that the gift was publicized as widely as possible; newspapers referred to 'the Welsh cottage'. 'The Duchess and I are especially pleased to know that the house should have been the means of raising funds for the relief of sickness and the terrible distress which has been so prevalent in these hard times,' the duke informed its donors.[40] Elizabeth did not receive her present until the middle of May. By then it had gone on show in a handful of locations between Cardiff and London. Its last stop before handover was the Empire Hall of the Ideal Home Exhibition. Its 100,000 visitors contributed £5,000 to charitable causes.

A doll's house version of the cottage, by Lines Bros, appeared in toy shops in 1933; Queen Mary claimed that Elizabeth had set a fashion for doll's houses. Each room was wired for lighting and included a tiny battery-powered bulb. These miniature Y Bwthyn Bachs gave lucky children across Britain tantalizing glimpses of a small corner of the princess's world. To these were added, in the years ahead, numerous photographs of Elizabeth at the cottage, sometimes alone, sometimes with Margaret, her parents, her grandparents. Like Adams's photographic portraits, Wales's gift came to symbolize the Yorks' cultivated ordinariness: a setting for family life on a diminutive scale, perfect in every detail, unshowy and necessarily informal given the restrictions of its size. Even the house's appearance, a country cottage that resembled the mock-Tudor semis of inter-war suburbia, chimed with contemporary aspirations. In the public imagination its royal chatelaine became an image of the wholesomeness of British family life, an association that would prove troublesome sixty years later with the unravelling of her own children's family lives. Less strenuously publicized by the Yorks was the present that stood in front of Elizabeth's thatched cottage at the Ideal Home Show: a miniature car 'worked on the pedal system despite its powerful-looking exterior', the princess's very own Rolls Royce.[41]

❦

At first, Elizabeth played in the cottage alone, dusting and washing up; Margaret was too young to join in her games. In the nursery she played schoolroom games alone, too, taking Alah's role as instructress, toys as her pupils, using the blackboard and easel bought for her by her mother. According to one account, 'when there [was] no other "class" to be had, a woolly toy terrier with a large tartan bow... ha[d] to sit up and be "instructed"'.[42] Instead Margaret joined her sister in her daily carriage rides in Hyde Park and Windsor Great Park; accompanied by Alah and Bobo MacDonald, she joined her on walks to see the ducks in St James's Park. These outings continued to attract interest, with no detail apparently too trivial for comment. Even a new hat with 'a shady [brim] of buttercup yellow', or rumoured fittings for new riding clothes ('brown breeches with a little velveteen jacket and cap'), merited mention.[43] Beagles issued a postcard of five-year-old Elizabeth driving in a carriage, dressed in a fur-trimmed coat and beret; opposite her, a bonneted Margaret sat on Alah's knee. Beagles captioned it 'a charming snapshot of the children of TRH the Duke and Duchess of York taken at Windsor whilst out for a drive'. In 1932, charm was their birthright as princesses. Photographers and postcard publishers were the price they paid for publicity they did not seek.

Elizabeth's socializing continued to be confined mostly to

members of her family. Bar Margaret, her principal contact with her own generation was her Lascelles cousins and, in lesser measure, the duchess's many nephews and nieces; each autumn in Scotland she attended the birthday party of her second cousin, James, Master of Carnegie, like Elizabeth a great-grandchild of Edward VII. In October 1931, she was one of twelve bridesmaids at the wedding in Sussex of Queen Mary's niece, Lady May Cambridge. Her fellow bridesmaids included members of the extended royal family: Princess Ingrid of Sweden, a granddaughter of Elizabeth's godfather the Duke of Connaught, and Princess Sybilla of Saxe-Coburg-Gotha, a great-granddaughter of Queen Victoria. From childhood this sorority of princesses has played a smaller role in Elizabeth's life than those of her predecessors. Most of her close friends have been British rather than royal, an outcome shaped in the first instance by her non-royal mother's preference for her own family. Preoccupied by royal genealogy, Queen Mary surely unpicked for her granddaughter the cat's cradle of her relationship to the other bridesmaids. Learning to be royal, and to recognize herself as such, was an aspect of Elizabeth's upbringing, and a significant contribution to her development on her grandmother's part. Elizabeth also played with the children of aristocratic London neighbours, like Lady Mairi Vane-Tempest-Stewart, or the Hon. Mary Anna Sturt, a god-daughter of the duchess's, whose parents' London house was at 13 Bruton Street. In May 1932, the return from the country to 144 Piccadilly of the Yorks' next-door neighbours, Lord-in-waiting Viscount Allendale and his family, was reported from Elizabeth's perspective: 'This will be good news for Princess Elizabeth. The Allendale children [the Honourable Wentworth, Ela and Richard Beaumont] are her playmates during the London season. She and they play in the railed-in garden which faces Hyde Park.'[44] At Elizabeth's sixth birthday party at Windsor the previous month, her guests were all family members: her parents and sister, the King and Queen, the Prince of Wales (her 'favourite' uncle), the Princess Royal and George and Gerald Lascelles. Elizabeth had sent out the invitations herself: her special treat was 'for the first time… to write little letters of thanks to her grandfather and grandmother, and to others who have sent her presents' in what was described as 'a very legible round hand'.[45] Hopefully, the pink-iced cake with six candles baked by the King's chef compensated for this corollary to what threatened to be a staid entertainment.

Elizabeth's presents from her family included a large doll – inevitably in her role as universal representative she was credited with 'all a little girl's love for dolls' – and a number of books for her to read to herself; Nannie B sent a knitted scarf.[46] Presents from members of the public unknown to her parents, 'in accordance with the invariable rule of the Royal Family', were returned to their donors. This year the rule was bent for a copy of *Alice's Adventures in Wonderland* signed for the princess by Lewis Carroll's model for Alice, the elderly Alice Hargreaves, but the lively, pony-loving Elizabeth did not enjoy Carroll's perplexing fantasy.[47] Writing in 1947, Betty Spencer Shew stated that the first book Elizabeth read to herself was 'a collection of simple stories bearing the appropriate title "Tales for Me to Read to Myself"'.[48] Like much in Elizabeth's early life, this was a late-Victorian offering, written, according to its preface, 'to supply the want which is sometimes felt, of a book sufficiently easy for this purpose, and yet more entertaining than the short sentences in spelling books'. Markedly more exciting was a new bicycle which replaced the tricycle on which the princess had first navigated Hamilton Gardens independently. It was a present from members of the British Cycle and Motor Cycle Manufacturers' and Traders' Union, and Elizabeth rode it in company with a new friend she had made for herself. Sonia Graham Hodgson was the daughter of George V's radiographer, Harold Hodgson. Elizabeth encountered her for the first time playing in Hamilton Gardens. 'One day this little girl came up to me and said, "Will you have a game with me?"' Sonia remembered.[49] They played French cricket for an hour, and Sonia became Elizabeth's 'particular girl friend... always invited by the Princess to her tea parties and... her companion on many occasions such as walks in St James's Park or a game in the gardens behind the Piccadilly House'.[50] Only eight months separated the girls. Sonia was the elder, she was taller and, in her own estimation, bossier. Quickly, princess and doctor's daughter began to see one another 'virtually every day, except for holidays' until Sonia went away to school.[51] Sonia wore white gloves to ride her bicycle, her clothes resembled Elizabeth's, but despite her father's professional connection with the royal family, her background, unlike that of the Bowes-Lyon cousins, rooted her outside the golden circle.

⸎

At Balmoral, late in the summer of 1931, Queen Mary had introduced her granddaughter to her newest woman of the bedchamber, Lady Victoria Forester. Elizabeth's reported response, 'Victoria? I seem to have heard that name before!', was widely quoted as an example of a witty bon mot on the part of the five-year-old princess.[52]

It was impossible that, even at five, Elizabeth should not have heard of her great-great-grandmother, Queen Victoria. In so many ways the old queen, dead only thirty years, imprinted her descendants' consciousness. Balmoral remained recognizably Victoria's Highland retreat; the calendar of the royal year was modelled on her own; her doctrines of moral rectitude and imperial unassailability continued to colour the royal outlook. To the King and Queen and a generation of courtiers and palace workers, memories of their redoubtable predecessor were still green. The Prince of Wales claimed that 'it was to her... that [the King] looked for a model of the Sovereign's deportment. His Court retained a Victorian flavour to the end',[53] while the prince's cousin, Lord Louis Mountbatten, denounced the King as 'bigoted... with his early Victorian ideas'. [54] It was not the case that the young Elizabeth's familiarity with Victoria's name represented a coded reference to dawning awareness of her destiny. Instead, the apparently self-assured princess, reported as 'rul[ing] her playmates with a firm will', put a number of those she encountered in mind of Britain's previous queen regnant.[55] The Duke and Duchess of York denied the possibility of the throne for themselves, but it was the duke who told writer Osbert Sitwell, 'giving me at the same time a very direct look, to see if I understood the allusion he was making to Queen Victoria, "From the first moment of talking, she showed so much character that it was impossible not to wonder whether history would not repeat itself."'[56]

The duchess had no intention of allowing such suspicions to cloud Elizabeth's horizon. Her ambition for both her daughters was altogether simpler: 'a happy childhood which they can always look back on... with lots of pleasant memories stored up against the days that might come'.[57] She was determined, wrote Cynthia Asquith in another royally approved account, that 'no shadow from the future should invade the bright present'.[58] Although she did not again confide in Queen Mary her concerns over public interest in Elizabeth, rumours circulated of her intermittent anxiety. 'The Duchess of York... is rather concerned at the unavoidable publicity which attaches to all the movements of little Princess Elizabeth,' wrote one columnist in the summer of 1932, citing no sources. 'The little girl is now old enough to be observant and she is getting somewhat self-conscious under the influence of all the lionising she encounters. Every time she goes out for a drive in the park everyone seems to recognise her and hats are raised and handkerchiefs waved from all quarters.'[59] The duchess may have tried to offer her daughter simple explanations, though her preference was for avoiding taxing subjects. Perhaps Alah, who, from Elizabeth's infancy, had instructed her when to wave at omnipresent bystanders, attempted a similar explanation or, indeed, Queen Mary, self-appointed custodian of royal mores. Elizabeth's subsequent behaviour, her refusal throughout a long life to court acclaim or publicity, suggests she learned early on that public interest was an adjunct of royal status. Her self-consciousness was not always obvious. In July, she visited the studio of portraitist Philip de László during his sittings with the duchess. 'There was no sign of shyness,' de László commented, 'and she was greatly interested in the portraits of her parents and made some very amusing remarks.' [60] Like her father, Elizabeth *was* shy, just as, like his, her temper was formidable. She would learn to copy his efforts in mastering both handicaps.

In the short term, there were two results of her mother's concern: conversations about the next stage in Elizabeth's education, and a deliberate decision that, despite the difference in their ages, Elizabeth and Margaret's upbringing be shared as closely as possible. The duchess was reported as hoping that Elizabeth beginning education proper would help in some degree to withdraw the Princess from so much public adulation', a hope that proved vain. [61] The second outcome was signalled visually. In May, a journalist calling herself 'Sylvia Mayfair' had introduced her readers to 'a Royal fashion lead that will undoubtedly be followed by many mothers': the duchess's decision to dress her two daughters alike. 'When I saw them driving in the Park,' Miss Mayfair offered, 'the two little Princesses were dressed in exactly similar raspberry pink serge coats with bonnets trimmed with rosebuds while neither wore gloves.' [62] They would continue to wear matching clothes for the next decade and beyond, one friend recording in her diary 7 June 1940 as the first time she saw Elizabeth and Margaret not dressed alike. [63] It was a decision that linked the sisters as siblings; as princesses, it suggested equality between them. It did indeed confirm a trend for sisters dressing alike, as Sylvia Mayfair had predicted, though their particular shared wardrobe nevertheless distinguished Elizabeth and Margaret from other little girls in 1930s Britain. In suggesting parity between the King's granddaughters, either of age or status, it perpetrated a kindly illusion. As a second son, the Duke of York had lamented the impact of an age gap of eighteen months in his own childhood. Even before their accession, neither he nor his wife meant their younger daughter to experience similar feelings of inconsequence. That they failed in the long term was not entirely their fault, albeit their determined overcompensating, which spoiled Margaret, engendered its own unhappy outcome, its consequences as troublesome for Elizabeth as for Margaret.

The princesses not only dressed alike, they did the same things, and not only at home. In July, Elizabeth attended a children's party in London given by Viscountess Astor. She was accompanied by Alah and Margaret. For Margaret, on the eve of her second birthday able to walk and talk, it was her first party outside the family circle. Invitations henceforth invariably included both princesses. From the outset Elizabeth's concerns were twofold: to enjoy herself and to look after her sister. The second would occupy her on and off until Margaret's death, her role as elder sister a facet of her identity. It was partly forced upon her. Anticipating the Yorks' departure for Glamis that summer, newspapers suggested, 'Princess Elizabeth is explaining to her sister the joys of a holiday in Scotland, where they can play as they please.'[64] Aside from its inference concerning the restrictions of the girls' London life, this explanation and others like it imposed on the older princess, still only six, the responsible role of tutor; protector and guardian would be added later. Elizabeth's enjoyment of the Astor party was described as more 'sedate' than Margaret's, 'as became the dignity of a lady of six'.[65] Margaret, observers decided, was 'naturally more impetuous and irresponsible than her more meditative elder sister had ever been'.[66] From first emergence of Margaret's capricious, quicksilver personality, this polarizing of the sisters' attributes, rooted in fact, justified Elizabeth's nearer proximity to the throne, with its requirements of good behaviour and self-discipline. A pattern had been set.

Elizabeth became aware of it only gradually; her life remained sunny. 'I have never met a child who seemed more in love with life,' wrote Cynthia Asquith.[67] Preparations for her grandfather's birthday parade, Trooping the Colour, had provided an exciting diversion at the beginning of June. Elizabeth's love of horses, shared with the King, was already deeply ingrained. From the windows of the day nursery she watched the mounted Life Guards passing down Piccadilly on their way to rehearse, in one account 'her face pressed close to the glass... She was so excited that she kept waving her hand and smiling at the soldiers.'[68] A fortnight later, the Yorks spent Ascot week on the Kent coast. The princesses played on the pebbled beach at Sandwich Bay; Elizabeth rode her bicycle.[69] Plans were afoot for the girls to have 'their own garden plots to tend'.[70] Here was the truth of the Yorks' 'ordinary' family life: horses, the seaside, bicycles and gardening. Elizabeth enjoyed them all.

❦

By 1932, however, one York family tradition was over. The duke had sold all six of his hunters. The previous March, her parents had taken an enthralled Elizabeth to a meet of the Pytchley Hunt at Kelmarsh Hall; they had been spending a number of weeks at Thornby Grange, near Rugby. But in the aftermath of an economically struggling Britain abandoning the Gold Standard that autumn and a decline in the value of sterling, George V had ordered a fifty per cent reduction in the Civil List moneys he received from the government, with cutbacks for other members of the royal family, including his sons. Hunting became too expensive for the Duke of York. He gave up his horses and the hunting boxes, like Thornby Grange, that he had rented in Northamptonshire and Warwickshire.

For Elizabeth, though she was too young to recognize it as such, it was a rare indicator of change in her parents' well-ordered and comfortable existence. So much in her upbringing suggested the survival of an inherited status quo, her grandparents' world of strict hierarchies, landed wealth, domestic staff: the assumptions and privileges of an aristocratic elite. The King's decision that his family participate in the national tightening of belts implied royal accountability and an acknowledgement that royal freedoms, notably of expenditure, were circumscribed. Over coming decades, the Yorks' world and the rarefied world of the Pytchley – also at the Kelmarsh meet were Grand Duke Michael of Russia, the Earl and Countess of Rosebery and the Yorks' London neighbours, the Allendales – would continue to overlap, but the social, political and financial hegemony of the landowning classes, in decline for decades, increasingly faltered. It was a change for which no one in Elizabeth's family thought to prepare her.

For the Yorks, however, there was to be a happy consequence of economic downturn: a house of their own in the country. This was Royal Lodge, in Windsor Great Park. In the autumn of 1931, it was offered to the duke and duchess by the King, following the death of its most recent occupant, the manager of the royal Thoroughbred Stud, Major Fetherstonhaugh. By royal standards it was a small house: its builder, George IV, had described it as a cottage. In 1931 it was ramshackle, ill-planned, inconvenient, partly demolished, added on to and altered, its chief beauty – Sir Jeffry Wyatville's long Gothic saloon or drawing room – divided any old how into three. It stood in large, unkempt gardens three miles from Windsor

Castle and a similar distance from the Prince of Wales's country house, Fort Belvedere; the overall impression was of neglect and want of comfort. To Queen Mary, the duchess described it as 'the most delightful place & the garden quite enchanting'. She decided 'it would be wonderful for the children, and I am sure that they would be very happy there'.[71] Briefly the Queen protested. Royal retrenchment notwithstanding, the duke commissioned a costly programme of knocking down and rebuilding. His aim, according to his official biographer, was to create a 'real home' for his tight-knit family of four.[72] It was an appropriate undertaking for the prince increasingly promoted as 'the "family man" of the Royal family'.[73]

By the New Year of 1933, work was complete, 'very 1930s, all cream and sweet pea colours', as it struck a later visitor.[74] In place of an old conservatory, a new wing had been added on to the south side of Royal Lodge, and two nurseries fitted up for Elizabeth and Margaret.[75] In a secluded corner of the grounds, in a garden neatly hedged, a site was chosen for Y Bwthyn Bach. The duchess made plans for a herb garden, modelled on the herb garden at Glamis; miniature garden plots were carved out for the princesses. Here the sisters' fifteen blue budgerigars found a home. Like Elizabeth's Welsh cottage, Royal Lodge provided a setting for the Yorks' glossy ordinariness: only its name asserted its occupants' rank. This was grandeur in miniature, and its small(ish) size and the duke and duchess's absorption in its garden perpetuated the myth of the King's second son, his wife and daughters as the archetypal inter-war nuclear family. Columnists who suggested 'the Duchess of York intends both her little daughters to have a thorough training in all housewifery arts' based their assumption simply on conventional appearances.[76] Elizabeth was happier riding than laying the table. Among her seventh birthday presents was a new, larger pony called Gem. 'And a real gem he is, too!' she declared.[77] A present to all the family was Rozavel Golden

Eagle, a Pembroke corgi puppy known as 'Dookie'; he was shortly joined by a second puppy, Rozavel Lady Jane, called Jane. For eight decades there would be at least one corgi never far from Elizabeth's side. Dookie and Jane joined the duke's golden labradors and Choo-Choo the Tibetan lion dog. All frequently featured in family photographs taken both at Royal Lodge and Y Bwthyn Bach, an aspect of the Yorks' easygoing intimacy reflecting the influence of the Strathmores.

In the autumn, the rebuilt Royal Lodge welcomed another new arrival, a recent graduate of Moray House teacher training college in Edinburgh. She received a bedroom and a sitting room of her own. Her name was Marion Crawford. She was twenty-two, the daughter of a mechanical engineer's clerk from Ayrshire, and her stay with the Yorks lasted fifteen years. They called her 'Crawfie'. Their delight in one another was sincere while it lasted.

It was unavoidable that Elizabeth's education should have become a topic of eager speculation: every aspect of her life was newsworthy. Briefly newspapers suggested a preparatory school on the Suffolk coast at Southwold; hastily the rumour was denied. 'There is no intention of the princess's elementary tuition being undertaken at a private school,' wrote the female author of 'Mayfair Gossip'. 'She is already being taught simple lessons in the three Rs, and in due course a governess will be engaged for her to have extended instruction. This plan is approved by the Queen, who takes the closest interest in the welfare and upbringing of her granddaughter.'[78]

Crawfie was the governess in question. She had made a trial visit to her would-be employers at Easter, before beginning work proper later in the year. Despite her youth, her references were of a sort guaranteed to appeal to the duchess: she had previously served as a temporary governess to the duchess's niece, Mary Leveson-Gower. 'I had certainly never intended to become a governess,' Crawfie wrote later; she had hoped to specialize in child psychology.[79] She had not counted on quirks of fate or the duchess's smiling determination. Her knowledge of English and the humanities was adequate, even enthusiastic. Less assured was her grasp of mathematics, which Queen Mary discounted as irrelevant in the circumstances, insisting that Elizabeth and Margaret 'will never do their own household books'.[80] The duchess would make manageable demands on Crawfie's abilities and her imperfect fund of knowledge. Even after her husband's accession, her focus was her daughters' happiness and physical wellbeing. She wanted for both girls an education like her own, intended as a preliminary to a suitable marriage, an unexacting requirement comfortably within Crawfie's capabilities. In the event, Crawfie's unambitious curriculum may have suited Elizabeth's future as a constitutional monarch in the second half of the twentieth century, a remit with little scope for inconvenient curiosity or imaginative flights. If so, this was as much a happy accident as a considered plan. As an approach, it would prove more frustrating for Margaret, whose future was less fettered than her sister's. Among key skills Crawfie taught Elizabeth was the ability to read quickly. Her youth made her an unintimidating teacher: she was only sixteen years older than her pupil. She appears to have taken pains to preserve Elizabeth's self-confidence.

At first Crawfie's appearance in the princesses' lives served to maintain the distinction between the two girls that the difference in their ages naturally imposed and to emphasize that Elizabeth was growing up. In 1933, Elizabeth, not Margaret, was Crawfie's pupil. Despite their wish that their younger daughter should not feel herself at a disadvantage, the Yorks themselves occasionally reinforced this discrepancy. The Master of the King's Music, Sir Edward Elgar, had dedicated to Elizabeth, Margaret and the duchess jointly a new composition to commemorate Margaret's birth. This was his 'Nursery Suite', performed at a concert on 4 July 1931 in front of an audience that included Elizabeth and her parents but not, inevitably, baby Margaret. The following autumn, Elizabeth went to a charity matinée with the duchess, with whom she also attended Sunday-morning church services. The *Daily Mail* described these outings as 'semi-public'.[81] To observers they were a reminder of Elizabeth's pre-eminence among the King's grandchildren. Newspapers delighted in mother and daughter's appearances together; they spared no truck for the duchess's anxiety about her daughter's lionizing. And, invariably, cheerful and polite Elizabeth acquitted herself commendably. 'The little Princess, who has been coached by her mother in the art of proper deportment, thoroughly enjoys being thus "taken out",' asserted the *Mail*'s 'Onlooker'.[82] Photographs of a smiling Elizabeth on her mother's arm point to the accuracy of this prim assessment. This was the happy, golden-haired child Crawfie inherited. At three, Margaret remained Alah's charge.

Crawfie recorded her first impressions of Princess Elizabeth in *The Little Princesses* in 1950. By then, almost two decades had passed since the evening she described. For much of this time, including at the time of writing, Elizabeth had been firmly established as heir to her father's throne. That this was not the case in 1933 does not invalidate the cosy glow of Crawfie's retrospective account of a 'small figure with a mop of curls', sitting up in bed driving an imaginary team of horses 'once or twice round the park', the cord of her dressing gown a substitute for reins.[83] 'From the very beginning I had a feeling about Lilibet that she was "special"... with so much character at so young an age,' Crawfie remembered, and her version of the seven-year-old princess aligns with other first-hand accounts.[84] Henry Owen, the duke's groom responsible for Elizabeth's riding lessons, wrote to Cynthia Asquith, 'Words really fail me to thoroughly explain how very nice Princess Elizabeth really is.'[85] That year, Philip de László painted Elizabeth's portrait and was dazzled by the child he described as 'a most intelligent and beautiful little girl'. He reported her telling him confidentially that, like him, she also painted, 'and I'm a very good painter. I'll bring some of my work next time and show you.' De László also explained, 'she is enormously popular and... at present looked upon as the future Queen of Great Britain'.[86] This last view was not one the duchess encouraged at 145 Piccadilly or Royal Lodge, and the portrait the Yorks commissioned from de László, a romantic exercise in chocolate-box prettiness akin to the best of Marcus Adams's photographs, excluded explicit markers of rank.

Crawfie's challenge was to fit into the relatively small number of hours the duchess allowed her elements of a rudimentary education. Sacrosanct in Elizabeth's days was the time mother, father and two daughters spent together: a post-breakfast romp in the duchess's bedroom, card games after tea (racing demon, rummy, happy families, snap), bathtime, nursery games like pillow fights, then bedtime with its ritual of story-reading. Everything else, lessons in particular, was liable to disruption. Hairdressers and dressmakers called at 145 Piccadilly, there were dental appointments to be kept. That winter, papers reported that the house had 'become the meeting place for a number of small people who attend a weekly dancing class there, and afterwards have tea with the little Princess'.[87] These sessions, shared with the Yorks' next-door neighbours and the three sons of the duchess's friend Lady Plunket, were led by Marguerite Vacani, 'famous teacher for the little people of society', recommended by the British-born Queen Ena of Spain. She directed her royal pupil 'to walk well, curtsey gracefully,... [and] dance on her toes' and later recalled her first impression of a 'little girl, bright blue eyes, smiling face and so pleased to see you'.[88] That Madame Vacani's lessons consumed an entire afternoon was of no consequence. Afternoons were for time off, preferably spent outdoors: drives in the park, feeding time for Elizabeth's

Japanese blue tortoise, Madame Butterfly, bicycle rides in the garden, including, in one account, a game Elizabeth and Margaret called 'pedestrians', in which Elizabeth rode up and down the gravel paths on her tricycle, watched by Margaret, until 'suddenly Princess Margaret steps forward and holds up her hand. Obediently Princess Elizabeth slows down and stops and Princess Margaret walks sedately across an imaginary pedestrian crossing in safety.'[89] There were weekly singing lessons at 32 Prince's Gate, the home of the Countess of Cavan, lady-in-waiting to both the duchess and the Princess Royal. Elizabeth shared her singing lessons with the countess's elder daughter, Lady Elizabeth Lambart, two years her senior and named after the duchess. Crawfie had no choice but to work around these distractions. In the short term, in the two and a half to three hours available to her each morning, she instructed Elizabeth in history, literature and arithmetic, 'the first two by far the favourite, as with all children'.[90] She took out a subscription to the *Children's Newspaper* (safely conservative with its mantra of Empire and Christian goodness); always to hand were copies of *Punch*. Her 'innovations' included 'dirty' playtime: games of hide-and-seek, sardines and Red Indians in shrubberies grubby with London soot. She writes dismissively of the 'quiet ladylike games in Hamilton Gardens, keeping to the paths', encouraged by Alah, for whom princesses 'should be princesses always... dear little figures like dolls', and the brief she set herself included encouraging her charges to be more than 'princess dolls'.[91] In London, Crawfie's lessons took place in a small room off the drawing room. There were plenty of opportunities for disturbances, including leisurely elevenses: for Elizabeth a special, and specially disliked, milk pudding. At Royal Lodge, the schoolroom was sunny, with bright chintz curtains, in line with the duchess's doctrine of joy. Occasionally Elizabeth's reward for 'working very industriously at her classes and... a good week's work' was permission to invite a friend to Royal Lodge for the weekend.[92]

The duke and duchess did not interfere ('No one ever had employers who interfered so little' was Crawfie's comment[93]): the value they attached to the substance of their daughter's learning, Crawfie suggested, was not always apparent to Crawfie. Since Elizabeth was taught alone, neither she nor her parents had any means of assessing her progress: as with other children educated similarly, direct comparison was impossible. This did not concern either duke or duchess. A rare opportunity for measurement against her peers was provided by Elizabeth's knitting. Her contribution of an orange and grey scarf she had knitted for an appeal for Queen Mary's Needlework Guild was reported in papers under the headline 'Boy Cousin Does Three'. Elizabeth disliked knitting, as she disliked the family hobby of needlework at which her father and her grandmother excelled; the scarf was 'the result of much patient work'. It was eclipsed by Gerald Lascelles's efforts. 'Not only has he knitted three scarves, but he has finished them with elaborate tassels,' the *Daily Telegraph* reported devastatingly.[94]

Crawfie's long stay with the Yorks is a measure of her liking for all four. As a teacher, she implied, she experienced frustrations. Unfairly her account deliberately portrayed Elizabeth's parents as uninterested in her education, more concerned, for example, with Elizabeth's 'promise of one day being an excellent dancer' and 'the grace and enthusiasm with which she perform[ed] Scottish dances', described as 'the admiration of all her friends'.[95] The education of aristocratic daughters by private governesses in this period seldom targeted academic distinction. The prominence in Elizabeth's patchy timetable of 'ladylike' accomplishments – dancing, drawing, riding – paralleled her contemporaries' experience, less surprising then than now. George V's best-known requirement of Elizabeth and Margaret's schooling was that they learn 'to write a decent hand', which both did.[96] Unsurprisingly, it closely resembled their mother's, the handwriting they saw most often. As long as Elizabeth remained an outside contender for the throne, with an assumption that a tardy Prince of Wales would do his duty and provide a male heir, the nation at large shared the duchess's pleasure in Elizabeth's 'extracurricular' diversions. And Crawfie was not to know that, more than once, dancing would prove a key skill in Elizabeth's arsenal later on. She was aware simply of the time denied her in the classroom and the progress hampered by parental laxness. Elizabeth's undoubted ability redoubled her governess's irritation. Crawfie commended her 'bright quickness of mind'; she noted that she 'was quick at picking anything up, and one never had to do a lot of explaining to her'.[97] She noted, too, a biddable quality in Elizabeth, 'from the start... a certain amenability, a reasonableness rare in anyone so young': under different circumstances, an ideal prescription. She would remain mostly amenable to what was expected of her.

Crawfie did not fight her battles single-handed. She discovered a supportive ally in Queen Mary. The attachment that both King and Queen felt for their elder granddaughter was genuine. Neither with his own children, nor any other grandchild, did the ageing sovereign retrieve on hands and knees hair clips lost beneath the royal sofas; he pointed out to her the crowded details of William Powell Frith's holiday panorama, *Ramsgate Sands*, hanging in his study. In Queen Mary's case, her attentiveness to Elizabeth transcended simple affection. The devotion to the British monarchy cherished by this great-granddaughter of George III was the guiding philosophy of her life. Any possibility of Elizabeth inheriting the throne placed her, in her grandmother's eyes, on the loftiest pedestal; her Olympian destiny required proper preparation. 'It would have been impossible', Lady Airlie wrote, 'for anyone so devoted to the Monarchy as Queen Mary to lose sight of the future Queen in this favourite grandchild.'[98] The Queen was 'very anxious for Princess Elizabeth to read the best type of children's books, and often chose them for her': Robert Louis Stevenson, Kipling, Austen.[99] She found herself 'more interested in the education of the two Princesses than she had been in her own children's'.[100] French lessons were an early focus. To follow Elizabeth's gramophone course, the Yorks employed a visiting mademoiselle; she insisted on the 'endless writing out of columns of verbs'. 'Goaded by boredom to violent measures', Elizabeth rebelled. She turned upside down over her head a large silver inkpot. The result was 'ink trickling down her face and slowly dyeing her golden curls blue' and the departure of the mademoiselle.[101] Queen Mary suggested a holiday governess: the duchess chose Georgina Guérin, her own French governess's daughter, who, from 1935, stayed with the family at Birkhall and Balmoral. (Elizabeth's response was less than enthusiastic. 'Mademoiselle arrived safely,' she wrote from Birkhall, 'which was a pity.')[102] The Queen encouraged learning poems by heart as 'wonderful memory-training'.[103] Elizabeth's repertoire included 'London Snow' by the recently deceased poet laureate Robert Bridges, Wordsworth's 'Daffodils' and a handful of poems by Walter de la Mare. But it was the duchess who requested Latin lessons for Elizabeth, beginning in 1935, and the duchess who insisted Elizabeth write thank you letters as soon as she was able. To her grandmother in February 1934, Elizabeth wrote with childish inconsequence, 'We loved staying at Sandringham with you. I lost a top front tooth yesterday morning. Margaret and I went to a fancy dress party at Lady Astor's.'[104]

Elizabeth herself was unaware of tensions surrounding her education, politely concealed below the surface. The duke and duchess did indeed create for their daughters the carefree family life on which they were set, as though, Crawfie commented unironically, 'the season was always spring'.[105] Happiness was consistently uppermost among the duchess's motives. It prompted the family's first trip to the circus, in

January 1934; it guided the duchess's choice of books and poetry to read aloud to Elizabeth and Margaret: 'Fairy stories... *Black Beauty*, *At the Back of the North Wind*, Peter Pan – anything we can find about horses and dogs, and gay poetry like "Come unto these yellow sands"'; she also read them Bible stories, as her mother had to her, first spur to Elizabeth's strong religious faith.[106] Together the sisters read Thackeray's fantastic royal dystopia, *The Rose and the Ring*. Among presents to his niece from the Prince of Wales were copies of A. A. Milne's Christopher Robin poems. Elizabeth's favourite was 'Buckingham Palace', about the changing of the guard, with its final question, funniest of all to this particular reader: 'Do you think the King knows all about me?' In the short term, Queen Mary mostly contented herself with a grandmother's treats, like the winter afternoon of brilliant sunshine when she and Elizabeth drove from Sandringham to Hunstanton beach and 'the little Princess, equipped with a toy pail, began collecting shells, and was helped by the Queen, who pointed them out to her, and they waded through puddles to secure them'.[107] She supervised the duke and Elizabeth stripping ivy from walls around the estate.[108]

❧

Her parents, her grandparents, baby Margaret, Alah, Bobo MacDonald, Owen the groom, Crawfie, Elizabeth Lambart to share her singing class, the Plunket boys in her dancing class: Elizabeth's was a tight-knit world full of a child's certainties. For the time being, it continued its accustomed round. Elizabeth's seventh birthday that spring had been celebrated as previously at Windsor. There were presents after breakfast, a morning's grace from lessons and the changing of the guard by the Welsh Guards in the castle quadrangle, watched not only by Elizabeth and her Lascelles cousins but 'a very large crowd... including a party of 200 Belgians who were visiting the Castle and Eton College'.[109] After an hour's riding, family tea – the King and Queen, the Princess Royal, the Prince of Wales – included the usual iced cake made by the King's chef. And there was an announcement, too, a rearguard action to safeguard for another year semblances of childhood. 'It was stated today that the Duke and Duchess of York have decided that their daughter is still much too young to take on public work. Not for another year at least is the Princess likely to be seen in public save on occasions like the Royal Tournament or the Royal Horse Show when she accompanies her mother.'[110]

CHAPTER III

'A delightful picture of English childhood'

THE FOREIGN PRINCESS whom an 'obviously excited' Elizabeth, in company with her parents, greeted on the platform of Ballater station on 17 September 1934 was Marina of Greece. Round and round on the red carpet the lively Elizabeth danced, 'until Princess Marina... stooped down to kiss her future niece'.[1] A cousin of Greece's deposed King George II, Marina was newly engaged to the youngest of Bertie's brothers, George, Duke of Kent. Seven years earlier, her haughty and ambitious mother, the former Grand Duchess Helen Vladimirovna, a granddaughter of Tsar Alexander II, had experienced fleeting excitement at the attentiveness towards her youngest daughter of the Prince of Wales. Nothing came of it. David's affections returned to the familiar embrace of his married mistress Freda Dudley Ward; he turned his back on Marina as he had any number of 'suitable' brides.

Alone in the family party gathered that autumn at Balmoral to welcome Marina and her parents, Elizabeth and Margaret were unaware of the 'problem' of Uncle David. As early as November 1924, the King had described his eldest son feelingly as 'very obstinate'.[2] Over the ensuing decade, exasperation had hardened into something more: the half fear, half conviction he communicated to his second son and daughter-in-law that David, who readily admitted his boredom with 'Princing', would never succeed to the throne. Time would prove George V nearly right. The working out of this royal prophecy was painful and dramatic, and changed the lives of many members of David's family, Elizabeth's most of all.

For his part David felt no regret over Marina's marriage to George. 'You know my views on "Royal Marriages",' he wrote to a friend; he described their courtship as 'so d – – d quick that one wonders how long it will last'.[3] Instead, on 29 November, with Bertie, he accompanied bridegroom George to Westminster Abbey. There the congregation included 'a very unattractive and common Englishman', Ernest Simpson, and his wife Wallis, 'an American 150 per cent', 'a jolly, plain, intelligent, quiet, unpretentious and unprepossessing little woman... [who had] already the air of a personage who walks into a room as though she almost expected to be curtsied to'.[4] This twice-married uber-American was, of course, David's latest mistress.

❧

For Elizabeth, her own role as bridesmaid made the two royal weddings of the following year memorable. Marina's bevy of attendants included a clutch of grown-up European princesses, all, bar Juliana of the Netherlands, flotsam of vanished thrones. Elizabeth and her second cousin Lady Mary Cambridge, a great-niece of Queen Mary's, carried Marina's silver-lined train. They wore white tulle frocks of the sort Elizabeth wore for parties and photographic sittings. For May Cambridge's wedding three years earlier, Elizabeth had worn her first long dress. To mark the occasion she sat for 'pottery artist' Phyllis Simpson for a six-inch-high ceramic sculpture commissioned by her parents.[5] On this later occasion her appearance did not excite the same degree of popular interest. Instead attention focused on Elizabeth's behaviour. Reviewing Marina's attendants, newspapers described Elizabeth approvingly as 'the most... earnest of them all', serious in her duties at the wedding rehearsal at Buckingham Palace as well as the service itself.[6] Her behaviour underlined again the age difference between Elizabeth and Margaret. Sitting with her parents, Margaret once 'endeavoured to exchange a sisterly greeting. She raised a little hand in front of her face and twiddled her fingers at Princess Elizabeth. Princess Elizabeth, however, was as dignified as anyone taking part in that ceremony of majesty and pomp, and she raised her eyebrows in a silent rebuke.'[7] Already each sister played her allotted role, Margaret puckish and spontaneous in her mischief, Elizabeth serious and precociously mature. Commendations of her earnestness and dignity – to modern ears, questionable virtues in an eight-year-old – inevitably shaped Elizabeth's understanding of appropriately 'royal' behaviour. The 'silent rebuke' would become a characteristic expression of disapproval.

Eleven months later, on 6 November 1935, Elizabeth was again a bridesmaid. The occasion was the marriage of Bertie's middle brother, Henry, Duke of Gloucester, to Lady Alice Montagu-Douglas-Scott, like the Duchess of York the daughter of a Scottish nobleman. Five-year-old Margaret joined her sister. Both were dressed for the first time by Norman Hartnell, who later designed the sisters' dresses for their parents' coronation, both their wedding dresses and Elizabeth's own coronation gown. Hartnell envisaged long dresses 'of a sophisticated Empire style'; he was foiled by the King's desire to see his granddaughters' 'pretty little knees'. Vain was his protest that 'they'll look like bloody little fairies':[8] a fairy-like appearance had been the duchess's aim since her daughters' birth. Fairies were prominent in the cultural diet of inter-war nurseries: in stories and poems, in the watercolours of Margaret Tarrant, like that in the day nursery at 145 Piccadilly. Elizabeth's Christmas present to Queen Mary in 1933 was her own painting of fairies; a gift of a woollen quilt to Elizabeth in January 1935 from 11,000 Australian girls also called Elizabeth was accompanied by a book 'decorated with drawings of native flowers and trees, with fairies and animals playing amongst them', including a picture of 'tiny sheep with fairies shearing them and busily sorting out the fleece'.[9] Fairies were dainty, sometimes whimsical, sometimes roguish, typical of the neverland of childish innocence: to enjoy and resemble fairies was proof of Elizabeth's wholesomeness. In fairy guise, she was photographed by Marcus Adams at the time of each wedding. A picture from November 1934 proved among Adams's most successful. It confirms the opinion of diplomat Miles Lampson, meeting Elizabeth at Balmoral in September, that he had 'seldom seen such an enchanting child as Princess Elizabeth', and the view of scullery maid Mollie Moran, who, from the upper deck of a bus in Park Lane, glimpsed both princesses playing in their parents' garden and 'stared, quite spellbound, at their pretty, peaches-and-cream complexions framed by soft fair curls'.[10] Resting her face on her left hand and leaning on a plump cushion, Adams's Elizabeth regards the viewer levelly. Her direct gaze suggests something of the fixity and coolness of appraisal observers would increasingly note. It is an image of self-assurance and possibly self-containment. Both were qualities repeatedly attributed to Elizabeth in the years ahead.

❧

The government's decision to celebrate the twenty-fifth anniversary of George V's accession in the form of a silver jubilee, the first commemoration of its sort in British history, made 1935 significant in the life of the royal family. During the celebrations themselves, Elizabeth was frequently at her grandparents' side. At first hand she experienced what the King called 'this personal link between me and my people', 'a spontaneous offering of loyalty – and... of love':[11] events and responses that cannot fail to have made a lasting impression on a serious-minded and observant child aware from infancy that her grandparents were also her sovereigns, their family life a focus of widespread interest.

In January, Elizabeth returned in kind the gift to her of a cake from the 'poor children of Battersea' at the time of her christening: she iced and decorated a cake for the boys of the Juvenile Instruction Centre, in the town of Blaina, South Wales.[12] Weeks later, following a visit by her father to its factory in New Southgate, she and Margaret were given their own telephones by the Standard Telephones and Cables company: 'ivory and gold-plated... two full-size instruments, each complete with a dial' and fully functional.[13] Here were two facets of royal life: the unearned tributes of high status and consideration for those less fortunate, increasingly identified as the grounds for such tributes. At eight and a half, Elizabeth did not recognize the two gestures as such. She would demonstrate convincingly over a long life her understanding of the 'contract' between royal family and people.

On 1 March a BBC official revealed that the corporation 'should very much welcome the opportunity of broadcasting the voice of the Princess to the children'.[14] It was the first time jubilee preparations focused on Elizabeth. 'It has been felt that special consideration might be given to the children in order to give them an interest all their own in the jubilee celebrations,' one newspaper explained.[15] But the idea of a jubilee broadcast by Elizabeth in a special edition of *Children's Hour* was not pursued, failing to win the sanction either of her parents or grandparents.

The suggestion nevertheless revealed Elizabeth's prominence. Just as Canadians had chosen Elizabeth to appear on a commemorative Silver Jubilee one cent stamp, it was Elizabeth whom the BBC identified as the royal grandchild to engage the interest of children nationwide. Elizabeth was most closely associated with her grandfather of any of the King's grandchildren: his chosen companion during his seaside convalescence, a frequent visitor to Windsor Castle. That spring, for the first time, she had been present when the King distributed the Royal Maundy Money in Westminster Abbey; she was reported to have 'caught her grandfather's enthusiasm and has started a stamp collection of her own', to which the King contributed. On 6 May, after the thanksgiving service at St Paul's Cathedral, Elizabeth stood between her grandparents on the balcony of Buckingham Palace to hear the cheers of a quarter of a million people. The Yorks' carriage had been first in the royal procession. Dressed like her sister in pale pink, 'Princess Elizabeth, serene and self-possessed, waved to the crowds with her tiny white-gloved hand', acknowledging what MP Chips Channon called 'thunderous applause'.[16] The bright sunshine, huge crowds, flags and fluttering decorations moved many that day to patriotic euphoria: one spectator described Elizabeth and Margaret as 'a delightful picture of English childhood'.[17] Inside St Paul's, Elizabeth may or may not have watched proceedings with 'her eyes wide with wonder'. Nor could she possibly have committed to memory the Archbishop of Canterbury's encomium. But the prelate's view of George V commanding the 'respect and trust' of his countrymen, his 'quiet dignity worthy of his high office' and his 'unselfish dedication to [the nation's] service' expounded a formula of monarchy that set the pattern for Elizabeth's father's reign and indeed her own. A week later, the King and Queen made a surprise visit to the East End. Accompanying them on their journey through London's poorest districts was their elder granddaughter. 'Everywhere in the narrow streets, through which news of their coming spread like wildfire, the King and Queen and little Princess were greeted with a wholehearted demonstration of affection unsurpassed in any quarter.'[18] More than once, the density of the throng brought the royal car to a standstill; crowds swarmed round it; men, women and children attempted to jump on to the running boards 'cheering and waving wildly'. The royal couple were moved but not alarmed. For Elizabeth it was an extraordinarily powerful demonstration, proof of a very personal dimension to the bonds of crown and country. Along the shabby flag- and bunting-strung streets rippled the loyalty on which thrones depend, a loyalty in the first instance not to the institution of monarchy but her grandparents personally.

The morning after her drive to the East End, the Court Circular recorded simply, 'Princess Elizabeth of York visited their Majesties and remained to luncheon.' Accurately newspapers described the relationship of king and princess as that of 'joyous friends'.[19] It was a claim none of George V's children could have made. In his diary that summer, the King wrote simply, 'All the children looked so nice, but none prettier than Lilibet and Margaret.'[20] To mark the occasion he gave both princesses pearl necklaces: three rows for Elizabeth, two for Margaret.

❧

For George V, the events of that sun-drenched May proved a swansong. In June he developed bronchial catarrh. A fortnight's unscheduled recuperation at Sandringham restored him to temporary health; he resumed the annual itinerary of Cowes Week, then Balmoral. In Scotland his guests included the Archbishop of Canterbury, to whom he talked 'a great deal about "this latest friendship of the Prince of Wales" [with Wallis Simpson], and was very concerned about it'.[21]

The Yorks remained in London or at Royal Lodge. In July, a Punch and Judy show in the grounds of Mount Clare in Roehampton provided Elizabeth and Margaret with a moment of unalloyed childish fun to offset earlier formalities. In late summer, they travelled north to Birkhall, the house on the Balmoral estate, still lit by oil lamps and heated by paraffin stoves, which the King had loaned them since 1929. Neither of her parents fully explained to Elizabeth her grandfather's worsening condition. Among treats was a birthday party at nearby Abergeldie Castle. It was given by the Earl and Countess of Shaftesbury for their granddaughter, Mary Anna Sturt. Despite a potentially inhibiting audience of the Queen, the duchess and the King of Greece, a children's entertainer called Mr A. Hay Prestowe performed magic tricks and ventriloquism. He invited Elizabeth to help him. Her debut as a magician saw her perform, inevitably, 'as to the manner born'.[22] In London at the end of November, she accompanied her parents to a matinée in aid of the National Theatre Appeal, three hours of scenes from Shakespeare; her parents took her away before the beginning of the murder scene from *Othello*. Her favourite moment was a slapstick performance by music hall comedian George Robey of a soliloquy from *Henry V*. Like her enjoyment of the Punch and Judy show, it was proof that, precocious dignity and earnestness aside, she was still a child, with a child's instincts and tastes.

At Christmas 1935, after a present-buying expedition to Woolworths ('china ornaments, sweets and pages of coloured stick-on scraps and transfers'),[23] Elizabeth and Margaret went to Sandringham without their parents. The duchess was suffering from pneumonia; she and the duke remained at Royal Lodge. The duchess wrote to her elder daughter. Her warning to be 'very polite to everybody. Mind you answer very nicely when you are asked questions, even though they may be silly ones!' is a reminder of the formality of the royal house party and the importance attached to good manners.[24] As in other years, the sisters helped their grandparents distribute presents to estate workers, this year dressed in the 'fairy' frocks they had worn for the Gloucesters' wedding. With the family party they listened to the King's Christmas broadcast, his description of the Empire's 'family of peoples' and his hopes for 'the blessing of peace'; they were too young to understand the old King's anxiety over Mussolini and Hitler. In the New Year, unable any longer to shoot, the King took sedate rides on his shooting pony instead. 'Out of the mist came the King, mounted on his white pony, Jock,' remembered a former member of the household, of a wintry, post-Christmas afternoon. 'Walking by the head of the pony as if leading it along was the little figure of Princess Elizabeth. She was taking her grandfather back to the house.'[25] Once before, at the seaside near Bognor, Elizabeth had cheered the King's recovery. There would be no getting better this time. The King's heart was weakening, he was short of breath, he walked with difficulty and struggled to remain awake. Perhaps, then, knowing, as he told old friends, that he was done for, he drew comfort from the small girl who accompanied his walks and saw him safely home. His estimate of her abilities was of the highest. He told Lady Algernon Gordon Lennox, 'I pray to God that my eldest son will never marry and have children, and that nothing will come between Bertie and Lilibet and the throne.'[26] For a man so conventional in outlook, with a conventional view of monarchy, such an irregular sentiment points to the despondency the Prince of Wales inspired in him.

Elizabeth sturdily rebuffed the efforts of the Archbishop of Canterbury to talk to her alone. In response to an invitation to accompany him on a walk, she asked him 'not [to] tell me anything more about God. I know all about him already.'[27] More appealing than the company of the elderly Lang was her snowman-building with Margaret on 17 January, or, the following morning, when 'in the spring-like sunshine, warmly clad, they romped in the snow, laughingly bombarding' their handiwork.[28] It was proof of Queen Mary's success in keeping up appearances that Elizabeth did not suspect the imminence of her grandfather's death: the first bulletin announcing the King's worsening condition was issued within hours of the princesses' snowman-building. Both girls were informed the next morning. They left Sandringham for London by train that afternoon, dressed in cherry-red coats and hats, Elizabeth unable to disguise her unhappiness.[29] Two days later, the King was dead. A lethal injection of cocaine and morphia into the jugular vein, administered by his doctor, hastened his end. It was a question of timing: his family's preference that first reports of his death not appear in the evening papers, with their jaunty raffishness, but the sober pages of the *Times*. Elizabeth and Margaret were told after breakfast. Later in the day, Uncle David, Prince of Wales no longer, announced his intention of reigning as Edward VIII. He had chosen the same name as his grandfather, Edward VII, whose easy philandering had long been among his fixations.

～～

Three weeks after George V's death, nine-year-old Kinara Kestyn from Derby received a letter from the Duchess of York's lady-in-waiting, Lettice Bowlby. 'I am desired by Her Royal Highness the Duchess of York to thank you very much for your kind letter of sympathy to Princess Elizabeth,' it ran. 'You will understand what it means to her, as she adored her grandfather.'[30]

The King's death was a watershed for all the Yorks save five-year-old Margaret, who was insulated by infancy. 'My life has been so bound up with yours the last twelve years,' the duchess wrote to Queen Mary.[31] For eleven of those twelve years she had been the King and Queen's only daughter-in-law, with an adroitness in managing that exacting couple that none of their own children possessed, and a privileged position at court. The births of Elizabeth, then Margaret, had strengthened this closeness. But while the duchess measured the King and Queen against the benchmark of her own parents and found them lacking, the King at times all but tyrannical as paterfamilias and, to his sons, 'not understanding and helpful', Elizabeth felt no such reservations about 'Old Man Kind'. She shared his love of horses, stamps and the Highlands; she would come to share his feeling for religion, 'impressive and appealing in its earnest simplicity';[32] grandfather and granddaughter shared a simple bond of affection. They had reputedly made an arrangement: every morning, at an agreed time, at the nursery window of 145 Piccadilly Elizabeth waved a white handkerchief in the direction of Buckingham Palace, where her grandfather also stood beside a window, watching for her greeting.[33]

By telegram, the duchess recalled Crawfie early to Royal Lodge from her Christmas holiday. Absent at the moment of the governess's return, she left her a message: a request that she not allow events to 'depress [Elizabeth and Margaret] more than is absolutely necessary... They are so young.'[34] Her kind intentions mistook the extent of Elizabeth's unhappiness. Elizabeth, Crawfie noted, 'in her sensitive fashion felt it all deeply'.[35] She was not to be hoodwinked from her grief. Even the toy horses provided faltering respite. 'I remember her pausing doubtfully as she groomed one... and looking up at me for a moment. "Oh, Crawfie... ought we to play?" she asked.'[36]

Elizabeth took part in a number of the King's obsequies, including the lying-in-state in Westminster Hall. Newspapers suggested 'it was Queen Mary's special wish': the widow kept her black-clad granddaughter at her side throughout a late-night vigil. 'The little princess gazed gravely on the bier and the statuesque groups of sentinels drawn from the Gentlemen-at-Arms, the Yeomen of the Guard and the Household Brigade of Guards.' The royal party were present for a changing of the guard, 'which the Queen also desired her granddaughter to watch': Guards officers' replacement by the dead king's four sons, the so-called 'vigil of the princes'.[37] Queen Mary explained to Elizabeth the significance of the lying-in-state and details of the regalia round the coffin. Elizabeth's presence was interpreted as a sign of the Queen's particular fondness, but the Queen's motives were mixed. The ceremonial of royal death represented history in the making. For the child now second in the line of succession, royal history, in her grandmother's view, was particularly her business. Elizabeth did not look for explanations of her grandmother's favour; her abiding impression was of Uncle David's stillness throughout the brothers' vigil and the overwhelming silence in the ancient building, as if, she said, 'the King were asleep'.[38]

To Paddington station, on 28 January, Crawfie took the nine-year-old princess to await the arrival of the gun carriage en route for burial at Windsor. In this gloomy, vaulted enclosure, 'packed with silent and often weeping people', Elizabeth struggled. She was 'very white... her small face quivered'. 'She did not much like all this,' Crawfie remembered, 'but she meant to go through with it, making no fuss.'[39] How often in the future would she act in just this way, this child raised in a world in which reserve and self-control were synonyms for good behaviour. But she would outlive that world. Sixty years later, following the death of Diana, Princess of Wales, the reserve Elizabeth learned in childhood, the instinct to eschew fuss, was seized upon by hostile crowds and an opportunist media as a cudgel with which to beat her most unkindly.

In the aftermath of the King's death, the Yorks continued to shelter Elizabeth from speculation about her future. Given Edward VIII's bachelorhood, such speculation was inevitable. The day after the funeral, the *Tatler* reproduced a full-page image of Elizabeth in her bridesmaid's frock from the Gloucesters' wedding. The magazine reminded readers that Elizabeth had taken another step closer to the throne; it indicated her fitness for the high office that might one day be hers. 'The delightful and beloved little lady,' it informed readers, 'as elder daughter of the Heir Presumptive to the Throne, is now second in the order of succession. Already an outstanding personality, Princess Elizabeth possesses a discernment remarkable in one so young, and her thoughtfulness for others is unfailing.'[40] That she was widely beloved was indeed the case. Overlooking the new king, whose film-star charisma inspired adulation, the *Sphere* told readers that 'of the Royal Family Princess Elizabeth probably commands the largest following of ardent "fans"'.[41] It was a verdict unlikely to recommend itself to the duke and duchess, to Crawfie, anxious to invest both sisters' upbringing with normality, or to the protective Alah. Nor did the duke and duchess comment on the visual symbolism of Frank Salisbury's official painting of the Silver Jubilee thanksgiving service when it was unveiled that spring. In Salisbury's processional image, only two members of the royal family directly regard the viewer: a querulous Prince of Wales and, behind him, his heir in the next generation, his niece Princess Elizabeth.

Too young to reflect on its larger implications, Elizabeth could not escape the short-term impact of George V's death. Even her wardrobe changed. In place of the cherry-red coat she had worn for snowballing at Sandringham was a new coat of grey flannel; she was fitted for linen summer frocks in mauve and white.[42] As ever, Margaret's clothes were the same. So were Mary Cambridge's: her new grey coat was 'cut on military lines, double breasted', to be worn with a matching grey beret. The princesses' mauve and white frocks were a concession, albeit drab enough compared with the flower-patterned cotton piqués the duchess usually chose: Queen Mary had 'expressed a wish that all the Royal children should wear light, half-mourning colours by Easter'.[43] Accompanying her parents on an engagement weeks later, Elizabeth wore a grey tweed coat with a mauve straw hat.

Before Easter 1936, however, came an escape from court mourning. At the beginning of March, the duke and duchess travelled to Eastbourne on the south coast and a month's recuperation for the duchess. Although Queen Mary had let it be known that, in her grief, 'her greatest joy... [was] the company of her granddaughters', Elizabeth and Margaret shortly joined their parents.[44] Their visits to the seaside were infrequent; at Eastbourne that spring, weather 'which would have done justice to June' and a beach chalet of their own gilded the lily.[45] The duchess complained about the crowds that dogged every excursion. To Queen Mary she wrote protestingly, 'Yesterday was divine, and in the morning we went down to the little "chalet" on the beach, and the sun was heavenly. The people were rather a bore, and though they stared quite politely, they <u>stared</u> & STARED.'[46] It was the princesses, not their parents, they wanted to see. The parish church was full for their first Sunday visit on 8 March, 'and outside the church the crowds increased in size when it was known that the Princesses had joined their parents at the service'.[47] A year before, watching the princesses playing in Hamilton Gardens from a passing bus, scullery maid Mollie Moran had described them as 'seemingly oblivious to the attention';[48] Lady Astor's niece Joyce Grenfell described them at a children's party as 'natural... always being watched and concentrated on'.[49] Obliviousness eluded the duchess. She arranged drives into the surrounding country, including to Winchelsea, where the rector showed Elizabeth the church. They went to Cooden Beach, '& the children enjoyed themselves enormously', and to Beachy Head. Sometimes their route was lined with wellwishers. In the privacy of Compton Place, loaned to them by the Duke of Devonshire, the duchess settled her daughters into the carefree routines that had always been her priority, the prying world shut out.

'he was popular with all classes because when he did a thing it was in the service of England'.[57] By contrast, the actions of his eldest son were widely condemned, including within the royal family, as a dereliction of duty, a sentiment Virginia Woolf discerned in letters to *The Times*: 'Our sons & brothers gave their wives & lovers & also their lives for the country. And can't the King even do this – ?'[58] The abdication threatened the stability of the crown and the unity of the country; at a critical moment in European affairs, it distracted the British from a full appreciation of the threat of Nazi Germany; and it altered royal lives for ever, Bertie's and his daughter Elizabeth's most of all. It became the Windsors' cautionary tale, the ex-king the dynasty's bogeyman; its narrative was of private inclination overwhelming public duty. The simplest explanation for Edward's actions was his preference for Wallis Simpson over lonely kingship. Officially the King chose love in place of sovereignty. His choice, stigmatized by Archbishop Lang as 'a craving for private happiness', cast a lasting shadow over Elizabeth's life and stamped indelibly her view of royalty's obligations.[59] Within Elizabeth's family, his choice demonized self-gratification. It confirmed this starchy family's fear of unchecked emotions. It also damned Mrs Simpson.

The abdication forced on Edward VIII by the actions of his prime minister, Stanley Baldwin, who consistently opposed marriage between the King and Mrs Simpson, and the hostility of dominion premiers and swathes of the press also highlighted the indivisibility for royalty of their public and private selves. The King was king at all times and in every aspect of his life. Given his position as supreme governor of a church that did not recognize divorce, his choice of life partner was potentially as trammelled as any other of his actions. Indeed all his choices were apparently circumscribed, any real power he possessed a will-o'-the-wisp without the bolstering of public endorsement and officialdom. At the eleventh hour, the King hell-bent on modernizing his father's 'Victorian' court, fell hostage to popular conceptions of royalty. As Woolf recorded, 'We can't have a woman Simpson for Queen, that was the sense of it. She's no more royal than you or me, was what the grocer's young woman said.'[60] From her elders, notably her grandmother, who, according to Osbert Sitwell, 'saw the world's moral and social problems in terms of black and white, with no gradation', Elizabeth absorbed the 'lessons' of the abdication.[61] Whenever she became aware of them, she did not allow herself to forget. Monarchy's fragility had been exposed to sneering view. How flimsy in the face of personal whim magic and mystique had proven.

❧

A month after George V's death, the *Yorkshire Evening Post* had informed its readers 'it is merely a coincidence that [Princess Elizabeth] has not seen her uncle, the new King, since his accession'.[62] Like other similar apologia, it fell wide of the mark. Mrs Simpson was the chief cause of strain in relations between the Yorks and Elizabeth's favourite uncle that lessened their time spent together; the duchess's antipathy pre-dated her brother-in-law's accession. It did not diminish over time. Discussing 'a certain person' in a letter to Queen Mary, the duchess claimed, 'I do not feel that I can make advances to her & ask her to our house, as I imagine would be liked, & this fact is bound to make relations a little difficult.'[63] To her mother-in-law the duchess did not need to explain further. From inception the King's relationship with Mrs Simpson had caused his parents dismay. In 1936 the unsuitability as royal consort of an American divorcee who would shortly have two living ex-husbands required no enumeration. The magpie-like Queen could not have made her disapprobation clearer than in a symbolic act of omission. Early in 1936, she divided up jewellery from the collection of George V's unmarried sister, Princess Victoria: pieces to the duchesses of York, Kent and Gloucester. To the new King, 'who might pass them on to Mrs Simpson', she gave nothing.[64]

Over the course of the year, Crawfie remembered, there were 'fewer occasions when [the King] dropped in for a romp with his nieces',[65] grounds for Princess Margaret – four years younger than her sister and with fewer memories before this date – telling biographer Christopher Warwick in 1981 that the closeness between Edward and the York princesses was apocryphal: 'We didn't know him.'[66] Unusually, the King was absent from Elizabeth's birthday tea party in April: when she cut her cake, she set aside a slice to be sent to him. He did, however, arrive at Royal Lodge the same evening with his present of a riding whip. Less happily he made an afternoon visit to Royal Lodge to show off a new American station wagon, taking with him a party that included Mrs Simpson. Whatever the declared purpose of that visit, it was Mrs Simpson who was scrutinized most closely by the duchess and Crawfie. 'I left with the distinct impression that while the Duke of York was sold on the American station wagon, the duchess was not sold on David's other American interest,' she wrote, and the visit, Crawfie noted, was never afterwards mentioned by her employers or the children.[67] Elizabeth saw the King again on her visit to the *Queen Mary* at the end of May. Although not reported, she was not alone in trying out the slide in the liner's nursery: her uncle tried it, too. Of course, Elizabeth remained unaware of royal concerns about Mrs Simpson's hold on the King, described that month as her 'absolute slave'.[68]

The autumn was to prove 'rather uneasy' for the adults in Elizabeth's life: Crawfie described it as an interlude of 'nervous tension'.[69] Metaphorically impermeable, the nursery walls immured Elizabeth from many warning signs. Her days retained their familiar pattern: the lightest timetable of lessons with Crawfie, twin-like playtime with Margaret, the familiar jockeyings with their parents, riding lessons, singing lessons, dancing classes. The foreign press made whoopee, agog at the King's relationship with his Baltimore broad; at home, newspapers kept a fragile silence. Court officials fulminated at the new King's shortcomings, his laziness, carelessness over state papers, calculated rudenesses. Already key players favoured his father's solution of the crown for Bertie, then Elizabeth. To Birkhall the duchess invited the Archbishop of Canterbury, repository of George V's anxieties. Approvingly the churchman watched Elizabeth at play with her sister and cousin, Margaret Elphinstone. 'They sang action songs most charmingly,' he recorded. 'It was strange to think of the destiny which may be awaiting the little Elizabeth, at present second from the throne. She and her lively little sister are certainly most entrancing children.'[70] In the event, Lang played no part in the abdication process, despite his partisanship behind the scenes and the newspaper seller reported by Chips Channon whose abdication day cry was 'The Church held a pistol to [the King's] head'.[71] Privately and publicly he championed Elizabeth's parents.

Elizabeth was still a little girl preoccupied by ponies. Towards her friends she displayed a tendency to bossiness, to her sister a strong protective instinct; she showed no interest at all in her clothes, save a favourite sapphire-blue velvet opera cloak. In Crawfie's descriptions she was still 'very farm-minded' and attached to her toy farm of animals bought from Woolworths, still the earnest, eager girl who had told her governess, 'If I am ever Queen I shall make a law that there must be no riding on Sundays. Horses should have a rest too.'[72] At the Royal Tournament, an annual highlight of horses and soldiers, she and Margaret 'sat forward, leaning on their elbows, watching every move'.[73] Photographs show Elizabeth standing at the front of the royal box: she clapped, she rocked with laughter, she was 'enthralled', 'delighted'. Crawfie was enlisted to join in pony games at home: ridden or driven by the princess, a string of Woolworth's pearls as reins. Elizabeth herself was a pony; she pawed the ground with a brogue-clad 'hoof', she snorted and whinnied; as a pony she ignored any questions asked her. In the evening, she and Margaret groomed the nursery's toy horses; they polished and cleaned immaculate tack. At length she quoted Henry Owen, the groom; she marvelled at his prowess. She felt keenly Ginger's mistreatment in *Black Beauty*. Horses dominated her memories of the Kents' wedding: 'she said that she could not bear to see the way the horses' manes had been tied up, nor the tightness of their bearing reins'.[74] In Scotland in September, riding alternated with tree climbing and learning to make pastry with Mrs McDonald, Birkhall's housekeeper. Elphinstone cousins came to stay. Horse games filled the long days, Elizabeth their instigator. 'We endlessly cavorted as horses,' remembered Margaret Elphinstone. 'We galloped round and round. We were horses of every kind: carthorses, racehorses and circus horses. We spent a lot of time as circus horses and it was obligatory to neigh.'[75] There were also picnics on an island in the River Muick, with competitions to eat as much brown bread and golden syrup as possible. When it rained the cousins played indoors, in a single-room annexe, rain drumming on the metal roof.[76]

Even as the King's reign entered its final febrile weeks, little altered in the routines of the nursery floor at 145 Piccadilly or at Royal Lodge. Elizabeth and Margaret loaned dolls to a forthcoming exhibition at Whiteley's department store in aid of Sunshine Homes for Blind Babies. Both were again knitting scarves for the annual clothing appeal organized by Queen Mary's Needlework Guild, and Elizabeth was busy making her grandmother's Christmas present: a linocut of a drawing she had already finished of a circus horse standing on its hind legs in the centre of the ring. Evolving plans for the coronation, scheduled for 12 May 1937, designated a role for Elizabeth but excluded Margaret: the lengthy ceremony was considered 'a too big demand upon the patience of the little Princess'.[77] Reports asserted then denied that Elizabeth would travel to Holland in January as a bridesmaid to Princess Juliana, her fellow bridesmaid at the Kent wedding two years earlier. More dramatic though less widely circulated was a rumour that Queen Mary had agreed to act as regent for her granddaughter.[78] On 17 November, David told the duke and Queen Mary of his resolution to abdicate in the event of being unable to marry Mrs Simpson. Three days later, a dazed Duke and Duchess of York left London for Wiltshire and a shooting weekend with Lord and Lady Pembroke at Wilton House, as ever leaving their daughters behind.

Stop-start discussions with the King and the pall cast by the increasing likelihood of the duke's own accession in David's place imposed an almost intolerable strain on Elizabeth's parents. The duchess lamented the horror of 'having to talk & behave as if nothing was wrong during these difficult days', but did just this: in public, in letters to her mother, at home.[79] That her daughters should be safeguarded from every shadow remained a primary concern. Looking back in 1950, Crawfie suggested, 'I do not know what we would have done at that time without the swimming lessons... The outings to the swimming club were the high spots of the week... and they helped a lot to take our minds off the clouds that were gathering about us all.'[80] Elizabeth knew little, and understood less, of the gathering clouds. Until the British press broke its silence on 3 December and billboards broadcast the King's dilemma, it is possible that her only warnings of things amiss were the haggardness of her father's appearance and, presumably, an atmosphere of something unspoken; at the eleventh hour the duchess again fell ill with influenza, her reaction more than once to unpleasantness. By early December both princesses had begun to notice the frequent comings and goings at 145 Piccadilly. To a question of Margaret's Elizabeth replied confusedly, 'I think Uncle David wants to marry Mrs Baldwin, and Mr Baldwin doesn't like it.'[81] (Another version has Margaret asking Elizabeth in the procession at her parents' coronation, 'Shall we see Uncle David today?', Elizabeth replying, 'Of course not, he's married Mrs Baldwin!'[82]) She was clearer in her excited response to the swimming lessons at the Bath Club in nearby Dover Street, under the tutelage of Amy Daly. In late November, a columnist calling herself 'A Woman in London' reported that the princesses were 'frequently to be seen at the Club. They are making excellent progress, their instructress tells me, and by what I saw of them they both seem to be enjoying the experience immensely.'[83] Sometimes their parents accompanied them. The duke marvelled at their progress; he marvelled at their lack of shyness and self-consciousness in the white-initialled blue bathing costumes that flattered Elizabeth but transformed Margaret into 'a plump navy-blue fish'; perhaps he marvelled at their absorption.[84] Anticipating the worst, he decided on a regnal name of 'George VI', a deliberate link with his father and more stable times.

'Princess Elizabeth's chance of sitting on Britain's throne in the future is a fairly long-odds chance,' the *Sphere* told readers on 22 February 1936. On 10 December, those odds unexpectedly shortened. At lunchtime the Act of Abdication received royal assent. The Duke of York succeeded his elder brother as king. On the former Edward VIII, he conferred the dukedom of Windsor. He initiated discussions of a financial settlement that swiftly became acrimonious. The ex-king departed for the Continent. His spectre loitered for years, cause of anxiety, anger and frustration to those left behind. His ire focused on a calculated omission: the new king's refusal to grant the Duchess of Windsor royal status.

Elizabeth learned what had happened from a footman. The noise of cheering in Piccadilly, a stream of cars arriving at and leaving the house, messengers with telegrams, delivery men with bouquets and an unexpected visit from the Duchess of Kent prompted her question. She told Margaret in the nursery.

'Does that mean that you will have to be the next queen?' her sister responded.

'Yes, some day.'

'Poor you,' said Margaret.[85]

From the nursery window the sisters watched the growing crowds with arms linked; the gesture was instinctive. Again and again they returned to their vantage point. By mid-afternoon, when Queen Mary visited their mother, the throng in the street below had swollen to several thousand. At each of the sisters' appearances at the window a cheer went up.

CHAPTER IV

'The delightful and beloved little lady... is now second in the order of succession'

❧

IN A SPEECH roundly applauded by his audience in 1932, at the opening of new headquarters of the British College of Obstetricians and Gynaecologists, Professor William Blair-Bell had celebrated the Duchess of York's contribution to British life. 'Your Royal Highness has given to us all a vision of the happiness of married life, and in a very beautiful way, through the little Princesses, the people have been permitted to share your joys and show their devotion to the Crown.'[1] On abdication day, newspapers reprinted Blair-Bell's encomia. The force of his remarks, commented one, 'is if anything even greater today'.

The beauty of family unity was a central theme of the reign begun in a spirit of make do and mend and characterized at its outset by the new King's apologetic note to his prime minister: 'I hope that time will allow me to make amends for what has happened.'[2] A bachelor king had abandoned duty for a *mésalliance*; in his stead appeared a readymade family of a sort that peopled children's reading primers. For the first time in history, a new sovereign and his consort were best known to their subjects as husband and wife, father and mother: lynchpins of a model family with happiness as its lodestar. In this light a disappointed nation tentatively embraced a second son 'less superficially endowed with the arts and graces that please', whose chief recommendations were a serviceable doggedness and successful domesticity.[3] Within weeks, loyal Cynthia Asquith had produced a new instalment of her heroine's story; it was published under the title *The Family Life of H M Queen Elizabeth*. 'No more homely British Family has ever ascended the throne than that of the Duke and Duchess of York,' asserted the *Daily Mirror* on 11 December; for the new King George VI homeliness took the place of divine right. Elizabeth and Margaret, the paper claimed, had inherited their mother's 'simple and homely ideas'.[4] Viewers of a Pathé Gazette newsreel were told that 'above all, King George VI and Queen Elizabeth receive our hearty and humble affection because they are true home-lovers in the sense most respected by every man and woman throughout the civilised world.'

The royal family rallied behind what appeared at first an unheroic cause. David's farewell broadcast trumpeted Bertie's single qualification for sovereignty: 'one matchless blessing enjoyed by so many of you and not bestowed on me, a happy home with his wife and children'. Queen Mary echoed the call, in a message ostensibly of thanks to the nation for its support and kindness to her personally. In words written for her by Cosmo Lang, the royal widow pledged her support for her second son; she commended his wife, she reminded his new subjects that they had already taken to heart his daughters. Newspapers published a photograph that made clear her role as royal matriarch, in her daughter-in-law's words 'a rock of defence':[5] the old queen seated centrally, flanked by Elizabeth and Margaret, on her knee Prince Edward of Kent, the newest royal baby, a visible linking of past and future, former glories and coming hopes. To Bertie himself, his opportunist cousin Lord Louis Mountbatten articulated the loyalist line: 'Luckily both you and your children have precisely those qualities needed to pull this country through this ghastly crisis.'[6]

Over time, a reeling nation mostly accepted the conjuring trick of the abdication by which domestic probity supplanted the legitimacy of primogeniture as grounds for kingship; even David himself had acquiesced. In this way, as in others, the accession of the family-minded Duke of York restored, rather than destroyed, continuity. The focus on family that characterized George V's later public utterances had won broad approval, like the letters the King received after his Christmas broadcast of 1934 with its reference to 'the marriage of our dear son and daughter', the Duke and Duchess of Kent: 'I think it was Lovely and Good of you... to think of your loving Son and Daughter in law'; 'it was most pleasing to us all to hear your loving remarks respecting Their Royal Highnesses the Duke and Duchess of Kent'.[7] Responses of this sort accounted for the successful reissue, the month after the abdication, of Michael Chance's syrupy *Our Princesses and Their Dogs*, illustrated with Lisa Sheridan's photographs of the new royal family taken in more carefree days. To this gossamer offering and other similar exercises a loyal press responded helpfully. 'You see what a cheery, natural kind of life these two little girls lead,' commented a columnist called 'Wendy'. 'They like to romp and play out of doors. They love the circus, they like to see a pantomime, and they simply adore parties. They can ride and dance, and Princess Elizabeth is learning to skate. They have to do lessons of course, though whether they like them very much I don't know!'[8] Here were the royal daughters as symbols of British orthodoxy: happiest out of doors, populist in their cultural choices, dog-loving, robustly unintellectual. 'Amid the delightful surroundings of Royal Lodge they live a happy, open-air life,' announced a cigarette card in Wills's commemorative coronation collection. It was as if Wallis Simpson's flaw was the time she spent indoors. She could not compete with the Yorks' absorption in their garden or the little girls' delight in their dogs and ponies.

On Elizabeth, though she was still too young to realize it, this compensatory approach to promoting the new reign imposed additional pressures: she must be happy at all times and conspicuously so in company with her family. Conveniently, happiness had been central to her public persona from birth. With the iron nib of the propagandist, Anne Ring acclaimed her as 'contented all day long' and 'passionately fond of her parents', in both instances truthfully.[9] For a public who still required from their royal family something more than ordinariness, the Yorks' storybook contentment elevated them above the common run. Uncle David had forfeited his throne by failing to find happiness in acceptable form; in December 1936, as the soon-to-be ex-king explained, such happiness was the Duke of York's trump card. As a rationale, its implications would be shared with both his daughters, as well as his wife. Time would show them well equipped to satisfy this particular expectation. 'Their joy in one another is complete and perfect,' the *Sunday Express* told readers before the coronation.[10] Unusually accurate for hyperbole, it was a view with which all four would have agreed.

They returned to Marcus Adams. Four days after the Duke of York became king, the family sat again for their favourite photographer, their purpose transmogrification into a 'Royal Family'. Again the princesses's frocks are whorls of pale organdie. Neither looks entirely at ease. Against the dark background an aureole of light illuminates the four faces. Four sets of linked arms communicate their closeness. Watching the family's arrival at a railway station soon afterwards, reporters noted that 'Princess Elizabeth held the hand of her sister,

Princess Margaret, when they stepped down from the Royal coach'.[11] Clinging on to one another was a metaphor of sorts for uncertain beginnings. Elizabeth would do her best to hold her sister's hand for much of the remainder of Margaret's life.

Yet no one but Elizabeth regarded these hand-holding sisters as equals, least of all in December 1936; Elizabeth's own behaviour indicates that she, too, recognized that their roles differed. The same reporter at King's Cross recorded that, prior to leaving the station, 'Princess Elizabeth left her sister, walked over to the group of [station] officials and shook hands with each.'[12] She was ten years old; she was now the heir to the throne and schooled in good manners. Elizabeth not Margaret was photographed by Adams on her own in a head-and-shoulders portrait striking in its maturity. She does not smile, and her gaze is unflinching: it was an image to delight her grandmother. The participation of Elizabeth, not Margaret, in her parents' forthcoming coronation, set for the date once fixed for Uncle David, consumed the curious with questions about her robes, coronet, attendants, whether or not 'she would lead the procession of the Princes and Princesses of the Blood Royal'.[13] Rumours that Elizabeth would attend a coronation durbar in Delhi did not extend to Margaret. Elizabeth's education would change; Margaret's need not. Elizabeth not Margaret would study constitutional history and economic theory with specialist tutors; Margaret would remain Crawfie's responsibility. In the abdication's aftermath, despite, Virginia Woolf noted, 'pictures of the Duke of York and the Princesses fill[ing] every [newspaper] cranny' for days beforehand, Elizabeth was the focus of most avid public interest.[14] It was Elizabeth's life that had changed irrevocably. 'With the heartfelt good wishes which pour out to her parents from millions of English-speaking people all over the world will go a hope that [Princess Elizabeth's] childhood may still be joyous despite the seriousness of the life that lies ahead,' offered the *Birmingham Daily Gazette* on 11 December.[15] It was her parents' hope, too. Thanks to a four-year difference in age, Margaret's life threatened no such 'seriousness'. What Elizabeth herself thought remains unknown. To her sister she did not again refer to her future role, nor did she, like the future Queen Victoria at a similar moment, utter any resolution concerning how she meant to set about it. Perhaps, in December 1936, it simply felt a long way off. If so, her equanimity would stand her in good stead. 'I'm afraid there are going to be great changes in our lives,' the new queen told Crawfie.[16] Both girls were too young to conceive any realistic view of the nature or impact of such changes, both, for the moment, young enough to absorb themselves wholeheartedly in the business of the present.

Elizabeth's behaviour in the coming months suggests Lady Strathmore's claim that her granddaughter had begun 'ardently praying for a baby brother', reported at second hand by Lady Airlie, was a fleeting response.[17] Nothing has emerged to indicate anxiety on Elizabeth's part, or that she protested against a fate beyond her control. 'Acceptance of inevitability', one of her cousins has claimed, seems always to have played its part in a character fundamentally pragmatic.[18]

❧

Elizabeth's position was unique. Her father had inherited the crown accidentally. By training and inclination he was unsuited to the task that confronted him; this was his own view and, overwhelmingly, that of members of the public canvased in Mass Observation surveys.[19] His first response to his altered state had been to break down in tears on Queen Mary's shoulder, an hour-long display of acute discomfort to this emotionally costive mother and son. In a calmer moment, he insisted his only knowledge was that of a naval officer. He was diffident and lacking in confidence. Although speech therapy had circumvented the worst of his stammer, public speaking frightened him; he lacked fluency. He lacked star quality, too, and, with his shy smile, slim figure and reputedly uneven health, any visible attributes of kingship. In the short term, his good fortune lay in his charismatic wife, in Queen Mary's assessment 'such a darling and... such a help to Bertie', and his pretty daughters.[20]

By contrast, Elizabeth at ten appeared to have been endowed with every quality of a princess. She was a beautiful child, her hair still flecked with gold, with an infectious zest for life, ready understanding, innate dignity and, in the eyes of many contemporaries, all the magnetism her father so conspicuously missed. Speculation that she would one day inherit the throne, beginning at her birth, seemed to strengthen the legitimacy of her post-abdication elevation. Her association with her royal grandparents worked to the same end. A picture of Elizabeth in Bognor in 1929, building sandcastles while nearby a convalescent George V reads a newspaper, featured in the special 1937 coronation number of the *Illustrated London News*; a more inventive writer likened Elizabeth to Queen Mary at the same age. 'She is today the image of her grandmother, Princess May of Teck, in 1877. There is the same fair colouring with its robust health. There are the same blue eyes that gain in apparent size by their setting and, above all, there is the same strength in the mouth and determination in the jaw.'[21] Where the new king was measured against Edward VIII and found wanting, his daughter – the inheritor of her grandparents' strengths – became a beacon of hope in whom commentators decided they had found the reassurance required by a shaken society. Fidelity to his father's values would be a guiding principle of the reign of George VI and, afterwards, shaped aspects of Elizabeth's own reign. In 1936, insistence on the princess's kinship with her grandparents seemed to suggest the long-term viability of the abdication settlement. In the House of Commons on 28

January 1937, in response to a backbencher query, the home secretary, Sir John Simon, ruled out the necessity of introducing legislation to formalize Elizabeth's claim to the throne, as an elder daughter, by an amendment to the Act of Settlement. No doubt existed, Simon suggested, that 'in present circumstances, Her Royal Highness Princess Elizabeth would succeed to the Throne as sole heir'. It was not a likelihood that provoked notable misgivings.

At ten years old, Elizabeth was heiress presumptive to the throne and a worldwide empire that still, in 1937, covered a quarter of the globe. Only the birth of a baby brother could unseat her claim. At the time, short-term concerns over her parents' suitability for sovereignty distracted attention from her own response to this daunting destiny discussed once with her sister Margaret, then set aside, unmentioned. Subsequent parliamentary discussion underlined her special status. Set before MPs in the context of a debate about the Civil List was the new king's intention to make provision for Elizabeth from his personal income of Duchy of Cornwall revenues. It was just one way in which George VI identified his elder daughter as his heir. For her part, Elizabeth's concerns were homelier. The death of Bobo's father in January had encouraged her to crayon a black edge on Sandringham writing paper. 'We are all very sad,' she wrote to a friend. She signed herself 'Lilibet (in mourning)'.[22]

※

'Dear Bertie and Elizabeth will carry out things in the same way that King George V did,' Queen Mary wrote to Lady Strathmore days after David's departure.[23] This widespread assumption proved largely correct; it extended to every aspect of Bertie's kingship. A party at Buckingham Palace early in the reign was described as 'on the same lines as the afternoon parties which were a regular feature of Buckingham Palace entertainment during the reign of King George V'.[24] 'The undoubted popularity of my brother Bertie, whose life is so much like that which my father led,' reflected the Duke of Windsor in 1951, 'suggests that... the British people are rightly pleased with his faithful carrying on of my father's ways.'[25]

To Winston Churchill, on 18 May 1937, the new king wrote, 'I fully realise the great responsibilities and cares that I have taken on as King.'[26] His solution, insofar as he was able, was to deal with them as his father had. The doctrine of continuity offered the clearest rebuttal of David's backsliding. Potentially it offered more: a conduit for inheritance of the father's popularity by the son. As a fourteen-year-old schoolboy wrote in an essay, 'I hope that the love of King George [V] will linger in the hearts of his people for a very long time and that they will try to love his successors.'[27] His successors hoped so, too. One consequence of the abdication in court circles was the hardening of a conviction that there was a single workable approach to kingship. Bertie's payback for greatness thrust upon him was the requirement that he behave like his father. In his case, the impulse fitted his instinctive conservatism and self-doubt: he did not consider behaving otherwise. One contemporary described him approvingly but not entirely accurately – Bertie was more sensitive, less confident – as 'an almost exact repeat of his father both in manner and in mind'.[28]

And a similar expectation was extended to his daughter. Below an uncharacteristically solemn photograph of Elizabeth, a coronation guide opined sententiously, 'In the event of her acceding one day to the Throne, there is little doubt that she will ably carry on the fine tradition established during a quarter of a century by her grandfather.'[29] Little wonder, then, that two decades later, Elizabeth as queen would be criticized as out of touch. Meanwhile to her son and daughter-in-law, Queen Mary wrote, 'What a joy it has been to me to feel that... you two dear beloved people will carry on the tradition which dear Papa & I tried to do.'[30] Elizabeth was too young, and her life to date had been too straightforwardly happy, to experience fully any dread of prison shades. The abdication had determined her future: as the *Western Mail* explained chillingly, 'so early in life, she has been dedicated to the service of an Empire'.[31] The attitude of key players closest to the little princess also sought to shape the manner of that future.

⁓

The new king and queen left 145 Piccadilly for Buckingham Palace in February, followed by their daughters, Alah, Bobo MacDonald and Crawfie.

Though she did not remember it, Elizabeth had lived in the palace before, during her parents' tour of Australia and New Zealand in 1927; the room chosen then for her nursery became her schoolroom now, full of sunshine on warmer days, with views across the large garden. Bedrooms for Elizabeth and Margaret were on the second floor, above their parents' rooms overlooking the Mall, quite different from Elizabeth's bedroom at 145 Piccadilly, with its large bay window above the quiet garden. Alongside day and night nurseries ('repainted and done up, and... bright and cheerful'[32]), and rooms for Alah and Crawfie, was also a sitting room for Elizabeth. Later, Margaret remembered the move as achieved with minimal disruption, though hers was the perspective of a six-year-old, after days spent carefully strapping saddles on to toy horses and packing into a large basket grooming brushes and polishing cloths. Crawfie's recollections were darker. Readers of *The Little Princesses* cannot mistake the recoiling the palace inspired in her: the 'wearing' distances; the 'menace' of vermin, especially mice; behind-the-scenes shabbiness; inconvenient plumbing, lighting, heating. Writing after the event, the ex-governess projects onto her charges her own intractability, but it is clear that the girls revelled in corridors long enough for bicycling indoors, the garden in which, the Princess Royal told them, their aunt and uncles had played summer games and the summer house, used by George V as a study, that became their outdoor schoolroom. In the centre of the garden was a large lake. Its resident population of ducks fascinated both girls. Searching for a nest, Elizabeth fell in. Dripping algae but soggily happy, she was smuggled back into the palace before her mother or Alah realized. On another occasion, Crawfie described Elizabeth's legs as brown and scratched. Her new garden suited tomboy instincts. On wet winter afternoons, the sisters amused themselves less boisterously, gazing through the lace curtains of upstairs windows at upturned faces in the crowds outside.[33]

'Sombre' was the adjective that Cynthia, Countess Spencer, one of the Queen's new ladies of the bedchamber, applied to the palace in 1937; the atmosphere in at least a handful of its more than 700 rooms changed surprisingly quickly.[34] 'Very little restraint placed on the children', who, with or without attendant corgis, raced along passages, 'one stoutish little girl panting "Wait for me, Lilibet, wait for me!"', and the Queen's genius, applauded by her husband and Lady Airlie, for making places 'homelike' wrought the difference.[35] More than ever, in the spring of 1937 the Queen's focus was her family life, which demanded, insofar as the aristocratic queen and her royal spouse understood it, a homely setting. 'Whatever the exertions of his great office, [the King's] natural taste for simplicity and family life will not be wholly starved,' Cynthia Asquith suggested, 'for, inspite of its immense size and vast staff, Buckingham Palace will remain as genuine a home as any cottage in the land.'[36] As at 145 Piccadilly, it was his wife's doing.

The Queen agreed to Margaret Lindsay Williams, responsible for her own portrait in Y Bwthyn Bach, painting a double portrait of her daughters. Three times, accompanied by Alah, the princesses visited the artist's studio in St John's Wood, happily distracted during sittings by her Sealyham terrier, Harriet. Newspapers mistook the Queen's intentions, suggesting she had requested from Lindsay Williams a picture of the two princesses to harmonize with her decorating plans: 'The white satin drapery behind the figures and the pale silvered frame will make the picture a feature in the Queen's sitting room in the palace, which is being redecorated in peach pink and white.'[37] In fact, the picture was not destined for Buckingham Palace but a gallery in South Africa. Nevertheless the Queen did ask that this latest portrait make no reference to her daughters' status. 'At the special wish of the Queen, neither child wears any jewellery, not even a ribbon in her hair... While the younger princess clasps a bunch of primroses, the elder has a few fallen flowers on her dress.'[38] The cosy but canny new queen commissioned an image of her daughters as harbingers of spring. For a decade Elizabeth's iconography echoed this theme. Stilted to the point of kitschiness to modern eyes, Lindsay Williams's picture – widely reproduced in women's magazines – achieved instant popularity. Like Lisa Sheridan's photographs, it played its part in consolidating support for the new regime with its 'simple' focus on family and home; it celebrated the little girls as icons of hope – in Christopher Hassall's poem 'The Princesses' of similar date, 'Two folded roses... Buds of a royal Spring', whom Hassall labelled unequivocally 'England's pride'.[39]

Yet at Buckingham Palace the illusion of ordinariness, so carefully fostered by the Queen as Duchess of York, could no longer be sustained. Here even private life was public, lived within sight of administrative as well as domestic staff, in a building that was simultaneously the headquarters of a worldwide empire, monarchy's offices and an official residence of the crown. Here there could be no chance acquaintanceships, like that Elizabeth struck up with Sonia Graham Hodgson, based on a meeting in

Hamilton Gardens, and little that was unregulated or unplanned. Here there were no next-door neighbours like the Allendales to encounter on terms of near-equality, nothing that suggested parity between Elizabeth and Margaret and any other children. At 145 Piccadilly and Royal Lodge, the Yorks had appeared to Crawfie to occupy an ivory tower, a term she imbues with nostalgia. It was at Buckingham Palace and Windsor Castle that the girls really became princesses in a tower. Equable Elizabeth does not appear to have been troubled; a friend of her own age shortly described her as 'above all untemperamental'.[40] Perhaps she had always understood, albeit unconsciously and only up to a point, that her 'ordinary' family life was at best a partial truth, this little girl photographed on every outing, to whom unknown bystanders had waved handkerchiefs and hats from her first ride in Hyde Park; who had stood between her parents and grandparents on the balcony at Buckingham Palace overlooking a sea of cheering faces; who had ridden through the crowds of the Silver Jubilee and driven along narrow East End streets crepitating with lusty cries for George V and Queen Mary; who had learned to wave before she could walk and to curtsey before she could read; who sat for portraitists and sculptors; whose birthdays were marked by messages of congratulations from unknown bodies, like the Chalfont St Giles Methodist Sisterhood, who sent 'hearty birthday greetings and love' in April 1937.[41] All of this Elizabeth knew.

At one end of the garden at Buckingham Palace was a hill. From its summit, Elizabeth, Margaret and Crawfie 'could look out into the wide world'.[42] Their view showed them cars, buses, 'people passing, and other children, with their nurses, bound for the park'. Sometimes, from beyond the garden walls, the trio heard snatches of conversation. 'These children were a source of interest,' Crawfie comments, like the crowds the girls watched from palace windows on rainy afternoons. She does not choose to offer further details. Elizabeth has remained interested in those beyond palace railings. 'I loved watching the people and the cars there in the Mall,' she told portraitist Pietro Annigoni in 1954. 'They all seemed so busy. I used to wonder what they were doing and where they were all going, and what they thought about outside the palace.'[43]

༄

Elizabeth's best-known comment on her parents' coronation in Westminster Abbey in May is the 'haze of wonder' she glimpsed covering the arches and beams of the roof at the moment of the King's crowning. This mystical response suggests the imaginative hold the coronation exercised over her, and perhaps, too, since the eleven-year-old concluded that it was 'all <u>very</u>, <u>very</u> wonderful', the degree of ease she felt at her family's change in fortunes. For the King and Queen and both their daughters, thoughts of the coronation had overrun their lives since December. Alongside coronation planning was a roster of special events. At a concert for children organized by philanthropist Robert Mayer on 6 April, the princesses heard a new orchestral fantasy, *Big Ben Looks On*, dedicated to them by its composer Sir Walford Davies. It began with 'two small dedicatory tunes, one for each Princess'; Elizabeth obligingly beamed when her own was played.[44] Like Davies's dedication, the size of the crowds at Windsor Castle later in the month for her birthday indicated Elizabeth's increased prominence as heiress presumptive. On this occasion, more than a thousand people gathered at the castle gates. They watched the changing of the guard; they cheered the royal family of four, visible in a doorway; and they cheered Elizabeth and Margaret, when, without their parents, they walked out into the Grand Quadrangle and 'stood in the centre of the lawn acknowledging the greetings'.[45] Elizabeth had taken part in a variant of this pageant since her third birthday; photographs suggest she felt almost comfortable. From it she absorbed an understanding of herself as public spectacle: her part was to respond appropriately to acclaim that was hers by dint of rank. Evidently she did so. Bystanders agreed she displayed 'a dignity which she seems to have got from her grandmother, Queen Mary... a very pleasing dignity, and with it there is a certain thoughtfulness'.[46] 'She has a quiet poise that makes her remarkable among... other children,' wrote another observer.[47]

Happily, dignity did not colour all of Elizabeth's existence; it never would. In the account of the coronation she wrote for her parents on sheets of lined paper tied together with pink ribbon, a sense of awe contends with puppyish enthusiasm and a prosaic diligence that may have been Crawfie's doing: a requirement that Elizabeth note and record every impression, regardless of relative significance. She describes her early awakening by the Royal Marines band; cosily crouching in the window with Bobo, wrapped in an eiderdown against the chill as both 'look[ed] onto a cold, misty morning' and the first spectators in the stands; the breakfast she was too excited to eat. She describes her dress: 'white silk with old cream lace and... little gold bows all the way down the middle... puffed sleeves with one little bow in the centre. Then there were the robes of purple velvet with gold on the edge.' She describes the 'very jolty' carriage that she and Margaret shared with the Princess Royal and the duchesses of Kent and Gloucester. And she describes the first instance that day of her public 'princessing', when the sisters 'showed ourselves to the visitors and housemaids', a spectacle once again. In Elizabeth's account, details trip over one another. In the rapturous wonder she felt at her parents' crowning is a sense of a personal epiphany. 'When Mummy was crowned and all the peeresses put on their coronets it looked wonderful to see arms and coronets hovering in the air and then the arms disappear as if by magic. Also the music was lovely and the band, the orchestra and the new organ all played beautifully.'

Fleetingly, wonder, magic and beauty combined to create a transcendent moment. For a child on the cusp of adolescence, it was a thrilling demonstration of the extraordinary power of royal theatre at its most sublime, and, for Elizabeth, its glory shimmered all the brighter when, bathetically, Queen Mary revealed to her granddaughter how little she remembered of her own coronation. Elizabeth was astonished. She enjoyed the picnic lunch eaten in a dressing room before departing the abbey more than the lengthy prayers with which the service ended. On the palace balcony, 'where <u>millions</u> of people were waiting below', her excitement was palpable.[48] In his diary, Chips Channon had recorded his view of the princesses arriving at the abbey 'excited by their coronets and trains'.[49] Excitement was the order of Elizabeth's day. Unlike her grandmother, she did not mean to forget a single detail. Her view resembled that of the *Times* writer who described Elizabeth and Margaret processing towards the Royal Gallery, 'all eyes... upon them, small figures advancing with a pretty wonder into a reality as fair as any fable'.[50] But footage and photographs reveal more than wonder in Elizabeth's demeanour. About her is 'an air of unwonted seriousness and quiet dignity'. As one observer suggested, the service brought home to her beyond doubt something of 'her realisation of the destiny awaiting her'.[51]

For Elizabeth, her parents' coronation occurred at exactly the moment likely to impress her most powerfully. She was young enough to be thrilled by its magic, old enough to grasp something of its life-changing significance. In witnessing her parents' ritualized transformation into anointed sovereigns, she surely glimpsed them in that moment heroically, as more than 'Mummie' and 'Papa'. Into their relationship crept at intervals a suggestion of reverence, a deeper respect than that of a child for parents, especially towards her father. Over time it increased her predisposition to follow in their footsteps, her values their values, her ways their ways, her view of monarchy shaped by their example. Her admiration for her king-father never wavered. In his coronation broadcast the new King told his subjects 'the highest of distinctions is the service of others, and to the Ministry of Kingship I have in your hearing dedicated myself... in words of the deepest solemnity', a sentiment that would reverberate through Elizabeth's thoughts of sovereignty ever after.[52]

Queen Mary, however, intended leaving nothing to chance. She embarked on a deliberate, partly covert process of supplementing Elizabeth's education: her particular focus was the princess's royal heritage. Through the intermediary of a lady-in-waiting, Lady Cynthia Colville, she had requested from Crawfie details of Elizabeth's timetable. More history, including genealogical and dynastic history, Bible reading, poetry learning and physical geography, especially of imperial possessions, were the dowager's suggestions. Ahead of the coronation, Crawfie read Elizabeth an account of her own coronation written by Queen Victoria; Queen Mary arranged for a coloured panorama of George IV's coronation procession to be displayed in the palace schoolroom, and explained to both sisters the role of its 700 participants and the traditions they represented.[53] By the time of the service itself, Elizabeth was steeped in coronation history. This picturesque immersion, in addition to her parents' apotheosis and less lofty thrills like her specially made lightweight coronet and, for the first time, her own train fringed with ermine, contributed to the potency of the spell cast over her.

After the hullabaloo of coronation summer, which included a visit to Edinburgh – 'The Royal Company of Archers are very picturesque in their green uniforms and big eagles' feathers,' wrote Elizabeth, with the family eye for details of uniform[54] – Balmoral's remoteness offered respite from constant attention. For Elizabeth there were friends to hand: daughters of members of the royal household Diana Legh and Winifred and Elizabeth

('Libby') Hardinge, in houses on the King's estate. The name chosen for the magazine the friends began together was *The Snapdragon*. Elizabeth wrote a piece about looking out of the window at Buckingham Palace during the changing of the guard, another instance of her curiosity about the world outside or perhaps her sense of herself as an observer behind glass.[55] The girls enjoyed time together without grown-ups nearby. 'Winifred made buttered eggs and the rest of us did odd jobs,' Elizabeth wrote. 'Libby and I fried potatoes and cooked sausages.'[56] When they stayed with the Elphinstones at Carberry Tower, there were pillow fights and sturdy nursery teas.

Back in London, both princesses were dragooned by Queen Mary into a series of visits to historic sights, including Hampton Court, Greenwich Palace and the Royal Mint. Their grandmother's intention was to increase the sisters' understanding of a royal past to which they themselves were linked by consanguinity and living tradition. Of an excursion in October to the Tower of London, the Queen wrote tactfully to her mother-in-law, 'the children were thrilled at the idea of going to the Tower, & I am sure, adored their visit there with you'.[57] Queen Mary described these Monday afternoon sallies as 'instructive amusements'. Less devoted than Elizabeth to her grandmother, Margaret would remember much instruction but little amusement, the sisters hurrying in the old queen's wake, 'absolutely exhausted by hours on end of walking and standing in museums and galleries'.[58] On Elizabeth the visits' effect or otherwise is unclear. Many years later, excusing a frail Frederick Ashton from standing in her presence, she explained, 'Our grandmother taught us to stand. We're used to it.'[59] The excursions did not diminish her love of history, which she described to Princess Marie Louise, a granddaughter of Queen Victoria known to her as 'Cousin Louie', as 'so thrilling'. Nevertheless, the pictures that most engaged her (and possibly

Queen Mary too) on a trip to the National Portrait Gallery were those of her immediate family: Lavery's group portrait of the family of George V and a bronze bust of George V, a Silver Jubilee commission by Felix Weiss.[60] At the same time, inspired by the glittering kaleidoscope of the coronation and its aftermath – a palace dinner for leading Indian princes, a naval review at Spithead, at which she was presented with an HMS *Victory* souvenir brooch – Elizabeth had conceived a romantic enthusiasm for the world she glimpsed around her: the time-warp lushness of her father's court *en fête*. Crawfie described both sisters' excitement at the evening courts at which debutantes were presented to the King and Queen. Through the window they watched arrivals in the palace forecourt; in their rosebud-patterned pink quilted dressing gowns, they watched their parents in full regalia lead the royal procession to the Throne Room. What Elizabeth called their 'fly's-eye view' was tantalizingly inadequate. With the reassurance that 'one day you and I will be down there sharing all the fun', she comforted herself as well as her sister. 'And I shall have a perfectly enormous train, yards long,' she added, a princess longing in that moment to be a grown-up princess.[61]

~~~

At Royal Lodge, where the Royal Family spent as many weekends as possible, the spirit of their former lives could be rekindled. 'Court etiquette was forgotten, and ceremony left behind. We were just a family again,' wrote Crawfie, suggesting solid foundations to the narrative of images like Lisa Sheridan's, taken the previous year in the grounds of Y Bwthyn Bach.[62] The King and Queen busied themselves with their garden; their daughters helped heap bonfires, assisted by the butler, chauffeur, Crawfie. The princesses rode their ponies, swam in the outdoor pool completed in time for Easter 1938, played with their dogs, played inside and outside Y Bwthyn Bach and, most of all, played with one another. On wet days, they rode the pair of rocking horses that stood outside the King's study, they painted, drew, read and knitted; there were jigsaw puzzles and, as previously, teatime games of Racing Demon and, appropriately, Happy Families. Elizabeth and Margaret were as devoted as their mother could have wished. Prominent in Elizabeth's feelings for her younger sister remained a protective instinct. She had been five and Margaret eighteen months old when an alarmingly buck-toothed clergyman called at Royal Lodge. Mesmerized, Elizabeth had gazed at the rise and fall of his jaw as he spoke. Eventually he had asked to see Margaret, a misplaced politeness. Firmly Elizabeth had refused. She had explained, 'I think your teeth might frighten her.'[63]

In Crawfie's account at intervals is a maddening superiority in Elizabeth's attitude: 'After all, she is very young for a Coronation, isn't she?' she supposedly asked her governess.[64] Despite this no doubt kindly condescension, at seven Margaret regarded her sister with an element of hero worship and a touching trust. In their daunting and highly unusual public lives, it was Elizabeth who guided her, their parents too often occupied elsewhere, Queen Mary a fearsome figure, for whom Margaret felt small attachment. The gossipy Crawfie recorded Elizabeth's instructions to Margaret on how to behave at a palace garden party: 'If you do see someone with a funny hat... you must *not* point at it and laugh. And you must not be in too much of a hurry to get through the crowds to the tea table. That's not polite either.'[65] By turns the sisters bickered and squabbled, no more strangers to sibling fractiousness than any other children; they fought over toys. Both hated wearing hats; elastic chin straps were pulled and painfully twanged. With her father's formidable temper, Elizabeth was not above a well-aimed punch. Margaret responded by biting. Although both

Crawfie and Queen Mary detected wilfulness behind Margaret's impish mischief, her parents placed responsibility on Elizabeth for maintaining harmony. 'You mustn't forget that [Margaret] is really very little, & sometimes you must control yourself when she is a little teasing. I know it is difficult, but you can do it, & I know you will,' the Queen wrote to Elizabeth when Margaret was eight.[66] Cynthia Asquith told a meeting of the Women's Institute in Sussex that 'from the time that the possibility of her future position dawned upon her, [Princess Elizabeth] was taught to prepare for it in every way, especially by self-control'.[67] Elizabeth's rare bursts of naughtiness increasingly gave way to the requirement that she always play the elder sister. Gently the Marchioness of Cambridge scolded her for cheating at cards. 'I can [cheat],' she responded, 'because I'm a princess.'[68] It was a rare instance of pulling rank. Acquired early, self-control became a defining characteristic.

The sisters were united by isolation. Formality, court etiquette, security measures and inexhaustible public interest in any and every aspect of their lives distinguished their everyday experience from that of their aristocratic contemporaries. They inhabited a world quite different even from that of their nearest royal cousins, Edward and Alexandra of Kent, both of whom, when old enough, attended conventional boarding schools and lived in a modest country house in the Home Counties. The traditionalism of George VI's court cocooned the King's daughters: princesses of the blood, they were set apart; in a culture of deference treated as royal rather than real. The journalist who, in April 1937, claimed that Elizabeth had already mastered 'the task of developing a kind of double personality... to keep her two selves quite separate. One is concerned with her important duties as princess and the other with her private life as a normal, happy little girl' cannot possibly have had access to Elizabeth's thoughts or observed her private life.[69] But the strangeness of both girls' lives since their father's accession made the development of compartmentalized on- and off-duty personae a realistic and almost certainly necessary mechanism. To herself and her family Elizabeth was 'Lilibet'; to the wider world, as she would become increasingly aware, she was next in line to the throne. In March 1937, the *Sketch*'s 'Mr Gossip' reported a rumour that plans were afoot to send the quinqualingual nine-year-old Princess Josephine-Charlotte of Belgium 'to be privately educated with our own Princesses' as a 'suitable' friend.[70] If there ever were such plans, they came to nothing. Neither Elizabeth nor Margaret had close royal friends whose experience of childhood mirrored their own. Instead, in a bid to maintain vestiges of normality, the King's private secretary Alan, or 'Tommy', Lascelles wrote to the editor of *The Times* asking that 'a concrete effort be made' to prevent press attention 'from spoiling these two, at present, delightful & sensible children'.[71] Press interest did not diminish, and only Elizabeth remained unspoiled, delightful and sensible.

The two sides of Elizabeth's life overlapped: her 'princessing' happened in a family context. At the end of October she attended the King's first State Opening of Parliament. Her parents travelled by coach, they were enthroned in the House of Lords in full royal fig; Elizabeth made the journey by car and watched her father's speech from the Lord Great Chamberlain's box as a spectator but not a participant. Reports of the ceremony noted that she did not occupy the chair of state reserved for the heir to the throne; her attendance was for her own interest and because the King was also her father. Again, in the middle of December, she iced the cake her mother sent to unemployed young men in the Welsh town of Blaina. The letter that accompanied the cake, although written by a lady-in-waiting, conveyed something of Elizabeth's liveliness and curiosity: 'The Princess Elizabeth asked me to tell you that Her Royal Highness did the icing entirely on her own account and also the decorations. Her Royal Highness would like to know how many people have slices of the cake at the tea and wish you to have a very happy time. I am sure she put many happy wishes into the cake, as she thoroughly enjoyed doing it for you.'[72] When Elizabeth and her mother attended a performance of the children's play *Where the Rainbow Ends* at the Holborn Empire at Christmas, the audience sang a special children's verse of the National Anthem in her honour: 'We who are children weak, We for the future speak'.[73]

So often the margins of public and private blurred. In September 1937, at his parents' house in Kincardineshire, Elizabeth planted an ash tree 'in honour of the Master of Carnegie's eighth birthday'.[74] Overseen by the head gardener and her fellow guests, and the moment obligingly recorded by a photographer, it was an out-of-the-ordinary coda to a family party. Earlier in the spring, Elizabeth's friend and cousin Lady Mary Cambridge had opened the Princess Elizabeth Boating Pool in Bognor Regis. The pool commemorated Elizabeth's visit to the seaside town with her grandparents eight years earlier.[75]

Much that happened was an inevitable consequence of the family's new position. From the outset, prompted partly by the King's conviction of his own unreadiness for high office, Elizabeth's parents recognized the importance of preparing her for what lay ahead: nothing diminished the Queen's determination that her daughters' happiness be sacrosanct. Fresh air and animals continued to feature largely in the princesses' days. They acquired a rabbit each; for her Christmas card in 1937 Elizabeth chose a pastel drawing by Lucy Dawson of Dookie the corgi; on 10 December, the girls and their mother enjoyed a 'cinema-lecture show' on Canadian wildlife by a 'Red Indian' naturalist called 'Grey Owl', who was later exposed as Archibald Belaney from Hastings.[76] And then Elizabeth became a Girl Guide and Margaret a Brownie. Crawfie claimed credit for the idea. Since the Princess Royal was president of the Girl Guides Association and, in 1920, the Queen had started a Guide troop at Glamis, the suggestion could just as easily have been their aunt's, their mother's or indeed their own. The plan almost failed to come off. The chosen company captain, future national Guide commissioner Violet Synge, queried the possibility of princess-Guides, given the movement's democratic principles: 'Guides must all treat one another like sisters,' she expostulated.[77] Her misgivings were overruled. Elizabeth and Margaret were enrolled by their aunt in the 1st Buckingham Palace Company of Girl Guides and Brownies, Elizabeth second in control of the Kingfisher patrol, under a cousin, Patricia Mountbatten. They met on Wednesday evenings at five o'clock in a variety of locations in and around the palace, including the swimming pool and George V's summerhouse; they practised fire lighting and laid tracking signs. Later they undertook expeditions in Windsor Great Park. Both sisters' enjoyment can be measured from the company's long survival.

As an essay in 'normal' girlhood, the palace Guides company is easily pooh-poohed. Even one of its own members decried her fellow Guides as 'all dukes' daughters and Mountbattens – it wasn't at all democratic'.[78] Social inclusion, as currently understood, was not among the King and Queen's aims: their focus was their daughters' inclusion, which was successfully achieved. Family, friends and daughters of members of the household made up the troop. Shared elite status undoubtedly helped these particular Guides to treat one another as 'sisters', though the failure to waive the requirement to curtsey to Elizabeth and Margaret was a stumbling block of sorts, and Crawfie noted among these courtiers' daughters 'a tendency to let [the princesses] have an advantage, win a game, or be relieved of the more sordid tasks', like washing up.[79] Fellow Guides included Elizabeth's cousins Lady Mary Cambridge, the Hon. Margaret Elphinstone and Patricia Mountbatten;

her former neighbour the Hon. Ela Beaumont; Lady Elizabeth and Lady Joanna Lambart, with whom the princesses had shared singing lessons in Prince's Gate, and the Hon. Alathea Fitzalan Howard; Winifred and Libby Hardinge, daughters of the King's private secretary, and Diana Legh, daughter of the master of the household; and Elizabeth's friend Sonia Graham Hodgson. Accurately, the *Tatler* described the royal troop as 'a special company formed of [the princesses'] personal friends'. It informed readers that 'they find this new play-time occupation very absorbing'.[80] Patricia Mountbatten described Elizabeth the Guide as 'really efficient, very organised and very responsible, keen and enthusiastic', a description that, in different contexts, others would echo over a long life with more than its share of responsibilities.[81]

∽∼∾

At the funeral of their grandmother Lady Strathmore, at Glamis in June 1938, was a wreath of blue irises and white carnations from Elizabeth and Margaret; the princesses remained in London. From Birkhall, their mother sent them a spray of heather, enclosed in a letter to Elizabeth, but it was a summer that would challenge the Queen's impulse to shield her daughters from shadows.

Day after day, the sun blazed. The King visited Cowes Week, the Queen showed her daughters Osborne House. At Portsmouth, all four boarded the royal yacht *Victoria and Albert* for a journey on millpond seas to Aberdeen and, from there, across country to Balmoral. 'All this week there have been war scares,' Chips Channon recorded in his diary on 8 August;[82] Hitler's unbridled aggression towards Czechoslovakia threatened the outbreak of Europe-wide conflict. Of the crisis averted, on 28 September, by the Munich Agreement and prime minister Neville Chamberlain's promise of 'peace for our time', the Queen wrote that it was 'a nightmare of horror & worry'.[83] With some success she concealed her anxiety from her daughters. Their timetable of morning lessons followed by reading was maintained by Crawfie; she was joined again by the girls' French holiday governess, Georgina Guérin. Elizabeth and Margaret rode their ponies. As long as he remained with them, they joined the King and other guns for lunch in the surrounding hills. They played barefoot in the haystacks; with their cousin, the Master of Carnegie, they attended the Braemar Gathering, an annual royal fixture. Respectful crowds tailed their shopping expeditions to Ballater and Aberdeen.

By long arrangement, the Queen was due to launch the world's largest ship, the *Queen Elizabeth*, named after her, on 27 September, in Glasgow. She carried out the engagement with her daughters. The King, who ought to have been with her, was in London, where preparations for war were hastily enacted: schoolchildren evacuated, air raid shelters dug in Hyde Park, the Privy Council summoned to agree the mobilization of the fleet. A nation overwhelmed by dread held its breath. In Glasgow the naming ceremony was filmed by Pathé. Commentary informed viewers that for many this was the first time they had heard the Queen's 'soft and mellow' voice. It was a moment at which softness and mellowness were at a premium. On the banks of the Clyde, 300,000 people came to witness the ceremony: a show of pride in the city's shipbuilding, as well as the reassurance of togetherness. The royals' noisy reception was one of heightened emotion. 'The great event for which the Queen had come to her native land was overshadowed by the thoughts surging through everybody's minds, but it provided the hour and the opportunity for her subjects to give expression to their emotions,' reported the *Northern Whig*.[84] After the Silver Jubilee and the coronation, Elizabeth walked beside her mother apparently undeterred by the crowd's scale. The Queen's speech included a message from the King that 'the people of this country... be of good cheer in spite of the dark clouds hanging over them and indeed over the whole world'. 'We cannot foretell the future,' she read, 'but in preparing for it, we show our trust in a divine providence and in ourselves.' Similar rhetoric would characterize royal pronouncements throughout the coming conflict. The princesses whom their mother had sheltered at Balmoral learned from her own lips of 'the dark clouds hanging... over the whole world'.

Five months later, the King launched the first British battleship built in over a decade. It was named after his father, *King George V*. Elizabeth and Margaret attended a march-past of a thousand Girl Guides at Windsor Castle. Elizabeth wore her Kingfisher Company blue tunic and dark-blue pleated skirt, Margaret her Brownie equivalent. In a sign of the times, press attention focused on the sisters' appearance for the first time in public in uniform.[85]

Elizabeth recognized war's imminence, like the abdication, in its impact on her parents. The King's workload escalated, he appeared tired but purposeful; there was a common theme to a number of royal engagements as well as visits to and from allies and would-be allies. In the early summer of 1938, the King and Queen made a state visit to Paris, its purpose Anglo-French amity; Elizabeth and Margaret remained at home. The French prepared a splendid gift for the absent princesses: a pair of dolls, 'France' and 'Marianne', each a metre high, with accessories including a florist's stall complete with watering cans and artificial flowers, and a wardrobe that, for sumptuousness, rivalled the Queen's: 'gowns for the morning, for the tea party, 5 o'clock aperitifs, for Ascot, for the opera, the theatre, smart tailor-mades for the shopping expedition, stout tweeds for the country, pyjamas for lazy mornings on the beach, mackintoshes for rainy days, bathing suits, lingerie, frocks for all sports, sunshades and umbrellas'.[86] The dolls had eight fur coats, including a baby leopard swagger coat, twenty bottles of scent, ostrich feather fans, embroidered scarves, gloves in a dozen colours and a jewel case each: in total, £5,000 worth of infant-size French finery. Elizabeth and Margaret formally accepted the present from the French ambassador at Buckingham Palace in November. As the *Daily Mirror* pointed out, it was their first official reception of an ambassador of a foreign power.[87] They thanked Monsieur Corbin in French; he complimented Elizabeth on her accent. 'I will now have to speak French to my Paris dolls,' she returned tactfully. Plans were made to exhibit the dolls the following month at St James's Palace in aid of the Princess Elizabeth of York Hospital for Children, Shadwell. Elizabeth described the encounter matter-of-factly in a letter to her grandmother: 'M[onsieur] Corbin came yesterday to hand over the dolls on behalf of the French people and we showed him all their clothes.'[88]

Foreign visits to the palace peppered the royal diary; their parents frequently introduced Elizabeth and Margaret to their guests. They were at their mother's side to welcome King Carol of Romania and his son, Crown Prince Michael, at the start of the king's winter state visit to London. The following spring Elizabeth joined the King and Queen for lunch with Poland's foreign minister, Colonel Beck; she talked to the colonel in French. In French she delivered a carefully rehearsed speech of welcome to President Lebrun and his wife, who, in March, returned her parents' visit. More informally, the princesses dipped in and out of the visit to Windsor Castle of the new American ambassador, Joe Kennedy. Their participation in their parents' official lives became a distinctive feature of the new court's entertaining. Part of the King and Queen's training for Elizabeth, with whom the King had begun discussing current affairs and politics, it was also a reflection of the King's view of his family as an indivisible unit, 'us Four' as he described them afterwards, a tight-knit quartet.

No one could doubt the strength of the bonds of affection between them. On 20 December 1938, Marcus Adams photographed the royal family for the first time at Buckingham Palace. In a country and empire on the brink of war, the resulting image achieved immense popularity. Framed in a doorway, Elizabeth and Margaret flank their parents, Dookie at Elizabeth's heel. All four figures are linked, arms intertwined, hands held, a more confident reprising of Adams's family portrait taken two years earlier. Against the magnificence of the palace – waterfall chandeliers, columns with gilded capitals – the pale frocks of the Queen and her 'fairy' daughters shimmer. Previously Adams had invested his royal sitters with would-be ordinariness; on this occasion they appear serene. To their contemporaries, it was an image to inspire pride as well as reassurance.

At the same sitting, Adams photographed Elizabeth alone with Dookie. As in Lisa Sheridan's photograph taken at Y Bwthyn Bach, the princess's attention is entirely and happily absorbed in the dog. Over time, such images would be interpreted as revealing the loneliness of Elizabeth's position, her turning to dogs and horses for companionship uncomplicated by the barrier of her rank. It was not true yet.

CHAPTER V

'She was truly in love from the very beginning'

❦

ELIZABETH'S NEW SILK STOCKINGS, worn at a family wedding in March 1939, caused ripples of excitement among women journalists. She wore them with a coat of 'pale geranium-coloured velvet', with a matching beret and low-heeled shoes; Margaret was still in white ankle socks and a bonnet.[1]

Elizabeth was weeks short of her thirteenth birthday. 'What a charming child she is,' wrote Joyce Grenfell, after seeing Elizabeth dressed as a 'Dutch Peasant' at a children's party of Grenfell's aunt, Lady Astor, in St James's Square. 'She has lengthened out a lot and has now got quite a lovely little face, really graceful arms and is generally very attractive.'[2] The stockings were a present from the Queen, an acknowledgement that, though she continued to be dressed like her four-years-younger sister, Elizabeth was growing up.

In other ways, nursery, schoolroom, even family routines remained unbending. Elizabeth's featherlight timetable had achieved competence in spoken French and an enthusiasm for history, the subject that surrounded her and inspired Crawfie's best, most dramatic efforts. As her grandfather had hoped, she wrote a confident, clear hand. Queen Mary's 'instructive amusements' continued on Monday afternoons; the old queen's conversation was full of instruction, much of it related to her favourite topic of royalty. In the Bethnal Green Museum, Elizabeth and Margaret saw a selection of their grandmother's toys, entrusted to curator Arthur Sabin. There were visits to the General Post Office in Mount Pleasant and to London Docks, including the head offices of the Port of London Authority. Margaret's relish for these heavyweight excursions did not increase; Elizabeth worked harder at interesting herself, training for what lay ahead. In May, after the King and Queen embarked on a lengthy visit to Canada and the United States, Crawfie took the girls to the YWCA Club in Great Russell Street. The visit's chief excitement was not tea in the self-service café, in itself a novelty, but their first, long-anticipated journey by Underground, from St James's Park to Tottenham Court Road, in a third-class smoking compartment. For much of their outing the party of the two princesses, Crawfie and the Queen's lady-in-waiting, Lady Helen Grahame, president of the YWCA, went unrecognized, a reminder that smartly dressed upper-class girls with their nannies were among the sights of inter-war London and that the poor quality of newspaper photographs sometimes permitted the sisters margins of leeway.

Elizabeth's letters to her parents included an account of a visit to London Zoo; she described a baby giant panda and riding an elephant. Affectionate and loving, her mother's replies were full of scenery and wildlife. 'What fun the Panda sounds,' she wrote. She was reading Hitler's *Mein Kampf*; to Elizabeth, in letters that skirted European politics, she described Canadian mountains like the hills around Balmoral, sightings of beavers, baby black bears and 'a great black shape in a little lake – a moose feeding on the water lily bulbs'. She asked about the rhododendrons in the woodland garden at Royal Lodge and new plantings of scented shrubs. 'I am absolutely longing to see you and Margaret again,' she told her daughter. 'What a hug you'll get when I get home.'[3]

Despite her best efforts, the Queen's letters transcended pleasantries. Canadians' enthusiasm convinced the royal couple of the value of dominion visits. 'One feels how important it is that the people here should see their King, & not have him only as a symbol,' she wrote on 27 May.[4] A week later she described to Elizabeth crowds in the country beyond Toronto: 'They are so happy to have "the King" with them, & sometimes I have tears in my eyes when one sees the emotion in their faces. It means so much to them to see the Sovereign who they are so loyal to.'[5] In time, overseas visits would play a key part in Elizabeth's promotion of the Commonwealth and her own international role, including as Queen of Canada. Her understanding of the ramifications of such trips began with her parents' example and their fidelity to the imperial orthodoxy of the crown as the living link between diverse territories and peoples.

The Queen's letters also touched on Elizabeth's education. At the time of her thirteenth birthday in April, Elizabeth had begun lessons in history and constitutional history with the vice-provost of Eton, Henry Marten. Marten was a contemporary of Queen Mary, with whom he shared an admiration for Queen Victoria, and a friend of Elizabeth's great-aunt, Princess Alice. He taught Elizabeth at weekends, when the royal family was at Windsor, with Crawfie in attendance. At first her enjoyment was limited: he remembered 'a somewhat shy girl... who when asked a question would look for confidence and support to her beloved governess'.[6] Her pleasure increased with increasing familiarity. Over six years princess and provost read together Sir William Anson's three-volume *Law and Custom of the Constitution*.

Marten outlined for the future queen the relationship between the monarch, parliament and the nation. In illustrations and digressions, he enlarged on Queen Victoria's example; he recommended a biography of her private secretary, Henry Ponsonby. He sketched for his pupil an overview of the monarchy's thousand-year history, beginning with Egbert. He drew her attention to current developments in the communion of sovereign and subject: the role of broadcasting pioneered by her grandfather in the Christmas addresses that the *Daily Express* likened to 'heart-to-heart Christmas talk[s]'; the emerging Commonwealth following the 1931 Statute of Westminster that had established 'autonomous communities within the British Empire' and made George V separately king of Canada, Australia, New Zealand, South Africa, Newfoundland and the Irish Free State.[7] The certainty 'that education broadly speaking was to help a student to learn to appraise both sides of a question, thus using his [or her] judgement' shaped Marten's teaching, a lesson in itself for the future queen.[8] 'I do hope that you are enjoying your Saturday evenings with Mr Marten,' the Queen wrote on 23 May with purposive underlining. 'Try & learn as much as you can from him, & mark how he brings the human element into all his history – of course history is made by ordinary humans, & one must not forget that.'[9]

A result of the family's seven-week separation – the longest they had been apart – was to bring the King closer to the Queen's view of Elizabeth's maturity. In Crawfie's account of their reunion on the *Empress of Britain*, ahead of the ship's arrival in Southampton, the Queen comments on the girls' growth, while the King gazes in silent wonder at Elizabeth. 'All the time the King could hardly take his eyes off Lilibet. I have a photograph which shows the Queen... holding Margaret's hand... and the King looking at Lilibet.'[10] Nevertheless, the reunion lunch was a reassuring combination of the childish and the rarefied, according to a member of the royal suite 'a glorious absolutely riotous lunch... complete pandemonium'.[11] To the girls' delight, the ship's pink-painted dining room was hung with streamers and balloons. The ship's orchestra, described by the Queen as 'the little band', played popular song tunes throughout: 'Jeepers Creepers' and 'Umbrella Man'.[12] At the King's suggestion, a sing-song before docking included his favourite 'Underneath the Spreading Chestnut Tree', with actions, and 'The Lambeth Walk'. The princesses released balloons out of portholes; in shops on the main deck they bought Canadian Mountie dolls and engraved penknives. Crew members presented them with panda-shaped nightdress cases. Elizabeth responded for both sisters. 'She has all the graces which will stand her in such good stead in the great position she must one day fill,' explained an unnamed 'friend of the family'.[13] Papers described a 'gala' atmosphere. It was typical of the ebullient family fun that was so important to both Elizabeth's parents.

A rapturous reception greeted the royal party on shore, at the end of a trip regarded as a diplomatic triumph ('If London was bombed USA would come in [to the war],' was the King's note on his conversations with President Roosevelt).[14] As when the Queen travelled to Glasgow for the naming of the *Queen Elizabeth*, uncertainty intensified the atmosphere, a 'horrible feeling', she wrote, 'of tension, rumour, and acute anxiety'.[15] A 'Welcome Home Pathé Gazette Special' acclaimed the homecoming King and Queen as 'the man and woman who have come to represent all our faith and ideals – of liberty, of peace, of toleration and freedom', in stark antithesis to the dishonest belligerence of Hitler and Mussolini. Something of these high-flown sentiments coloured the crowds' noisy response, as the royal family drove through packed streets to Southampton station and the train for Waterloo. In the car, a fidgety Margaret sat between her parents. Elizabeth was on her own in a row of seats in front, composed despite the cheering: as her parents recognized, older.

Just how much older, however, neither quite suspected. Within less than a month, a combination of good looks, gymnastic prowess, a heroic appetite for shrimps and, perhaps, the skirl of sea breezes set Elizabeth on the path of a love affair that would prove of remarkable longevity.

The object of her admiration was a portionless royal exile, five years her senior, 'a fair-haired boy, rather like a Viking, with a sharp face and piercing blue eyes': Prince Philip of Greece and Denmark, like Elizabeth a great-great-grandchild of Queen Victoria.[16] Their paths had crossed before, at the wedding of Philip's cousin Marina to Elizabeth's uncle George, Philip on that occasion one of 'various small Eton-suited Princes from abroad', Elizabeth a diminutive bridesmaid.[17] Neither took note at the time. Looking back in 1947, Elizabeth wrote, 'We may have met before at the Coronation or the Duchess of Kent's wedding, but I don't remember.'[18] On 22 July 1939, at the Royal Naval College in Dartmouth, by Philip's standards Elizabeth was still diminutive, months past her thirteenth birthday, dressed in the same clothes as her younger sister. Philip's abiding impression, according to a conversation overheard by his cousin Queen Alexandra of Yugoslavia, was of her shyness.[19] Elizabeth's impressions of Philip were quite different.

The timing of the royal family's visit to the college was fortunate for young love. Discovered at the eleventh hour, an outbreak of chickenpox and mumps prevented the princesses from accompanying their parents to a service in the college chapel. Instead, in the house of the captain of the college, they were offered as diversion a train set; there were ginger biscuits and lemonade, then there was Philip. He ate, drank, played, grew bored, suggested the tennis courts. Crawfie bridled at something brisk in his manner, but Elizabeth made up her own mind. Philip was eighteen, not an ideal age for humouring a shy, earnest, sheltered thirteen-year-old still invariably referred to as 'little'. At the tennis courts he enjoyed himself in his own fashion, jumping over the nets. Crawfie thought he showed off: to her chagrin 'the little girls were much impressed'.[20] Philip teased Margaret. Elizabeth gazed at Philip. 'She never took her eyes off him the whole time,' Crawfie remembered sourly.[21] To her governess Elizabeth marvelled, 'How good he is, Crawfie. How high he can jump.'

Philip was still in swaggering attendance at lunchtime. In the evening, he dined on the royal yacht. He did not see Elizabeth, who had gone to bed early, according to nursery routines. They met again the following day. At teatime Elizabeth played hostess. Her repeated enquiry – 'What would you like to eat? What would you like?' – sounds excitable. Nothing in her manner put Philip off his food: he ate 'several platefuls of shrimps, and a banana split'. Elizabeth relapsed into contented silence, 'pink-faced, enjoying it all very much', watching.[22] Crawfie stored up her irritation for *The Little Princesses*.

Her last chance of winning over Elizabeth to her own view of Philip as 'a rather bumptious boy' was defeated by a valedictory gesture of dashing bravado.[23] At the end of the visit, 'while their Majesties, accompanied by Princess Elizabeth and Princess Margaret Rose, stood on the top deck waving farewell, the royal yacht was escorted into the Channel by an armada of 400 vessels, including every available craft from the Royal Naval College, which were manned by nearly 500 cadets'. Among this cockleshell flotilla was Philip. 'While the green valley of the Dart resounded with storm after storm of cheering, the royal yacht steamed slowly out to sea surrounded by sailing-boats, rowing-boats, pleasure steamers, cutters, dinghies, speed-boats and motor-boats.'[24] One small craft continued to tail the royal yacht long after the others had turned back. At its oars was a single rower: Philip. 'The young fool!' the King shouted. 'He must go back!'

Through her field glasses Elizabeth watched her hero's progress. For her there would be no going back.

For at least one jobbing seer, it had been written in the stars. The unnamed astrologer quoted in the *Woman's Magazine* in March 1932 foresaw it all. His or her prediction for six-year-old Elizabeth was 'an alliance after her own heart at the age of eighteen, eventually leading to one of the oldest European thrones'.[25]

Elizabeth married Philip, of a cadet branch of the Danish royal house of Schleswig-Holstein-Sonderburg-Glücksburg, months after her twenty-first birthday, in November 1947, Philip by then a naturalized British subject. With her parents' consent she would have done so sooner. Chips Channon considered the match a given as early as January 1941, when Elizabeth was not yet fifteen, a view shaped by gossip in Continental royal circles.[26] Philip's own memories parried any such suggestion. Afterwards, he dismissed the whole of his fitful wartime acquaintance with the princess: 'I thought not all that much about it. We used to correspond occasionally... If you're related... it isn't so extraordinary to be on kind of family relationship terms. You don't necessarily have to think about marriage.'[27] It was a characteristically brisk evasion on the part of a man disinclined to explain himself to third parties, and at odds with Elizabeth's authorization in 1958 of a statement by her father's official biographer that she had been in love with Philip 'from their first meeting'.[28] 'She was truly in love from the very beginning,' remembered her cousin Margaret Elphinstone.[29] 'Mummy never seriously thought of anyone else after [their] encounter when she was 13!', one of Philip's family explained later.[30] The astrologer had been correct at least in predicting 'an alliance after her own heart'.

Accounts of Elizabeth's marriage to Philip typically identify a puppetmaster's role for Philip's uncle, Lord Louis Mountbatten, known as Dickie, the younger brother of his mother, Princess Alice of Battenberg. In attendance on the King at Dartmouth on 22 July 1939, Mountbatten emerges from this version of events as a man of Brobdingnagian ambition, who orchestrated the meeting of these high-ranking teenagers with the sole aim of gratifying his own overweening family pride, the participants themselves powerless against his plotting. And indeed a letter written later by Philip to his uncle specifically warned him against overplaying his hand in this way: 'It is apparent that you like the idea of being General Manager of this little show, and I am rather afraid that she might not take to the idea quite as docilely as I do... don't forget that she has not had you as Uncle loco parentis, counsellor and friend as long as I have.'[31] By 1947, the year of Philip's letter, Mountbatten was exceedingly anxious that the marriage come off. His family pride was also excessive, as the eleven years he devoted to the privately printed *The Mountbatten Lineage: The Direct Descent of the Family of Mountbatten from the House of Brabant and the Rulers of Hesse* indicates. In 1939, Mountbatten may have entertained only the germ of an idea. In his diary, in the briefest of references, he links Philip with both Elizabeth and Margaret: 'Philip came back aboard V and A for tea and was a great success with children'.[32] That he drew no distinction between the sisters, despite the discrepancy in their age and prospects, does not suggest he identified either at this stage as a romantic lead in a drama of his own devising. Perhaps his aim was simpler then: advancement of any sort for a penurious nephew. It was Mountbatten who, ahead of the royal visit, had suggested the 'messenger' role that kept Philip continually in the royal line of vision.

There is no reason to assume that Elizabeth required the prompting of her father's worldly kinsman to fall in love with Philip. Boys had played scant part in her life: they were creatures, Crawfie explained, out of another world.[33] Teenagers fall in love: Elizabeth had had neither opportunity nor focus for her affections. Philip was strikingly handsome, funny and boisterous, 'Prince Charming in every sense of the word' according to Elizabeth's elderly cousin Princess Marie Louise.[34] Towards the sombre princess he was neither deferential nor tongue-tied by shyness. He was royal and a distant relative. Lady Anne Glenconner described him later as 'ideal – good looking and a foreign prince'.[35] Her view that Philip's royalty qualified him as a partner for Elizabeth was one that Elizabeth, at thirteen, could share. Until her parents' generation, most members of her family had married within the royal fold. Only five years earlier, she had been a bridesmaid at the wedding of her father's youngest brother to the glamorous foreign Princess Marina, Philip's cousin. In 1939 'royal marriages' were still usual among European dynasties, grounds for Philip's inclusion, in January 1937, in a list of possible suitors for the then eleven-year-old Elizabeth compiled by *Literary Digest*.[36] Frequently the parties were related, like Elizabeth's grandparents, both great-great-grandchildren of George III.

The handsome, brisk 'Viking' was both more and less royal than Elizabeth, whose mother was a British noblewoman: her superior in bloodlines, his royal prospects negligible in comparison with those of Britain's heiress presumptive. Recent family history linked Philip to reigning and exiled dynasties across Europe. On his father's side he was the nephew and grandson of kings of Greece, a great-grandson of Christian IX of Denmark and the great-nephew of Britain's Queen Alexandra; on his mother's side a nephew by marriage of Gustav VI Adolf of Sweden, a great-nephew of the last Tsarina of Russia and a great-great-grandson of Queen Victoria through the marriage of Victoria's second daughter Alice to Grand Duke Louis of Hesse. When Philip was twelve, the headmaster of his British preparatory school concluded that he 'would make a good king', as he had 'two vital qualities, leadership and personality'. He based his view on Philip's family background: he was thinking of him then, he explained subsequently, not as a husband for Elizabeth but 'as King of Greece'.[37]

It was an unlikely outcome, especially for the youngest child of a hapless fourth son. In the first half of the last century, few thrones teetered as precariously as that of Greece. A suitcase ready-packed, claimed one member of Philip's family, was a prerequisite for every Greek royal. Philip's own exile had begun when he was months old: in 1922, the family was rescued by a British battleship at the request of George V. He spent the early part of his peripatetic childhood in St Cloud, outside Paris, in a modest country house provided by a wealthy aunt, Princess Marie Bonaparte. Seven years younger than the youngest of his four sisters, Philip lived in a household dominated by women and financial anxiety. He was educated in Paris, England, Germany, then Scotland, and holidayed across the Continent with Romanian, Hessian and British royal relatives. His parents, Prince and Princess Andrew of Greece, lacked fortune and influence, lucky to have escaped revolutionary Greece with their lives. In material terms, Philip's 'royalty' had a threadbare quality, fragile as cobweb. Splendid connections and astrological predictions aside, the eighteen-year-old naval cadet who leaped tennis nets for the British princesses possessed few solid expectations; even his scant wardrobe had been provided by his extended family. His principal legacy was emotional and deeply chequered. For much of his childhood his mother had been absent, confined to an asylum following a nervous breakdown in 1929 when she declared herself a saint and 'the bride of Christ'; she did not communicate with her son at all, not even birthday cards. His father withdrew to the French Riviera, later settling on a yacht with an actress-mistress who called herself Comtesse Andrée de la Bigne. Unlike Elizabeth, Philip was of his own making, a survivor of family wreckage and royal dispossession, stateless, throneless and homeless, orphaned by circumstances: determined, strong and forward-looking, encased in the thickest skin, self-contained, a sensitive bully, ripe for iconoclasm. To the Queen he explained elliptically that he 'had always played a lone hand, and had had to fight [his] own battles'.[38]

～～

In London in July 1939, Elizabeth and Margaret returned to 145 Piccadilly. Their visit with Crawfie and one of the Queen's ladies-in-waiting to see an exhibition of 'royal treasures' in aid of the Heritage Craft Schools in Chailey lasted an hour. Like a detail in a children's story, Elizabeth picked up a bracelet of Queen Victoria's and found it fitted her perfectly; she admitted she had tried on the old Queen's spectacles before. The sisters revisited their night nursery. In Elizabeth's former bedroom at the back of the house was a collection of their favourite toys. Exhibits were insured for an estimated £1 million.

For the princesses, the display, like works in a museum, of toys so recently cast aside offered further proof of the public aspect of their childhood – like Queen Mary's toys arranged in glass cases in Bethnal Green Museum when they visited in February. For a modest fee even their former bedrooms were available to view. But escape from prying eyes was not the only reason for their particular concern that their Scottish holiday go ahead as usual this year. Balmoral inspired feelings of security, remote from London and the shadows that had continued to cluster all summer. Europe shuddered on the brink of war. After some uncertainty, the royal family departed London for the Highlands, arriving on 7 August. For the King it would be a sadly brief stay.

CHAPTER VI

'A simple, united family life, whatever calls there might be to duty'

❦

'I HAD A MOST beautiful birthday present,' eleven-year-old Betty Murphy wrote to her mother in November 1939. 'Princess Elizabeth's coat. She said she had grown out of it and that if it fitted me I could have it. It is fawn and has wee tyers to tie inside. It is double-breasted, has a half-belt at the back and an inverted pleat. It is lined with fawn satin and has two pockets, but not for putting your hands in. I'm going to write to Princess Elizabeth and thank her for her lovely present.'[1]

Betty Murphy was an evacuee. While her mother stayed behind in the family's Glasgow tenement, she was living at Craigowan Lodge on the King's Scottish estate, among a large group of Glaswegian evacuees, in some cases mothers as well as children. Also separated from their parents, though there the similarity ended, Elizabeth and Margaret had moved from Balmoral to the smaller house of Birkhall. Convinced until the last minute that war would be avoided, the King had nevertheless been forced to cut short his Scottish holiday and return to London, followed, on 28 August, by the Queen; as late as 27 August, he had written to the exiled Queen Ena of Spain about her visiting the family in Scotland.[2] Instead, their cousin Margaret Elphinstone kept the girls company. When war was declared on 3 September, all three were at Crathie church. 'The Minister, a small, spare man called Dr Lamb preached a highly emotional sermon and told his flock that the uneasy peace which had prevailed since the end of the First World War was now over,' remembered Margaret Elphinstone.[3] In the evening the King broadcast to the nation. Despite warning signals for some time, Elizabeth may still have been surprised, misled by her father's conviction that Hitler would relent and both her parents' determined concealment from their daughters of their 'deepening sense of crisis'.[4] In the event Elizabeth's concerns mirrored those of her sister, whose response to their parents' return to London was the unvarnished question, 'Do you think the Germans will get them?' 'I hope he won't come over here,' Elizabeth said simply of Hitler.[5] The Queen wrote to her sister Rose Granville, asking that she look after Elizabeth and Margaret in the event of anything happening to her and the King, her letter a measure of her concern. 'I would give up everything to try & make the two darlings happy,' Lady Granville replied on 6 September.[6] As in the aftermath of George V's death, Crawfie was recalled early from her holiday. She joined Alah, the French holiday governess Georgina Guérin and lady-in-waiting Lettice Bowlby; her presence mitigated the animosity between the mademoiselle and the courtier.

Elizabeth and Margaret and their small party of attendants remained at Birkhall until Christmas, despite nights so cold in the unheated house that, to their delight, sponges and flannels froze solid and windows glittered with a lacework of frost. Sometimes they wore their Guide and Brownie uniforms; they attended Guide meetings joined by Glasgow evacuees. Crawfie went out of her way to fill the girls' days, denying them insofar as possible time for anxiety over their parents. She introduced initiatives she labelled 'war work', inspired by similar innovations of the Queen at Buckingham Palace. At sewing parties in the schoolroom for 'crofters' wives, farmers' wives, wives of estate employees', the princesses handed round teacups and cake, 'talked away happily to the various women' and entertained them with records on an immensely loud, old-fashioned horn gramophone; they knitted for the Red Cross; there were 'hikes and tea parties and outings', the last to include the evacuees.[7] Brought up among adults and trained in good manners, the sisters fared better at the sedate tea parties. 'We have got hundreds all around about from Glasgow,' Elizabeth had written to Crawfie ahead of her return.[8] She may have felt overwhelmed by these children whose lives were so remote from her own; their discomfort in one another's company was mutual. More successful were the princesses' donations of discarded clothes and toys, like the coat given to Betty Murphy. In Betty's letter to her mother a sense of wonder permeates the careful itemization of each hand-stitched detail. The coat's decorative pockets are a reminder of the formality of Elizabeth's life. Only in her nineties was she photographed for the first time with her hands in her pockets. Even then she knew that, had she been alive, her mother would have disapproved.

To Elizabeth her parents explained the necessity of the war that the Queen described in a letter to Prince Paul of Yugoslavia as 'a struggle of the spirit, evil thinking, arrogance and materialism, against truth, liberty & justice'.[9] Crawfie 'read the newspapers to the children after tea, trying as far as possible to give them some idea of what was happening without too many horrible details'; patriotically she read them Milton, including 'At a Solemn Musick', with its invocation to 'sirens' that gave rise to amused misunderstanding. They listened to the radio. The girls jeered Lord Haw-Haw, throwing books and cushions at the set; they enjoyed comedian Arthur Askey in a weekly programme called *Band Waggon*. On the Queen's instructions, Crawfie did her best to restore schoolroom routine at the end of an unsettled year.[10] The princesses' distance from their parents and the distractions of peacetime London proved unexpectedly beneficial. Even Elizabeth's lessons with Henry Marten continued after a fashion, essays posted, marked, returned. Hanni Davey, the princesses' German teacher, also sent exercises by post. Georgina Guérin returned to France to join the French Resistance; French lessons were entrusted to a Mrs Montaudon-Smith, called 'Monty'. The King and Queen telephoned at six o'clock each evening, their calls eagerly awaited by both sisters. In the middle of September, the Queen arrived for a week. She visited the evacuees and showed an enthusiastic Elizabeth how to make up roller bandages for ambulance supplies.[11] Elizabeth in turn taught Margaret. She wrote regularly to her grandmother Queen Mary, in reluctant exile at Badminton House with her niece, the Duchess of Beaufort. Elizabeth may or may not have known that the list of serving officers for whom Queen Mary knitted woollen scarves and pullovers included Philip of Greece.[12]

Crawfie organized picnics, the girls rode a pony called George, on long autumn walks they looked out for hares and geese, they tramped high on the moors and sometimes through the darkness of the woods; they were thrilled by the first white frosts on stubble fields and early falls of snow. There were special evening screenings, on a borrowed projector, of Laurel and Hardy and Charlie Chaplin films and, occasionally, weekend visitors. A dentist in Aberdeen oversaw Elizabeth's braces; in Woolworths the sisters shopped for Christmas presents. In the safety of the Highlands, parted from their parents but cosseted by their nurse and governess, the princesses' 'evacuation' differed markedly from that of children like Betty Murphy, sent to unfamiliar surrounds, uncertain of their reception, cut off from anything they had previously known. Aspects of her wartime experience shaped Elizabeth: that autumn at Birkhall cemented her love of the Highlands and her hermetic companionship with Margaret. It did not expand her understanding of many of those who would one day be her subjects. Instead, the first months of conflict increased Elizabeth's isolation. Newspapers lamented 'the restriction of intercourse with girls of her own age which Princess Elizabeth enjoyed so freely when living in Buckingham Palace', an exaggeration of her erstwhile freedoms that also discounted the Glaswegian girls billeted nearby.[13] The walls of the sisters' ivory tower did not crumble yet.

After Christmas at Sandringham, made possible by the non-events of the Phoney War, Elizabeth and Margaret moved to Royal Lodge. Five months later, on 12 May, they moved again, this time into Windsor Castle itself. The five-room 'royal nursery' in the Augusta Tower was their home for the remainder of the war. Elizabeth shared with Bobo MacDonald the bedroom that had always been hers. Alah and Margaret were next door, Crawfie accommodated at a remove in the Victoria Tower. Newspapers explained to their readers the inconveniences of Birkhall, too far from affairs of state for the King to visit; 'another place nearer London, but in the "safety area"' was obviously more practical.[14] The princesses' whereabouts – their 'country evacuation home' – were kept secret.[15] In his diary, the King stated 'at their age, their education is too important to be neglected'.[16] In fact, Crawfie's programme at Windsor did not differ materially from the routine she had re-established at Birkhall in the war's first weeks, though Henry Marten was nearby, and Elizabeth's lessons resumed, sometimes in Marten's rooms at Eton, complete with his pet raven, Marten addressing Elizabeth and Crawfie absentmindedly as 'Gentlemen'; their studies included the world's great explorers, beginning with Columbus, and the history of America. There was still a weekly dancing class with Miss Vacani. In place of the singing classes of pre-war London were afternoon cookery lessons;[17] Queen

Mary's 'instructive amusements' were replaced by tours of the castle with the royal librarian, Owen Morshead; in his house in the castle cloisters, Elizabeth and Margaret visited the organist of St George's Chapel, Dr Harris, for weekly conversations about the lives and works of prominent composers. In addition, Crawfie referred to 'numerous other children staying in and around Windsor', including Owen Morshead's daughter Mary and Libby Hardinge.[18] One in particular shared much of the princesses' war. 'One of the closest companions of Princess Elizabeth – the sixteen-year-old daughter of an old family friend – is living close at hand,' reported the *Sunday Mirror*.[19] She was Alathea Fitzalan Howard, who had also been evacuated from her parents' house in London, like Libby Hardinge a member of the palace Guide company. She spent the war at Cumberland Lodge in Windsor Great Park, with her grandfather, Viscount Fitzalan of Derwent, and an unmarried great-aunt, only too happy to flee this repressive, elderly household for the sunshine world of the princesses and Crawfie, whom she loved.

Officially in hiding, Elizabeth experienced a greater degree of privacy than at any moment to date. Concealed from the world at large, she escaped temporarily the ever-present bystanders and photographers, cocooned with Margaret in a small but busy world of Crawfie, Monty, Alah and Bobo, friends like Alathea Fitzalan Howard, castle staff and household officials. From a distance, newspapers selected details of their sequestered existence to demonstrate the royal children's participation in the collective war effort. As throughout the difficult decade of the 1930s, with or without their parents Elizabeth and Margaret embodied a family ideal that was also a national ideal. Stories illustrated their concern for the plight of others, small-scale kindnesses, patriotic frugality, and, whenever possible, reunions with their parents: riding with the King, picnic teas at Frogmore in Windsor Great Park, a film together, like the evening of the King's birthday when they watched Charlie Chaplin in *The Great Dictator*. In public the King and Queen dedicated themselves to national morale; in private, according to Lisa Sheridan, they battled 'to maintain a simple, united family life, whatever calls there might be to duty'.[20] The princesses' contributions to the war effort were assiduously publicized: presents of chocolate to evacuated French children; donations to the Over-Seas League Tobacco Fund to supply servicemen with 18 million cigarettes on Empire Day 1940; 'a gift of sweets... received at the Army Comforts Depot, Reading, for distribution to some of the British and French troops who have returned from Dunkirk'; the royal Christmas tree passed on to the Mayor of Windsor for use at children's parties.[21] Improbably, an appeal for aluminium by the Women's Voluntary Service elicited a veritable royal ironmongery: 'saucepans and frying pans that have cooked many a royal meal' and utensils from Y Bwthyn Bach: a miniature kitchen measure and a stock pot.[22] At Queen Mary's suggestion and to assist the government's salvage scheme, the sisters became 'keen collectors of tin foil', a thrifty impulse in line with Elizabeth's years of saving wrapping paper and ribbons.[23] None of this, in truth, consumed much of Elizabeth's time, as she would become increasingly aware. Her life retained a leisurely quality. Crawfie referred to 'monotonous days' and 'long slow months';[24] Marcus Adams photographed the sisters occupied with a large jigsaw puzzle in an incongruously splendid interior, an image released as a wartime postcard. Conscientious, and recognizably the same child who had jumped out of bed to straighten her shoes, Elizabeth wore her gas mask, as officially instructed, for ten minutes a day, then 'carefully clean[ed] the eyepiece every evening with the ointment provided'.[25] The sisters drove a pony cart. *The Times* explained that the cart had been brought back into use 'in view of the need for saving petrol'.[26] Photographs suggest their enjoyment of their new conveyance, which they drove themselves, accompanied by a corgi. Attended by an equerry, Elizabeth had a handful of carriage driving lessons with the royal riding instructor, Horace Smith, owner of a nearby riding school, who also taught her to ride side-saddle. It was Smith who received her much-quoted confidence that 'had she not been who she was, she would like to be a lady living in the country with lots of dogs and horses', a statement invariably interpreted as suggesting a craving for ordinariness. It may simply have been a conversational politeness to highlight common ground – their love of the country – between instructor and pupil.[27] Elizabeth's experience of country life – at Royal Lodge, Balmoral and Sandringham – was far from typical, as she may have been old enough to understand.

In March 1940, society magazine *Queen* lamented 'we have seen very little of the Princesses for such a long time that new pictures of them would be very much appreciated by everybody.'[28] A sitting with Marcus Adams in April reflected the altered mood of the time. In place of their fairy frills, the girls wore tweed jackets and kilts. Elizabeth appears serious, as indeed she was, 'very matter of fact' in Alathea Fitzalan Howard's verdict.[29] Examining Adams's pictures, loyally the *Sunday Mirror* enumerated wartime changes in the royal sisters' lives: 'There are fewer frocks, fewer parties and fewer outings... Jerseys and skirts are the order of the day, except when the hot weather has made a change into cotton frocks necessary.'[30] For a sugary picture book called *Our Princesses at Home*, Lisa Sheridan photographed the sisters outdoors at Royal Lodge 'in their natural home life away from the public eye':[31] gardening, knitting, playing with their dogs, still dressed alike, though Elizabeth wears stockings in place of Margaret's ankle socks and bare legs. Even Elizabeth's fourteenth birthday conformed to the new narrative of cheerful stoicism: her birthday cake was a plain sponge and her presents included a gift of £100 that was only nominally hers. In his accompanying letter, the governor of Jamaica explained, 'The children of Jamaica wish Her Royal

Highness Princess Elizabeth many happy returns... and submit with their humble greetings a draft for £100, which they hope Her Royal Highness will donate to her favourite war charity.'[32] When Margaret's birthday arrived in August, much was made of the lack of icing on her cake. Frances Towers, the author of another paean, *The Two Princesses*, wrote that the sisters 'try to be useful, make their own beds, wrap up and address their own parcels', again small-scale inroads into long days.[33]

Over the course of 1940, as war escalated with the fall of Denmark, Norway, the Netherlands, Belgium and France, the King and Queen were frequently at Windsor, spending nights at the castle, though the Royal Standard flew at Buckingham Palace to maintain the illusion of their presence in the capital. For Elizabeth and Margaret, 'no longer... allowed to appear in public for reasons affecting their own safety', their lives resembled those of their aristocratic contemporaries: educated by their governess in a large country house, with plenty of fresh air and more time with their nurse than their parents.[34] Alah's unquenchable instinct for royal state went some way to maintaining pre-war levels of ceremony, including meals served by the nursery footman, Cyril Dickman, with rigid punctuality. Over time the pudding of stewed bottled plums from the garden was always the same, the regime increasingly spartan, despite venison and game to supplement rations, the rooms often unpleasantly cold. Nothing indicated to Alah grounds for lowering standards. Neither sister protested. Alah's attitude reflected the Queen's, itself shaped by Queen Mary's view of appropriate royal behaviour. It was all the princesses knew.

The suggestion that the princesses spend the war in Canada like members of the Dutch and Norwegian royal families and several of their friends was firmly rebuffed by the Queen, a popular decision, not least with the girls themselves. But the plan had not simply been concerned with their safety. 'If the Nazis got hold of their Persons,' wrote a former Lord

Chancellor to Winston Churchill, 'they would be able to bring tremendous pressure to bear on the King and Queen to accept intimidation by threatening death and even worse things.'[35] Mischievously, German radio reported the sisters living in Montreal and, later, New York.[36] Instead, an air raid shelter was made under the Brunswick Tower, with reinforced walls and a four-feet-thick roof of concrete and girders, and, in time, subterranean bedrooms and bathrooms for all the royal family. Throughout the castle low-wattage light bulbs replaced brighter peacetime lighting ('it seemed to be perpetual twilight,' Margaret Elphinstone remembered),[37] chandeliers were taken down to eliminate the threat of splintering crystal and, as thoroughly as possible in a house of a thousand rooms, the blackout enforced. Paintings were removed from their frames to safe storage, cabinets and vitrines emptied or turned to face the wall to protect their contents. Barbed wire circled the ancient stronghold. In their underground shelter, Elizabeth and Margaret stowed away their personal treasures, using the blue and pink jewel cases that belonged to the dolls Marianne and France. They kept a selection of books in the shelter, too, and the diaries they wrote daily. After a delay in their appearance below ground during Windsor's first air raid, caused by Alah insisting they change out of their nightclothes, they were provided with siren suits for convenience.

Despite considerable anxieties – unusually, in this period she found herself waking early and lying in bed worrying – the Queen remained successfully dedicated to her daughters' happiness. As a young woman, Elizabeth would tell George V's biographer Harold Nicolson that 'all the happiest memories of her childhood were associated with [Windsor] Castle and the Park'.[38] The sisters found the war exciting as well as alarming. On a visit to bomb craters in the autumn of 1940, agog, both 'expressed a desire to have a souvenir of the raids'; each was rewarded with her own bomb fin.[39] Months later, at RAF

Coastal Command, they enjoyed watching planes landing and taking off, exploring a Hudson aircraft with its New Zealander pilot and listening to pilots' messages through headphones. When bombers targeted Windsor on consecutive nights in October 1940, both girls had been 'wonderful', their mother wrote. It was 'the first time that the children had actually heard the whistle & scream of bombs'.[40] Neither expressed fear. On the contrary, Crawfie described Elizabeth as 'troublesome' during air raids: '"*Do* let me see what is happening," she would beg, her eyes very large.'[41]

Again a Guide company was formed. Evacuees from Stepney, billeted in Windsor, swelled its numbers. Crawfie detected a wartime spirit of democracy in the cries of 'Wait for me, Lilibet' in Cockney accents and the Eastenders' lack of special treatment of the princesses; she records the sisters' response as one of fascination, like their absorption in a world beyond their own, standing on the hill in the garden of Buckingham Palace, hearing fragments of conversations over the garden wall.[42] At a concert in aid of the Minesweepers' Comforts Fund, this democratic spirit failed. Elizabeth and Margaret were acclaimed 'the stars'; 'the other performers' were village children and the London evacuees.[43] Each princess performed a solo dance, they danced together, then, with the 'other performers', they took part in a scene written for them by Hubert Tanner, headmaster of the Royal School at Windsor. In 'An Apple for the Teacher', Elizabeth was the teacher in mortar board and gown, recalling her play-acting with miniature blackboard a decade earlier, Margaret one of a quartet of tap-dancing pupils. At Christmas the sisters appeared in a nativity play, *The Christmas Child*. An unnamed mother quoted in the *Daily Herald* praised Elizabeth for setting an example: 'During the rehearsals Princess Elizabeth tried hard to be word perfect, and all the other children followed her example.'[44] It was the role thrust upon Elizabeth by Anne Ring ten years earlier. Appropriately she played the part of a king. In the audience, her father wept throughout. This modest man discerned in both his daughters something miraculous. The emotional glue that bonded the family of four was of the tightest.

A starring role on an altogether bigger stage, however, had been Elizabeth's in the autumn. A week after its announcement, and after much rehearsing of phrasing and breathing, on 13 October, in the BBC's *Children's Hour*, Elizabeth made her first radio broadcast. With some hauteur the palace had declined all previous requests that she broadcast. By the autumn of 1940, opinions had changed. In September, the Blitz began – seventy-six consecutive nights of German bombing of ports and cities the length and breadth of Britain that killed 40,000 civilians and destroyed more than a million homes, including 145 Piccadilly and 32 Prince's Gate, where Elizabeth and Margaret had shared singing classes with Elizabeth and Joanna Lambart. Elizabeth's speech addressed the children sent away from their families to places of greater safety, including those who had gone abroad; she spoke to them as one who '[knew] from experience what it means to be away from those you love most of all'. She referred to her sister 'Margaret Rose... by my side', and Margaret had joined her in wishing the unseen childish millions goodnight. Older courtiers considered it mawkish. The response of audiences globally was overwhelmingly positive. Joyce Grenfell wrote to her mother, 'It was one of the loveliest things I've ever heard. So young, so true – so touching in its innocence and wisdom... Whoever thought up the whole idea was a genius; whoever wrote that little speech couldn't have done it better... you can't possibly defeat what that little talk stood for. The love and generosity and warmth of it.'[45] In her diary, a South African novelist, Sarah Gertrude Millin, described it as 'perfectly done' and prophesied, 'If there are still queens in the world a generation hence, this child will be a good queen.'[46] Even the *International Women's Suffrage News* congratulated Elizabeth 'on the manner in which she has performed her first public service', which it considered 'typical of a generation of children confronted with adult cares'.[47] In February of the following year, the Princess Elizabeth of York Hospital Shadwell received a cheque for 25 guineas from the proceeds of a gramophone record of the speech.

Listeners to Elizabeth's broadcast, including her father, noted how like the Queen she sounded, 'that little voice, so like her mother's, so strong and clear'; like Joyce Grenfell they noted that she sounded very young.[48] As previously, Elizabeth's double life as princess and daughter required her to be simultaneously adult and child, like the three-year-old who had revelled in feeding biscuits to George V's Cairn terrier and, on her birthday, taken the salute at the changing of the guard in her honour. Alathea Fitzalan Howard described a Sunday in July 1941 typical of Elizabeth and Margaret's storybook childhood: punting on the water close to Frogmore, a picnic with Crawfie, Monty, the corgis and ginger beer drunk straight from the bottle; feeding flies to the princesses' pet chameleon. Ten days later, Elizabeth was on parade as royal hostess. She joined her parents at Buckingham Palace for an afternoon party for 200 heads and representatives of Allied states living in Britain, and helped the King and Queen to receive guests including the rulers of Norway, Yugoslavia and the Netherlands, the presidents of Poland and Czechoslovakia and the Soviet ambassador. As so often in the past, public and private blurred. Photographs released to mark Margaret's eleventh birthday in August showed the sisters dressed identically in summer frocks and straw hats playing with their chameleon in the garden and Elizabeth netting lettuces and strawberry plants. The princesses were symbols of hope; an immaculately dressed Elizabeth dug, weeded, netted for victory. Matching clothes emphasized their relationship: as always, the sisters embodied affectionate family ties, a powerful message at a time when casualties, conscription, women's war work and evacuation had done so much to disperse many families. The pictures excluded jarring notes. They presented the princesses in a self-contained world of sunshine, occupied with an everyday routine whose orderliness defied war's tumult, 'a "governess & schoolroom" atmosphere' in the Queen's words, 'which, in these days of war, is very healing'.[49]

The Queen took Elizabeth and Margaret with her on hospital visits, aware of the tonic qualities of her pretty, prettily behaved daughters. Although it was the Queen who was the star of the trio, Joyce Grenfell decided, after witnessing one such visit in August 1940, Elizabeth caught her imagination. 'Princess Elizabeth is going to be lovely,' she wrote to her mother. 'One can suddenly see her as she will be. She's got her mother's smile and Queen Mary's colouring so she'll do.'[50] The Queen agreed to Elizabeth lending her name to a new flag day for children's charities. In June, the first Princess Elizabeth Day raised £19,962, a record for initiatives of its sort, with 3 million Princess Elizabeth Day emblems, the forerunner of today's charity ribbon knots or rubber wristbands, sold in the London area alone.[51] The following year, the total reached £23,588. As throughout her childhood, the princess's imprimatur yielded profits for others.

The day after Elizabeth's sixteenth birthday, the *Tatler* printed a full-page photograph of Lady Mary Cambridge in her VAD uniform. Lady Mary, it told readers, 'though only seventeen years of age... for some time past has been doing Red Cross work at a convalescent home in Gloucestershire'.[52] At eighteen, George Lascelles had joined the Grenadier Guards. Waiting to follow him, his brother Gerald, a year younger, had spent the last year working in a munitions factory under an assumed

name. 'He has not waited until old enough (officially!) to do
his bit,' the illustrated paper trilled.[53] Winifred Hardinge, who
had edited *The Snapdragon* during pre-war summers at Balmoral,
was in the WRNS; Elizabeth's friend and singing partner Lady
Elizabeth Lambart was taking lessons in French and cookery
in Oxford. Also at Windsor Castle was Margaret Elphinstòne,
who travelled daily by bus to the Queen's Secretarial College
in Egham, assuming that she, too, would join the WRNS
when the course ended (in fact she joined MI6); her eldest
sister Elizabeth was a VAD. Within weeks of Elizabeth's
birthday, Wentworth Beaumont, the eldest of the six children
of the Royal Family's Piccadilly neighbours the Allendales,
was reported missing on operations and shortly confirmed as
a German prisoner of war. He was a pilot officer in the RAF
Volunteer Reserve. Sonia Graham Hodgson would take a job
in a Polish government office in London.

Elizabeth was growing up. As recently as 1940, headlines
had called her 'the world's most famous little girl', but she was
no longer a little girl.[54] Photographs taken by Lisa Sheridan in
1941 showed that she was as tall as her mother.[55] One by one her
friends were leaving the schoolroom behind, making first steps
towards adulthood and, in most cases, war work. It was not the
King's plan for the elder daughter on whom he doted. Elizabeth,
a friend considered, was 'relatively young [for her age]'.[56] A
result of her parents' decision to treat their two daughters as
equals, it suited the King.

Instead, on 28 March 1942, Elizabeth was confirmed in
the private chapel at Windsor Castle, by the same Archbishop
Lang who had christened her. The congregation included her
aunt, the Princess Royal, and her grandmother. Queen Mary
praised Elizabeth's composure: the service was a rite of passage
of particular significance for a communicant destined to be
the Church's supreme governor. Excitedly, Mabell, Countess
of Airlie, noticed something more in the princess, a quality

she identified as regal. 'I saw a grave little face under a small white net veil, and a slender figure in a plain white woollen frock,' she wrote. 'The carriage of her head was unequalled, and there was about her that indescribable something which Queen Victoria had. Although she was perfectly simple, modest and unselfconscious, she gave the impression of great personality.'[57] The King had made the same comparison to Osbert Sitwell years earlier. It was quite safe now. No one expected the Queen to give birth again at the age of forty-one. If a technicality forced upon Elizabeth the label heir presumptive rather than heir apparent, there could be no real doubts that she would succeed her father as Britain's first queen regnant since her great-great-grandmother.

In February, the King gave his daughter an early birthday present, appointing her colonel of the Grenadier Guards after the death of her great-great-uncle and their shared godfather, the Duke of Connaught. Elizabeth inspected the regiment for the first time on her birthday. 'Slowly and with dignity' she walked along the line of troops, followed by her parents and Margaret, before making her way to a dais for the march past, all in view of the inevitable flotilla of reporters and photographers.[58] A *Daily Mail* reporter detected 'no sign of nervousness';[59] photographs tell a different story. Elizabeth herself described the experience as 'a bit frightening... but not as bad as I expected it to be.'[60] She carried out a second inspection weeks later, wearing a hat shaped like a service cap to which was fastened a Grenadier badge, on the lapel of her coat a brooch in the form of a regimental cipher, given to her by the brigade's officers. Little details suggest the eager earnestness with which she approached her task (so, too, the thoroughness of her 'inspection' that overlooked no minor details; she had inherited the family's attachment to minutiae of dress and decorations). She was photographed wearing hat, badge and brooch in October by Cecil Beaton, an engagingly sympathetic image that captured Beaton's delighted response to his first encounter with the sixteen-year-old and turned Elizabeth's hat into a fashion sensation, copied, according to the *Sunday Post*, in 'tens of thousands'.[61] 'I was enthusiastic to see how very much more charming Princess Elizabeth has become than any of the photographs I have seen of her. She has her mother's smile,' Beaton wrote in his diary.[62] At the same sitting he also photographed Elizabeth and Margaret together. The pictures copied a portrait by Gainsborough of the painter's daughters. They are romantic, even theatrical images. More than the 'Grenadier' portrait, with its Girl Guide sweetness, they depict Elizabeth on the cusp of womanhood.

The weekend after her birthday, accompanied by her mother and wearing her Guides uniform, Elizabeth reported to the local Labour Exchange and registered for the government's youth service scheme. It was the first time, newspapers reported, that 'a Princess of the reigning house and a future Queen' had done so (it was the first time such an opportunity had existed for a future queen).[63] Of course, her services were not called on. Only three years later did she embark on the sort of war work undertaken by her peers, as Second Subaltern Elizabeth Alexandra Mary Windsor in the Auxiliary Territorial Service (ATS). By then, the King had marked Elizabeth's eighteenth birthday by outlining for her work of a different variety. He appointed her a counsellor of state, authorized to carry out many of his own official duties in his absence overseas. Since counsellorship had previously been restricted to those over the age of twenty-one, this required an amendment to the Regency Act, which the King successfully pressed Churchill's government to pass. Her father's response to Elizabeth's wartime desire to 'do as other girls do' and join one of the women's service organizations suggests a rare breakdown in understanding between them: the King regarded Elizabeth's destiny as specifically royal, her training for the crown more important than any possible role in ordinary national service. In the spring of 1942, father and daughter were photographed together by Lisa Sheridan at the King's desk at Royal Lodge. Beside a vase of flowering forsythia stand the red boxes of daily government despatches. Over the King's shoulder, Elizabeth reads the same document as her father, his heir in training. She had been encouraged to listen carefully to BBC news bulletins. Her father discussed the mechanisms of kingship with her. And he continued to introduce her to high-ranking visitors. 'Part – and an important part – of Princess Elizabeth's training is for her to meet outstanding figures of the day,' explained *The Tatler*.[64] Among those she impressed with her knowledge and serious-mindedness was the US president's wife, Eleanor Roosevelt, staying with the King and Queen in the autumn of 1942. Elizabeth 'asked her many questions about the youth movements of America' and showed her footage she had taken herself with her cine camera of 'home life scenes of the Royal Family', including the King stalking at Balmoral with Margaret.[65] 'She asked me a number of questions about life in the United States,' Mrs Roosevelt recorded, 'and they were serious questions.'[66]

❧

The King and Queen considered that the war had denied their daughters fun. 'What a beastly time it is for people growing up,' the Queen wrote.[67] She also had her reservations about Windsor Castle as a permanent home for the frequently parentless princesses, describing it as 'not really a good place for them, the noise of guns is heavy, and then of course there have been so many bombs dropped all around, & some so close'.[68] Neither was Elizabeth's view. 'Oh, Crawfie, *do* you think we are being too happy?' she asked in the spring of 1941.[69]

That Elizabeth could ask such a question – characteristic of her desire to behave in a manner exactly 'right' – points to the success with which the miniature court at Windsor managed the princesses' lives. 'Sometimes one's heart seems near breaking under the stress of so much sorrow and anxiety,' the Queen wrote to Eleanor Roosevelt.[70] None of this did she communicate to her daughters. From infancy she had nurtured their happiness; to the best of her ability, she did not let Hitler deflect her from her purpose now. Sorrow and anxiety there had undoubtedly been: the relentless setbacks of the war's first years; the bombs that destroyed 145 Piccadilly and, in repeated attacks, parts of Buckingham Palace, including the private chapel in which Elizabeth had been christened; and, in August 1942, the death in an accidental plane crash of her brother-in-law, George, Duke of Kent, only seven weeks after the birth of his youngest child, Michael. 'I cannot & will not accept any idea of defeat,' she wrote to her mother-in-law, her bravado stiffened by the deep religious faith that she shared with her husband.[71] This kindliest of warrior spirits coloured her daughters' lives. When Elizabeth grieved over the deaths of her pet chameleon and the corgi Jane, killed by a car in Windsor Great Park, the Queen encouraged her to maintain a sense of proportion at what was, after all, the height of a world war. Had Elizabeth's life been less happy, the reminder would have been unnecessary, 'but there was no feeling of doom and gloom' according to a palace insider.[72] Artist Rex Whistler described the King and Queen in May 1943, giving the impression 'they hadn't a care in the world!'[73] It was not achieved without considerable effort.

If the war had permitted few of the splendid court entertainments that Elizabeth and Margaret had once watched in their dressing gowns with their 'fly's-eye view', or the lunches and cocktail parties and balls of the London season, there were more intimate occasions instead. Among them were small-scale fortnightly dances held in the Bow Room at Buckingham Palace and the dance the King and Queen gave at Windsor on 26 March 1943, ahead of Elizabeth's seventeenth birthday, with Guards officers, including subalterns from the Grenadiers, and a handful of American officers. Country life provided quieter treats. At Balmoral in the autumn of 1942, the King took Elizabeth stalking. Her bag of three included a ten-pointer and kindled an enthusiasm shared by neither Margaret nor Crawfie. She caught her first salmon; she visited the royal racehorses in training at Beckhampton; the following year she hunted with the Garth Foxhounds and the Duke of Beaufort's Hounds. 'The strong inherent love for country life is a marked characteristic of Princess Elizabeth,' commented a Pathé news bulletin. Although the big house at Sandringham was shut up at the outbreak of war, the royal family used nearby Appleton House, previously the English home of George V's sister, Queen Maud of Norway; Elizabeth joined the local Women's Institute in March 1943, after paying her annual subscription of two shillings. Her favourite recreation, according to Pathé, was 'to ride her brown pony Jock in the lovely surroundings of Sandringham'; idyllic end-of-summer photographs showed the family inspecting the harvest, the Queen driving a pony trap across flat, tree-studded fields, Elizabeth, Margaret and the King following on bicycles. At Windsor, officers of the Castle Company of Grenadiers, tasked with guarding the royal family, provided male companionship for Elizabeth and Margaret drawn from the same elite background as their Strathmore cousins. This group of men, whom Queen Mary called 'the body guard', included the Earl of Euston, heir to the Duke of Grafton, afterwards a candidate for Elizabeth's husband, Lord Rupert Nevill and Mark Bonham Carter. Officers joined the princesses for lunch and what Crawfie called 'clump parties', with hide-and-seek, treasure hunts and sardines; they sang madrigals with the princesses, their numbers supplemented by Etonians and, sometimes, the Eton choir.

Once Elizabeth's interest was engaged, claimed Horace Smith, it did not 'wane with the passing of time or the claim of other new matters upon her attention'.[74] She was diligent, thorough, conscientious. What was true of all things equine proved equally true of the princess's affections.

Elizabeth did not forget the handsome blond cadet at Dartmouth. Afterwards, sporadically, they exchanged letters, cousinly on Philip's part, for Elizabeth was only fifteen when, in Cape Town, in June 1941, his own cousin, Princess Alexandra of Greece, interrupted him writing to her. She was still too young for him to consider her in any other light when he spent a weekend's leave at Windsor in October. Later he described his response to wartime weekends with the royal family as 'the simple enjoyment of family pleasures and amusements'.[75] It was an affectionate but unromantic remembering.

Elizabeth almost certainly took a different view. Philip was an *idée fixe* for her, her fidelity to her obsession stiffened by a drip feed of reminders of him: his attendance at the funeral of the Duke of Connaught in January 1942; the mention in despatches a month later of 'Midshipman Prince Philip of Greece and Denmark, serving in HMS *Valiant*';[76] his regular visits to his cousin, Princess Marina, at her house, Coppins, in Buckinghamshire, after his posting in June 1942 to 'E-boat Alley': convoy duty the length of the east coast from Sheerness to Rosyth. By September of that year Elizabeth's mind was made up: in a letter to Crawfie she suggested that Philip was 'the one'. She was sixteen years old. She had told Alathea Fitzalan Howard that 'P[hilip] was her "boy"' as long ago as April of the previous year.[77]

The princesses' nativity play had been followed by an annual pantomime, beginning in 1941 with *Cinderella*, staged in the castle's Waterloo Chamber, with proceeds used to buy wool for knitting for the troops. Elizabeth took the part of the principal boy, Prince Florizel; Margaret was Cinderella. This allocation would be repeated. It appears to have reflected Elizabeth's own view of the sisters' relative attractions ('Princess Margaret does draw all the attention and Princess Elizabeth lets her do that,' wrote a concerned Crawfie).[78] Less flatteringly, Alathea Fitzalan Howard found herself cast as an ugly sister, Agatha Blimp. If reliable, Crawfie's account of a disagreement between Elizabeth and Margaret over ticket prices illustrates Elizabeth's unassumingness, a characteristic she would retain, and a measure of unworldliness. 'You can't ask people to pay seven and sixpence, Crawfie. No one will pay that to look at us!' protests Elizabeth. Crawfie's Margaret replies more knowingly, 'They'll pay anything to see us.'[79] *The Sleeping Beauty* followed in 1942, then, in 1943, dressed in breeches and silk stockings, Elizabeth took the lead in *Aladdin*. In the front row on the last night sat Philip.

For seventeen-year-old Elizabeth it was a particular boon. Flu had kept Philip away from the dance the King and Queen had given for their daughters days before; he recovered in time for the pantomime's final performance. She was unable to conceal her excitement. 'Who *do* you think is coming to see us act?' she asked her governess; Crawfie described her as 'rather pink'.[80] Her animation coloured her performance. Crawfie recorded that 'there was a sparkle [about Elizabeth] none of us had ever seen before. Many people remarked on it.' Philip laughed loudly at each bad joke; coyly Lisa Sheridan remembered that 'he thoroughly entered into the fun, and was welcomed by the princesses as a delightful boy cousin'.[81] And then he stayed for the weekend. And then he stayed for Christmas, too, a boisterous, ebullient interlude quite different from earlier wartime Christmases, 'a very gay time', according to Elizabeth, with a film show, dinner parties and dancing to the gramophone.[82] There were Boxing Day charades; the young 'capered and frisked away' into the early hours; Philip worried afterwards that his behaviour had got out of hand.[83] The King and Queen's invitation to this royal rolling stone perhaps challenges Harold Nicolson's assessment of their first reaction: 'The family were... horrified when they saw that Prince Philip was making up to Princess Elizabeth. They felt he was rough, ill mannered, uneducated and would probably not be faithful.'[84] For some time, 'rough, ill mannered [and] uneducated' would certainly be courtiers' verdict. 'He was new-broomish... and no respecter of the status quo,' remembered one.[85]

Elizabeth was untroubled, unaware or impervious to their view. She was in love and happy. Queen Mary traced her affection to Philip's first Windsor stay.[86] The Dartmouth *coup de foudre* notwithstanding, Elizabeth's feelings had developed over time. Crawfie described an altered Philip in December 1943: grave and charming, no sign of erstwhile bumptiousness. The greater change was in Elizabeth. At Dartmouth, Philip had encountered a child. The sparkling Elizabeth Philip saw at Windsor was closer to the 'sweet little Princess Elizabeth' artist Rex Whistler described to writer Edith Olivier in May of the following year, 'sweet-natured *charming*... and a little demure from shyness but not *too* shy, and a delicious way of gazing – very serious and solemn – into your eyes while talking but all breaking up into enchanting laughter if we came to anything funny'.[87] One of Elizabeth's Grenadiers found himself similarly enchanted, transported, according to the Queen's private secretary Arthur Penn, to 'a state which I can best describe as exaltation': 'it was a new experience... to find friendliness so allied to dignity and kindness to a perfect naturalness'.[88] Philip would find that he disagreed with the view of Elizabeth formed earlier in the year by novelist Rebecca West, who met the whole royal family at Buckingham Palace. West considered Elizabeth 'too good, too sexless', deciding 'she may be the one who falls in love and is too innocent to be loved'.[89]

Her parents' focus was not Elizabeth's romantic life. In March 1944, the King wrote to his mother that Elizabeth was 'too young for that now, as she has never met any young men of her own age'.[90] Instead the King and Queen concentrated on Elizabeth's royal vocation. Rumours in 1942 that the imminent appointment of a lady-in-waiting of her own signalled her entry into public life remained unrealized for two more years. At eighteen Elizabeth was a 'grave girl with honest blue-grey eyes', president of the National Society for the Prevention of Cruelty to Children and the Royal College of Music, a counsellor of state, colonel of the Grenadier Guards and an enthusiastic Sea Ranger.[91] She was also still a pupil of Henry Marten. Marten's later lessons examined the evolution of 'responsible government' and details of parliamentary procedure; topics included 'National Expenditure before the War of 1939' and 'National Expenditure during the War'; ahead of their discussions on current affairs, Marten sent Elizabeth newspaper cuttings.[92] In addition, Elizabeth studied Continental history with an émigré Belgian aristocrat, the Vicomtesse de Bellaigue. Antoinette de Bellaigue, known to the sisters as 'Toni', had joined the household in 1942 to improve Elizabeth and Margaret's French conversation. She interpreted her task as raising their 'awareness of other countries, their way of thought and customs', a comment on the insularity of the Crawfie/Alah regime.[93] Henry Marten set essays on Toni's teaching; Elizabeth wrote her answers in French. When, on 30 January 1945, Elizabeth broadcast a message of thanks to Belgian children for Christmas toys sent to Britain, she did so in French under Toni's direction. Horace Smith considered that the teenage princess possessed 'a keen and retentive mind':[94] in meticulous pencilled notes, Elizabeth set about the considerable task of retaining as much as possible of Marten's training for her future. Newspapers referred to her 'serving the apprenticeship which will fit her to rule Britain', a sentiment that mirrored in its seriousness her own and her parents' view of the preparation for sovereignty Elizabeth received both from Marten and her father's dogged example.[95] Marten's teaching emphasized the importance of royal flexibility. From her father's exhausted and overtaxed record, Elizabeth absorbed lessons in duty. Even the royal pantomimes came to be seen as part of Elizabeth's training. 'How thankful I am too for those pantomimes,' she reflected later. 'They taught me so much about speaking in public.'[96]

Wartime restrictions and the King's patriotic austerity curbed celebrations of Elizabeth's eighteenth birthday in April 1944, despite flurries of congratulatory telegrams and offerings like F. H. Shilcock's 'To The Royal Princess Elizabeth' that again linked Elizabeth with spring: 'Oh glorious spring / Let your sweet flowers bring / Gladness and pleasure / To our Royal princess'.[97] Rumours that the princess would make a nationwide 'independent tour' came to nothing, and, in February, the King had acted decisively to overrule suggestions that Elizabeth be created Princess of Wales, his decision guided by precedent and the belief he expressed in his diary that 'her own name is so nice'. On the day itself, with George and Gerald Lascelles overseas, Margaret was Elizabeth's only contemporary at a family lunch at Windsor. The dance given by the King and Queen early in May was considered 'a comparatively small affair' with just 150 guests.[98] That Elizabeth and Margaret danced on that occasion 'till the gunpowder ran out at the heels of their shoes' around three o'clock in the morning reflected both their enjoyment and the paucity of such treats.[99] To Queen Mary, the Queen had written, 'I am giving Lilibet a small diamond tiara of my own for her 18th birthday [the halo tiara given to the Queen by her husband in 1936], & Bertie is giving her a little bracelet to wear now.'[100] Although the Queen explained the impossibility of buying 'anything good', husband and wife found a Cartier aquamarine and diamond clip brooch, which Elizabeth has continued to wear; they also gave Elizabeth a corgi puppy, Susan, to replace Jane. Among presents from members of the public was a photograph from a resident of Newton Abbot of her grandparents as the Duke and Duchess of York on a visit to the town in 1899, another reminder of her place in the royal continuum. In similar spirit, the *Sketch* produced a montage of photographs of Elizabeth and her mother at similar ages from infancy to eighteen, entitled 'Our royal Elizabeths in Childhood and Youth', its purpose to enable readers 'to trace the likeness between mother and daughter'.[101] A Pathé newsreel, 'Many Happy Returns', described Elizabeth as 'the gracious young lady in whom there reposes the endearing charms of her parents'. Again, there were comparisons to Queen Mary.[102] More straightforwardly, the crew of *President III*, the Sea Ranger vessel of which Elizabeth was bosun, gave her a copy of John Masefield's 'A Sailor's Garland'.

Elizabeth's parents marked the milestone by sharing with her for the first time their concern for their own safety, after Germany launched the pilotless VI flying bomb in June with raids in central London. The King wrote an explanation of the terms of his will for Elizabeth, while the Queen, admitting 'it seems silly', concerned herself with how most fairly to divide her jewels between her daughters.[103] Less morbidly, they sanctioned her first steps in public life, including making speeches at the Queen Elizabeth Hospital for Children and on behalf of the NSPCC. Then, in July, the King confirmed the appointment of Elizabeth's first lady-in-waiting, Lady Mary Palmer, like the princess an ex-Guide with a taste for dancing. The youngest daughter of the Earl of Selborne, twenty-three-year-old Lady Mary, was drawn from the same aristocratic circle as Elizabeth's childhood friends. As so often, there was a Strathmore connection: Lord Selborne worked alongside the Queen's brother David Bowes-Lyon at the Ministry of

Economic Warfare. 'She seems a most charming girl, well-educated, poised, intelligent and delightfully natural & unshy,' the Queen wrote.[104] Six years older than Elizabeth and already engaged to be married, she accompanied Elizabeth on her early engagements. On these occasions the princess's public wardrobe closely resembled her mother's, partly a result of her lack of interest ('she accepted the fitting as part of her official duties but one did not feel that she was interested in clothes as such,' Norman Hartnell wrote of the making of an early evening dress).[105] The combination of 1940s tailoring, heavy stuffs for coats and the princess's large bust gave her a less than youthful appearance. 'Now that Princess Elizabeth is being dressed ten years above her age she looks the image of her mother,' Sheffield housewife Edie Rutherford recorded in her diary.[106] Tactfully reporters drew attention to her hats. After a series of autumn appearances in Scotland, the *Perthshire Advertiser* announced, 'Princess Elizabeth's loveliness and charm are now known and acknowledged in the north. From pictures, from reports and from descriptions of those who have seen her, there is now no question on the subject. She is fair and beautiful, fresh and altogether delightful.'[107] A lady-in-waiting described her then as 'very charming, but very quiet and shy'.[108] For contemporary commentators, her shyness contributed to her charm, considered appropriate for her age and sex.

Elizabeth won plaudits for the conspicuous diligence with which she carried out the duties assigned to her, the earnestness of her desire to do her very best at all times; she always would. Among her tasks as a counsellor of state during her father's visit to the Eighth Army in Italy in July 1944 was the granting of a reprieve in a murder case. In her discussions with Crawfie afterwards, her response mixed puzzlement with a determination to understand better, her own equivalent of the teenage Queen Victoria's resolution to be 'good'. 'What makes people do such terrible things?' she asked her governess. 'One ought to know. There should be some way to help them. I have so much to learn about people!'[109]

The difficulty of learning about people – then and ever since – was the impossibility of encountering her contemporaries on an equal footing. Elizabeth's social exposure had been narrow, markedly more so than that of her father or grandfather, both of whom, at naval college in their teens, had encountered boys of backgrounds different from their own. Elizabeth and Margaret had grown up in an aristocratic world in which the courtier's code of honeyed deference dominated social interaction. Even as a Guide, Elizabeth was still a princess, surrounded by the children of courtiers and aristocrats, and none of her fellow Guides treated her, as the movement required, quite as a sister. It was not stand-offishness on Elizabeth's part that imposed a barrier between her and those she encountered, although her upbringing's lack of rough and tumble with girls outside her family created a reserve: at Guide camps at Frogmore she found excuses to avoid sharing a tent, retreating instead to private quarters. In her photograph albums were pictures from a Sea Rangers camp in the summer of 1944. Elizabeth labelled one 'In the trench during an alert for flying bombs'. On it she identified each of the eight girls with her, as if this meticulous recording of their names brought her closer to them.

It was camaraderie of a sort, as Elizabeth experienced again the following year when, in March, after repeated entreaties, the King capitulated, aware now that the end of the war was approaching, and she began an NCO cadre course for the Auxiliary Territorial Service at No. 1 Mechanical Transport Training Centre, Camberley. Crawfie recorded Elizabeth's pride in her uniform of belted khaki and 'in the fact that she was doing what other girls of her age had to do'; Elizabeth herself later told politician Barbara Castle that her ATS training represented a sole instance in her life of testing herself against people of her own age.[110] It was nearly the case. Initially, over-attentive officers all but screened Elizabeth from the eleven other girls on her Vehicle Maintenance Course; she lunched in the officers' mess and returned to Windsor Castle every evening while her classmates slept in dormitory huts. Mischievous reports in the *Daily Mail* of special treatment for the princess heralded a shake-up. 'She is very interested in us,' wrote Corporal Eileen Heron, an observation that would not have surprised Crawfie.[111] Remembering fifty years later, Elizabeth said she had 'learned a little about driving and the workings of the combustion engine and much about the strength and happiness of comradeship'.[112] Her classmates, of course, were equally interested in her. Like the *Perthshire Advertiser*, they reached flattering conclusions about her appearance: 'Quite striking... Short, pretty, brown, crisp, curly hair. Lovely blue-grey eyes and an extremely charming smile, *and* she uses lipstick!'[113] Elizabeth relaxed with them, something that was easier for her than for them, and Corporal Heron recorded her 'talk[ing] much more now she is used to us and is not a bit shy'.[114] Five years later, during a visit to a Wills cigarette factory in Bristol in March 1950, Elizabeth encountered one of her fellow ATS trainees, Elsie Huff, working as an operator of machines producing filter- and cork-tipped cigarettes.[115]

Alah wrote that 'Princess E enjoyed every minute of her course in the ATS.' Her letter expressed her own nervousness at her charge's very grown-up adventure: 'You can take it I worried when she was taking her night driving tests when the rockets used to be falling about!'[116] To a friend Elizabeth wrote, 'Everything I learnt was brand new to me – all the oddities of the inside of a car, and all the intricacies of map reading. But I enjoyed it all very much and found it a great experience.'[117] The Queen described Elizabeth's 'really hard work at the Motor Company' to Queen Mary as 'such a success', adding rather vaguely, 'the experience will be of use to her in the future'.[118] Neither mother nor daughter commented on the number of times Elizabeth was photographed during the three-week course: photographers were among the norms of the daily experience of both. A studio portrait of a uniformed Elizabeth by Dorothy Wilding, responsible for a similar portrait two years earlier of Elizabeth in her Sea Rangers uniform, presented the servicewoman-princess as chicly efficient. Newspapers preferred images of Elizabeth uncharacteristically dishevelled, dressed in trousers, hair awry, busy with spanner or motor parts. And Elizabeth, not imaginative, learned about more than car maintenance. During visits by the Princess Royal and then her parents, she glimpsed the other side of the royal experience. To Crawfie she reported, 'Aunt Mary is coming down on an inspection. You've no idea what a business it has been. Everyone working so hard – spit and polish the whole day long. Now I realise what must happen when Papa and Mummie go anywhere. That's something I shall never forget.'[119]

There was to be no corollary to Elizabeth's ATS training. The King and Queen marked her nineteenth birthday with a particularly feminine present, a Cartier brooch in the shape of a flower sprig, with petals of pink and blue sapphires, and within weeks of her return to Windsor, the Queen's private secretary, Arthur Penn, had written to the pretty, twenty-two-year-old widow of Guards officer Captain the Hon. Vicary Gibbs, inviting her to become an extra lady-in-waiting to the princess. The invitation was symbolic, a sign that Elizabeth's royal duties were set to expand: the end of her career in the ATS. The day after Jean Gibbs joined the princess, Britain celebrated victory in Europe. On 8 May, amid unprecedented public outpourings of relief and joy, the royal family appeared on the balcony of Buckingham Palace, alongside prime minister Winston Churchill. Elizabeth wore her ATS uniform.

That night Elizabeth and Margaret left their parents to join the crowds beyond the palace railings. With them were

Margaret Elphinstone and Jean Gibbs, Toni de Bellaigue, a clutch of Guards officers and the King's equerry Peter Townsend. Among sardine-packed crowds, the gaggle of sixteen danced the conga, the Lambeth Walk and the hokey-cokey up St James's Street and along Piccadilly, 'all of us', in Elizabeth's words, 'swept along by tides of happiness and relief'; later she told the novelist Hammond Innes that she had knocked off a policeman's helmet.[120] They pushed forwards to the palace forecourt and someone, probably Townsend, smuggled a message inside to the King and Queen, who reappeared on the balcony following chants of 'We want the King! We want the Queen!' in which their daughters joined. 'It was a view of their parents that the princesses had never before experienced,' suggested Margaret Elphinstone, of the girls gazing distantly at the tiny figures on the balcony.[121] In fact it confirmed the view of the King and Queen as heroic, out-of-the-common-run, more than human that Elizabeth had conceived at their coronation. Decades later, she remembered it as 'one of the most memorable nights of my life'.

Like princesses in a fairy tale, who had once tasted freedom, the sisters escaped again the following evening. 'Out in crowd again,' Elizabeth wrote in her diary, 'Trafalgar Square, Piccadilly, Pall Mall, walked simply miles. Saw parents on balcony at 12.30am – ate, partied, bed 3am!'[122] On the first night, according to Madame de Bellaigue, they went unrecognized, despite an officer in the party stuffily refusing to allow Elizabeth to break King's Regulations and pull her cap low on to her forehead as disguise. On 9 May fifteen-year-old Ronald Thomas recognized the princess. For a fraction of a minute he danced with Elizabeth in Trafalgar Square. She denied her identity; he promised to say nothing. Swiftly their companions moved the princesses on. Policemen, *The Times* reported, told merry-makers that the princesses 'wished to be treated as private individuals, and they were allowed to go on their way'.[123] Margaret Elphinstone described the experience as 'a unique burst of freedom' for her cousins, 'a Cinderella moment in reverse, in which they could pretend that they were ordinary and unknown'.[124] On VJ Day and the night that followed it, Elizabeth and Margaret relived their adventure, including running through the Ritz.

Recognized by strangers, protected by police intervention, accompanied by her lady-in-waiting and her father's equerry, prevented even from wearing her uniform cap in the way she wished, Elizabeth could not deceive herself that she was either unknown or free. Her willingness, at the age of nineteen, to settle for so brief and qualified a 'burst of freedom' is proof of the extent of her acceptance of the fate thrust upon her in December 1936. Within a decade her life was already settling into the groove of her parents' making. On her behalf the King or Queen decided on her patronages and nominated her ladies-in-waiting; the King's private secretary accepted or declined her engagements. Her nearest attendants were chosen for her, her home life regulated by Bobo MacDonald and Cyril Dickman, the nursery footman promoted to Elizabeth's service. Her clothes were made by her mother's dressmakers, including Miss Ford of Albermarle Street, who had made clothes for the princesses as children, and her rooms decorated according to her mother's choices (in her sitting room at Buckingham Palace, even her favourite pink carnations in the vase on her desk matched the Queen's preferred colour scheme of pink and fawn). 'The greater part of her day she gave up to performing what must often have been pretty dull duties, and she did this quite as a matter of course. Like her parents she considered it her job, and it never struck her to try to avoid it,' reflected Crawfie.[125] Alah described Elizabeth in 1945 as 'a nice girl, with a beautiful character'.[126] Compliance was key to the character of this girl encouraged from childhood to emulate her parents and grandparents. Only in one way would she defy their expectations.

CHAPTER VII

'Are we being got ready... for the betrothal of the heir to the throne?'

❧

IN MAY 1946, bridesmaid Elizabeth was photographed with Prince Philip of Greece at Jean Gibbs's wedding to the Queen's nephew, the Hon. Andrew Elphinstone. The previous month Elizabeth had included Philip in the party of six she took to John Patrick's wartime drama, *The Hasty Heart*, at the Aldwych Theatre. So widespread were rumours of a royal engagement by the autumn that, on 7 September, the King's private secretary, Sir Alan Lascelles, known as Tommy, issued a categorical denial: 'Princess Elizabeth is not engaged. The report is incorrect.' At the time Philip was a guest of the King and Queen at Balmoral. Before his three-week stay ended, it seems likely that he proposed to and was accepted by Elizabeth, in her own words, according to Philip's cousin Alexandra, 'beside some well-loved loch, the white clouds sailing overhead and a curlew crying just out of sight'.[1] In his thank you letter to the Queen, Philip wrote, 'I am sure I do not deserve all the good things which have happened to me... The generous hospitality and the warm friendliness did much to restore my faith in permanent values... Naturally there is one circumstance which has done more for me than anything else in my life.'[2] Inevitably Lascelles's denial proved counterproductive. A housewife in the north of England commented on 'the rumoured engagement to Philip of Greece... I imagine they have little scope in finding her a husband who would be considered worthy of the job.'[3] She had reached her own conclusion, based on Elizabeth's clothes. 'There are comments on all sides about the too-grown-up way she has appeared since the Victory parade,' she wrote. 'Are we being got ready, as an Empire, for the betrothal of the heir to the throne, and is she being made to look of marriageable age, so that no one can think what a kid she looks, given as a lamb to the slaughter?'[4]

The King and Queen were tired, in the Queen's words 'absolutely *whacked*'.[5] Six years of war had taken their toll on the monarch and his consort. Their reward was popularity verging on adulation, but it was to Elizabeth and Margaret, rather than their parents, that a nation weary of austerity, its main topics of conversation, according to the King, 'food, fuel and clothes', looked for vicarious excitement.[6] The palace responded by releasing a series of photographs of the royal sisters. Lisa Sheridan pictured Elizabeth in the gardens of Royal Lodge, a wholesome girl-next-door, and in her sitting room at Buckingham Palace reading, busy with her stamp albums, smilingly business like at her large, orderly desk, and noted the new encroachments of Elizabeth's public life: 'constant interruptions... while we worked parcels, packets and letters were slowly mounting up on a table beside the door'.[7] Quite different were dream-like pictures taken by Cecil Beaton in March 1945 and held back till war's end: Elizabeth in the same Hartnell pre-war crinoline dress of the Queen's she had worn as Lady Christina Sherwood in the 1944 pantomime *Old Mother Red*

Riding Boots; in long-sleeved, flower-patterned chiffon in front of a painted backdrop depicting winter, harbinger of spring again; with Margaret at the foot of a palace staircase, butterfly princesses amid the glittering gilt, an updating of Marcus Adams's soufflé vision. The wartime popularity of the royal family had confirmed Elizabeth's status as a nation's darling – as the Duchess of Windsor called her spitefully, the royal Shirley Temple. Unlike the American child actress, Elizabeth had not outgrown her ability to enthral. In 1946, *The Times* estimated an enormous crowd of 40,000 to witness Elizabeth's traditional birthday celebrations at Windsor, while her two-day visit to Exeter in November attracted the largest crowds for any royal visitor in the town's history. In April, thirteen-year-old Harvey Blackett met Elizabeth when she opened the Sir John Priestman Durham County and Sunderland Eye Infirmary. His eyes bandaged after a squint operation, he told reporters afterwards, 'I would love to have seen her, her voice is so lovely.'[8] Violet Bonham Carter described Elizabeth as 'much prettier than any photograph because she has real bloom of youth'.[9] In the grey, exhausted, impoverished world of peacetime Elizabeth found herself a romantic heroine by accident.

Or perhaps not. From infancy, she had existed on one level as a figment of the popular imagination, a construct of newspapers' mythmaking and delicious photographs. By 1945 this 'Princess Elizabeth' possessed every blessing but romantic love: the queen-in-waiting's single requirement was a husband. Even the timing was right. Alah's death, at the relatively young age of sixty-seven, in January 1946, forced a break with Elizabeth's childhood. Schoolroom lessons also ended. In May, the King underlined his elder daughter's status as a full working royal by appointing a third lady-in-waiting, Lady Margaret Egerton, one of six daughters of the Earl of Ellesmere. Elizabeth, wrote Dermot Morrah, 'moved into her place in the main stream of the national life as the daughter of victory'.[10] To gossips and journalists, her coming of age presented an irresistible challenge.

It would not be long before they linked Elizabeth's name with Philip's, but they were several steps behind the couple themselves. In the spring of 1944, Philip's uncle, George II of the Hellenes, discussed with the King Philip's hopes of being Elizabeth's suitor, an infelicitous impulse on the Greek king's part that confirmed George VI's conviction of Elizabeth's youth and emotional inexperience. The royal reaction to Dickie Mountbatten's Svengali-like manoeuvrings on behalf of his handsome, rootless nephew was similar. Nevertheless, Elizabeth's fixed purpose compelled her parents to acknowledge the relationship and, in March 1945, more than a year before the press 'revealed' an engagement, the King instructed Tommy Lascelles to find out from the Home Office the stages by which Philip could become a British subject (part of his 'campaign' for Philip with which Mountbatten had been concerned for some time). In May 1946, Philip told his youngest sister Sophie that he was 'thinking about getting engaged'.[11] With his return to Britain from the Far East and humdrum peacetime deployment in naval training in North Wales, Philip had recognized both Elizabeth's feelings and his own.

Philip's naturalization that, late in February 1947, officially transformed him from a foreign prince, in the line of succession to the Greek throne, to Lieutenant Philip Mountbatten RN, subject of the British crown, occupied the energies of those concerned for some time, including the College of Heralds, which first coined the name 'Philip Oldcastle', and the home secretary, James Chuter Ede, who pressed for something 'grander and more glittering';[12] latterly it preoccupied Elizabeth. Philip suggested afterwards that there had been no formal proposal at Balmoral the previous autumn: instead 'one thing led to another. It was sort of fixed up.'[13] If true, it sounds an unsatisfactory impasse, especially for a girl deeply in love, and may explain why Elizabeth attached significance to Philip's change of nationality, viewing it as a necessary preliminary to their formal engagement. Philip's calculated disingenuousness was one aspect of his response to the King's requirement, following the royal family's acceptance earlier in 1946 of an invitation to visit South Africa the following spring, that any arrangement remain secret at least until the family's return.

The King's condition was not a mark of his opposition to the match, or indeed to Philip himself, whom he described as 'intelligent, [with] a good sense of humour & thinks about things in the right way';[14] afterwards he insisted he had not been hard-hearted in forcing Elizabeth to wait. Rather, this uxorious, affectionate man experienced an overwhelming aversion to changes to the tight-knit, supportive family unit he later described to Elizabeth as 'us four, the "Royal Family"'. Instinctively conservative, and dependent on his wife and daughters for happiness and the day-to-day emotional support that made kingship bearable, he considered it imperative, he wrote, that they 'remain together'.[15] Their comfortable shared dynamic was threatened by any addition to their ranks – in particular, a forthright young man of independent views, with a stranglehold on Elizabeth's attention and, already, a suggestion of impatience at the court's Victorianisms. Although the King gave every evidence of being dazzled by his younger daughter – her ravishing beauty even in her mid-teens, her laughing mischief and general air of an *enfant terrible* – he looked to reticent, steady Elizabeth for something more substantial. Elizabeth, Lady Airlie recorded, was his 'constant companion in shooting, walking, riding – in fact in everything. His affection for her was touching';[16] a visitor to Sandringham described their happiness in each other's company, 'talk[ing] together eagerly and animatedly'.[17] 'As a family we enjoy things so, and have that saving gift of laughter which lightens any burden,' the Queen told Ena von Coller months later.[18] For the King, the family who brought him enjoyment and laughter and lightened his burden was too precious a resource to jeopardize lightly. Quite to his liking was James Gunn's group portrait, *Conversation Piece at the Royal Lodge, Windsor*. Although at the time of its commission in 1950 the King had both a son-in-law and a grandson, it depicts only 'us four', seated or standing around a tea table, re-enacting a domestic ritual they had performed together on numberless weekends.

Opposition, however, there undoubtedly was to the match, especially in court circles. Usually accounts trace this hostility to the Queen and a coterie of courtiers. According to this theory, the Queen hoped for a homegrown candidate for Elizabeth's hand, a British aristocrat of her own background and outlook, like the members of the Windsor 'body guard', and was supported in this leaning by her favourite brother, David Bowes-Lyon, and courtiers including the Earl of Eldon and Lord Cranborne. The Queen, claimed the King's assistant private secretary Edward Ford, 'wanted to introduce her daughter to a wide range of possibles from the higher flights of the British aristocracy... [She] wanted Elizabeth to see a lot of young men, any of whom might have been suitable if they fell for each other';[19] it was the King who took pleasure in Philip's royal birth. A handful of factors lent credence to the theory. Given the Queen's antipathy to Germans, Philip's standing with his mother-in-law-to-be gained little lustre from the marriages of all four of his sisters to German princes, including, in the case of his youngest sister's former husband Christoph of Hesse, a high-ranking Nazi officer said to have boasted of his desire to bomb Buckingham Palace. Nor did Philip benefit from the Queen's ambivalent attitude to his cousin the Duchess of Kent, who was inclined to patronize her non-royal sister-in-law and, like Dickie Mountbatten, encouraged Philip's suit. Accustomed to acquiescence, the smilingly determined Queen did not relish the challenge of a brisk, brusque princeling who devoted scant energies to courting her good opinion and lacked the emollient good manners of her favourites. In fact the Queen's letters offer no grounds for this interpretation: she wrote that she thought Elizabeth had made the right decision; to Arthur Penn she joked 'how annoyed the Grenadiers will be!'; she described Philip to Osbert Sitwell as 'a very nice person'.[20] Whatever the truth of her view, she was defeated by a combination of Elizabeth's single-mindedness and the errant emotions of the young men she might have chosen in Philip's stead: over the course of 1946 a tiny field narrowed with the marriages of the Earl of Euston, the Earl of Dalkeith (heir to the Duke of Buccleuch), and the Duke of Northumberland; 'body guard' Lord Rupert Nevill had married Elizabeth's friend Lady Camilla Wallop a year before. At Sandringham in the New Year, Lady Airlie had noted the joshing nature of the relationship between Elizabeth and Margaret and the hand-picked young men who made up their party, surprised by the way 'both sisters teased, and were teased by, the young Guardsmen'.[21] Such light-hearted teasing was not a hallmark of Elizabeth's behaviour towards Philip. Its superficial intimacy was proof of her detachment.

It may or may not be true that, at a meeting arranged by Mountbatten in November 1946, Philip told executives of Express Newspapers 'how deep was his affection for the Princess and hers for him' (Mountbatten vigorously denied this statement by John Gordon, editor of the *Sunday Express*).[22] If so, Philip did not mention it again in public and the newspaper men were equally (and surprisingly) silent. To all save her family and Crawfie, Elizabeth kept silent, too.

❧

'You are always such an unselfish & thoughtful angel to Papa & me,' the Queen wrote to Elizabeth late in 1947.[23] Elizabeth had proven her unselfishness earlier in the year. On 31 January, with her parents and Margaret, she had sailed for

Above: A doting Duchess of York and her daughter, Princess Elizabeth, May 1926.

Above right: An early royal wave: the princess acknowledges bystanders, riding in a carriage of the Royal Mews.

Dressed in the 'dainty, fairy-like' dress her mother preferred, Elizabeth with her grandmother, Queen Mary, photographed by Marcus Adams on 31 March 1927.

On 24 October 1931, wearing her first long dress, five-year-old Elizabeth was one of twelve bridesmaids in attendance on her second cousin, Lady May Cambridge, at her wedding to Captain Henry Abel-Smith.

Elizabeth standing outside Y Bwthyn Bach, the miniature thatched cottage presented to her on her sixth birthday by the people of Wales and constructed in the gardens of the Royal Lodge, Windsor Great Park, c.1933.

Although portraitist Philip de László painted six-year-old Elizabeth without any markers of her royal rank, he was quite certain, he wrote, that she was 'the future Queen of Great Britain'.

From C. Edmond Brock, whose father built the Victoria Memorial in front of Buckingham Palace, the Duchess of York commissioned this 'family picture of myself and our two daughters', completed in 1936. Brock's several images of the princesses were favourites of their father's.

Above: Elizabeth on a tricycle, 1933.

Left: Elizabeth in a carriage with, from left, her father, the Duke of York, King George V and the Duchess of York, on the way to Crathie Church, Scotland, 26 August 1935.

Wearing dresses of 'white silk with old cream lace and... little gold bows all the way down the middle... and robes of purple velvet with gold on the edge', Elizabeth and Margaret joined their parents and grandmother on the balcony of Buckingham Palace after George VI's coronation, 12 May 1937.

Marcus Adams's first photograph of the new Royal
Family at Buckingham Palace, taken on 20 December
1938, proved immensely popular. The following
year Elizabeth's parents used the picture as their
Christmas card.

Above: Elizabeth was sixteen when Cecil Beaton photographed her in the Bow Room at Buckingham Palace, wearing a pink dress with blue pearl bows.

Left: A smiling Elizabeth at Sandringham in 1944.

Below: Second Subaltern Elizabeth Alexandra Mary Windsor of the ATS, busy with vehicle mechanics, 1945.

Margaret and Elizabeth travel on the footplate of a steam engine towing the royal train across South Africa, February 1947. On the right is F. C. Sturrock, the South African Minister of Transport.

Elizabeth married Lieutenant Philip Mountbatten, formerly Prince Philip of Greece and Denmark, created HRH The Duke of Edinburgh by George VI, on 20 November 1947. She borrowed the diamond fringe tiara from her mother; her earrings were twenty-first birthday presents from her grandmother, Queen Mary.

Elizabeth and Philip watching a cricket match at Windsor, 1948.
Philip is about to bat for Windsor Great Park Team A.

A beaming Elizabeth and Philip with six-month-old
Prince Charles Philip Arthur George, 27 April 1949.

South Africa. The tour's purpose was respite for the King and Queen after the strain of the war years, and a gesture of thanks to the dominion for its contribution to the Allied victory; that Elizabeth would celebrate her twenty-first birthday in South Africa was an added compliment. Crawfie noted nevertheless Elizabeth's lack of enthusiasm for the tour. While the King fretted at abandoning Britain in a state of near-bankruptcy, severe fuel shortages worsening the coldest winter on record, Elizabeth braced herself for the effort of separation from Philip and dissembling her feelings over three months of public scrutiny, their engagement still a secret. On the eve of departure was a conventional fillip: an early birthday present in the form of a pair of diamond and pearl cluster earrings from her grandmother, previously part of a larger pair of earrings inherited by Queen Mary in 1897. Elizabeth would wear the jewels on her wedding day ten months later and during her honeymoon. Throughout the tour she wrote to Queen Mary, as well as to Philip, whose photograph in a silver frame she took with her; she also wrote to Crawfie, a habit begun in childhood.

If there was to be little relaxation for the King and Queen during a visit that criss-crossed southern Africa in a crowded programme of 7,000 miles of near-constant travel on the specially built gold-and-white White Train, there was at least, after the separations of the war, the compensation of being together. The family's pleasure in one another was genuine and wholehearted. Currents of affection, noted the King's equerry, were palpable 'between father and mother, between sister and sister, between parents and their daughters'.[24] For Elizabeth, secretly plighted to Philip, as well as for her parents and sixteen-year-old Margaret, poignancy surely tinctured this easy togetherness: the certainty that this was to be a last adventure for the close-knit family of four. And yet, despite Elizabeth's misgivings, moments of carefree delight marked this first overseas visit. It shaped her lifelong. Many years later, remembering, she claimed, 'South Africa is in my blood.'[25] It introduced her to a fragmenting Empire and emergent Commonwealth; it revealed an unhappily riven society, the politics of race omnipresent if sometimes unspoken, black and white Africans segregated, nationalist Afrikaners stubbornly hostile to the royal junketings; at first hand she glimpsed the affection inspired by her family among many of the dominion's diverse communities.

Even the voyage out, after early stormy seas, provided flashes of joy. Gliding towards the tropics, the royal family 'danced under an awning on the quarterdeck beneath a star-studded sky'; Elizabeth partnered her lady-in-waiting Margaret Egerton in 'vigorous deck tennis' with the King and an equerry; there was shooting in the ship's miniature rifle range and a treasure hunt in which Elizabeth and her midshipman partner came second.[26] In place of the traditional ducking and shaving ceremony at the Equator, sailors dusted Elizabeth and Margaret's noses with powder. One of the best-known photographs of Elizabeth as a young woman shows her in a printed frock, breezes tugging her hair, twisting as she runs in a lively deck game with the ship's white-uniformed officers, among whom she identified for Crawfie 'one or two "smashers"', eyes closed in a smile of unaffected bliss. Rounding the Cape, she and Margaret, who were sharing a cabin, opened the porthole only to be doused by an incoming wave. During the tour itself were similarly relaxed interludes, albeit snatched from an unrelenting itinerary that both her parents found punishing: travelling on the footplate of the train's engine carriage; early-morning canters with Margaret on borrowed horses, like their very first ride, at Sandfontein, 'for an hour through desolate country studded with prickly pear', the sisters once again dressed identically in 'jodhpurs, bright-yellow shirts and wide-brimmed hats', or along the shore at Bonga Bay.[27] Close to Port Elizabeth, Elizabeth and her father swam in the Indian Ocean. A reporter's description of Elizabeth in her bathing costume as having curves in all the right places marred the King's pleasure in retrospect.[28] 'Oh, the poor King and Princess, bathing with hundreds looking on,' commented housewife Edie Rutherford. 'Well, I call it bad management. There are heaps and heaps of lovely bathing spots round the coast and it should have been possible to whisk the whole royal family by car to some secluded cove... Human nature is the same the world over, we MUST gawp at Royalty.'[29] To Queen Mary, reflecting on the contrast between the warmth of South Africa and Britain's punishing winter, Elizabeth described a sense of discomfort 'that we had got away to the sun while everyone else was freezing... We hear such terrible stories of the weather and the fuel situation at home... I do hope you have not suffered too much.'[30]

For the princess there were to be rigours of a different sort. 'Princess Elizabeth will take her full share in the functions and engagements and will relieve the King and Queen of some of the arduous work of such a busy programme,' British newspapers announced on the day of departure.[31] For the most part, the sisters' role was to walk in their parents' shadow, dressed alike in Molyneux frocks of contrasting colours, the gay, smiling, youthful faces of the royal fairy tale. On 3 March, however, without her parents Elizabeth opened a new graving dock at East London in front of a crowd of 30,000 (and, as thanks, received with 'unaffected exclamations of delight' five large diamonds, 'flawless stones exquisitely cut').[32] And then, in Cape Town on 21 April, she celebrated her twenty-first birthday with a day of public engagements. It was a coming of age among strangers, shared for public consumption like so many milestones that lay ahead. Celebrations culminated in two large dances: a public subscription ball for 3,000 at City Hall and a more select affair at Government House. At the second Elizabeth was presented with what she described to her jewellery-loving grandmother as her 'biggest and most striking' birthday present, a necklace of twenty-one exceptional graduated diamonds.[33] But the most significant event of the day took place before Elizabeth changed into her dazzling Hartnell evening gown of sequinned white tulle. At seven o'clock she made a special radio broadcast. Heard by an estimated 200 million people worldwide, it would become the defining speech of her life. For more than seven decades she has kept faith with its uncompromising avowal of service.

In the ballroom at Government House that evening, Elizabeth responded to her dancing partner's question of whether she was overawed by the portraits of her ancestors that surrounded them with a brief 'Not a bit.'[34] This matter-of-fact reply may have been intended to deflect further questions; it was also the response of a young woman at ease with her own prospects. To a friend Elizabeth admitted, 'I lie in my bath before dinner and think, oh, who am I going to sit by and what are they going to talk about? I'm absolutely terrified of sitting next to people in case they talk about things I've never heard of.'[35] She worried about gaps in her knowledge; she felt less anxiety about her royal calling. 'Your daughter already seems to be a queen, because she has so much dignity,' the Regent of Basutoland, Mantsebo Seeiso, had told the Queen days earlier.[36] Happy with her family, happy in love, schooled in her royal destiny by Queen Mary and Henry Marten, gazed upon, waved at and cheered from infancy, Elizabeth at twenty-one was no longer the earnest schoolgirl who, five years earlier, had carried out her first hesitant inspection of the Grenadier Guards. She lacked her mother's extraordinary charisma and her happy spontaneity, described by Lady Harlech as the Queen's 'sixth sense' for 'someone... feeling hurt or left out or frightened'.[37] 'She was a shy girl who didn't find social life easy' in the words of a friend; 'not easy to talk to, except when one sits next to her at dinner' according to her future private secretary, a verdict others have echoed; in 1949, photographer Cecil Beaton noted her 'hesitancy'.[38] She felt most at ease in small, private gatherings, like Laura Grenfell's coming-out dance in a house in Chesham Place in February 1946: Laura described her then as 'so absolutely natural – very dignified while you are doing presentations etc and then she opens with a very easy and cosy joke or remark and you find yourself talking more naturally than at any ordinary set piece dinner. She had everyone in fits talking about a sentry who lost his hat while presenting arms.'[39] Alongside the glamour of her royal birth, she possessed qualities encapsulated in the South African prime minister Jan Smuts's description of her as 'so human and sincere and modest'.[40] It was clear that she also possessed an unshakeable determination to be worthy of the examples of her father and grandfather. Although written for her by Dermot Morrah of *The Times*, a former Oxford fellow turned royal speechwriter, her birthday broadcast was her own idea. Its sentiments both expressed and shaped the conviction of her royal mission. Afterwards Elizabeth wrote to Queen Mary, 'I felt sad when I realised that I would not spend my coming of age at home, but now I think it forms a very happy link with South Africa.'[41] Even in private letters, already duty preceded self. How accurately Morrah judged her character in coupling joy and obligation: 'This is a happy day for me; but it is also one that brings serious thoughts,' she told invisible listening millions.

The speech was nearly lost, mislaid in the plushness of the White Train until rediscovered among bottles of spirits. The King had told Lady Airlie a year before that Elizabeth helped him with his Christmas broadcasts. On this occasion, the King and Queen, alongside Frank Gillard, in charge of BBC coverage of the tour, spent two hours working with Elizabeth on Morrah's first version, lightening its tone. All were delighted with the finished draft; like many of Elizabeth's listeners, they were deeply moved. 'The speaker herself told me that it had made her cry,' wrote Tommy Lascelles to Morrah on 10 March; Lascelles himself, 'dusty cynic though I am', felt similarly. 'It has the trumpet-ring of the other Elizabeth's Tilbury speech, combined with the immortal simplicity of Victoria's "I will be good."'[42]

That Elizabeth was moved to tears by the broadcast's text is a measure of her sincerity, and one reason its avouchments resonated so powerfully with listeners, including the formidably self-controlled Queen Mary, who recorded in her diary, 'Of course I wept.'[43] 'It left an impression of sincerity and high resolve that was deeply moving,' commented a paper at home, 'especially when it was remembered that this young woman was standing on the threshold of a life that must necessarily be extremely exacting in its demands.'[44] Elizabeth addressed herself to an audience of all races and nationalities. She felt as much at home in Cape Town, she said, as the country of her birth. She asked to be allowed to claim her place as the representative of 'the youth of the British family of nations'. She expressed the love she felt for 'this ancient commonwealth' and a vision of its 'powerful influence for good in the world'. And then, thrillingly, she positioned herself in the long continuum of England's monarchs, invoking the motto borne by many of her ancestors: 'I serve.' She could not, she said, make a 'knightly dedication' similar to that of her forebears, but went on to do something remarkably like: 'I declare before you all that my whole life whether it be long or short shall be devoted to your service and the service of our great imperial family to which we all belong.' It was a simple promise of self-sacrifice. On 21 April 1947, few doubted the earnestness of her desire to make it good. A lifetime later, it is a promise she has yet to break.

Elizabeth almost certainly derived greater satisfaction from the knowledge that the important broadcast had been accomplished successfully than pleasure in the glamorous but sweltering scrimmages of the two Cape Town balls. At the end of a day of receiving the birthday congratulations of well-meaning strangers, she was reunited with Margaret and her parents. The King and Queen departed the Government House ballroom at midnight. The last recorded sight of Elizabeth on her birthday has her sitting on the ballroom staircase with Margaret. The two sisters are giggling, taking off their shoes to relieve feet tired after a day on parade and an evening of being trampled on by the nervous dancing partners mustered for them by the governor-general's wife, Mrs van Zyl. It is the early hours of Tuesday morning. Two days later, the royal party departed for home.

The trip, Lascelles wrote, was 'an immense success and amply achieved its only object... to convince the South African people that the British monarchy is an investment worth keeping.'[45] The King's private secretary was mistaken. The victory of the Afrikaner-led nationalists in elections the following year opened doors to both republicanism and the evils of apartheid. More accurate was Lascelles's suggestion that 'the most satisfactory feature of the whole business is the remarkable development of Princess Elizabeth'.[46] He noted her 'healthy sense of fun' and 'astonishing solicitude for other people's comfort'; such unselfishness, he commented dryly, was 'not a normal characteristic of that family'.[47] In more than one sense, Elizabeth had come of age.

⁓

To Lady Airlie, Queen Mary had described 'something very steadfast and determined in [Elizabeth] – like her father'; Rebecca West had concluded she was 'sweetly dutiful, possibly with her father's obstinacy'.[48] In the summer, her steadfastness and determination were rewarded. At midnight on 8 July, Buckingham Palace announced her engagement to Philip. (The same day the palace had informed Lady Serena James that she need not invite Philip to accompany Elizabeth to her daughter's coming-out dance that evening as the engagement 'wasn't official till midnight'.[49]) She 'has thought about it a great deal, and had made up her mind some time ago', the Queen wrote.[50] Public and press reaction, after lengthy, rather hectic speculation, was mostly positive. 'Enthusiasm and affection boiled over,' wrote Mary Grieve, editor of *Woman* magazine.[51] 'There is a special place in English hearts for a sailor and a sailor's bride,' the *Spectator* commented, and the newly engaged couple appeared on the balcony of Buckingham Palace to acknowledge cheering crowds, who had waited all afternoon for a glimpse of them.[52] Reporters quoted golden opinions from across the globe: the *New York Times*, *Melbourne Herald*, *Sydney Sun*. Most overlooked views like that of the *Chicago Tribune* that the engagement was 'fraught with dark political implications', though at least one opinion poll registered significant disapproval of Philip as 'a foreigner'.[53] Slushier reports focused on the couple's appearance, casting them as figures of filmstar glamour. 'Looks as if our future Queen is going to be a humdinger for the looking part,' wrote housewife Edie Rutherford in Sheffield.[54]

'Not long before the engagement was announced,' Elizabeth told Betty Spencer Shew, Philip gave her an engagement ring made of diamonds from a tiara belonging to his mother, centred on a three-carat solitaire. 'I don't know the history of the stone, except that it is a very fine old cutting,' she wrote proudly.[55] The stones' provenance was a reminder that, with or without Philip's princely title, Elizabeth was marrying within the royal fold. Queen Mary worked out the exact nature of the couple's consanguinity: third cousins through Queen Victoria, fourth cousins once removed through collateral descendants of George III, second cousins once removed through Christian IX of Denmark.[56] These were details for private consumption: in 1917, Elizabeth's family had sought to blur their own German heritage and did not intend to trumpet Philip's. The *Scotsman* informed readers that Elizabeth's fiancé was 'young and handsome, a sportsman and a good dancer, unassuming by nature but allied by birth to several of the Royal families of Europe, and with active service with the Royal Navy in war-time to his credit... he has spent most of his life in this country'.[57] Potted accounts of Philip of this sort cut their cloth in line with the prevailing emotions of a population still suffering the after-effects of six years of war against Nazi Germany. Soft-pedalled were Philip's close kinship with the recently deceased Greek king, George II, and his unpopular authoritarian regime, as well as the family name of Schleswig-Holstein-Sonderburg-Glücksburg. A Press Association court correspondent quoted widely reported 'on the highest authority' that 'when Princess Elizabeth marries she will retain her surname of Windsor as a daughter of the reigning house. Thus any children of the marriage... would be Princes or Princesses of the Royal House of Windsor.'[58] Philip's three surviving sisters, all married to German princes, would not be invited to the wedding. Nor would the Duke of Windsor, with whom relations were mired in painful recrimination, an inability on either side to forgive or move on. 'This one subject of the abdication never seems to lose its anguish & misery for us,' the Queen wrote.[59]

Post-war Britain remained in the darkest economic slough. Attlee's Labour government, in power since Churchill's electoral defeat in 1945, had embarked on the far-reaching, costly social reform that created the Welfare State. Partly funded by stringent taxation of the rich, its spirit was at odds with royal pomp. The King experienced pangs of nervousness, unsettled by his own fears of republicanism. Nevertheless, a jubilantly happy Elizabeth, reluctant to wait until the promise of good weather in the spring, pressed her father for an early wedding. King and prime minister agreed a venue of Westminster Abbey, a green light to large-scale celebrations, and a date of 20 November. The palace made nods towards current austerity: Elizabeth's choice of the same frock that she had worn to review troops on her birthday in Cape Town for family photographs by Dorothy Wilding to mark the engagement, a wedding breakfast modest by royal standards using game from the royal estates. For the most part, it would be, said Churchill, 'a flash of colour on the hard road we have to travel'. 'Only a curmudgeon', offered one paper, 'would have us match an occasion like this with the greyness of the times.'[60] Edie Rutherford recorded her husband's cynical view that '[the betrothal] is only being done to boost public morale in the coming bad winter'.[61] The princess whose birth had offered distraction at the time of the General Strike again inspired escapism, extensive coverage a gooey sort of popular opiate. Again Elizabeth embodied fairy-tale ideas of royalty, in love with her square-jawed Viking prince from across the seas, radiant in her happiness and everything, Duff Cooper wrote, 'that a princess in a fairy tale ought to look like on the eve of her wedding'.[62] She, too, played her part in promoting Philip's distinguished war record and enthusiastic 'Britishness'. In October she launched the White Star liner *Caronia* in Glasgow, with Philip at her side. Her speech informed her listeners, 'He has served with the Royal Navy in war and peace, so that I need not dwell on his love of the sea and of all that belongs to it', a statement greeted gratifyingly by cheers.[63]

In the spring, 'by gracious permission of His Majesty the King', author of Elizabeth's Cape Town speech Dermot Morrah had marked her twenty-first birthday with an illustrated version of her life story. Morrah expounded a version of Elizabeth acceptable to post-war readers: he stressed her ordinariness in an extraordinary position. In Morrah's account Elizabeth is modest, friendly, kind, shy, humorous, simple, hard-working and, above all, unpompous. 'The King and Queen have never encouraged her to regard herself as anything but an ordinary person, and as such she sees herself still,' he wrote. 'It is her position, not her personality, that she knows to be exceptional;

and she fully understands that by showing the capacity of an ordinary woman to play an extraordinary part in the national life she best discharges the high task of royalty.' For good measure, Morrah pointed out that this quality in Elizabeth was genetic. 'Her father and grandfather before her have proved that men of normal capacity, normal tastes and normal training are equal to the highest demands of exalted rank, provided only that they are willing to devote themselves unsparingly to public service; and it is already clear that Princess Elizabeth's direct and simple character is of a kind that fits her to walk in their footsteps.'[64] In the summer of 1947, with memories of Elizabeth's broadcast still green, this philosophy of unremarkable, dedicated royalty won broad approval. The appointment, in June, of Elizabeth's first private secretary, John Colville, called 'Jock', the son of Queen Mary's lady-in-waiting, Lady Cynthia Colville, appeared to confirm her earnestness in embracing public duties.

Throughout the four-month engagement, an eager readership devoured royal tidbits: the names of Elizabeth's eight bridesmaids, including her cousins Princess Alexandra of Kent, Margaret Elphinstone and Lady Mary Cambridge, and her childhood friend Elizabeth Lambart; the honeymoon destination of Broadlands, the Mountbattens' house on the Test; the silk specially woven in Scotland and Kent for Elizabeth's Hartnell-designed wedding dress; ingredients for the wedding cake donated by Australian Girl Guides. Violet Bonham Carter expressed her horror at the King's gift to his daughter of a cumbrous grace-and-favour house close to Ascot: she referred to it in inverted commas, 'Sunninghill Park'; others were less critical.[65] (Obligingly the house burned down a fortnight later.) Accounts luxuriated in wedding presents from across the globe: an 'all-wool, ice-blue Australian cloak' promised within days of the engagement by 84,000 rehabilitation trainees in Sydney;[66] from the richest of India's princes, the Nizam of Hyderabad, a magnificent Cartier-designed diamond necklace and tiara;

a fine Hepplewhite mahogany chair from the Girl Guides'
Association; and the Sultan of Zanzibar's ebony-and-silver
cigarette box for the bride who did not smoke. At home, the
purchase of presents by public subscription puffed civic pride.
Of the eighteenth-century porcelain dessert service presented
by the people of Cheltenham, the town's mayor wrote, 'Certainly
it is a gift of which [we] can be proud... The service is not likely
to be one of those presents that after the initial inspection are
left in their packing cases – as with so many wedding presents.'[67]
From 'the citizens of York' came nine pieces of historic silver
made as a wedding present for an earlier Princess Elizabeth,
George III's second daughter; Edinburgh's gift of 450 pieces of
crystal copied the design of crystal in use at Holyroodhouse.[68]
In a sign of straitened times, there were practical presents:
a refrigerator from the United States; a length of furnishing
fabric of Elizabeth's choice and 'a coat length of pure camel
hair' woven by Miss Gertrude Frimstone and Miss Edith
Williams of Holywell Textile Mills; food parcels amounting
staggeringly to more than 2 million pounds in weight.[69] A
handful of presents were overtly political, a reminder that the
bride was also a ruler-in-waiting, like the engraved silver loving
cup filled with soil from Independence Square, Philadelphia,
from the American town's Jewish community. The publisher
of the *Philadelphia Jewish Times*, Philip Klein, explained that the
gift was intended 'to dramatise the present Palestine crisis
to Britain's future ruler'.[70] Other presents had a charitable
purpose, like Elizabeth's fourteenth birthday gift of £100 for
distribution to wartime causes: £5,500 from the government
of the Bahamas to endow British hospital beds; blankets from
Kenya. Of the twenty-five gowns presented to Elizabeth by the
New York Institute of Dress Designers, twenty were offered to
brides also called Elizabeth, also twenty-one and marrying on
20 November; the Women's Voluntary Service administered
the lottery. Tinned food came from overseas: from Toronto

and Ontario and the British community in Buenos Aires; the government of Queensland sent 500 cases of tinned pineapple. Its distribution among the needy, like Mrs Stanton, a widow in Lincolnshire, who received nine tins of fruit, soups and meat, or pensioners Mr and Mrs Kenyon, of Brierfield, Pendle, whose parcel included tinned plum pudding, prunes, corn syrup, chicken stew and spinach, was accompanied in each case by a letter from Elizabeth: 'Many kind friends overseas sent me gifts of food at the time of my wedding... I therefore ask you to accept this parcel with my very best wishes.'

The wedding presents were catalogued and placed on display at St James's Palace. From her parents and her grandmother Elizabeth received a foretaste of her glittering inheritance. A cascade of jewels from Queen Mary included pieces she herself had received at the time of her own wedding in 1893: a large diamond bow brooch and the 'Girls of Great Britain and Ireland' tiara, which Elizabeth has continued to wear. From her parents came the crown pearls, two single-row pearl necklaces that had belonged to Queen Anne and to George II's wife, Queen Caroline, diamond chandelier earrings, a Victorian necklace of rubies and diamonds and another of similar date of large sapphires; the King gave his daughter a pair of Purdey shotguns. Like Elizabeth's engagement ring, Philip's present of a diamond bracelet was made up of stones from a tiara belonging to his mother.

Of course, there were dissenting voices: Labour MPs, frazzled housewives interviewed by the forerunner of modern polling, Mass Observation, and, in James Lees-Milne's diary, a company of Coldstream Guards, half of whom refused to contribute towards a present for Elizabeth on grounds that 'the Royal Family did nothing for anybody, and... the Royal Family would not contribute towards a present for their weddings'.[71]

As the day approached, the carping dwindled. The autumn's drip feed of trivia had heated public interest to fever pitch.

When Elizabeth attended a ball at the Savoy Hotel, a week before the wedding, in aid of the Exeter-based St Loye's College for the Training and Rehabilitation of the Disabled, extra police were deployed to control crowds at the hotel entrance; ahead of publication, Liverpool's *Daily Post* reported 'keen demand' for its illustrated wedding souvenir. To Elizabeth, brouhaha on this scale was part of the royal spectacle, among her memories of her grandfather's Silver Jubilee, her parents' coronation, VE Day. Philip could not be expected to adapt so quickly, and did not.

From across Europe and beyond appeared a cavalcade of foreign royalties, the kings of Norway, Romania and Iraq, the King and Queen of Denmark, the Queen of the Hellenes, the ex-queens of Spain and Romania, the ex-King and Queen of Yugoslavia, the Princess Regent of the Netherlands and her husband, the Prince Regent of Belgium, members of the grand ducal family of Luxembourg, related and interrelated, a gathering rare in the post-war world to add glister (threadbare or tarnished as may be) to the government's celebrations. 'People who had been starving in little garrets all over Europe suddenly reappeared,' Margaret commented; the King and Queen contributed to their travel expenses.[72] Rowdily the royal mob crowded the corridors and dining room of Claridge's. In their travelling cases were the impedimenta of rank: jewels, uniforms, orders. Things were not quite as they would once have been – Juliana of the Netherlands exclaimed at her fellow guests' 'dirty' jewellery. 'It must have been a nice outing for all those decayed old royals – the poor little Yugoslavs were thrilled & spent happy weeks having their jewels re-set,' wrote Nancy Mitford; their mustering rooted Elizabeth and Philip in a distinctively royal cousinhood.[73] The gathering served, too, to emphasize the pre-eminence of Elizabeth's family among ruling and exiled dynasties: as Jan Smuts told Queen Mary, their status was that of big potatoes among the little potatoes, a quality identified by playwright Noël Coward at a pre-wedding ball at Buckingham Palace as 'something indestructible'.[74] In time for the wedding, the King conferred on Philip a roster of titles: Duke of Edinburgh, Earl of Merioneth, Baron Greenwich. After some discussion, including, of course, investigation of precedents, he bestowed upon him Royal Highness status; he made him a Garter knight exactly a week after admitting Elizabeth to the ancient order of chivalry, careful to maintain his daughter's seniority. To Queen Mary he commented with qualified confidence in his decision that it was a lot for a man to receive in a single swoop.

This phoenix-like royal re-emergence within months of setting aside the Greek title of his birth did nothing to diminish wariness of Philip among courtiers of the Eldon/Cranbourne ilk: doubters inside the palace queried the sincerity of his affections. Something undemonstrative about both partners encouraged speculation. At Balmoral, Jock Colville recorded 'sunshine and gaiety... picnics on the moors everyday; pleasant siestas... songs and games',[75] but physical reserve was ingrained in Elizabeth's psyche, despite her overtly affectionate upbringing, a characteristic she shared with her grandmother. Margery Roberts had noticed her dislike of physical contact during Elizabeth's visit to Brighton in December 1945. Roberts, the daughter of the curator of historic Preston Manor, remembered, 'As we walked along the corridor [to tea], the Mayor went to put his arm round the Princess's waist. She made no comment, but obviously stiffened.'[76] It was an aversion Philip shared. In surviving newsreel footage of the couple, Elizabeth's incandescent smile tells a story of its own.

As she had on the morning of her parents' coronation, on her wedding day Elizabeth looked out of the window on to a Mall already dense with crowds, in this case streaked with the pewter shadows of a dull, cold day. By six o'clock, 'a spiv could not have sold you an inch of kerbstone': thousands had spent the night under the bare November trees, and 'many women had slept peacefully in the gutter on blown-up rubber mattresses, in sleeping bags, swathed in travelling rugs or blankets'.[77] Bobo MacDonald busied herself, Crawfie hovered, in her own account overwrought at her sense of an ending. There was no Alah now, and Margaret, always Elizabeth's closest companion and today her principal bridesmaid, is absent from records of this last unmarried awakening. Available sources do not reveal whether Elizabeth's thoughts returned to her parents' coronation, whether remembrances of Alah or any of the family weddings in which she had played her part as bridesmaid dimmed her view. In Crawfie's version, she is excited, pinching herself to prove the reality of her dream come true.[78] Letters she wrote afterwards to her mother make clear that she understood the certain effect of her marriage on her immediate family. 'As you say,' her mother replied, '"we four" have had wonderful fun & much laughter even through the darkest times.'[79] Her dressing, helped by Hartnell's fitters, occupied her for more than an hour; she wore the earrings Queen Mary had given her for her twenty-first birthday and appeared to at least one of Hartnell's *vendeuses* 'so solemn'.[80] Her mother loaned her a fringe tiara made for Queen Mary in 1919, using diamonds from a wedding present from Queen Victoria: something borrowed. With it Elizabeth wore the crown pearls. Her jewels formed a link with her mother, her grandmother and her great-great-grandmother, with the last of the Stuarts and the first and greatest of the Hanoverian consorts.

Piccadilly, Regent Street, Trafalgar Square, Whitehall 'and many streets miles from the route [were] gay with flags and bunting' as Elizabeth drove with her father in the Irish State Coach to the abbey.[81] Powerful emotions stirred the King: in truth he was not ready to lose this daughter so like him in outlook and temperament, whose companionship suited him so well. Walking beside her in the abbey, he described himself as proud and thrilled, Elizabeth as 'so calm and composed';

Crawfie detected no sign of nervousness in either. Meagre sunlight through the abbey windows transformed Elizabeth into a shimmering white vision. 'The wedding was most moving and beautifully done,' wrote Noël Coward.[82] 'I have had really touching & wonderful letters from people saying how deeply moved they were, and even people who one might have thought would not have been touched by beauty or religious feeling,' the Queen wrote afterwards to Elizabeth.[83] Both the King and Queen Mary came close to tears during the signing of the register: to the Archbishop of Canterbury the King explained, 'It is a far more moving thing to give your daughter away than to be married yourself.'[84] Aspects of these heightened emotions swayed the crowds who lined the streets, starved of spectacle and unalloyed hopefulness through almost a decade of deprivation and fear. Elizabeth's dress induced trance-like wonder, 'a gown which was a mist of dewy satin... minute pearls and crystals afire and shimmering in the soft light... a swirling skirt designed in all the beauty that Botticelli could bring to a canvas': it invested its wearer with the same magical aura.[85] On this occasion it was Elizabeth's elderly cousin, Princess Marie Louise, who made the inevitable comparison: 'No fairy Princess could have been more lovely than this young girl in her bridal beauty.'[86]

'It is lovely to think that your happiness has made millions happy too in these hard times,' wrote the Queen, '& it is a wonderful strength to the country that we can feel like one big family on occasions.'[87] Happiness was bittersweet for the King. In the letter he wrote to Elizabeth following her departure for her honeymoon, he told her that when he gave her hand to the archbishop he felt he 'had lost something very precious'.[88] Elizabeth, by contrast, excused herself as 'so happy and enjoying myself so much', fearful she had behaved selfishly in her joy.[89] But she was quite sincere in telling the Queen, 'I think I've got the best mother and father in the world, and I only hope that

I can bring up my children in the happy atmosphere of love and fairness which Margaret and I have grown up in.'[90] The following year, she told listeners in Cardiff, 'I can speak with feeling of the advantages which a happy family life can bring to a child.'[91] Had she read the diary of a thirty-something writer in Berkshire, she would have felt no shadow of apprehension: 'One wishes them a long and happy life together, to set an example to the nation of what marriage *can* be like.'[92] Elizabeth had been setting an example for as long as she could remember.

~⌒~

More than three hours before it opened to the public, queues eventually extending to several thousands began to form outside Westminster Abbey the morning after Elizabeth and Philip's wedding. They came the next day, too, and the following week to see the signatures of husband and wife in the abbey register, and to look at Elizabeth's bouquet of white orchids, laid at her request on the Tomb of the Unknown Soldier. Until the end of February, daily crowds of several thousand people converged on St James's Palace for the exhibition of the royal wedding presents. They were mesmerized by Elizabeth's dress and her jewels and, in a sign of the times, the kitchen and labour-saving equipment.[93]

Wedding mania was slow to subside: Elizabeth would remain the fairy-tale princess of that vivid November pageant for years to come. So often she had been associated with spring: in her marriage she seemed to embody for willing millions a spring-like spirit of renewal and rebirth, a pennant of hope. At Broadlands, sightseers laid siege to house and gardens. Philip reacted in a manner characterized by Jock Colville as querulous. Without his exasperation, Elizabeth may have been better able to ignore the snoopers in shrubs and hedgerows or perched on tombstones, chairs, ladders, even a sideboard in the churchyard for their Sunday attendance at Romsey Abbey; later she acquired for the Royal Collection one of the snooper's photographs: herself, Philip and Susan the corgi walking through wintry sunlight and a silver palimpsest of dry leaves underfoot. In letters to her parents she expressed the depth of her contentment and the wonder of first togetherness: 'Philip is an angel – he is so kind and thoughtful, and living with him and having him around all the time is just perfect.'[94] She expressed her gratitude for the family life of 'us four' in which, Crawfie claimed, 'no doors banged, and voices were never raised in anger'.[95] 'No parents ever had a better daughter,' the Queen replied feelingly, '& we are so grateful for all your goodness and sweetness.' The Queen's letter acknowledged the extraordinariness of Elizabeth's position, in which the choice of a spouse had involved unique considerations: 'Papa & I are so happy in your happiness, for it has always been our dearest wish that your marriage should be one of the heart, as well as the head.'[96]

Harried by sightseers, the couple remained at Broadlands less than a week, before travelling north to a snowy Birkhall, stopping en route in London. Elizabeth collected from the palace a favourite dog lead; jointly they issued a statement. 'We want to say that the reception given us on our wedding day and the loving interest shown by our fellow countrymen and well wishers has left an impression which will never grow faint. We can find no words to express what we feel, but we can at least offer our grateful thanks to the millions who have given us this unforgettable send-off in our married life.'[97] It bore Philip's imprint. That ironic 'loving interest' found no echo in the stately blandishments of the King and Queen's public pronouncements or in Elizabeth's well-mannered compliance. That the husband's should be the whip hand is not a surprise. Opening a new women's college at Durham University in October, Elizabeth had reminded listeners of women's 'traditional duties in the home', warning that her sex 'must not forget that before all else we are women'.[98] Instinctively conformist in a conservative era, Elizabeth inevitably gave ground within her marriage. With hindsight the couple's honeymoon statement sounds a note of warning. Elizabeth's submission to Philip's testiness compromised her own politeness, for the subtext was discourteous, lacking royal restraint, a 'them and us' mentality none in Elizabeth's family would find they could cultivate safely. As she had vowed in her wedding service, Elizabeth intended to 'obey'. The statement was signed 'Elizabeth and Philip'. But she, not Philip, was the heir to the throne.

CHAPTER VIII

'A new combined existence'

❧

'IT IS SOMETIMES the case, even when our sorrows are most hard to bear, that misfortune is opportunity in disguise.' It was 22 May 1948, and Elizabeth was in Coventry, devastated by wartime bombing, opening the first phase of rebuilding in the city centre. Her speech combined comforting balm with brisk encouragement and she ended with the hope that, before many years, she would return to see new development 'as fine as modern taste and craftsmanship can build it'.[1] The day was a resounding success. The *Coventry Telegraph* reported that 'from the youngest to the oldest the hearts of the many thousands who greeted her were captured by Princess Elizabeth'. They responded to Elizabeth's instinctive combination of willingness and gravity, 'a most charming mixture in her expression of eagerness to please and yet a serious awareness of her rank and responsibility' in the verdict of a diplomat's wife.[2] In her letter of thanks to the Mayor – written, like her speech, by Jock Colville – Elizabeth commended 'flawless arrangements which made what would have been a long and tiring day into one that was a real pleasure'. She had remembered, as she had told her parents she would, observing preparations for the Princess Royal's visit to the ATS training camp, the painstaking efforts made by visits' organizers.

From Laura Knight, *Coventry Telegraph* proprietor Lord Iliffe commissioned a painting of Elizabeth at the moment of cutting the ceremonial ribbon; Elizabeth gave Knight sittings at Buckingham Palace. The artist placed the princess centrally amid a camarilla of civic worthies against a backdrop of the city's ruins. She appears a messianic figure, in one hand a pair of scissors, the other raised in a gesture like waving, but her face lacks any trace of expression: grave, composed, impassive.

Here, then, was a template, and one to which Elizabeth would adhere for the remainder of her public life: words of reassurance and fellow feeling, and benignity that was no less sincere for a certain detachment in her manner. In the same year she visited Coventry, Attlee's Labour government passed the National Health Service Act and the National Assistance Act, making free healthcare universal and extending financial provision for the needy. The new Welfare State assumed responsibility for the nation's wellbeing. It was a development with implications for the royal family. Previously private philanthropy, particularly fundraising for hospitals, had looked to royal patronage for endorsement and support. At a stroke, this role potentially disappeared. Elizabeth's approach to her nascent public duties registered no change: she appeared to reconsider neither the focus nor conduct of her engagements in an altered world. In a devastated city centre, what 'touched the heart of Coventry was the winning smile of a young woman – and the many sincere indications of a deep and kindly interest in the people'.[3] It was an old-fashioned recipe for royal interaction that had sufficed for generations in a hierarchical society in which members of the royal family were seen to combine intimations of divinity with the glamour of high birth. And in 1948, for many people, it was still enough. In March, a letter printed in the *Sunday Mirror*, a paper with a large working-class readership, suggested Elizabeth 'should visit some of the very poor areas and show what charm and breeding can do to bring a little sunshine into drab lives', an endorsement of feminized paternalism by a representative of its beneficiaries.[4]

❧

To Laura Knight Lord Iliffe explained his commission: Elizabeth's opening of the new Broadgate symbolized Coventry's rebirth. Within a fortnight of the royal visit, Elizabeth's own pregnancy was announced by Buckingham Palace. She would give birth a week before her first wedding anniversary.

Philip had written affectionately of his young bride to his mother-in-law, 'My ambition is to weld the two of us into a new combined existence.'[5] So long as he remained a serving naval officer, occupied during the week, the couple's existence included separate working lives; a number of Elizabeth's engagements were undertaken without her husband. As in Coventry she exercised a hypnotic effect over many she encountered. 'A visit by a young princess with beautiful blue eyes and a superb natural complexion brought gleams of radiant sunshine into the dingiest streets of the dreariest cities,' Jock Colville noted.[6] He did not agree that this 'princess effect' invested Elizabeth's public life with purpose or sterling value. At the time of the couple's engagement, Queen Mary had discussed with him the narrowness of Elizabeth's social exposure, indicating 'the necessity of travel, of mixing with all the classes (HRH is inclined to associate with young Guards officers to the exclusion of more representative strata of the community) and of learning to know young members of the Labour Party'.[7] Colville could not direct Elizabeth's social life: he was anxious to familiarize her more closely with the business of government and its current practitioners. With the King's agreement he arranged that she receive Foreign Office telegrams. She read them diligently but without marked interest: in the words of Dermot Morrah, loyal and emollient, 'she found it rather heavy going, for her natural tastes are not political; but she grappled with the task with perseverance'.[8] Colville suggested a visit to a foreign policy debate in the House of Commons. 'These visits by the heir to the Throne are part of their education for the high responsibilities they will eventually have to assume,' reporters dutifully noted.[9] It was unfortunate that the debate in question was 'perhaps the most gloomy that has taken place in the life of the present Parliament'. In the face of Elizabeth's inscrutable good behaviour in the Speaker's Gallery, attention focused on the fur cape she wore over her blue dress.[10] More successful was a visit to a juvenile court three weeks later. The hearing concerned the case of a fifteen-year-old girl found drunk in the street 'with her arms round a lamppost'. Elizabeth was visibly moved by the unhappiness of the girl, who burst into tears, crying, 'The real trouble is my home life.'[11] Colville regarded exposure of this sort as constructive. Like a number of letters addressed to Elizabeth, it revealed stark inequalities among her father's subjects and the very real tribulations of many lives.

Colville's concern that Elizabeth visibly engage with life outside the palace had been sharpened by difficulties surrounding the Civil List allowance granted to the couple at the time of their marriage. On her twenty-first birthday, Elizabeth's income had increased from £6,000 to £15,000. Only after a degree of wrangling and the timely resignation of chancellor of the exchequer Hugh Dalton, who dug in his heels over a considerably lower sum, did parliament agree to the King's request of a further increase to £50,000, to include £10,000 for Philip. 'A royal family that did not maintain a certain ceremonial would ill please a people that loves a show as much as the average Englishman (and woman) does,' commented a relieved *Spectator*, reminding its readers that the purpose of Civil List payments was the maintenance of royal bread and circuses.[12] As even the *Spectator* noted, the outlook of the post-war world had changed. 'That the royal couple should be spoken of commonly by the people and sometimes by the press as simply Philip and Elizabeth is symptomatic... The spirit of egalitarianism is in the air. To that even royalty may in some degree have to adapt itself.'[13] Colville's 'education' of Elizabeth was his own contribution to this process of adapting. In the short term its success was qualified; later Elizabeth simply side-stepped egalitarianism in order to survive in a society in thrall to the tenets (if not the reality) of meritocracy. In London again in the autumn, Eleanor Roosevelt noted her keen interest in governments' responses to social problems, but at a dinner party given by the prime minister, Hugh Gaitskill, minister of Fuel and Power, who spoke to her for fifteen minutes, recorded that Elizabeth 'had a very pretty voice and quite an easy manner but is not, I think, very interested in politics or affairs generally'.[14] It was fortunate, as she demonstrated on the couple's four-day official visit to Paris in May, that Elizabeth was capable of dazzling simply by dint of youthful good looks, evident good intentions and her status as a princess. (On this occasion, Elizabeth's determination to acquit herself as well as she possibly could overcame a combination of acute morning sickness and the highest May temperatures on record.) 'Wildly cheering crowds' accompanied the royal couple; Pathé referred to Parisians' 'spontaneous display of affection', and an estimated half a million people lined the riverbanks when Elizabeth and Philip took to the Seine in a motor launch.[15] On the part of the president, Vincent Auriol, was also a considerable degree of ceremony and deference in his treatment of Elizabeth, a foretaste of what lay ahead and perhaps the explanation for the more 'queenly attitude' that members of Elizabeth's household thought they identified afterwards.[16] Elizabeth put to good use the French lessons with Monty and Toni de Bellaigue. When she opened an exhibition on British Life at the Musée Galliera, she delivered her speech in French. 'In four hectic days the Princess conquered Paris,' concluded Jock Colville.[17] It was a claim that would be repeated throughout her life, of locations across the globe.

Like her parents at the time of her own birth, Elizabeth and Philip were homeless as her November due date approached; like her parents they were blissfully happy. To the Queen Philip wrote straightforwardly, 'Lilibet is the only "thing" in this world which is absolutely real to me';[18] Chips Channon's verdict, after watching the pregnant Elizabeth dance 'until nearly 5 am' at a party of the Duchess of Kent's, was that husband and wife 'seemed supremely happy'.[19] Clarence House, close to St James's Palace, had been chosen as their London home. Eighteen months of renovation delayed their occupancy until the summer of 1949. In the interval, like the Yorks in Bruton Street, they lived with Elizabeth's parents, in the Buhl Suite in Buckingham Palace; for an interval they borrowed from the Athlones the Clock House at Kensington Palace, densely furnished with big game trophies. They spent weekends in 'a moderate-size creeper-clad house, about a quarter of a mile off the road, near Sunningdale': Windlesham Moor, rented part furnished from a Mrs Warwick Bryant. 'In modern taste and... of two floors, with a large attic storeroom above', it was a replacement for Sunningdale Park, which had been left a virtual shell.[20] Philip hung pictures, Elizabeth directed him moving furniture. Although smaller than she had been used to, the staff of six, including Mrs Barnes the cook and a steward appropriately called King, guaranteed the seamless housekeeping to which Elizabeth was accustomed. In London, Elizabeth tried her hand at mixing green paint for her new dining room. Husband and wife delighted in the cosiness of homemaking that Elizabeth took for granted but which was quite new to Philip. If either was concerned by criticism of the costs of renovation by a team of fifty-five workmen, they did not reveal it beyond maintaining a careful silence over Mountbatten's offer of a private cinema. At the private view of the Ideal Homes Show in March 1949, a tangle of protesters greeted the couple with shouts of 'Houses for the working people and not for the rich'. From a balcony, they showered a confetti of leaflets produced by the London Young Communist League, entitled 'Ideal Homes – Ideal Dreams – Unless'. Elizabeth did not react. With minister Aneurin Bevan she looked at furnished rooms in a Ministry of Health house display. Her response was a practical 'Yes, but where do you keep the pram?'[21]

The couple's happiness owed much to Philip's forbearance. Buckingham Palace was not only home to his parents-in-law, but a number of courtiers and staff still unreconciled to Philip, among them the influential Tommy Lascelles. Possessive, unyielding and, according to Philip's equerry, tyrannical, Bobo MacDonald continued her bossy and unrelenting ministrations to her 'little lady'. 'When Elizabeth was changing for dinner and having a bath,' remembered Patricia Mountbatten, Bobo 'would be in and out of the bathroom, so Philip couldn't share the bath with her. Elizabeth didn't feel she could say, "Bobo, please don't come in," so Philip had to go off and have a bath on his own.'[22] Philip did not complain. He was surely aware that, while his own life had been transformed by marriage, Elizabeth's had scarcely altered, her working life identical, still surrounded at home by familiar attendants, still in thrall to her parents, with whom, Crawfie claimed, she 'continued her childhood's habit, and always went down to the Queen to ask, "Shall I do this?" or "Do you approve of that?"[23] In his own case, experience had not prepared Philip for the reality of the change. A child of impoverished royal exiles, his formative years scarred by pervasive uncertainty, the breakdown in his mother's mental health and the collapse of his parents' marriage, he was as unaccustomed to the extreme formality of the royal family's life as to its charades-and-singsong chumminess; his background of German castles, Gordonstoun and the navy set him apart from the ranks of Etonian ex-Guardsmen courtiers, too; emotional neglect and indigence had taught him self-reliance from childhood. Some of this Elizabeth saw. A letter written to her mother on her honeymoon made clear that she recognized grounds for friction: 'Philip is terribly independent, and I quite understand the poor darling wanting to start off properly, without everything being <u>done</u> for us'; she told the Queen how much she hoped Philip could be 'boss in his own home'.[24] In many ways unimaginative, Elizabeth possessed a degree of shrewdness, though she failed to create under her parents' roof the setting for their married life that either partner had anticipated, and Philip's desire to 'weld' their existences into one, for all the dominance implied by his choice of verb, would be forced to wait.

Elizabeth's public life placed additional hurdles in the path of married bliss. Debate among politicians and outside parliament about the kind of monarchy best suited to the post-war world had not altered Elizabeth's understanding of royalty or its mission, shaped by her parents and grandparents. As recently as her engagement, the King had written, 'My father set before me and my family a high standard of duty. I am sure that our daughter will always keep King George's lofty ideals before her and endeavour to follow his example of constant service.'[25] In practice, fidelity to George V's example, emphasized throughout Elizabeth's growing up, rated public service above the claims of private life (the lesson the royal family drew from the abdication); it served as a cornerstone of what Colville labelled the family's 'semi-divine interpretation of Monarchy', which he considered distinct from Philip's 'hail-fellow-well-met' approach.[26] Even when she was a child, observers had applauded Elizabeth's dignity and those closest to her, like Crawfie, her determination to do what was expected of her to the best of her ability: marriage did not dispel either her public reserve or her conscientiousness. The combination delighted her contemporaries. Diplomatist's wife Cynthia Jebb referred to Elizabeth's 'charming diffidence' as 'very appealing'; she explained that 'a touch of genuine gravity was always the barrier which separated royalty from the common herd, warning them that no liberty should be taken. But all this with a sweet smile, a very pretty soft voice, and a certain gaucherie in her walk, showing her to be still just a young girl.'[27] 'Semi-divinity' inferred a gulf between the royal family and the King's subjects, Jebb's 'barrier'. In their sittings at Buckingham Palace, Elizabeth told Laura Knight, 'I love looking at the crowds gathering when I myself am out of sight,' a statement that echoes her fascination since childhood with the multitudes beyond the palace railings and embodies this notional separation. In the first year of her marriage, Elizabeth sat for photographs at the Elysée Palace in Paris, wearing full evening dress, including her grandmother's tiara and her South African birthday necklace; she sat for Hon. Mountstuart Elphinstone dressed in furs and wearing Philip's diamond bracelet; in mid-December she sat for Cecil Beaton, against a painted backcloth in a gilded chair that resembled a throne. Still homeless but happy, Philip could be in no doubt that the woman he had married was also a princess whose identity, model of behaviour and earnest sense of purpose were wrapped up in her royal status.

In a more leisurely age, Elizabeth attended her last official engagement in July. As her confinement drew closer, she received from members of the public at home and abroad presents and torrents of advice. Among presents that were not returned were a baby's coat, cardigan, bootees and gloves knitted by a Mrs Seager, living in Wells's renamed workhouse, from wool contributed by her fellow inmates. In her letter of thanks, Elizabeth's lady-in-waiting explained that Elizabeth accepted them gladly 'as a token of your good wishes'.[28]

She gave birth to her first child, a son, at 9.14 p.m. on 14 November 1948 in a room specially prepared on the first floor of the palace overlooking the Mall, 'after a hard time... 30 hours in all'.[29] Her parents awaited the good news nearby. Philip played squash to relieve nervous impatience during what his mother called 'the anxious trying hours of the confinement'.[30] Close at hand were Bobo MacDonald and Elizabeth's lady-in-waiting, married now as Lady Mary Strachey. The King and Queen greeted their first grandchild in evening dress, Philip hot from the squash court, a polarity of sorts: on the one hand formality and tradition, on the other restless energy. As at every juncture of her life, Elizabeth had done what was expected of her with the minimum of fuss; her father's press secretary commented 'I knew she'd do it! She'd never let us down', as if the baby's sex had been a simple matter of choice for the dutiful Elizabeth.[31] Ahead of the birth, the King had departed from tradition in countermanding the attendance of the home secretary, James Chuter Ede; he had approved letters patent to ensure the child held the rank of royal prince or princess. Newspapers reported that instead Chuter Ede 'was the first person to be notified of the birth by a telephone message' (from Tommy Lascelles) and that the new arrival was the first royal birth at Buckingham Palace since that of Princess Patricia of Connaught in 1886; Queen Mary and Margaret, who was away, were also informed at once. The new great-grandmother arrived at the palace an hour later, accompanied by her brother and sister-in-law, to much cheering. Cheering on the part of large crowds continued into the early hours, despite pleas for quiet. In Trafalgar Square, water in the fountains ran blue in honour of the prince christened, after a month and a day, and for no other reason, his parents claimed, than that they liked the sound of the name and Philip 'wanted to break away from the more obvious family names', Charles Philip Arthur George.[32] To mark the occasion the King and Queen gave their daughter a brooch in the form of a diamond basket of jewelled flowers. She wore it for her first official photographs with her son.

~~~

Crawfie suggested on Elizabeth's part a business-like attitude to imminent motherhood, apprehension dismissed with an unprotesting 'After all, it is what we're made for.'[33] Elizabeth wrote to her piano teacher, Mabel Lander, whom she had known most of her life, describing for the pianist the baby's hands: 'rather large, but fine with long fingers – quite unlike mine and certainly unlike his father's. It will be interesting to see what they will become.' With a mixture of wonder and astonishment, she added, 'I still find it difficult to believe I have a baby of my own.'[34] Like her parents in 1926, she authorized the release of mother-and-child photographs, on this occasion taken by Cecil Beaton. With grand afflatus *The Times* had described Charles's birth as 'a national and imperial event which can for a moment divert the people's thoughts from the acrimonies of domestic argument and the anxieties of the international scene', investing Elizabeth's child with the role she herself had repeatedly embodied of national, even international panacea. At the same time the paper explained the birth's strengthening of the bond between crown and country, calling it a 'simple joy... [to be] shared by all'.[35] After a month, Queen Louise of Sweden, Philip's aunt, described Elizabeth 'looking so well & fresh, a good recovery'.[36] Photographs support her view. The *Illustrated London News* chose a photograph of Elizabeth and her baby that it described as 'not only one of the most charming of Princess Elizabeth ever taken, but one of the most radiant studies of a young mother with her baby son. No mother, whether of royal or humble birth, who treasures the first photograph of her child for the memories it bestirs can look at it unmoved.'[37] Motherhood brought Elizabeth closer to her father's subjects; maternal joy took no account of rank, and Elizabeth marked Charles's birth, like her wedding, with food parcels distributed among other mothers of children born on the same day. But no one in Charles's family overlooked his unique status. Among those invited to be godparents to the infant prince were the King, Queen Mary, the King of Norway and Prince George of Greece, all of them related. Queen Mary glimpsed a resemblance to the Prince Consort; she did not refer to the prince's namesake, the only English King to be executed by his subjects. She found the baby, Elizabeth wrote, 'a very lovable creature'.[38]

For two months Elizabeth breastfed, until, at Sandringham in late January, she contracted measles, and mother and child were separated. Although Elizabeth labelled it 'a horrid illness', her recovery, under Sister Turner, was straightforward, and she did not pass the illness on to Charles, who was moved to Windlesham Moor and visited by his parents at weekends.[39] Of more pressing concern was the King's health. In the last weeks of her pregnancy, at his own request, Elizabeth had been shielded from doctors' concerns for her father's worsening condition. Privy to their diagnosis of arteriosclerosis caused by a lifetime of heavy smoking and view that amputation of the right leg offered the surest means of avoiding gangrene, the Queen described to Winston Churchill 'experiences & emotions during the last months... that... have been almost <u>too</u> vampire & have drained away something of the joy of living'.[40] Eight hours a day with his legs clamped in a device called an occluder went some way to restoring the King's circulation and staved off amputation. He was instructed to rest. A royal tour of Australia and New Zealand was cancelled; for the foreseeable future, the King would carry out only light public engagements. The implications for Elizabeth and Philip were clear. Temporarily Philip scaled back his naval commitments. In a contemporary account, he 'shar[ed] with the Duke of Gloucester many duties as an understudy for the King'.[41]

From modeller Doris Lindner the Queen had commissioned a china statuette of Elizabeth in her uniform as colonel of the Grenadier Guards, riding side-saddle at the King's birthday parade the previous year. In the late autumn of 1948, Royal Worcester released a hundred of Lindner's equestrian figures. Perhaps the Queen regretted the timing of the release that, at such an unhappy pass in the King's life, so obviously marked out Elizabeth as sovereign-in-waiting. Elizabeth took on a number of the King's more symbolic engagements, including the service of distribution of the Royal Maundy the following Easter. Her concern was for her father's wellbeing and for her mother's anxiety, palpable below the surface despite, a courtier noted, the Queen's refusal to allow anyone 'to contemplate the fact of the King's illness'.[42] Nothing dented her happiness. She celebrated her twenty-third birthday in April with a theatre visit, dinner at the Café de Paris and dancing at a nightclub afterwards. To Vivien Leigh, who, with her husband Laurence Olivier, had been of the party, she wrote, 'I did so enjoy my visit to "School for Scandal" and it was a wonderful birthday party – I am so glad you were both able to come as well.'[43]

In time the King's partial recovery lightened the mood at court and, in early July, a year and a half after their wedding, Elizabeth and Philip, with baby Charles, moved into Clarence

House. Here at last was a home of their own, its lengthy renovation overseen by the couple jointly, its furniture mostly wedding presents, with pictures borrowed from the Royal Collection. They had significantly overspent the government's £50,000 budget. The result, in one account, was 'a cheerful, light, modern house, not overcrowded, but each room furnished with taste and distinction'.[44] On architectural historian Christopher Hussey, who visited in the autumn, the effect was alternately giddying and underwhelming. Lyrically he described Elizabeth's chosen colour scheme for her private sitting room as 'catching the sensation of an early morning in September, when the sky is of a pale cloudless blue, but when the sun is still veiled by a thin haze and the lawn is silvered with dew'.[45] Tactfully he explained an impersonal quality to the decoration, only partly attributable to ongoing restrictions: 'As the years pass, and Their Royal Highnesses have the leisure to exercise their tastes in supplementing the present collection, most of the components of which have been gifts, no doubt personal preferences will become more marked.'[46] For all Philip's fondness for new technology, the radios and a 'sleek, white, very futuristic television set' in the comfortable staff quarters, corners of Elizabeth's new home suggested the patrician timelessness of her mother's interiors: handsome eighteenth-century mahogany, a chintz-covered armchair in front of an antique Chinese screen that had been a wedding present from Queen Mary, the Hepplewhite breakfront bookcase given to her by a group of cousins, including Princess Marie Louise and her sister Helena Victoria and the King of Norway, a quartet of red Chinese porcelain cockerels, the gift of an army regiment. Like her parents and many upper-class couples of the time, Elizabeth and Philip had adjoining bedrooms. These were decorated in markedly different manner in line with views about the distinct roles of men and women, Philip's sleekly panelled in white Scottish sycamore, Elizabeth's pink and blue, the bed with a draped canopy. In each room, the dressing table stood in reach of the communicating door, allowing husband and wife to talk to one another as they dressed. Philip hung a new portrait of Elizabeth by Russian watercolourist Savely Sorine; the picture, commissioned by the Queen, closely resembled Sorine's portrait of the Queen as Duchess of York, once displayed in the drawing room at 145 Piccadilly. Acquiescence in this copycat commission said much about Elizabeth's indifference to evolving a new royal iconography. A year later, despite Deputy Keeper of the King's Pictures Benedict Nicolson informing Elizabeth that portraiture in Europe was dead, the newlyweds were painted by Edward Halliday, a romantic, full-length double portrait, its arrangement reminiscent of Gainsborough's *Duke and Duchess of Gloucester*.[47] Nicolson recommended instead 'excellent photographers'.[48]

In Clarence House, Elizabeth settled into a way of life that resembled her parents' as Duke and Duchess of York. In Elizabeth's case, residence in a substantial London mansion, with a comfortable indoor staff, set her apart from her contemporaries. Swingeing taxation sped the death throes of the aristocratic townhouse and its hierarchy of servants; there would be few equivalents for little Charles of the Allendales, the Cavans or the Londonderrys, close at hand in splendour equivalent to his parents'. Without rancour diplomatist's wife Cynthia Jebb identified this imperviousness to change as an aspect of post-war royalty: 'they continue to live the life they have always led, to keep up as much ceremony as modern times permit'.[49] Elizabeth was served by her private secretary, her ladies-in-waiting, her comptroller, or treasurer, General Sir Frederick 'Boy' Browning, recommended by Mountbatten and married to the popular novelist Daphne du Maurier, as well as secretaries known as 'lady clerks'. Bobo MacDonald was indispensable. There were four Clarence House footmen, Mr Bennett the butler, an under-butler, four housemaids, a separate kitchen staff, two chauffeurs and Elizabeth's detectives, an equerry for Philip (Michael Parker, an Australian friend from the navy), his valet John Dean, Charles's nurse Helen Lightbody, inherited from the Gloucesters, the nurserymaid Mabel Anderson and a nursery footman, John Gibson, to deliver Charles's meals and maintain his navy-blue pram, which was washed and polished, including wheels, tyres and hood, every day. This 'princely' establishment perpetuated aspects of the pre-war world in which Elizabeth had grown up: levels of service were of the highest – even the soles of shoes were polished – and long working hours for the servants afforded little time off: half a day a week and every other Sunday. The clockwork regulation of Elizabeth's life had as much to do with a well-trained staff as with her royal duties: breakfast of scones, eggs and bacon served by a footman in blue livery with Edinburgh green epaulettes, eaten with the newspapers; half an hour with Charles, already washed, dressed and fed; time for correspondence with her lady-in-waiting; a walk with her dogs in St James's Park, shadowed by her detective, and, engagements permitting, an hour and a half with Charles every evening, 'romping on the nursery floor, bathing [him] and finally tucking [him] up in bed'.[50] Elizabeth's dog walks took little account of the weather. She wore an old raincoat and a headscarf, schooled from childhood in an upper-class conviction of the unassailable virtues of time spent outdoors. As she wrote once to a friend, 'Now that we have got some good weather, one might as well make use of it.'[51] It was the mindset that made Balmoral bearable. At teatime, Elizabeth fed the corgis, mixing together meat, vegetables and gravy from dishes delivered on a silver tray by a footman.

Despite her lack of political engagement, Elizabeth went about her public duties assiduously. To Helen Hardinge, whose daughters Winifred and Libby had been members of the palace Guide company, she explained that 'life is very hectic, with every day mapped out to the second'.[52] She and Philip undertook visits together: to the Channel Islands, the West Riding of Yorkshire, Macclesfield, Nottingham, Harlech and, of greater personal significance, Dartmouth. Everywhere huge crowds turned out for them, apparently spellbound by this most rarefied of love matches. Such was the interest in the couple that, ahead of their return rail journey from Harlech to Paddington, the *Banbury Guardian* informed its readers of the royal train's scheduled halt at Banbury –'on Friday evening at 8.41 pm... for four minutes' – so that readers could make their way to the platform in the hope of seeing the couple even though 'the Royal passengers [were] not expected to alight'.[53] Even Chips Channon, urbanest of royal hangers-on, and waspish Cecil Beaton were dazzled by Elizabeth and her husband. 'They looked divine,' Channon wrote, of their 'somewhat late appearance' at a ball at Windsor Castle in June 1949. 'She wore a very high tiara and the Garter... They looked like characters out of a fairy tale.'[54] Beaton rhapsodized in Elizabeth's case 'the effect of the dazzlingly fresh complexion, the clear regard from the glass-blue eyes, and the gentle, all-pervading sweetness of her smile'.[55] None of this went to their heads. Shy Elizabeth told Laura Knight that her only way of withstanding the constant attention of crowds was 'to dismiss it entirely from your mind or you could not possibly continue', and neither she nor Philip enjoyed public speaking.[56] 'When they are on their way to an important function together,' one of their household told Dermot Morrah, 'they are apt to sit in the car holding hands in severe nervous tension which may burst out in a sudden explosion over some trivial mishap on the way'.[57] Elizabeth took pains that she overlook no one involved in any detail of an engagement. Organizers of her visit to Plymouth in October 1949 failed to present to her church organist Dr Harry Moreton. Later, she learned that the octogenarian Dr Moreton had composed music in honour of Queen Victoria's

Diamond Jubilee as well as for her own visit. Elizabeth made good the oversight with a longer than usual letter dictated to her lady-in-waiting: 'The Princess was most impressed by the beauty of the anthem which you composed specially for the occasion, and... would like to thank you for the pleasure which it gave her. Princess Elizabeth was very much interested to hear of your long association with the Royal Family and bids me send you her good wishes.'[58] Closer to home, her 'kindness' suggested the limits of her social awareness lamented by her grandmother. Jewelled and gowned for an evening engagement, she remarked to the female staff invited to line the staircase at Clarence House for a ringside view of her finery, 'It's fun to dress up sometimes, isn't it?'[59]

The photograph Elizabeth and Philip released to the press in September was taken at Clarence House. Elizabeth wore a simple silk frock, Philip his lieutenant's uniform, and Philip, not Elizabeth, is the picture's focus. Following improvements in the King's health over the summer, the release marked Philip's return in October to full-time naval duties as first lieutenant on a destroyer called *Chequers*, stationed at Malta. Elizabeth would join him later, a week after Charles's first birthday, leaving Charles behind in the care of Nanny Lightbody and Mabel Anderson. Ahead of Philip's departure, mother, father and baby were photographed by Baron (Sterling Henry Nahum). Released by Raphael Tuck & Sons as postcards, Baron's pictures capture Elizabeth's unaffected delight in her new baby. Before her own departure, like her parents in 1927, she and Charles sat for Marcus Adams. Nevertheless Elizabeth was away for five weeks, including Christmas. Unlike her own mother, she was apparently untroubled by the separation, though one of the Maltese house party, shown films of Charles that Elizabeth had taken herself, recorded her pride in the little boy 'who was now walking and was very sweet'.[60] In Malta, she stayed mostly with the Mountbattens. Despite the attendance of a lady-in-waiting, Bobo and a detective, a gun salute to acknowledge her arrival on this island, 'the Legislative Assembly carr[ying] by acclamation a resolution extending a hearty welcome to her' and a handful of engagements, including an official visit to the Malta Industrial Exhibition and lunch with Archbishop Gonzi, on Malta Elizabeth came as close as she ever would to living like other naval wives.[61] Only Mountbatten appeared unable to forget her rank: he was predictably attentive to his royal houseguest and swiftly smitten. 'Lilibet is quite enchanting and I've lost whatever of my heart is left to spare entirely to her,' he told his elder daughter.[62] Princess and ambitious kinsman played their respective parts. 'I think she's so sweet and attractive,' continued the zealous Mountbatten. 'At times I think she likes me too, though she is far too reserved to give any indication.'[63]

Possibly her reserve enabled Elizabeth to manage the separation alternately from Philip and Charles. To her mother she had written of her desire to recreate in her own family the 'happy atmosphere of love and fairness' to which she had been accustomed as a child. But she was also in thrall to her strong-minded and adored husband and, as she indicated in a controversial speech to a Mothers' Union rally shortly before leaving London, she disapproved of divorce. Later Elizabeth's parenting would be criticized. In the autumn of 1949, weighing all in the balance, she may have estimated Philip's need for her as greater than that of the year-old baby son attended by his own staff of three and his doting royal grandparents. Certainly the Queen detected no detachment in Elizabeth's attitude to Charles and appeared to endorse her decision. To Prince Paul of Yugoslavia she had written in January, 'The baby is so sweet, & Lilibet & Philip are enchanted,' while to Elizabeth herself, on 21 December, she described her decision to spend Christmas with Philip as 'quite right to be with the hub of your universe!'[64] Elizabeth returned to Britain a week later. She remained at Clarence House alone until New Year's Eve, when she went racing at Hurst Park to see her horse Monaveen win the Queen Elizabeth Chase. Flushed with success, she made the journey to Sandringham, her parents and, belatedly, Charles. Edwina Mountbatten would describe seeing Elizabeth off on her homeward journeys from Malta as 'like putting a bird back into a very small cage'.[65] Three months later, Elizabeth returned to the island. To Queen Frederica of the Hellenes, the German-born wife of Philip's cousin King Paul, in a matter-of-fact statement that suggests her ease with her divided domestic life, she described moving between London and Malta as like having 'a flat in London and a house by the sea'.[66]

Again she left Charles behind. Again she delighted in her reunion with Philip. Again the fleeting taste of what passed for normality thrilled her. 'It's lovely seeing her so radiant and leading a more or less human existence for once,' wrote Edwina Mountbatten.[67] Philip's valet John Dean remembered the couple on the island as 'so relaxed and free, coming and going as they pleased'; in retrospect friends considered it the happiest period in their lives.[68] Their wedding present from the Chinese government of green, gold and aubergine porcelain was decorated with a motif of five bats to indicate five supreme happinesses round the double Hsi character for married bliss.[69] On Malta, its auguries were realized. Elizabeth drove herself along the winding, chattering streets, she visited shops and the hairdresser; with Philip or the Mountbattens she swam in secluded coves and picnicked in the shade of orange trees. She watched Philip play polo. From her vantage point on Fort St Elmo she filmed the fleet with her cine camera, eyes screwed tight behind her sunglasses to make out Philip's figure on deck. Together she and Philip danced in local restaurants.

At the Phoenicia Hotel, the Jimmy Dowling Band played their favourite song, 'People Will Say We're in Love', from *Oklahoma!*. 'She and the Duke used to dance a lot. She was always so beautiful and always so nice and kind,' remembered a band member.[70] Maltese shopkeepers noted her slowness in handling money. She stayed six weeks. At some point, for the second time, Elizabeth fell pregnant.

❦

Elizabeth had reasons other than Philip to be happy to be away from home in the spring of 1950. The popular weekly magazine *Woman's Own* had begun serialization of a sentimental and adoring version of Elizabeth's childhood that angered and appalled her parents. Its hapless author was the recently retired Crawfie, the book *The Little Princesses*, trumpeted as a 'loving, human, authentic' account of their story. Serialization began first in an American magazine, the *Ladies Home Journal*, whose shark-like editors, Bruce and Beatrice Blackmar Gould, had gulled Crawfie into believing she could tell all with impunity, retain the royal family's friendship and even advance the cause of Anglo-American relations by bolstering Americans' respect and affection for the monarchy. The Queen believed she had made clear her horror at the prospect, writing to Crawfie in April 1949, 'I do feel most strongly that you must... say No No No to offers of dollars for articles about something as private & precious as our family.'[71] She did not count on the Goulds' determination or the greedy bullying of the man Crawfie had married in the autumn of 1947, Major George Buthlay. Crawfie completed her manuscript in August 1949; the Goulds devoted a month to rewriting it, and Crawfie submitted it to the Queen. As the Goulds had always intended, publication proceeded inexorably, regardless of royal ire or misgivings at the palace. Lady Astor described Elizabeth as 'deeply shocked

& hurt & furious'.[72] She did not add, since it was not necessary, impotent in her rage.

As a child Elizabeth could not have understood the ramifications of a life that was both public and private. By 1950, she had learned to navigate her hybrid existence. Successfully, she and Philip had concealed the secret of their engagement; unprotestingly, she had agreed to government and royal household plans for her marriage: wedding guests unknown to her, public exhibition of her wedding presents and, in time, her dress, snoopers on her honeymoon. Increasingly practised as a public performer, she remained nevertheless shy and unusually reserved. She attached a high value to the privacy permitted her. For all its oozy celebration of Elizabeth herself, *The Little Princesses* made public the family life that she and Margaret and their parents considered sacrosanct, and focused even greater public attention on Elizabeth and her sister. Crawfie had described their lives as bound by an ivory tower, but it was she, however artlessly, who tore down the tower's walls. The Queen's response to Crawfie's act of betrayal would prove as unequivocal as her view of the abdication. Given the shock, hurt and fury glimpsed by Lady Astor, Elizabeth could not be expected to dispute her mother's line.

Three months into serialization in the *Ladies Home Journal*, another American magazine, *Pageant*, ranked Elizabeth eighth among women internationally who 'exert[ed] the greatest influence on modern life'.[73]

❧

More to Elizabeth's liking that summer was the gesture of the commander of an American Air Force unit stationed close to London who instructed his pilots not to fly over Clarence House until Elizabeth's baby was born. Elizabeth gave birth to her only daughter on 15 August 1950, again attended by maternity nurse Sister Helen Rowe, inevitably called 'Rowie', who had been present at Charles's birth; thriftily, she reused the layette made for Charles. Police marshalled into orderly crocodiles the crowds who had massed outside Clarence House for days: two by two they filed past the official bulletin. At the Oval an announcement of the baby's birth interrupted the fourth Test match against the West Indies before play stopped for lunch. Philip was with his wife; the Queen had remained in London after the King's departure for Balmoral and arrived almost immediately. As at the time of Elizabeth's birth, newspapers attributed interest in baby Anne Elizabeth Alice Louise to their affection for the royal mother: 'The warmth of London's greeting to the youngest Princess', the *Scotsman* informed readers, 'is some measure of the pride and pleasure with which we regard all our memories of this daughter of a Scottish Queen.'[74] Elizabeth described herself as 'very thrilled about the new baby': 'We are very delighted and proud to have a little girl as well as a boy – and it will be such fun when they are older.'[75] She was concerned that Charles, until recently living on his own without siblings or indeed either parent, 'take kindly to it'.[76] She reported that he 'appear[ed] fascinated by her and treats her with great care and affection – so far!'[77]

As after Charles's birth, Elizabeth's recovery was leisurely. On 20 September, Clarence House issued a statement: 'Princess Elizabeth has been advised by her doctors that her programme of engagements for this autumn is too heavy, and she has found it necessary to make alterations to her plans.' The first cancelled engagement was the opening of the International Motor Show, scheduled for 18 October; commentators noted that this was only two months since Anne's birth and that Elizabeth had rested for three and a half months after Charles was born. Instead, as autumn turned to winter, Elizabeth rejoined Philip in Malta. She would again be away for Christmas, leaving

Charles and Anne with their grandparents, as she and Margaret had spent Christmas 1935 separated from their parents by their mother's illness; Nurse Lightbody insisted that travel upset small children. Her visit on this occasion included six days spent in Athens with King Paul and Queen Frederica. As at home, public interest levels were high. British newspapers reported crowds outside the royal palace, factory workers rushing to line processional routes and 'the Greek press... full of the visit. Photographs of Princess Elizabeth are published, with articles on her childhood and marriage.'[78] Despite – or because of – Philip's Greek heritage, Elizabeth proved the main attraction. Observing the couple at close quarters, the British ambassador, Sir Clifford Norton, discerned Philip's part in his wife's success, noting that, while she was 'very shy, rather withdrawn, a bit of a shrinking violet in fact', Philip was 'young and vigorous and jollied her along. He didn't actually say, "Come on, old girl!" but it was that sort of thing.'[79] The combination of Elizabeth's newsworthiness and Philip's 'jollying' set a pattern that would not change. In December, Margaret joined them in Malta, bringing with her new photographs of Charles and Anne; with Elizabeth she flew to Tripoli, where Elizabeth reviewed the 1st Battalion Grenadier Guards. 'Margaret simply <u>adored</u> her visit to you,' wrote the Queen, concerned to maintain her daughters' closeness in the face of the separation caused by Elizabeth's marriage.[80]

Elizabeth did not return to Clarence House until the middle of February 1951. She had been away from her children for eleven weeks. While the press at home were mostly silent on this aspect of her absences, overseas comment was less favourable. In a case of having its cake and eating it, the *Sunday Mirror* attributed criticism to the French paper *Samedi Soir*. 'A certain section of British opinion started to whisper that she was a bad mother,' the paper quoted. *Samedi Soir*, it wrote, claimed that Philip was to give up his naval command and return to England 'so that Elizabeth does not become a bad mother'.[81] Five months would pass before Philip stepped down from his naval command. The cause was not anxiety about Elizabeth's parenting, but a sharp decline in the King's health afterwards traced to a malignant tumour that would eventually necessitate the removal of his left lung on 23 September 1951. In the meantime, again without the children, Elizabeth returned to Malta for Easter. She and Philip went to Italy, staying with Philip's cousin Queen Helen of Romania outside Florence and at the British embassy in Rome. 'We are living like gypsies,' Elizabeth wrote home happily.[82] Back at home she gave Philip a painting of the harbour at Valletta.

To Elizabeth fell much of her father's workload, to a philosophical Philip, certain this spelled the end of any independent career, the task of supporting her that would continue for the remainder of his long life. 'The prince who won [Elizabeth's] hand has proved himself a ready and willing support in her manifold duties,' intoned a Pathé announcer months later; readiness almost certainly exceeded willingness as he surrendered the naval man's life he loved.[83] They replaced the King and Queen on a five-week tour of Canada in the autumn of 1951. In style the visit resembled the earlier tour of South Africa: almost half the 10,000-mile itinerary was undertaken in a private train with an observation platform at the rear to 'give thousands of Canadians the chance to see the Princess as she passes and the Princess the opportunity to acknowledge their cheers'.[84] In Elizabeth's luggage was mourning for her father; her new private secretary, the Hon. Martin Charteris, Jock Colville's successor and a nephew of Cynthia Asquith, carried with him draft accession documents. The spectre of the King's death hovered. Elizabeth could not lightly shrug off the memory of Holy Communion with the Archbishop of Canterbury at Lambeth Palace the morning of her father's operation: herself, Margaret and the Queen. She told listeners at a state banquet in Ottawa on 10 October, 'The anxiety of these last two weeks has seemed endless', before reassuring them of the King's slow improvement. At stopping points, telephone calls were arranged to her father at Buckingham Palace, as if she could make him better by encouragement or force of will. Flashes of lightheartedness punctuated the tour nevertheless. Perhaps there was an ostrich-like quality to the couple's enjoyment, each of them unwilling to countenance the possibility of the King dying. Elizabeth described as 'a magnificent experience' the fourteen miles from Yates to Peers, Alberta, when she and Philip drove the train, Elizabeth as engineer, Philip as fireman, and puzzled crowds lining the track scanned in vain the observation platform for the royal travellers busy in the engine carriage.[85] On their second night in Ottawa they danced till midnight at 'a gay informal square dance', for which Elizabeth wore '"Cinderella" clothes': 'a brown checkered blouse, blue dirndl skirt embroidered with beads and Cuban square-heeled shoes', a tribute to the resourcefulness of John Dean, who also bought blue jeans, a check shirt, loafers and a cowboy belt for Philip.[86] Philip 'jollied' Elizabeth in private as well as public, chasing her along a corridor of the train wearing false teeth or tricking her with a joke tin of nuts from which, on opening, a toy snake sprang. Elizabeth protested at criticism in Canadian newspapers that she did not smile enough; her 'sullen' expression would remain cause for adverse comment, later explained by a cabinet minister as arising 'when she is deeply moved and tries to control it': 'very often when she's been deeply touched by the plaudits of the crowd she merely looks bad-tempered'.[87] For the most part, large crowds – an estimated 170,000 on the couple's arrival at Ottawa and 500,000 in Quebec – responded excitedly, especially to Philip, who 'smiled more, waved more, unbent more'; at one railway station, crowds sang 'Will ye no come back again?' after the departing train.[88] At home the Queen distracted herself with chatty letters full of news of Charles and Anne; she worried over the declamatory quality of Elizabeth's delivery of her speeches: 'Don't forget to put a bit of <u>inflection</u> into your speeches, especially for coming over the radio, darling,' she wrote.[89] Elizabeth and Philip travelled south of the border for a flying visit to President Truman, taking with them presents from the King. In Washington were no complaints about Elizabeth's dour expression. The *New York Herald Tribune* acclaimed 'the world's most interesting couple' and enthused that 'Princess Elizabeth, attractive as she is in photographs, is altogether devastating in person'.[90] 'Certainly movie stuff' was the *Washington Daily News*' description of Philip, who was reported as causing stenographers to swoon. Truman resorted to a familiar conceit. 'When I was a little boy,' he said, 'I read about a fairy princess, and there she is.'[91] Adulation on this scale, albeit expressed less fulsomely at home, had become a feature of Elizabeth and Philip's shared engagements and would colour the first years of Elizabeth's reign. Back on British soil, the behaviour of their countrymen echoed Canadians'. The *Rugby Advertiser* reported that, when the homeward-bound royal train passed through Rugby station on its way to London, 'several hundred people lined the southbound platform' and were rewarded with 'a glimpse of Their Royal Highnesses having lunch' at thirty miles an hour.[92]

During Elizabeth's absence, the King cancelled for the second time a tour of Ceylon, Australia and New Zealand planned for the spring. It was not a surprise to Elizabeth, who had set in motion preparations for such a contingency prior to departure, writing to her dressmaker Norman Hartnell on 24 September, 'I would very much like you to prepare some sketches for me to see... as a precaution against any sudden decision for us to go in the King's place.'[93] In the event, neither Elizabeth nor her parents would visit Australia in 1952.

'February 3 to February 7, rest at Royal Lodge,' ran the official programme of Elizabeth and Philip's visit to Kenya at the start of their four-month overseas tour. On the slopes of Mount Kenya above the Sagana River, in ten acres of immaculate garden green with Ugandan turf, Royal Lodge was the couple's wedding present from the colony. Photographs show Elizabeth smiling on the threshold of the timber-clad single-storey house: she had waited four years to see for herself this grown-up version of Y Bwthyn Bach complete with uniformed sentry, accommodation for a lady-in-waiting and, in Philip's dressing room, curtains patterned with famous ships from history.

From Royal Lodge, late in the afternoon of 5 February, Elizabeth and Philip, with lady-in-waiting Henriette Palmer and Michael Parker, drove to a wooden tree house raised on stilts in a wild fig tree in the Aberdare Forest. The Treetops Hotel was an observation post with three bedrooms, a dining area and a viewing platform constructed alongside a lake with a salt lick where big game came to drink. It was a fantastical place, remote and dangerous. 'Visitors are brought by car to within a quarter of a mile of the post and then go by foot through a jungle full of rhino, elephant, leopard and various poisonous snakes,' explained the *Illustrated London News*. 'Along the path are numerous ladders in case of any attack. From the comfortable "hotel" observation post, visitors can watch the life of the jungle at close range, but in perfect safety.' [94] As afternoon turned to evening, Elizabeth watched with fascinated absorption, filming with her cine camera as long as the light lasted. Afterwards the group discussed what they had seen. They talked about the King; Elizabeth described his improvement. 'Clearly from the tone of her conversation,' remembered Treetops' owner Eric Sherbrooke Walker, 'she was hoping for a complete recovery'.[95]

Instead, George VI died in his sleep of a coronary thrombosis in the early hours of 6 February, at Sandringham, while Elizabeth was out of reach in her jungle eyrie. The circumstances of her accession, once known, seemed to add another fairy-tale detail to her already fabled existence: the young woman who climbed a tree a princess and descended it a queen. She did so unaware of her altered state, cut off by African forest from radio or telegrams. She rose early, watched the swooping and soaring of an eagle overhead, baboons, a rhino at the salt lick. The party breakfasted on eggs and bacon and coffee, and returned to Royal Lodge, Elizabeth 'looking wonderful in blue jeans, talking about the rhinoceros'.[96] Before lunch they fished; afterwards they rested. It was Martin Charteris, at a nearby hotel, who heard the news first, from a local journalist. He telephoned Michael Parker at Royal Lodge. Parker told Philip. Philip told Elizabeth, now his sovereign as well as his wife. He took her out into the garden where they walked slowly up and down, 'while he talked and talked and talked to her' – intently, as Cynthia Jebb remembered them talking under such different circumstances at a party at Sandringham three years before. [97] Elizabeth was not crying when they returned to the house: Henriette Palmer described her as 'very magnificent and strong'.[98] 'She bore her bereavement with queenly courage (the report published in some journals that she broke down in tears was quite unfounded),' according to the authors of *The Coronation Book of Queen Elizabeth II*, published the following year; her self-control resembled her mother's, which a lady-in-waiting called 'supreme'.[99] By the time Martin Charteris arrived at Royal Lodge, she was 'seated at her desk, very upright, high colour, no sign of tears';[100] she appeared to him 'absolute master of her fate'.[101] To her lady-in-waiting, Lady Pamela Mountbatten, Dickie's younger daughter, Elizabeth apologized for the immediate cancellation of the remainder of their tour, an example under extraordinary circumstances of that 'solicitude for other people's comfort' that Tommy Lascelles had noted in

South Africa; at her desk she wrote letters of apology to others involved in the tour. Charteris asked what she was going to call herself. 'My own name, of course – what else?' she replied. It was the only possible answer for the young woman whose royal destiny, calmly accepted long before, was central to her identity, a young woman, an elderly courtier would claim, who 'always [did] the right thing instinctively'.[102]

CHAPTER IX

'History's bride, anointed, blessed'

✠

'I AM SURE SHE is going to be a tremendous influence for good,' Arthur Grenfell had written of Elizabeth in February 1946, after observing her effect on her fellow guests at his daughter's coming-out dance.[1] On that occasion he described 'everyone at her feet' within half an hour of her arrival.

The same excitement greeted Elizabeth's accession six years later. Mourning for the King was sincere and widespread. At his lying-in-state in Westminster Hall more than 300,000 people queued to file past the coffin. Another 200,000 criss-crossed the lawns of St George's Chapel, Windsor to see laid out there wreaths and flowers from individuals, communities and organizations large and small; 'subdued floodlighting' mitigated latecomers' disappointment on dark February afternoons.[2] Without exaggeration, Elizabeth described to a friend of Alah from 145 Piccadilly days 'the volume of affection from all over the world for the King'; to the wife of schoolmaster Hubert Tanner, contributor to the Windsor pantomimes, she wrote of 'the countless numbers who have written to say they all feel the loss of a friend as well as their King'.[3] Yet eagerness tempered this sadness, a buoyant anticipation. 'With a queen to rule, Britain has always known greatness,' Pathé told viewers of an accession newsreel released on 11 February; she shared 'the name that once before spelled glory for Britain'.[4] The sentiment echoed the broadcast made on the day of Elizabeth's return by Winston Churchill, prime minister again at the age of seventy-seven: 'Famous have been the reigns of our Queens. Some of the greatest periods in our history have unfolded under their sceptre.' A grieving nation, stirred by grandiloquence and an irresistible urge to banish post-war doldrums by grasping this nominal link with former greatness, embraced the 'Princess Elizabeth' who, from birth, in countless editorials and illustrated papers, had provided sunshine diversion from the humdrum and the mundane: as Pathé acclaimed her, 'the princess we knew as a girl and watched in the even growth of her stature'. Expectation was heartfelt, though unrealistic. Commentators talked of 'new Elizabethans'. The elderly poet laureate, John Masefield, invoked Shakespeare's *Richard II*: 'May this old land revive and be / Again a star set in the sea'.[5] That Elizabeth had come to symbolize renewal, the victory generation and the wholesomeness of an idealized British way of being was in truth little of her own doing. She had blossomed as wife and mother as the King's health visibly declined. Opening the Festival of Britain in May 1951, George VI had appeared to be fading and failing. By contrast, Elizabeth positively glowed at the inaugural concert at the Royal Festival Hall the same evening. Her matchless complexion, full bust and tiny waist, exaggerated by bright lipstick, the Nizam's diamonds and sumptuous evening frocks, were all that contemporaries admired. For many of her new subjects, accustomed to Queen Mary's ramrod majesty and the late King's diffidence, Elizabeth's earnestness and gravity – subsequently censured as remoteness – constituted dignity appropriate to her high calling. A third of those polled considered her divinely ordained for sovereignty, and a supportive parliament voted Elizabeth a Civil List settlement of £475,000 a year with, in addition, a ninth of the net revenue of the Duchy of Cornwall to provide for her heir.

For Elizabeth, Philip suggested, her father's death, less than a week since he had waved her off, was 'the most appalling shock'; King Peter of Yugoslavia recorded husband and wife '[telling] me they felt anaesthetised'.[6] Like her mother and Margaret, Elizabeth thought the King 'most wonderfully better', 'so full of ideas & plans for the future'; she considered that 'he died as he was getting better'.[7] In few ways was she surprised by the burden of sovereignty that was bereavement's immediate corollary. The inescapability of this moment had been felt, if lightly, in so much of her growing up: the changing of the guard at Windsor Castle in honour of her birthday; her grandmother's fetishistic dynasticism; lessons with Henry Marten, knighted by the King for his efforts; the King's elision of 'us four' and 'the royal family'; her own designation as 'heir' or 'heiress presumptive'; and, latterly, the Foreign Office telegrams on which Jock Colville had insisted and, from the summer of 1950, on Martin Charteris's initiative, cabinet minutes and memoranda, and deputizing for the King through the chapters of his illness. Above all were the conversations between father and daughter, that gentle but diligent apprenticeship that Lisa Sheridan had set out to capture at Royal Lodge in 1942, the King photographed at his desk, Elizabeth reading over his shoulder, boxes of state papers neatly stacked. Behind the self-immolation of Elizabeth's Cape Town speech was no flippant surety that the call to serve lay decades away, though she could reasonably have assumed as much and must have hoped so. The King's death at the age of fifty-six, as Elizabeth said later, happened 'much too young'; its prematurity merely hastened a destiny she had already acknowledged and would never shirk.

Both the 'theatre' and the mechanics of monarchy were familiar to her: she had taken the salute at the Trooping the Colour ceremony, witnessed the distribution of the Royal Maundy, laid wreaths at the Cenotaph on Armistice Day; at the age of eighteen she had acted as a counsellor of state.

Precisely what her royal destiny entailed was in some ways ill-defined. Beyond its executive and constitutional role, monarchy's less tangible purpose had not occupied Henry Marten. For Elizabeth's family, sovereignty was an amalgam of abstract ideals demanded by birth and precedent, an intensely serious inheritance; the experience of the abdication had hardened its focus on duty. The familiar formula was reiterated within days of the King's death by his widow, now styled Queen Elizabeth the Queen Mother, in a message to the nation: 'No man had a deeper sense than [the King] of duty and of service, and no man was more full of compassion for his fellow men'; she recalled 'the great task of service that was laid upon us'.[8] In February 1952, 'the great task of service' became Elizabeth's. Compliant with a lifetime's teachings, it was inconceivable she would interpret it otherwise than as a continuation of her father's example, itself a deliberate extension of George V's model of kingship, embraced in the traumatic uncertainty of December 1936. Observation of her father, dogged but highly strung, had shown her the arduousness of sovereignty, and her later statement that she had 'always assumed people wanted her to look solemn most of the time' reveals both Queen Mary's strictures on royal dignity and a view shared by Elizabeth and her father of the seriousness and rigours of their lofty office.[9] In her Christmas broadcast at the end of the year, Elizabeth recalled 'my father, and my grandfather before him': 'I shall strive to carry on their work,' she promised. She had made the same vow in her Declaration of Sovereignty in front of 175 privy councillors at a meeting at ten o'clock on 8 February, when she asked for God's help in 'this heavy task that has been lain upon me so early in my life'. In this, the first address of her reign, she pointed to her purpose, sanctioned by family practice: 'I shall always work, as my father did throughout his reign, to advance the happiness and prosperity of my peoples, spread as they are the world over.'[10] The promotion of happiness and prosperity was to be the aim of her great task of service, and the outlook of this daughter and granddaughter of Empire was global. Colonial Secretary Lord Chandos described it as 'one of the most touching speeches to which I have ever listened, and I, like many others, could hardly control my emotions'. At locations across London she was proclaimed in the meeting's aftermath 'Queen Elizabeth the Second, by the grace of God Queen of this Realm and of all her other Realms and Territories, Head of the Commonwealth, Defender of the Faith'.

Signs of fidelity to what had gone before emerged swiftly. On 26 February, Elizabeth sat for portraits on which to base her image on stamps, coins and banknotes; she followed her father's choice of photographer Dorothy Wilding and wore the same diamond diadem chosen by Queen Victoria for her Penny Black portrait. A week later, a date for Elizabeth's official birthday was announced. 'In deciding that her official birthday should be observed in June,' explained the *Daily Telegraph*, 'the Queen is following the custom of her father.'[11] The following week came the news that, on 10 April, Elizabeth would take up residence at Windsor, 'following the practice of King George VI in making the traditional Easter visit to the Castle'.[12] She held an investiture for 360 soldiers and sailors involved in the King's funeral 'as a gesture to the memory of her father' on 2 April.[13] Despite rain, and dressed in inky black, Elizabeth celebrated her twenty-sixth birthday, as always, with a review of the Grenadier Guards at Windsor. She made appointments to her household, including, as a woman of the bedchamber, her mother's elder sister Mary, Lady Elphinstone. Court functions perpetuated a familiar round. Although court mourning caused the postponement of debutantes' coming-out dances planned for May, in early summer Elizabeth held the traditional presentation parties, including at Holyroodhouse in Edinburgh, at which daughters of the upper classes curtsied to the monarch in a formal rite of passage that signalled, as it always had, their adulthood and availability for the right sort of marriage. At her Accession Council, she had made clear her understanding that, despite first steps towards the dismantling of Empire – Indian and Burmese independence in 1947, final severing of links between Britain and Eire a year later – she inherited a crown imperial in reach. Her messages of 'good wishes' to the new Nigerian House of Representatives on its formal opening in Lagos on 10 March and, in the same month, 'deep sympathy' to the administrator of the Ceylonese government following the death of the prime minister, Don Stephen Senanayake, suggest her awareness of her international role as a symbol of association in the new Commonwealth, explained to her by her father and Henry Marten.

The new queen felt none of Edward VIII's impatience with her royal inheritance. In the summer of 1952, architect Hugh Casson judged her 'interested and excited about everything and not worried by the load of her responsibility'.[14] Later Elizabeth described her accession as 'a matter of... accepting your fate'.[15] Instinctively conservative, she bore the imprint of an old-fashioned upbringing. Princess Marie Louise had noticed 'the value that [Elizabeth] placed on tradition and all that it contributes to the life of a nation' as early as Christmas 1946.[16] Elizabeth had been devoted to her father, whom she admired; the habit of deferring to her ultra-conservative mother was deep-rooted and would persist in matters large and small: Hugh Casson described an argument between Elizabeth and Margaret over whether their mother's attendance at a picnic necessitated saucers as well as cups, Elizabeth overruling Margaret's brisk instruction 'Don't pander.'[17] Although it would become so before the decade ended, attentiveness to the received wisdom of the older generation was not a mindset that, in the spring of 1952, invited criticism. Conservatism characterized much mainstream post-war thinking, a reassertion of social, sexual and religious mores after the maelstrom of the war. It was an outlook in which female submissiveness remained the norm and youth culture had yet to challenge the equation of age and knowledge. In a book called *Britain's Royal Family at Home*, published in 1950, author Margaret Saville had claimed, 'In common with many young wives, Princess Elizabeth enjoys deferring to her husband's tastes and making them her own when they are together.'[18] (Philip himself would later corroborate what Saville almost certainly surmised.) Deferring to what was expected of her came naturally to Elizabeth. For as long as she could remember, she had been encouraged to follow her parents' and grandparents' example as her lodestars – and successfully so: playwright Christopher Fry described her as 'bearing by inheritance the simplicity which was her father's and her grandfather's also'.[19] She had been praised for her resemblance to her mother and to Queen Mary, and for sharing her father's steadfastness; Queen Mary had encouraged her to share her own love for the throne, a feeling both intense and reverent. As expected by those closest to her, she approached the task of sovereignty determined to master the formula she had inherited and to do so to the very best of her ability. She showed little interest in innovation; approvingly her private secretary noted that she was not 'steamed up on reforms'.[20] She would be assisted by her elderly prime minister and his cabinet and by members of her court, all of them men closer in age to her father: her seventy-four-year-old lord chamberlain, Lord Clarendon, the grandson of a lord-in-waiting to Queen Victoria; the sixty-five-year-old Lascelles; her assistant private secretary Michael Adeane, a grandson of George V's private secretary Lord Stamfordham, who, in 1917, had suggested the dynasty's new name of Windsor. In charge of her domestic affairs were staff (never 'servants') familiar from her childhood, including Bobo and the nursery footman Cyril Dickman, whom Elizabeth later promoted to palace steward. Both were her parents' appointments.

In the febrile atmosphere of sadness at the King's death and excitement at Elizabeth's promise of a new beginning were adjustments and uncertainties. If Elizabeth was surprisingly prepared for her compulsory burden, her mother, husband and sister all found themselves temporarily cast adrift. Sovereignty supplied unbidden Elizabeth's identity and purpose and greedily consumed her days, but the public roles and private lives of Queen Elizabeth and Margaret had pivoted on the King. While Elizabeth was granted insufficient time to grieve, forced back on the self-control that Cynthia Asquith had once suggested was her chief preparation for her role, Margaret and her mother had too much. Margaret remembered later 'an awful sense of being in a black hole'; in the vicarage of St Paul's, Knightsbridge she attended post-confirmation classes and a series of talks about eternal life by the Bishop of Kensington.[21] Her mother oscillated between devastation and, more challenging for Elizabeth, a prickly reluctance to relinquish her pre-eminence.[22] In Philip's case there were few clear duties for a male consort. He was granted no apparent autonomy or sphere of activity in an existence in which virtually all of those with whom he found himself in daily contact focused exclusively on Elizabeth, their treatment of Philip high-handed and, in some instances, scarcely tolerant. As queen regnant, Elizabeth assumed both the male role of royal power (such as it was) and the female or consort's role of soft power, domestic nurturing and visual pzazz. Philip was constitutionally superfluous; he had already fulfilled his reproductive function in enabling Elizabeth to guarantee the succession with the births of Charles and Anne. First informed of the King's death, Philip had looked 'as if the whole world had dropped on him'. In fact much of his world had simply fallen away – 'the whole thing changed very, very considerably,' he said later – and his response to the King dying was more traumatized than Elizabeth's.[23] Presciently his mother had written to him, 'I think much of the change in your life this means. It means much personal self-sacrifice for you.'[24] That Philip had known what lay ahead did not diminish its impact. King Peter of Yugoslavia described him as like a volcano that had been covered: 'I don't know how long he can last... bottled up like that!'[25] Keenly he felt the loss of his naval career and would continue to do so. His present to Elizabeth on their fifth wedding anniversary in November was a bracelet of his own design, made by Boucheron. It was decorated with flowers and crosses of rubies, sapphires and diamonds, but at its centre, set with diamonds, was his naval badge of a crowned anchor. Alongside her grief were Elizabeth's concerns for those closest to her. She worried about the unhappiness of her mother and sister. To her cousin Margaret Elphinstone, married now as Margaret Rhodes, she described as 'ghastly' her absence at the time of the King's death: 'the feeling that I was unable to help or comfort Mummy or Margaret, and that there was nothing one could do at all'.[26]

Her relief is palpable in a letter written five months later, following the Queen Mother's first return to Sandringham: 'I had been in a fever in case it would prove too much agony for you.'[27] It was to Elizabeth more than Margaret that their mother turned to talk about her feelings. 'I can't tell you how much I miss you, darling, it's awful having nobody to talk to about things,' the Queen Mother wrote during one of Elizabeth's absences.[28] Elizabeth worried about Philip, too. She was not immediately aware of the extent to which, as Michael Parker saw it, he was 'constantly being squashed, snubbed, ticked off, rapped over the knuckles' by courtiers: thwarted, frustrated and diminished.[29] 'I was told "Keep Out" and that was that,' Philip remembered later.[30] And unwittingly she contributed to

Philip's disaffection. The family's move to Buckingham Palace at the beginning of May, insisted on by Churchill and leading courtiers but inevitable anyway, represented for Philip the loss of the only home of his own he had ever had. In place of an environment of his own shaping, run ship-like along lines of his own devising, was a building of more than 600 rooms still redolent of his parents-in-law. His suggestion that Elizabeth use the palace as an office, while continuing to live at Clarence House, points to his horror; her tears on leaving Clarence House for the last time indicate how close her own feelings were to his. Philip sought no part in Elizabeth's discharge of the sovereign's role, pointedly opposed to any title for himself of the 'prince consort' variety. Elizabeth's punctilio and that of senior officials, including a rigid Tommy Lascelles, whom she had inherited as private secretary, necessarily excluded him. On 18 March, for example, Elizabeth received the Italian ambassador in the morning; in the evening she held her weekly audience with Churchill. Philip was present for the diplomatic pleasantries of the first appointment, absent from the more serious business of the second. Nor did Elizabeth form the King's habit of discussing with her spouse her response to the contents of such meetings. This separation at the very heart of her existence offered further proof of her self-discipline – or grounds for a view of Elizabeth expressed later by Lady Selina Hastings as 'cold, competent and incorruptible'.[31] No trace of former 'rogueishness' lingered to compromise the sovereign's integrity.

The snub that a cousin described as 'the final insult' to Philip arose thanks in part to Mountbatten's braggadocio. It seemed to illustrate the impossibility for Elizabeth of reconciling her public role with Philip's seniority within their marriage, which she had always acknowledged, and the personal cost of adhering to the constitutional requirement that she follow ministerial advice.[32]

Philip's uncle acted unwisely in boasting, within days of the King's death, that 'the House of Mountbatten now reigned'. The reaction of Queen Mary, informed of his puffery by Prince Ernst August of Hanover, forced the involvement of the prime minister. Churchill neither liked nor trusted Mountbatten; Queen Mary's loyalty was to the memory of her son and husband, responsible for changing the dynasty's name to 'Windsor'. Churchill informed the cabinet of Mountbatten's vainglory; he made clear his own views. A united cabinet 'was strongly of the opinion that the Family name of Windsor should be retained'.[33] So were Queen Mary, the Queen Mother and, indeed, many in the royal household, the view conveyed by Churchill to Elizabeth. The prime minister's persuasion, a memorandum from the lord chancellor reminding Elizabeth that 'permanence and continuity are valuable factors in the maintenance of a constitutional monarchy',[34] Mountbatten's indiscretion and the animosity he inspired among leading players combined to force Elizabeth's declaration, early in April, that her family's name remain unchanged. In vain an angry Philip had suggested 'Edinburgh' as an alternative; he probably considered himself the victim of a stitch-up. For a torn Elizabeth the struggle was deeply upsetting. She interpreted her first loyalty as to her predecessors: both her inclination and her preference were to uphold their legacy. It was inconceivable that, in the first weeks of her reign, she would challenge the memory of her grandfather in open opposition to her grandmother. Not for the last time, faced with a conflict between family and royal family, Elizabeth honoured the latter. Later she would suggest that the decision had been made for her 'and that she accepted [it]', but she did not accept it 'in spirit'.[35]

Nevertheless, the decision once taken won widespread approval. Valentine Heywood, author of *The Use and Misuse of the Titles of Peers and Commoners*, published the previous year, wrote that 'the Queen's proclamation has quickly disposed of the argument... that she would be the last sovereign of the House of Windsor [and] that the surname of the Royal Family was now Mountbatten. Those who advanced that contention ignored the obvious spirit of the proclamation which, in 1917, King George V issued dealing with the names and styles of the Royal Family.'[36] For those of her contemporaries concerned by such matters, Elizabeth had acted in line with 'Her Majesty's hereditary sense of duty'.[37] She heaped honours on a disgruntled Philip. She invested him with the insignia of a knight of the Order of the Thistle; she supported his chairmanship of the Coronation Commission, which met for the first time in May; on 18 September she was 'graciously pleased to declare and ordain that HRH the Duke of Edinburgh should henceforth have, hold and enjoy the Place, Pre-eminence and Precedence next to Her Majesty'; over the course of the year she appointed him colonel-in-chief of the Army Cadet Force, admiral of the Sea Cadet Corps and air commodore-in-chief of the Air Training Corps, with weightier, though unearned, appointments the following year: admiral of the fleet, field marshal, marshal of the Royal Air Force; in November 1953, in a message to the House of Commons, she requested his replacement of Margaret as regent-designate for Charles under the terms of the 1937 Regency Act. Philip's challenge, similar to that of the Queen Mother and Margaret, was to find an outlet for considerable energies and frustrated leadership instincts. Whatever her inclinations, Elizabeth was unable to restore the earlier status quo, in which, in his own words, Philip's had been 'the principal position'.[38]

At the end of May, medical journal the *Lancet* issued a warning against overtaxing Elizabeth's strength. Its irony could not have been lost on Philip. 'As mother of a young family and mistress of a home, she has a life of her own whose happy fulfilment her subjects would place first... As doctors we should have special reason to welcome an assurance that, by deliberate decisions taken in advance, Her Majesty's health and vitality will be protected.'[39] But sovereignty suited Elizabeth. She was blooming, in her own words 'strong as a horse'. To a friend she described, with some surprise, changes in herself that she traced to her accession: 'I no longer feel anxious or worried. I don't know what it is – but I have lost all my timidity and somehow becoming the Sovereign and having to receive the Prime Minister, for instance...'[40] She was no longer the 'sweet but sort of shy' young woman Boy Browning's wife Daphne du Maurier described shortly after Elizabeth's marriage.[41] Approvingly her staff noticed the change in her; they noted, too, her efficiency, a methodical thoroughness, her orderliness, patience, perspicacity, the same qualities Patricia Mountbatten had seen in Elizabeth's Guiding. Trained by her father, 'she was conscientious, she was well-informed, she was serious-minded,' remembered Martin Charteris.[42] For Princess Marie Louise, these were the King's qualities, including 'her thoroughness in making herself fully acquainted with every subject placed before her'.[43] Never under Elizabeth's watch would government papers appear dog-eared, ringed with cocktail glasses and late, as they had from Fort Belvedere during Uncle David's brief tenure. Her assistant private secretary Edward Ford called her 'a bureaucrat's dream': she did not baulk at the desk work of monarchy. Ford found her decisive and 'very clear in her own opinions'.[44] That she appeared to enjoy routine was another aspect of the self-discipline encouraged since childhood and a reflection of that tidiness that had her jumping out of bed to straighten pairs of shoes in the night nursery at 145 Piccadilly. First views of Elizabeth as little more than a 'sweet girl', like that of politician Harold Nicolson, were swiftly dispelled.[45] Even Churchill, who lamented the King's passing, would conclude that 'all the film people in the world, if they had scoured the globe, could not have found anyone so suited to the part'; he called her splendid, reminded perhaps of her childish 'air of authority and reflectiveness' that had astonished him at Balmoral a quarter of a century earlier.[46] In the summer of 1952, it was not Elizabeth but Philip who was treated for jaundice and for three weeks remained in bed at Buckingham Palace while Elizabeth travelled north to Scotland. Happily for Elizabeth, Ford claimed that, 'except for big tours and speeches, she didn't depend on him', a view of questionable accuracy.[47]

<hr />

It was a dry November day, with clear skies over London, when, for the first time, Elizabeth opened parliament. With Philip beside her, she drove in state from Buckingham Palace. She wore a dress of gold brocade and the diamond diadem she had inherited on her father's death that she would wear for the journey to every subsequent state opening. In the royal robing room, the young woman who had once longed for 'a perfectly *enormous* train' put on her great-great-grandmother's. Against the crimson and gold of the Upper Chamber, 'she was the person on whom all the traditional ritual converged', as Helen Hardinge had written of her stand-in appearance at the King's last Trooping the Colour; in her Victorian robes, the weight of inheritance was as reassuring as daunting.[48] In the now familiar comparison, reporters likened the royal couple to 'two figures in a fairy tale, with the Queen in a glistening gold lace gown... and the long trailing robe Queen Victoria had worn on state occasions'.[49] Inside the House of Lords, the silence, in one account, was 'of respect, not untouched by wonder'.[50] Not content with her own assurances on this score, Churchill had included in Elizabeth's speech from the throne a statement of intent that provoked a single instance of her faltering: 'My father set an example which it will be my constant endeavour to follow.' Pathé filmed the procession coming and going and its culmination in a balcony appearance. Outside Buckingham Palace, a crowd of 20,000 spectators cheered. To a triumphant roar, the royal parents were joined by Charles and Anne. The newsreel commentary was unequivocal: 'Even the spectacular procession that has gone before is outshone by the radiance of their family affection.' 'Radiance' was a favourite concept associated with the new queen. It suggested the happiness with which she had embraced her destiny and a more-than-human quality that illuminated both her own beauty and the continuing dinginess of the post-war outlook. A conservative era required its female monarch to combine the roles of sovereign and domestic paragon, 'a wise Mother, Wife and Queen' as she was acclaimed in an amateur poem published on the eve of the coronation.[51] Before the decade ended, adulation would mellow. The appearance of a model family, 'radiant' in its affection, was slower to fragment. Its terrible unravelling would provide Elizabeth with some of the most serious challenges of her reign.

Sooner, however, came the death of Queen Mary, on 24 March 1953. She herself had anticipated it, leaving instructions that court mourning not hinder coronation plans. In the aftermath of the King's death, she had made a new will. To Elizabeth she bequeathed quantities of magnificent jewellery, including the pearl-and-diamond brooch she had worn at Elizabeth's christening and for their first photograph together; she bestowed on her granddaughter the bulk of what she called 'my interesting things': precious *objets de vertu*, like the Fabergé paper knife decorated with rose diamonds that had belonged to her spendthrift mother. Weeks after the King's death she had distracted herself by visiting Kensington Palace to examine Queen Victoria's coronation robes as a model for her granddaughter's. In her last letter, written six days before she died, she dwelt on a painting by Goya of his grandson. 'I particularly like the portrait of Marianito Goya with the silk hat – as one sees it was painted with great love.'[52] Great had been Queen Mary's love for her first royal granddaughter, who visited her, with Philip and Margaret, shortly before she died. Her influence would prove significant and long-lasting: the fears of her comptroller, Sir John Coke, that 'now that she was gone there was no member of the Royal Family to keep the rest of them up to the mark, no one now to prevent the Queen from having meals with people like Douglas Fairbanks, from motoring in a jeep without wearing a hat, etc' would, in the short term, prove mostly unfounded in Elizabeth's case.[53] The greatest bequest of George V's widow to Elizabeth, inculcated from infancy, was reverence for the crown and her indomitable conviction of royalty's uniqueness. Elizabeth reciprocated her affection. 'I cannot imagine a world without her,' she said simply.[54] She approved a lying-in-state for her grandmother, the first consort in memory to receive such an honour. At Balmoral in the summer she invested Lady Airlie, her grandmother's lady-in-waiting of half a century, whom she herself had known all her life, with the Grand Cross of the Royal Victorian Order, her personal tribute of family piety.

~

'The coronation of Queen Elizabeth on 2 June will undoubtedly be the outstanding event of the twentieth century,' wrote a popular astrologer, offering as explanation that 'by the planetary configurations at the time of her birth, Queen Elizabeth is shown to be a veritable Queen of Destiny.'[55]

It was a moment for hyperbole. The wartime efforts of Elizabeth's parents had strengthened bonds of feeling connecting crown and country; from her childhood, Elizabeth had been presented to cinema-goers and the reading public as an object of affection. Now, with no holds barred, the *Daily Express* celebrated her as universally beloved, with a stake in every loving impulse: 'Every British lad sees the Queen in his girl and his girl in the Queen, every father sees there his daughter, every infant his mother.'[56] Churchill told listeners at a dinner in Westminster Hall that monarchy provided 'the central link in all our modern changing life... the one which above all others claims our allegiance to death'; he described Elizabeth's throne as 'broadly and securely based on the people's love and the nation's will'.[57] In the summer of 1953, for a nation still battling the terrible costs of victory, monarchy supplied grounds for pride. The turkey-cock boast of the *Yorkshire Post* was typical: 'Our monarchy today, in an age when crowns have fallen all around us, remains probably more secure than at any time in our long history.'[58] That the throne's incumbent was a dedicated young woman described by her elderly cousin Princess Alice as 'a young and beautiful Queen and sovereign who looked like a debutante',[59] married to a go-ahead war hero, with two small children to people the myth of idealized royal domesticity, contributed to the nation's euphoria. In his diary, BBC commentator Richard Dimbleby would recall 'those hours in the Abbey, when the whole nation was swept by the same sense of love and pride that filled those of us standing so near the Queen'.[60] In the early 1950s this combination of love and pride was more readily manufactured for Elizabeth than it would have been for a male counterpart. In the prayer of thanksgiving for her accession included in church services the Sunday before the coronation was the hope that she 'always possess the hearts of her people'.[61] Something else was in the atmosphere, too: a sense of rebirth, what Margaret called 'a phoenix time'. In the coronation's immediate aftermath, historian C. V. Wedgwood suggested that 'Britain has regained in the past few days that spiritual and moral ascendancy in the world which was hers in 1940'.[62] It was an illusion, and in time even the 'sense of love and pride' would alter, diminishing in fervour. Briefly, the coronation provided a magnificent tonic for a country struggling with the unpalatability of grinding economic anxiety and apparently inexorable eclipse on the world stage. 'What a day for England, and the traditional forces of the world,' crowed Chips Channon.[63] But imperialism in the second half of the twentieth century would belong to the United States, a frequently brash affair of expansionist commercialism and capitalist neurosis. The coronation did nothing to check its juggernaut progress. For an instant, it offered Elizabeth's subjects across the globe the exhilaration of forgetfulness. The focus of their heightened emotions was not an abstract concept – nation, crown, Empire or Commonwealth – but Elizabeth herself.

It was to be a national and patriotic celebration. In November, a spokesman for Ede & Ravenscroft, entrusted with making Elizabeth's coronation robes, announced that 'all the materials used will be British': handmade silk velvet from Warner & Sons of Braintree, satin made by Stephen Walters & Sons of Sudbury and, in a loose interpretation of 'British', 'miniver from the best Canadian ermine'.[64] The Worshipful Company of Gardeners suggested English flowers for Elizabeth's bouquet: 'little white orchids which will come from Crowbrough and Tunbridge Wells; lily-of-the-valley from Bromley, Kent; white roses from Cheshunt, Hertfordshire; and white carnations from Eton, Buckinghamshire'.[65][66] Carpet for Westminster Abbey was specially woven in Glasgow, velvet for the congregation's stools and chairs made to order in Bradford. The first eight designs for Elizabeth's gown submitted by Norman Hartnell featured the floral emblems of England, Scotland, Ireland and Wales. (Elizabeth's requested inclusion of emblems of the fledgling Commonwealth, symbols of Ceylon, Pakistan, South Africa, Canada, Australia and New Zealand, sent Hartnell back to the drawing board.) Hartnell's white satin, like the velvet of Elizabeth's robes, was of British manufacture, from Lady Hart Dyke's silk farm at Lullingstone Castle. Over 3,500 hours English embroiderers would work the thread of gold on her velvet robes. Such painstaking preparations appealed to Elizabeth's eye for detail as well as the mood of patriotic renaissance.

For gainsayers, the year-long build-up to the ceremony was too long. Novelist Ivy Compton-Burnett complained afterwards, 'We seem to have been crowning her for a whole year. I was bored with it long ago, and so relieved to know it really is done at last.'[67] But Compton-Burnett's view was out of the ordinary: that fellow novelist Elizabeth Taylor remarked on the older woman's lack of coronation decorations suggests this was unusual. For the majority, the interlude of expectancy, stoked by newspapers, magazines and the radio, fermented astonishing levels of anticipation; a commemorative issue of the *Radio Times* sold 9 million copies. 'Never has there been such excitement,' wrote Jock Colville.[68] This feeling was shared across the globe, even in countries outside the Empire and Commonwealth, enabling Christopher Fry to claim in his narrative for the coronation film *A Queen Is Crowned*, 'the day of the crowning... finds a people and a world in waiting'. Colville suggested that no monarch had ever received such adulation. In their eve-of-coronation sermons, two vicars in West Sussex invited their congregations to offer 'prayerful support' to 'the most precious lady in the world'.[69] Novelist Paul Gallico wrote a series of reports for American readers; he outlined 'the tremendous and almost unprecedented outpouring of love from the people of Great Britain for their Queen. This Coronation is being called the greatest love affair in the course of history and it may well be so.'[70] Even Elizabeth's own family was not immune. A former equerry to Queen Mary claimed that the Queen Mother's attitude to her daughter was 'one of adoring admiration'.[71]

As the date approached and rehearsals began in the specially refitted abbey, crowds gathered outside to catch a glimpse of Elizabeth entering or leaving. With no appetite for other stories, newspapers recorded her visits in novelettish detail: on 21 May, in 'a light-coffee-coloured shanting two-piece costume, with a flared skirt, the whole in a design of white polka dots', with a matching straw hat with two white feathers, and carrying a red-covered copy of the service; five days later 'in a dove-grey white spotted taffeta two-piece suit with a fully flared skirt'.[72] When Elizabeth arrived with Philip for a rehearsal of the forty boys chosen to act as pages – 'all between twelve and fifteen and not more than 5 feet 6 inches tall'[73] – police linked arms to keep at bay the adoring crowds, estimated at 2,000 strong.

Much of Elizabeth's preparation happened in private. Michael Parker's wife Eileen remembered that, at Buckingham Palace, 'the ballroom was marked with tape to indicate the approximate shape of Westminster Abbey. Household members assumed the role of the chief actors, and the Queen herself, with a sheet pinned to her shoulders, went through tiring rehearsals time and again.'[74] Elizabeth listened to recordings of her father's coronation; she practised wearing the heavy St Edward's Crown. The Archbishop of Canterbury suggested prayers. He expounded his exalted view of her calling in a series of pre-coronation sermons in which he celebrated the throne's 'possibility of a spiritual power': 'the power to lead, to inspire, to unite, by the Sovereign's personal character, personal conviction, personal example'.[75] Elizabeth, he told congregations, increasing the burden upon her with every sonorous period, would leave the abbey after her crowning 'to face for the rest of her life the demands of Christian duty in her high calling'. Given such a weight of expectation, how could Elizabeth's feelings not differ from of those of the million sightseers in London to view coronation decorations, or the eager thousands who bought their commemorative folding periscopes called Coronation Copescopes, or the hardy loyalists who, for forty-eight hours, staked out their places along the processional route, sleeping in plastic mackintoshes and wrapped in newspaper against an unseasonable chill? Elizabeth's feelings seesawed between exhilaration and fretfulness; she worried about the new postage stamps, Philip's new passion for flying, the expense of curtains and carpeting for the new royal apartments.[76] Of her father's coronation, she remembered the 'haze of wonder' she had glimpsed at the moment of crowning; she remembered the King's subsequent recital of the service's blunders and bunglings.

～～

On the most important day in Elizabeth's royal life, its date chosen for its likelihood of sunshine, cold continuous rain cast a pall. 'The weather could not have been viler as apart from wet it was very cold,' wrote Violet Bonham Carter, who was in her seat in one of the timber-built stands along the Mall by 7 a.m.[77] Neither rain nor cold deterred the crowds. Among the 13,000 soldiers in the procession were British, colonial and Commonwealth troops, Scots, Irish, Pakistani and Gurkha pipers, dominion policemen and the red-clad pantomime figures of the Queen's bargemen: as Noël Coward described it, 'the English State Ballet at its best'.[78] In borrowed carriages came exotically clad sultans of half-remembered tiny territories: Lahej, Selangor, Johore, Perak, Kelentan. A rainbow of faces and overseas uniforms brought a last imperial huzzah to wet London streets. The wet crowds cheered them all. They cheered Churchill; they cheered the mammoth wet figure of the Queen of Tonga, who refused to spoil their view of her by raising the carriage hood; rain turned the plume in her headdress into a stiff, wet aerial. Last of all appeared the remarkable golden coach made two centuries earlier for the coronation of George III. Let diarist James Lees-Milne make the inevitable comparison on this occasion, watching on television in the morning room at Brooks's. He remembered it as 'like something out of a fairy tale, Cinderella's [coach], drawn by six [greys] with grooms in eighteenth-century livery; and inside the Queen... and the handsome Duke in a cocked hat by her side.'[79] 'A huge wave of cheering travels with her, pouring along the Mall as though it would lift her up and carry her on her way,' runs the narration of *A Queen Is Crowned*; 'the tumult of love surrounds her.'

Like children starved of sweet things, diarists, letter-writers and journalists inventoried the Byzantine glitter of Elizabeth's crowning. Among jewelled details were the blue and gold copes worn by the canons of Westminster, each one appliquéd with images of the lion and unicorn from the royal coat of arms, gifts from Elizabeth. At the centre of the brilliant harlequinade was a solitary figure, dressed in the gown Hartnell himself described as 'shimmering and sparkling [with] its gold, its crystal, its diamonds, and the muted colours of God's rainbow in the emblems which festooned [the] wide spreading skirt';[80] or the simple white shift in which, at the service's most sacred moment and part hidden by a canopy of cloth of gold, she was anointed with holy oil on her hands, her forehead and her breast; or the belted golden Supertunica worn to receive the royal regalia, and the shimmering golden cloak, called the Imperial Mantle, in which she was crowned with St Edward's Crown to the thunderous cry of 'God save the Queen' from a congregation mostly drawn from the peerage. In long white gowns and long white gloves six maids of honour attended her, the daughters of leading peers. She was escorted by ecclesiastical 'supporters', the bishops of Durham and Bath and Wells. Her principal attendant was her mistress of the robes, the Dowager Duchess of Northumberland, magnificent in diamonds and her own lengthy train. Precedent had fixed their complex choreography, the suggestion of an early planning meeting 'Let's look at an old copy of the *Illustrated London News* and see what they did last time'.[81] In a radio broadcast to the nation that evening, Elizabeth spoke of ancient ceremonies 'and some of their origins are veiled in the mists of the past... the splendid traditions... of more than a thousand years'. For everyone present and the millions who watched on television or afterwards in cinemas, the supernumerary players in their *Alice in Wonderland* motley could not distract from the new queen, high priestess in her hieratic vestments, sacrificial victim as she knelt in prayer or received from elderly men the golden emblems of kingship, 'bending under the weight of the glittering crown... almost a living sacrifice', wrote Edna Healey, 'very tiny and fragile' as a maid of honour remembered her, or, in the words of a later poet laureate, 'history's bride, anointed, blessed'.[82] For Elizabeth herself, as for her father, the experience of her coronation, with its act of lifelong consecration, was transformative; she approached it in a spirit of humility and high seriousness, qualities that shaped her personal conduct of sovereignty ever after. Watching her, her cousin Princess Alice, witness of former coronations, commended her 'dignity and modesty', her combination of majesty and simplicity; Arthur Grenfell had observed her ability to '[draw] herself up with great and natural dignity' long before.[83] Other observers were moved by 'the young Queen so calm, grave and sure of every movement, and so palpably serious and intent'.[84] 'How serious, how absorbed, how carried out of herself she looked,' recorded Viscountess Pakenham, the same impression she had registered at Elizabeth's marriage.[85] Now Elizabeth was married twice over: not only to a man but to a nation. The seriousness of the ceremony and its intense personal resonance for Elizabeth were not lost on television viewers. A secretary in Bournemouth wrote to a friend, 'Towards the climax of the Communion, I began to feel most embarrassed, as though I were eavesdropping, or looking through a keyhole.'[86] Watching the procession from a first-floor window on St James's Street, Sonia Graham Hodgson described her former playmate as 'very calm and happy and dedicated, as she always is'.

There is a black-and-white photograph of the newly crowned Elizabeth entering Buckingham Palace from the inner courtyard at the end of the procession from the abbey, still carrying orb and sceptre and smiling as she negotiates shallow steps. At some point after her return she looked in on a party to which Charles had invited children of the household. A little girl, aged four, was asked what Elizabeth looked like. She answered simply: 'Mummy, she *sparkled*.'[87] And so she did. Standing close to King Edward's Chair at the moment of Elizabeth's anointing was Dermot Morrah, on this occasion in the guise of Arundel Herald Extraordinary. His memory was of 'the sense of spiritual exaltation that radiated from her'.[88] On the palace balcony, the Duchess of Gloucester's train bearer Lady Caroline Gilmour had 'looked along the balcony and [seen] the Queen really shining – it was really quite remarkable as she was surrounded by all her very pretty Maids of Honour and yet she made them look nothing at all'.[89] That night, Churchill described Elizabeth II to the nation as 'the gleaming figure whom Providence has brought to us'.[90]

CHAPTER X

'A thunderous progress... lit to incandescence by the affection and enthusiasm of... devoted subjects'

～⌇～

THE 'COURAGEOUS SPIRIT of adventure that is the finest quality of youth' earned Elizabeth's commendation in the first Christmas broadcast of her reign. Under the circumstances, it was an ambiguous attribute.

A pragmatic Philip had been quick to separate the early frustrations of his consort's role from his love for Elizabeth, steadying for the time being the marital ship. In her coronation broadcast, Elizabeth described to listening millions her sense of their partnership: 'I have my husband to support me. He shares all my ideals.' The Queen Mother had 'screw[ed] [her]self up a good deal' to re-enter public life and, at the end of June 1953, departed for an official tour of a new African federation created from Northern and Southern Rhodesia and Nyasaland.[1] Only in Margaret's case did equanimity remain a distant aspiration. With a heavy heart she accompanied her mother to southern Africa, nurturing in her breast a youthful spirit of adventure destined to be thwarted: an overwhelming longing for a war hero-turned-courtier who, before her return, had been exiled with Elizabeth's agreement to a sinecure in Brussels.

From the King's introspective cult of 'us four' emerged the same short-term beneficiary and long-term victim: Margaret. The youngest of the quartet, Margaret benefited as a child from adoring parents and an equally adoring sister. Her education was lighter even than Elizabeth's, with no requirement to unravel constitutional complexities with Henry Marten and none of the weight of expectation Queen Mary lavished on her elder sister. As a result, her upbringing also lacked that single guiding purpose that ultimately shaped Elizabeth's outlook and stamped her character. Margaret was both blessed and cursed in her miraculous beauty that did not appear to have been inherited from either of her pleasant-looking parents. She was charmingly decorative – and trained to be nothing more. But unlike Elizabeth she was also capricious and self-willed and required by none of her immediate family to check these shortcomings. The little girl whom her mother had extricated from the more arduous of Queen Mary's 'instructive amusements' grew up intent on cherrypicking diversions: as one of her future hostesses noted, 'she is not prepared to stick to the rules if they bore or annoy her'.[2] She basked in the King's wondering delight, shielded by the excuses that Elizabeth made for her from childhood. Then Elizabeth married, and what Lisa Sheridan had described as 'the harmony which exists between the royal sisters' necessarily changed, leaving Margaret, aged seventeen, alone in the palace. A letter she wrote to the American ambassador's wife in October 1950 reveals the royal family's pleasure in one another, even after Elizabeth's marriage, and the rarity then of this sort of time alone: 'It was such fun just being your family and my family! We all loved it, I can assure you, and it was so nice to be able to spend a delicious quiet talky evening with you.'[3] Then the King died. Elizabeth emerged elated from her coronation; Margaret wept. To maid of honour Lady Anne Coke, she explained, 'I've lost my father, and I've lost my sister. She will be so busy. Our lives will change.'[4]

Flotsam in the family shipwreck of her father's death, Margaret clung to the familiarity of the old life. Over time she clung particularly to her father's former equerry and deputy master of the household, Group Captain Peter Townsend, a wartime flying ace whom she met, as Elizabeth had Philip, when she was thirteen. The same year Margaret had met novelist Rebecca West. Of the young princess encountered so briefly, West concluded she possessed a 'shrewd egotism': 'when she grows up people will fall in love with her as if she were not royal'.[5] It was true of Peter Townsend, who fell in love with Margaret apparently heedless of complications. A sheltered and unhappy Margaret returned his feelings. In the spring of 1953, Margaret told Elizabeth. Townsend told Elizabeth's private secretary Tommy Lascelles, whose response of cold fury was that he was 'either mad or bad'. Elizabeth and Philip invited Margaret and Townsend for dinner the evening of Margaret's revelation. Philip pointed out objections to the match; a sympathetic Elizabeth, for whom Townsend was associated with happy last years of 'us four', appeared not to commit herself either way. Unsupportive, Lascelles was equally opaque. Townsend was fifteen years older than Margaret. He was also divorced. Neither Margaret, brought up in the shadow of the abdication, nor the deeply religious Townsend appeared to conceive the scale of the difficulties they faced. A distraught Queen Mother discussed the relationship with Elizabeth, described herself as 'quite shattered by the whole thing', but otherwise looked away, 'completely unapproachable and remote' according to one of Margaret's friends.[6] Taken by surprise, itself a measure of the separate lives of the once inseparable sisters, Elizabeth asked Margaret and Townsend to wait a year. It was her own equivalent of her mother's avoidance. The Queen Mother reflected that Elizabeth 'minded what happened to <u>people</u>', but any hope that time would bring about an easy resolution proved vain.[7] A positive result of Elizabeth's sympathy was a rekindling for the moment of the sisters' closeness.

In this instance, however, Elizabeth could not count on Margaret's caprice. The couple apparently took heart from the failure of any of those party to their secret to spell out to them the impossibility of their relationship, given Margaret's proximity to the throne and Elizabeth's position as head of a church opposed to divorcees' remarriage. Leaving Westminster Abbey after the coronation, Margaret's unhappiness was briefly deflected. 'A great crowd of crowned heads, of nobles and commons – and newspapermen, British and foreign – were gathered in the Great Hall,' Townsend remembered. 'Princess Margaret came up to me; she looked superb, sparkling, ravishing. As we chatted she brushed a bit of fluff off my uniform. We laughed and thought no more of it...'[8] But Margaret had been observed in her gesture of careless intimacy. So lightly was their secret revealed, and soon they would be forced to think much more of it. Eleven days later, 'rumours' appeared in the first British newspaper. The *People* explained as 'quite unthinkable' any suggestion 'that a Royal Princess, third in line of succession to the throne, should even contemplate marriage with a man who has been through the divorce courts' and encouraged its readers to think about this very contingency.[9] In that climate of royal fever, the story caused a sensation that refused to abate, until, as Noël Coward recorded in his diary the following month, 'everyone is clacking about it from John o' Groats to Land's End'.[10]

⁓

Theatrical impresario Emile Littler commissioned a coronation portrait of the new queen for the Palace Theatre, Shaftesbury Avenue. Grace Wheatley's congested pictorial fantasy of

1959, subsequently familiar to a generation of theatre-goers, surrounds a sun-kissed Elizabeth with people, plants and animals of the Commonwealth. It expresses a vision of an overseas role for Elizabeth that she herself shared.

In November 1953, Elizabeth and Philip departed for a five-and-a-half-month tour of the Commonwealth. An expression of the spirit of the times, the poet laureate commemorated their departure with a prayer, 'On our Queen's Going to Her Peoples'; he prayed for a safe return and 'a gladness in all days and in all woes'.[11] They flew to Bermuda in the Caribbean; in Jamaica they boarded SS *Gothic*. Through the Panama Canal they sailed to Fiji and Tonga, and onwards to New Zealand, Tasmania, Australia, the Cocos Islands, then homewards via Ceylon, Aden, Uganda, Malta, Gibraltar and, on the new royal yacht *Britannia*, at last to London. The first circumnavigation of the globe by any monarch, this epic royal odyssey consolidated Elizabeth's sense of herself as sovereign and demonstrated beyond any doubt her role, if she wished it, as symbolic lynchpin of the sprawling global agglomeration transitioning from Empire to Commonwealth. On the eve of departure, Lord Salisbury told the House of Lords, 'Without the strong cement which is provided by loyalty to the Crown, it would, I believe, be only a short time before the British Commonwealth dissolved into its constituent parts.' In the Commons, the Labour leader Clement Attlee described Elizabeth as the Commonwealth's 'symbol of unity'. Newspapers took their cue from a loyal parliament. 'It may well be,' commented one, that 'this Royal tour [will] cement the bonds of fealty among the Queen's lieges overseas.'[12] 'Let us recognise how immeasurable a responsibility rests upon the shoulders of our young Queen,' Salisbury concluded, 'for on the personal loyalties of her peoples the whole future of a free world may depend.'[13]

Like Archbishop Fisher's claims at the time of the coronation, it was a considerable burden to impose on Elizabeth. The zeal of old men in predicting at the outset of her reign national revival, spiritual regeneration and Commonwealth unity as a bulwark against the threats of the Cold War both reflected and promoted widespread dizzy optimism. Such extravagant ambitions, the chimera of 'new Elizabethanism', underpinned the exaggerated and hagiographic response to Elizabeth herself, and proposed for her reign a programme almost certainly impossible to achieve. No evidence suggests that the modest and pragmatic Elizabeth tried, although her dedication to Commonwealth unity would survive the variable enthusiasm of governments at home and abroad and her own religious faith was central to her understanding of her role. For over a year, in a 'courageous spirit of adventure', Elizabeth had looked forward to her journey of more than 43,000 miles, a version of the tour twice planned for her parents and once before for herself, distracting herself at Balmoral with atlases and charts in the sad summer of 1952. Her behaviour during the tour itself suggests she was neither daunted nor deterred by ministerial puffery: in her Christmas broadcast, made at Government House in Auckland, she distanced herself from 'the hope that my reign may mark a new Elizabethan age', insisting that she did not feel at all like her great Tudor forebear, 'who was blessed with neither husband nor children, who ruled as a despot and was never able to leave her native shores'. Henry Marten had outlined the limits of her office; she knew from long ago that the throne she inherited spanned continents – from her grandfather's Christmas broadcasts and the wooden building blocks given to her as a birthday present by Queen Mary; from her mother's letters from Canada, written on the brink of war, with their descriptions of remote settlements, black bears and moose, and the personal attachment of dominion subjects to their distant sovereign; from Marten's explanation of the 1931 Statute of Westminster; from the royal family's tour of South Africa, when Elizabeth had dedicated herself to the service of a 'great imperial family'; from her own visits to Canada and, fleetingly, Kenya.

Her mother wrote to Elizabeth on the day of departure, 'It must be a ghastly day for you, poor darling.'[14] Like her mother as Duchess of York in 1927, Elizabeth was leaving behind Charles and Anne. For the third time, she would be separated from five-year-old Charles at Christmas. She and Philip had remained at Sandringham, finalizing plans, while Charles celebrated his fifth birthday with the Queen Mother at Windsor, but their final parting proved a strain. Elizabeth burst into tears after putting the children to bed for the last time for nearly six months on 22 November; it was a still tearful Elizabeth who, the next day, acknowledged waiting crowds at London Airport. Elizabeth almost certainly rationalized the prospect of separation as compelled by duty; that her mother anticipated its ghastliness in her letter to her suggests something of Elizabeth's own feelings. Twice during their parents' absence, Charles and Anne sat for Marcus Adams; photographs, including the children flanking a measuring stick to show how much they had grown, were despatched to Elizabeth and Philip overseas. At intervals parents and children spoke by 'radio-telephone'; Elizabeth spoke to her mother, too. How much Charles and Anne missed their parents can be judged from the Queen Mother's description of them 'poised to snatch the receiver' whenever she herself tried to speak to her daughter.[15] Elizabeth wrote 'family' letters to her mother for reading aloud. Like her holiday letters to Crawfie twenty years before, these would become part of her on-tour routine; the Queen Mother called them 'lovely "diary" letter[s]'.[16] She responded with bright, lively anecdotes of the curious five-year-old and his robust and loud-voiced little sister. At Sandringham with their grandmother, Margaret and the Gloucesters, the children listened to Elizabeth's Christmas broadcast, but the tour was a test of stamina that could not easily have accommodated them.

The *Daily Telegraph* explained the parents' separation from their children as 'a real privation': an idea of Elizabeth as a mother missing her children was interwoven into the tour's addresses and speeches.[17] At Wanganui on New Zealand's North Island, mayor Edward Millward referred to 'the great sacrifice you are making in the prolonged absence from your children enforced upon you by this visit.'[18] Elizabeth told 600 guests at a women's lunch in Melbourne that she and Philip were 'greatly looking forward to seeing our children again'.[19] The following day she described to her mother her excitement that she would see the children three weeks earlier than planned: they were to meet in Tobruk, in Libya.[20] 'The Queen thought it a wonderful idea, her eyes quite shining,' wrote a friend.[21] In the latest book in preparation by photographer Lisa Sheridan, *Playtime at Royal Lodge*, the children's relationship with their grandmother took centre stage. Missing his parents, Sheridan's Charles presses the Queen Mother, 'Tell us a story, Granny, about how Mummy and Margot [Margaret] played in this garden when they were little girls.' It was, wrote Sheridan, in text authorized by Elizabeth's mother, 'the story that the children are never tired of hearing'.[22]

Triumphs balanced the tour's hardships, just as gentle days aboard SS *Gothic* offset Elizabeth's 102 speeches and, by one calculation, 13,213 handshakes, granting husband and wife shared reprieve and rekindling the relaxed intimacy of vanished days in Malta.[23] Wraparound coverage of the coronation had galvanized popular interest on a scale never to be repeated; limited television ownership made it imperative to see Elizabeth in the flesh. Turnout in Australia and New Zealand was on a vast scale. Of the million people who lined Elizabeth's nine-mile drive through Sydney, an estimated half had slept out overnight. A million people cheered the royal arrival in Melbourne. Smaller centres saw similar levels of engagement. At Wollongong on the south coast, the crowd of 120,000 was almost double the town's population, while 250,000 people clustered along the fifty-mile route of Elizabeth's drive there, including a farmer who tied a cow by the roadside in a harness of red, white and blue ribbons (in a similar gesture in New Zealand, one farmer tethered sheep dyed red, white and blue within sight of the rail tracks). Greetings everywhere were rowdily affectionate, proof of the intense personal loyalty inspired by the figure of the sovereign in these dog days of Empire. New Zealand's high commissioner referred to 'adulation' for Elizabeth;[24] a commemorative account of the visit published in Australia described 'a thunderous progress through thousands of miles lit to incandescence by the affection and enthusiasm of nine million devoted subjects'.[25] Despite the experiences of coronation year, Elizabeth and Philip were astonished. 'The level of adulation, you wouldn't believe it,' Philip commented later.[26] A photographer described Elizabeth's arrival in New Zealand as 'like the second coming'.[27] No detail was too small for rapture: the *Sydney Morning Herald* described the unremarkable frock Elizabeth wore to visit the Blue Mountains as 'as blue as the Jamieson Valley... as blue as her eyes'.[28]

None of this went to Elizabeth's head. 'It would have been very easy to play to the gallery, but I took a conscious decision not to do that,' Philip said.[29] For Elizabeth, no conscious decisions were necessary. Rapacious and uncritical public interest had been a feature of her life from birth. She was only six when the *Tatler* told its readers that, if she were old enough to have her head turned by national adulation, 'it would have happened long ago'. Early exposure to the unremitting attention of strangers safeguarded her from egotism: an expectation, she regarded it as neither reward nor commendation. She was unlikely to forget a childhood visit with Queen Mary to a concert at the Queen's Hall. Her grandmother had offered a fidgety Elizabeth the option of leaving early. A swift departure was indeed the outcome of Elizabeth's hapless response: 'Oh, no, Granny, we can't leave before the end. Think of all the people who'll be waiting to see us outside.' Vulgar enjoyment of crowds smacked of actresses. Her grandmother's stern rebuke taught Elizabeth the impropriety, as she saw it, of crowd-pleasing. Queen Mary practised public reserve, Elizabeth public humility. At her own request, her cars and trains proceeded slowly, to allow those who had travelled long distances or endured lengthy waits the best possible view of her: only fear of the car's engine overheating prevented her chauffeur from driving at less than ten miles an hour through a thronged Sydney. Making herself visible in this way, regardless of the discomfort of high temperatures and the strain of smiling continually, was key to Elizabeth's understanding of her purpose. 'What's the point in coming unless they can see me?' she repeated. [30]

In her speech to the New Zealand parliament in Wellington, she echoed the familiar theme of service, linked as so often to fidelity to her father's memory: 'My constant prayer is that I may in some measure carry on that ideal of service of which he gave so outstanding an example'; in an equivalent speech in Canberra she announced her 'resolve that under God I shall not only rule but serve'.[31] At such moments Elizabeth brought conviction and sincerity to sentiments written for her by courtiers who, like her crown, she had inherited from her father, including her new private secretary, Michael Adeane, who had replaced Tommy Lascelles. And there were gentle reminders from close to home that ecstatic public tributes were paid to the monarch not the individual. The sovereign was a conduit for popular feeling, her mother wrote to Elizabeth in March: 'how moving & humble-making, that one can be the vehicle through which this love for country can be expressed'. [32]

Instead Elizabeth learned important lessons about the physical and emotional demands of overseas tours. She was the same young woman who had found excuses to avoid sharing a tent with fellow Guides or Sea Rangers at Frogmore and whom Margery Roberts had witnessed shrink from the mayor's touch in Brighton in 1945. Yet for nearly six months, save intervals at sea, she was continuously on view, continuously required to satisfy the expectations of those whom she knew would remember their encounter for the rest of their lives. At a children's rally in Brisbane, a determined four-year-old broke through the security cordon to jump on Elizabeth's lap. On this occasion a surprised Elizabeth chatted to the girl until a bodyguard removed her. Less fugacious were relentless mayoral receiving lines and the stilted small talk of unvarying civic receptions: required to initiate every conversation, Elizabeth faced a problem familiar to her great-great-great-great-grandmother, Queen Charlotte, that she 'not only has to start the subject but commonly entirely to support it'.[33] At least once her composure faltered. 'Why is everyone so boring, boring, boring?' she demanded of Philip tearfully.[34] Elizabeth might have taken comfort from an entertainment provided early in the tour in Fiji. Fijian schoolgirls staged 'a fairy tale in which [Elizabeth] is Fairy Queen and the Duke of Edinburgh Prince Charming'.[35] It included an ode of loyalty sung to 'Elisipeti our Queen' and the Duke of 'Edinibara'. The song, Elizabeth learned, followed a traditional melody; the movements of the dance, much like the pattern of her own life, had been passed down from generation to generation.

As in South Africa, there were sporadic, uncomfortable reminders of empire's exclusions: in Australia and New Zealand the tour's organizers made few efforts to satisfy Elizabeth's requests to meet Aboriginal and Maori communities. And there were foreshadowings of a new world, in which local sensibilities could not be ignored, including the call by Buddhist monk Thalpawila Seelawansa that his fellow monks 'stand outside the temples at Kandy during the Queen's visit to Ceylon and show that they do not wish her to occupy the temple octagon unless she pays homage to the Buddha's tooth'.[36] (In the event Elizabeth did visit the Sacred Shrine at the Temple of the Tooth at Kandy without the embarrassment of a monks' boycott, removing her shoes to do so.) As she would throughout her reign, Elizabeth used dress to woo and flatter her hosts. Included in her eight tonnes of luggage for the tour was a Hartnell gown of mimosa gold tulle with sparkling embroidery of wattle flowers, Australia's national flower. Elizabeth wore it on her first and last evenings in Australia. It was one of her favourites, Bobo revealed. It was one of Australians', too, and Elizabeth wore it again that winter for sittings at Buckingham Palace with Australian painter William Dargie. Dargie's 'Wattle Portrait', one of the most successful of the reign, became an Australian icon. It was reproduced on the naturalization papers of a generation of Australian immigrants and displayed as a print in schools, libraries, hospitals, church halls and local, state and federal government offices across the country; the painting itself was exhibited at Sydney's David Jones department store. Australia returned the compliment by presenting Elizabeth with a wattle flower brooch of white and yellow diamonds.

~⁀~

The fervour of Elizabeth's welcome home, wrote the *New Yorker*'s London correspondent Mollie Panter Downes, might have encouraged an uninformed observer to conclude 'she had returned from a voyage of six years, not six months, and that her land had been under foreign occupation in her absence'.[37] A Pathé newsreel, 'The Queen Comes Home', showed banks of the Thames dense with crowds and the dark river pocked with little craft like a view by Canaletto, for the first appearance in British waters of the new royal yacht *Britannia*, carrying the royal family. Parents and children had been reunited in Libya, after a courtesy call on King Idris; together they visited Malta and Gibraltar. 'The children are enchanting and it is so wonderful to be with them again!' a relieved Elizabeth wrote to her mother; like her mother before her, she had worried they would not recognize her.[38] Off the Isle of Wight Churchill joined the royal party: nearing home, he described the Thames to them as 'the silver thread which runs through the history of Britain'. Seeing it as a 'dirty commercial river', Elizabeth concluded 'one was looking at it in a rather too mundane way'.[39] She was neither fanciful nor imaginative and she did not, she knew, regard the world in the 'very romantic and glittering way' of her elderly premier. But her own 'mundane' way was useful as well as limiting, one of her shields against adulation and flattery. Waving from the palace balcony at the end of a procession through decorated London streets in a landau drawn by six Windsor greys, Elizabeth appeared relaxed and happy. Criticism had been nugatory compared with her extraordinary success in stimulating sentimental bonds of loyalty and embodying for distant subjects a concrete understanding of royalty, in her sumptuous Hartnell evening gowns, with the sash of the Order of the Garter and magnificent jewellery, what Charles would later describe as 'dressing up and Queening it'. In December, Labour MP Cyril Bence had questioned the expense of equipping SS *Gothic*; inevitably journalists criticized the cost of the new royal yacht. For the majority, Elizabeth's tour had been a triumph, extensive coverage at home a reminder of how far across the globe British influence still stretched, and the fulsome encomium of society magazine *The Queen* did not provoke raised eyebrows: 'Millions of her subjects all over the world have recently been made aware... of the sincerity with which that wonderful dedication was made in her twenty-first birthday speech at Cape Town in 1947, so selflessly implemented as her reign continues.'[40] For Elizabeth, 173 days away had given her, she said, 'visible and audible proof' that monarchy was 'living in the hearts of the people'.[41] The Queen Mother and Margaret, who had never previously been parted from her sister for so long, hosted a welcome-home party at Royal Lodge.

❧

The intense, idolatrous affection of coronation summer lingered yet awhile. At the Royal Academy's Summer Exhibition in May 1955 were new portraits of Elizabeth by Pietro Annigoni and Simon Elwes, and Terence Cuneo's painting of the coronation. Popular and critical opinion favoured the first. This was posterity's verdict, too, for its combination of 'queenly dignity with youthful freshness and sincerity', its depiction of its subject as 'regal, natural and the essence of youthful dignity'.[42]

That Annigoni had revealed little of Elizabeth's interior life beyond her evident ease with her position and the curiosity about the world glimpsed through palace windows that, in French, artist and sitter discussed together, as Elizabeth had with Laura Knight, did not provoke comment. Elizabeth's inscrutability, giving nothing of herself away, was not yet established as a given; for a still deferential society hauteur was part of the royal condition. Elizabeth herself admired Annigoni's picture, content that it play its part in shaping public perceptions. In the year since her return, the qualities of detachment and regal self-containment highlighted by the Florentine portraitist had shaped her behaviour twice over.

Irresolution had awaited Elizabeth on that cold May morning in 1954, when *Britannia* passed through Tower Bridge and bunting fluttered on barges and the royal aunts lined up to greet her. Unresolved were Margaret's romantic dilemma and a question over the future of the ailing and aged Churchill, contentious issues at the heart of Elizabeth's family and her government. Elizabeth did not initiate the unravelling of either; in each case ideas of her wellbeing were invoked. Churchill left office in April 1955; at the end of October Margaret renounced Peter Townsend. Both decisions were overdue. In each case, Elizabeth might have acted decisively or sooner to precipitate the necessary closure.

Churchill had suffered a stroke in June 1953, three weeks after the coronation. Secretly Jock Colville, once Elizabeth's private secretary, now Churchill's, informed the palace. If, as expected, Churchill had died, Elizabeth's right was to choose the candidate to succeed him to ensure continuity of government. Instead, against the odds, Churchill rallied. Elizabeth invited the Churchills to spend their forty-fifth wedding anniversary with her at Doncaster races; she invited them to Balmoral afterwards. Kindly overtures were not an endorsement of her faith in his continuing ability, although they could be construed as such; as much as his cabinet and his doctors, Elizabeth expected Churchill's resignation, even if, on a personal level, she did not wish it. No resignation was forthcoming. With Elizabeth's departure in November, Churchill postponed any relinquishing of power until her return. She returned, and he did not resign. Early in 1955, cabinet hostility appeared to force his hand; he made up his mind, wavered, then resigned on 5 April. 'I've had my turn – a good turn. I can't keep others waiting about for ever,' he told Violet Bonham Carter with partial conviction.[43] Sincerely Elizabeth conveyed 'the greatest personal regrets'; Michael Adeane wrote on her behalf that 'she would especially miss the weekly audiences which she had found so instructive and, if one can say so of state matters, so entertaining'.[44] His resignation accepted, Churchill declined to recommend a successor, mindful of constitutional proprieties and the prerogative right that belonged to Elizabeth, not the outgoing prime minister, of nominating a new leader. Elizabeth 'chose' foreign secretary Anthony Eden, in line with assumptions within the Conservative Party, as well as those of Eden himself and indeed Churchill (Eden had described himself as the party's 'crown prince', while Churchill labelled him his 'Princess Elizabeth'). It was another instance of Elizabeth's compliance with expectation. The royal line was unassertive and, in its predictability, non-interventionist. It appeared to express no view of matters on Elizabeth's part: instead it legitimized assumptions made by those more closely involved. Elizabeth had exercised her prerogative power with the same apparent detachment with which Annigoni's Elizabeth stares beyond the canvas, a butterfly touch whose lightness might in future spark questions about the need for her involvement. A courtier of the time described her as 'a person who accepts what has to be done with so little question'.[45] Ideally suited to the limitations of smoothly functioning constitutional monarchy, it is an approach liable to falter in a crisis.

On his last night in office, Churchill hosted a farewell dinner for the sovereign with whom, Colville claimed, he was 'madly in love'. Photographs taken at the end of the evening show a genial premier escorting Elizabeth to her waiting car. His expression is avuncular, admiring, affectionate. He had told her that 'never have the august duties which fall upon the British monarchy been discharged with more devotion than in the brilliant opening of Your Majesty's reign'.[46] From the outset, Elizabeth had visibly embraced devotion to her 'august duties': neither she nor those closest to her had countenanced an alternative. It was the path she would tread for seven decades. Her understanding of those duties was traceable to the fearful embarrassment that, in the wake of the abdication, shook both her father and the whole royal apparatus.

❦

Were memories of the abdication at the forefront of Elizabeth's mind in the slow unravelling of Margaret's relationship with Peter Townsend? Certainly those closest to her who opposed the marriage, beginning with Tommy Lascelles, invoked that dread spectre, albeit with careful obliquity; Lascelles wrote to both Elizabeth and Margaret of the possibility of Commonwealth governments' hostility. Margaret can be forgiven if she failed to take fully seriously warnings of opposition. All her life, she had overturned unpleasantness through charm and what Queen Mary called her 'espièglerie' or roguishness; twenty-three is a late age at which to learn the inevitability of thwarting. If Elizabeth had hoped that Townsend's overseas posting would lessen either Margaret's attachment or press fascination, she was mistaken. Attention focused on Margaret's twenty-fifth birthday in August 1955. It was the age at which she could marry without Elizabeth's agreement, according to the terms of the 1772 Royal Marriages Act. As the anniversary approached, the Queen Mother forced herself to discuss matters with her headstrong daughter. 'I feel such a deep sense of responsibility as your only living parent,' she wrote to Margaret. Margaret almost apologized for 'hav[ing] blown up at intervals when we've discussed the situation'.[47] She told Anthony Eden that she would finalize any decision only after Townsend's return from Brussels in October and in the meantime would remain at Balmoral, valued by the royal family for its 'soul-refreshing quality', where a clamorous posse of up to 300 journalists maintained a mawkish, sometimes sanctimonious vigil.[48] Eden and his wife Clarissa – ironically his second wife, following a divorce in which, like Townsend, he was the innocent party – travelled to Balmoral in October. Elizabeth and Philip discussed the princess's predicament with the prime minister, discussions that would inform a later conversation between Elizabeth, Philip and Margaret that left Margaret 'in great distress' and almost certainly impacted on her final decision.[49] Elizabeth's distress may well have equalled Margaret's. She remained devoted to her sister and had been determined 'that nobody should influence [Margaret] over her decision, and that she should be free to make up her own mind'.[50] As Establishment opposition to the marriage coalesced, it seems likely that Elizabeth's conviction grew that Margaret would resolve for herself in the only way permissible the conflict between personal fulfilment and the dictates of duty. It was an assumption based on the closeness of the sisters' shared upbringing and Elizabeth's belief that both had absorbed similar lessons from their parents' example.

Margaret and Peter Townsend were reunited at Clarence House on 24 October, Margaret still shaken by her conversation with Elizabeth and Philip at Windsor the day before. They knew now that the cabinet would not support their marriage: Margaret's only option was to renounce her royal status, including her place in the line of succession and her Civil List income. Afterwards both were at pains to stress that their decision was mutual; together they wrote the statement that Margaret released to the press on 31 October. The interval between its writing and public release confirmed their certainty that their decision was the right one; Margaret wrote to a sympathetic Toni de Bellaigue that the outcome was of God's ordaining.[51] Publicly, she explained her decision: she was 'mindful of the Church's teachings that Christian marriage is indissoluble, and conscious of my duty to the Commonwealth'.

To Elizabeth, the outcome could only have come as a relief. On a personal level, in stating her willingness to put duty first, Margaret appeared to validate the beliefs that were cornerstones of Elizabeth's existence. Her decision, which won widespread approval, also had a public dimension. As the crisis gathered pace, a stentorian *Times* had described Elizabeth as the 'universal representative in whom her people see their better selves reflected'; it had insisted that Elizabeth's family had a part to play in a popular ideal of family life. It was, said the *Daily Mirror*, a 'bullying ultimatum' from 'a dusty world and a forgotten age', but Margaret played her part, hostage to the legacy of the royal sisters' assiduously publicized happy childhood: Marcus Adams's *sfumato* vision of the devotedness of 'us four', the winsome domesticity of Lisa Sheridan's photographs of Royal Lodge and Y Bwthyn Bach. Elizabeth was enabled to continue to reflect the 'better selves' of her people.[52] Margaret paid a high price for her proximity to the throne: in the event, five years of what she described as 'travell[ing] unhappily, bumping about' until she married in 1960.[53] Elizabeth would not always be so well served by her family. In the meantime, Margaret ensured that her sister did not forget the sacrifice made on her behalf: sniping rudenesses, omissions interpretable as snubs. Her nemesis Tommy Lascelles claimed she became 'selfish and hard and wild'.[54]

~~~

In an emerald-green coat with a black astrakhan collar, Elizabeth was in Birmingham the week after Margaret's announcement. The city was *en fête*. Streets along the royal procession 'were gaily decorated with flags, bunting and garlands'. In a special detail, lampposts were topped 'with models of galleons and jet aircraft to depict the two Elizabethan eras'.[55] In Bristol the following April, where Elizabeth opened new council offices and a reservoir, the plans of local officials echoed Elizabeth I's visit four centuries earlier. 'Following the example of her illustrious namesake,' reported the *Illustrated London News*, 'Her Majesty... arrived in the centre of Bristol by water... The royal party landed at the Narrow Quay, where the first Queen Elizabeth had disembarked during a visit to the city in 1574.'[56]

The achievements of the new Elizabethans had yet to match those of England's golden age. News that a Commonwealth expedition had successfully scaled Everest, the world's highest mountain, had been released on coronation morning, and Elizabeth herself had captured hearts at home and across the globe. Churchill's last premiership suggested superficial links with imperial glories, but British power globally was illusory, and the domestic economy remained fragile to the point of collapse. Yet in Birmingham on a wet November morning and in spring sunshine in the southwest, the illusion of this second age of progress held. It did not matter that Elizabeth had denied any personal connection in her Christmas broadcast in 1953; in other ways she played her part. Her new private secretary, Martin Charteris, described as 'just what we want for Nigeria' photographs taken by Cecil Beaton in November. Beaton had been pessimistic about the sitting. It was a cold, dull day. 'There was not only no sunshine filtering through the windows to give a lift to the scene, but there was an ugly foggy pall coming into the Palace rooms,' he recorded in his diary. 'The Queen brought no sunshine with her... In the cold afternoon light the Queen looked cold. Her complexion extremely white – her hands somewhat pink. She did not look her best.'[57] He photographed Elizabeth in three-quarters profile, wearing her coronation necklace and earrings, the George IV diamond diadem, Garter sash and family orders, in a chair of state in the palace ballroom. The photograph was released the day of Elizabeth and Philip's departure for Nigeria in January 1956. It was an appropriately 'royal' image for a tour in which, it had been announced, 'at ceremonies which the Queen attends on foot... a standard bearer will walk immediately behind her carrying a silk standard'.[58] There were visual affinities between Beaton's portrait and images of an elderly Queen Victoria, and the presence of a uniformed bearer carrying the royal standard brought to Nigerian garden parties the bright flummery of the coronation. But the world had changed since Victoria's reign. At the Oji River Leper Settlement, where, Victoria-like, Elizabeth was greeted with a traditional welcome, 'Our Mother is coming', she shook hands with Nigerian lepers who had been cured.[59] 'We cannot express enough our joy and happiness at seeing you here,' one of them, John Aguh, told her. Elizabeth shaking hands was a progressive, modern gesture that contributed to changing attitudes about this contagious and frightening disease, and she and Philip also each financially adopted a leper child. But there was no suggestion, as in centuries past, that Elizabeth's touch could cure. Nor would her nominal leadership, despite her qualities of dedication and personal grace, halt the decline in British fortunes at home or overseas. The *Daily Mail* had suggested at the time of the coronation that 'with Elizabeth as our guiding star... there is every prospect that this island and its sister countries will go forward into a future better even than the best of the past', but by instinct as well as training Elizabeth inclined not to guide but to follow.[60]

Elizabeth flew to Corsica shortly after her return from west Africa. She went to join Philip, busy on fleet exercises in the Mediterranean, for a week-long cruise of appalling weather on *Britannia*. As in their Malta days, she did not take with her Charles and Anne. In their place was her nineteen-year-old cousin, Philip's first cousin once removed, Princess Alexandra of Kent. Alexandra would become one of Elizabeth's closest friends in the royal family. Rumour of the sort that clung to Philip through the second half of the 1950s would claim, without proof, that she played a part in Philip's life, too.

CHAPTER XI

'Still the age of the golden cobwebs'?

❦

'RATHER WISTFULLY ALONE, and very solemn, no doubt owing to the gravity of world events' was 'Jennifer' of the *Tatler*'s description of Elizabeth at the State Opening of Parliament in November 1956.[1]

Elizabeth certainly had reason for solemnity as autumn gave way to winter; she also had grounds for loneliness. On 15 October, Philip had set off for a four-month Commonwealth tour without her. The next day, in the short service of dedication that followed her opening of a new reservoir in the Lowther Hills, she joined in a prayer for Philip, 'as he travels across the world'.[2] She was accompanied to the State Opening by Margaret. After the tensions of the previous year, it appeared a show of sisterly unity that reduced a number of onlookers to tears. At no point had Elizabeth had such need of her husband as trusted and confidential adviser. Decisions taken by Anthony Eden, with many of which he had familiarized Elizabeth in advance, shortly earned Britain resounding international condemnation.

On Coronation Day,
2 June 1953, Churchill
hailed Elizabeth as 'the
gleaming figure whom
Providence has brought to
us', seen here, with Philip,
on the palace balcony after
the ceremony.

'Mummy, she *sparkled*,'
said a little girl, who saw
Elizabeth at close quarters.
Here, a sparkling Elizabeth
is photographed by Cecil
Beaton holding the orb and
sceptre, in front of what
Beaton called 'my Abbey
background'.

In 1955, critics applauded Pietro Annigoni's depiction of Elizabeth as 'regal, natural and the essence of youthful dignity'. A picture she herself admired, it has proved enduringly popular.

On Suva Wharf in Fiji, Adi Kainona curtsies after presenting
Elizabeth with a bouquet of Fijian flowers, during Elizabeth's
epic 173-day tour of the Commonwealth, 1953–4.

Elizabeth was joined on the Royal Yacht Britannia by Charles, Lord
Mountbatten and Anne, for a review of the Western Fleet, 30 July 1969.

Elizabeth broke the old miner's superstition of not allowing a woman to visit a pit when she donned a white boiler suit and hard hat to visit the Rothes Colliery in Fife, 1 July 1958.

In 1956, Elizabeth took Charles, Anne and a brace of corgis to watch Philip play polo in Windsor Great Park.

Elizabeth and Philip during a visit to Schefferville, Quebec, during a tour of Canada in 1959.

The strength of Elizabeth's affection for her sometimes difficult younger sister is evident in this photograph of Elizabeth with Margaret and Tony Armstrong-Jones, 1960s.

This dazzling photographic portrait, by Anthony Buckley, from October 1960, bears out a journalist's verdict of Elizabeth: 'She looks a Queen and obviously believes in her right to be one. Her bearing is both simple and majestic – no actress could possibly match it.'

'The person on whom all the traditional ritual converged', in the words of a courtier's wife: above, Elizabeth leaving the State Opening of Parliament in 1964 and, below, two years later, uniformed and mounted side saddle to take the salute at the Trooping the Colour ceremony.

Sovereign, dynast and mother: Elizabeth presents Charles to the people of Wales following his investiture as Prince of Wales at Caernarvon Castle, 1 July 1969.

Elizabeth as Head of the Commonwealth, visiting the Bahamas in the spring of 1966. Seven years later, Elizabeth became queen of the newly independent Bahamas, one of fifteen overseas Commonwealth realms of which she is monarch.

The Suez Crisis resulted in an enforced British volte-face that served as an act of national humiliation, a threnody for empire and a jolt to the sunshine complacency of the dawn of the second Elizabethan age. Privy to Foreign Office and intelligence agencies telegrams, Elizabeth knew more than most the strength of opposition across the Commonwealth and the severity of threatened Soviet hostility in the wake of British aggression. Alone within her family she shouldered her anxiety.

She had agreed to the extended tour on *Britannia* that Philip would justify as his 'personal contribution to the Commonwealth ideal'.[3] Within her marriage acquiescence was her default setting, established in her wedding vow of obedience and her reminder to the young women of Durham University of women's place within the family; if she had misgivings, she shared them with no one but Philip, perhaps not even very strenuously with him. Observers noted her seriousness at the airport with Charles and Anne for Philip's departure. Subsequently, her failure to muster a smile would be interpreted as evidence of her marital unhappiness. Philip opened the Olympic Games in Melbourne in November; he travelled to New Zealand, Norfolk Island and Antarctica, where he visited British scientific stations. In her Christmas broadcast Elizabeth described his journey as encompassing 'some of the least accessible parts of the world, those islands of the South Atlantic... linked to us with bonds of brotherhood and trust', including the Falkland Islands and Ascension Island. Philip travelled on to Gambia, the Canary Islands and Gibraltar. On their ninth wedding anniversary in November, he sent Elizabeth white roses and a photograph of two iguanas embracing, but before their reunion in Lisbon in February, Elizabeth had authorized her antediluvian press secretary, Commander Richard Colville, to issue a terse statement about her marriage: 'It is quite untrue that there is any rift between the Queen and the Duke.' The tour was dogged by speculation about the reason for Philip's solo adventure and lurid surmise about his activities ashore. News that Michael Parker's wife Eileen had initiated first steps in a legal separation electrified the press, the marriage of Philip's right-hand man easily presented as a reflection of the royal marriage. Parker offered to resign to spare Philip's embarrassment. Philip demurred, but Parker resigned anyway. In 1982, Eileen Parker claimed, 'I started to wonder if his resignation was a smokescreen for something, or somebody else.'[4] Newspapers overseas concluded that Parker's removal had been forced in order to prevent him from leading Philip astray.[5]

Domestic disharmony real or imaginary contributed to Elizabeth's intense unsettlement in the wake of the Suez Crisis. In the summer of 1956, anger at nationalization of the Anglo-French-owned Suez Canal Company by the new Egyptian president, Gamal Abdel Nasser, and concerns over its impact on British shipping and oil transportation, had ultimately inspired a response on the part of Eden's government that was both short-sighted and illegal. Secretly Britain, France and Israel plotted joint action: an attack on Egypt by Israel and, subsequently, military occupation of the Canal Zone by British and French forces to reclaim control under the guise of international policemanship. Eden did not consult or inform Britain's allies, notably US and Commonwealth leaders. Their condemnation was swift, mirrored by that of the Soviet Union and states across the Arab world, for British actions that included bombing Egyptian airfields. Eden claimed afterwards that Elizabeth had been fully apprised of his plans, although he also acknowledged that she did not actively support the line taken; he may well have kept from her the full duplicity of the British-French-Israeli Sèvres Protocol, which would have troubled her on account of its dishonesty – those nearest to Elizabeth have always esteemed her honesty.[6] Undoubtedly she knew more of the prime minister's purpose than several members of his government. British responses to Nasser's nationalization in July had been mixed; responses to Eden's actions three months later were less so. Noël Coward recorded a popular view that 'Anthony Eden has gone round the bend'.[7] Martin Charteris believed Elizabeth felt the same; one palace source suggested she regarded the undertaking as 'idiotic'.[8] Her role, she knew, was not to voice disapproval, nor to direct the prime minister: the sovereign's constitutional entitlement is to be consulted, to encourage and to warn. In the fourth year of her reign, schooled in political unassertiveness, it was unlikely that Elizabeth should have considered herself equipped to restrain a prime minister twice her age whose parliamentary career had included serving three times as foreign secretary. As the week-long crisis lurched towards ignominious curtailment, she described herself as 'having the most awful time'.[9] Philip, she suggested, would have been 'impossible to live with' had he been at home. Perhaps she meant to reconcile herself to his absence from a divided country and a divided court. She noted that her milkman strongly supported Eden's policy.

In January, Elizabeth reacted tactfully to Eden's resignation in the crisis's wake, reassuring him that his political record, 'written in tempestuous times, is highly valued and never will be forgotten by your Sovereign'.[10] It was evidence of Cynthia Gladwyn's assessment of Elizabeth's 'very fine character, simple, kind and good... a person who would never let anyone down'.[11] In response, Eden thanked her for her kindness. He described having looked forward 'to my weekly audience, knowing that I should receive from Your Majesty a wise and impartial reaction to events, which was quite simply the voice of our land'.[12]

In public, Elizabeth's reaction differed. Her Christmas broadcast, written in Philip's absence and without the help he had previously given her, celebrated the Commonwealth as 'a "family of nations"' and acknowledged the inevitability of family disputatiousness. 'Deep and acute differences... are bound to arise between members of a family,' she told her global radio audience of 150 million. 'In all such differences, however, there comes a moment when, for the sake of ultimate harmony, the healing power of tolerance, comradeship and love must be allowed to play its part'; she described 'a love that can rise above anger and is ready to forgive'. Her ostensible prompt was Commonwealth denunciation of Britain over Suez. Elizabeth may not simply have been thinking of foreign policy in commending tolerance and forgiveness in love. She was, Cynthia Gladwyn would write, 'quite shrewd and quick about all that is going on'.[13]

Elizabeth had suggested for herself the role of representative of 'the youth of the British family of nations' in her twenty-first birthday speech. Hers had never been Eden's 'voice of our land'. Save as royal figurehead, she was scarcely representative even of her own generation, despite good intentions and her determination to embody to the best of her ability values of timeless Britishness and the possibilities of peacetime after war. In the lapsarian, post-Suez world, Elizabeth would not escape the scepticism towards authority that was the coda to Eden's devastating miscalculation and his subsequent lying to parliament. Intense adulation did not evaporate overnight. Three years later, a left-leaning Sunday paper described 'reverence for royalty' as 'the national religion', but over time claims made on Elizabeth's behalf would forfeit something of their earlier triumphalism.[14]

Elizabeth was vulnerable to change. Her upbringing and training for the throne had emphasized the importance of continuity. As her father had consciously perpetuated his own father's model of sovereignty, Elizabeth sought to do the same. In this she was encouraged by assumptions made within her family, as well as the interventions of court and household officials, and helped by a (characteristic) attitude of acceptance of the ceremonial side of monarchy, undertaken unshowily but with conviction – former *Punch* editor Malcolm Muggeridge described 'a certain sleepwalking quality about the gestures, movements and ceremonial'[15] – which obviated any pressing need for reappraisal. In the short term, no one appears to have questioned the compatibility of Elizabeth's equable conservatism with the aspirations of new Elizabethanism that championed revival and fresh beginnings. In September 1956, even before the Suez watershed, a series of articles by Keith Waterhouse, published over three days in the country's biggest-selling tabloid, the *Daily Mirror*, signalled stirrings of disappointment. 'In four-and-a-half years the hope that a young reign of a Queen in her twenties would mark a new era for the Royal Family has been destroyed,' asserted Waterhouse.[16] His agent of destruction was the group of friends and courtiers surrounding Elizabeth, Philip and Margaret, whose aristocratic credentials (and overlaps of family and clan) he enumerated in some detail. Elizabeth had passed her thirtieth birthday in April; the landmark signalled the end of her 'young' reign, providing Waterhouse's prompt for stocktaking. Unhappily he concluded that it was 'still the age of the golden cobwebs'; he described Elizabeth's advisers and friends as 'much the same as... in Queen Victoria's palmier days'.[17] Importantly, he refrained from direct criticism of Elizabeth herself.

Disparagement of courtiers and palace flunkeys was to become a stock gripe. Elizabeth had taken tentative steps towards innovation: the short-term appointment of a Nigerian equerry, Major Aguiyi-Ironsi, two months ahead of her visit, and, in May, at Philip's suggestion, the first of a series of luncheon parties, at which men and women prominent across many fields, irrespective of background, joined the royal couple (potentially a challenging prospect for the woman who had admitted her terror of sitting next to people who might talk about topics outside her ken). Waterhouse suggested 'this should have been the age when kings mixed with commoners'. In principle Elizabeth was doing just that, though a courtier's explanation of the lunches as providing opportunities for 'feeling the pulse of the nation by contact with ordinary men and women in all walks of life in the community' was misleading: none of those invited was 'ordinary', and eight months passed before the first invitation was extended to a woman. It was small beer. When the vacancy arose for a new deputy master of the household in 1954, Elizabeth made a youthful appointment. Thirty-one-year-old Patrick Plunket was an Eton-educated ex-Irish Guardsman and Anglo-Irish peer, a friend since childhood, member of Elizabeth's dancing class and a former equerry to her father, described by the Queen Mother as 'someone I have known and loved since I held him in my arms soon after he was born'.[18] Public engagements brought both Elizabeth and Philip into contact with subjects of diverse backgrounds, but Elizabeth's immediate coterie remained as uncompromisingly patrician as the palace Guides company; a decade on, Queen Mary's warning about the narrowness of Elizabeth's circle had not yielded any noticeable response. In her Christmas broadcast in 1954, Elizabeth paid tribute to the unseen masses whose work was so essential to the country's economic wellbeing. Her Olympian tone, in addressing 'those of you whose lot is cast in dull and unenvied surroundings', whose 'monotonous' lives consist of 'dull repetitive work and... constant small adversities', suggested the gulf between her own life and theirs, an example of the 'very condescending and hieratic way [of talking]' that would shortly goad a Tory radical into devastating criticism.[19] After Elizabeth's visit to Paris in April 1957, Cynthia Gladwyn would conclude, 'she is quite a "chip off the old block", in that there is much like Queen Mary or the Princess Royal about her, for she is definitely royal'.[20] This was not the new way the

Daily Mirror wanted Elizabeth to embrace. 'The scientists, the writers, the designers, the explorers. They are the true new Elizabethans. They are the people who belong in the modern court of a modern Queen,' wrote Waterhouse.[21] It was not to be. Elizabeth's cousin, the Earl of Harewood, responsible for a new opera by Benjamin Britten staged six days after the coronation, attributed its failure to its 'unworthy' audience, including Elizabeth's court. 'Would the Queen's ministers and the diplomats and the court of Gloriana's day have proved so unreceptive to a grandiose new work as their counterparts in our second Elizabethan age?' he asked.[22] For the foreseeable future, the 'modern' aspect of Elizabeth's court was a question of manner, and set by Philip, who was described as 'handsome and informal, creating an easy democratic atmosphere in the wake of the Queen. He likes to pick out people at a party; to ask who they are, find out about them himself, crack jokes with them, get lost in the general melee... He shines out as a breezy sailor who has known what it is not to be a royalty.'[23]

In the wake of the *Mirror*'s criticisms, which echoed earlier, less widely publicized comments by Malcolm Muggeridge in the *New Statesman*, Elizabeth was poorly served by Conservative Party leadership procedure. Like Churchill's retirement, Eden's precipitate resignation necessitated the choice of a new prime minister. As previously, *The Times* explained, 'the ultimate responsibility... is the Queen's alone. It is a hard and heavy duty to discharge.'[24] That the same responsibility would not have been Elizabeth's under equivalent circumstances in the case of a Labour government, given differences in the way the Labour Party went about such things, consolidated for those so minded the conviction of Elizabeth as hand-in-glove with an old-fashioned (Tory) Establishment. Elizabeth took soundings from a senior party figure: her parents' friend, Lord Salisbury, the same aristocratic mandarin who had doubted Philip's suitability as a husband and threatened to resign from government in the event of Margaret marrying Townsend; he had been recommended to Michael Adeane by Eden. She also consulted Churchill. With the lord chancellor Lord Kilmuir, Salisbury offered cabinet ministers a choice of two candidates, Harold Macmillan and R. A. 'Rab' Butler. Most chose Macmillan, a view seconded by Churchill. Macmillan therefore was Elizabeth's choice. Neither backbench MPs nor party members had been consulted. The party was for Butler; so, too, were the press. Elizabeth's 'choice', which had involved no independent judgement, suggested she was the puppet of a grand (and elderly) cabal, at odds with grass-roots opinion.

Labour leaders, claimed the *Daily Herald,* considered that the Conservatives had 'brought the Crown into party politics by forcing the Queen to choose not only a new Prime Minister but a new leader of the Tory Party'.[25] Criticism focused on the process of leadership selection, with its requirement of royal involvement, rather than Elizabeth herself. Elizabeth had acted correctly, assisted by an assiduous Salisbury, though her decision-making pointed to a rubber-stamp quality to the royal prerogative. Together, monarch and ministers had selected the old guard's favourite, a son-in-law of the Duke of Devonshire, a man of patrician inclinations, albeit his background was less illustrious than his tweedy outdoorsiness implied. A complacent *Times* reported that Elizabeth had discharged her responsibility well.[26]

❧

As ever, Pathé cameramen were on hand to record Elizabeth's departure for Lisbon. She would be reunited with Philip ahead of their joint arrival in the Portuguese capital for a four-day state visit. In its commentary, Pathé wished Elizabeth 'God speed... on her double mission of private reunion and international good will'.[27] On both counts Elizabeth would succeed. Husband and wife alighted smiling from the Portuguese state barge, rowed by forty liveried oarsmen, that carried them across the Tagus on 16 February 1957. They had met two days earlier, out of sight of crowds, at Montijo military airfield, Elizabeth and her lady-in-waiting sporting false beards, after a bevy of photographs of a bearded Philip had accompanied his solo tour (an amused Philip, by contrast, was clean shaven for the reunion). Their visit was notable for the crowds' enthusiasm and the warmth of Elizabeth's response. Wherever husband and wife travelled, their motorcade was slowed and, frequently, stopped by onlookers who broke through police cordons; in Lisbon, half the city's population 'jammed the pavements to watch the Royal parade. Many fainted in the crush'; others, crowding mud flats alongside the river, waved as they sank up to their knees.[28] Elizabeth and Philip's evident enjoyment refuted suggestions of discord. At home again, Elizabeth honoured her husband publicly. Mountbatten had written to his sister, Queen Louise of Sweden, 'Lilibet has got the new Prime Minister – in consultation with Commonwealth colleagues – to ask for Philip to be made "The Prince" on return from this tour.'[29] Created Duke of Edinburgh and a Royal Highness by his father-in-law in 1947, Philip now became a prince of the United Kingdom, the grant gazetted on 22 February. Four days later, Elizabeth formalized his entitlement to a full verse of the National Anthem, an honour he shared with only his wife and mother-in-law. A decade after their marriage, Elizabeth's bestowal and Philip's acceptance showed husband and wife in public accord. 'Action belies rumours of a rift,' conceded the *Daily Mirror*.[30] 'In our eyes she was first and foremost the wife of her husband and the mother of her children,' Nikita Khrushchev had concluded after meeting Elizabeth the previous April.[31] Their visit to Portugal and its aftermath enabled Elizabeth and Philip to give substance to half of the Soviet leader's assessment.

Rumours did not, of course, disappear at once. Philip's fidelity remained a favourite subject for speculation, fuelled by the separations of the couple's lives, their lack of physical demonstrativeness and the respectfulness of Philip's behaviour towards Elizabeth in public. (Even in private, there were anomalies: Philip's brisk, unconcealed irritation at moments; the bottles of Chanel scent given to Elizabeth as birthday presents not by Philip but, at Philip's suggestion, by his comptroller, Boy Browning: 'You have discovered just the very thing I particularly wanted... I am already using it and, I hope, smelling all the better for it!!' Elizabeth had thanked Browning in April 1955.[32]) In the short term, stories about Philip's imagined liaisons with actresses and showgirls dwindled. The death in September of the photographer Baron and Parker's resignation helped. Baron had been a driving force behind a Soho-based bachelor lunch society called the Thursday Club, attended by Philip with Parker. Partly on account of its raffish locale, the Thursday Club inspired colourful gossip. But stories that Philip used an apartment loaned him by Baron for assignations with an unnamed 'party girl' were harder to countenance with Baron dead.

Visiting Elizabeth in May, Eleanor Roosevelt described her as 'still more serious, as one might expect her to be under the burden of her duties'.[33] Elizabeth's grounds for seriousness were not confined to her public life: one observer referred tactfully to the royal couple's 'ups and downs'.[34] French magazine *Point de vue* captioned a sombre photograph of Elizabeth on its cover in 1959 'Sick? Disappointed Wife?' Two years later, another French magazine, *Noir et blanc*, reproduced an even less happy image under the headline 'Elizabeth jealous...' Such conjecture accounted for Mountbatten's entry into the fray. In the guise of an unnamed 'lifelong friend', he told journalist Audrey Whiting in December 1962 that, for Elizabeth, life without Philip was unimaginable, she was more in love with him than she had ever been and without him she would 'retire to the country for a very long time'.[35]

⌘

In August 1957, an Italian monarchist, Commendatore Renato Marmirol, requested from the British ambassador in Rome a travel visa for Britain. His purpose, he explained, was to fight a duel.[36] His intended victim was an improbable villain, a thirty-three-year-old Conservative peer of unorthodox opinions, John Grigg, Baron Altrincham.

The forum for Altrincham's unorthodoxy was a magazine of small circulation, the *National and English Review*, which he edited, and an essay he contributed to a monarchy-themed issue in which he revisited Waterhouse's protests about the exclusivity of Elizabeth's court and her immediate circle of friends. Altrincham argued for a less socially lopsided royal establishment, a 'truly classless and Commonwealth Court'; he rejected Dermot Morrah's version of Elizabeth's role, suggesting instead that she perform the 'seemingly impossible task of being at once ordinary and extraordinary'; and, unlike Waterhouse, he criticized Elizabeth herself as ultimately responsible for employing the advisers who crafted for her a public persona that was prim, remote and aloof. Altrincham focused on Elizabeth's style of public speaking and her apparent narrowness of outlook. Significantly in light of Elizabeth's own view of her task, he compared her unfavourably with her grandfather. In George V's scripted speeches and broadcasts he identified an 'authentic', personal quality. Of Elizabeth he wrote, 'the personality conveyed by the utterances which are put into her mouth is that of a priggish schoolgirl, captain of the hockey team, a prefect, and a recent candidate for Confirmation'. Later he would argue that 'she had tended... to deliver her speeches monotonously, mechanically and with an absence of expression', a reaction that may have been hinted at in the Queen Mother's warning to Elizabeth in Canada in 1951 that she deliver her radio broadcasts with 'inflection'.[37]

Altrincham's was a balanced thesis. Elizabeth, he wrote, possessed 'dignity, a sense of duty, and (so far as one can judge) goodness of heart'. Her public manner as queen, however, isolated her from the majority of her subjects, distancing her from current concerns – playwright John Osborne would suggest that, under Elizabeth, monarchy had become 'a splendid triviality'. Altrincham's criticisms echoed the anxieties of Jock Colville, and even Queen Mary, a decade earlier; encountering Elizabeth in August, James Pope-Hennessy noted 'perfect debutante manners'.[38] Altrincham's view of starched-shirt courtiers was probably Philip's, too.

In the post-Suez climate of embattled national humiliation, the insider attack on Elizabeth on the part of the Etonian peer whipped up a fury. In Altrincham itself, the town council convened an extraordinary meeting and, on 7 August, issued a statement 'most strongly deplor[ing] the article written by Lord Altrincham'. The council wanted, it wrote, 'to dissociate this borough from the comments contained in that article. At the same time, we desire that it should be known by Her Majesty the Queen that no town has a greater sense of loyalty and devotion to the Crown than the borough of Altrincham.'[39] The Archbishop of Canterbury rallied to his sovereign's cause, insisting that 'her subjects feel that the Queen fulfils their highest ideals in her combination of a proper formality and restraint on the one hand and of a full, intelligent and happy relationship with as many of her subjects as possible on the other'.[40] Altrincham himself was physically attacked by a member of the right-wing League of Empire Loyalists; letters sent to him included razor blades and faeces. But neither the newspaper-reading public in its entirety nor all of those closest to Elizabeth shared this hifalutin' outrage. Both Elizabeth's assistant private secretaries,

Martin Charteris and Edward Ford, privately acknowledged grounds for Altrincham's comments, judging them 'the best thing that happened to the Palace for years'.[41] The twenty-year-old Marquess of Londonderry went a step further in a letter in Altrincham's defence published in the *New Statesman*. Lord Londonderry, the nephew of Elizabeth's childhood friend Lady Mairi Vane-Tempest-Stewart, dismissed as 'ludicrously and nauseatingly incongruous in a modern democracy' the idea 'that the Monarchy is a sacrosanct head of the [national] family'.[42]

Altrincham was unrepentant. In an interview with Pathé, he pursued his attack, reiterating that 'the trouble about the Court is that it's all drawn from one small section of this country. It should be drawn from every country of the Commonwealth and every section of the community.'[43] At the end of the month he insisted 'the Queen's choice of official advisers must surely be open to comment and criticism', untroubled that such criticism could only be directed at Elizabeth herself for placing her trust in second-rate employees.[44] In a second essay, 'The Rumpus and After', Altrincham underlined his own position as constructive critic and committed monarchist. Elizabeth, he wrote, 'must know that she is loved, but if her character is what I believe it to be she will not mistake adulation for the loyalty that stands all tests'.

At Balmoral Elizabeth reacted angrily to Altrincham's appraisal; she would never have any truck with Londonderry's challenge to her symbolic role as head of the national family. James Pope-Hennessy's description of her that August as 'a little careworn, with lines from nose to mouth' reflects her strain. 'She is clearly living at great tension and does not give an impression of happiness,' he concluded. 'Her hands are thin and worried-looking... One feels that the spring is wound up very tight.'[45] Elizabeth could not be expected to agree with her plausible and mild-mannered critic. She had modelled her behaviour on the example of a father whose memory she revered; among the courtiers Altrincham deplored were those who had served her parents before her. Her mother was still alive and deeply protective of George VI's memory. Elizabeth was not imaginative. As the Dowager Duchess of Devonshire described her, 'she was <u>very</u> practical'.[46] Diligently and undemonstratively, she undertook the business of monarchy as understood by her immediate predecessors, an approach shaped by her personal modesty, which made her unassertive, and her royal dignity that discounted playing to the gallery. While the hullabaloo lasted, she did nothing at all. Instead, she postponed a decision she and Philip had already taken to discontinue debutantes' presentations in favour of more socially inclusive royal garden parties; the lord chamberlain's announcement made clear that 'for some time – in fact since 1954 – the Queen has had in mind the general pattern of official entertaining at Buckingham Palace, including the problem of Presentation Parties'.[47] Court presentations continued for a further year – 'just to show', a courtier explained, 'that she wasn't going to bow to Altrincham'.[48] It was Elizabeth's version of the stubborn mantra of her great-great-grandmother, 'The Queen will not be dictated to', in line with Macmillan's view that she 'mean[t] to be Queen and not a puppet'.[49] Unsurprisingly, remembered Martin Charteris, courtiers criticized by Altrincham 'disliked it very much'.[50] Elizabeth countenanced an innovation of Philip's: she agreed that the Maundy Thursday service take place in alternate years in cathedrals outside London.

Altrincham had asked if Elizabeth would 'have the wisdom to give her children an education very different from her own'. Charles had already spent a year at Hill House, a private school in Knightsbridge. It was an escape from the royal schoolroom quite different from Elizabeth's sequestered schooling by Crawfie, although his visits to museums and London monuments resembled Elizabeth's outings with Queen Mary (albeit his grandmother did not accompany Charles). Altrincham's point was that Charles should mix 'with children who will one day be bus drivers, doctors, engineers, etc'; that a third of Hill House's pupils were of overseas origin was diversity of a different sort. Weeks after Altrincham's attack, Elizabeth and Philip moved Charles to Cheam in Surrey, the same preparatory school Philip had attended. It had once been known as 'The Little House of Lords'. Philip explained their hope that Charles 'go to school with other boys of his generation and learn to live with other children, and to absorb from childhood the discipline imposed by education with others', a rationale of superficial plausibility that appeared to ignore the uniqueness of Charles's position and Elizabeth's own remarkable discipline that owed nothing to being educated alongside her peers.[51] It was a choice that did nothing to placate Altrincham et al. and did not suit the shy and sensitive Charles.

But 'Moucher' Devonshire had been correct in her assessment of Elizabeth's nature as practical. Elizabeth took steps to improve her public speaking, including guidance from the prime minister, and to forge at least the semblance of a closer bond between monarch and people through the use of television. In March, ahead of the controversy, she had agreed to the televising of her Christmas broadcast, setting aside a deep-rooted antipathy; at the beginning of October, she made known through Commander Colville her willingness that her speech from the throne at the State Opening of Parliament also be filmed; incorporated in the programme of her visit to Canada the same month was a live television broadcast watched by 14 million Canadians. At the same time, the courtiers responsible for the speeches derided by Altrincham took opportunities to remind Elizabeth's listeners of the loving nature of the relationship between subjects and their young sovereign. Opening the Canadian parliament in Ottawa in October, in her coronation gown and the towering kokoshnik-style Russian fringe tiara that had once belonged to her great-grandmother

Queen Alexandra, Elizabeth quoted Elizabeth I: 'I count the glory of my crown, that I have reigned with your loves'. She added, 'Now here in the New World I say to you that it is my wish that in the years before me I may so reign in Canada and be so remembered.' On Elizabeth's part it was as much a reminder of what was due to her as a request, though in keeping with the language of service and public humility that she embraced lifelong; the following week, she reported later, she was surprised on her visit to the States by what she interpreted as Americans' need to be liked and the apparent lack of self-confidence of the president, Eisenhower. Unelected and at ease in her position despite the summer's well-publicized criticism, Elizabeth knew that she could count on more solid foundations than the short-term loyalty of voters. The wife of one of Eisenhower's staff in Washington described her as 'very certain, and very comfortable in her role'.[52] Pope-Hennessy had observed 'that she clearly does not *feel* inadequate'.[53]

Elizabeth's Christmas broadcast, filmed in the Long Library at Sandringham, offered a careful riposte to recent scrutiny. 'I am not an actress,' Elizabeth repeatedly told the BBC producer Peter Dimmock and, at the end of a challenging year, the text of the seven-minute broadcast, though mostly Philip's wording, was a sincere reflection of her feelings requiring no dissembling.[54] A nervous Elizabeth stared directly at the viewer. She acknowledged that she must seem 'a rather remote figure'. Pointedly she talked of 'withstand[ing] the subtle corruption of the cynics so that we can show the world that we are not afraid of the future'; she castigated 'unthinking people who carelessly throw away ageless ideals', and she commended honesty and the value of self-restraint over self-interest. In place of the promises of duty and dedication which had characterized earlier speeches, she offered her audience 'my heart and my devotion', a more intimate connection than her natural inclination, which Pope-Hennessy assessed as a 'kind and business-like, and somewhat impersonal' engagement.[55] She reminded viewers of the affection she inspired across the globe as their queen: the tumultuous welcome she had received on her visits to Portugal, France, Denmark and the United States; 'the loyalty and enthusiasm of my Canadian people', by which she had been 'overwhelmed'. She ended with a quotation from Bunyan's *Pilgrim's Progress*: 'My marks and scars I carry with me, to be a witness for me that I have fought his battles who will now be my rewarder.' Her delivery was livelier than often in the past. With dignity and apparent candour, Elizabeth had articulated a straightforward manifesto that for many of her audience was deeply moving, her commitment to 'religion, morality in personal and public life... [and] honesty'. Less discreet than its British counterpart, the American press interpreted it as a direct – and successful – response to her critics. Typical was the verdict of the *New York Herald Tribune*: 'Against the background of recent critical comment and discussion of her conduct of the monarchy, the thirty-one-year-old Queen rose serenely to the occasion.'[56] Boosted by the broadcast, crowds outside Sandringham's church of St Mary Magdalene on the first Sunday after Christmas reached a record 10,000.

Of course, discussion was not quelled indefinitely. Ahead of Elizabeth's state visit to the Netherlands in the spring of 1958, the *People* returned to the fray. It made much of the contrast between British royal formality and the seeming ordinariness of Queen Juliana's life, her enjoyment of shopping for bargains, her daughters' bicycling and seaside holidays, her decision to do away with curtseying. For the *People*, the tour offered Elizabeth an opportunity for a 'close-up peep at a really democratic monarchy'. 'One thing is certain,' it told readers. 'When the Queen comes back from Holland she will realise that, by contrast with Queen Juliana, her life at Buckingham Palace and Windsor Castle is surrounded by Victorian pomp and ceremony.'[57] It was what the Queen Mother labelled 'headliny, gossipy, untruthful kind of writing' and overlooked any possibility that Victorian pomp and ceremony did not concern Elizabeth unduly: adjuncts of her life since childhood, she was happy to retain them as long as they contributed to royal dignity and were not excessively impractical.[58] In 1958, however, there were few serious calls to reform the monarchy in line with the bicycling Dutch. Instead, later in the year, semi-official commentator Dermot Morrah published *The Queen at Work*. It revealed 'the Queen as a woman trained and dedicated to a unique and lonely and exalted office, and her day's round to be as arduous as that of any of her most industrious subjects'; it restated the importance of her overseas role as 'a symbol of unity' to 'each independent nation, and indeed to each dependent colony' of the Commonwealth.[59] Serialization in the *Daily Express* suggests Morrah's thesis was a popular one. It refuted aspects of Altrincham's attack, but neither Morrah nor the Elizabeth of the television screens dispelled adverse comment that had seized on royal philistinism and showed no sign of abating. For the foreseeable future, Elizabeth's principal interest remained racing, Philip's sailing and polo. 'I cannot help regretting that she has not got more interesting interests,' Cynthia Gladwyn had lamented in Paris the previous spring. 'Apart from horses and racing I could not discover anything that interested her, such as the arts, or gardens, or books. This seems to apply equally to Prince Philip.'[60] A keen-eyed television viewer at home noticed Elizabeth's response to paintings in the Louvre during her Paris visit. 'Added to those paintings the Queen [had said she] wanted to see, a couple by Degas showing horses! The Queen... seemed delighted by this. She went round the others quite sombrely... and coming to the end, the President, Monsieur Coty, came up to her and, quite suddenly, the Queen was lit up – lively and loquacious and full of spirits.'[61] Harold Nicolson concluded that it was true 'that the Queen was dull and surrounded by dull people and that she only cared for horses'.[62] Less waspish than Nicolson, Macmillan considered the shortcoming largely irrelevant in the face of Elizabeth's appetite for service: 'She does not enjoy "society". She likes her horses. But she loves her duty.'

In January, Elizabeth agreed to be photographed working at her desk at Buckingham Palace. Under an anglepoise lamp, amid a clutter of photographs and a vase of rusty chrysanthemums, she opens a brimming leather despatch box, one aspect of the arduous round applauded by Morrah. The boxes arrived daily. Daily, dutiful Elizabeth read their contents, annotating and commenting where necessary. Macmillan admired her consistency and assiduity; he admired the accumulation of political experience absorbed so quickly from so many documents read, noted, remembered; he admired her level of knowledge that would compel successive prime ministers to value their weekly audiences – as the French president, de Gaulle, concluded a year later, 'she was well informed about everything'.[63] Macmillan admired the 'brightly shining eyes which are her chief beauty' and treated her with avuncular gallantry, delighting in her sympathy, neither the first nor the last of Elizabeth's ministers to be dazzled by their royal mistress.[64]

ॐ

'It would be so marvellous if you thought of having more children,' the Queen Mother had written to her daughter on 12 April 1956.[65] As so often, Elizabeth would find herself in agreement with her mother, despite statements by Philip which appeared to indicate his preference for a small family. She fell pregnant in the late spring of 1959, ten years after her last pregnancy, and gave birth to her third child, Andrew Albert Christian Edward, the following February. It was not, as a section of the public assumed, an accident. Elizabeth told Martin Charteris, 'I am going to have a baby, which I have been trying to do for some time,' probably since Philip's return from his tour of the southern hemisphere in early 1957.[66] She shared her news with Macmillan at an audience on 15 June, then, despite morning sickness, carried out as planned a six-week visit to Canada. She did, however, cancel a visit to Ghana in October. Instead, she invited the Ghanaian leader, Kwame Nkrumah, to Balmoral.

It was an unusual invitation on Elizabeth's part, the first she had issued to a Commonwealth leader. Two years earlier, Ghana, formerly the Gold Coast, had become the first of Britain's tropical African colonies to achieve independence. At its helm was Nkrumah, its prime minister since 1951, accused by Lord Salisbury of 'crude, barbaric nationalism'.[67] Nkrumah's instincts were republican – later he made a series of speeches denouncing imperialism – but he felt a strong personal attachment to Elizabeth, reportedly telling his private secretary, 'It would be too bad for that young girl if we left the Commonwealth.'[68] The 'young girl' herself certainly shared his views. She made Nkrumah a privy councillor. This double compliment of a personal invitation to one of Elizabeth's private homes and membership of the Privy Council reaped dividends: in January 1960, Macmillan told Elizabeth that Nkrumah had indicated Ghana's willingness to recognize her as head of the Commonwealth even were it to become, as it shortly did, a republic, the precedent already established by India.[69] His stay at Balmoral recalled visits to Windsor in the previous reign: a kilted Charles and Anne accompanied their parents and Nkrumah for walks along the terrace. The family context prevented Elizabeth's diplomatic overtures from appearing coercive.

Thoughts of family preoccupied Elizabeth as she prepared for her newest baby. The week before her confinement, her visitors at Buckingham Palace included 'a smiling Lord Mountbatten'. 'There is much speculation about the reason for the visits,' papers reported.[70] The reason concerned the vexed question of the royal family's name. In the seven years since Churchill and Queen Mary outflanked Mountbatten at Philip's expense, Philip's resentment had remained a source of tension between husband and wife, and Mountbatten had continued to plot and push. After visiting the royal family at Sandringham after Christmas, Macmillan referred in his diary to Philip's 'almost brutal attitude to the Queen over all this'; he relished a Colonel Blimpish anecdote in which a flustered Duke of Gloucester had told him that Elizabeth was 'in a terrible state' because 'Prince Philip's in the library wanting to change the family name to Mountbatten'.[71] In staunching this running sore, Elizabeth was at pains that all concerned understood not only that the decision had been her intention for some time and was her own (explanations of the Duke of Gloucester's notwithstanding), but that it would give her particular personal pleasure. In late January, Rab Butler had reported to Macmillan that it was a change 'on which she absolutely set her heart'. This was justification enough for the prime minister, who, with an old-fashioned view of marriage, recorded, 'The Queen only wishes (properly enough) to do something to please her husband – with whom she is desperately in love.'[72]

What Elizabeth did for her husband – clearly at his instigation, if Macmillan's view of Philip's 'brutality' on this score is reliable – was to incorporate the name 'Mountbatten' within her family's names, without changing the dynasty's name from Windsor. It was a tactful compromise by which Elizabeth satisfied the claims of both family and royal family, and made easier by the death of her grandmother and James Pope-Hennessy's suspicion, in the summer of 1957, that Elizabeth had taken a step away from Queen Mary.[73] Elizabeth's statement to the Privy Council made clear her even-handedness and the double nature of the pressures upon her: 'The Queen has always wanted, without changing the name of the Royal House established by her grandfather, to associate the name of her husband with her own and his descendants.' That Philip should have drawn pleasure from a decision that placed Elizabeth under considerable strain, to perpetuate *ad aeternum* a name he had held for nine months prior to his marriage, says much about his disgruntlement within the palace, or perhaps the persuasiveness of his fanatically ambitious uncle's lobbying. Butler revealed Elizabeth's tearfulness during discussions; Macmillan's cabinet reacted with ambivalence. Nevertheless, on 8 February, Elizabeth's statement granted the name 'Mountbatten-Windsor' to those non-royal descendants who lacked the style 'Royal Highness' and to 'female descendants who marry and their descendants'. Public reaction was mixed. Staunchly anti-Mountbatten, the *Daily Express* suggested that, under family pressure, Elizabeth had had no choice: 'she sympathises with her husband's feelings and more particularly with the overtures of his uncle.'[74]

Eleven days later, after private antenatal classes with former nurse Betty Parsons and with expectant crowds outside Buckingham Palace, thirty-three-year-old Elizabeth gave birth to her third child, to whom, as a boy, the changes would not apply. She named him Andrew, an anglicization of Philip's father's name, Andrea, as well as a tribute to Scotland. Reaction was positive at home and abroad. For the Commonwealth queen, the premier of Queensland, Frank Nicklin, chose locally grown Cooktown orchids, which were flown to London by jet and delivered to the palace.[75] Elizabeth described the baby as 'adorable and... very good, and putting on weight well. Both the older children are completely riveted by him and all in all, he's going to be terribly spoilt by all of us, I'm sure!' Her delight in Andrew and happiness with Philip are clear on contact sheets in the archives of the Victoria & Albert Museum, from a sitting with Cecil Beaton weeks later. Anne, Elizabeth, Charles and

Philip surround Andrew's cot. In a picture that was not released to the public, Elizabeth beams at her smiling husband.[76] Of a sitting marred by his dislike of Philip ('this hearty naval type') and Anne, with her 'high fog horn voice', 'shrewishness' and 'minny mouse feet', a crotchety Beaton recorded that Elizabeth 'seemed affable enough but showed no signs of real interest in anything... Not one word of conversation.'[77] It was Cynthia Gladwyn's lament of the paucity of Elizabeth's interests again, and it would recur over succeeding decades.

❧

Elizabeth met Margaret's future husband at least a year before her sister. In October 1957, Antony Armstrong-Jones, previously one of Baron's assistants, photographed Elizabeth and her family in the garden at Buckingham Palace. The best-known image from that sitting is both idyllic and poignant, the family of four arranged around a stone bridge, autumn sunlight in the trees' sparse branches. Charles and Anne sit on a shelf of rock, looking at a book, their parents looking down at them from the bridge. Elizabeth wears a smart frock and, four rows of pearls. Philip is smiling tentatively; Elizabeth's expression is harder to read. Only Anne appears entirely at ease and happy. In another picture taken at the same time, Elizabeth and Anne ignore the book open on Elizabeth's lap and gaze adoringly at Philip. Without much conviction, Charles, isolated in the centre of the shot, strokes a corgi. Both are picturesque images of separation. In the first, though the parents' focus is undoubtedly their children, the distance between the two pairings cannot be scaled by parents or offspring. Hard to discern are the currents of affection once noted of Elizabeth and Margaret and their parents: between father and mother, between siblings, between parents and children. It is a curiously formal image, despite its outdoor setting and elegant domesticity. Philip's frozen stance never-theless conveys formidable energy. There can be no doubt of the family's guiding spirit.

With the announcement of his engagement to Margaret on 26 February 1960, Armstrong-Jones's role shifted from that of external observer. He had been invited to Balmoral in the summer and, on the pretext of designing a pergola, to Sandringham in January. There, despite having proposed and been accepted the previous month, he formally asked Elizabeth's permission to marry her sister. A public announcement was postponed until the week after Andrew's birth. On Elizabeth's behalf Commander Colville then announced that 'Both the Queen and Prince Philip said they are delighted because this is such an obviously happy match.' Their delight was quite different from the reaction of Tony's father and a handful of his close friends, who questioned his suitedness to royal life and its constraints. Elizabeth was no less aware of the gulf between her sister and the photographer, but either buried – or did not conceive in the first place – similar reservations, relieved at Margaret's happiness, reassured by the couple's shared interests in art and the performing arts, charmed by Tony himself, determined not to provide grounds for a second disappointment for Margaret. Her reaction mirrored her mother's. Describing Margaret as 'so serenely happy', the Queen Mother did not look for worms in the bud.[78] Her reward was closer, better relations with her younger daughter than for some time, Margaret later thanking her 'for being so absolutely heavenly all the time we were engaged, you were so encouraging and angelic'.[79] The wedding was fixed for the beginning of May, and a decision taken that, like the coronation, it should be televised. In her father's place, Philip led Margaret down the long abbey aisle.

More than any other member of her immediate family Margaret had married outside the royal fold. Her choice of a professional photographer, albeit the Etonian son of a successful lawyer and, through his mother's second marriage, stepson of an Irish peer, brought the crown into contact with the creative meritocracy identified by Keith Waterhouse four years earlier as appropriate courtiers of the new Elizabethan age. It did not lead – nor did anyone by now anticipate it leading – to an efflorescence of court culture or a realigning of the court at the centre of the nation's cultural life. At a stroke the marriage of the sovereign's sister offered a possible response to Elizabeth's detractors, yet the contrast between Elizabeth's court and the miniature court afterwards centred on Margaret and Tony at Kensington Palace seemed to emphasize the free-spiritedness of one and the traditionalist aspic of the other. Unabashedly, or with simple lack of imagination, Buckingham Palace had announced Elizabeth's first public outing after Andrew's birth: with Philip, the Queen Mother, Margaret and Tony, she was to be the guest of the Duke of Beaufort for the annual Badminton horse trials that began on her birthday. Before that date arrived, however, plans were revealed 'to display masterpieces from the royal private collections in a gallery adapted from the bombed-out chapel of Buckingham Palace'. It was described as 'a departure from tradition'.[80] In making accessible to the public treasures from the world's finest royal collection, in a sophisticated exhibitions programme that began in 1962, it became one of the great innovations of the reign of horse-loving Elizabeth.

CHAPTER XII

*'Her time and energy divided between three duties –
those to her country, her husband and her children'*

❧

'ALREADY THE PEOPLE sense that Her Majesty is in sympathy with their aspirations and hopes,' a Pathé newsreel told cinema-goers, describing early encounters during Elizabeth's rescheduled visit to Ghana over twelve days in November 1961. Commentary did not explain the nature of Ghanaian aspiration, nor grounds for Elizabeth's sympathy.

An exuberant response to Elizabeth's visit on the part of Ghanaians, including the 350,000 who lined her route from the airport, made the statement plausible. It was a visit that had come close to cancellation. The previous week, bomb explosions in Accra provoked fears for Elizabeth's safety; within parliament a groundswell of opposition to Nkrumah's authoritarianism questioned the wisdom of appearing to endorse his undemocratic regime. Macmillan was anxious that the trip proceed, Elizabeth too. Speeches made in September by Nkrumah in eastern Europe and China gave rise to concern that the strutting president felt closer to the Eastern bloc than the Commonwealth. The possibility of communist footholds in Africa troubled Macmillan and the new American president, John F. Kennedy, as much as Elizabeth.

Elizabeth's feelings, as they survive in available sources, reveal the importance she attached to her Commonwealth visits and her view of their purpose. She had made clear to Macmillan her frustration at parliamentarians determined to keep her at home. The prime minister told his press secretary that Elizabeth's response to the idea of cancellation was indignation. 'The House of Commons, she thought, should not show lack of moral fibre in this way. She took very seriously her Commonwealth responsibilities'; she did not wish to be considered a mascot, she resented decisions taken on the basis of her sex and, presumably, womanly fragility.[1] On 10 November, the Queen Mother wrote to Elizabeth, 'I am sure that you were right to go, & I am sure that if one listened to all the faint hearts, one would never go anywhere.'[2] In his diary, Macmillan described Elizabeth – the 'splendid girl' – as 'absolutely determined'. Accurately assessing her confidence in her own role, he recorded, 'She has great faith in the work she can do in the Commonwealth especially.'[3]

Welcoming Elizabeth to Washington in 1957, Eisenhower had told her, 'Even more than the pleasure which your visit brings us, we're conscious of its importance because of its effect in strengthening the ties of friendship that bind our two countries together.' This was the light in which Elizabeth had been encouraged to regard royal tours since her parents' pre-war visits to France and Canada. In Paris and Washington in the wake of the Suez Crisis, she had seen for herself the power of the royal presence to bolster faltering international relations. For Elizabeth, travelling to Ghana represented the fulfilment of a promise made to Nkrumah at Balmoral two years earlier and her own opportunity to woo a politician susceptible to communist flattery. 'How silly I should look if

I was scared to visit Ghana and then Khrushchev went and had a good reception,' she told Macmillan. Like her premier, Elizabeth understood that Nkrumah's defection could weaken the Commonwealth, especially after South Africa's departure in the spring in the face of fellow members' horror at apartheid. Australian prime minister Robert Menzies had claimed in 1954 that her presence in the country stirred 'the most profound and passionate feelings of loyalty and devotion'. In Ghana, despite Nkrumah's declaration of a republic the year before and saddened by events in the country in which she had celebrated her twenty-first birthday, Elizabeth intended to stir loyalty and devotion to the Commonwealth ideal.

Her confidence in her ability to achieve her end did not arise from egotism. Across the globe she had won golden opinions. In the spring, a million Indians had welcomed her to New Delhi; later in the month, as queen of the newly independent Sierra Leone, she would be received rapturously in Freetown, the *Guardian* describing *Britannia*'s arrival 'followed by a sort of waterborne riot. Dozens of small fishing boats were being furiously paddled in the wake of the yacht... they gathered at her stern, some in real danger of being crushed, bumping wildly together, and the ceremonies at the quayside were conducted against a cheerful background of strident shouting and an occasional song'.[4] Past experience encouraged Elizabeth to trust her reception by the Ghanaian people, and she was determined to win over Nkrumah, which she did. Photographs of the jewelled Queen dancing with a grinning president splashed newspapers across the globe. Subsequent American finance of Ghana's Upper Volta dam project successfully trumped Soviet overtures.

The strength of Elizabeth's commitment to the Commonwealth, evident in her obduracy over Ghana despite concerns for her safety, has been variously interpreted. Macmillan himself claimed that 'the responsibilities of the UK monarchy had so shrunk that if you left it at that you might as well have a film star'. The Commonwealth, by contrast, maintained Elizabeth's globalism, even as the tendency through the 1960s for newly independent colonies to become republics, rejecting Elizabeth as head of state, challenged the idea of the crown's centrality to the fledgling association. Elizabeth had inherited the grandest monarchy in Europe, in trappings, rhetoric and popular acclaim still a largely Victorian conception. Her attachment to the Commonwealth that replaced her father's and grandfather's empire, and her decision to embrace a central role as mediator and torchbearer, endowed her personally with vestiges of similar grandeur even as the monarchy itself declined in splendour with Britain's eclipse as a world power during the second half of the twentieth century. That this should have been her principal aim, however, would be uncharacteristic. More than other children of her generation, Elizabeth had grown up feeling a personal connection to the Empire: at the time of her father's accession, one newspaper considered her already, 'so early in life', dedicated to its service. She felt a loyalty to her inheritance; an understanding of the Commonwealth as a worldwide family of nations linked by loyalty to the monarch was part of her ideological bequest from her father. It was inevitable she would seek to preserve it and regard this preservation as part of her duty. In Australia in 1954, she had described her hope that her visit had 'demonstrated that the Crown is a human link between all the peoples who owe allegiance to me – an allegiance of mutual love and respect, and never of compulsion'.

Shrewdly Elizabeth assessed her Ghanaian host. She was surprised, she wrote to Henry Porchester, by Nkrumah's combination of vainglory and naivety. More revealing of her personal outlook was her view of his perspective as short-term. To her aristocratic correspondent, himself the heir to a hereditary peerage, England's forty-first monarch since Alfred noted that Nkrumah did not look beyond his own lifetime – with surprise, disdain or envy on her part?[5]

While sovereignty was not for sharing, Elizabeth entrusted a key aspect of her own long-term planning to her husband. In decisions affecting her family life, Philip's was the casting vote. His choices more than Elizabeth's shaped the upbringing of the heir to the throne, Charles. Not all proved serendipitous.

Received wisdom on the post-abdication monarchy argues that the shadow of that cataclysm has continued to imprint royal thinking. It may be that Edward VIII's perceived choice of self over service sanctified the doctrine of duty embraced apologetically by George VI and with zeal by his daughter. If so, his successors have devoted less thought to the underlying causes of Edward's disaffection. Exemplary public servants, they have successfully kicked over his traces. Aided by Queen Mary, George VI took steps to ensure that his own heir rejected her uncle's primrose path; she in turn proved less assiduous in providing Charles with the bedrock of untroubled happiness that was the source of her own early confidence in her position, or the conspicuously close and loving relationship between parents and child that, in contrast to Edward, played a part in her desire to follow in her father's footsteps. In his abdication broadcast, Edward had described as Bertie's 'one matchless blessing' a 'happy home'; at the same time a Sunday paper celebrated the 'joy in one another' of the new family on the throne, and, in the provinces, a journalist spared a thought for ten-year-old Elizabeth: that despite the seriousness of the life ahead, hers would be a 'joyous childhood'. As a young mother, Martin Charteris suggested, Elizabeth was 'always... doing her duty'.[6] The duty in question was not primarily domestic or maternal. It lay outside Charles's nursery – in the Villa Guardamangia on Malta and her round of public duties; after her accession, in the red boxes of Whitehall documents, audiences, investitures and the lengthy overseas visits that consumed weeks and months of Charles's childhood. As queen, Elizabeth was too busy to make her children's 'joy' her priority, busier than her own parents had been during her childhood. She spent time with Charles when she could; at other times, even her racehorses made more pressing claims on her attention. Years later, the Queen Mother would write to Elizabeth about photographs of foals in the royal stables, 'I like to think of you poring over them & dreaming dreams!'; she made no equivalent comment about photographs of Charles or Anne.[7] 'She treated Charles very nicely,' remembered a member of the royal household in 2002, 'but she was never warm. There were no open arms, no hugs. I can hardly ever remember her kissing him.'[8] For a child, emotional reserve can appear remarkably like lack of affection. Anne would suggest that Elizabeth's children comprehended and accepted the unusual circumstances of their upbringing: 'we understood what the limitations were in time and the responsibilities placed on her as monarch in the things she had to do and the travels she had to make, but I don't think that any of us, for a second, thought she didn't care for us in exactly the same way as any mother did'.[9] 'I miss them when I'm away for long,' Elizabeth told scientist Niels Bohr, during her state visit to Denmark in May 1957, 'but they understand why I have to go.'[10]

Elizabeth had been sincere in the hope she expressed to her parents on her marriage, of bringing up her children in a happy atmosphere of love and fairness. Fairness was a quality she possessed in abundance; those who knew her best acknowledged her intense love for Philip and her pleasure in her children. For the most part she struggled to give expression to her feelings, stamped indelibly with a mindset that elevated emotional continence above every spontaneous effusion. The little girl 'bright as an atom of radium' had grown into a woman who restrained emotion in order to behave as uncontentiously as possible. It was a family trait from which she would never depart.

Lord Harewood discerned the same rigid self-discipline in his mother, Elizabeth's aunt the Princess Royal, whom he described as 'conditioned to communicate only on as uncontroversial a level as possible... the result of an upbringing which discouraged direct discussion or any display of emotion'.[11] At first Elizabeth's habit of dispassionate detachment won universal commendation: in 1954, the colonial secretary, Lord Chandos, stated that 'the Queen discharges her [responsibilities] as nearly to perfection as a mortal can';[12] the same habit seemed to disqualify her from participating fully in her marriage or her family. She 'found her time and energy divided between three duties – those to her country, her husband and her children', wrote Lady Peacock in 1955, ordering Elizabeth's obligations as perhaps she did herself.[13] 'Each one of us has a primary and personal responsibility for our own children,' Elizabeth would tell viewers of her Christmas broadcast many years later.[14] At the time, her primary responsibility seldom appeared either Charles or Anne. Among predictable results, as Martin Charteris remembered, was that 'she really had very little to do with Charles', a view apparently borne out by a letter Elizabeth wrote to one of her mother's ladies-in-waiting, in which she admitted 'it was a great relief to me when church was over as I've never taken Charles to a service before, it's always been his grandmother who has taken him!'[15]

It was an outcome as obvious to her contemporaries as to subsequent generations privy to the revelations of royal biographers (and their subjects). In sympathetic vein in October 1961 the *People* explained, 'Undoubtedly the Queen is devoted to her children and would like to be with them like an ordinary mother is with her family. But the hundred and one duties which occupy her working day leave her no time to prepare their meals, see to their clothes – and check that they brush their teeth and wash behind their ears.'[16] It was a well-intentioned misreading of what Charteris estimated as the 'terribly old-fashioned upper-class upbringing' Elizabeth gave Charles and Anne.[17] Elizabeth's own pre-war upbringing had been leavened by her parents' cosy insularity: the early-morning romps, games of snap and Happy Families, the action songs like 'Underneath the Spreading Chestnut Tree', Balmoral picnics and Sandringham bicycle rides, the overt affection of 'us four' grounded in flower-filled rooms at Royal Lodge. Elizabeth's mother retained this outlook. Thanking Elizabeth for a visit to Balmoral in the summer of 1960, the Queen Mother inventoried the joys of family life under a familiar roof: 'well remembered smells of stone & stocks, & children's feet running by, & that delectable baby [Andrew], & the door opening & you staggering into my room with that heavenly creature in your arms... & the picnic & the card games & the cinema, & especially being with my children. That is always the real treat.'[18] Elizabeth shared these feelings unreservedly: later she described 'the God-given love that binds a family together'.[19] Hugh Casson recorded a cosy family scene at Balmoral in 1952, Elizabeth 'in a blue woollen frock and sitting on a fireside stool in her private sitting room while Prince Charles "cut" her hair with white plastic scissors'; he described family weekends at Windsor, Elizabeth, Philip, Charles and Anne watching *Muffin the Mule* at teatime, Philip organizing treasure hunts, with clues drawn rather than written as the children were too young to read.[20] Margaret's lady-in-waiting Lady Elizabeth Cavendish saw clearly that Elizabeth 'adored' Charles.[21] But 'the Queen is not good at showing affection,' said gossipy Charteris, and Charles would not always be certain that he was adored. In 1954, several years after their last meeting, Crawfie described Elizabeth as 'Elizabeth the Homemaker'. She suggested she knew 'that in a world of changing values, some things remain constant; and the greatest of these, is the home'.[22] Nevertheless, Elizabeth entrusted much of the homemaking for her own family to the husband, who, though close to his sisters, had scant experience of a conventional childhood. The nursery regime of Nanny Lightbody, assisted by Mabel Anderson, also contributed tensions, given the very different outlooks of the two women. Only Mabel Anderson, less rigid in her viewpoint, would remain in position long term.

The choice of Cheam as preparatory school in the autumn of 1957, with Gordonstoun afterwards, was Philip's; with marked success he had attended both. His were the shibboleths that shaped Charles's childhood. Differences in temperament between father and son, later identified by Philip as pragmatist versus romantic, underlay uneasiness in a relationship in which, nevertheless, Charles admired the intimidating, often bullying Philip; by forcing Charles to follow in his own footsteps, Philip seemed to guarantee his son's discomfort. Unconfrontational and unprepared to challenge her husband's authority in this sphere, Elizabeth did not effectively arbitrate a middle way. Philip's iron resilience was one result of his own emotionally barren childhood, with its lengthy separations from his estranged parents; Elizabeth was as powerless to oppose her husband as Charles was (she was reported as saying, 'My view has to be checked over'.[23]) Almost from Charles's birth, newspapers reported his father's hope that he should grow up a man's man, tough, energetic and resourceful. Instead, the son who at first saw so little of Philip was shy, sensitive and painfully polite, physically maladroit, tending to chubbiness. It was Anne who was 'intrepid, venturesome and agile', a delight to her father.[24] 'Whenever I have seen the whole family on the screen,' wrote Frances Woodsford, a secretary in the Public Baths Department of Bournemouth Town Council, 'the Duke of Edinburgh is invariably looking after his daughter, and leaving Charles severely alone.'[25] 'Charles will hang back,' stated a Sunday paper when he was twelve, 'while his sister rushes in where angels fear to tread.'[26] Anne would surely have thrived at (the all-boys) Cheam and Gordonstoun; Charles was singularly unsuited to both and predictably unhappy. He made no attempt to conceal his unhappiness from his parents; Philip did not revise his plans. 'Charles is just beginning to dread the return to school next week – so much worse for the second term,' wrote Elizabeth, who had never been to school or suffered homesickness or been bullied by classmates or even shared a tent with fellow Sea Rangers or a dormitory with other ATS trainees.[27] The sentence sounds like repeating something a friend had told her, casually unfeeling in its easy acceptance of the inevitability of Charles's unhappiness. Philip's view, expressed in 1974, that 'children may be indulged at home', points to a conviction likely to have overruled every objection.[28] 'School is expected to be a spartan and disciplined experience in the process of developing into self-controlled, considerate and independent adults,' he wrote. Both parents set store by self-control and consideration. Part of Charles's training in independence included his parents' absence through a series of childhood ailments. In 1959, when he contracted chicken pox, which she had never had, Elizabeth's doctors forbade her seeing him. Three years later, suffering from acute appendicitis, Charles was taken late at night by ambulance from Cheam to Great Ormond Street Hospital. Elizabeth remained at Windsor, visiting the following day; Philip was in Venezuela. The conflict in Elizabeth's life that arose from her multiple roles appeared to be symbolized by her decision, in the summer of 1958, to confer on Charles the title of Prince of Wales without any warning to Charles himself. He learned of it in the headmaster's study at Cheam, in company with a group of classmates, watching on television the closing ceremony of the Empire and Commonwealth Games in Cardiff. Elizabeth's pre-recorded message was roundly applauded in Wales and beyond. Charles's reaction was of acute embarrassment.

Encountering eleven-year-old Charles in February 1960, Cecil Beaton concluded that he was the most considerate member of the family. He also suspected paternal bullying. 'Poor little Prince Charles... [has] a perpetually hunched effect of the shoulders and a wrinkled forehead and pained look in the eyes as if awaiting a clout from behind, or for his father to tweak his ear or pull the tuft of hair at the crown of his head... I realised soon that he was nice and kind and sensitive – but that he has to be hearty – to be in a perpetual rugger scrum because that's what Papa expects of him.'[29] Tabloid journalists scented something similar. The following summer, the *Sunday Mirror* claimed that Charles's parents had told him to '[pull] his socks up': he had 'so far disappointed his father by showing a marked preference for sports like shooting and trout-fishing rather than the athletic activities at which Prince Philip excels'.[30]

Charles was only two when his grandmother cautioned Elizabeth, 'He is a brave little boy, but I think he's sensitive, & you will have to see that he doesn't get frightened by silly people.'[31] From childhood the Queen Mother provided Charles with respite from 'silly people'. For Elizabeth, the chasm between her mother's view of what was best for Charles and her husband's was an embarrassment and a strain. In vain, the Queen Mother championed Eton for her grandson; she was firmly opposed to Philip's insistence that Charles follow him to Gordonstoun. In its favour she offered Eton's proximity to Windsor Castle, the presence there of 'all your friends' sons' and its 'staunchly protestant' chapel.[32] Elizabeth had resolved Philip's longstanding anger over the family name only a year before. Even had it been in her nature, she could not have been expected to oppose him again so soon, especially in a choice that pitted Philip against the palace old guard, most of whom were Etonians. The reappearance of Lord Altrincham, on this occasion writing in Sydney's *Sunday Mirror News Pictorial*, did not contribute to family consensus. Altrincham dismissed Gordonstoun – 'I doubt it would be the right choice' – and argued that 'it would not be fair... to dump

[Charles] in surroundings entirely unfamiliar and daunting'.[33]

This, however, is precisely what did happen on 1 May 1962. Predictably Gordonstoun proved a frightful experience for Charles, its bear-baiting atmosphere of bullying and physical intimidation as unsympathetic as any school could possibly have been. After two terms, Charles pleaded with his parents to take him away. A former tutor from the palace schoolroom concluded he was 'simply not a rough and tumble sort of chap' and would certainly have fared better at Eton or Westminster.[34] Charles's letters home spared his parents none of his misery. Perhaps Philip persuaded Elizabeth that the challenge of so unforgiving an environment would transform him into the king-in-waiting they wanted. It seems unlikely that she was fully convinced, and Charles's letters must have upset her deeply. In her son's absence, however, although she maintained a habit begun much earlier of writing to him regularly, she did not resist her refractory spouse. For all her dismay at Nkrumah's short-term perspective in November 1961, by acquiescing in Charles's unhappiness, Elizabeth unwittingly took her own risks with the dynasty's future, apparently heedless that her own compliance with her royal destiny had arisen at least in part from the closeness of her relationship with her father and the confidence he placed in her. The Queen Mother kept her counsel. At a lunch party in 1968, after Charles had left Gordonstoun, her host noted 'perhaps just a suspicion of criticism for his father sending him to a tough school. "Now he doesn't need to be toughened any more."'[35]

With unintended irony, Lisa Sheridan's *A Day with Prince Andrew*, 'published with the authority of H. M. The Queen', had appeared as Charles headed north for his first term in Scotland. The slim volume of photographs of the two-year-old captured a warm and easy relationship between Elizabeth and her youngest child. Elizabeth had determined to spend more time with Andrew than she had spared Charles and Anne. But she and

Philip were the same parents they had always been. 'Prince Andrew is fortunate in having parents who do not hamper his eager boisterousness,' Sheridan offered. 'When he climbs he is encouraged to be self-reliant; if he falls there is no anxious rush to soothe and examine for hurts.'[36] Time would prove the veracity of Sheridan's assessment that characterized aspects of Elizabeth and Philip's relationships with all their children.

❧

'Insecure, sad, ambivalent and melancholy' was one critic's view of Elizabeth as presented in a new portrait exhibited at the Royal Academy in 1965. The two-and-a-half-metre-high *Study for a Portrait of Her Majesty the Queen*, painted the previous year by Royal Academician Peter Greenham, depicted Elizabeth in a simple evening gown of her favourite lime green, with the Garter ribbon and Queen Alexandra's kokoshnik tiara. Impressionistic and gauzy, it is an uncertain image. It garnered mixed reviews from a public resentful of its inferences concerning the corrosive anxieties of sovereignty; it provoked what newspapers called a 'royal controversy'.

Greenham's was evidently not Elizabeth's view of herself. The following year, she agreed to Canadian photographer Yousuf Karsh reprising Beaton's 1955 studies of her seated on a chair of state in the palace ballroom. Images of severe and uncompromising grandeur, they belie any suggestion of their subject querying her role or questioning her purpose. Yet the first half of the new decade had undoubtedly brought Elizabeth concerns quite different from the sunny optimism with which her reign began. The memory of personal criticism lingered – first salvos by Malcolm Muggeridge and Keith Waterhouse escalated by Lord Altrincham; Muggeridge had quoted sneering views of Elizabeth as 'frumpish' and 'banal'. There were differences of opinion between Commonwealth leaders and Westminster over Britain's proposed entry to the Common Market. In 1963, during a state visit by the unpopular King and Queen of the Hellenes, Elizabeth herself was booed, unthinkable a decade earlier. Political scandal accelerated Macmillan's resignation, while hostile debate surrounding nomination of his successor did not spare Elizabeth. She worried about an unhappy Charles. In 1964, she made her first appearance in a newspaper cartoon – her head on a postage stamp to commemorate the 400th anniversary of Shakespeare's birth, yawning with boredom, the old criticism of philistinism.[37] In her Christmas broadcast in 1961, the thirty-five-year-old monarch – so recently associated with renewal and rebirth – had distanced herself from 'the younger generation'. Above all, Greenham's portrait was an image of an older Elizabeth.

Elizabeth's personal star had not dimmed. At home and abroad, enormous crowds flocked to gaze and wave and cheer. 'A million smiles greeted the Queen today in the most memorable drive she has made since her Coronation,' the *Sunday Express* reported of Elizabeth's arrival in Delhi in January 1961. 'And keeping pace with her along these opening miles of her Indian tour, one word swept through the jam-packed crowd: "Khubsurat" – Hindi for beautiful.'[38] Although the magistrate who fined Altrincham's assailant was mistaken in his claim, in August 1957, that 'ninety-five per cent of the population of this country were disgusted and offended by what was written' – a third of respondents in a *Daily Mail* poll had agreed with Altrincham – respect for Elizabeth herself remained high, with criticism mostly directed at the court.[39] Deference would linger yet, despite the ebbing of earlier reverence – what Cecil Beaton labelled 'the *Woman's Own* gush about the glorious little lady of the throne'.[40] A Mass Observation survey concluded in 1964 that 'in the 1960s there is widespread support in this country for the royal and monarchical system... The royal idea appears as vital and compelling in the sense that it provides strong psychological securities... It is an important, and perhaps an increasingly important, symbol of national prestige.' The thirty per cent of those polled for whom Elizabeth was 'especially chosen by God' had not changed since the accession.[41] Overwhelming evidence of her popularity and her continuing prominence in national life did not encourage Elizabeth to make sweeping changes to her conduct of monarchy. A politician's secretary visiting Buckingham Palace noted the prevalent tweediness of royal equerries: 'the conversation centred on horses. Perhaps it was assumed that everyone was interested in horses.'[42] One of Elizabeth's personal benefactions in 1962 was the purchase of one of four remaining Cleveland Bay stallions in Britain in order to promote the endangered breed. Elizabeth's mother continued to exert a powerful influence. The Queen Mother reflected on her own 'distaste' for aspects of modernity, describing 'modern novels... so loathsome, & so perfectly horrible, that I felt quite sick... I think that we must be living through a moment of bad taste in many forms of art'.[43] In 1993, Charles would refer to 'the more ludicrous frontiers of the 60s in terms of education, architecture, art, music, and literature', a response almost certainly shaped by his grandmother's views and indicative of views surrounding Elizabeth at the time.[44] Of the concrete-framed Hilton Hotel, on a site once occupied by Londonderry House, Elizabeth told John Betjeman and Ted Hughes, 'I wish they'd spend as much pulling it down as they spent putting it up', though her objection was as much to its location, overlooking the north corner of the palace, as its unlovely appearance.[45] The cultural shifts of the 1960s were overwhelmingly initiatives of the young. Their impatience and irritation were directed at an older generation, notably the traditional power-brokers of the Establishment. At a moment of iconoclasm, Elizabeth's challenges included retaining the affection and loyalty of this generation in revolt against a world that overlapped so closely with her own.

In the autumn of 1962, Elizabeth confronted a dilemma of divided loyalties. Macmillan had earlier set in motion a bid for British membership of the Common Market. In April 1960, Elizabeth had hosted a state visit by the French president, Charles de Gaulle; for Macmillan's government, its chief aim was to persuade de Gaulle of the wholeheartedness of Britain's commitment to a European trading zone. Every possible diplomatic blandishment greeted the former leader of the Free French in what Pathé described as 'the most popular and successful state visit to Britain this century'. Yet the visit would shortly prove anything but successful. De Gaulle's reservations concerned the closeness of British links to the United States and Britain's attachment to the Commonwealth; at the beginning of 1963 he vetoed Britain's application. In the meantime, disgruntled Commonwealth leaders observed British overtures to Europe and, ahead of a Commonwealth conference in September 1962, discussed their anger with Elizabeth, an early instance of her role as sounding board that came to play a key part in the organization's smooth running. In a pointed statement, Elizabeth told Macmillan she was 'worried about Commonwealth feeling'.[46] She was almost certainly worried about the complexities of her own position as queen of Commonwealth realms, and concerned by divisions within an organization she was determined to nurture. Macmillan apologized to Elizabeth, but damage had been done. Despite de Gaulle's veto, Britain's 'disloyalty' to Commonwealth trading partners sowed seeds of mistrust. In her Christmas broadcast, in an optimistic statement of unity, Elizabeth appealed over the heads of politicians: 'In spite of all the changes of the modern world and the many stresses and strains involved, the feeling of a special relationship between the ordinary people of the older Commonwealth countries will never be weakened.' Within weeks of de Gaulle's decision, Elizabeth and Philip embarked on a second tour of Australia and New Zealand. The 100,000 people who packed Sydney's Circular Quay for the royal arrival, reported the *Canberra Times*, formed 'the biggest crowd seen there since the opening of Sydney Harbour Bridge in 1932'; in the west coast town of Geraldton, the entire population of 12,000, swollen by a further 4,000 from surrounding areas, turned out to cheer. Loyally Pathé reported, 'Of all Her Majesty's tours none can have been more brilliantly successful than this one.'[47] But the atmosphere was not that of Elizabeth's previous visit. Increased television ownership lessened the need to see Elizabeth in the flesh and eroded royal mystique; perceived British perfidy over Europe also curbed enthusiasm. A critical note crept into reports. Of a rainy royal garden party in Sydney, the *Adelaide Advertiser*'s Shirley Stott described the dampening effect of royal aides' heavy-handedness, with 'lessons in elementary etiquette' relayed by loudspeaker, instructing guests to bow, curtsey, avoid staring. It proved, wrote Stott, the 'final dismal straw which seemed to break the spirits of guests who had braved rain and chill to see the Queen... By the time the Queen arrived, the guests looked like schoolchildren who had been browbeaten into submission by a disciplinarian headmaster.'[48] It made, Stott claimed, for 'the dullest occasion'.

At home, dullness was in sadly short supply. A sex-and-spies scandal engulfed Macmillan's government with the revelation that the war minister, John Profumo, had lied to the House of Commons about an affair with show girl Christine Keeler, whose other lovers included a Russian military attaché. 'Everyone talks excitedly about the great Profumo scandal, which may even bring the Conservative Party toppling,' noted the Labour-leaning diarist Frances Partridge.[49] Macmillan reformed his cabinet and wrote apologetically to Elizabeth of the damage caused by a government minister's 'terrible behaviour'; the *Daily Mirror* announced that Profumo had 'ended up in a morass of lying and dishonour that has not seen its like this century'.[50] Elizabeth's response was sympathetic.

Her position was powerless, though she understood the danger to the crown of association with unpopular or disreputable politicians. Macmillan worried about the scandal touching Elizabeth's family. Stephen Ward, a fashionable osteopath and artist, who produced portrait sketches for the *Illustrated London News* and the *Daily Telegraph*, was found guilty of brothel keeping: among those invited to his weekend cottage on the Cliveden estate, where Profumo met Keeler, was Keeler herself. Subjects of Stephen Ward's sketches included a handful of Elizabeth's relatives; Ward had been among Philip's fellow Thursday Club members. With palm-rubbing sanctimony, the *Mirror* told readers, 'The Royal Family have been dragged in... by the fact that [Profumo's] one-time friend, the osteopath Stephen Ward, is well known to Royalty, having painted Princess Margaret, Prince Philip, Tony Armstrong-Jones, the Duke of Gloucester, Princess Marina and Princess Alexandra.'[51] A fortnight later the paper reported ghoulishly, 'the foulest rumour which is being circulated about the Profumo Scandal has involved the Royal Family. The name mentioned in this rumour is Prince Philip's', underneath the headline 'Rumour is utterly unfounded'.[52] Attempts were made to sell Ward's sketches to fund his legal fees. The surveyor of the Queen's pictures discreetly purchased the drawings in question and, despite the *Mirror*'s best efforts, rumours of Philip's involvement stalled.[53]

It was not the Profumo Affair but a prostatectomy and hypochondria that, in October 1963, three months earlier than the date he had already discussed with Elizabeth, forced Macmillan's resignation, at the age of sixty-nine. Faced with this prospect, an older, more experienced Elizabeth reacted warily. Twice before, a Conservative prime minister leaving office had necessitated her involvement in the process of appointing a successor. Through Adeane, she made clear her reluctance for more than a nominal role; she had indicated already, Macmillan wrote later, 'the great importance' she attached 'to maintaining the prerogative intact'. Party rules, unreformed despite criticism in 1957, offered her no escape. The vice chancellor of the University of Cambridge, Sir Ivor Jennings, explained, 'her concern is to find somebody who will be a good Prime Minister and acceptable to Conservative MPs'.[54] The Countess of Longford suggested that 'whoever she entrusted with the task would succeed, simply by being her nominee';[55] it was not in Elizabeth's nature to think so, nor was her choice as untrammelled as this (retrospective) assessment might indicate. The problem was twofold: not only did a handful of potential successors present themselves (unlike in 1955 and 1957), Macmillan himself had a clear preference that he intended to impress upon Elizabeth.

He was able to do so since, despite incapacity, he did not immediately tender his resignation: so long as he remained prime minister, he remained Elizabeth's chief adviser. As such, from his hospital bed, he initiated the party soundings that would identify the new leader. As interpreted by Macmillan, soundings yielded his preferred outcome: most marked support for the foreign secretary, Lord Home, whom he determined to recommend to Elizabeth. He did so in a meeting in the boardroom of the King Edward VII Hospital, still confined to his bed, shortly after his letter of resignation had been delivered to Buckingham Palace on the morning of 18 October. He knew that Elizabeth would ask his advice. To this end he had prepared a memo, which he read aloud in a meeting that he characterized afterwards as impossibly romantic, monarch and minister both deeply moved. It was Macmillan's personal Melbourne/Victoria fantasy of the elder statesman forsaking his youthful sovereign to the regret of both.

In truth, there was little romance in Macmillan's manipulation of Elizabeth's strong desire to avoid any statement of preference. Buckingham Palace had announced his resignation soon after receipt of his letter. As Adeane told Elizabeth, she was not constitutionally bound to accept the advice of a prime minister who, hours earlier, had resigned from office: her sole obligation was to find a replacement able to command a majority in the House of Commons. In Elizabeth's eyes, acquiescence in what she may not have suspected was Macmillan's legerdemain was the swiftest way of extricating herself from the internal politics of the Conservative Party. All the better that the candidate in question was entirely sympathetic: a Scottish earl of conventional outdoorsiness. 'She loved Alec,' remembered Martin Charteris. 'He was an old friend. They talked about dogs and shooting. They were both Scottish landowners, the same sort of people, like old school friends.'[56] 'There are many doubts in the Conservative Party whether it would be wise to appoint a peer who, simply because he was a peer, would provide the Labour Party with a ready-made election target,' reported one newspaper.[57] Predictably, but not unjustifiably, the Labour leader Harold Wilson referred to the workings of an 'aristocratic cabal'. Elizabeth appears to have been an unresisting victim. To a far greater extent than in 1957, she found herself unable to satisfy what had become the contradictory impulses of exercising her prerogative without 'choosing'. Ultimately her readiness to accept Macmillan's advice was itself a choice, albeit she faced considerable pressure to act quickly, even the *Mirror* conceding that 'she cannot allow the government of the nation to drift indefinitely while the Tories fight among themselves'.[58] Her invitation to try to form an administration to a family friend, the 14th Earl of Home, would confirm a growing view of Elizabeth and her court as out of touch with the decade's democratic spirit.

༺ཨ༻

Elizabeth granted access to Pathé cameramen at Easter in 1965. Brief footage entitled 'Royal Family at Windsor' showed Elizabeth, Philip, Charles, Anne and Andrew walking in the gardens of Frogmore. Elizabeth pushed a pram. In it was her fourth and last child, Edward Antony Richard Louis, born weeks short of her thirty-eighth birthday, on 10 March 1964, for the first time with Philip present in the delivery room. Commentary revisited familiar themes. Still in tone eulogistic, it acknowledged the near-impossibility of combining motherhood with sovereignty. On this occasion 'Her Majesty was seen in the role of mother' only because she was able to enjoy 'a few days respite from all cares of state'. 'The pleasures of family life are enjoyed by the baby's parents less frequently than by ordinary parents,' viewers were told. 'To be Head of the Commonwealth entails long absences abroad... How prized are these days, comparatively few, when they are all together.' 'Respite from the cares of state' was necessarily brief and infrequent, but Elizabeth would take pains to play 'the role of mother' more vigorously than a decade earlier. 'Goodness, what fun it is to have a baby in the house again!' she told a friend after Edward's birth.[59] Her delight in her newest child emerged in a letter to her midwife, Helen Rowe, when Edward was six months old: 'The baby is wonderful – good as gold, trying to sit up and weighing 15 lbs 12! He smiles and giggles at everyone, and makes everyone happy!'[60] In a leatherbound appointment book she had pencilled time to spend with Andrew as a toddler and defended it against encroachments; she brought forward her Tuesday-evening audiences with the prime minister in order to be free for Edward's bathtime, and both younger boys, their sister Anne suggested later, were spoiled by their parents compared with their elder siblings' treatment. Timothy Knatchbull, one of Mountbatten's grandsons, described 'how quickly [Elizabeth and Philip] adopted some of the new ideas of the Swinging Sixties, including new ideas of parenting, which is that you spend masses of time with your kid. Which is what

Prince Edward got.'[61] In her Christmas broadcast, Elizabeth described a young family as a blessing; she determined to shield Andrew and Edward from the media intrusions of Charles and Anne's childhood and had withheld from public release photographs of Andrew's christening. 'More and more,' claimed a deferential account published afterwards, 'the Queen is insisting on a stouter, tougher wall of privacy around her closer personal affairs.'[62]

But it was Elizabeth herself, encouraged by Philip and new blood in the palace, who first breached the wall.

CHAPTER XIII

'No one wants to end up like a brontosaurus'

'WHEN SHE HAS lost the bloom of youth the Queen's reputation will depend, far more than it does now, upon her personality. It will not be enough then for her to go through the motions,' Lord Altrincham had suggested. After a sitting in September 1968, Cecil Beaton noted the bloom of youth clouded by 'signs of suffering, of past anxieties. The Queen has bloodshot eyes, [the] blue glass eyes of her father.'[1]

The warning signs of the late 1950s had not been banished. In place of earlier criticism were more worrying signs of indifference and even disaffection. In 1967, the *Sunday Telegraph* announced that 'most people' now cared much less about the monarchy than previously; at a moment of youth-driven cultural shift, it explained that this applied 'particularly among the young, many of whom regard the Queen as the arch-square'.[2] Royal historian Sir Charles Petrie informed readers of the *Illustrated London News* that 'the British monarchy is not as firmly vested in the hearts of the people as was the case even a generation ago', while Queen Mary's biographer, James Pope-Hennessy, startled a dinner party in January with his announcement that 'of course what we must do [is] get rid of the royal family': it was 'no good to man or beast'.[3] Among certain courtiers arose genuine anxiety, including the private secretary who reflected afterwards, 'We had to change because we were getting so boring,' 'we' apparently referring to the royal family rather than their attendants. But the nature of any change was not straightforward. In 1964, Philip had pointed out that 'the monarchy... has to be all things to all people. Of course, it cannot do this when it comes to being all things to people who are traditionalists and all things to people who are iconoclasts.'[4] Three years later, his position had shifted: 'No one wants to end up like a brontosaurus, who couldn't adapt himself, and ended up stuffed in a museum,' he told a news conference in Canberra.[5] Elizabeth's response to conductor Sir John Barbirolli, who told her he reacted to adverse criticism by doing nothing, was a pensive 'I wonder if that can be really possible...' Later, informed by an outgoing minister that 'there had been moments where I'd been nervous about what was happening [politically]', Elizabeth asked him if he had felt so nervous that he wanted to give it all up.[6] It was an option denied to her.

Her decision in 1968 to take part in a fly-on-the-wall television film was not motivated by panic. Far from currying favour with a rebellious younger generation, Elizabeth's expectations of the young, as she pointed out in her Commonwealth Day address in 1969, remained those that she herself had shouldered: 'In the... Commonwealth we have a ready-made opportunity to give expression to that concern for others, that desire to serve and to help, which I regard as one of the great characteristics of the young people of all our countries.' She knew the residue of feeling for her at grass-roots level across the country. 'If you go to the East End they

wave their little flags and they are very keen on the monarchy,'
Philip told a Labour politician.[7] Large crowds at the opening
of the Severn Bridge in September 1966 typified the response
Elizabeth continued to inspire. She was greeted enthusiastically;
threatened demonstrations by Welsh Nationalists did not
materialize. 'Along the M4 London–South Wales motorway
towards the bridge, there were long ranks of cars and thousands
of spectators who cheerfully defied the prohibition against
pedestrians on the motorway and cheered and waved flags as
the Queen's entourage sped past.'[8] She had not yet forfeited her
fairy-tale aura. At a reception at Schloss Augustusburg, Brühl,
in Germany in May 1965, Elizabeth had worn a blue and white
embroidered dress inspired by the castle's rococo decoration.
'The Queen dazzles them' trumpeted the front page of the next
morning's *Daily Express*, above a picture of 'a gown that stunned
a nation'.[9] Abroad, there had even been praise for Elizabeth's
modernity and cultural engagement. One particular outcome
of her state visit to Ethiopia at the beginning of the same year,
at the invitation of Emperor Haile Selassie, was unexpected.
The *Guardian* reported that 'the Queen's arrival has inspired
the capital's only daily newspaper to inaugurate a women's
page, and in this the Queen is praised as a monarch who has
shown interest in industry and patronised the arts.'[10] Even her
response to the horrific collapse of a colliery spoil tip in the
Glamorgan mining village of Aberfan, which killed 116 children
and twenty-eight adults in October 1966, was not regarded at
the time as ruefully as Elizabeth herself came to consider it.
She did not visit the village until rescue work ceased, eight days
after the disaster. Advisers pressed her to make the journey
sooner. Concerned that her visit would interfere with rescue
operations, Elizabeth stalled. Margaret launched an appeal for
toys for the children who had survived the disaster; Elizabeth
insisted that the toys sent from Andrew and Edward's nursery
were given anonymously, the palace explaining she 'felt it best

that there should be nothing to indicate where they came from'.[11] Her reaction suggests an aversion to easy gestures, dismissed as 'stunts', and genuine humility; it points to a lack of understanding of the succour offered by her presence, an idea as old as kingship of the healing power of the anointed sovereign. She may have been concerned about her response to such raw suffering; she certainly acknowledged the possibility of intruding on private grief. In the event, Elizabeth's week-delayed, hour-long visit lasted two and a half hours and left her, in one account, 'pale with emotion, her eyes dark with distress and often, it seemed, on the verge of tears'.[12] Newspapers cast her presence in Aberfan as that of a wife and mother 'linked by a common bond of understanding with the [village's] bereaved mothers';[13] local memories suggest catharsis in the visit's aftermath. It was the kind of visit the King and Queen had repeatedly made during the Blitz, but Elizabeth knew that she lacked her mother's ease with those whose lives were so different from her own, as well as her capacity for detachment that was an aspect of the Queen Mother's more theatrical public manner; both factors encouraged her to hang back. As it happened, those she met drew considerable comfort from Elizabeth's distress on their behalf, visible despite her self-control; they did not clamour, as would a later generation, for a masquerade of public grief. In following decades, Elizabeth would return on four subsequent occasions, her personal atonement for what she regarded as an error of judgement, but Aberfan was not a turning point in her public life. She would continue to respond to unforeseen challenges cautiously.

~~~

More than a year in the planning and making, *Royal Family* is a film conceived as memories of former triumphs were dimming. Like Elizabeth herself it lacked bombast or bravado.

Its thesis is unpompous and, as Altrincham might have wished, one of its achievements was to reveal to viewers facets of Elizabeth's personality. She emerged, in the verdict of one television critic, as 'a warm, friendly person, with a thoroughly engaging sense of humour',[14] though her discreet gift of a replacement necklace to a crew member from whom, during filming, a necklace of sentimental value had been stolen, went unpublicized. In keeping with the spirit of the times, it sought to present Elizabeth from a human perspective, Morrah's idea of an exalted ordinariness rather than what Jock Colville had labelled a 'semi-divine interpretation of monarchy'. As its title indicated, there was an emphasis on family. Publicity material described 'a closely united, warm family, with a sense of humour and fun as well as a strong sense of duty'. Commentary was written by Antony Jay, who would write another television documentary about Elizabeth in 1992; the director of the joint BBC–ITV production was Richard Cawston. Jay's contribution added ballast. On its first showing on 21 June 1969, the film's 22 million viewers may have been more interested in the ingredients of the royal salad dressing or Elizabeth's skill in not flinching at the American ambassador's verbosity, but they also learned key facts about Elizabeth's position and her working life: 'while the Queen occupies the highest office of state, no one else can. While she is head of the law, no politician can take over the courts. While she is head of state, no generals can take over the government... Monarchy does not lie in the power it gives to the sovereign, but in the power it denies to anyone else.' This negative defence of monarchy, which echoed the denials of Elizabeth's first televised Christmas broadcast – 'I cannot lead you into battle. I do not give you laws or administer justice' – suited a rebellious decade. In the Cold War Swinging Sixties, menaced by the possibility of nuclear war with the Soviet Union, 'arch-square' Elizabeth as barrier to political extremism was a more persuasive argument to many than the more fulsome commendations of the previous decade. Cecil Beaton – sympathetic to the royal cause – considered this one of the film's successes: 'The point being so well taken that the Queen with this tremendous job was herself without power, but was a bulwark against dictators or others usurping power and doing it badly.'[15]

The film was not Elizabeth's idea. She was a reluctant innovator. Her aversion to television was of long standing. Initially she had resisted television cameras at her coronation. Until 1957, she resisted televising her Christmas broadcast, and she held out against colour filming for another decade. *Royal Family* involved living in range of television cameras for seventy-five days. It was a full-scale embracing of the medium many in court circles continued to regard warily as both dangerous and cheapening. It could not have taken place without the retirement, the year before, of the palace's obstructive veteran press officer, Commander Colville, known with good reason as the 'Abominable No Man', a man of old-fashioned outlook determined to resist media intrusion on all fronts and the inspiration for Malcolm Muggeridge's criticism of royal press officers as 'quite exceptionally incompetent'. The project was the brainchild of Colville's eventual replacement, Elizabeth's assistant press officer, an Australian called William Heseltine, and Mountbatten's son-in-law, Lord Brabourne, a film director. Martin Charteris claimed that the film arose from their shared feeling 'that the Royal Family was almost too dull, and one ought to lift the curtain of obscurity'.[16] Such a rationale could not have borne fruit without Philip's enthusiastic endorsement and the support of Mountbatten himself. It happened at a moment when 'the curtain of obscurity' had already begun to be tweaked. At the beginning of October 1968, French magazine *Paris Match* published eight stolen photographs taken by Philip four years earlier, of Elizabeth in bed with the newborn Edward;

the following day two of the pictures appeared in the *Daily Express*, including on the cover. 'Since the photographs are of such a personal kind, the Queen would naturally prefer that they had not been published,' commented a palace spokesman with characteristic understatement and the baleful impotence that would increasingly characterize royal relations with muscle-flexing media.

Nevertheless Elizabeth's agreement ought not to be taken for granted. She involved herself closely with aspects of her public image within her control. Elizabeth annotated photographs taken by John Hedgecoe on 22 June 1966 for use by sculptor Arnold Machin in creating a new bust portrait for postage stamps: 'Good', in the case of her preferred study and, in capital letters, 'NO', on an image she disliked; she annotated designs submitted to her by her dressmakers with suggestions for alterations. In other instances she gracefully bowed to the inevitable, as she has continued to do, especially where clear benefits to the monarchy are discernible: having agreed to film her Christmas broadcast, for example, she initiated filming of her speech at the State Opening of Parliament and, in 1969, of a palace banquet during the state visit of President Saragat of Italy. But *Royal Family* resembled none of these initiatives: it was neither scripted nor an exercise in traditional pageantry. Rather than satisfying pre-existing expectations, it sought to create new impressions. 'Royal Family at Windsor', of 1965, had replicated the kind of newsreel footage Elizabeth's parents had sanctioned three decades earlier, the royals themselves silent, filmed at a respectful distance, their moods and actions carefully interpreted for the viewer in reverent commentary; fly-on-the-wall coverage was quite different. The niggling carping of a recent royal-themed television documentary – a programme about the royal palaces written by ex-Surveyor of the King's Pictures Kenneth Clark – had so angered Elizabeth that, after a private screening, 'the Queen rose to her feet with a face of iron, K Clark approached, hand outstretched, waiting for congratulations, to be met with an irate, "Did you *have* to be so sarcastic?"[17] Elizabeth's green light to *Royal Family* was an act of faith; its participants enforced a degree of control through an editorial committee headed by Philip and the involvement as intermediary of William Heseltine, who kept a foot in both camps. At one level a measure of Elizabeth's self-assurance, her agreement showed, too, the progress of her own ideas. By her grandparents' standards, this palace-generated public unbuttoning looked like deliberate crowd pleasing, known by some in the family as 'Mountbattenism'; its apparently unfiltered viewpoint and *cinéma vérité* style set aside the careful artifice of the visions conjured for Elizabeth's parents by Marcus Adams and Lisa Sheridan. Only Elizabeth's commendation of Queen Victoria's iron self-control, over lunch with Philip, Charles and Anne, recalled the atmosphere of her childhood. Even after a lifetime as an object of scrutiny and curiosity, she found unnerving the experience of being filmed continually, though she relaxed by stages.

Her courage – and acquiescence – were rewarded with an overwhelmingly positive response to the film. One newspaper described it as a personal triumph for Elizabeth.[18] Cecil Beaton's view was not unusual. 'The Queen came through as a great character, quite severe, very self-assured, a bit bossy, serious, frowning a bit... Her sentences are halting. She hesitates mid-way, you think she has dried up, you prompt her but she goes on doggedly. She came out on top as the nice person she is.'[19] For the first time, Elizabeth's subjects saw her almost as she was in private, as Noël Coward described her, 'easy and gay and ready to giggle'.[20] If popular views of Elizabeth had been in danger of mirroring the lithograph *Elizabeth I*, made in 1966 by German artist Gerhard Richter, in which Richter reproduced a black-and-white press photograph of Elizabeth and blurred it until it lost all definition, *Royal Family* reinstated Elizabeth's crisp outlines and her reality. 'We're getting on for middle age,' Philip had told a television interviewer the year the plan was conceived. 'I would have thought we were entering the least interesting period of the kind of glamorous existence... There used to be much more interest.'[21] *Royal Family* successfully re-engaged public interest in Elizabeth and her family. It played its part in dispelling the *Sunday Telegraph*'s prediction of gloom – 'The British monarchy... could well be swallowed up in a great and growing yawn' – and in shaping the findings of the Gallup poll that, in 1969, established support for the monarchy at a reassuring sixty-nine per cent, with less than twenty per cent in favour of a republic.

The film showed Elizabeth juggling her public and private roles: royal, connubial, maternal. By merging Elizabeth's roles as sovereign and matriarch in scenes in which, accompanied by her eldest children, she greets statesmen and public servants, embodying both roles simultaneously, it set ticking a time bomb. Not only could the public reasonably expect both aspects of Elizabeth's life to be equally successful, if they were to be equally prominent, many viewers felt the film gave them assurances of precisely this. With the help of Cynthia Asquith and Beryl Poignand, Marcus Adams, Lisa Sheridan and Cecil Beaton, Elizabeth's mother had popularized a view of idealized family harmony centred on the strong and loving marriage of the King and Queen. *Royal Family* appeared to do the same. The difference was the medium chosen, television bolder in its promise of 'reality' and truthfulness. Even an astute viewer like *Evening Standard* columnist Milton Shulman would suggest 'it is fortunate that at this moment of time we have a royal family that fits in so splendidly with a public relations man's dream', a view with which the family-minded Elizabeth could have been persuaded to agree.[22] The danger lay in the extent of the claims made by *Royal Family*. Elizabeth's parents' vision had embraced only 'us four', a quartet as happy as photographs, newsreels and the

Queen Mother's pet writers insisted. Cawston's film included three generations, spouses and an extended cousinhood. In this populous domestic neverland, divorce was the wolf at the gate, the ultimate denial of harmony, blackened by its association with the abdication. Two years earlier, the divorce of Elizabeth's cousin Lord Harewood had foreshadowed the impossibility of Cawston's cumbrous group sustaining such exacting illusions. The break up of the Harewood marriage was sensationally reported as 'the third time within living memory that divorce has rocked the Royal Family' (Wallis Simpson and Peter Townsend were listed as forerunners).[23] It was unrealistic not to anticipate a fourth time.

Affection between Elizabeth and Charles emerged in the flick of a glance mother to son, the exchange of smiles, touchingly gentle on Charles's part, impossible for the camera to counterfeit. They are preparing salad while Philip barbecues. It suggests that Violet Bonham Carter's conviction of a gulf between the prince and his parents, observing them while staying at Windsor Castle in April 1968 – a conviction repeatedly shared by Charles himself – was overstated. 'Prince Charles... [is] quite unlike either parent... He is so different from his parents that one wonders where he has come from,' she wrote. She had been told that Elizabeth and Philip 'would like him to be quite different – keen on Polo and Sailing like Princess Anne – tougher & rougher –... they are not understanding & often critical. To send such a boy to Gordonstoun rather bears this out – a school of toughness, hardening, where people are expected to practise "adventurousness". To have to be "adventurous" as a duty & not from an impulse would be a nightmare. He would I imagine have been far happier at one of the traditional schools like Eton or Winchester.'[24] Charles was the film's main focus after Elizabeth: among its hooks were his forthcoming investiture as Prince of Wales and his twenty-first birthday in November 1969. His presentation to the people of Wales, as

Elizabeth had promised in 1958, took place within a fortnight of *Royal Family*'s first screening – watched by so many that a loo break intermission caused a temporary water shortage in London – in a theatrically conceived, made-to-order, pseudo-medieval ceremony at Caernarvon Castle, complete with slate 'thrones' and a modern princely crown.

Like *Royal Family*, Charles's investiture, designed and overseen by Tony Armstrong-Jones, was devised specifically as a small-screen extravaganza: the response of its television audience of 500 million was acknowledged as more important than that of the gathering within the castle walls or indeed the ceremony's main participants. Successfully, if surprisingly, it persuaded many of its spectators that its new-minted 'ceremonial rites... ha[d] scarcely altered over six and a half centuries'.[25] Elizabeth had requested from Norman Hartnell a simple silk coat and frock, with a striking hat that Hartnell called her 'medieval helmet'; shortly before the procession began she complained of a dressmaker's pin that had to be hastily removed.[26] Presenting monarchy afresh to television viewers across the globe, Elizabeth had returned to the dressmaker discovered by her mother a lifetime ago, who had created clothes for more than thirty state visits and overseas tours and every key ceremony in Elizabeth's public life. As with her coronation, she practised her part in the investiture beforehand. At the dress rehearsal, she remembered, Charles's coronet – too large for the prince's head – 'extinguished him like a candlesnuffer'.[27] His oath of fealty recalled Philip's at the coronation. Unlike Cawston's film, with its focus on royal 'ordinariness', Charles's oath was a reminder that, even in the bosom of her family, Elizabeth was also – and always – the Queen, and that the family in question was a dynasty bent on survival. The Marquess of Anglesey noticed 'a little bickering' between Elizabeth and Philip before the ceremony began. In a response that points to perceptions of the royal marriage,

Lady Gladwyn blamed Philip: 'probably cross because he was not in the limelight'.[28]

❧

Much in *Royal Family* was familiar to readers of the Court Circular or illustrated papers like the *Sphere* or the *Illustrated London News*: Elizabeth processing with knights of the Garter, taking the salute at Trooping the Colour, unveiling a statue, riding in a carriage, visiting a factory, meeting sportsmen, presenting the Queen's Medal for Poetry. There were glimpses of the executive side of Elizabeth's working life, previously confined to photographs of her seated at her desk: the daily delivery of red boxes, even at Balmoral; despatches of Foreign Office telegrams; audiences with the prime minister and overseas ambassadors. That the woman who navigated this unforgiving daily round appeared at the same time wry and fully convinced of its importance achieved the aim shared by Philip and William Heseltine of countering arguments that Elizabeth and her family were 'out of touch'; the impression conveyed, wrote Milton Shulman, was of 'homeliness, industry and relaxation'. Yet the film did not conceal the splendour of much of Elizabeth's existence, the shimmering glamour of interiors at Buckingham Palace and Windsor, a floating home-from-home in the form of the royal yacht, the swan-like progress of a routine oiled by domestic help on a scale that, in the interval since Elizabeth's childhood, had virtually disappeared elsewhere: carrots for the royal horses presented by a footman on a silver salver; Elizabeth's lady's maid, Bobo, on hand to discuss the possibilities of a magnificent ruby necklace. If, as critics then and since have argued, *Royal Family* let daylight flood the royal magic, it also reminded viewers of the magic's existence and Elizabeth's status as the inheritor of a millennium-long tradition, a powerful endorsement of her legitimacy. The film was a careful publicizing of royal continuity and Elizabeth's committed busyness, supported by her family; it gave substance to her statement that she survived 'by enjoying myself every moment of the day'. It was not a rebranding akin to the streamlined monarchies of Scandinavia and the Netherlands, which has never been Elizabeth's aim.

Royal Family showed something of the extent to which, in the second decade of her reign, Elizabeth's life adhered to a calendar that would have been recognizable to her grandparents as well as her parents. Neither the social shifts of the 1960s nor Elizabeth's first socialist government, under Harold Wilson, elected in 1964, had disrupted the time-honoured round of the royal year: the court's annual progress from wintry Sandringham to Windsor for Easter and late-summer family holidays at Balmoral, including an annual visit, on *Britannia*, to the Queen Mother at the Castle of Mey. A clutch of engagements were immoveable: the Holy Week distribution of the Royal Maundy, the Birthday Parade on Elizabeth's official birthday in June (the only occasion on which she rode side-saddle, which she disliked), the Garter Service, State Opening of Parliament and Act of Remembrance at the Cenotaph. The reception held for members of the diplomatic corps, accredited to the Court of St James's, was the grandest party in the royal calendar; there were garden parties at Buckingham Palace and the Palace of Holyroodhouse in Edinburgh; Elizabeth and Philip continued to invite distinguished subjects to 'informal' lunches – beards, hypnotism and the blind had been among uncontroversial conversational topics at the lunch attended by the actress Flora Robson in the spring of 1958.[29] In the racing calendar, the Derby and Ascot week were non-negotiable. Every year, in the early years of her reign, at Ascot, Elizabeth, members of her family and house party guests enjoyed a late-morning race of their own on the empty course, Elizabeth, as on the beaches of South Africa with Margaret, hatless and exhilarated. Long-haul

Commonwealth visits took place in the winter; there were state visits overseas and official visits hosted at Buckingham Palace and, in time, Windsor Castle. Simply by showing Elizabeth off script, in a variety of domestic settings, *Royal Family* convinced its viewers of her connectedness to the here-and-now; a Mass Observation survey in its aftermath showed a rise from sixty-nine to eighty-one per cent in those who considered her 'in touch with what is going on'.[30] With its curious dichotomy of extreme material comfort and the pervasive helpless concern that was one potential response to her privileged access to government reports, including Foreign Office papers, Elizabeth's life had little in common with that of most of her subjects beyond its family relationships. Bar transport methods, a more clamorous media and the particular fears of the Cold War, the affinities of her day-to-day existence were overwhelmingly with those of her immediate predecessors. In 1947, disappointment underpinned the reaction of a snobbish Edinburgh antiques dealer to photographs of the royal family in South Africa: 'my name for them, "the Smith family", is more than ever suitable now... The King and two princesses are exactly like the average person one sees in any street, on any day, at any time, in any town in Great Britain.'[31] By 1969, responses of this sort, encouraged by *Royal Family*, were part of Heseltine's purpose.

For the moment, few of the film's viewers heeded Milton Shulman's warning that 'every institution that has so far attempted to use TV to popularise or aggrandise itself, has been trivialised by it.'[32]

❧

'She is not clever, but she is reasonably intelligent and she is experienced: she has been involved in government now for eighteen years,' wrote Labour MP Tony Benn in July 1969, after accompanying Elizabeth to the Steam Generating Heavy Water Reactor at Winfrith in Dorset.[33] Grudgingly, anti-monarchist Benn acknowledged the thoroughness of Elizabeth's preparation for her visit, which he attributed to her diligence in reading cabinet papers or her private secretary's diligence in briefing her.

Elizabeth had evolved a working method, at first based on observation of her father, in which both played their part: she relied on her private secretaries, she was scrupulous in the time she devoted to government papers. In the interval since her accession, her confidence in this modus operandi had grown. She discovered that she *was* interested in politics, including political gossip. Labour minister Roy Hattersley would describe her as 'interested in the machinery of government'.[34] She was passionately interested in the Commonwealth, of which she received information from the governors-general that they did not share with her prime minister or members of the cabinet and the Commonwealth secretary-general; she trusted her closest advisers and attendants, most of whom were her own appointments; she was helped by Philip's trenchancy and intelligence. By 1969, she had surrounded herself with a reliable team. Michael Adeane and Martin Charteris had been her private secretary and assistant private secretary from the beginning of the reign; since 1954, Patrick Plunket had brought style and wit to the role of deputy master of the household; Bobo MacDonald, tyrannical in her dealings with members of the household and palace staff, remained passionately devoted to the 'little lady' she had served and protected since babyhood. 'Always when she is at home Her Majesty fulfils her role as mistress of the house, deciding details of the domestic work, changes of furniture and furnishings, selecting menus,' wrote Brigadier Stanley Clarke in 1958.[35] In fact, much of this remit fell to Plunket, whose glamorous arrangements of table settings and lighting and banquets and flowers, his engaging manners and light touch in all his dealings added lustre to Elizabeth's court. Among Elizabeth's ladies were long-term associates, like former lady-in-waiting Jean Elphinstone, now a woman of the bedchamber. In 1960, Elizabeth had appointed two further women of the bedchamber, Hon. Mary Morrison and Lady Susan Hussey, described by Joyce Grenfell as 'tall, dark, elegant, domesticated... and a creature of spirit and understanding'.[36] Seven years later, on the Duchess of Northumberland's retirement as mistress of the robes, Elizabeth invited the Countess of Euston, afterwards the Duchess of Grafton, married to former Windsor 'body guard' Hugh Euston, to succeed her. All three women would remain in post for more than half a century. Their long service points to the loyalty Elizabeth inspires and a level of harmony within her household. None satisfied earlier pressure to broaden the social base of Elizabeth's court; their shared background contributed to smooth working practices. Given Gallup's endorsement a decade after Altrincham, Elizabeth, who had lived her whole life among an aristocratic clique, did not reform this particular aspect of the royal machinery. Her ladies were drawn from the traditional courtier class. 'If you live this sort of life,' Elizabeth explained in 1992, 'you live very much by tradition and continuity.' Elizabeth's instinct remained to look backwards. It was an aspect of her family piety, loyalty to the King's memory, and almost certainly shaped by her mother's aversion to change. Like her father, Elizabeth made sense of monarchy through reference to precedent. In May 1955, she had presented to the Aga Khan the insignia of Knight Grand Cross of the Order of St Michael and St George. 'Her Majesty', the Aga Khan explained, 'observed that, since I was a prince myself and the descendant of kings, she would not ask me to kneel to receive the accolade... but would simply hand the order to me.' It was, he noted, as Elizabeth was aware, the same courtesy extended to him by Queen Victoria, conferring his first knighthood almost sixty years before.[37]

By the time of *Royal Family*, Elizabeth's confidence extended to her relationship with many in the Labour government that, in October 1964, had replaced Home's brief ministry. Born in 1916, Harold Wilson was the first of her prime ministers to be too close to Elizabeth in age to play the role of elder statesman or *preux chevalier*. Instead he allowed himself to fall in love with an idea of Elizabeth; over time his aides would worry about the extent of his besottedness. Elizabeth had kept to herself her response to Wilson's electoral victory. The defeat of the 14th Earl of Home by the man he called 'the 14th Mr Wilson' was characteristic of the country's altered mood. Wilson's cabinet was known to include republicans, although he himself shared little of their radicalism – one Labour supporter reported the view of party faithful that 'Wilson is too much of a Conservative.'[38] If Elizabeth's own views were apolitical, those of her mother, who remained a central influence in her life, were less so; both royal women understood the importance of Elizabeth establishing effective and harmonious working relations with her latest premier. To the surprise of Elizabeth's courtiers, Wilson arrived at the palace for his first formal meeting with a phalanx of his family. Elizabeth saw him alone. She questioned him about cabinet minutes relating to the Milton Keynes New Town project and found him unprepared. With some embarrassment, he learned the truth of his predecessor's verdict that 'the Queen... is always up to date and fully versed in the niceties of every national and international problem', and swiftly, given his willingness to acknowledge and remedy his mistake, minister and monarch achieved an easy, even cosy, rapport.[39] On the surface, Wilson conceded to Elizabeth a flattering degree of parity. Their relationship went further. Awareness of the gulf between them sharpened their mutual curiosity. Wilson represented a class Elizabeth scarcely knew, modest in background, proudly provincial and grammar school-educated, but as traditional as Elizabeth in his taste for pageantry and his old-fashioned patriotism. One of Elizabeth's ladies-in-waiting remembered her announcing, after their first audience, 'We have to work very hard on him.'[40] She soon achieved the desired outcome. Among Elizabeth's surprises for her new prime minister was her interest in back-to-back housing in Leeds, where she had opened a new housing estate.[41] Wilson discovered he could talk to Elizabeth less guardedly than to many of his colleagues; he described her as 'very informal, very well informed, and always very *interested*'.[42] She in turn responded to his loquacity, flattered, Edward Ford claimed, 'that he appeared to want to inform her about what he intended to do'.[43] The length of their audiences stretched. Wilson smoked his pipe; Elizabeth took the unusual step of asking him to stay for drinks.

Undoubtedly the contempt of members of his government spiked Wilson's partisanship towards Elizabeth: Housing Minister Richard Crossman, Postmaster General Anthony Wedgwood Benn, Minister of State for Economic Affairs Anthony Crosland, and backbencher Emrys Hughes, whose proposed Abolition of Titles Bill moved Elizabeth to behind-the-scenes protest in 1967. Crossman in particular was fascinated by the monarch even as he protested his distaste for monarchy; he and Benn delighted in small-scale discourtesies towards Elizabeth, who, understanding, mostly avoided responding. Staunchly socialist Barbara Castle, the Minister of Overseas Development and afterwards Minister of Transport, discovered common ground with Elizabeth and Margaret as women in the public eye. She admired what she considered Elizabeth's professionalism and the conscientiousness that had first impressed Wilson; her concern that Elizabeth 'never relaxed for a moment' was sympathetic as well as regretful.[44] She interpreted as a very human reaction Elizabeth's 'obvious pleasure' in a compliment on her dress;[45] she was amused by the accuracy of Margaret's impersonation of Crosland and her support for the abolition of the death penalty. Ideological opposition at the heart of the ministry heightened the need for Elizabeth and her advisers to establish trust with Wilson himself. In the face of her success, Richard Crossman would lament the government's 'working class socialists who are by and large staunchly monarchist. The nearer the Queen they get the more the working class members of the Cabinet love her.'[46] It was an effect of which Elizabeth was fully aware, a variant of Philip's Eastenders 'wav[ing] their little flags' and the more marked because of Elizabeth's sex. On the letters page of the *Illustrated London News* bubbled a very British spat about a misrendering of the final line of the National Anthem as 'God save *our* Queen'. A reader in Shropshire suggested it arose from 'the natural protectiveness her male subjects feel towards a Queen... More warmth and less austerity would seem naturally to colour people's feelings towards a "sovereign lady", and to awaken the kind of gentle possessiveness... that "our" suggests.'[47] The same protectiveness would tincture attitudes among Wilson's cabinet.

Yet opposition remained, exemplified by Wedgwood Benn's well-known campaign to dislodge Elizabeth's head from commemorative stamps. In January 1965, artist David Gentleman wrote to Wedgwood Benn, 'I'm convinced that the main single drawback to the realisation of unified modern designs is the monarch's head, not merely the unsatisfactory angle of the present photograph but the traditional inclusion of the head at all.'[48] It was music to the politician's ears. He encouraged Gentleman to produce designs omitting Elizabeth's head and, in March, presented a selection to her. A polite, embarrassed Elizabeth expressed interest. In Wedgwood Benn's account she 'indicated that she had no personal feeling about it at all'.[49] He concluded that she had agreed to his plan, which he disguised to himself as 'popular clamour for change'.[50] Unlike Wedgwood Benn's Elizabeth, Michael Adeane did have strong personal feelings about the matter. So, according to Margaret, did the Queen Mother when Elizabeth showed her Gentleman's proposals, as she did all new stamp and coin designs. The Queen Mother's emphatic reminder, 'You are the Head of *State*!' precluded the possibility of ambivalence on Elizabeth's part.[51] Elizabeth spoke to Wilson; they discussed the new stamps for more than an hour. Wilson told Wedgwood Benn 'that she didn't want her head removed from the stamps. "She is a nice woman," he said to me, "and you absolutely charmed her into saying yes when she didn't really mean it,"' Wedgwood Benn recorded in his diary. 'He went on, "I don't think you ought to go back and argue it out with her again because I'm sure you would win and she really wouldn't be happy."'[52] The minister admitted defeat, choosing to blame 'Adeane and all the flunkies at Buckingham Palace'.[53] Elizabeth's head remained on commemorative stamps. In addition, a new portrait of Elizabeth was commissioned for definitive stamps (Machin's sculpted relief, based on the Hedgecoe photographs that Elizabeth authorized). First issues appeared under Wedgwood Benn's successor Edward Short in June 1967. As if to banish the spectre of philatelic insurrection, Short was lavish in his praise of both Machin's image and Elizabeth herself: 'This stamp will rank with the classic Penny Black, one of the most beautiful stamps we have ever had – but, of course, we have one of the most beautiful queens.'[54] Never subsequently updated, Machin's portrait has since become the most reproduced work of art in history as well as an omnipresent aspect of Elizabeth's iconography.

～～～

Uniquely there was to be no Christmas broadcast in 1969. After *Royal Family* and the televised investiture ceremony, Elizabeth issued a written Christmas message instead. 'My thoughts', she wrote, 'are with my older children who are entering the service of the people of this country and the Commonwealth.'[55] At key moments in her children's lives, including long after they had grown up, Elizabeth, whose prestige always outstripped theirs, commended them to her subjects. In her last public statement of the 1960s, she made on their behalf the pledge of service that had formed the core of her own coming-of-age speech more than twenty years earlier. Service was the inarguable justification for immense privilege and unearned office. By 1969, it felt a more old-fashioned ideal than it had in 1947; it would continue to serve as a *raison d'être* of Elizabeth's welfare monarchy. Her own dutifulness was widely acknowledged and successfully showcased in *Royal Family*. She assumed the same of her children and encouraged subjects across the globe to share this assumption. The decision not to make a Christmas broadcast, following the year's television spectaculars, suggests an accurate assessment of the public mood: a Gallup poll published on 2 November found fifty-two per cent 'not disappointed' by Elizabeth's call.

There was nothing misleading in *Royal Family*'s presentation of Elizabeth's life as family-focused. By upbringing and inclination she was family-minded. Mountbatten's secretary noticed that she found it 'very difficult to relax unless she is surrounded by those with whom she feels at home';[56] Alathea Fitzalan Howard had described her twenty-five years earlier, as 'always happy in her own family'.[57] From her mother, as well as Queen Mary, she had absorbed a sense of family from infancy; 'I have always been a "family" person,' the Queen Mother wrote to Elizabeth. The distinct pressures of royal life encouraged Elizabeth's family to trust one another more readily than outsiders: the shadow of Crawfie's betrayal lingered. Only among her immediate family was Elizabeth treated with a degree of normality. Daphne du Maurier, Elizabeth's hostess on a handful of occasions as the wife of courtier Boy Browning, recorded her surprise in 1962 at her own inability to speak normally and behave sensibly towards Elizabeth: 'I don't know what was talked about, I heard sounds coming from my mouth I didn't recognise!'[58] Composer Benjamin Britten remembered visits to Sandringham as potentially 'dire... with everybody keeping their mouths shut for fear of saying something that might give offence, or prove controversial or indeed just interesting'.[59] At the Oxford Union, in May 1968, 800 students were emasculated by Elizabeth in their midst. 'When the cheering stopped,' wrote one in his diary, 'a sudden chill filled the atmosphere. There was silence, and a palpable awkwardness, in the hall... because of the presence of the Queen none of us could be "normal".'[60] Writer Jonathan Gathorne-Hardy recorded an alternative but no less unnatural response: being 'engulfed by a wave, a tsunami, of sycophancy and showing off'.[61] Even before her accession, Elizabeth had become accustomed to distorted encounters with those overcome by nerves, excitement, silliness or fawning, reactions that were all but universal. Her social exposure as a child had been dominated by family members: her royal aunt, uncles and her Lascelles cousins at the birthday parties hosted for her at Windsor Castle by George V and Queen Mary; riding with her Uncle Harry, the Duke of Gloucester, in Windsor Great Park; any number of Bowes-Lyon cousins in Scotland. In the short term, Elizabeth had remained close to the Duke of Gloucester and his wife, Alice – Elizabeth and Philip spent their seventh wedding anniversary at the Gloucesters' house in Northamptonshire; among the adult Elizabeth's close friends were her Elphinstone cousins Margaret and Jean and their husbands, Denys Rhodes and John Wills. Family provided Elizabeth with the dominant metaphor of her speech-making; it supplied her recurring image of the Commonwealth, 'rather a special family – a family of nations', as she called it in 1971, the same image her father and grandfather had chosen for the Empire. For Elizabeth – conveniently overlooking the ongoing feud with the Duke and Duchess of Windsor, one of several areas in which she had no appetite to challenge what she imagined was her mother's implacability – 'family' was synonymous with unity, happiness and as much as her life allowed her of normality.

Much of Elizabeth's time off duty was spent with relations. In the small private dining room at Windsor Castle, she had watched *Royal Family* with Philip, Anne and Philip's youngest sister Sophie, Princess George of Hanover, called 'Tiny'. Sophie was a favourite sister-in-law and a regular visitor: she and George of Hanover, her second husband, had first been invited to stay with Elizabeth and Philip at Birkhall in 1948. Anti-German feeling in the aftermath of the war demanded a degree of discretion about their early visits; that Elizabeth agreed to be godmother to the couple's youngest daughter, Friederike, in 1954, and three years later, Philip became godfather to Princess Maria Tatiana of Yugoslavia, Sophie's granddaughter by her Nazi first husband, Christoph of Hesse, went largely unpublicized. Even years later, a newspaper could ask rhetorically, 'Who were the guests accompanying the Royal Family, on holiday at Deeside, to morning service at Crathie Church yesterday?', before informing readers of their identity: Sophie, her son Welf and nephew Albrecht of Hohenlohe-Langenburg, the youngest son of Sophie and Philip's eldest sister, Margarita.[62] Since May 1967, Philip and Sophie's mother, Princess Andrew of Greece, had lived at Buckingham Palace. Political turmoil in Athens, which would shortly force into exile the new Greek king, Constantine, prompted Elizabeth's invitation to the ailing, lonely and impecunious princess. Wearing the full-length grey nun's habit she had adopted since founding a religious sisterhood in 1948, chain-smoking and with a hacking cough, Alice was an exotic houseguest. Previously Elizabeth had contributed to her religious charities; now she treated her with great kindness and relished her memories of Queen Victoria.

Andrew and Edward played halma with their throaty-voiced grandmother; with a hearth brush in place of a cricket bat, Andrew attempted to return the soft balls Alice bowled along the palace corridors. All contributed to the contentment of Alice's final years. A decade earlier, a similar compassionate instinct had prompted Elizabeth's invitations to her youngest cousin, Prince Michael of Kent, whose father had died when he was seven weeks old. In August 1955, thirteen-year-old Michael boarded *Britannia* to sail with Elizabeth, Philip, six-year-old Charles, five-year-old Anne and Philip's mother, from Portsmouth to Weymouth, Milford Haven, the Isle of Man and eventually to Scotland, to share the family's summer break at Balmoral; he had spent the week before departure sailing at Cowes with Philip.

In November 1969, Elizabeth's family feelings became a matter for public debate with Philip's announcement on American television of the precariousness of royal finances. Since the accession, Elizabeth's Civil List payment – the money she received from the government for official expenses, in return for surrendering the income of the Crown Estates – had remained fixed. Inflation throughout the 1960s, rising consumer prices and salaries had incurred an inevitable shortfall. Philip told American viewers he had been forced to sell his ocean-going yacht, *Bloodhound*, 'and I shall probably have to give up polo fairly soon'; the royal family, he explained, would shortly go into the red. Flippant or simply ill-judged, his comments focused attention on an area of considerable sensitivity: the cost of the monarchy. More circumspectly, Elizabeth had already initiated a dialogue about royal finances with Harold Wilson. She cannot have welcomed her husband's comments, which earned Philip the disparaging moniker 'the royal shop steward' from former unofficial leader of the London dockers Jack Dash, and placed what Wilson described as 'this important... and delicate matter' indelicately on newspapers' front pages, where it would remain on and off for the next three years. Elizabeth's reputation for frugality counted for little in the face of Philip's own goal over his yacht and polo ponies. Among calls on the Civil List were allowances for those family members not funded by government grant but engaged in public duties whose support extended the reach of Elizabeth's own endeavours and whose efforts enabled Elizabeth's monarchy to maintain a formidable workload at home and abroad: her cousins Alexandra and Edward, Duke of Kent, and his wife Katharine. The accession grant, Wilson explained in the House of Commons, had included an allocation of £95,000, of which £25,000 was available 'for provisions by the Sovereign to members of the Royal Family for whom Parliament had not specifically provided'. 'The balance of not less than £70,000', said Wilson, 'was to provide a surplus for investment to provide for deficits which were expected to accrue later in the reign.' Deficits had accrued since 1962, and £25,000 no longer funded three additional members of the royal family. It was not Elizabeth's fault and even her most vocal critic, republican Labour MP William Hamilton, did not accuse her of personal extravagance (he preferred to accuse her of chutzpah for requesting what he determinedly called a pay rise at a time of ongoing economic slump).

Wilson called an election for the following year. In the meantime he made arrangements for a bipartisan select committee on royal funding to begin work afterwards. Although he lost the election to the Conservatives under Edward Heath, Wilson headed the committee's Labour MPs and was party to its scrutiny of royal finances, which proved anything but a formality. Given his deep attachment to Elizabeth, the ex-prime minister took no pleasure in Hamilton's vituperative comments about Margaret and the Queen Mother – *The Times* described his attitude as 'protective' – nor in the committee's close examination of two aspects of Elizabeth's financial position guaranteed to prove contentious then and afterwards: the monarch's tax exemption and the extent of her private fortune. The Select Committee made awkward recommendations, including an annual salary for Elizabeth and a halving of Philip's award; Elizabeth's refusal to disclose details of her personal wealth, supported by the committee's Tory chairman, prompted fetid speculation. Largely thanks to Labour abstentions, parliament passed an act the following year that almost doubled Elizabeth's annual Civil List allowance to £980,000. It sought to set this figure for the next decade, and increased the allowances made to other members of the royal family, including Philip, Margaret and the Queen Mother. It also established the principle of regular review.

For the palace, it was success at a cost. It had been a surprisingly confrontational process, and the disquiet it caused Elizabeth may account for her only partly flippant comment to Lord Cottesloe that she 'very much doubted' whether she would still be queen in five years' time.[63] In forcing the monarchy to justify its contribution to the life of the nation, the Select Committee did more than *Royal Family* to strip away its magic. There is no mystique in royal value for money. But Elizabeth had shown stubbornness and flashes of Hanoverian spleen. She had no intention of revealing her personal wealth, a refusal that inevitably gave rise to unhelpfully exaggerated estimates. Only Mountbatten's forceful intervention, in a plea to Philip in June 1971, quashed the press's wilder guesses: on palace instructions, Jock Colville, now at Coutts, told *The Times* that Elizabeth's fortune amounted to about £12 million. To the Select Committee Michael Adeane had let slip her attachment to the royal tax immunity. It was an exemption by which her father had set store. For as long as possible, Elizabeth intended to retain her privileged position.

The commission entrusted in 1960 by Elizabeth and Philip to architect Sir Hugh Casson, professor of interior design at the Royal College of Art, to remodel rooms in the Edward III Tower at Windsor 'made... quite clear that they wished to see within the Castle one suite of rooms that would be as typical of this time as other suites have been of times past'.[64] Philip rather than Elizabeth instigated this up-to-date brief: Casson was responsible for the earlier redesign of Philip's study at Buckingham Palace and, previously, *Britannia*'s interiors. Elizabeth, however, had her own views on paintings for the new rooms, to be hung against wallpaper by Edward Bawden. From the selection of works by living artists assembled by Patrick Plunket and, with some disdain, by the surveyor of the Queen's paintings, Anthony Blunt (not yet unmasked as a Soviet spy), Elizabeth's choices included drawings of surgeons' hands by Barbara Hepworth and eight landscapes empty of human figures. 'Elizabeth has brought the sun in and chased out the clustering shadows,' was the verdict of Queen Ena of Spain.[65]

Her father had worried that sovereignty would impose on Elizabeth a lifelong burden of loneliness. At times she craved the solitude of an empty landscape, with no smiling faces and no hands to shake. In the year of *Royal Family* and Charles's investiture, Elizabeth sat again for Annigoni, a commission for the National Portrait Gallery. In Annigoni's portrait of 1954, the isolation of her position had appeared romantic, even poetic. Over eighteen sittings he revisited the same theme. 'I saw her as a monarch, alone in the problems of her responsibility,' he said. In a magazine interview, he explained his view that 'over the past fifteen years her devotion to duty and service has led, in my eyes, to great solitude'; on a lighter note, he suggested that 'her disarming frankness never failed to surprise and fascinate me'.[66] Annigoni's second portrait of Elizabeth succeeded in its aim: in place of an individual, the stiff, red-cloaked figure has the monumentality of an institution. After a lengthy press build-up – itself proof of the success of recent initiatives in rekindling interest in Elizabeth and her family – many visitors to the gallery reacted furiously. Privy to Elizabeth's frankness, or what he took to be such, Annigoni had painted a woman who accepted the loneliness of sovereignty as unprotestingly as any of its burdens. In a television interview the week before his investiture, Charles had commended his mother as 'terribly sensible and wise'.[67] In Annigoni's portrait unveiled three months later, good sense and wisdom overmaster sprightlier impulses. Its bleak vision, the artist claimed, was of a woman who 'has become aware of her limits'. In truth, Elizabeth had always been modest, personal humility among the lessons she absorbed from her parents and grandparents, consolidated over time by her religious faith. To a twenty-three-year-old American Rhodes Scholar at Oxford called Bill Clinton, Elizabeth appeared, from a distance, 'elegant and stoic'.[68]

Happily, the decade ahead would convincingly challenge one tabloid's conclusion that Annigoni's latest portrait proved Elizabeth's world was 'no longer an enchanted royal playground'.[69] It began with another innovation on William Heseltine's part: Elizabeth's first walkabout, in Wellington, in March 1970, during a seven-week tour of dependably loyal New Zealand and, afterwards, Australia. Unlike the anti-climax of 1963, this was a visit of buoyant atmosphere. 'There is a feeling of eagerness that was lacking before the [last] visit,' one newspaper claimed.[70] It was partly the effect of *Royal Family*, including its revelation of Elizabeth's modernity. On-message Elizabeth commissioned from Norman Hartnell a mimosa-yellow coat and frock to team with Australia's wattle flower brooch: skimming her knees, it was considered daringly short for the forty-four-year-old monarch. Excitement had been generated, too, by Elizabeth's decision that Charles and Anne, twenty-one and nineteen respectively, accompany their parents.

Joyce Grenfell suggested that Alexandra was the real inventor of the walkabout, on a tour of Australia in 1959.[71] In Elizabeth's case, her agreement to step, even fleetingly, across the invisible margin that separated sovereign from subject was an important one. Neither her father nor her grandfather had walked among their people and spoken to them directly in this way. Often stilted, such exchanges nevertheless suggested on Elizabeth's part interest in the world and the people around her.

In the summer, Elizabeth made her first walkabouts at home, in Coventry and Manchester. A cabinet minister told Elizabeth 'you are so much closer to the people than we are, you know how the people feel', a sycophantic statement given substance by the casual encounters of the new walkabouts.[72] *Royal Family* had invested Elizabeth and her family with 'ordinariness'; the 1971 Select Committee attached a price tag to their actions. Lasting transformation came with the walkabout. Its chance exchanges, never forgotten by those singled out, made Elizabeth real.

CHAPTER XIV

'A love affair with the country'

～～～

MIDDLE AGE AND economic collapse are a surprising recipe for apotheosis. In the celebrations surrounding her Silver Jubilee in the summer of 1977, a mostly grateful nation repaid Elizabeth's twenty-five years on the throne with an enthusiastic demonstration of affection and admiration. In an echo of her grandfather's response four decades earlier, Elizabeth was both astonished and moved. To a courtier she repeated over and over again, 'I am simply amazed, I had no idea.' 'Why me?' she asked a friend, without disingenuousness. 'I'm just an ordinary person.'[1]

Without disappearing, the iconoclasm of the previous decade had dwindled. In 1975, a correspondent in the north of England had written to royal scourge William Hamilton, 'I think that our dear Queen does a wonderful job and cannot be praised too highly.'[2] Three years earlier, in November 1972, commentary accompanying television footage of Elizabeth and Philip's silver wedding anniversary procession to Westminster

Abbey had acclaimed Elizabeth as both loved and esteemed. In contrast to the rebellious spirit of the 1960s, which castigated Elizabeth as out of date and 'square', it identified as praiseworthy her very unchangingness: 'In an age of rapid change in which many ancient institutions, including marriage, have been questioned,' viewers learned, 'the Royal Family has set an example of stability and respect for the basic simple values of human relations that has inspired even the sceptics.'[3] It was a sentiment championed by rearguard comment in the *Daily Telegraph* as early as 1969, when the paper insisted 'there is really no need for continuous change in all things... what ordinary people desperately need in this age of swirling dissolution and transformation is something constant and durable to hang on to. Is it not part of the Monarch's high function to supply this?'.[4] Slogans on banners confronting Elizabeth on a visit to the University of East Anglia the year before had included 'No to Anarchy, Yes to Monarchy'. Both might have served as mission statements for Elizabeth, and the *Telegraph*'s plea for constancy did indeed later become one. For the moment neither William Heseltine nor Martin Charteris, appointed Elizabeth's private secretary on Adeane's retirement in April 1972, intended to forfeit the hard-won claim to being in touch that was among outcomes of *Royal Family*. And so a forward-thinking Elizabeth, describing herself and Philip, had told guests at the Guildhall lunch for her silver wedding anniversary, 'Neither of us are much given to looking back.' It was not true of her attitude to monarchy; it accurately expressed her pragmatic acceptance of a life of restricted freedoms and tyrannous diary planning. To her ladies-in-waiting was entrusted the task of acknowledging anniversary presents: red rose bushes from Lancashire County Council, a baby elephant from the president of Cameroon.

Elizabeth's Guildhall speech included a statement that ought to have surprised her husband: 'We had the good fortune to grow up in happy and united families.' This had been her own experience of the life of 'us four'; it was misleading as a description of Philip's fractured growing-up. Throughout the 1970s, Elizabeth continued to promote a vision of Britain's monarchy as a happy, unified family, an example of domestic probity to encourage and inspire. 'If I am asked today what I think about family life after twenty-five years,' she told Guildhall guests, 'I can answer with... simplicity and conviction. I am for it.' On Boxing Day, with nineteen family members, including all four of her children, her mother, sister, Kent cousins and their children, she and Philip had posed for official silver wedding photographs by Patrick Lichfield, himself a cousin through her mother's family. Several are strangely messy images. Elizabeth is seated centrally, her family sitting or standing round her heavy giltwood chair, would-be informality at odds with a backdrop of painted and gilded panelling and towering portraits of George III and Charlotte of Mecklenburg-Strelitz. The photographs' message was apparently simple, grounding a smiling Elizabeth within the family circle; the portraits recalled an earlier happy royal marriage, George and Charlotte parents to fifteen children. But Lichfield's photographs had a wishful as well as a celebratory quality. Both Margaret and Tony Armstrong-Jones had already embarked on the series of affairs that spelled out for each of them their long-term incompatibility. Elizabeth disliked gossip and inclined to ignore family difficulties, but the Snowdons' differences had ceased to be palace secrets. A book published in 1970 had informed readers that 'endless rumours circulate about Tony and Meg... When is Tony going to leave? Or vice versa'; among the author's interviewees were Margaret and Tony.[5] That children emulate their parents, faithful to family models, was a cornerstone of Elizabeth's beliefs and true in her own case. In her Christmas broadcast in 1971, she expressed her view of parents' responsibility towards their children: 'We... leave them with a set of values which they take from our lives and from our example.' It would hardly be true of her own children, and only a determinedly optimistic Elizabeth could have hoped that loyalty to their parents' ideals and the memory of 'us four' would continue to bolster Margaret in her increasingly acrimonious marriage.

In the spring of 1972, during a tour of France, Elizabeth visited the Duke of Windsor. Their meeting moved her to tears. Ten days from death, wasted by cancer and racked with pain, the duke had passed beyond high emotion. Interest in the family he had cast aside, who had punished his defection with private recrimination and icy public indifference, was consigned to memory. Elizabeth had already agreed to his request that he and the duchess be buried at Frogmore; their meeting so close to the end was for Elizabeth's benefit not his, a closing of a rupture of four decades' standing, at a point at which all that remained for the duke were his concerns for the wife he left behind. Despite being attached to a drip, he was dressed; he left his bedroom for an upstairs sitting room, his doctor close by. Somehow he summoned the energy at Elizabeth's entry not only to stand but to bow. In his gaunt, lined face were reminders of her father that shook Elizabeth deeply. To those who chose to interpret it as such, her visit was a sign of the family unity for which commentators like historian Sir Charles Petrie had been calling for a number of years. Following the duke's death ten days later, his coffin was placed on display in St George's Chapel, Windsor. At the funeral Elizabeth's behaviour towards the duchess was solicitous, even, in one account, touchingly maternal; the day after, she instructed her lord chamberlain, Lord Maclean, to accompany the duchess to Heathrow Airport for her return flight to Paris. None of the royal family joined Maclean, an absence noted by newspapers. It was an arid sort of reconciliation, evidence that, in some ways, Elizabeth did indeed, as she had told Guildhall guests, lack the appetite for looking back.

Divisions within Elizabeth's wider 'family' of the Commonwealth proved similarly challenging. In 1947, Elizabeth had dedicated herself for life to Britain's 'imperial family'; she had used her Christmas broadcasts to promote an ideal of Commonwealth unity. The Commonwealth was integral to her royal identity. She regarded it as a cornerstone of her inheritance. As late as 1970, in a speech in Hobart, she referred – either proprietorially or with old-fashioned paternalism – to '*my* Tasmanian people' (author's italics). She was Queen of the United Kingdom and former imperial territories large and small; on 16 September 1975, she had acquired an additional realm when the newly independent Papua New Guinea invited her to become its queen. In Britain, the passage of time had eroded popular imperialism, leaving a void that, for most of Elizabeth's subjects at home, the Commonwealth did not fill. In April 1962, cabinet secretary Norman Brook had asked 'What is the significance and purpose of the Commonwealth in the years ahead? What function and value will this new Commonwealth have in the modern world?'; writing in *The Times* in 1964, Conservative MP Enoch Powell described the grouping unambiguously as 'a gigantic farce'.[6] Wilson's replacement in the summer of 1970 by Conservative prime minister Edward Heath made clear to Elizabeth the peripheral status of her cherished family of nations for many of her countrymen. Heath was an ardent Europhile, committed to British entry to the Common Market; he accorded a much lower priority to the Commonwealth. Martin Charteris claimed that Elizabeth found him heavy going. His lack of concern for the Commonwealth, absence of small talk or perceptible humour and any chivalrous impulse towards Elizabeth personally, and his interests in sailing and classical music, which she did not share, made theirs a more socially sterile relationship than Elizabeth had enjoyed with Heath's predecessors. Heath subsequently described his punctilio in his dealings with Elizabeth, the agenda for their weekly audiences drawn up in advance and shared with Elizabeth's private secretary, much as Wilson had done, his determination to conceal nothing from her. Theirs were not, however, the easy, discursive exchanges Elizabeth had enjoyed with Wilson or Churchill, or Macmillan's wide-ranging disquisitions, though a practised Elizabeth quickly established trust between them, and Heath, who was unmarried, valued the possibility of unburdening himself in meetings that were reliably confidential. He discovered the full extent of Elizabeth's impartiality, noting that she never voiced opposition to government policy: her method was to probe him about the merits of a decision while withholding any indication of her own views. He did not treat Elizabeth with discourtesy, nor did he fail to support her. The Civil List settlement of 1970 was as favourable as Wilson or the palace could have wished. A letter leaked in December 1973 revealed that, like Elizabeth, Heath attached 'great importance to arrangements which protect the Queen's private share holdings from disclosure'.[7]

More than any previous prime minister, however, Heath made clear his distinction between the government's priorities and Elizabeth's. Each might have argued that their concern represented the nation's best interests, but it was Heath not Elizabeth who wielded ultimate power. His decision to resume selling arms to South Africa, overturning Wilson's embargo in protest at South African apartheid, angered black Africa: among those who threatened to leave the Commonwealth were Tanzania and Zambia. Elizabeth could not make public her sympathies any more than she could have ignored Heath's advice, amounting to an instruction, that she not attend the first Commonwealth Heads of Government Meeting in Singapore in January 1971, at which opposition to his policy was expected to be vocal and energetic. Elizabeth communicated to Heath's advisers her deep unhappiness and her feelings about his 'undisguised disrespect' for Commonwealth sensibilities and its leaders; she was more cautious about her views on his setting aside any role for her at the gathering.[8] That Heath's administration did not resolve the question of Rhodesia, which, in 1965, had declared itself independent under white rule, while attempting to retain Elizabeth as head of state, was unsurprising. The prime minister was simply not interested enough. Elizabeth's anxiety that the continuing political exclusion of Rhodesia's black majority anger other African nations to the extent of fragmenting the Commonwealth was one her premier apparently failed to share. Economic crises at home were more pressing; more immediate redress was demanded by escalating violence in Northern Ireland. In January 1972, the Bloody Sunday killing of thirteen unarmed civilian demonstrators by British paratroopers in Londonderry ushered in a year of frightful sectarian violence in which as many as 479 people would be killed and 4,876 injured. In the first instance, its likely effect on the Commonwealth, more than threats to national sovereignty, which did not emerge immediately, coloured Elizabeth's attitude to Britain's joining the EEC, which came into effect on 1 January 1973. This was the rationale behind her Christmas broadcast of the preceding week: carefully emollient, mindful of Commonwealth reactions to Macmillan's entry bid in 1960. Elizabeth suggested that 'new links with Europe will not replace those with the Commonwealth'; she prayed for peace in Northern Ireland. In both aspirations she would be thwarted. In December, she had accepted an invitation from Canadian prime minister Pierre Trudeau to attend the 1973 Commonwealth Heads of Government Meeting in Ottawa. She had responded to the invitation as Queen of Canada, without consulting Heath, sidestepping the possibility of a second veto. Plans were made for goodwill visits to Australia in October and, early in 1974, to New Zealand. On 3 January, Elizabeth and Philip joined Edward Heath at the Royal Opera House for a gala celebration, 'Fanfare for Europe'. The prime minister described his heart as 'full of joy... at the recognition which Her Majesty had given to our country's great achievement', but a Gallup poll had found only thirty-eight per cent of respondents in favour of joining the EEC and angry protesters heckled the royal arrival.[9] Three months before, at Stirling University in October, Elizabeth had experienced similar jeering, 'obscenities... and ribald songs' by students protesting at the cost of her visit there.[10] At Covent Garden, phlegmatic and tactful, she was well served by what she had once lamented as her 'rather too mundane' way of looking at things. Her tiara broke en route to the gala. Patrick Plunket came to her rescue and, in place of the broken jewel, Elizabeth wore Plunket's own family tiara, which he had hurriedly retrieved from his London home nearby. Anyone more fanciful might have been tempted to interpret it as an omen.

Public reaction in May 1973 to Anne's engagement to Mark Phillips, an officer in the Queen's Dragoon Guards and, like Anne, an international equestrian, focused on Phillips's lack of a title, like Tony Armstrong-Jones. More than Margaret's marriage, however, Anne's husband-to-be appeared on the surface a man of the sort Elizabeth herself might have chosen had she realized the childhood ambition she confessed to Horace Smith of living in the country with lots of dogs and horses. Phillips's father and grandfather had served as officers in the same Guards regiment. From 1947 to 1950, his maternal grandfather, Colonel John Tiarks of the Royal Armoured Corps, had served as aide-de-camp to George VI. At a photocall in the garden at Buckingham Palace, the newly engaged couple were joined by their black labradors. Debrett calculated that Anne and Mark were thirteenth cousins three times removed through a shared forebear in the early sixteenth century, a detail more likely to have amused than impressed unsnobbish Elizabeth. Colonel Tiarks's royal service overlapped with the first years of Elizabeth's marriage and the move to Clarence House, and the personal connection between the families was slender. Elizabeth was sceptical about the match, despite

Mark Phillips's prowess as a rider and interests confined to horses and the army. Her family, including Charles, shared her reservations, but Elizabeth did not intervene. She had never offered family leadership save by her own uncomplicated example in which dedication to her non-family role as sovereign overrode conventional maternal impulses. Anne was strong-willed; she expected to get her own way. Time would suggest with devastating clarity that Elizabeth's inclination to endorse her children's wilful autonomy was a lapse in the good sense and wisdom that Charles had praised at the time of his investiture.

Despite the clear unsuitedness for such a role of blunt, brusque Anne – the first British princess to command a Centurion tank – journalists determined to transform her into the heroine of a fairy-tale romance. Only a year before, Cecil Beaton had described Elizabeth at forty-six as 'positively dazzling... her eyes flashed like crystal, her teeth dazzling, her smile radiant... at the peak of her looks,... a work of art'; in the summer of 1971, the Earl of Longford had insisted she was 'wonderful, beautiful'.[11] With Anne's engagement, the Elizabeth of writers' and journalists' imaginations at last ceased to play the part of fairy-tale princess they had forced upon her for so long; the baton passed to a younger generation. The palace conspired in the improbable illusion. Norman Parkinson had photographed Anne for *Vogue* to mark her twenty-first birthday in 1971. In 1973, he was summoned again. He successfully created a rosy backlit vision of a jewelled and frilly-frocked princess, with her loving Guardsman, that helped stoke considerable public interest in their November wedding, on Charles's birthday, at Westminster Abbey. The ceremony was attended by a clutch of European royals, all of them bar Beatrix and Claus of the Netherlands and the Prince and Princess of Monaco relatives of the bride's. But attitudes had changed over Elizabeth's twenty-year reign. A film released after the ceremony, *Princess Anne – A Royal Romance*, informed viewers, as it might have done at the time of Elizabeth's own wedding, 'In all the best fairy stories the princess marries the man she loves.' On this occasion a note of equivocation unbalanced glib certainties: 'Let us hope that in this story too they all live happily ever afterwards.' It was also Elizabeth's hope. In a pattern that would characterize her dealings with her grown-up children, the hope proved sterile.

Gossip at court suggested that Elizabeth's hopes for Margaret's marriage were running thin. At the ball at Buckingham Palace on the eve of Anne's wedding, Cecil Beaton failed to see Margaret's husband. In his diary, Beaton, who disliked Tony Armstrong-Jones, reflected with some pleasure, 'It is said that the Queen would be willing to let P[rince]ss M[argaret] get rid of him but Tony won't go'; as always, Elizabeth's feelings towards her sister included an element of protectiveness.[12] The couple lived separate lives. Earlier that year, Margaret had been introduced to Roddy Llewellyn, a willowy young man seventeen years her junior; their relationship would ultimately test Elizabeth's tolerance and precipitate the end of Margaret's marriage. Margaret's susceptibility contrasted with the settled quality of Elizabeth's own domestic life, as Elizabeth was surely aware. Rumours of Philip's roving eye, gossip-writers' preoccupation in the 1950s, never entirely disappeared. He was flirtatious and energetic in his attentions to a handful of attractive, well-born women, but Elizabeth's public reaction was serene. Philip contributed a dash of mustard to the couple's family life; the strength of their shared affection was acknowledged by their closest friends. In the case of Margaret and Tony, love had ceased to season antagonism. Anne's brief transformation into the family's fairy-tale princess and Margaret's midlife waywardness seemed to legitimize Elizabeth's headscarf-wearing middle age: with the spotlight elsewhere, Elizabeth no longer needed to concern herself with Altrincham-style criticism of her tweediness, if indeed she ever had. After a performance at Windsor Castle by

Joyce Grenfell the summer of Anne's engagement, Elizabeth, who had chosen Grenfell's programme – 'All the numbers were comedy; that is what the Queen specifically wanted the programme to be'[13] – wrote to thank her. Elizabeth 'hoped they had not been a very "stuffed shirt" audience'.[14] Significantly, it was neither an apology nor a justification.

For Grenfell it was a golden evening, 'gloriously grand'. She was dazzled by the beauty of her surrounds, like poet Ted Hughes visiting Elizabeth at Buckingham Palace a year later, finding it 'more palatial than anything I had imagined possible... Everything gleaming & glittering under the chandeliers.'[15] Grenfell described it as 'managed with the superb order that only the British now seem capable of achieving... [an occasion] of real style to lift the heart, gladden the eye, and nourish the spirit'.[16] The superb order of Elizabeth's formal entertaining was mostly Patrick Plunket's doing. Grenfell marvelled at 'visual pleasures' she termed 'endless': 'eight-foot-tall standard fuchsias... all at their exact point of perfection', 'an exuberant flower arrangement, on a scale that made me gasp', the ballet-like procession into dinner. She did not see Plunket's imprint on the mix of Elizabeth's guests, his inclusion of those outside the tight-knit circle of traditional court aristocrats, or his solicitude for Elizabeth's own enjoyment; she did not know that it was Plunket, more than Queen Mary, who had engaged Elizabeth's enthusiasm for the dazzling art treasures by which she was surrounded. Unmarried and of easy charm, imaginative and deft, Plunket contributed harmony as well as style to Elizabeth's court. His combination of intense admiration for the woman he had known since childhood, adroit administrative skills in overseeing a wide-ranging remit and his readiness to have with her the difficult conversations others avoided made him invaluable and irreplaceable, as Elizabeth knew. The *Daily Mirror* suggested that Plunket would emerge from Elizabeth's official biography as 'her eyes and ears on a world that is often denied to her'; it described their low-key visits to the ABC Cinema on London's Fulham Road, followed by supper nearby at San Frediano or Spot 3, and cosy TV dinners in Philip's absence watching *Mastermind* or *Till Death Us Do Part*.[17] Plunket rode with Elizabeth, shot with Philip, fished with the Queen Mother and Charles, played the piano with Margaret. His diagnosis of inoperable cancer of the liver, followed by his death on Easter Sunday 1975, shook Elizabeth; an unnamed 'close friend' described her two months later as still 'very miserable'.[18] His death robbed her court of a senior official whose respect for tradition was neither pompous nor inflexible; he had leavened the staidness that was inevitable in an environment shaped by caution and precedent. Unusually Elizabeth attended both his funeral and memorial service. His family believed she had a hand in his obituary in *The Times*; she agreed to his burial at Frogmore, where she also contributed to a memorial in the form of a pavilion. A lady of the bedchamber described Patrick Plunket as 'the one person who could talk to [Elizabeth] on equal terms'.[19] It has become a biographical commonplace to liken the relationship of monarch and courtier to that of siblings, but even in one of Elizabeth's last letters to him she maintained her distance, signing herself formally 'Yours sincerely, Elizabeth R'.[20] On this occasion she accompanied the note, delivered on Plunket's breakfast tray, with a posy of miniature spring flowers.

Plunket's bequest to Elizabeth of the small seascape by early-nineteenth-century landscapist Richard Parkes Bonington that had previously hung above the chimneypiece in his drawing room in the country testified to his affection. An image of English coast and sky, it was a reminder too of the solace of wide-open spaces away from the hurly burly.

The plan conceived by London Transport in the summer of 1976 to mark Elizabeth's Silver Jubilee a year later with twenty-five silver-painted buses included a hope that advertisers would be found to sponsor the buses' new livery. The country's economic condition remained parlous. A month after Anne's wedding, in the face of dwindling fuel supplies, union militancy and steeply rising costs of living, including a seventy per cent increase in oil prices, Edward Heath had imposed a three-day week and power cuts. A second Wilson premiership, following two elections in 1974, failed to redirect the tide. Within a year, inflation hit twenty-five per cent. Strikes multiplied, dividing popular sympathies. There were, wrote Philip, 'many worms in the fruit'.[21] Elizabeth's engagements accommodated pressing concerns. Among iconic images of the mid-1970s were photographs of the royal visit to Silverwood Colliery in South Yorkshire: in snowy white overalls and wearing a hard hat over her headscarf, Elizabeth smiles dazzlingly as she talks to miners. In 1976, Britain applied to the International Monetary Fund for a £2.3 billion bail-out. Two years earlier, Elizabeth herself had been forced to request a similar bail-out: a second increase in the Civil List, to an annual £1.4 million. Agreed by a disgruntled parliament, the request at such a pass was not guaranteed to bolster popular support either for Elizabeth or the monarchy more generally. In an atmosphere of grumbling discontent, William Hamilton's republican philippic, My Queen and I, was widely publicized; his targets included Margaret, wintering on Mustique, derided for 'her expensive, extravagant irrelevance'.[22] Elizabeth's personal economies were less widely circulated, though her decision in 1975, explained to dressmaker Hardy Amies, that her wardrobe for tours to Mexico and Japan would need to include 'my last year's dresses' in order to cut costs, could not have gone far to counter Hamilton's criticisms, well-informed as they were given his place on the 1971 Select Committee.[23] 1974 had been a successful year for Elizabeth as a racehorse owner. Her filly Highclere won the 1,000 Guineas at Newmarket, the Prix de Diane at Chantilly and the King George VI and Queen Elizabeth Diamond Stakes at Ascot. It was the first time in nearly two decades that one of Elizabeth's horses had won a classic title, and her winnings, in the year of her second requested Civil List increase, amounted to £140,000.[24] Two years later, to her considerable pleasure, it was another of Elizabeth's horses, Goodwill, that Anne rode in the Montreal Olympics as a member of the British equestrian team.

Plans for local celebrations of Elizabeth's Silver Jubilee, only the second in British history, occupied communities across Britain throughout a year's lead-up. As expected there were dissenters: Labour councillors in Knowsley, for example, pressed instead for celebration of May Day as Labour Day. 'No matter how much the children would enjoy the celebrations for the Queen, I think it would be more appropriate to have them on May Day. It would be better than celebrating this outmoded institution,' insisted Councillor George Howarth in December.[25] The same month Charles gave up his command of minesweeper HMS *Bronington*, leaving the navy to head the committee organizing official jubilee celebrations. He gave his navy severance pay to the new Prince's Trust, which he had launched in June. Elizabeth requested that a proposed jubilee scheme 'help young people help others' by encouraging voluntary service by the young within their own communities.

It was not in Elizabeth's nature to anticipate the approaching celebrations as a personal endorsement, though for the most part her staff, led by Martin Charteris, were both determined and quietly confident. With the exception of silence on the part of the poet laureate, John Betjeman, who excused himself as lacking inspiration, responses to Elizabeth's fiftieth birthday in April 1976 had offered grounds for optimism. 'At a time when the country needs all the encouragement it can get,' *The Times* had told readers, 'it is a strength and reassurance that the central institution of the monarch is so sound.'[26] With Britain close to bankruptcy and forced to cut public spending as a condition of IMF aid, government bodies were more apathetic than the palace or the provincial scout groups and Women's Institute branches whose plans filled local papers. Unlike protracted anticipation of the coronation, interest in the Silver Jubilee was slow to gain momentum. In this instance, Charles forced Betjeman's hand. The poet's lacklustre offering provoked derision, though its reference to 'That look of dedication / In her trusting eyes of blue' came close to how Elizabeth may have wished to be commemorated, and suggests the open gaze of Michael Noakes's enigmatic portrait of Elizabeth, painted at the time of her silver wedding anniversary, which Charles, who acquired it, later included in an exhibition of his favourite works of art.

In the prayers led by the Bishop of London in the service of thanksgiving at St Paul's Cathedral on 7 June 1977, at which Elizabeth appeared markedly happy, was the hope that she 'always possess the hearts of her people'. Demonstrations of the extent and sincerity of popular affection dominated jubilee summer. Elizabeth's visits to thirty-six counties of the United Kingdom were greeted by enormous crowds: in Bristol city centre, a quarter of a million people clustered to see her; some 40,000 children filled a stadium in Leeds. Tributes were fond and eccentric in equal measure, a distinctively British gallimaufry. In Cricklewood, firemen were required to assemble the twenty-five tiers of jubilee cake baked and iced over six months by a local electrician; half a million rose petals, collected from the city's gardens, rained on Elizabeth's drive through Bath; in still working-class Fulham, kerbstones were painted red, white and blue and house fronts extravagantly strung with bunting. A million people thronged the Mall to watch the royal procession that culminated in the golden state coach in which Elizabeth and Philip had last ridden in 1953; the size of the crowds equalled those of the coronation. The Archbishop of Canterbury celebrated 'service untiringly done, duty faithfully fulfilled, and... a home life stable and wonderfully happy'. Elizabeth wore a dress and matching coat of bright pink, the same colour she had worn forty-two years earlier for her grandfather's silver jubilee. Even its designer, Hardy Amies, admitted its costliness, the coat 'lined with the same material as that of the dress. This was extravagant because the heavy silk crepe was very expensive.'[27] In a nod to straitened times, it was not a new outfit: she had worn it a year earlier, to open the Olympic Games in Montreal.

Commentators acclaimed the 'ecstatic ovation' that accompanied the gold coach on its journey. Martin Charteris detected a similar response throughout Elizabeth's extensive travels, which encompassed every part of Britain, despite the dangers in Northern Ireland, where over 30,000 police and troops were on alert throughout her two-day visit, and journeys of 56,000 miles around Commonwealth countries. 'She had a love affair with the country,' Charteris suggested; Philip Ziegler noted that, as she walked among the crowds, 'their hands stretched out to her as if she were a medieval monarch whose touch would cure'.[28] It was a very personal triumph at a low point in the nation's fortunes, proof of a theory expounded thirty years earlier in John Masefield's poem written to commemorate Elizabeth's wedding: 'A Crown shines,' the poet had claimed, 'when hope is dim and luck is out of joint... There a land's spirit finds a rallying point.'[29] Fervent, fleeting expressions of mass affection are typical of royal celebrations. In the summer of 1977, a continually smiling Elizabeth appeared to return the warmth of feeling she encountered in walkabouts the length and breadth of the country. Robert Lacey recorded a brief exchange in which a young woman told Elizabeth, 'We've come here because we love you.' It was not the sort of statement with which Elizabeth typically engages, but she responded in kind, revealingly: 'I can feel it, and it means so much to me.'[30] By the end of her reign, such statements had been overused by those in the public eye to the point of meaninglessness. This was not the case in 1977, and Elizabeth did not dissemble her feelings. That she allowed herself such candour suggests how moved she was. Throughout her life, lustily enthusiastic crowds had played their part: at her grandfather's silver jubilee, her parents' coronation and her own, on her visits overseas, both within and outside the Commonwealth. Elizabeth did not take for granted the feelings that drew people to the streets in jubilee summer; the most controlled of women, she was touched by a celebration that, as in her grandfather's case, became a robust thanksgiving for her twenty-five years' service. On its front page on 8 June, the *Daily Mail* quoted Elizabeth asking, 'Is everybody happy? I am!'[31] Her happiness both fed off and fed the warmth of public acclaim. Two days later, she took part in the final set piece of London celebrations, a river procession; she made her last appearance after midnight. In one diary account she was all but pushed on to the palace balcony by Margaret, who alone 'grasp[ed] the fervour of the crowd'.[32] Her cousin's wife, the Duchess of Kent, described her as 'totally bewildered and overwhelmed by this huge flood of affection directed towards her'.[33] 'The roar [of the crowd] was deafening. The Queen had only to lift her hand a little for a tide of fervour to ripple through the masses looking up.'[34] As Elizabeth had always acknowledged, she did not possess her mother's ability to respond with spontaneity to public displays. It was Margaret, less reserved, unconstrained by the experience of sovereignty, who understood instinctively what the public mood required and applied a firm sisterly push.

In each of her two key jubilee speeches, Elizabeth sounded an uncharacteristically personal note. Her response to parliament's loyal addresses in Westminster Hall in May was notable for its opposition to devolution at a time of strident regional nationalism, especially in Scotland: 'I cannot forget', she asserted, 'that I was crowned Queen of a United Kingdom.' Only a diplomatic 'perhaps' softened the force of her words in the interests of diplomacy: 'Perhaps this Jubilee is a time to remind ourselves of the benefits which union has conferred... on the inhabitants of all parts of this United Kingdom.' No one present doubted her seriousness. In her Christmas broadcast at the end of the year, she returned to the fray, opposed to any shrinking of her kingdom: she suggested that jubilee crowds had 'revealed to the world that we can be a united people'. In her speech at the Guildhall, at lunch following the service of thanksgiving, Elizabeth recalled her act of dedication made in Cape Town in 1947. 'Although that vow was made in my salad days, when I was green in judgement, I do not regret nor retract one word of it,' she announced with absolute conviction. Those closest to her witnessed the effect on her of her own words. Her mouth was working as she sat down after speaking. She seemed to smile, but struggled to suppress the smile. Often, when most moved, she conceals the strength of her emotion behind a thunderous expression. On jubilee day, grim composure failed her. What moved her so greatly? The success of her speech? The success of her walkabout en route to the Guildhall? Memories, like magic lanterns slides, of the quarter century now consigned to history? Or the pleasure she took in her own words, with their reaffirmation of her strongest statement of belief, her fidelity to the promises of her crowning? Was she most moved by the force of her own conviction, this woman whose commitment to her lifelong calling outstripped lesser bonds?

Like the coronation and the Commonwealth tour that followed it, Elizabeth's Silver Jubilee represented a personal high-water mark. It was a tribute to Elizabeth herself: although Philip was continually at her side, it did not emerge as a celebration of their joint achievement. It represented a decisive moment in public perceptions of a monarch who, unlike her grandfather in 1935, was assumed (correctly) to have many years still to reign. Up and down the country, Elizabeth embodied the remit for queenship that Michael Adeane had tried to explain to the 1971 Select Committee: 'Taking a lively interest in everything, saying a kind word here and asking a question there, always smiling'.[35] The huge crowds who turned out for her applauded her resilience; in a grinning summer of street parties and children's teas, they rejoiced in the survival of a vanishing Britain, the confident, decent, more neighbourly world of Elizabeth's parents. They knew her better than her predecessors, thanks to television and *Royal Family*. For a season their enthusiasm elevated her to the focus of national life. Postcards, children's scrapbooks, biscuit tins and mugs bore pixelated images of Elizabeth and Philip, as Victoria's jubilees had been marketed a century earlier. The British knew that Elizabeth was not like them, with her formal manners, her formal style of speech and dress (the hats and gloves that had all but vanished from ordinary wardrobes). Despite walkabouts, 'Liz rules OK' on banners and T-shirts and graffiti in shabby 1970s city centres, her formality preserved the distance between sovereign and subjects. The scale and magnificence of her life was unimaginable to many. In the year of her silver wedding anniversary, she had bought Polhampton Lodge Stud in Berkshire to expand the breeding and training programme of her racehorses carried on at Sandringham and Hampton Court; she added to her collection of tiaras in 1973, with a new ruby and diamond diadem made by Garrard; to Hugh Casson in 1974 she wrote, 'I hope Sandringham doesn't break us', as Casson's colleague David Roberts proceeded with an ambitious remodelling of the ungainly Victorian mansion that included pulling down one wing, constructing new areas and updating the main house, at a cost to Elizabeth of

£200,000.[36] After the maelstrom of the 1960s, Elizabeth's 'square' but sumptuous formality could be celebrated as dignity. Long forgotten were the embarrassing prognostications of new Elizabethanism, their only echo Benjamin Britten's decision to base his jubilee commission, the *Welcome Ode*, around a handful of Elizabethan lyrics. In Silver Jubilee year, Elizabeth was praised instead for steadfastness, the quality that would come to define her reign, and an instinctive understanding of what her countrymen expected of her. 'Since her reign began,' a television commentator informed viewers, 'the years between have known happiness and tragedy... and through it all she has kept the soul of Britain and the Commonwealth together with a modest but regal dignity.' The BBC's decision to ban from the airwaves the Sex Pistols' 'God Save the Queen', which coupled Elizabeth with 'a fascist regime', suggested survival of earlier protective instincts towards her. Even the former Lord Altrincham, now John Grigg, was moved to praise. Grigg identified as Elizabeth's most important quality her 'exceptionally steady character'.[37]

A queen with little appetite for change was praised for not changing. 'Through a period of fluctuating fashion and considerable moral disintegration, she has lived up to her own high standards and, in doing so, has set an example which has been grudgingly admired even by those who have not followed it,' Grigg wrote.[38] The poet Philip Larkin acclaimed similar qualities in Elizabeth. Conceived in retrospect, his was a shorter but more distinguished poem than Betjeman's official offering: It praised 'one constant good': her unchangingness at a time when everything around her 'worsened, or grew strange'.[39]

Twenty years had passed since Altrincham's attack in the *National and English Review*. After the cataclysms of the 1960s, the Fourth Estate apparently accepted Elizabeth on her own terms. For the most part, this would remain their verdict. 'While all else has changed, she has been unchanging,' noted one paper on

Unhappy family? Observers noted Elizabeth's concern for the newly widowed Duchess of Windsor at the Duke of Windsor's funeral in June 1972.

Happy family: Elizabeth and Philip with all four of their children at Balmoral the previous summer. From left: Anne, Charles, Edward, Andrew, Elizabeth and Philip.

Elizabeth on duty, with President Gerald Ford and Betty Ford, at a banquet in Washington, D. C. in July 1976. 'British royalty', the *New York Times* told readers, 'still has a fairytale glamor'.

Elizabeth off duty, riding at Balmoral in September 1971, one of several images released to mark her Silver Wedding Anniversary the following year.

A thoughtful Elizabeth with her second cousin once removed – and Philip's uncle – Dickie Mountbatten, in July 1979, the month before Mountbatten's assassination by the IRA.

'A love affair with the country', according to Martin Charteris: Elizabeth in Silver Jubilee year, with the Lord Mayor of London after the Service of Thanksgiving at St Paul's Cathedral, 7 June 1977.

'I survive by enjoying myself every moment of the day,' Elizabeth is reported to have commented: above, on a walkabout in New Zealand, in the spring of 1977, wearing the Maori cloak first given to her in the 1950s; and, below, at the Epsom Derby, in 1978, with Lord Porchester, her racing manager from 1969.

A lifelong bond: Elizabeth with her mother and sister,
photographed by Norman Parkinson in 1980.

With members of her immediate family, and children of her cousins, on
the balcony at Buckingham Palace after Trooping the Colour, 15 June 1985.
From left: Philip, Lord Frederick Windsor (Prince Michael of Kent's son),
Edward, Elizabeth, Anne, Charles (holding Harry), William, Diana, Lady
Rose and Lady Davina Windsor (daughters of the Duke of Gloucester)
and Anne's daughter Zara Phillips.

'Truly in love from the very beginning', according to Elizabeth's cousin, Margaret Rhodes – as they remained: Elizabeth and Philip at the Royal Windsor Horse Show, 16 May 1982.

Elizabeth's relationship with her first female prime minister, Margaret Thatcher – seen here with US president, Ronald Reagan, in June 1984 – provoked widespread speculation. Elizabeth's attachment to 'things going on as they are, tolerance, good manners, Christian behaviour, doing the right thing' was not always Thatcher's first priority.

Elizabeth admires some of the Terracotta Army soldiers at Qin Shi Huang's Museum of the Terracotta Warriors and Horses, during a state visit to the People's Republic of China, 1986.

In her own words 'a humbling experience', Elizabeth's Diamond Jubilee in 2012 included a pop concert in the gardens of Buckingham Palace. One performer acclaimed her as 'a living testimony to the power of dedication, kindness, tolerance and loyalty'.

In a marriage that lasted more than seventy-three years, until his death in April 2021, Philip proved, as Elizabeth called him, her 'strength and stay', 'a constant strength and guide'.

In isolation at Windsor Castle during the pandemic, Elizabeth's weekly audience with the prime minister, Boris Johnson, took place by telephone.

the thirtieth anniversary of her accession in 1982.[40] Wilson's successor, James Callaghan, attributed to Elizabeth's deliberate efforts the monarchy's continuing prestige.[41]

❧

Elizabeth celebrated more quietly a second, less public anniversary: Bobo MacDonald's fifty years of personal service. From Garrard she commissioned a flower-shaped brooch of twenty-five gold stamens set with twenty-five diamonds.[42] The bond between the two women was among the closest in Elizabeth's life, a relationship based on unwavering trust and a familiarity that Elizabeth shared only with her husband, her mother and her sister. In her early seventies, Bobo did not mean to leave her 'little lady' yet. Despite her high-handed behaviour towards other royal servants and members of the household, Elizabeth did not hasten her retirement, especially in the aftermath of Patrick Plunket's death and Martin Charteris's notice of his decision to retire in November. There had never been a time when Bobo had not been integral to the smooth running of Elizabeth's life. Like her parents, Elizabeth valued the stability of attendants of long standing. As she told Labour politician Richard Crossman, in any context she disliked the business of getting to know quantities of new people.

Yet she was powerless to prevent the diaspora of the late 1970s, including changes in her working life and her family life, with three of her four children grown up. That she anticipated the loss of Martin Charteris personally as well as professionally explained Anne's accompanying her to their farewell audience. Elizabeth presented Charteris with an engraved silver tray; she thanked him very simply 'for a lifetime'. It was quickly over. Charteris cried, as he had known he would; from the outset he had admitted falling in love with the woman he had served for twenty-seven years. Anne's unsentimental presence kept a check on her mother's emotions. Charteris had been the architect of many of the jubilee's successes, and his departure contributed to the inevitable sense of anti-climax that followed a strenuous year; Elizabeth comforted herself that 'he was still around if I needed to ask anything difficult'. [43] Like Patrick Plunket's death, his going also diminished the levity of Elizabeth's court and any sprightliness in her public speeches. His successor, Philip Moore, lacked both his puckishness and his romantic devotion to Elizabeth. It was left to William Heseltine, assistant private secretary since 1972, to continue to imbue Elizabeth's public life with traces of humour. At Elizabeth's instruction, Heseltine wrote to the mayor of Reading thanking him for a royal visit, 'The amenities of the new Magistrates Courts may not be appreciated by all who use them, but these... are clearly a marvellous addition to the civic buildings of Reading.'[44]

In February 1976, newspapers' exposure of Margaret's affair with Roddy Llewellyn and, in its wake, a formal announcement of the Snowdons' decision to separate had brought that 'moral disintegration' identified by John Grigg to the heart of Elizabeth's family. On the day of the royal announcement, after less than two years in office, Harold Wilson had announced his resignation from his second term as prime minister, concerned by his worsening health, including a fear of the 'premature senility' from which he claimed his mother had suffered (he subsequently developed Alzheimer's disease). Loyal Wilson may have hoped that his resignation would distract attention from Elizabeth's troubled sister. It didn't, and Margaret's black sheep newsworthiness would never disappear entirely. 'The hideous coverage really tarnishes,' director of the National Portrait Gallery, Roy Strong, recorded in his diary.[45] Elizabeth knew it and had feared something like it for some time. Happy in her own marriage, partly constrained by post-war sexual politics, which had expected her to combine the roles of queen and domestic paragon, like her parents she had promoted a vision of the post-abdication monarchy centred on family values; twenty years before, Margaret herself had chosen royal duty over her love for Peter Townsend. In April, the Queen Mother had written to Elizabeth that 'the three months after Christmas had been very difficult, what with one thing & another'. [46] Elizabeth's own response was less understated: she described herself to Tony as devastated by the marriage's breakdown. Again Elizabeth experienced divided loyalties as sister and sovereign, but she did not abandon Margaret. In June, at a state banquet for the new French president, Valéry Giscard d'Estaing, Elizabeth placed the statesman between herself and her sister. Margaret was with her for the opening of the new National Theatre in October, as well as jubilee celebrations the following summer. Historian Jack Plumb's observation at a royal dinner at Brooks's that 'the way to the "Headmistress" is through her sister' suggests an understanding among those on the fringes of the court of Elizabeth's continuing closeness to Margaret. [47] Elizabeth's support, however, neither ameliorated Margaret's difficult temper, which did not always spare her older sister, nor resolved the disorder of Margaret's life, which tabloid newspapers served up salaciously as a helter-skelter of torrid self-indulgence. Margaret's relationship with Llewellyn continued, despite Elizabeth's disapproval. Both sisters were troubled by the spiritual implications of Margaret's divorce, in May 1978, though Margaret did not regret Tony's departure. Elizabeth's anxiety was wide-ranging: for the sister she loved immoderately, for the damage inflicted on the monarchy and for Margaret's children. 'Nobody ever stops to consider what effect all this publicity about Princess Margaret Rose's malarkey with "Roddy" Llewellyn might have on her young children, the Viscount Linley, aged 16, and the Lady Sarah Armstrong-Jones, who was 14 on May Day,' Auberon Waugh wrote in his *Private Eye* diary.[48] A *Times* editorial on 20 May 1978, stating that 'divorce is now increasingly regarded as a matter for commiseration rather than for criticism, unless it is accompanied by a public parade of private bitterness', offered crumbs of comfort to Elizabeth, as well as a prescient warning that not all her children would heed. Tony Snowdon remained on good terms with both his sister-in-law and his mother-in-law partly by avoiding any such parade of private bitterness. Instead he remarried within three months of his divorce and was invited by Elizabeth to take her photograph with her first grandchild, Peter Phillips, born on 15 November 1977. Snowdon's comfortable pictures contrast with Beaton's of Elizabeth with her own babies and, even more strikingly, with first images of baby Elizabeth with her grandmother, Queen Mary. Intimate and classless, they pointed to the extent of change within the monarchy and the nation at large. Public pleasure in Elizabeth's untitled first grandson went some way to balancing adverse comment on the latest Civil List increase to £1,905,000, which had been announced in the House of Commons the week before the birth.[49]

Just as Elizabeth's marriage to Philip had thrust Margaret's romantic life onto the front pages, Anne's apparently settled domesticity contrasted with the single status of her elder brother Charles. If Elizabeth delighted in becoming a grandmother, her pleasure did not lessen her concern at Charles's continuing bachelorhood on the brink of his thirtieth birthday. Undoubtedly, Charles had felt a special closeness to his mother at the time of his investiture. This particular intimacy, of sovereign and heir, which Elizabeth herself had enjoyed with her father, had lessened over the course of the decade, with Charles's emergence as a full-time working royal and the inevitable separations of the family's working lives. Elizabeth remained affectionate but preoccupied and, if it ever crossed her mind that her father had died in his fifties, she did not take pains to prepare Charles for a similar contingency. 'My great problem in life is that I do not really know what my role in life is,' Charles told an audience of students in November 1978, a partly disingenuous statement.[50] His parents, by contrast, had very clear ideas of his role.

So did his great-uncle, Lord Mountbatten. Mountbatten's enjoyment of the part he had allotted himself of *éminence grise* to Elizabeth and her family made him more forthcoming in his dealings with Charles than the costive Elizabeth or vigorously decisive Philip. To his grandmother Charles looked for affection of the sort he believed Elizabeth withheld; Mountbatten offered him the guidance more usually provided by parents. He was a forceful but sensitive adviser and, by the time of Charles's landmark birthday in 1978, as concerned as Elizabeth at Charles's extended bachelorhood, haunted for the older man by the spectre of a previous unmarried, philandering Prince of Wales. Like Great-uncle David, Charles had discovered the easy sexual perquisites of his position. Mountbatten's misgivings focused on the coarsening effects of Charles's casual romantic life, which the older man dismissed as 'popping in and out of bed with girls', as well as the corrosiveness of high rank.[51] He warned Charles of 'the downward slope which wrecked your Uncle David's life and led to his disgraceful Abdication and his futile life ever after'.[52] Not quite accurately, Martin Charteris described the prince's life as 'hunting, shooting, polo and fornicating'.[53]

Charles himself was every bit as preoccupied by the need to find a wife as his parents and great-uncle. To a friend, he wrote, 'I'm told that marriage is the only cure for me – and maybe it is!', but did not, apparently, discuss his impasse with either Elizabeth or Philip.[54] Mountbatten's solution was characteristic: he championed the cause of his granddaughter, Amanda Knatchbull, who subsequently declined Charles's proposal. Elizabeth reputedly favoured Lady Leonora Grosvenor, a daughter of the Duke of Westminster. Sections of the public preferred the romance of an old-fashioned royal marriage; newspapers informed readers that Elizabeth seconded their choice of Princess Marie Astrid of Luxembourg, eldest daughter of the former Princess Josephine-Charlotte of Belgium, now Grand Duchess of Luxembourg, who, in the spring of 1937, had been rumoured as joining Elizabeth in the Buckingham Palace schoolroom. 'Beautiful, poised, selfless, "liked" by the Queen – she seems the ideal daughter-in-law,' suggested one, though the idea was a fanciful one.[55] A handful of the young women with whom Charles's name had been linked were invited to the thirtieth birthday ball hosted by Elizabeth at Buckingham Palace in November 1978, among them Lady Jane Wellesley and Lady Sarah Spencer, a granddaughter of one of the Queen Mother's former ladies of the bedchamber, Cynthia, Countess Spencer, and her lady-in-waiting, Ruth, Lady Fermoy. Also present was Sarah Spencer's younger sister, seventeen-year-old Diana. Excluded on Elizabeth's instructions was the wife of a handsome Guards officer with whom, six years earlier, Charles had fallen in love. She had been unmarried then. Despite her marriage, Charles had lately resumed their relationship, as fellow officers had informed Elizabeth. The former Camilla Shand was now Mrs Andrew Parker Bowles. Elizabeth discussed neither his affair, nor her omission from the royal guestlist, with Charles.

❦

In June 1972, Mountbatten had despatched to the lord chamberlain, Lord Maclean, his 'great funeral letter', including 'suggestions' for his funeral service that, if followed, would guarantee an event both magnificent and costly. He made his plans at Maclean's invitation, though mostly confident that they would not be called upon for some time. In this he was correct. In the event the circumstances of Mountbatten's funeral seven years later were unexpected and tragic in equal measure.

Mountbatten had questioned the Cabinet Office concerning the safety of his August visits, with his daughters and grandchildren, to Classiebawn Castle in County Sligo as early as 1972; each year he renewed his enquiries. Since 1961, plain-clothes policemen had discreetly guarded Elizabeth and Philip's kinsman during his Irish holidays; by 1974, twenty-eight policemen were on duty around the castle. At the end of August 1979, they were not enough to prevent the planting of a bomb by the IRA in Mountbatten's fishing boat, *Shadow* V. It exploded as the boat approached a lobster pot, killing Mountbatten, an Irish crew member and one of his grandsons immediately, injuring his elder daughter Patricia Brabourne, her husband, her mother-in-law and her son Timothy. The terrorists' aim had been to '[bring] home emotionally to the English ruling-class... that their government's war on us is going to cost them as well'.[56] In this it succeeded.

None felt the shock more powerfully than Elizabeth, in the distant fastness of Balmoral, where a visit with her niece Sarah Armstrong-Jones to Crathie church's sale of work, to which she had donated a set of Stuart Crystal whisky glasses, was an event among quiet days on the moors. For Elizabeth and her family, Mountbatten's loss as exasperatingly meddlesome but wise, kindly and wholly committed would-be paterfamilias deprived them of a key adviser, Elizabeth of a living link with the family's recent past, and Philip and Charles, in different ways, of a surrogate parent, a source, Charles claimed, of 'the wisest of counsel and advice'.[57] In October, while his mother, Patricia Brabourne, one of Elizabeth's oldest friends, remained in hospital, Elizabeth invited fourteen-year-old Timothy Knatchbull, with his sister Amanda, to Balmoral to recover. Later he remembered her greeting, arriving at the castle in the middle of the night, 'this sort of feeling of a mother duck gathering up her lost young... [her] default setting of love and care, of asking us about family, of plying us with soup and sandwiches and wrapping us up in a sort of motherliness'. He remembered 'a strange warm glow that's really never left me... the care, the loving tender care that the Queen [has] as a mum'.[58] It was typical of the depth of concern and affection Elizabeth was capable of expressing towards those outside her immediate family circle, especially those with a connection to her own past. A similar spirit coloured her sporadic correspondence with the wife of Hubert Tanner, the Windsor schoolmaster instrumental in the princesses' wartime pantomimes. 'I do hope you are keeping quite well, and managing all right, as I know you had a horrid time last year. I trust you will always tell me... if you need anything,' Elizabeth wrote to Mrs Tanner, thanking her for a birthday present.[59]

With Mountbatten's murder, only the Queen Mother remained of the principal players of the royal inner circle in which Elizabeth had grown up. Her advice, rooted in tradition and a heartfelt attachment to royal dignity, lacked Mountbatten's keenness and imagination. Plunket, Charteris and Mountbatten never exercised over Elizabeth an influence as powerful as her mother's, but these trusted insiders had offered her a connection of sorts with worlds beyond the court and intermediaries in her dealings with her children. Elizabeth's father had worried about republicanism. For Elizabeth, as the IRA's message made clear, the threat was not chiefly to her throne but her personal safety.

CHAPTER XV

Moderation in all things

Praise of Elizabeth was not the primary aim of the *Zambia Daily Mail* when, in August 1979, the newspaper described 'the extraordinary loving heart of the Queen'.¹ Its purpose was criticism of Elizabeth's latest prime minister, whom African statesmen agreed conspicuously lacked the monarch's affection for their continent and its causes.

In the aftermath of the Silver Jubilee, the secretary of state for the environment, Peter Shore, discerned at home 'a genuine English nationalist feeling, a deep feeling about the English and how they see themselves in terms of their own history'. He suggested that the politician who reflected this feeling was the leader of the opposition.² Fifteen months after Shore's warning, Callaghan's Labour Party was defeated in an election, following a vote of no confidence, by the Conservatives under Margaret Thatcher, 'the most right-wing Conservative Government and Leader for fifty years', as Tony Benn noted in his diary.³

In her third decade on the throne, Elizabeth was at ease

in her position. A television producer on assignment at Buckingham Palace in November 1976 had witnessed her return after the State Opening of Parliament. Elizabeth was bright and animated; the rigours of the ceremony and longueurs of the speech written for her by the government had left no trace. Her mind was full of horses. 'Did you see that horse?' she asked. 'He came to a full stop a dozen yards before he should. Gave the coach a frightful jerk. The coachman was trying to make him go, but he wouldn't budge. The other horses had to drag him with them. He just slid along, all four feet down.'[4] Over the coming decade, Elizabeth would find she had more to think about than horses. Her experience of the 1980s was shaped by the proximity of two women with whom, in character and outlook, she was repeatedly at odds. One was her prime minister. The other was the pretty, blushing teenager chosen for Charles's wife.

❧

'Friendliness without friendship' had been James Callaghan's verdict on his dealings with Elizabeth. It would be doubly true in the case of Elizabeth's association with Margaret Thatcher. At the time and since, their relationship inspired widespread speculation. Within a year of Thatcher taking office, her manner provoked a pithy riposte from one tabloid: 'There is still only one woman who wears the Crown in this country, whatever the other woman may think.'[5] Despite long association, neither reached an understanding of the other. Like her relationship with Edward Heath, Elizabeth's dealings with Margaret Thatcher lacked intimacy: Heath betrayed limited interest in Elizabeth beyond her role in the machinery of government, while the depth of Thatcher's reverence for monarchy prevented any near approach to Elizabeth on a personal level. Instead, '[holding] royalty in almost God-like awe', according to her press secretary, exaggeratedly but sincerely deferential, performing floor-skimming curtsies, Thatcher treated Elizabeth as the embodiment of an inherited ideal.[6] Six of her seven prime ministers to date had leavened respect for Elizabeth as sovereign with protective gallantry or flashes of humour. In her own words a 'plain, straightforward provincial', Thatcher lacked Elizabeth's dry wit and there was no room in the relationship of woman-to-woman for gallantry. Suggestions that Elizabeth disliked Thatcher's tendency to lecture her may well be true; it seems less likely that she was troubled, as sometimes claimed, by her premier sitting on the edge of her chair during their meetings or her habit of running one sentence into another, limiting any possibility of interjection, since Elizabeth was more inclined to listen than to speak – as she explained later, 'One's a sort of sponge.'[7] In the summer of 1985, Baroness-in-Waiting Lady Trumpington reported Elizabeth commenting on her audiences with Mrs Thatcher, 'She stays too long and talks too much. She has lived too long among men.'[8] Recorded at second hand, Elizabeth's comment has become detached from the intonation that would have made clear its prompt: wryness, exasperation or puzzlement. Given the strength of her prime minister's conviction of their relative positions, only Elizabeth could have bridged the gulf between them, but mostly failed to do so. At one level, it was a rerun of the story of the teenage princess and the Glasgow evacuees at Craigowan. Elizabeth is all but absent from Thatcher's autobiography. The women's behaviour to one another was consistently correct. Thatcher respected Elizabeth as her sovereign but evidently did not always give ground to her in the private recesses of her imagination.

Patriotism united monarch and premier: both longed for revived British fortunes at home and prestige abroad, and Thatcher's particular brand of patriotism, the 'English nationalism' Peter Shore had discerned, would contribute to the royal family's prominence throughout her premiership. The lives of both women were in thrall to vocations that overrode conventional domestic ties, played out in male-dominated arenas, but they differed in manner. Apolitical, centrist and studiedly uncontroversial, Elizabeth regarded the throne as a unifying force; her outlook was pragmatic, her manner emollient. Thatcher meant to wrest a floundering Britain from trade unions' clutches and the wastefulness of state funding. Although her own behaviour would become increasingly regal over time, she mistrusted the old-fashioned Establishment, of which Elizabeth was the apex, as much as she disliked socialist collectivism; she admired thrusting vigour like her own. Private enterprise and hard work lay at the heart of her philosophy, and she thrived on the abrasiveness of confrontation that was anathema to Elizabeth. Elizabeth's focus was a country united, neighbourly and civic-minded, her view conservative, with an understandable attachment to the status quo. 'What she's interested in', reflected a prime ministerial aide, 'are things going on as they are, tolerance, good manners, Christian behaviour, doing the right thing.'[9] Thatcher's radicalism and apparent intractability would exacerbate fissures in an already divided nation. The first years of her premiership were marked by riots in Bristol, Brixton and Toxteth, hunger strikes in Belfast and sharp rises in unemployment and homelessness. Elizabeth, observed Alvilde Lees-Milne to the Duchess of Beaufort, frequently looked sad. She *was* sad, 'it was the times,' explained the duchess, the former Lady Mary Cambridge, Elizabeth's cousin and occasional hostess.[10] But Elizabeth continued to relish her twofold role as British sovereign and head of the Commonwealth; Commonwealth affairs played a significant part in her working life. By contrast Thatcher inclined to discount the Commonwealth, doubting its economic benefits to Britain, and regarded its leaders with disdain; her brief was specifically British and did not encompass an equivalent of Elizabeth's international remit. From starchy beginnings, observers agree, the women's relationship became one marked by fondness on Elizabeth's side and admiration on Thatcher's, but it was a journey that included bumps along the way.

Events within months of Margaret Thatcher taking office indicated which of the women was the more sure-footed international statesman. The palace's 'unusual step', at the beginning of July 1979, of announcing Elizabeth's 'firm intention' of attending the Commonwealth Heads of Government conference in Lusaka, heralded what would become one of her key interventions. The announcement's purpose was to circumvent repetition of the previous Conservative government's veto of Elizabeth's attendance, given the prime minister's own lack of appetite for the conference and the excuse of escalating guerrilla violence in the region jeopardizing Elizabeth's safety. Newspapers responded as the palace intended: 'The Queen now seems certain to carry out her "danger mission" – the opening of next month's Commonwealth conference in Zambia,' stated the *Daily Mirror*.[11] Elizabeth was determined to exert her influence on those African leaders whose angry outspokenness at Thatcher's reluctance to impose sanctions on Rhodesia threatened to overwhelm the conference. She fully intended to foster cooperation between Rhodesia's neighbours and Britain's new prime minister over the issue of Rhodesian independence and its future government and, in doing so, to prevent any splintering of the organization itself.

'When she arrived, she found it a very tense situation,' remembered Zambia's president, Kenneth Kaunda. 'But, mainly because of her own personal involvement, tempers cooled.'[12] Elizabeth carried out her task in the back of a presidential limousine and, reported newspapers, from the unlikely base of 'a small suburban villa', 3 Mulungushi Village, outside Lusaka. In the first, she travelled from the airport with her host, Kaunda.

Over the course of their journey she persuaded him to amend his proposed speech for the evening's state banquet, removing passages antagonistic to Mrs Thatcher and Rhodesia's white minority as an essential preliminary to constructive discussion later. In the second, she held informal meetings with heads of government. 'As the hectic world of Commonwealth politics buzzed about her, the Queen was working quietly behind the scenes, seeing... heads of delegations... She acted as umpire between warring factions... encouraging positive thinking.'[13] It was a definition of a role within the Commonwealth that was both proactive and discreet. Elizabeth did not attend the meeting's discussions and played no part in the formal debates that led to the agreement of unanimous commitment 'to genuine black majority rule' for Rhodesia. She did not advise, nor did she directly offer suggestions. Her contribution, during the reception and banquet she hosted for heads of government and through her meetings with each of them over a space of three days, was to create a climate of willingness. She set greatest store, as did the leaders themselves, by the one-to-one meetings in her suburban villa, 'just them and me, with nobody else listening, which is very useful,'[14] as she described similar meetings in 1985. Unanimity led to the emergence of an independent Zimbabwe within less than a year, its baleful future then unsuspected. The significance of Elizabeth's behind-the-scenes diplomacy, including her intervention with Kenneth Kaunda, was not only in the outcome to which it contributed, but a conviction among key players that, without her, agreement would not have been reached. 'The very act of living a decent and upright life is in itself a positive factor in maintaining civilised standards,' Elizabeth claimed the following year.[15] Guilelessness and decency were among the gifts she took to Lusaka; unlike other members of her family, her support for black majority rule had never wavered. On the eve of her arrival, Botswana's president, Sir Seretse Khama, praised her 'great personal courage and commitment'.[16] Kenneth Kaunda acclaimed her afterwards as 'a great person... a leader among leaders... Because we all realise her commitment to the Commonwealth, we all respond to her message of conciliation.'[17]

༄

From Zambia Elizabeth retreated to the familiar routines of Balmoral: grouse shooting, stalking, riding; picnics and barbecues eaten outside or in wooden cabins across the estate; 'the beauty of the hills, and the peace of mind that comes when one walks on them, no screaming police sirens & no hurry hurry'; time to read, like the autumn she told Ted Hughes she had read his poem 'An Otter'.[18] Her private secretary Philip Moore wrote a firm letter to the Foreign Office pointing out the nature of her contribution to the Lusaka Accord.[19] If it was proof of royal pride, it was unusual on Elizabeth's part and illustrates the significance she attaches to her Commonwealth role and, in this instance, her pleasure in the achievement of her preferred outcome. More typical was her attitude towards celebration of her mother's eightieth birthday the following summer. Together Elizabeth and Margaret had involved themselves in planning a programme that culminated in a gala at the Royal Opera House. The three women sat for Norman Parkinson at Royal Lodge, in one image identically dressed, the Queen Mother flanked by her daughters, an updating of Marcus Adams's pre-war photographs. On each celebratory occasion, Elizabeth happily ceded place of honour to the Queen Mother. At Covent Garden, Roy Strong noted 'flashes of pleasure' from Elizabeth throughout the evening. 'Tough to have the competition of her mother but she was a genius at stepping back on this occasion.'[20] The sisters bought their mother a fur coat, 'the biggest & most exciting surprise of my life', as she described it in her thank you letter to Margaret.[21]

Her thank you letter to Elizabeth prompted a characteristic response. The whole family, Elizabeth replied, had 'rejoiced in the huge and loving feeling of thanksgiving for all that your life represents which has come from all walks of the people who make up this country and Commonwealth, and especially your own family. I hope you have been buoyed up by knowing what people feel.'[22] None rejoiced more wholeheartedly than Elizabeth, a devoted and indulgent daughter, who undoubtedly shared the loving feeling of thanksgiving.

It was to be a decade of ceding the limelight. The 1980s saw the thirtieth anniversary of Elizabeth's accession, her sixtieth birthday and her fortieth wedding anniversary. For a public distracted by tabloid sensationalism and increasingly garish royal coverage, only her bravery in reacting to a gunman's attack during Trooping the Colour in 1981, and a palace break-in the year after, rivalled the romantic, and unromantic, antics of her grown-up children and a prime minister apparently determined to bestride the political world like a Colossus.

❧

The role of fairy-tale princess had never suited Anne, who, since her wedding, had become established as one of the family's least popular members with the public (this would later change). In the autumn of 1980, journalists were pleased and relieved to discover more promising material in the form of an aristocratic ingénue, Lady Diana Spencer. Sarah Spencer's youngest sister, a nineteen-year-old of whom her stepmother claimed 'She's got nothing to say! Once you've finished talking about Duran Duran, that's it,' Diana was the unlikely new girlfriend of the heir to the throne. Charles was twelve years her senior, an introspective, thoughtful man of old-fashioned upbringing, quick-tempered and emotionally rudderless. Wounded by her parents' divorce during her childhood, Diana had dreamed of escaping into marriage with a duke; her step-grandmother, romantic novelist Barbara Cartland, told Mountbatten's private secretary that 'she had set her heart on Charles from an early age'.[23] Her prettiness belied a streak of selfishness; she was strong-willed but emotionally fragile. Charles appeared overwhelmed by his duty to marry; Diana was well-born, with no romantic past to cast a shadow. Charles was in love with Camilla Parker Bowles, and Mountbatten, who might have counselled him, was dead. Neither he nor his parents discussed his particular challenge in finding a wife who was also a suitable future queen. Culpability was shared. 'One must long... to have been able to talk freely about the things that matter deeply, but one was too inhibited to discuss,' Charles reflected in 1987, and he consigned even relatively neutral topics, like his views of Australia, to letters to his grandmother rather than his mother.[24] In her previous Christmas broadcast, Elizabeth had suggested, 'Let us... stop to think whether we are making enough effort to pass on our experience of life to our children.' Even at so critical a juncture, the woman who disliked articulating her feelings did not pass on to the child who was also her heir the experiences of her own emotional life or her marriage, which had successfully withstood extraordinary scrutiny and pressures of a sort to which his marriage would also be exposed. 'He is encouraged to be self-reliant,' Lisa Sheridan had written in 1962 of Elizabeth and Philip's parenting of two-year-old Andrew. So it was with Charles two decades later, and the press, getting wind of the scent, through the simple expedient of column inches seemed to force Charles's hand. By mid-November, leading royal journalist Audrey Whiting felt sufficiently sure of her ground to describe Diana unequivocally as 'an identikit picture of everything [the Royal Family] want in a future Princess of Wales'.[25]

For Whiting, Diana's suitability lay in her aristocratic background and the Spencers' connections to Elizabeth's family.

Diana's father, the 8th Earl Spencer, had served both Elizabeth and her father as equerry; both Diana's grandmothers and four of her great-aunts were members of the Queen Mother's household, while her middle sister Jane was married to Robert Fellowes, Elizabeth's assistant private secretary since 1977, and her only brother, Charles, was Elizabeth's godson. Diana had known Andrew and Edward as children; as a child she had lived at Park House on the Sandringham Estate. The marriage was championed by her surviving grandmother, Ruth, Lady Fermoy, who helped secure the Queen Mother's approval, a weighty consideration for Elizabeth as well as Charles. To a friend, Elizabeth wrote, 'She is one of us. I am very fond of all three of the Spencer girls.'[26] As her grandmother and Jock Colville had observed forty years earlier, Elizabeth moved in a narrow aristocratic clique. It is unsurprising if, in her concern for Charles's predicament, she took comfort from the familiarity of Diana's background. In choosing Diana, Charles proposed exactly the kind of marriage many had suspected the Queen Mother had wanted for Elizabeth, in the days when members of 'the body guard' appeared more to her liking than energetic, free-thinking Philip. Diana's background resembled the Queen Mother's, and Elizabeth could testify to the success of the marriage of the former Lady Elizabeth Bowes-Lyon to another future king. Like all concerned, Elizabeth *wanted* Charles to make the right choice. Later, Diana suggested Elizabeth was exasperated by her son's vacillations.

With speculation mounting – 'as things get worse and worse the royalist cult accelerates,' wrote Roy Strong, noting the link, played out repeatedly in Elizabeth's life, of dire economic prospects and escapist fantasies centred on the royal family – Philip wrote to Charles, partly prompted by Elizabeth's irritation at press intrusiveness. Philip's intention was to make clear to his son the danger to Diana's reputation of so public a relationship in the event that marriage was not his aim; Charles interpreted his father's letter as an ultimatum. Unsuspected by journalists like Whiting, Charles and Diana were virtual strangers to one another. Charles was beset by misgivings, but Philip encouraged him to act decisively. Charles did not directly address his concerns in conversations with his mother, though a rumour recorded in Hugo Vickers's diary that Charles had 'told the Queen angrily: "My marriage and my sex life have nothing to do with each other..."', if true, suggests an exchange, however oblique, about Camilla Parker Bowles.[27] Charles spoke more candidly to friends. Their responses, including, in a minority of cases, opposition to the marriage, were equally candid. Charles proposed to Diana and was accepted. Their engagement was announced on 24 February 1981. Public reaction was for the most part ecstatic. By contrast, a laconic Margaret described the royal family as 'all extremely relieved'; she also revealed to friends that Camilla 'ha[d] no intention of giving him up'.[28] She did not mention happiness, either the couple's or the royal family's. Charles and Diana were photographed with Elizabeth. They gave a televised interview remembered subsequently for Charles's infelicitous response to a question about his feelings: 'whatever "in love" means'. 'There is something sad about a girl of 19 being led into royal captivity,' observed historian and journalist Kenneth Rose.[29] He did not comment on the interviewer quizzing Charles about the state of his emotions, a question that encapsulated new levels of intrusiveness unanticipated at the time of Elizabeth's marriage in 1947. The Queen Mother hosted a dinner at which she presented Diana with a large sapphire brooch, which Diana subsequently had reset as the centre of a choker. At the considerable cost of £28,000, Elizabeth bought Diana's engagement ring of an oval sapphire surrounded by diamonds. Publication weeks later of Jock Colville's *The Churchillians* reminded readers that Elizabeth, too, had once been a romantic heroine. In an extract quoted in several newspapers, Colville wrote: 'There was one lady by whom, from 1952 onwards, Churchill was dazzled. That was the new Queen… At a respectful distance, he fell in love with the Queen.'[30] For the foreseeable future, it was Diana not Elizabeth who occupied readers of the more clamorous press.

Nothing in Elizabeth's life since her accession had deflected her from the business of state: nor on the surface did Charles's engagement to Diana Spencer. In May, as planned, she and Philip made a state visit to Norway, where they were greeted by placards protesting at Thatcher's treatment of hunger strikers in Northern Ireland; they would visit Tunisia in the autumn, once wedding brouhaha subsided. Off duty, her family occupied Elizabeth. In March, she and Philip flew to Gordonstoun to watch Edward in a school production. As she had since childhood, she celebrated her fifty-fifth birthday in April with a family party at Windsor. Two days before the wedding, on 27 July, at the reception after the christening of Anne's second child, Zara, it was Elizabeth who carried the baby; godparents on that occasion included Andrew Parker Bowles. The same year, Denys Rhodes was diagnosed with inoperable lung cancer. Elizabeth offered Rhodes and his wife, the former Margaret Elphinstone, a house in Windsor Great Park where, frequently, she visited her after church on Sunday mornings, happy and relaxed in the company of the cousin she knew so well. Also close at hand at Windsor, at Adelaide Cottage, was Libby Hardinge, another link with Elizabeth's childhood. A letter Elizabeth wrote to a friend after Diana moved into Buckingham Palace suggests she was aware of the younger woman's belatedly mixed emotions: 'I trust that Diana will find living here less of a burden than expected.'[31] How sympathetic uncomplicated Elizabeth felt towards her soon-to-be daughter-in-law is unclear. If she shared Charles's nervousness, she concealed it. Charles's staff, surprised by Diana's oscillating moods and her obsessive interest in Camilla Parker Bowles, which emerged soon after the engagement, kept their own counsel. Elizabeth attributed Diana's unsettledness to pre-wedding nerves.

On the day of the wedding itself, in St Paul's Cathedral, Elizabeth's happiness appeared to match that of the global television audience of 750 million viewers. Diana included in her bouquet stems of a new bright-yellow rose named after Mountbatten, a symbolic gesture to appeal to the royal family. 'Watching the Queen returning from the royal wedding... in an open landau to the cheers of a delighted throng', writer Alan Bennett observed Elizabeth navigating an experience that was simultaneously private and public, a distinctive royal conundrum: 'trying to manage the happy chatting of Earl Spencer on the one hand and acknowledging the frenzy of the crowd with the other'.[32] Crowds delighted in the newlyweds' kiss on the palace balcony, and both Elizabeth and Philip greatly enjoyed the party at Claridge's that followed their departure for the first stage of their honeymoon. But in Patrick Lichfield's behind-the-scenes photographs of Diana and her bridesmaids after the ceremony, Elizabeth appears tired and pale, excluded by age, even marginal, and Philip is nowhere to be seen. With devastating consequences, this would be the view taken by a handful of determined, abrasive, aggressive tabloid editors for the next decade and beyond. Their unrelenting focus on Diana and other younger family members, which became the dominant royal narrative, would reap a most unhappy harvest.

The next day Elizabeth spent several hours in fittings with her dressmaker Hardy Amies. Amies thanked her for making time to see him so soon after the busy mêlée of the wedding. Elizabeth's reply was that of countless mothers after large-scale family celebrations: she told Amies 'she was pleased to have something to do, as life seemed rather flat now that the wedding was over'.[33] More surprisingly, she remarked on her amazement at the size of crowds in the Mall and in front of Buckingham Palace, proof, if it was more than a conversational commonplace, that she did not take for granted such demonstrations of public affection.[34]

Perhaps there was an idolatrous quality to the immoderate royal worship of the summer of 1981, when prelates and newspapermen vied to celebrate in loftiest encomia the virtues of Elizabeth's family. If so, Elizabeth had contributed to the sentimental euphoria in a manner she would happily have forsworn. At 10.57 on the morning of Saturday, 13 April, her black mare, Burmese, bolted on the Mall. Within a handful of paces, Elizabeth regained control and calmed the frightened horse. Leaning forward, she patted Burmese's neck. Possibly she spoke to her as well. Elizabeth's face was very pale. She had survived six blank shots aimed directly at her as she rode to Horseguards for Trooping the Colour, mounted side saddle on the horse given to her by the Canadian Mounties. The culprit was seventeen-year-old Marcus Serjeant, known to 'friends and neighbours... as a quiet loner who spends most of his time on his hobbies of fishing and butterfly collecting'.[35] His shots disturbed Elizabeth's horse, but apparently not the sovereign herself; their echo was heard in the crowd's angry dismay. In one account, 'there were cries of "Lynch the bastard" as the young man was hauled away to the ambulance tent in the Mall'. The *Sunday Mirror* reported that 'the festive mood of the crowd turned to fury after the shots'.[36] Elizabeth became a nation's hero. Sentencing Serjeant to five years' imprisonment under the Treason Act 1842, judge Lord Lane explained, 'The public sense of outrage must be marked.'

Above all, praise targeted Elizabeth's sangfroid. In the days that followed, she did not alter her planned engagements or the style of those engagements. As headlines acclaimed her, she was 'resolute'. Observing her at close quarters at Windsor that week, Elizabeth Longford concluded that she was both mentally and morally tough; watching footage of the shooting many years later, Charles described his mother as 'made of strong stuff'.[37]

Newspapers quoted a source identified variously as a palace or a police spokesman: 'The Queen feels that if she is going to do an engagement, then the public must be able to see her.'[38] It was her own version of the spirit attributed to her parents during the Blitz and supported her motto that she must be seen to be believed. Thames Valley Police asked racegoers at Royal Ascot the next week to be 'on the alert for anything suspicious' in order to 'act as security guards – and help protect the Queen'.[39]

Although no one could have known it at the time, it was a summer when polarized outlooks converged. An innocent-looking but self-absorbed young woman became an international icon, while her doughty soon-to-be mother-in-law inspired universal praise for unselfconscious bravery and stoical endurance. Elizabeth had behaved instinctively. Afterwards she was at pains to exonerate Burmese's skittishness. But her instinct for good behaviour, which she equated with self-control and absence of fuss, would not always win plaudits from a public whose heads had been turned.

On 5 November officials made a public announcement of Diana's pregnancy. Inevitably it served to magnify interest in the new Princess of Wales, although she herself was struggling with the realities of her position, including loss of privacy; her grandmother, Ruth Fermoy, noted 'how much [she] had yet to learn'.[40] For Elizabeth, who had agreed the previous month to Diana receiving psychiatric counselling in London, the prospect of a child offered hope for Charles's marriage and Diana's happiness, as well as future guarantees for the dynasty. To smooth Diana's transition to royal life, Elizabeth had requested the youngest of her ladies-in-waiting, Susan Hussey, to help her. In age Lady Susan was closer to Charles than Diana; Charles's fondness for her was of two decades' standing, and he had written to her during miserable years at Gordonstoun. Elizabeth's good intentions suggest how far she was from understanding Diana's condition. Reliable, scrupulous, loyal and witty, Susan Hussey was too 'correct' for the volatile, fragile Diana and, like many of Diana's relationships within the palace, their association soured over time. At the beginning of December, Elizabeth held a drinks reception for newspaper, television and radio news editors, at which her press secretary, Michael Shea, indicated the corrosive effect on Diana of unrelenting scrutiny, a royal plea for abatement and clemency. Elizabeth suggested to Diana that she always feel free to see her. The possibility that she frightened her daughter-in-law did not occur to her. Those who observed the two women together argued that Diana's view of Elizabeth resembled Roy Strong's, expressed the following year after an encounter at Royal Lodge: 'The Queen is always, I find, very formidable and frightening and it is impossible to drift up to her.'[41] Elizabeth had taken steps to help Diana, but Diana's particular needs lay beyond Elizabeth's experience, and Elizabeth's failure to discuss with Diana her unhappiness, though characteristic, was wrongly interpreted by Diana as proof of her indifference.

❧

Sovereignty can be a dangerous calling. In October 1982 Elizabeth had again been the target of a gunman's shots, in Dunedin in New Zealand. Frightened that news of an attempt on her life, albeit unsuccessful, would mean the end of royal visits, the New Zealand government colluded in a cover-up that lasted four decades; the seventeen-year-old gunman, Christopher Lewis, committed suicide in 1997 on a subsequent trial for murder. Elizabeth herself may not have known what happened: New Zealand officials explained the distant sound of gunshot as a falling council sign. In exploring the theme of bravery in her Christmas broadcast months later, Elizabeth's focus was not herself but those living with disabilities, to mark the United Nations' International Year of Disabled Persons.

The year ahead tested Elizabeth's courage nevertheless. The thirtieth anniversary of her accession generated praise for her personal qualities as well as the smooth working of monarchy as an institution. In a series of interviews, Harold Wilson attributed the monarchy's success to 'the nature and steadfastness of the Queen herself'. In the kind of statement that presages disaster in Greek tragedies, he claimed that, thanks to her exemplary record, Elizabeth was 'in an invincible position'.[42] For Elizabeth, the anniversary was also, as always, that of her father's death, and she spent it quietly at Sandringham. It was not, however, to be a spring of quiet reflection. At the beginning of April, Tony Benn described the House of Commons as 'in the grip of jingoism'.[43] For seventy-four days, Britain waged war 8,000 miles from home, following Argentina's occupation of the Falkland Islands and South Georgia, a British crown colony since 1841. The decision to respond to Argentinian aggression was Margaret Thatcher's; in her capacity as queen of the islands, head of the Commonwealth and head of the armed forces, Elizabeth described the conflict as 'go[ing] to the rescue of the Falkland Islanders... in defence of basic freedoms'.[44] Among the troops was her middle and favourite son, Andrew, then a twenty-two-year-old helicopter pilot on HMS *Invincible*. A palace statement that Elizabeth supported Andrew's deployment in the conflict was her own equivalent of her parents' well-publicized wartime residence in London and earned her sympathy as a mother. Thatcher seized the opportunity to present herself in the combined roles of Boudicca and Britannia, and an upsurge in patriotic feeling boosted her popularity. Her belligerence suggested Queen Victoria's attitude at such moments. By contrast, Elizabeth was markedly less gung-ho, 'perhaps... a little wary of the role that Mrs Thatcher was assuming', according to Thatcher colleague and apologist Alan Clark.[45] David Cannadine described Elizabeth throughout the conflict as 'curiously low-key, an absentee'.[46] It is hard to see what alternative her prime minister gave her, and Elizabeth visited casualties following troops' return and afterwards led the nation's tributes at the Falklands memorial services held annually at St Paul's Cathedral. The conflict had momentarily sidelined questions of her possible abdication in Charles's favour, aired only months earlier at the thirtieth anniversary of her accession. Then Harold Wilson had offered what became the accepted explanation: Elizabeth, he stated, was 'conscious of her duty in a religious way' and lifelong promises made before God.[47]

Weeks after Argentina's surrender on 14 June, Elizabeth faced an invader of a different sort. It was an incident described in the *Illustrated London News* as a 'saga, teetering on the edge of farce, [that] could well have turned to tragedy'.[48] In a summer of terrorist violence, with two IRA attacks on troops in central London within a fortnight, it would raise protests that the state of royal security had become a national crisis. Michael Fagan was unemployed, footloose, miserable in the aftermath of his wife's desertion, an old-fashioned ne'er-do-well, scruffy and feckless. He broke into Buckingham Palace, clambering over a garden wall, for no more compelling reason than that he knew he could, having done so undetected once before. His accounts of his actions early that July morning varied over time, as anniversaries of his daring renewed his fleeting newsworthiness. He said he had meant to find Elizabeth's room; he said he found his way there by accident. Whatever the truth, he stood at Elizabeth's bedside, despite her protests, one hand bloodied by a broken ashtray. In vain she summoned help, neither her alarm button nor the palace telephone eliciting any response, Philip absent, after leaving the palace early for an out-of-town engagement. The appearance of Elizabeth's chambermaid, Elizabeth Andrew, with an unguarded 'Bloody 'ell, Ma'am, what's 'e doing 'ere?', lessened tension. First a footman, then policemen came belatedly to Elizabeth's rescue. Fagan does not appear to have intended her any harm. His descriptions of Elizabeth's Liberty print nightdress and her 'little' bare feet suggest he was charmed by her. Elizabeth denied that she had been afraid; as planned, she went ahead with an investiture ceremony hours later. Undoubtedly she was shocked. Many years later, Fagan would claim that their encounter had lasted no longer than seconds; at the time accounts agreed that monarch and miscreant were alone for up to ten minutes. A level-headed Elizabeth valued her privacy but had not previously had grounds for suspecting her own vulnerability when alone. After Marcus Serjeant's gunfire and Mountbatten's murder, Fagan's break-in was unsettling.

The incident shocked many across the country as well as Elizabeth. There were indications, however, of the continuing sea change in attitudes. Thirty years earlier, a similar breach would have been greeted by a storm of chivalrous protest. In 1982, even the respectful *Illustrated London News* appeared uncertain in its response, unsure whether to characterize events as farcical or tragic. Again Elizabeth's bravery won praise, but the heat of early adulation had burned out, that torch passed now to Charles and, especially, Diana. Like praise for Elizabeth's steadfastness, it was sincere, but more respectful than impassioned, although a survey conducted in the autumn by Market Research Enterprises confirmed Elizabeth's place as 'most liked' member of the royal family, with thirty-seven per cent of votes polled.

On 21 July, the birth of Charles and Diana's first child, a boy christened a fortnight later William Philip Arthur Louis, provided Elizabeth with her second grandson and, in her own words, 'another heir'.[49] As sovereign she could not discount the dynastic significance of the birth; her twofold pleasure as grandmother and monarch recalled her dismay twenty years before at the short-term empire-building of Kwame Nkrumah. Elizabeth did not deceive herself that William was the panacea required by Charles and Diana's troubled marriage, even though she was unaware of the full extent of the couple's difficulties only a year after their wedding, but his birth distracted her briefly from her unhappiness at the death, two days earlier, of Rupert Nevill. Nevill had served latterly as Philip's private secretary; he was a godfather of Margaret's son, David. Like Patrick Plunket, he was a friend of Elizabeth's youth: trusted, discreet, like-minded. Nor were Charles and Diana her only source of anxiety within her family. The official release in the autumn of photographs of Anne and Mark Phillips, to coincide with Phillips's thirty-fourth birthday, was interpreted as an attempt on the palace's part to put paid to rumours about the state of their marriage; Elizabeth knew of Anne's relationship with her protection officer Peter Cross.[50] Meanwhile Andrew's transformation, in his own assessment, from boy to man, as a result of the experience of the Falklands, did not add up to a constructive role for Elizabeth's middle son. Andrew embarked on a series of widely reported short-term relationships that, despite public support – 'nearly all those questioned think he should be allowed a "fling"' – were at odds with ideas of a model royal family, lacking either romance or dignity.[51] A light biography of the prince published the following year suggested that the initials HRH 'stand for His Royal Heart-throb'.[52] Elizabeth's autumn Commonwealth tour, which included her first visit to far-flung islands of the South Pacific, was presented to newspaper readers as a 'great adventure'.[53] It offered Elizabeth welcome respite and an opportunity to set aside her concerns temporarily. Four years earlier, she had been created queen of the newly independent Tuvalu, which became her smallest realm. Her arrival on the tiny island was like no other in her reign, seated in a gold and turquoise canoe decorated with tropical foliage and flowers and carried by twenty-six 'warriors' dressed in grass skirts. Afterwards, at a traditional feast whose menu included barbecued bat, Elizabeth wore a mother-of-pearl necklace and a simple headdress of stephanotis flowers given to her by the islanders. Her appearance suggested a degree of unbending she seldom allowed herself at home and contrasted with signs of strain when, immediately after her return, she opened parliament at Westminster.

Elizabeth's enjoyment of her Commonwealth tours had not dimmed. Her attachment to this key facet of her inheritance was unflagging, though the African independence movements of the 1950s and 1960s, sporadic republicanism in Canada and Australia and the pan-European initiatives of the 1970s had loosened the Commonwealth's imaginative hold on many of her British subjects. In 1953, Elizabeth's symbolic Commonwealth role as unifier was widely accepted in Britain; thirty years on, sceptics queried the value of her globe-trotting much as they queried the value of the Commonwealth itself. Of Elizabeth's visit to Canada in March 1983, the BBC's unconvinced court correspondent Kate Adie reflected 'there was no evidence that a tour did harm; to the contrary, most of the events brought pleasure to those attending, satisfaction to small towns and thrills to those who shook hands, and confirmed that civilised behaviour supports a thousand causes and charities and enterprises'.[54] Adie was dismissive of what she saw as Elizabeth's dowdiness; she concluded that 'worthiness and duty were on show'.[55] It was a reiteration of the gulf that had opened between Elizabeth and sections of the popular mindset as long ago as the mid-1950s. Elizabeth was proud to embrace worthiness and duty and to celebrate those qualities in others, as she made clear in her Christmas broadcasts and her conversations with voluntary-sector workers recognized at palace investitures. Ideals of civic-mindedness held limited appeal for journalists in pursuit of a story at a moment when royal reporting was increasingly personality-focused and less and less concerned with monarchy's daily round. Home-grown reaction to Elizabeth and Philip's three-day visit to British

Columbia was mostly more affectionate. Contra Adie, a report in Canada's *Maclean's* magazine acclaimed Elizabeth as 'a *real* superstar', with a 'legendary power to dispel gloom'.[56] Famous across the globe from birth, Elizabeth did not aspire to be a superstar; her eminence was of a different variety. She did expect her role to be taken seriously and accorded an appropriate level of respect. Among causes of her considerable fury at an American-led invasion of Grenada on 25 October 1983 was her own sidelining as Queen of Grenada by the US president, Ronald Reagan. Reagan's government did not inform Elizabeth of its intentions, grounded in American fears of communism in the region, nor discuss them with her advisers. Elizabeth's pointed reference two years later, in a speech on neighbouring Barbados, to 'the vulnerability of small [Caribbean] states', proved the strength of her indignation.

❧

In 1985, a photograph by Peter Grugeon, taken at Windsor Castle ten years earlier and used as Elizabeth's official Silver Jubilee portrait, was reworked by American artist Andy Warhol. Warhol was preoccupied by fame. 'I want to be as famous as the Queen of England,' he said. For the fame-loving Warhol, Elizabeth was synonymous with celebrity. Warhol's four boldly coloured screenprints reduced Grudgeon's portrait of her to a doll-like mask. They celebrated Elizabeth as a global brand, as instantly recognizable as Campbell's Soup; they suggested the artifice of royal iconography.

Wittingly or otherwise, Warhol successfully captured Elizabeth's understanding of the importance of what Charles had called 'dressing up and Queening it'. Repeatedly since her accession, she had been painted and photographed in full royal fig, complete with orders and jewels. In doing so, she projected one version of royalty. She gave away nothing of herself, her own personality secondary to the signifiers of royal status, the public image a neutral mask. Novelist Anthony Powell was astonished by private snapshots of Elizabeth taken by portraitist Rodrigo Moynihan in November. Powell described them as 'different from any photographs I have seen of her. Much more convincing in the way her character was suggested.'[57] In Warhol's images is nothing of the 'real' Elizabeth glimpsed by Moynihan and Powell: he reduces her to an empty template, like an actress posing for the camera.

Warhol's view, however, was not Elizabeth's. For Elizabeth monarchy was a sacred trust, its stock-in-trade public service. Stiffened by her mother, she had opposed Tony Benn's plans for removing her portrait from postage stamps, aware that ubiquitous royal iconography was key to sustaining the idea of monarchy subliminally in the popular imagination. Warhol's focus was Elizabeth's fame: his vivid 'portraits', undertaken without sittings, presented her as a royal 'star' in an emerging celebrity culture that would overwhelm the second half of her reign. This happened by stages and posed challenges for Elizabeth and her family. A hereditary monarchy cannot exist as an aspect of celebrity culture, since its members are required to command public approval lifelong, while celebrity is too often temporary, based on public curiosity rather than respect. 'Celebrity' has never shaped Elizabeth's view of her position: she absorbed from Queen Mary an understanding of royalty that was both sterner and more rarefied. Younger members of Elizabeth's family colluded in blurring boundaries between royalty and celebrity, talking to journalists, interviewed on chat shows. A hungry press rewarded their efforts by cutting them down to size as players in what Malcolm Muggeridge had derided thirty years earlier as a royal 'soap opera'. Inevitably, Elizabeth resisted intervening to direct her children's behaviour. For the time being, remote as Warhol's gaudy poster girl, she herself escaped the press's downgrading.

Elizabeth's reluctance to gainsay her family was an inherited weakness. Worldwide attention greeted the Queen Mother's eighty-fifth birthday in August 1985. Coverage on television news programmes included an interview with biographer Christopher Warwick. Elliptically he referred to 'problems in the lives of her daughters, problems within her family groups', before stating, 'she won't accept problems, you can't go to her with problems... she just pretends that problems don't exist.' Large crowds greeted the royal family outside church at Sandringham on the morning of the birthday itself. It began to rain, and Margaret arranged a raincoat around her mother's shoulders. Attentive as always, Elizabeth helped her mother with the many posies of flowers offered by children. 'For once the Queen played the role of floral assistant,' noted a television journalist. A birthday concert on Radio 4 that evening took its title from Tennyson's letters to Queen Victoria: 'Dear and Honoured Lady'. At her own request it included a short exchange from Noël Coward's *Private Lives* that appeared to encapsulate the Queen Mother's problem avoidance: 'Let's be superficial and pity the poor Philosophers. Let's blow trumpets and squeakers, and enjoy the party as much as we can... Let's savour the delights of the moment.' Whether or not Elizabeth chose to reflect on her mother's choice is impossible to say. Serious and dutiful from childhood, she had never allowed herself to enjoy the party at the expense of other calls on her attention.

She marked her own sixtieth birthday, in April 1986, with the release of a new photograph, taken by Andrew at Sandringham: a kindly, strikingly relaxed image of a happy, smiling Elizabeth, arms crossed in a comfortable twinset, more mumsy than regal. Postage stamps and television documentaries commemorated the milestone; Elizabeth was photographed by the Bank of

England's in-house photographer for an updated portrait for banknotes to replace the image by Harry Ecclestone that had been in use since 1971. Commentary on the milestone was overwhelmingly favourable. The assessment of former arts minister Norman St John Stevas that Elizabeth's achievement was a 'stronger, more stable, more popular' monarchy, 'more appreciated than at any time in our history', was widely shared.[58] At Edward's request, Andrew Lloyd Webber and Tim Rice wrote a new short musical, called *Cricket*; it included a part for Edward himself and was performed at Windsor Castle in June. Elizabeth's enjoyment suggests she did not draw any parallels with the predicament of the hero and heroine, cricketer Donald and his girlfriend, earl's daughter Emma, whose relationship threatens to unravel thanks to Emma's belief that Donald is more attached to his cricket team than to her. The royal household's birthday present of two paintings of the budgerigars in the Windsor aviary, descendants of the birds Elizabeth had been given as a child, connected past and present; Elizabeth described the pictures as 'an inspired choice for a special birthday'.[59] Among highlights of a Royal Opera House gala on 21 April was a performance of Elgar's *Nursery Suite*, dedicated in 1930 to the then Duchess of York and her daughters. On this occasion, the suite was performed as an eight-minute-long ballet, choreographed by royal favourite Frederick Ashton. Ashton was inspired by a memory of 145 Piccadilly. Like scullery maid Mollie Moran, he had seen Elizabeth and her sister as children in their London garden and never forgotten the sight. 'I was on the number 19 bus going home and we stopped and there they were, the two little girls playing.'[60] *Nursery Suite* presented Elizabeth and Margaret dressed in the frilly frocks of the Marcus Adams years, tied with coloured sashes, playing together outdoors with balls and hoops and skipping ropes used as reins in one of Elizabeth's favourite pony games. Ashton had discussed his idea with Margaret. She talked to him about the sort of games the sisters played together and gave him photographs; knowing her sister, she warned him not to make it 'too whimsical'. The first movement captured the sisters' absorption in one another in their self-contained world of Alah and Crawfie; in the last, the Elizabeth dancer puts on a cloak handed to her by Margaret, symbolically embracing her destiny, her childhood over. Afterwards, Margaret told Ashton she had worried about the commission. 'I thought it would make both The Queen and my mother sick,' she wrote, 'but we all ended up in floods of tears.'[61] She thanked him for his 'miraculous re-enactment' of her childhood, a feeling that the enthusiasm of her letter suggests Elizabeth had shared. 'How you got that child to act the last bit in the cloak... It was wonderful and my mama was blubbing like anything.' No one was more accustomed than Elizabeth to the fictionalization of her life story. From childhood she had provided copy for writers, hacks and panegyrists. Ashton had done something different. Fleetingly he rekindled the particular magic of Elizabeth's very happy upbringing. That she should have been moved, seated in the royal box close to Margaret and her mother, is only a measure of her affection for the two women to whom, alongside Philip, she remained closest. Remembering ought to have been bittersweet – 145 Piccadilly had been destroyed by bombs; the world to which it belonged had succumbed to stealthier opponents, but was equally irretrievable – but there is no evidence that Elizabeth considered it so. At the time of her silver wedding anniversary, she had denied any impulse to dwell on the past. A decade on, in a private conversation, she suggested this was no longer strictly accurate. At a party hosted by booksellers Hatchard's she admitted she had kept 'a lot' of the letters sent to her by family and friends and that she reread them. 'I don't find it sad,' she said.[62] She valued long-term relationships; the past was comprehensible, coherent in ways not true of the present, and her own past had included great happiness.

The Opera House had been garlanded for the evening with spring flowers, an evocation, after a cruelly cold winter, of Elizabeth's role of long ago as harbinger of spring. Springtime was doubly represented in the royal box. At the furthest corner of the front row, a bouncy young woman, sparkling in diamonds, sat beside Andrew. Weeks before, she had joined the royal family for the Easter break at Windsor. 'I thought Sarah fitted in very happily, didn't you?' the Queen Mother had written to Elizabeth on 10 April. 'She is such a cheerful person, and seems to be so thankful & pleased to be part of a united family, & is truly devoted to darling Andrew. It seems most hopeful which is a comfort.'[63] The palace had announced the engagement of Elizabeth's roving-eyed second son to Sarah Ferguson on 17 March, almost a month after Andrew's proposal. Elizabeth was pleased with his choice. Two years had passed since Princess Michael of Kent, married to Elizabeth's youngest cousin, had described Elizabeth as 'withdrawn' from the troubles of Charles and Diana's marriage; in Andrew's case, Elizabeth shared her mother's hopefulness.[64] Like Diana Spencer, Sarah Ferguson was connected to the court: a cousin of Robert Fellowes, her father a polo associate of Philip's and Charles's; she shared Elizabeth's fondness for country life. The couple were cheerfully rumbustious, and a chummy press nicknamed Sarah 'Fergie'. Like Diana, her childhood had been marred by painful marital break-up; as in Diana's case, her mother had abandoned her marriage and her children. It was not a point on which anyone chose to dwell. Elizabeth was both sufficiently humble and sufficiently serene to overlook implied criticism that, in her fourth decade on the throne, a Tigger-ish young woman, lacking dignity or any compelling sense of duty, was the 'breath of fresh air' the monarchy needed.

Elizabeth recharged her batteries in May with a private visit to the United States. For the second time, she stayed with William and Sarah Farish at Lane's End Farm, near Versailles, Kentucky. At the time of her previous visit, an unnamed courtier quoted in the *New York Times* had explained her decision to stay with the Farishes in overtly snobbish terms: 'They are "old money" not new, and they are not what you Americans would call "prominent socialites".'[65] The arrangement was suggested by Anglophile thoroughbred breeder Paul Mellon, whose stallion Mill Reef had featured in Elizabeth's breeding programmes since 1974. William Farish was vice president of America's Jockey Club; conversation revolved around horses and dogs. As on her previous visit, in October 1984, Elizabeth's purpose was to visit Kentucky stud farms, where, a palace spokesman explained archly, she 'ha[d] mares of her own visiting American stallions'; her goal was to breed and train a Derby winner.[66] Despite careful planning, both visits were markedly informal. Sarah Farish had described her first experience of accommodating the world's most high-profile monarch as 'the most wonderful week either of us had ever had... it was almost beyond words'. The Farishes saw at first hand Elizabeth's eagerness to enjoy herself, her passion for horses, which they shared, her lack of affectation. The winter after her first visit, Elizabeth had responded to a family member's question about her Christmas present with a down-to-earth request for a dressing gown that was machine washable. It was duly made by the Emmanuels, designers of Diana's wedding dress, with practical fabric-covered buttons.

Andrew and Sarah Ferguson were married at Westminster Abbey on 23 July 1986. Elizabeth bestowed on Andrew the title Duke of York, associated with second sons, which had belonged to both her father and her grandfather. She wore a blue coat and dress by Hartnell-trained Ian Thomas, who had begun making clothes for her in 1969. Thomas recorded a compliment from Philip, who came into Elizabeth's dressing room during a fitting, that made her flush with pleasure. During the wedding itself, the fidgetiness of four-year-old William of Wales attracted his grandmother's irritated attention, so different from her own earnest good behaviour as a bridesmaid to Lady May Cambridge in October 1931, when she was five. That it did not mar her enjoyment of an ebullient occasion was confirmed in her subsequent Christmas broadcast. With uncharacteristic whimsy, Elizabeth suggested that 'even the horses in their stables' had been aware 'that something quite special [was] happening... on that happy day back in July when my son and daughter-in-law were married, and they drew the carriages through the cheerful crowds thronging the London streets'.[67] Watching the wedding on television, veteran novelist Anthony Powell judged it more simply an 'unusually good show'.[68]

Journalists outside the abbey combed the crowds for any shard of opinion to distinguish their gushing copy from other front pages. The *Sunday Tribune* found a trio of friends from Cheshire. Obligingly, Winifred Mould shared her opinion that 'she personally never believed that the Queen and Mrs Thatcher has ever got on'.[69] It was not a random statement on Mrs Mould's part. Days before the wedding, quoting 'sources close to the Queen', the *Sunday Times* had informed readers of Elizabeth's view of Thatcher's style of government as 'uncaring, confrontational and divisive'.[70] Initial reactions of Elizabeth's advisers, among whom the story's source was at first unsuspected, were of horrified astonishment. From Windsor Castle, Elizabeth agreed to telephone an upset Thatcher; she commiserated with her, presumably over press perfidy, and reassured her that 'the story bore no relation to the facts'.[71] Within a week, the 'sources close to the Queen' were identified as Elizabeth's press secretary Michael Shea, who denied making the offending statements in anything resembling the form in which they were published; he had responded to a telephone interview, he claimed, in anodyne fashion. Readers were sensibly sceptical that Elizabeth, after thirty-four years of oyster-like political discretion, should express herself so unguardedly, an argument expounded by William Heseltine in a letter to *The Times*, in which he also defended Elizabeth's right to form opinions on government policy. Thatcher exonerated Elizabeth from blame; she worried that rumours of royal disapproval would undermine her own grass-roots support. The danger to Elizabeth was significant. Partiality was not permitted to a crown above politics. Differences of opinion between Elizabeth and her prime minister over Commonwealth affairs were already suspected. Three days earlier, the Commonwealth Games had opened in Edinburgh in disarray. Thirty-two black nations boycotted the competition, angry at Thatcher's resistance to sanctions against South Africa's apartheid regime. As at Lusaka, Elizabeth was anxious to facilitate compromise in the interest of the organization's continuance. She understood the pitfalls of any suggestion that her roles of head of state and head of the Commonwealth conflicted. A consensus emerged that the opinions were Michael Shea's own; months later he left royal employment. Nevertheless a view persisted that, in so serious a matter as Elizabeth's relationship with her prime minister, there could be no press smoke without fire. Winifred Mould was not alone in her conclusion.

~~~

As long ago as December 1937, the *Spectator* had noted of the royal family, 'with all that needs to be known about their private lives the public is quite adequately familiar. Tissues of trivialities about what Prince Someone's chauffeur or Princess Somebody's hairdresser said of them do small service to their reputation.' The writer concluded that 'the highest 'compliment' the British public could pay its royals was 'to treat them as they would obviously desire to be treated'.[72]

In the summer of 1987, quite how Elizabeth's family desired to be treated became a moot point. In June, Elizabeth conferred on Anne the title Princess Royal. Twenty-two years had passed since the death of the last Princess Royal, Elizabeth's aunt, Princess Mary. Although the title was reserved for the sovereign's eldest daughter, the award to Anne was explained as a recognition of her public service, notably her work as president of Save the Children. It was an old-fashioned royal gesture that gave particular pleasure to both Elizabeth and Philip, glossed in terms acceptable to 1980s meritocrats. The same month, however, against the advice of all her senior staff, Elizabeth permitted a televised fundraising initiative that ultimately cocked a snook at notions of royal status. It was the brainchild of her youngest son, Edward, who earlier in the year had left the Royal Marines midway through training, to his mother's disappointment. Edward's aim was to raise £1 million to be divided between four charities, each charity the beneficiary of a team led by a member of his own family, in a royal version of a popular game show called *It's a Knockout*. Anne, Andrew and Sarah would join him as team leaders; Charles had declined to take part and had vetoed Diana's participation. In an interview ahead of the event, Edward offered, 'I hope I didn't twist anybody's arm. It was completely up to them and luckily they all thought it was a good idea.'[73] That it was not a good idea to combine royalty with a slapstick outdoor game show in a pastiche medieval setting, or to encourage television and sports personalities to indulge in a pantomime version of a courtly tournament, complete with exaggerated gestures of mock deference to the royal team leaders, ought to have been obvious. Deference is not a safe subject for royal-led public satire; boisterousness sits uneasily with inherited ideas of royal dignity. 'Monarchy is the manipulation of illusion...

Royals of old saw it as their duty to present an image of propriety,' a provincial newspaper reminded its readers with a sniff of disapproval.[74] *It's a Royal Knockout* stripped its royal participants of the possibility of inspiring illusions. Only Anne, conspicuously uncomfortable, emerged mostly unscathed; her newest sister-in-law had abandoned propriety gleefully. An on-site press conference ended unhappily with Edward's stormy departure, after journalists failed to praise the day's events. As hoped, a significant sum had been raised for a quartet of charities, but this was overlooked in the subsequent fallout. A resoundingly negative response to the enterprise was a reminder, too late, that public expectations of the royal family were conservative: a well-respected novelist would suggest that 'in return for privilege, wealth and adoration, [they] must... indicate from time to time that they are subject to burdensome duty'.[75] On this occasion, Elizabeth's children could not blame the media for a failure of judgement and ill-advised behaviour that were all their own. A royal official described the programme as 'a step down the slippery slope. It brought ridicule on the organisation.'[76] Elizabeth's reluctance to halt Edward's plans had enabled her headstrong brood unwittingly to inflict unnecessary damage on the institution to which she had dedicated her life. Only a year before, biographer John Pearson had claimed that Elizabeth had 'surrendered nothing of the essence of the royal myth which she accepted as a sacred trust from that dedicated king, her father', but the royal myth was fragile in the face of rapidly changing attitudes and her children's folly.[77] Elizabeth would describe herself as 'like Queen Victoria... a believer in that old maxim "moderation in all things"', a claim supported by her iron self-control and frugality: hotwater bottle covers used until threadbare, electric lights assiduously turned off; but neither she nor Philip, who Andrew identified as the instigator of duty and discipline in his own and his siblings' upbringing, had enforced moderation on their children.[78] In a book published five years earlier, Philip had set out his belief in the importance he attached to 'the responsibility [the individual] takes for his own attitudes and his own actions'.[79] In practice, it was a laissez-faire doctrine and, seconded by Elizabeth, afforded all four royal children considerable scope for error.

In the week of *It's a Royal Knockout*, an embarrassment of royal-themed riches was available to television viewers. Without enthusiasm the *Daily Mirror* noted 'thirteen major programmes on the BBC alone'.[80] If it was a warning about over-exposure, it was one that both the paper itself and members of Elizabeth's family ignored.

~~~~~

At Balmoral, on 30 August 1987, Elizabeth and Philip were photographed by Canadian-Armenian photographer Yousuf Karsh, for whom Elizabeth had first sat in 1943, surrounded by their grandchildren. Months later, the release of official photographs by Tim Graham marked their fortieth wedding anniversary. After the indignities of the summer, Elizabeth and Philip appeared at their most formal, in the Green Drawing Room at Windsor Castle. From the same sitting were pictures of Elizabeth alone. She appears austere, stern-featured and formidable, armoured against the unpredictability of the present by accoutrements of the past: the Royal Family Orders of George V and George VI worn against the Garter ribbon and, appropriately for the occasion, the Girls of Great Britain and Ireland tiara, a wedding present from her grandmother. The pictures bear out Lady Selina Hastings's view of Elizabeth, expressed a year before: 'The Queen has no desire to participate in ordinary life... There she is up on her cloud and on her cloud, she knows very well, it is essential she remain.'[81] In her Christmas broadcast, Elizabeth referred to the hundreds of letters she received daily, including, she acknowledged, those 'full of frank advice for me and my family'. 'Some of them do not hesitate to be critical,' she said truthfully.

CHAPTER XVI

'How long to reign over us?'

Elizabeth's decision, announced in the last week of November 1987, to overturn a historic restriction against women's membership of the Orders of the Garter and the Thistle was part of an evolving process of modernization. The less frivolous press applauded it as a removal of sex discrimination, albeit one unlikely to affect many of its readers; the tabloids stuck to their pursuit of Elizabeth's daughters-in-law. At a private lunch, Martin Charteris described himself as 'worried about the younger ones'. Roy Strong reported him 'stress[ing] the need to put the mystery back as they had been virtually "stripped naked"'.[1] But the time was out of joint for royal mystique: at odds with Diana's growing embitterment, which would lead her into a damaging alliance with the press against her husband; beyond Sarah's careless bunglings.

Elizabeth, however, had been encouraged to recognize an equally pressing need to rationalize the mysterious workings of her own household. More than thirty years earlier, Philip had wrestled with the stubborn inertia of palace and court machinery; loyal to her father's memory and concerned not to upset her mother, Elizabeth had sanctioned only piecemeal change. The architect of more sweeping updates in the mid-1980s was a childhood friend of impeccable court credentials, David Ogilvy, 13th Earl of Airlie. Lord Airlie was the eldest grandson of Queen Mary's devoted lady-in-waiting, his father the Queen Mother's former lord chamberlain; his wife was Elizabeth's only American lady-in-waiting, and his younger brother, Angus, had married Elizabeth's cousin Alexandra. The retiring chairman of merchant bank Schroders, described as 'part Wall Street executive, part Highland chieftain', Airlie was invited to succeed Chips Maclean as Elizabeth's lord chamberlain while shooting at Sandringham.[2]

Her private secretaries had noticed a meticulous orderliness to Elizabeth's working life from her accession: the girl who neatly lined up her toy horses on the landing at 145 Piccadilly and followed to the letter government instructions on the daily use and cleaning of her gas mask grew into a monarch diligent in her turnaround of state papers. Elizabeth was practical and, if need be, pragmatic, as David Airlie discovered quickly; as he knew already, she was a careful innovator. He observed the mechanics of Elizabeth's household, noting the smooth working of the private secretaries' office and the assurance of ceremonial aspects of royal life. Elsewhere, Airlie discerned grounds for full-scale internal review in line with the sort of restructuring processes sweeping through so many organizations; he noticed the dependence on government and the Civil Service in areas including maintenance and transport. Elizabeth accepted his suggestion of an efficiency review by an outside consultant: the 'outsider' in question, Etonian Michael Peat, had 'inside' form as a partner in accounting firm Peat Marwick McLintock, the royal auditors. Peat's 1,393-page report was a year in the making; it included almost 200 suggestions for change, all of which Elizabeth accepted, the majority implemented over the next three years. Airlie involved Elizabeth as much as he felt necessary. It is unlikely that she relished the process, which caused consternation among old hands and considerable unhappiness. Peat's reforms overturned assumptions and working practices that had survived since the nineteenth century unchallenged by Elizabeth's father, grandfather and, until now, Elizabeth herself. That they pointed the way to greater cost efficiency, a necessary bulwark against the monarchy's detractors, was their principal recommendation: the 1971 Select Committee had revealed the contentiousness of royal finances. Through the remainder of the decade the engagement of monarchy and media grew increasingly torrid, inflamed by behaviour interpreted as extravagant, self-indulgent or outspoken on the part of Elizabeth's children and their spouses, as well as escalating rumours of marital discord; attempts to curb expenses held out a promise of protection against mounting criticism; they also offered leverage with the Treasury. Evidence of the palace's ability to manage its finances, including addressing the £92,000 annual cost of changing light bulbs identified by Peat, contributed to government willingness to negotiate a new long-term funding plan for the monarchy.[3] The result, in 1990, was an increase in Elizabeth's annual Civil List allowance to £7.9 million, this figure fixed for ten years. Although she could not have known it at the time, as a result Elizabeth would be spared embarrassing and controversial annual requests for additional funding during the most difficult and dangerous decade of her reign.

It was Thatcher's last significant tribute to the institution she revered and a sovereign she admired. In November, a leadership challenge from within the Conservative Party forced her resignation eleven and a half years after she became the country's first female prime minister; John Major replaced her. Thatcher's public humiliation at the hands of her own party distressed Elizabeth, who, in a show of sympathy, invited the ousted premier to the races, as she had once invited a struggling Winston Churchill. Thatcher declined but was touched nevertheless. Part of her pleasure in Elizabeth's award to her of the Order of the Garter and the Order of Merit – both nominations within Elizabeth's own giving – was the gifts' implied rebuttal of the rumoured rift between the women four years earlier. Since there was no established tradition of departing prime ministers automatically joining the exclusive Order of Merit, the decision could be interpreted flatteringly.

                                           ∾

At a children's concert at the Royal Albert Hall in December 1989, Elizabeth described the crown, in answer to a child's question, as 'quite heavy: you don't really want to walk about very long in it'. She paused. 'It's meant to be heavy, I think,' she added.

She had never regarded sovereignty as less than a weighty burden, but for much of her four decades on the throne her behaviour had suggested an overwhelming enjoyment of its exactions. A chapter that had begun with such promise, in the carnival whoopee of Charles's marriage to Diana, gave way to years of unprecedented strain that included press attacks on Elizabeth herself, as well as a brutal dismantling of the Victorian ideal of a family on the throne. Sections of the media and public explained the collapse of Anne, Charles and Andrew's marriages in the early 1990s as a direct consequence of Elizabeth's distant parenting, and Elizabeth's suffering was not lessened by the irony that those who condemned her self-restraint as coldness were those who, with equal vehemence, criticized her children and their spouses for lack of self-control. When the going was good, Elizabeth had sensibly put one of her houses in order, greenlighting the Airlie/Peat reforms that between 1991 and 2000 would shave nearly £30 million from the monarchy's annual running costs.[4] The behaviour of younger members of her family was less easily resolved, particularly by a woman who had inherited her mother's aversion to confrontation. An increasingly hardline approach to a mischievous press pointed to Elizabeth and her advisers' understanding of the maelstrom that threatened her: in January 1987, Philip brought legal proceedings for breach of copyright against the *Sun*, after the paper published a leaked letter he had written to Edward's commanding officer in the Royal Marines. Royal retaliation of this sort was sporadic, and tabloids were undaunted. The fierce, often cruel, frequently invasive spotlight of an irreverent, contemptuous Fleet Street was not easily deflected. Criticism of Elizabeth herself was desultory at first, though the puzzled observation that 'the Queen never, ever, visits the scenes of disasters', citing her failure to rearrange her schedule after the Lockerbie air crash in December 1988, the earlier Piper Alpha disaster and the Zeebrugge ferry sinking, suggested disappointment that little had changed since Aberfan.[5] In the short term, in a survey conducted by the Barbican's Royal Britain tourist attraction, Elizabeth and her mother emerged as the royal family's most popular members. Her three-day visit with Philip to the Channel Islands in May was notable for large crowds throughout. Walkabouts remained good-naturedly stilted, provoking in those singled out what Alan Bennett categorized as 'fatuous smile[s], any social awkwardness veiled in nervous laughter so that the Queen moves among her people buoyed up on waves of obliging hilarity'.[6] Despite his reputation for tactless gaffes – in his own terminology 'dontopedalogy... the science of opening your mouth and putting your foot in it' – Philip was skilful in noticing those Elizabeth overlooked; on occasions he lifted disappointed children over the safety barrier to deliver their wilting posies.

In the same survey, Anne had polled more votes than either Diana or Sarah, despite the announcement that year of her separation from Mark Phillips, following tabloids' revelation that one of Elizabeth's equerries, Commander Timothy Laurence, had written love letters over a period of eighteen months to the married princess. In a sketch of the time in satirical television puppet show *Spitting Image*, Diana asks Edward, 'What do you do?' After the disillusionment of *It's a Royal Knockout*, Edward's response of 'Nothing. No one does. Everything is provided' encapsulated a growing view of the younger royals. It was easy to accuse fashion-conscious Diana of extravagance. Sarah was too guileless to disguise her enjoyment of living high on the hog, with frequent holidays abroad. She and Andrew had built a new house, Sunninghill Park. Astonishing in its ugliness, it nevertheless gobbled up £3.5 million, provided, apparently uncomplainingly, by Elizabeth. So entrenched was the idea of Sarah's financial fecklessness by 1991 that the *Guardian* could claim the Yorks' new house had in fact cost £5 million.[7] And despite the births of William and, two years later, Harry, and Andrew and Sarah's daughters Beatrice and Eugenie, in 1988 and 1990, both marriages had come adrift.

Repeatedly in Elizabeth's life, economic downturn had prompted an embattled public to look to the monarchy for uplift; this had been the case at the time of Elizabeth's wedding and again at her Silver Jubilee. In the second half of 1990, unemployment rose, and the economy contracted; in January 1991, John Major's government officially declared a recession. The Queen Mother's ninetieth birthday in August had provided an opportunity for affectionate tributes, but there would be no comparable public rallying behind the royal family in the year ahead. Newspapermen continued to luxuriate in the anguished private lives of Elizabeth's three elder children; most sensational was the bitter collapse of Charles's marriage to Diana. Domestic squabbling did not dignify the monarchy. Elizabeth and Philip understood its potential to undermine their own record of forty years' making, Philip commenting in private 'Everything I have worked for for forty years has been in vain.'[8] The death of her retired mare Burmese, to whom she was deeply attached, added to Elizabeth's unhappiness. On 2 August 1990, Iraq invaded Kuwait; Allied forces responded five months later. Britain played a much smaller part in the liberation of Kuwait than in the Falklands War, and Andrew, though still a serving naval officer, did not see active service in the conflict. The dangers faced by British troops offered newspapers a stick with which to beat Elizabeth's apparently self-absorbed family, several of whom were on holiday. Columnists berated the 'apathetic behaviour of the Royal Family'; a television poll found eighty-three per cent of respondents 'disgusted by their behaviour'.[9] On 7 February, a mortar attack on 10 Downing Street by the Provisional IRA prompted a last-minute forceful rewriting of the speech Elizabeth delivered at the Royal Brompton National Heart and Lung Hospital later in the day: 'This morning we have had a reminder at home that there are those who seek to undermine our democratic system and way of life. I would like to take this opportunity to remind them that they will not succeed.' A fortnight later, Elizabeth made a televised address to the nation, her first of its kind. It was a moderate, prayer-like hope for swift success with minimum loss of life and, given the war was not a British initiative, it lacked any sort of rallying note. Under the circumstances, there was an effete quality to its blandness that contrasted poorly with the less publicized vigour of her speech at the Royal Brompton. Two days later, in something surprisingly close to self-justification, Elizabeth's private secretary announced the monarch's close consultation with senior government ministers about the war's prosecution.[10]

Elizabeth could have been justified in a sense of grievance. As she had since her accession, she, like Philip, maintained a full and busy schedule of engagements, almost 600 over the previous year; on the evidence of media reports, the nation was indifferent to the couple's efforts. In the querulous spirit of the times, it was the old bugbears of Elizabeth's personal fortune and her tax exemption that attracted public comment. Mountbatten had warned Elizabeth and Philip twenty years before that concealment would prove inflammatory, and so it turned out. Glossy magazine *Harpers & Queen* claimed that Elizabeth was the richest woman in the world, with private assets valued at a colossal £6 billion. A recession-hit public read that Elizabeth's wealth had increased by a quarter in the previous year and that, even through 1991, a huge portfolio of blue-chip investments would earn her interest of £1 million a day. Other sources computed markedly lower figures. In every case, they suggested that Elizabeth was well able to pay the income tax on her private fortune that she had been spared since 1952. A clamorous campaign to this end offered distraction of sorts from forensic unpicking of Charles and Diana's frigidly separate lives, including rumours of Charles's rekindled relationship with Camilla Parker Bowles.

In the summer of 1976, Elizabeth had visited the United States as part of the country's bicentenary celebrations. In a speech in Philadelphia, she had told her American audience that Britain 'lost the American colonies because we lacked the statesmanship to know the right time and the manner of yielding what is impossible to keep'. Yet media carping did not immediately have the effect of convincing Elizabeth that the right moment to yield her tax exemption was at hand. Not until February 1992 did the palace approach the Treasury over the issue. Even then, nothing was made public. Secrecy about Elizabeth's wealth was a habit long ingrained. In this instance, silence makes possible a parallel with the royal response to

Altrincham's criticisms in 1957, when Elizabeth withheld cancelling debutantes' presentations for one more year to quell suggestions of royal kowtowing. If so, the approach proved counterproductive.

Margaret Rhodes suggested that Elizabeth had inherited her mother's ability to set aside the unwelcome and the unpalatable. 'She is very lucky in having a sort of compartmentalised brain, which means that she can switch off from a particular worry, shut the door and carry on in a light-hearted and happy way.'[11] Beginning in October 1990, with a particular end in view, Elizabeth took time to switch off from murmurous discontent and worries about her children's private lives. In this she was helped by the patchiness of her knowledge of Charles and Diana's marriage, although details of the couple's squabble over Diana's thirtieth birthday party in July 1991, leaked by Diana to the *Daily Mail*, were readily available. Elizabeth, of course, could have approached either or both of them, but that was not her way. She remained closer to her mother and her sister than any of her children, and Diana's tearful private visits to her left Elizabeth drained but incapable of answers. Charles still resisted any approach to his parents. 'Trouble lies in fact that the Queen, Prince Philip and P of W [Prince of Wales] all find it very difficult to talk to each other,' explained Charles's friend the Duchess of Devonshire to guests at Chatsworth.[12] Like Charles, Elizabeth was unaware that Diana was about to shatter every code of her polite, decorous world: in audio recordings entrusted via an intermediary to a tabloid journalist in the summer of 1991, Elizabeth's daughter-in-law had embarked on a secret unburdening of her private woes that would claim Elizabeth among its victims – her self-restraint and good behaviour, which Diana characterized as unfeeling. Instead, while she and Philip maintained the routines of a lifetime, Elizabeth also looked ahead to 1992 and the fortieth anniversary of her accession. The milestone would be marked, *inter alia*, by a documentary chronicling a year in her life. Its title, *Elizabeth R*, made clear its focus and its purpose. The programme's makers were granted closer access to their subject than at any point since *Royal Family*. In a sombre mood of public disapproval, the camera lens tracked only Elizabeth.

Of the twelve possible producers sent by the BBC to Buckingham Palace in the second half of 1990, Elizabeth's near-contemporary Edward Mirzoeff won the commission. Mirzoeff had made a trio of films with the former poet laureate John Betjeman and, a decade earlier, a documentary after Elizabeth's own heart, *The Englishwoman and the Horse: A Kind of Love Story*. On this occasion, the filmmaker would discover that his task involved more than documentary-making. In 1969, Elizabeth had found that she enjoyed the experience of *Royal Family*. More than twenty years later, journalistic deference had all but vanished, and Elizabeth had her own views on the perils of media access. 'My impression', Mirzoeff remembered, 'was that she needed to be convinced that it was a good idea.' From the outset he did not make his task easier: Mirzoeff wanted to accompany his behind-the-scenes footage with voice-over commentary provided by Elizabeth. Negotiations over the commentary lasted six months. 'The Queen just doesn't do that sort of thing, which is why it took so much [persuasion]. And she was nervous about it.' Elizabeth is not introspective, she does not talk about herself and has never felt comfortable speaking publicly without a script. In 1957, James Pope-Hennessy had categorized her conversation as not 'memorable, interesting, or worth the paper it could be typed upon'.[13] For the majority of viewers, her voice-over proved the film's highlight, described by diarist James Lees-Milne as 'her little understated asides of wit... humorous, sensible, wise, wise'.[14]

As with *Royal Family*, Elizabeth agreed to filming in a number of locations over twelve months: Buckingham Palace, Windsor

Castle, Sandringham, Holyrood and Balmoral, her private box at Epsom races, the royal train. She was filmed on and off duty, though Mirzoeff would conclude that her attitude to sovereignty meant she was never in fact off duty. His assessment that 'there isn't a moment where she can say, "Well, that's it. I can stop being the Queen now and start having fun"' matched that of friends and family; Harold Wilson's wife, Mary, had reached a similar conclusion. In a poem called 'The Opening of Parliament', Mary Wilson recalled Elizabeth at Balmoral, 'walking free upon her own estate'. 'Still in her solitude she is the Queen,' she wrote.[15] Though Mirzoeff permitted none of Elizabeth's family to obtrude more than fleetingly on the viewer's consciousness, his Elizabeth is family focused; a junto of officials, ladies-in-waiting, private and press secretaries invariably more poker-faced than the monarch herself surrounds her. Family troubles do not ruffle the seamless narrative. Mirzoeff captured Elizabeth's conscientiousness, the effort behind each public encounter, her enthusiasms, a serene indomitability. His Elizabeth 'has a great sense of fun and enjoyment... It's almost girlish – terribly attractive.'[16] Overwhelmingly, viewers agreed.

The surge reported by electricity and water companies following the film's screening on 6 February 1992, the fortieth anniversary of Elizabeth's accession, proved the size of its audience – at the time, the largest recorded for a documentary – and Elizabeth's enduring hold on the public imagination. Afterwards it became the nation's fastest-selling video. As such it represented a high point in a year the Queen Mother subsequently described to Elizabeth without exaggeration as one of 'ghastly happenings':[17] Diana's carefully staged solo photograph in front of the Taj Mahal and, as she intended, predictable brouhaha in its wake; announcement of Andrew and Sarah's separation in March, giving the lie to Elizabeth's statement in *Elizabeth R* that naval wives 'are given some extra sort of strength to be able to cope'; Anne's divorce in April. In her Christmas broadcast, Elizabeth had drawn attention to the anniversary in characteristic terms, explaining that, for forty years, she had tried 'to follow my father's example and to serve you as best I can'. In the sullied atmosphere of 1992, hers would echo as a voice from another world. Save in her own doggedness and her mother's iron-willed continuance, the King's record of steadfastness and service was all but obliterated. Elizabeth's statement of family piety seemed to underline her helplessness in the face of her children's fragmenting lives. Perhaps listeners were surprised that, after the longest reign of the century, she continued to draw inspiration from her father. Was it the security of 'us four' she craved, or the reassurance that her father, unprepared for the challenges he faced, had succeeded through fixed purpose? At its simplest it was a statement of straightforward truthfulness, proof of Elizabeth's modesty and a reminder at a difficult moment of the monarchy's historic roots. At the same time planning for *Elizabeth R* began, Elizabeth invited Cyril Woods, who had taken part with the princesses in the Windsor pantomimes, to make a written record of his memories of the wartime productions. It was in Elizabeth's nature to ensure that such personal records were not lost, attentive to the historic value of royal lives; there was comfort, too, in recalling past happiness. Woods sent copies of his eighteen-page 'Memories of The Royal Pantomimes' to Elizabeth and Margaret in January 1991.

Elizabeth had begun 1992, as always, at Sandringham. The family party included her mother. Together they walked in the garden; they picked branches of flowering witch hazel, which the Queen Mother took with her to Clarence House. She did not remain with her daughter for the anniversary of the King's death and Elizabeth's accession; without her, Elizabeth went to church early in the morning and afterwards visited cancer patients in a local hospital. The Queen Mother described her long stay in Norfolk as 'better than ten bottles of tonic or twenty bottles of Arnica'.[18] For both women this feeling would vanish as the year unfurled its inventory of wretchedness, beginning with a rash of spiky anniversary articles at odds with fulsome responses to the silver jubilee or Elizabeth's thirtieth anniversary ten years before. The *Daily Telegraph* published poet laureate Ted Hughes's official anniversary offering, a five-part poem called 'The Unicorn' that included in its survey 'the tabloid howl that tops the charts'. A plan to erect a commemorative twenty-five-foot bronze unicorn fountain in Parliament Square had been postponed indefinitely. 'I thought of filling the gap, provisionally, with a Unicorn in verse,' commented Hughes.[19]

Diana's revenge on Charles was public and deeply damaging. First extracts of *Diana: Her True Story* appeared in the *Sunday Times* on 7 June; a further instalment followed a week later. Philip was not alone in suspecting Diana's own part in Andrew Morton's book; to her brother-in-law Robert Fellowes, Elizabeth's private secretary, Diana denied collusion. For Elizabeth, Morton's revelations were unprecedented, and her response was more complex than the fury Crawfie's tale-telling had inspired a lifetime earlier. She worried for her grandchildren; she worried for the awful toll on the monarchy. Her concern and Philip's insistence prompted a meeting between Charles and his parents, at which Elizabeth, always cautious, advised her son to wait before committing himself to separation. After the paper's second extract, Elizabeth and Philip met both partners in Elizabeth's private sitting room at Windsor Castle. Courtiers have suggested that a passive quality in Elizabeth exasperates her husband: 'she's much better at knowing when it's right to say no, than at taking the initiative and saying yes. So he'll say, "Come on, Lilibet. Come on. Just do it!"'[20] On this occasion, Philip spared his wife by firmly advising both Charles and Diana to consider their children and the monarchy in place of personal unhappiness. Self-abnegation in the interests of duty had been a central tenet of Elizabeth and Philip's married lives: of their son and daughter-in-law they asked only the compromise they themselves had embraced. Although Diana did not attend an agreed second meeting, Elizabeth chose to believe that both she and Charles intended to follow advice to take stock before moving forwards. Philip wrote to his daughter-in-law, a correspondence they maintained for four months, the prince, as he explained, like Diana, a Windsor outsider who had married the heir to the throne and been forced to make adjustments. Sometimes his sentiments were evidently Elizabeth's, too, indicated by plural pronouns; Diana understood as much, replying with 'much love to you both'. Philip's warning that she could not content herself with 'simply being a hero to the British people' fell on deaf ears: she had no appetite for paternal advice of this sort and did not wish to be reminded of her duty to the royal family or her 'proper' role towards the country at large. Diana's attitude towards her father-in-law hardened, which distanced her from Elizabeth. The revelation that Diana had indeed collaborated with Morton and lied about involvement with *Diana: Her True Story* ranged Elizabeth's family against her. Margaret's reaction was especially clear cut, as her sister soon understood. With no alternative and something like relief, Elizabeth maintained her summer programme of engagements: she opened Manchester's £130 million Metrolink 'super tram' system; in North Wales she planted a yew tree to celebrate the 700th anniversary of the granting of a royal charter to Overton-on-Dee. She was outwardly untroubled, giving credence to the view of her lately retired Archbishop of Canterbury, Robert Runcie, that 'she is in a league by herself in terms of rising above calamity or changing fortune. She's very much in control of her emotions about these things, just as she is about almost everything. With her, duty comes first, even above family problems.'[21] On a three-day visit to Canada, the prime minister, Brian

Mulroney, assured her that Canadians 'regard you with loyalty and affection, and they stand by you and the Crown', comfort in a comfortless season.

'I think as a human being one always has hope,' Elizabeth had offered in *Elizabeth R*, but she had little reason for optimism as the summer pursued its bloody course. Martin Charteris's fears of the younger members of the royal family being 'stripped naked' by folly and a caustic press were fully realized in August when photographs of a topless Sarah lying beside a swimming pool in the South of France splashed front pages. Licking her toes was a Texan millionaire the hapless duchess insisted was her financial adviser.

That morning Sarah was at Balmoral with her husband's family. Already despondent about Charles and Diana, Elizabeth reacted with a fury that was all the more powerful for its quiet control. Days later the *Sun* published a transcript of a telephone conversation between Diana and a lover, James Gilbey. It was not enough that Elizabeth's children's marriages should fail. A ravening press and its equally hungry readers revelled in lewd and petty details, and the family who, in *It's a Royal Knockout*, had assumed the status of television celebrities, was treated with the scurrilous disrespect that Robert Runcie had warned 'befalls the fashionable personality who is played out after ten years or so in the public eye'.[22] Like discarded toys, the comfortable promises of Cynthia Asquith and Lisa Sheridan and the doll's house domesticity of Y Bwthyn Bach were consigned to history. A. N. Wilson labelled them 'strange times... with their ineluctable tendency to turn their events into farce and... [their] dramatis personae... into clowns', the fate that summer of Andrew, Sarah and Charles.[23] Not so Diana, who worked hard to lodge herself in the public mind as a victim. Nor Elizabeth, unassailable in the straightforwardness of her own private life. Those closest to her saw and admired her steadiness in the face of her family's relentless public baiting, much of it, as she knew, the family's own doing ; they regretted her suffering. 'The Queen was grey and ashen and completely flat,' remembered one senior courtier. 'She looked so awful, I felt like crying.'[24] Evanescent as summer rain was the short-term impact of *Elizabeth R*. James Lees-Milne recorded the Earl of Westmorland talking as early as April 'of the perilous state of the monarchy. If a referendum took place now, it would just scrape through; doubtful a generation hence.'[25] Again, Elizabeth's exemption from taxation raised its head. In fact, plans for Elizabeth to pay tax voluntarily on her private income were almost complete. At the same time, in discussions with the prime minister during the summer break at Balmoral, the palace evolved a sop to public hostility: amendments to the Civil List, so that Elizabeth personally would fund the public activities of all her family bar her husband and her mother. Sections of the media scoffed at news of Elizabeth's likely tax payments, intransigent in their cynicism. The palace did not mention the Civil List.

≈≈≈

Equably, matter-of-factly, Elizabeth replied to a letter of sympathy about the fire that, on 20 November, spread through more than a hundred rooms of Windsor Castle, destroying St George's Hall and a sequence of state rooms, and filling the dank, late-autumn sky for miles around with an angry orange glow that seemed to most who witnessed it a powerful symbol of the House of Windsor's year of disasters. Elizabeth's correspondents were Cyril Woods and his sister Iris. Elizabeth's letter was friendly; it lacked self-pity. 'In some respects we were very lucky as in spite of the serious structural damage, the part that was burned was virtually empty of furniture and pictures due to the re-wiring programme,' she explained. She thanked the Woods for their part in the hasty, improvised removal operation organized by helpers including Andrew that filled the quadrangle with paintings by Rubens, Van Dyck and Gainsborough, eighteenth-century furniture and Sèvres porcelain. 'I hope that memories of rooms in the past will be translated into reality before too long,' Elizabeth wrote; she expressed a hope that the restoration 'will make this very special place better than before'.[26] To her sister Margaret, she expressed her view that there had been three 'miracles' about the fire: no lives were lost; there was no wind; and many of the rooms' contents had already been removed as part of the rewiring process.[27]

Almost a month had passed before Elizabeth wrote to the Woods. Her restored composure was remarkable nevertheless. Her belief in the possibility of phoenix-like renewal was sincere: it shaped her thoughts about the home she loved and surely her prayers for the wounded dynasty that bore its name. Reaction to the fire had revealed continuing affection for Elizabeth as well as the bitterness of current disillusion. And for once setting aside the passivity that Philip deplored, Elizabeth had acted decisively to tip the balance favourably.

She was a forlorn, apparently lonely figure in news footage, surveying the fifteen-hour-long conflagration, dressed in a hooded mackintosh, her expression of overwhelming tiredness, Philip overseas on this most dramatic of forty-fifth wedding anniversaries. On television, Andrew described her as 'shocked and devastated'. Later, those at Windsor that day wished they had told her how sorry they were, engulfed by smoking apocalypse, but no one did, the barrier of sovereignty as unbreachable then as on happier occasions. The length of her telephone calls to Philip, as the fire burned through the night, was a measure of Elizabeth's distress. Britons had watched in horror and disbelief, but a hasty misjudgement by an unpopular government to meet the enormous cost of restoration from the public purse transformed sympathy into outrage, and the tom-tom drums sounded again, again angry at Elizabeth's tax position. Elizabeth caught a cold, worsened by inhaling smoke. By the time of a lunch at the Guildhall four days later, with a temperature of 101°F, she could hardly speak. 'The Queen broke with tradition yesterday by publicly admitting the human frailties of members of the Royal Family and requesting moderation from their critics,' reported the *Daily Telegraph*, beside a photograph of an inexpressibly sad Elizabeth.[28] Two days later, John Major announced her decision to pay tax, first considered in happier days – in the estimate of *The Times* 'a response to a chasm of distrust that has been dug between people and palace by junior royalty and competitive newspapers'[29] – and the ending of separate Civil List allowances for Margaret and all four of her children. Both appeared concessions forced by panic. But Elizabeth's words at the Guildhall would resonate longer than the smallness of press reporting. In the fire's aftermath, her former assistant private secretary Sir Edward Ford had written to her commiserating that, deserving an *annus mirabilis*, she found herself mired in an *annus horribilis*. The sentiment struck a chord and would make its way into Elizabeth's speech, alongside a plea for kindlier consideration. Elizabeth acknowledged the monarchy's accountability, with a caveat: 'we are all part of the same fabric of our national society and... scrutiny, by one part of another, can be just as effective if it is made with a touch of gentleness, good humour and understanding.' Among lunch guests Conservative MP Gyles Brandreth described it as 'the most wonderful speech – wry, personal and very moving', a response that was widespread.[30] Elizabeth's authority is inherited; her moral authority is of her own shaping. 'I do think that you have been marvellous,' her mother wrote to her months later, reflecting on a tumultuous year.[31] Among the voiceless majority were many who shared this view. A republican novelist imagined the creation of a British republic, with the royal family consigned to semi-detached council houses in Hellebore Close, but the portrait of Elizabeth at the centre of Sue Townsend's comic *The Queen and I* was an affectionate one, a woman who 'talked of homeopathic medicine and dogs and the problems of adolescent children', preferred jam sandwiches to broth and kept faith with Crawfie's maxims.

On 9 December, Elizabeth was out of London, at Wood Farm on the Sandringham estate, the five-bedroom cottage with views of the sea that family members had used since the late-1960s for informal visits and entertaining. To a sombre House of Commons the prime minister announced Charles and Diana's separation. Reflecting royal concern about the constitutional implications of their failed marriage, he added puzzlingly, 'There is no reason why the Princess of Wales should not be crowned queen in due course.' With old-fashioned royal understatement, which had been lacking over the last twelve months, Elizabeth and Philip were described as 'saddened'. Elizabeth's feelings encompassed much more than sadness, and she did not watch the announcement on television; she took the dogs for a walk, a sign of her unsettlement. Bookmakers William Hill changed their odds on Charles renouncing the throne from 10-1 to 6-1. 'I can't see Prince Charles becoming King Charles,' a Labour backbencher told American journalists.[32] Others came to share this opinion after publication six weeks later of transcripts of a compromising and undignified telephone conversation between Charles and Camilla, recorded in 1989. According to one account, Elizabeth's response, when told of tabloids' decision to publish, was 'Just when we thought things couldn't get any worse.'[33] She was worried about her mother, who had comforted her after the fire at Windsor, the Queen Mother and Margaret anxious that Elizabeth, and later Philip, join them at Royal Lodge; friends would trace the slow decline in the Queen Mother's health to the summer of Morton's Diana book.[34] With mixed success both Elizabeth and Margaret pressed their mother to use a walking stick they gave her: 'It has a magic handle which fits one's hand like a glove and therefore gives one confidence in movement, especially when feeling dizzy! Just at this moment, it would make... me very happy and relieved if you would rely on its support!' Elizabeth wrote in the summer of 1993, with concern and good-humoured exasperation.[35] Her present of a golf buggy the following year proved more welcome. At the same time, in her rooms above Elizabeth's in Buckingham Palace, relieved of her duties for several years and tended now by nurses, Bobo MacDonald was fading. She died on 23 September 1993, at the age of eighty-nine. As if for a family member, Elizabeth broke her holiday at Balmoral to attend Bobo's funeral at The Queen's Chapel, St James's Palace. Her death spelled the loss of Elizabeth's earliest confidante and one of her staunchest defenders, Bobo's unswerving loyalty matched only by Philip's and her mother's.

❧

The 'rather too mundane' way of looking at things she had observed in herself forty years before bolstered Elizabeth in the tense, uncertain period between Charles and Diana's separation and the princess's death five years later. Elizabeth did not respond to Diana's revelations made public by Morton, nor did she answer her own critics beyond commending moderation in her Guildhall speech. She simply carried on with the task of royalty: engagements, audiences and investitures, which she rated the most important aspect of her public life and for which she prepared with briefing lists of biographical information on recipients, committed to memory over diligent weekends at Windsor. 'The Queen must have been desperately worried and unhappy,' reflected Lady Kennard, a friend since childhood, who had shared Elizabeth's swimming lessons at the Bath Club, 'but you would never know it because she has this iron self-discipline.'[36] Concern for other people's troubles, and the example of philanthropist Leonard Cheshire, who had lately died, were at the heart of her 1992 Christmas message. Elizabeth's reference to 'some difficult days this year' overshadowed another element of her broadcast. The recording had been made at Sandringham. It was the house, Elizabeth reminded viewers, bought by Edward VII more than a century ago; it was the place from which her father and her grandfather had made their Christmas broadcasts. As she had made clear a year earlier, Elizabeth considered herself a monarch forged in the image of her forebears. One year on, she reminded her audience of the monarchy's deep roots, stretching back through generations beyond living memory. In the house in which she herself had been a granddaughter, building snowmen with Margaret during George V's final illness, she now, she explained, entertained her own grandchildren. 'To me, this continuity is a great source of comfort in a world of change, tension and violence.' In the annual public statement that most closely reflects her own thoughts, Elizabeth set out a new personal rhetoric. It built on ideas of her constancy celebrated as long ago as her silver wedding anniversary, but went further in linking continuity with comfort as shields against change and violence. Elizabeth could not mend Charles and Diana's marriage and she correctly feared the ability of both to damage her family's standing, but she could, as she always had, embody living tradition, a dependable still point in a vortex that, with technological advances, would whirl ever more dizzyingly in the years ahead. In practice, this meant continuing in familiar fashion, an approach that suited her conservatism, but her dutiful round would have a low-key quality, and much of what she did went unrecorded outside local papers. Elizabeth's unshowy doggedness was eclipsed by press excitement at Charles and Diana's point-scoring and by bigger arguments about the monarchy both at home and abroad, notably in

Australia, where a Labour government under prime minister Paul Keating planned to sever ties with the crown by 2001. In June 1993, the fortieth anniversary of her coronation offered no respite. Interviewed as part of a television news item, one middle-aged woman remembered the thrill of being taken to watch the coronation procession, at the age of nine, 'because the Queen in those days was a very magical and revered figure'. The *Mirror*'s front page posed a stark question: 'How long to reign over us?' To the poet laureate, Ted Hughes, the Queen Mother expressed her family's view of itself as 'battered by tragic happenings'.[37] The Queen Mother did not support Elizabeth's decision to open Buckingham Palace to the public that summer, though the initiative was successful commercially and contributed significantly to restoration costs at Windsor. It worked on a symbolic level, too, suggesting accessibility on the royal family's part. There were shreds of comfort for Elizabeth in buoyant visitor numbers, proof despite current doldrums of an interest in the monarchy that transcended tabloid prurience.

In May 1993, Elizabeth made her first state visit to the former Eastern bloc, when she and Philip spent four days in Hungary. It was a successful preliminary to a visit to Russia the following October, during which she told the Russian president, Boris Yeltsin, that he and she had both 'spent most of our lives believing such a visit could never happen'. With France's President Mitterrand, Elizabeth opened the Channel Tunnel in May 1994; a month later she returned to France for the fiftieth anniversary of the D-Day Landings. On the beach at Arromanches, she took the salute from more than 7,000 veterans. The warmth of Elizabeth's reception by survivors of her own wartime generation, which moved both them and her, did not deceive her about the scale of the challenge confronting her family. Elizabeth had invited the American president, Bill Clinton, and his wife, Hillary, to spend the previous night on *Britannia*. Clinton was impressed by a diplomatic quality to Elizabeth's charm, as well as her love of her country and its history. It was the same month in which, after lengthy discussions, Elizabeth reluctantly accepted government plans to decommission the royal yacht.

That Elizabeth's family occupied so many of her thoughts was inevitable at a point of continuing crisis. Instinctively conciliatory, Elizabeth had overruled Philip's objections to Diana joining the family party at Sandringham for Christmas 1992 and, to the fury of her mother, her sister and her daughter, she continued to allow Diana, at her own request, to take part in a handful of state occasions, like the banquet held in April 1993 in honour of President Soares of Portugal.[38] But it was Charles, not Diana, who first dealt more unexpected blows. A documentary broadcast on 29 June 1994, days before the twenty-fifth anniversary of Charles's investiture as Prince of Wales, showcased his wide-ranging charity work. The programme took the form of an extended interview with journalist Jonathan Dimbleby, whose father had provided commentary on royal ceremonial, including Elizabeth's coronation, a generation earlier. For radio listeners and television viewers, Richard Dimbleby had invested Elizabeth and her family with an aura all but divine, born of his own romantic reverence for monarchy; his son facilitated Elizabeth's heir's admission of adultery in front of an audience of 14 million. He also probed Charles's spiritual views, offering the prince the opportunity to alienate the Anglican establishment with a statement that his preference was to be 'Defender of *Faith*, not *the* Faith'.

The programme was the fruit of a two-year collaboration, and Charles had informed his parents of its outline. Their response had been to caution discretion on the subject of his private life. Charles ignored them, anxious to rebut Diana/Morton suggestions that his relationship with a former lover had nullified his marriage from the outset. His parents' warning proved astute. The Dimbleby documentary did remind viewers of Charles's public service, but its most memorable takeaway was an unprecedented confession of infidelity on the part of the heir to the throne. Like his mother, Charles prizes honesty, but in Philip's old antithesis of pragmatism and romance, the parents' pragmatism, shaped by a pre-war code of silence, was better guaranteed to dampen the flames. Correctly Charles wrote to a retired royal servant, 'I suspect it is what is called "living dangerously".'[39] Her son's behaviour stunned Elizabeth. So did further shocks, delivered in the form of a biography of Charles, also by Dimbleby, that drew on sources including Charles's diaries and private letters. Like so many brickbats hurled at Elizabeth's family, it emerged first in the pages of the *Sunday Times*, in the middle of October, a day ahead of Elizabeth's arrival in Moscow. The book explored Charles's upbringing as well as his marriage. It described Elizabeth and Philip's 'deep if inarticulate love for their son' and Philip's 'inexplicably harsh' behaviour towards Charles growing up; Dimbleby's Elizabeth is 'not indifferent so much as detached', and he notes, at key moments, the absence of a mother's 'protective word or gesture'.[40] The book's publishers boasted of a 'uniquely authoritative account of the man born to be king', and Charles's acquiescence in his biographer's cool portraits of his parents sensationalized every claim. Only in the aftermath of Philip's death almost thirty years later would an alternative publicizing of the parent-child relationship emerge as a belated corrective.

It was not the fanfare Elizabeth would have chosen for an important overseas visit and it offered stark testament to the worsening of her relationship with Charles in the quarter century since his investiture. Angrily, Anne, Andrew and Edward hastened to their parents' defence. 'We did our best', was Philip's terse rejoinder; as ever, Elizabeth kept her own counsel.[41] She had no choice but to immerse herself in diplomatic niceties. She established a quick rapport with Yeltsin; in Moscow and St Petersburg, she and Philip were greeted by cheering crowds 'less interested in the newest palace dust-up than in the glamour of having royalty here again'.[42] At the state banquet in the Kremlin, Yeltsin praised Elizabeth for 'bearing your mission with dignity'; he told her 'you confirm an important idea: monarchy can be an integral part of a democratic system of government, an embodiment of the spiritual and historic unity of a nation'. Advised in advance that Russians would expect her to look the part, Elizabeth obliged by wearing quantities of jewellery for evening engagements, even when Philip and Yeltsin wore lounge suits. Left at home were jewels that Queen Mary had acquired from exiled Romanovs in the wake of the Bolshevik Revolution. Her only Russian jewel was a large sapphire and pearl brooch from the collection of Nicholas II's mother, the Empress Marie Feodorovna; it had been a wedding present to the former Danish princess from Elizabeth's great-grandfather, Edward VII. Yeltsin told his British visitors, 'In Russia, the Queen is seen as the personification of state wisdom, continuity of history, greatness of the nation.' Elizabeth's appearance of thoughtfulness at intervals during the visit ought not to give grounds for surprise.

Among the decade's inconsistencies was the success of significant overseas trips, which in turn played a part in reminding Elizabeth's countrymen of the esteem and affection with which she was regarded internationally. At home her path remained thorny. In March 1995, six months after IRA and loyalist ceasefires, Elizabeth visited Northern Ireland. Security was tight for her first walkabout in Belfast. Newspapers published in London applauded 'her courageous mission of faith in the Ulster peace progress' as well as her doughtiness: 'She has made it clear that she will not be intimidated by threats.'[43] Republican opinion was less easily swayed. In a divided province, Elizabeth could not embody Yeltsin's 'spiritual and historic unity', the history of British Ireland too often one of disunity. Describing her visit to Armagh, the Republican *Sunday Tribune* presented Elizabeth's formality as coldness, the nervous silence of schoolchildren as indifference. The paper's unlovely portrait of Elizabeth was of 'a small compact woman, lightly painted with rouge, powder and lipstick [with] lines under her small dark eyes and a tracery of fine lines on her skin'.[44] It was an accurate if dispassionate summing up of the sixty-nine-year-old monarch, and devoid of magic, mystique or warmth.

In South Africa two months later, Elizabeth appeared unconcerned by questions of security. Indeed, to a remarkable extent she appeared unconcerned by anything beyond her happiness in returning, and discounted security advisers who cautioned the royal party against visiting black townships. Exactly a year before, Nelson Mandela had been elected president of a new democratic South Africa; to Elizabeth's considerable pleasure, the country rejoined the Commonwealth. Elizabeth described the new South Africa as 'little short of a miracle'. Unusually she played a central part in initiating her visit. She explained to foreign secretary Douglas Hurd, 'Mr Mandela is getting advice from lots of people but no one's actually giving him any help. He needs physical assistance and he needs a show.'[45] Her own visit would be the show the fledgling regime required. It was not a boastful rationale, simply a recognition based on experience that her presence in South Africa would serve as an endorsement internationally and a means of bolstering domestic support. Concerned by public opinion at home, she planned regretfully to travel to South Africa by plane, in order to prevent criticism of the expense of *Britannia*. In the event, her fears were overruled by the trip's organizers, who arranged commercial events on *Britannia* to offset travel costs. Elizabeth and Philip flew to South Africa, then transferred to the royal yacht for their official arrival in Cape Town. With Nelson Mandela, Elizabeth established one of her strongest Commonwealth friendships; she bestowed on him the Order of Merit, afterwards she commended him as 'the most gracious of men'. A courtier explained their fondness for one another as based on shared understanding: both had led lives of restricted freedoms – 'You see, they've both spent a lot of time in prison.'[46] It was too pat an explanation, and Elizabeth did not make light of Mandela's incarceration on Robben Island or compare sovereignty to imprisonment. She admired Mandela's hopefulness, his lack of bitterness towards past opponents. At a state banquet, she wore the diamond necklace that had been the dominion's twenty-first birthday present on her previous visit. A Zulu king presented her with a stuffed lioness, and everywhere she went black and white South Africans thanked her for returning. The British high commissioner, Sir Antony Reeve, wrote to Douglas Hurd, 'For most black people, the Queen must have been an unknown quantity, but they turned out with exuberance in their thousands. They were overjoyed, too, by the heavy and much-needed rain which led Deputy President Mbeki to bestow on Her Majesty the title "Motlalepula, she who brings the rain".'[47] Reeve described the visit as 'a touch of forgotten splendour'. In speeches throughout, Elizabeth celebrated the country's transformation, which many had doubted was possible. 'The world has its share of cynics and pessimists,' she told listeners on the eve of departure. As always her delivery was studiedly unemotional in its lack of inflection.

Foreign successes, of course, did not address the more pressing issue of Charles and Diana, for which neither Elizabeth nor Philip had solutions. Elizabeth understood only the probable toll on her grandsons and the continuing erosion of respect and affection for the monarchy. Her relationship with Charles was inevitably strained after the Dimbleby disclosures: Pamela Hicks repeated a conversation in which Alexandra claimed Charles 'never consults the Queen. "There has been a complete break."'[48] Outsiders reached their own conclusions, Robert Runcie convinced by the end of May 'that the Prince of Wales must divorce to avoid even more catastrophic consequences'.[49] Elizabeth was supported by her mother and her sister. On 8 May, all three re-enacted their balcony appearance on VE Day, fifty years earlier. Elizabeth's concern that the public would stay at home proved unfounded, and large crowds gathered outside the palace, partly on account of the Queen Mother's enduring popularity, which current scandals had not diminished. One of her ladies-in-waiting recorded that Elizabeth's eyes were brimming with tears as the three women re-entered the palace.[50] In part a measure of her relief, it was proof of the extent of her concern, as well as her pride in her mother. Even within the relative privacy of a small gathering, she was quick to brush aside her feelings. On and off throughout the morning, Elizabeth had stared out of the window to see if crowds were mustering. How much her life had changed and how distant was the fleeting freedom of her escape into joy- and song-filled London streets fifty years before, dancing with uniformed strangers, running through the Ritz.

But in one matter she would make her feelings all too clear. Diana gave her mother-in-law's advisers six days' notice of her latest and, as it turned out, her last deliberate public act of revenge against her estranged husband. This was an hour-long interview for the BBC current affairs programme *Panorama*, shown to an audience of 23 million people on 20 November 1995, the night of Elizabeth's forty-eighth wedding anniversary, while she and Philip dutifully endured the Royal Variety Performance. In different accounts, filming at Kensington Palace on 5 November, in utmost secrecy using a single cameraman, had taken anything from three to seventeen hours. 'She did each bit again and again until she had achieved the right degree of spurious sincerity,' noted Kenneth Rose tartly.[51] Diana's bravura performance carefully placed blame for her failed marriage on Charles and his mistress; she denounced the royal household and their perception of her 'as a threat of some kind'; and, in criticizing the royal family's engagement with the nation, she made her first implied attack on Elizabeth herself. 'Someone's got to go out there and love people, and show it,' the renegade princess told viewers. She had accused Elizabeth's family of coldness before. The would-be 'queen of people's hearts' pitted the heart on her sleeve against Elizabeth's ramrod back and white gloves.

Elizabeth let it be known that she *never* watched *Panorama*; her advisers took stock of public reaction. Although many viewers expressed their support for Diana, Elizabeth's primary concern was no longer her son or the daughter-in-law to whom she, alone in her family, had remained sympathetic. 'What game is the monarchy playing now, tit for tat, is that the sort of game they're playing now?' asked an audience member on a daytime chat show a day later; it was a moment when patience snapped.[52] Tony Benn noted without pleasure that, in fifty-five minutes, Diana had done great damage to the monarchy.[53] Indeed, Charles and Diana's antipathy had become a campaign for the soul of the monarchy that Elizabeth could not safely countenance. Three weeks later, after discussions separately with Philip and the prime minister, and pressed by her private secretary, Robert Fellowes, Elizabeth wrote to both partners, requesting their agreement to an 'early divorce... in the best interests of the country'.[54] She also entrusted her Christmas broadcast for the first time to ITV. Members of Parliament had called for cancellation of the BBC's Royal Charter; a former BBC governor, crime novelist P. D. James, argued that trust between the corporation and the palace had been deliberately broken. The view of Diana's step-grandmother, romantic novelist Barbara Cartland, that Diana's aim was 'to bring back love' was a picturesque sideshow.

Elizabeth had already met Diana on her own to discuss her requirements of a divorce settlement when, on 13 March 1996, a gunman entered a primary school in the Scottish town of Dunblane and opened fire, killing sixteen children and their teacher. Elizabeth chose Mother's Day for her visit, accompanied by Anne. Her walkabout included laying a wreath of flowers, she met grieving relatives in Dunblane Cathedral and, in Stirling Royal Infirmary, she visited children injured in the attack. Consultant paediatrician Dr Jack Beattie described Elizabeth's encounter with the children in hospital as like a grandmother with her grandchildren; those in the cathedral congregation described her as visibly moved.[55] It was Elizabeth's nearest approach to Diana's cherished role of 'queen of hearts', though she went about it unostentatiously, her purpose to acknowledge Dunblane's suffering and express the nation's sympathy. Elizabeth's presence indicated that lessons had been learned. The primary lesson, belatedly, was that of Aberfan, rather than Diana's charismatic public healing.

Five months later, on 28 August, Charles and Diana's divorce was finalized. As in 1992, in the year of her seventieth birthday Elizabeth had again been denied an *annus mirabilis*. Even in the *Daily Telegraph*, loyalest of broadsheets, an apologetic quality coloured celebration of the royal milestone, which the paper described without gusto as presenting 'a chance to put a long life of service into a wider context, to recall the happy times of the past'.[56] In his diary, Alan Bennett described himself 'sometimes feeling I am the last person in the country to believe in the monarchy'.[57] Not quite the last. Royal determination to survive had inspired an 'in-house' focus group, the Way Ahead Group: Elizabeth, Philip, their four children and senior advisers. At meetings at Sandringham, Balmoral or Buckingham Palace two or three times a year the group discussed policy – from the geographical reach of the family's engagements to the social inclusivity of royal garden parties. It discussed far-reaching changes like alterations in the laws of succession in favour of first-born royal women and the royal tax position; the former became law in the 2013 Succession to the Crown Act, which also permitted marriage with a Roman Catholic. The group's aim was clear: according to Elizabeth's press secretary, Charles Anson, to 'make sure that the monarchy remained relevant in a modern society'. In this forum of opinionated men – Philip, Charles, Andrew, Edward – Elizabeth listened and took stock. She had formulated her own views, briefed in advance. Much of what was discussed, recalled Anson, 'had probably been fairly precooked: the Queen would have been consulted way ahead of a Way Ahead Group meeting'.[58] Her thoughts were of the future.

Elizabeth was at Balmoral on Sunday 31 August 1997, when Diana died in the early hours of the morning in a Paris hospital. She was killed in a car crash in an underpass below the Place d'Alma, fleeing paparazzi with her newest lover, Dodi Fayed, playboy son of Mohammed al-Fayed, owner of Harrods. Diana was thirty-six. Her fifteen- and thirteen-year-old sons William and Harry were also in Scotland with their father and grandparents. There all five would remain for six days, to the rising consternation of significant numbers of Elizabeth's subjects, whom a noisy press goaded to ugly disaffection. It was a decision that brought Elizabeth's monarchy to the brink of crisis.

Elizabeth owed her throne to divorce, her father's accession determined by her uncle's unsuitable choice of bride. The ramifications of Charles and Diana's separation had threatened to split the nation into two camps and tar Elizabeth with Diana's criticisms of Charles; Diana's death did just this. Public reaction to Elizabeth and to her family's response to the tragedy in Paris revealed the consensual nature of modern monarchy and how easily the throne's security could be imperilled by a royal family at odds with the prevailing public mood. 'Not since the abdication of Edward has such damage been done to the folks who live on the Mall,' claimed one newspaper at the time of the Gulf War, criticizing apparent royal indifference to British troops' suffering.[59] An exaggeration in 1991 proved less so six years later. An outpouring of grief convulsed a once stoic nation. Closer to the Queen Mother in age than Diana, James Lees-Milne expressed the view of those who regarded the collective misery with bemusement: 'The grieving over Princess Diana is beyond all belief.'[60] Mourners gathered outside Kensington Palace; they clustered in front of the railings at Buckingham Palace. And swiftly they realized that they alone had come to grieve in London's royal heartlands: Elizabeth and her family were absent.

In Dunblane the previous year, and in Aberfan before that, Elizabeth had embodied a nation's response to tragedy. In the wake of her visits, those affected experienced comfort. Her recognition of their suffering – formally as queen and on a personal level as a mother and grandmother – was an act of sharing and, in its way, alleviating grief. In both instances, Elizabeth had participated in her subjects' sorrow: her grief was on their behalf, an expression of sympathy. On 31 August 1997, the grief was her own and that of her family. She did not feel moved to share it with those who had not known Diana, any more than she had shared her reaction to any family bereavement. The palace's statement that 'The Queen and Prince of Wales are deeply shocked and distressed by this terrible news', issued on the morning of Diana's death, was a truthful expression of Elizabeth and Charles's reactions. It made no mention of their feelings towards Diana and it took no account of the reactions of the nameless millions who considered themselves equally shocked and distressed. Elizabeth's focus was William and Harry. Although advisers claimed she and Philip did foresee public grief, since this was how they felt themselves, they did not anticipate the scale of the response to Diana's death, which found its only parallel in public devastation at the death of George IV's daughter, Princess Charlotte, almost two centuries earlier. Elizabeth compounded her misjudgement of the national mood by a failure to change tack once it became clear what was afoot. Through five decades, she had acknowledged the prior claims of country: queen-wife, queen-mother, queen-sister. On this occasion, she put family first. She approved plans for the return to Britain of Diana's body and its removal with full royal honours to the Chapel Royal, St James's Palace. And she conceded the right of Diana's family thereafter to organize the private family funeral that was the express wish of Earl Spencer and his mother, Mrs Shand Kydd. For William and Harry there was to be time outdoors, fresh air – and no prying cameras or newspapermen.

Elizabeth also agreed that morning to a public statement on the part of her new prime minister, Tony Blair. Blair's short address hailed Diana as 'the People's Princess', a label formerly applied to Elizabeth's great-grandmother, Princess Mary Adelaide of Teck; he explained that 'people everywhere... regarded her as one of the people'. At one level profoundly misleading, both statements caught the popular mood. More than this, Blair had pinpointed Diana's view of herself. In the last years of her life, this aristocratic daughter of a family of court intimates had ranged herself against the royal family, whom she believed had rejected her. Now the prime minister divided the country into non-royals – 'the people', including Diana – and royals. It was a chivalrous send-off for Diana, whom the less temperate were already lamenting as a martyr and a saint. But Blair's crowd-pleasing did not serve Elizabeth well. In this equation, royals were hopelessly outnumbered. Elizabeth and her family, all of whom had altered their plans to remain at Balmoral with William and Harry, went to Crathie church. There were no prayers for Diana, in order, the minister explained afterwards, to avoid further upsetting her sons, and no visible expressions of grief, just as there had been none on his family's part following the King's death or, more recently, Mountbatten's. And so, unwittingly, the royal family conformed to the stereotype so disliked by Diana. By the end of the day, Elizabeth had agreed that the scale of mourning made it imperative to overrule Spencer wishes for a private family funeral. By nine o'clock on Monday morning, she had approved David Airlie's plans for a full-scale funeral at Westminster Abbey.

Forty years before, Elizabeth had inspired adulation. Cards and messages amid the cellophane-wrapped sea of flowers outside Kensington Palace may have saluted Diana as a saint, but in 1954 Elizabeth's arrival in New Zealand had been described in messianic terms as a second coming. Neither Elizabeth nor Philip had courted such responses, which they interpreted as adjuncts of their remarkable position rather than personal tributes. Of his sternly unboastful grandmother, William has said, 'She cares not for celebrity, that's for sure.'[61] Reaction to Diana's death, so different from the quiet grief usually associated with royal deaths, was beyond Elizabeth's ready understanding, like semaphore from a distant planet: it did not lessen her certainty that her duty was her grandsons' wellbeing. As her staff and the prime minister were forced to persuade her, this was not the view of crowds in the capital. Days passed, and their mood shifted between grief and a sullen anger at the monarch's continuing absence. Charles Spencer had blamed the media for his sister's death; the media found an easy scapegoat in its seventy-one-year-old queen. The empty flagpole at Buckingham Palace became an object of overriding concern. In Elizabeth's absence from the palace no flag was flown; the flagpole had not flown the Royal Standard at half mast for her father, she would not expect it to fly at half mast for herself. Against her instincts, Elizabeth was forced to authorize a Union flag. 'The world has lost the plot,' wrote Gyles Brandreth.

'The issue of the hour appears to be the Buckingham Palace flagpole... The tabloids... are baying for blood. [The Queen] has bowed to public opinion and the union flag is now flying over Buckingham Palace at half mast.'[62] Elizabeth also agreed to leave Balmoral sooner than planned and, once in London, to make a special address to the nation. She had been bullied by the tabloid press, with emotive headlines demanding a statement of grief, and, on television news, hatchet-faced women plucked from the crowds by presenters, who disgracefully berated their monarch; more persuasive were the arguments of her own staff in London. She had stayed away too long. Tony Blair had defended her and, with Charles's help, added his own voice to those who persuaded her to make concessions, but her decision, supported by Philip, to shield her grandsons, had prevented her from fulfilling a primary duty as a focus and conduit for the nation's feelings. Her assistant private secretary Robin Janvrin judged her 'composed but distressed by the way the nation assumed she did not care'.[63] Another staff member described her in less stately terms as 'like a stunned fish'.[64] A MORI opinion poll commissioned by American television network ABC found almost one in four Britons persuaded that the country would be better off without the monarchy.

Yet Elizabeth's return to Buckingham Palace on the afternoon of Friday 5 September proved that she, too, like Diana, inspires powerful emotions in her countrymen. The royal car stopped short of the palace gates. Her expression uncertain, Elizabeth stepped out of the car with Philip. In place of Alan Bennett's 'waves of obliging hilarity', a ripple of applause greeted her, polite but modest in scale. She examined the banks of flowers in front of the black-painted railings, then made her way towards the crowds. They had not expected her car to stop and they had not expected Elizabeth to speak to them. Notable all afternoon had been the surprising quiet of those waiting and watching. This disconcerting silence, heavy with recrimination, was broken first by the clapping, then the conversations initiated by monarch and consort. It was a lessening of tension, and it found ultimate release following Elizabeth's live broadcast from the palace's Chinese Dining Room. Elizabeth spoke in front of an open window, the Victoria Memorial visible behind her and around it some of the same crowds she had encountered earlier. Perhaps her colour was fractionally heightened; she was not as still as usual when broadcasting, but her manner was assured, and she spoke with her customary authority, apparently unruffled despite her shaken state. She praised Diana as 'an exceptional and gifted human being'; she expressed admiration and respect for her. She did not mention love. She suggested there were lessons to be learned. Some viewers interpreted this as a promise to copy Diana; Elizabeth may have had in mind her detractors of the preceding week or the media more generally. And she suggested that Diana's funeral, held the following day, offered an opportunity for national unity. Reaction to the broadcast was overwhelmingly positive. Its masterstrokes included the suggestion of Tony Blair's press secretary Alastair Campbell that Elizabeth describe herself as both queen and grandmother. Elizabeth was praised for her sincerity. The morning after, she was equally sincere in a final public tribute to Diana. She led a family party to the palace gates to await the gun carriage's passing. At the appearance of Diana's coffin, draped in her personal standard and crowned with flowers, Elizabeth bowed her head.

After the funeral, in which neither Elizabeth nor Philip betrayed any response to the stinging criticisms of Earl Spencer's eulogy, Elizabeth returned to Balmoral, pensive but relieved nonetheless. The experience of the Highlands was restorative. She had approved a standard typed acknowledgement to letters of condolence about Diana's death. To one such, to lady-in-waiting Henriette Abel Smith, she made a brief addendum:

'Emotions are still so mixed up but we have been through a very bad experience!'[65] It was no less than the truth, but the exclamation mark was expressive – as far as she would allow herself in confiding the full horror of recent days and a sign, too, of her tentative hope that the worst of the crisis had passed. Received in audience, the prime minister, still finding his way with Elizabeth after only four months in office, noted 'a certain hauteur' in response to his suggestion that events offered lessons to be learned: he acknowledged later that Elizabeth had already begun the process of reflection and looking forwards. With time, he would discover, as others had before him, the seriousness with which Elizabeth approached her calling: impossible that she would not reflect on the most dangerous week of her reign. A letter from Margaret, expressing 'my loving admiration for you', was a fillip: 'how you kindly arranged everybody's lives after the accident and made life tolerable for the two poor boys... there, always in command, was you, listening to everyone and deciding on the issues... I just felt you were wonderful.'[66] Margaret's loyalty was important to Elizabeth. No one but Philip and her mother were as close to her, no one else so privy to Elizabeth's feelings or able – when she chose to – to understand so well Elizabeth's outlook that was embedded in the shared experience of their childhood. In her handbag, always with her, was a small gold box given to her by Margaret; it contained her sweeteners.

❦

Margaret had refused to attend the decommissioning ceremony of the royal yacht *Britannia* in December. For Elizabeth, it was a moment of extraordinary sadness, on a bright but cold day, on South Railway Jetty in the Royal Navy's base in Portsmouth Harbour. In accepting the government's decision to retire *Britannia*, rather than approve costly refurbishment, this practical woman had accepted the limits of her choices. Her tears highlighted the understatement of her admission – characteristic in its crisp formality – that 'it is with sadness that we must now say goodbye to *Britannia*'. For all her efforts, the tears rolled freely. She tried to distract herself with a bright aside to Charles, but succeeded only briefly. Courtiers believed she cried for the lost freedom of her seaborne hideaway, for the only home that had ever been truly *hers*, for memories that encompassed the forty-three years of *Britannia*'s service (most of her marriage and her children's lives), for the ship's overseas role in Elizabeth's Commonwealth mission; for the cruises round the Western Isles that were part of Balmoral summers. Monarch's and yacht's had been a partnership, both emblems of the country Elizabeth had been brought up to love with a deep and abiding intensity. Now, both Britain and Elizabeth were diminished by the loss of this symbol of national pride.

Two years before, in a letter to the Cabinet Office, Elizabeth's deputy private secretary, Sir Kenneth Scott, had made clear the importance to Elizabeth of a royal yacht: 'I have deliberately taken a back seat in recent correspondence, since the question of whether there should be a replacement yacht is very much one for the Government and since the last thing I would like to see is a newspaper headline saying "Queen Demands New Yacht". At the same time I hope it is clear to all concerned that this reticence on the part of the palace no way implies that Her Majesty is not deeply interested in the subject; on the contrary, the Queen would naturally very much welcome it if a way could be found of making available for the nation in the twenty-first century the kind of service which *Britannia* has provided for the last forty-three years.'[67]

Elizabeth's 'deep interest' yielded no outcome. In so many ways it had been a decade without rewards.

CHAPTER XVII

'The people's affection for the Queen...
appears indelible'

❧

THE SETTING FOR the ball held at Windsor Castle on 20 November 1997 was the rooms destroyed by fire five years earlier and now dazzlingly restored. The occasion was Elizabeth and Philip's golden wedding anniversary. A gala concert at the Royal Festival Hall, a Guildhall lunch the day before, and a service of thanksgiving at Westminster Abbey followed by a government-organized 'people's banquet' also marked the milestone. Philip celebrated Elizabeth's abundant tolerance, Blair acclaimed her as 'the essence of dignity... unstuffy, unfussy, indeed unfazed by anything, with a keen sense of humour and a mean ability for mimicry'. Of her husband of half a century, Elizabeth told lunch guests he was her 'strength and stay all these years'; on another occasion she would resort to racing imagery and equated a happy marriage with 'the winner's enclosure'. Philip had not faltered in what Michael Parker called 'his constant job [of] looking after the Queen in first place, second and third'.[1] Celebrations saw the largest gathering of European royalty in London since the coronation, including Philip's sister Tiny, the Kings and Queens of Spain, Norway, Sweden, Greece, Bulgaria and Romania, Elizabeth's fellow reigning queens Beatrix of the Netherlands and Margrethe of Denmark with their consorts, and the King and Queen of Jordan. In the months that followed all sat for portraitist Andrew Festing, for a conversation piece set in Windsor's newly restored Green Drawing Room that also includes a full roster of Elizabeth's royal cousins. Inspired by the populous royal tableaux commissioned by Queen Victoria from Danish painter Laurits Tuxen, the painting was the royal household's wedding anniversary present to Elizabeth and Philip. It is displayed prominently in the entrance hall at Sandringham. Elizabeth sits centrally, like her great-great-grandmother, 'the doyenne of sovereigns'. Beside her is her sister Margaret. Margaret's is the largest of the seventeen female portraits in Festing's painting. Hers is also the only figure Festing depicted in heavy shadow.

It proved a presentiment of sorts. Within months of the anniversary celebrations, sixty-seven year-old Margaret suffered a mild stroke. 'Is it forty years of fags and whisky taking its toll?' asked Roy Strong unsympathetically.[2] Margaret's health had been variable since the 1970s, in contrast to that of her sister, who was described as 'strong as a yak'. Bar a degree of forgetfulness, she recovered sufficiently well to pick up where she left off, even returning to the Caribbean island of Mustique a year later. Her stroke, however, had happened shortly after the Queen Mother fell and broke her left hip visiting the stables at Sandringham. She, too, made a convincing and, under the circumstances, quick recovery, resuming public engagements at the end of March, but Elizabeth did not deceive herself that her ninety-eight-year-old mother could continue to hold time at bay, or that her troubled, often lonely sister desired to match their mother's longevity. Given the strength of the bond between the women, for Elizabeth it was an unsettling start to the year.

The change in royal style demanded by the response to Diana's death revealed itself in shifts of emphasis in Elizabeth's diary. Engagements and events sought to bring the monarch closer to her subjects or, in the terminology of the Blair government, 'the people'. On 27 March, Elizabeth visited a Devon pub, the Bridge Inn in Topsham, which was celebrating 101 years of ownership by the same family. A local newspaper had reported the anniversary. A telephone call from Buckingham Palace followed, and afterwards, to finetune details of the visit, 'all manner of folks with shiny shoes and clipboards descended on sleepy Topsham'. Among the pub's decorations were flags purchased for George VI's coronation in 1937. Elizabeth talked about the flags and accepted a crate of commemorative ale for Philip. During her state visit to Malaysia in September, she signed a football for children. She travelled to Harrogate, where she met the cast of the Christmas pantomime, *Aladdin*; press coverage included photographs of Elizabeth and Margaret's own wartime *Aladdin*. She remained clear that she would not be party to what she labelled 'stunts' – 'I am not a politician' – but a handful of instances suggested deliberate, post-Diana 'rebranding' by Elizabeth's staff. On other occasions, Elizabeth achieved the desired level of connection without contrivance. Days before his death, she presented the poet laureate, Ted Hughes, with the Order of Merit at Buckingham Palace. Hughes gave her a copy of *Birthday Letters*, his poems addressed to his first wife, Sylvia Plath, '– and she was fascinated. I told her how I had come to write it, & even moreso how I had come to publish it. I felt to make contact with her as never before. She was extremely vivacious & happy-spirited – more so than ever before. I suppose, talking about those poems, I was able to open my heart more than ever before – and so she responded in kind.'[3]

Hughes found Elizabeth 'extremely easy to speak to quite intimately'. In this he likened her to the Queen Mother and Charles. To the sadness of both, neither Elizabeth nor Charles found it easy to speak intimately to one another. Diana's death had not effected a rapprochement. Events suggest mistrust, unsurprising following the Dimbleby accusations and the questionable role of Mark Bolland, appointed Charles's deputy private secretary in the autumn of 1996, in promoting Charles at the expense of Buckingham Palace and, by implication, Elizabeth: in the week after Diana's death, Bolland leaked to press contacts details of emerging funeral plans, crediting Charles, not Elizabeth's advisers, with the touchy-feely developments likely to win acclaim. Elizabeth's bridge-building included the visit she and Philip made in May 1998 to the new model town of Poundbury, built by Charles in Dorset. Elizabeth's enthusiastic response did not satisfy Charles, for whom his parents' twenty-minute visit was an insufficient acknowledgement of 'the project of my lifetime'.[4] Further setbacks emerged from commemorations of Charles's fiftieth birthday in November. The makers of a documentary, *Charles at Fifty*, claimed, 'We have been told by a senior aide that Charles believes the monarchy needs radical modernization. He is impatient to get on with the job. And that's why, the aide said, the prince would be "privately delighted" if the Queen were to abdicate.' Hastily Buckingham Palace and St James's Palace issued a joint statement explaining that Charles had telephoned Elizabeth to express his distress; in fact a furious Elizabeth had tracked him down on an overseas visit to discover that he knew nothing of the allegations. A dutiful Charles responded by describing the suggestion publicly as 'deeply offensive', 'hurtful' and 'completely wrong'. Elizabeth was indeed hurt: rumours inside the palace suggested that the subject of her abdication had arisen at private dinner parties. Days later, her composure was unruffled at the birthday party she gave for Charles in the ballroom at Buckingham Palace, attended by the Queen Mother with the Gloucesters and Kents, alongside representatives of his many charities; she praised his 'vision, compassion and leadership'. Charles's reply – that he 'enormously appreciated' his parents' tolerance over fifty years – had acquired added piquancy over the preceding week. The following night, neither Elizabeth nor Philip accompanied Margaret to a party at Highgrove,[5] attended by European royals and members of Elizabeth's own inner circle, including Susan Hussey, the Airlies and the Brabournes. Charles had expected as much, and delivered his invitation to his mother via an intermediary.[6] The party's hostess was Camilla Parker Bowles, divorced since 1995 and now 'non-negotiable' in Charles's life. She had been excluded from Elizabeth's guest list for twenty years. Elizabeth would not agree to meet her for another eighteen months.

At the State Opening of Parliament two weeks later, Elizabeth delivered the royal address, as always written on her behalf by the government. For the first time in living memory, her speech was not received in respectful silence. Labour MPs greeted with 'Hear, hears' her announcement of 'the first stage in a process of reform to make the House of Lords more democratic and representative': for the majority of hereditary peers the loss of an inherited right to sit in parliament's upper chamber. Elizabeth was not deflected by the interruption. Nothing in her manner indicated her view of this assault on the hereditary principle, to which she owed her throne; few if any who were present remembered her determined behind-the-scenes response to Emrys Hughes's Abolition of Titles Bill in 1967. In the year ahead she would open a new Welsh assembly in Cardiff and a Scottish parliament in Edinburgh, both invested with devolved powers. Her own position remained constitutionally inviolate.

A striking new portrait of Elizabeth by twenty-seven-year-old painter Justin Mortimer, unveiled in January 1998, provoked strongly negative responses across middle England. Mortimer's accomplished painting separated Elizabeth's head from her body. His 'guillotined' queen was widely regarded with incomprehension and distaste.

~~~

More than the populism of Elizabeth's pub visit or her football autograph, or the spin doctoring of Charles's aides at St James's Palace, Edward's wedding to Sophie Rhys-Jones at St George's Chapel, Windsor, in June 1999 appeared to represent the post-Diana monarchy embracing a simpler way forward. Sophie was Edward's girlfriend of seven years. Of unremarkable background, she had none of Diana's or Sarah's connections to Elizabeth's court. She met Edward in 1993; for part of their long relationship, she had lived in apartments of her own in Buckingham Palace. The *Sun* greeted their engagement with an eight-page 'Sophie' supplement and warning noises that it was preparing to welcome Edward's fiancée as a new Diana, to whom she bore a passing resemblance. It was an impulse Sophie, Edward and the palace united in resisting. Edward told reporters, 'We are the very best of friends and that's essential, and it also helps that we happen to love each other as well very much.' Commentators noted that the couple's relationship had already lasted longer than the marriage of Andrew and Sarah or 'the brief happy period enjoyed by Charles and Diana'.[7] The couple outlined plans to continue after marriage with their non-royal working lives, Edward as a television producer, Sophie in public relations, a decision that, in the face of poor professional judgement, they were subsequently forced to rescind.

Elizabeth bestowed on Edward the title Earl of Wessex; on his wedding day she announced that, in due course, he would inherit Philip's title of Duke of Edinburgh, a reflection of the closeness between Philip and his youngest son. She had agreed to Bagshot Park as the couple's married home, a fifty-six-room 'Tudor Gothic' mansion eleven miles from Windsor Castle, tactfully described by the royal editor of *The Times* as 'a much more modest home than Buckingham Palace'.[8] Built for Queen Victoria's third and favourite son, Elizabeth's godfather Arthur, Duke of Connaught, Bagshot was considered by Elizabeth's advisers too large, and too expensive to run, for the monarch's youngest child. Elizabeth had bought costly Gatcombe Park[9] for Anne, she had met the considerable costs of building Sunninghill Park for Andrew and Sarah. To Edward fell Bagshot. He contributed significantly to renovation costs and later extended his lease, at a cost of £5 million, to 150 years.

Edward's wedding was an interval of celebration for Elizabeth; from the outset her relationship with her newest daughter-in-law was more straightforward than those with Diana or Sarah. She took pleasure, too, in the presence at the service of her ninety-eight-year-old mother and her sister. In February, in her house on Mustique, Margaret had so badly scalded her feet that, four months later, and despite more than a month's medical treatment after Elizabeth organized her emergency return to Britain, the burns had still not healed. Margaret was a reluctant convalescent: to her family's distress she betrayed little desire to get better. Weeks before Edward's wedding, it was unclear whether or not she would be well enough to attend. Impatient of illness but devoted to her sister, Elizabeth was partly comforted by Margaret's return to a sort of normality and, in the autumn, her resumption of a limited programme of public engagements.

For Elizabeth, phlegmatically accustomed to the pressures of her position, there were more grounds for apprehension than there had once been. Tony Blair was the first of her prime ministers to be born after her accession and her first middle-class Labour premier, with none of the instinctive deference of Wilson or Callaghan. His government was impatient of inherited formalities, including the constitutional courtesies owed to the monarch, like the failure to request from Elizabeth a dissolution of parliament in order to call a general election in 2001. In time, Blair learned to value his relationship with Elizabeth to the extent that his aides teased him about a suspected tendresse. Within a year of taking office, their audiences lasted longer than Elizabeth's audiences with Margaret Thatcher or John Major, although, unlike John Major, he was not invited to stay for drinks afterwards. But their outlook significantly differed. Like Heath and Thatcher, Blair had little interest in the Commonwealth. The hundreds of hours of parliamentary time devoted to banning hunting suggested a lack of sympathy with the country and country life; Elizabeth's explanation of the broad demographic of those involved in hunting surprised him. The Blair government's pursuit of the new and the smoke and mirrors of 'Cool Britannia' threatened to marginalize the woman who represented old Britannia. Even to her apologists Elizabeth appeared against the backdrop of Blairite novelty 'increasingly to be a relic from another era'.[10] Regional devolution threatened to loosen the bonds of the united kingdom that, in 1977, Elizabeth had asserted as her inheritance. Reform of the House of Lords, with its explicit overturning of the hereditary principle, unnerved the head of a family whose right to reign rested on inheritance. A civil servant characterized the Blair government's attitude to the monarchy as cheerfully arrogant. Within the palace were suspicions of presidential aspirations on Blair's part and his desire for a monarchy modernized in line with reactions to Diana's death. Elizabeth is too cautious for knee-jerk responses of this sort; her knowledge of Diana did not encourage her to believe that her former daughter-in-law's record offered all the answers. Blair was in a hurry to make changes, but Elizabeth's outlook is long-term. It was the story of Kwame Nkrumah all over again. Philip described Blairite modernizing as 'buggering about with things'.[11] Encounters between the Blairs and the world of the Windsors had an uncomfortable quality. 'I found the experience of visiting and spending the weekend [at Balmoral] a vivid combination of the intriguing, the surreal and the utterly freaky,' Blair wrote, in a statement stripped of the respect that usually colours prime ministers' memories of Elizabeth and her family.[12] For Anne Glenconner, detailed to look after the prime minister's wife in the Highlands, Cherie Blair 'didn't give the impression she was overly pleased to be there'.[13] Elizabeth evidently found her guests equally disconcerting: biographer William Shawcross explained his invitation to Balmoral in September 2003 as 'to help create a more informal atmosphere, where people can help to talk to the Blairs'.[14] And it was impossible to pretend that New Year's Eve 1999, when Elizabeth opened the unsuccessful Millennium Dome and welcomed the new century and a new millennium with a notably joyless rendition of 'Auld Lang Syne', holding her prime minister's hand, her lips unmoving, was anything but miserable. It was a rare instance of Elizabeth's public mask slipping. Embedded in her Christmas message had been a plea not to discard the past, of which she was the living representative. She enlisted Churchill to strengthen her cause, telling viewers, 'Winston Churchill, my first prime minister, said that "the further backward you look, the further forward you can see".' It was not a Blairite sentiment.

⟨⟩

In November 1999, an Australian referendum had voted to retain Elizabeth as head of state. Monarchist prime minister John Howard offered the electorate in Elizabeth's place a non-elected, non-royal head of state chosen by the Australian parliament. Primarily a rejection of Howard's alternative (as he had intended), the vote changed the complexion of

Elizabeth and Philip's visit to Australia in March 2000, which many had anticipated as a farewell tour. Elizabeth did not exult in the referendum's outcome. In a carefully moderate speech at Sydney Opera House, she described her continuing commitment as Australia's queen, taking as always the long view. She restated her conviction that 'the future of the monarchy in Australia is an issue for... the Australian people'. She looked back over her long association with her distant realm. 'Since I first stepped ashore here in Sydney in February 1954, I have felt part of this rugged, honest, creative land. I have shared in the joys and the sorrows, the challenges and the changes that have shaped this country's history over these past fifty years.' And she remembered her father: 'I cannot forget that I was on my way to Australia when my father died.'

Elizabeth had reached a moment for retrospection. The vituperation of the summer of 1997 had receded, redressed were toxins of the *annus horríbilis*, like Elizabeth's tax exemption; Windsor Castle was rebuilt, Sarah excluded from the royal fold, Diana's memory less raw with the lapse of time. In Charles's office in St James's Palace, a campaign to rebuild his tattered reputation was making gains; so, too, an effort to win public acceptance of Camilla Parker Bowles. Rightly Elizabeth's own standing benefited from comparison with the short-term goals and, in some instances, self-seeking of politicians. 'No Head of State in the world embodies the notion of incorruptible public decency better than Queen Elizabeth II,' the *Tablet* told readers in October 2000.[15] Plans progressed for a costly memorial to Diana in Kensington Gardens; at its opening, Elizabeth would be able to tell those present, 'Of course there were difficult times, but memories mellow with the passing of the years.' Elizabeth was seventy-four, but seemed younger, active and spry, forced into the illusion of protracted middle age by the survival of her centenarian mother. In a year of anniversaries – the eighteenth, fortieth, fiftieth and seventieth birthdays respectively of William, Andrew, Anne and Margaret – her mother's hundredth birthday in August overshadowed other celebrations; again Elizabeth and Margaret joined her on the palace balcony. In two years' time, Elizabeth would have reigned for half a century. That summer planning began for celebrations of her Golden Jubilee, overseen by Robin Janvrin, her private secretary since Robert Fellowes's retirement a year before. At the same time, Elizabeth also gave her first sitting to Lucian Freud for a portrait that would become among the best-known images of the ageing monarch. Artist and subject shared a passion for racing, but Elizabeth's schedule limited the number of their sittings. In December 2001, Freud presented the painting to the Royal Collection – a gift in honour of the Golden Jubilee, though not one that flattered its subject, whose gaze is empty, the firm snap of her lips misleadingly without benignity, lower portions of her face blue-shadowed.

Shortly before Freud's gift was a family celebration of a bittersweet nature for Elizabeth: the hundredth birthday of her aunt by marriage, Princess Alice, Duchess of Gloucester. At Kensington Palace, Elizabeth and Margaret joined their Scottish aunt to watch a short military parade, with pipers and a specially composed birthday march. Seven decades earlier, the sisters had been Alice's bridesmaids at her wedding in the private chapel of Buckingham Palace, dressed in the pale-pink satin and tulle frocks that an irritated Norman Hartnell had been forced to shorten to show off their knees. Now Margaret was wheelchair bound, black glasses partly concealing a face that was puffy with medication, only her hair stubbornly resisting time's depredations, still richly coloured. On the site of the bombed chapel stood a public gallery. For Elizabeth, remembering was poignant.

There was worse to come. Elizabeth was on her own at Sandringham the following week when, from the helicopter that landed in a blizzard of snow, emerged her mother and sister, both in wheelchairs, both to spend much of Christmas in their rooms. Margaret could eat little and was all but blind; she hardly spoke, distraction in listless, painful, reluctant days provided by Charles or a lady-in-waiting reading aloud, or falteringly attentive to the television. The Queen Mother's condition was less melancholy, but a virus and weariness of spirits kept her at Sandringham after Margaret's departure for London, followed by Elizabeth's. It was a sombre Christmas, its uncertainty not yet dispelled by the time of Elizabeth's Accession Day, which was also the anniversary of her father's death. Three days later, Margaret died. Heart problems had followed another stroke. At half past two in the morning on 9 February, she was taken from Kensington Palace to hospital. Elizabeth was notified. Through a sleepless night she was informed of developments – and of Margaret's death, her children at her bedside, four hours later.

No spasm of public grief followed the announcement that Elizabeth's 'beloved sister Princess Margaret died peacefully in her sleep this morning'. Coverage was mixed. The BBC reminded viewers that, in her youth, 'Margaret's royal status and considerable glamour made her a major star equal to anything in terms of public interest that was achieved a generation later by Diana, Princess of Wales'. 'If she had died in the middle of the 1960s,' noted one diarist, 'the response would have been akin to that on the death of Diana.'[16] Instead, reaction was subdued, and commentators underestimated the impact on Elizabeth of her sister's death, focusing on Margaret's high-handedness and hauteur, which Elizabeth, modest and conciliatory, had accepted and endured. Elizabeth carried out pre-arranged engagements before the private funeral at St George's Chapel, Windsor, on 15 February, the fiftieth anniversary of the King's funeral. On the steps of the chapel, watching Margaret's coffin lifted into the waiting hearse, she faltered; with a black-gloved hand she wiped away tears. In public, she kept pace with the business of the unfolding jubilee year; in private her thoughts were full of Margaret. A poem by the poet laureate, Andrew Motion, published on the day of Margaret's funeral, drew attention to Margaret's unhappiness; among Elizabeth's memories were joy and enchantment and, at times, the closest companionship. Three days later, she and Philip left for Jamaica on the first of her Commonwealth Golden Jubilee visits. From Jamaica, New Zealand and Australia, Elizabeth telephoned her mother daily. Dreading more bad news, she found the sight of members of her household answering mobile phones consistently unnerving; it was harder than usual to compartmentalize public and private in the name of duty. The tour generated less interest than her visits fifty years earlier, with republican debate prominent in all three countries, though a Jamaican poll after her departure found that fifty-seven per cent of those questioned considered the royal visit important and news commentary in Australia concluded that 'the people's affection for the Queen... appears indelible'. Elizabeth's behaviour was characteristic, with no evidence of personal strain. To Australia's governor-general, mired in controversy over accusations of mishandling child sex offences in the church, Elizabeth spoke publicly about Wellington's cathedral; she was predictably disconcerted by the little girl who gave her a bottle of grape juice on a walkabout; in Adelaide she relaxed meeting members of the Welsh Corgi Club of South Australia.

The Queen Mother died on Easter Saturday, a month after Elizabeth's return and seven weeks after Margaret's death. Doctors told Elizabeth of her mother's worsening condition; in her riding clothes, she arrived at Royal Lodge. She spoke to her mother as long as she remained awake, left, changed her clothes, returned. She was at her side when the Queen Mother died at quarter past three in the afternoon. Elizabeth's cousin, Margaret Rhodes, was also at Royal Lodge, and Margaret's children, David Linley and Sarah Chatto. Elizabeth broke the news to Charles, skiing with his sons in Klosters; she invited

Margaret Rhodes to spend the night at the castle. Later the Queen Mother's chaplain, Canon John Ovenden, celebrated Evensong for Elizabeth and her family in the nearby Royal Chapel, where Elizabeth also attended Easter Matins the following morning and where the Queen Mother's coffin remained for two more days. Few royal funerals had ever been planned more thoroughly: from the coffin's removal to London, its ceremonial procession to Westminster Hall, the lying-in-state, state funeral in Westminster Abbey and final committal in St George's Chapel, all was accomplished with flawless magnificence. A flag flew at half mast above the palace. On the eve of the funeral, Elizabeth made a televised address from Windsor. Significantly, she used the first-person pronoun throughout – 'I' in place of 'one'. Her broadcast combined celebration of the Queen Mother's long life with thanks for support and sympathy shown to Elizabeth in the nine days since her death. In the message's simplicity lay its power to move: 'I thank you... from my heart for the love you gave her during her life and the honour you now give her in death.' For Elizabeth herself, still mourning Margaret, had been moved by the response to her mother's death. In Westminster Hall, she and her family had gathered for prayers, led by the Archbishop of Canterbury. She left with Philip for the short return journey by car to Buckingham Palace. The car turned from Parliament Square into Whitehall, in the full gaze of silent crowds; and then the crowds began to clap, and applause, spontaneous and heartfelt, accompanied Elizabeth for the remainder of her journey. It was, she said, one of the most touching things that had ever happened to her.[17] It was proof that the affection Elizabeth inspired, like that felt for her mother and Diana, was personal. Crowds of mourners celebrated her stoicism and her endurance; they applauded her humanity, a daughter without her mother, a sisterless sister, sole survivor of that intensely loving quartet of 'us four'. Their applause made good the inscription on a commemorative Golden Jubilee coin: '*amor populi praesidium reginae*', 'the love of the people is the Queen's protection'. 'Grief is the price we pay for love,' Elizabeth had told the people of New York seven months before, in a much-quoted message written for her by Robin Janvrin and read in her absence by the British ambassador at a memorial service for victims of the September 11 terrorist attack. On the same day, she had been devastated by the death of her racing manager and close friend since the 1940s, Henry Carnarvon. If the words were Janvrin's, the sentiment was Elizabeth's. It took her mother's death for many of her subjects to acknowledge the reality of her suffering.

∿

'People thought, my goodness, she's been on the throne for fifty years and I've not realised it's been that long,' remembered Elizabeth's press secretary, Charles Anson, of the public response to the Golden Jubilee. A decade after the *Mirror*'s 'How long to reign over us?', the *Daily Mail* replaced a question with a prayer: 'Long to reign over us'.[18] In what Elizabeth called 'about as full a year as I can remember', she had criss-crossed her united kingdom, from the isles of Lewis and Skye to Anglesey, from Portsmouth on the south coast to Scunthorpe on the east, visiting seventy towns and cities. She had opened new museums, attended celebratory services in cathedrals in Glasgow, Belfast, Bangor and Manchester; she had hosted a garden party for guests born on Accession Day, and concerts of pop music and classical music in the gardens of Buckingham Palace. On the day of the National Service of Thanksgiving at St Paul's, from a palace balcony draped with a special hanging, Elizabeth looked out over a crowd estimated at a million people. 'Palace fears Jubilee flop,' *The Times* had informed readers in January. London Transport revisited the

Silver Jubilee, painting a clutch of double-decker buses gold, and members of the cabinet contributed £200 each towards the traditional piece of silver, in this case a signed silver-gilt platter. Across the country, twenty-eight couples included 'Jubilee' among the names given to their newborn babies.

At Windsor Castle, as at the time of her golden wedding anniversary, Elizabeth marked her jubilee with a party for her fellow reigning sovereigns in Europe: the rulers of Belgium, the Netherlands, Spain, Denmark, Norway, Sweden and Luxembourg. Five of them shared Elizabeth and Philip's descent from Queen Victoria; it was a gathering to have thrilled Elizabeth's grandmother, Queen Mary. At dinner in the Waterloo Chamber, her grandmother's spirit hovered within reach: on the bodice of a gown embroidered with floral symbols of the Union, Elizabeth wore a large diamond stomacher, a wedding present from Queen Mary and too large to wear often. But the triumph of the jubilee was not its affirmation of Elizabeth's place within the royal fraternity. Celebrations looked forwards as well as back, inwards as well as across the Commonwealth, now astonishingly expanded to fifty-four members. After the most difficult decade of Elizabeth's reign, events across the country restated the bond of affection between crown and country that Philip's uncle, Prince Christopher of Greece, had described at the time of George VI's accession as 'a personal love of the Sovereign... deeply ingrained in the hearts of the people'.[19] In her speech at the Guildhall, Elizabeth had articulated her feelings for the country over which she had reigned for half a century: 'Gratitude, respect and pride, these words sum up how I feel about the people of this country and the Commonwealth – and what this Golden Jubilee means to me.' With zealous single-mindedness, she had followed her father's example in embracing duty as her vocation: at the Guildhall she gave thanks for the opportunity to serve. Months before, Andrew Motion had described Margaret as 'a woman in possession of the fact / That duty and love speak two languages'. Not in Elizabeth's case. Her duty remained a defining passion. After the devastating grief of the spring, the warm glow of the jubilee acted as a tonic, reinvigorating Philip as well as Elizabeth. 'The Jubilee has been a most interesting experience,' Philip wrote to a friend; 'it's impossible not to be stimulated by the enthusiasm of the crowds.'[20]

Only at one point on 4 June 2002 did the deafening cheers beneath the palace balcony rise in a crescendo of screaming: at the appearance behind Elizabeth of her elder royal grandson, William. At twenty, William bore a gazelle-like resemblance to his beautiful mother. Media arrangements agreed in the aftermath of Diana's death had shielded him far more than any of Elizabeth's children, or Elizabeth herself as a child, from intrusion and excessive exposure. Famous across the globe, William was nevertheless little known, a focus of widespread fascination. Elizabeth did not react to the burst of shrieks that greeted him. In a more decorous age, she had inspired the same response as a young woman. She gave her attention to the crowds below, to the celebratory flypast, the coloured umbrellas twirling above the sea of faces and the Union Jacks that lined the Mall.

William had been the focus of his grandmother's attention for several years. With greater emotional insight than is usually accredited to either, Elizabeth and Philip had recognized the devastating impact on William of his parents' acrimonious separation. Philip nudged Elizabeth to intervene; she initiated regular Sunday lunches on weekends when William did not see Charles or Diana, William walking the short distance across the river from Eton to the castle. Their lunches took place in the Oak Room, where Elizabeth had opened birthday presents as a child and, each year, celebrated with her royal uncles and aunts, the Lascelles boys and her grandparents, and pink-iced birthday cakes made for her by George V's chef. In the same room, lunch over, she talked to William. Later he remembered her serenity. Perhaps he, too, derived comfort, as Elizabeth had suggested, from continuity, in the setting in which she in turn had imbibed ideas of royalty from her grandparents. For William was both grandchild and future sovereign. Elizabeth, he explained at the time of his twenty-first birthday, had shown him that the monarch's role is 'about helping people and dedication and loyalty', focuses more insistent – and more enriching – than personal anxieties.[21]

He stood close to Elizabeth at the service held in Westminster Abbey on 2 June 2003 to commemorate the fiftieth anniversary of her coronation. Elizabeth had asked for a 'quieter, more reflective' celebration than the gorgeous jamboree of the previous summer. Dressed in one of the blue copes given by Elizabeth to Westminster Abbey in 1953, the Dean of Westminster led a service that invited its congregation to share the ideals to which Elizabeth had dedicated herself – as themes go, observed Roy Strong, who was present, 'about as good as you could get'.[22] 'We shall not place on her renewed responsibility for all the duty and service to the nation,' the dean informed a congregation that included more than 200 coronation veterans, former choristers, thirty-four 'coronation babies' and conqueror of Everest Sir Edmund Hillary, who, to Elizabeth's delight, flew in specially from Kathmandu. 'On this significant anniversary, with quiet but deep respect and affection, we stand with our sovereign and each and all of us commit ourselves anew to that duty and service which are both hers and ours.' Afterwards Elizabeth unveiled a plaque to mark the Golden Jubilee extension of the Jubilee Walkway in the Mall. Nine-year-old Louisa Harrington presented her with a crown-shaped bouquet. Through a charity for children with life-threatening illnesses, Louisa, who suffered from restrictive cardiomyopathy, had written to Buckingham Palace, asking if she could meet Elizabeth and 'be a princess for the day'. 'I want to meet this little girl during the anniversary celebrations,' Elizabeth told Robin Janvrin.[23] It was not 'Diana-speak' or a politician's stunt, nor the cold formality of which Diana had accused her husband's family; not the rigid adherence to precedent that, five years before, stiffened Elizabeth's resistance to a flag for Diana on the palace flagpole.

In the abbey's quire stalls on that 2 June, separate from the royal family, was Camilla Parker Bowles. Three years had passed since Elizabeth had acknowledged her son's mistress, at a sixtieth birthday party for former King Constantine of Greece, hosted by Charles at Highgrove. Their encounter was deliberate on Elizabeth's part. Charles remained firm in his insistence that Camilla was an essential element of his life; a diligent Mark Bolland had devoted considerable energy to achieving public acceptance of their relationship, including careful press leaks and equally careful picture opportunities. In meeting Camilla, Elizabeth acknowledged the relationship; she was encouraged by members of her staff and her family, including her niece Sarah Chatto. She went no further. Palace staff described her policy as 'acknowledging but not accepting' Camilla. A courtier labelled their exchange at Highgrove 'very brief, very formal'; one of Charles's staff described it as 'merely a cracking of the ice rather than a breaking of it'.[24] As so often, Elizabeth's motives balanced public and private concerns: she cared for Charles's happiness, although she could not understand his decision to jeopardize the monarchy's stability in pursuit of self-fulfilment. Her outlook bore the imprint of the abdication, especially while her mother was alive; the success of her own marriage gave fewer grounds for empathy. Deliberately uncontroversial herself, she recognized the extent to which Charles's private life continued to polarize opinions. In the short term, the meeting between monarch and mistress at Highgrove made easier a more public role for Camilla in Charles's life. Elizabeth, as so often, proceeded cautiously.

Loftily the palace dismissed as speculation claims in the *Spectator* in August 2001 that Elizabeth had agreed to Charles and Camilla's marriage. The magazine quoted a 'well-informed Palace observer' saying that Elizabeth 'accept[ed] that the last great thing she has to do in her reign is to sort out the relationship between Charles and Camilla, and in practice that means to smile on a marriage'.[25] Of course, Elizabeth realized that the monarchy's wellbeing demanded a solution for a relationship that had already caused so much damage; she would take time to agree to marriage. The appointment early in 2002 of Michael Peat as Charles's private secretary, a move suggested to Elizabeth by David Airlie, and the departure the following month from Charles's office of Mark Bolland, improved relations between Buckingham Palace and St James's Palace. Elizabeth did not dislike Camilla, who, more than Diana, shared her own country interests and brisk, wry outlook. In June, she made possible Camilla's first public appearance alongside the royal family, when Camilla was invited to both Golden Jubilee concerts; she also invited her to the family dinner she held at the Ritz following the jubilee's success. Elizabeth was aware of opinions like those expressed in a *Panorama* documentary in October, that found only forty-two per cent of people in favour of the couple's marriage and fifty-two per cent opposed to Camilla becoming queen. Unnervingly for Elizabeth, the recently retired vicar of Tetbury, close to Highgrove, presented Charles's predicament as a revisiting of Uncle David's unhappy dilemma: 'I think that Charles has got to make a decision on where his duty lies. Does it lie with the woman he undoubtedly loves? Does it lie with his position as future monarch?'[26] As supreme governor of the Church of England, and a woman of deep faith who shared her parents' belief in the sanctity of marriage, Elizabeth could not easily discount clerical opinion. She could, however, seek guidance. Both George Carey and his successor as Archbishop of Canterbury, Rowan Williams, supported Charles and Camilla's marriage; Williams advised against a religious ceremony as divisive among Anglican clergy. At Sandringham at Christmas in 2004, Elizabeth agreed to Charles's remarriage. Months before, a message tied to railings at Kensington Palace for the seventh anniversary of Diana's death, had read 'No to Queen Camilla'.[27]

Elizabeth did not attend the civil marriage ceremony in Windsor's Guildhall on 9 April 2005. She and Philip were among the congregation of more than 700 in St George's Chapel for the subsequent service of prayer and dedication. As on other occasions, her decision acknowledged the claims of traditional orthodoxies and her position not simply as mother but the established church's supreme governor. Behind closed doors, in the castle's state apartments, Elizabeth was notably cheerful at the reception she hosted for Charles and his new Duchess of Cornwall, and in June, she and Philip accompanied Charles and Camilla to William's graduation ceremony in St Andrews, though she had not attended similar ceremonies for Charles or Edward. At last was an opportunity for respite from family troubles. Testaments to family harmony peppered extensive celebrations of Elizabeth's eightieth birthday, beginning the following spring. Elizabeth's updating of the Order of Precedence 'on blood principles' gave prominence to her closest relations: neither her daughter Anne nor her cousin Alexandra was required to curtsey to Camilla in Charles's absence; in Alexandra's case Elizabeth had already rewarded the 'wonderful service to this country... of her beloved cousin' with the Order of the Garter.[28] At a Guildhall lunch, Elizabeth thanked Charles as well as Philip for 'all the support they give me each and every day', while a televised birthday tribute to his mother by Charles praised her for showing 'the most remarkable steadfastness and fortitude, always remaining a figure of reassuring calm and dependability, an example to so many of service, duty and devotion in a world of sometimes bewildering change and disorientation'. Charles invested his mother at eighty with her father's attributes of steadfastness and bravery; he celebrated as a strength her stasis in the face of change that forty years before had appeared a weakness. A birthday poem by Andrew Motion, discussed by Motion with Elizabeth and Charles, sounded a similar note. Each stanza ended with a refrain-like 'The golden rule, your constancy, survives.' For official birthday photographs, Elizabeth chose fellow octogenarian Jane Bown, whose career, like her own, had begun in the late 1940s: benign, comfortable, serene images with none of the malignancy of Freud's portrait. Celebrations concluded with a belated birthday dinner at the Ritz in December, to which Elizabeth invited not only her own ladies-in-waiting, but those of the Queen Mother and Margaret, attentive to the claims of the past. Before then Elizabeth had hosted a lunch for ninety-nine people from across the country who shared her birthday: in a speech of welcome she addressed them as her 'exact twins'. When identical twins Keith and Jack Hurst told her they hoped she would live as long as her mother, her reply was unexpected. 'Do you really want to live that long?' she asked.[29]

Elizabeth's own death was apparently anticipated by the letters sent in October to privy councillors, reminding them that 'on the death of the sovereign the Accession Council meets within twenty-four hours to proclaim the new sovereign'.[30]

⁘

In May 1977, Philip wrote sympathetically to Daphne du Maurier, widow of his former comptroller Boy Browning, lamenting Boy's depiction in Richard Attenborough's film

A *Bridge Too Far*: 'it really is monstrous the way film-makers re-write history for the sake of entertainment'.[31]

Elizabeth's own history would be rewritten by a number of film-makers, as well as playwrights and producers of television drama. In 2006, a film called *The Queen* revisited dark days after Diana's death. It would become, newspapers argued, a film that 'changed public perceptions of the woman who has reigned for fifty-five years'.[32] It starred Helen Mirren as Elizabeth. Elizabeth has small cinema rooms at Balmoral, Sandringham and Buckingham Palace, but is not, according to friends, 'a great "film person"'. She told Tony Blair that she did not intend to watch the film. It was not a week on which she cared to dwell, even had she inclined to watch an actress playing her. Elizabeth is an accomplished mimic. In a life in which she is so often forced to suppress her responses to people or happenings, mimicry – of the silly, sycophantic or self-important – offers a release of tension after the event. But she had always denied being an actress, transforming the theatre of monarchy into more than empty spectacle through her sincerity and seriousness. The same gravity of purpose denied that her life was substance for fiction. A palace spokesman described her as pleased by Helen Mirren's Oscar success nevertheless: in her Oscar acceptance speech Mirren had 'salute[d] [Elizabeth's] courage and her consistency'. Later Elizabeth invited Mirren for tea in her box at Ascot. The film's impact was entirely positive. The *Daily Telegraph*'s claim that 'the Queen has emerged from the movie of the same name as caring, calm and dignified' was widely shared.[33] In truth, Elizabeth had been caring, calm and dignified, courageous and consistent for the last fifty-four years.

CHAPTER XVIII

'She has made her public happy'

～⚬～

'Over the years those who have seemed to me to be the most happy, contented and fulfilled have always been the people who have lived the most outgoing and unselfish lives,' Elizabeth told viewers of her Christmas broadcast in 2008. It was the end of a year in which, at the age of eighty-two, she had carried out more than 400 British and overseas engagements. More relentless than that of any of her predecessors, her public life satisfied her sense of duty. In old age, as throughout her reign, it included longueurs. To French president Nicolas Sarkozy's unguarded question of whether she ever got bored, at a state banquet in his honour in March, Elizabeth had replied 'Yes, but I don't say so.'[1]

For twenty years, the strength of her self-discipline had distinguished Elizabeth from younger members of her family. American photographer Annie Leibovitz left a sitting with the monarch in April 2007 impressed by Elizabeth's 'resolve, her devotion to duty'. 'There's absolutely and precisely no training scheme whatsoever,' Edward told documentary makers in 2007, discussing the royal 'job'.[2] With mixed results, Elizabeth and Philip had consistently sought to lead by example: observation of their parents' unflagging appetite for public service and, in Elizabeth's case, her public humility, provided their children's 'training scheme'. Elizabeth's speech at a sixtieth birthday party for Charles in November 2008 praised his fidelity to the royal couple's 'guiding principles of public service and duty to others'. In her ninth decade Elizabeth continued to dedicate herself to the same principles. She did not contemplate abdication, she told her cousin Margaret Rhodes, 'unless I get Alzheimer's or have a stroke'; on his retirement as Archbishop of Canterbury in 2003, she explained to George Carey 'that's something I can't do. I'm going to carry on to the end.' 'I sometimes think her advisers don't realise she is eighty-three years old. Maybe she doesn't want them to slow her down,' Margaret Rhodes reflected after Elizabeth's return from a Caribbean tour in November 2009.[3] It was indeed the view shared by her advisers. Long ago, Elizabeth had learned to pace herself; she did not squander her energies. In 2007 she gave two sittings to Chris Levine for her first three-dimensional holographic portrait, commissioned to celebrate the 800th anniversary of Jersey's allegiance to the crown. Levine produced a second photographic portrait, which he entitled *Lightness of Being*. It captured the inevitable fatigue of age. Resting between shots, Elizabeth had momentarily closed her eyes.

Slowing down happened gradually – not until 2016 did Elizabeth hand over a number of her patronages to her children and grandchildren; it did not affect her role within her family. 'Friendly, authoritative control over each and every one' was how, in 2016, animal psychologist Dr Roger Mugford characterized Elizabeth's relationship with her dogs. Friendly and authoritative would – mostly – be her watchwords in her dealings with her family, with Philip's firm, sometimes combative support. Elizabeth did not try to control them, and they did not always heed wise counsel. In the first years of the new century, however, emerged a sense of the royal family's smooth running as an organization. The Queen Mother's death had elevated Elizabeth at last to the position of matriarch. Although she missed her mother's advice, and the easy companionship of gatherings at Royal Lodge after church on Sunday and their morning telephone calls, she benefited from release from the habit of deferring to the strong-minded former consort. In the Golden Jubilee's aftermath, royal aides revealed that thoughts within the palace were already turning to 2012 and a diamond jubilee, for which planning began as early as 2009. Events of 2002 would not prove Elizabeth's swansong. Given the robustness of her health and high levels of public support – in 2006, a MORI poll found eighty-five per cent of respondents satisfied 'with the way the Queen is doing her job as Monarch' – there was little that was valedictory about the next ten years. Both Elizabeth and Philip maintained a schedule of engagements heavier than those of any of their family save Charles and Anne. This included overseas visits – to Norway, France, Germany, the United States, Belgium, the Netherlands, Turkey and the Baltic states – and incoming visits, like that in 2009 of new American president Barack Obama and his wife Michelle, with whom Elizabeth swiftly struck up a relationship that was notably warm and informal. Elizabeth continued to attend biennial Commonwealth Heads of Government Meetings: in Australia, Nigeria, Malta, Uganda and Trinidad and Tobago. Her affection and concern for the Commonwealth had not dimmed: in 2008, in protest at the corruption and brutality of his regime, she agreed to the removal of the honorary knighthood that, in 1994, she had bestowed on Zimbabwe's president, Robert Mugabe.

Conscientious Elizabeth, imbued with her grandmother's sense of dynasty, looked to the future. In the summer of 2008, she appointed William to the Order of the Garter, the thousandth knight in the order's nearly 700-year history. His early appointment mirrored her own in 1947, when she was twenty-one; four years later she invested him with the Order of the Thistle. As she had with Charles and Camilla, she also sanctioned a key relationship in William's life. Walking beside his father in the traditional Garter procession from Castle Hill, William was watched by his girlfriend of six years, Catherine Middleton. She had been invited to join the royal fold for the day and, on her first appearance at an official royal public event, stood beside Camilla and Sophie Wessex, whose unshowy public work Elizabeth would shortly reward with her highest seal of approval, the Grand Cross of the Royal Victorian Order. The following year, William and Harry set up a shared household independent of Charles's. Elizabeth took a careful interest. The part-time, unpaid appointment of 'wise man' and former diplomat Sir David Manning was made at her suggestion. A royal official made clear the source of Manning's authority: 'Sir David meets the Princes from time to time. He also meets the royal household more frequently.'[4] In January 2010, he accompanied William to New Zealand and Australia, William's first foreign tour representing his grandmother. Manning's role was to guide the future king, the nature of this guidance shaped by his understanding of Elizabeth's wishes. Also present at William's opening of Wellington's new Supreme Court building, although he insisted his presence was unofficial, was Elizabeth's private secretary, Sir Christopher Geidt. In the case of Elizabeth's senior grandson, she appeared at pains to provide the 'training scheme' that Edward had denied existed.

❧

The honours list issued to mark Elizabeth's eightieth birthday had included membership of the Royal Victorian Order for Angela Kelly, a chirpy, quick-tempered Liverpudlian divorcee born the year of Elizabeth's accession. The order recognizes personal service to the monarch or the monarch's family; a year later, at her own suggestion, Kelly was awarded the panjandrum-like title Personal Assistant, Adviser and Curator to Her Majesty the Queen (Jewellery, Insignias and Wardrobe). For more than a decade, she had been Elizabeth's senior dresser, following the retirement after more than thirty-five years (and only two years after Bobo's death) of Peggy Hoath. The two women developed an affectionate bond. Footage of Kelly helping Elizabeth with her Garter robes during a photographic sitting for Annie Leibovitz showed her gently patting Elizabeth on the shoulder; Kelly cheerfully admitted being regularly moved to tears by the sight of Elizabeth wearing the Imperial State Crown for the State Opening of Parliament. Although she lacked the long history Bobo shared with Elizabeth, Kelly had come to occupy a position of trust and intimacy nearer to Bobo's than that of other servants, an occasional source of jealousy within the household. She denied that her relationship with Elizabeth became closer following the deaths of Margaret and the Queen Mother in 2002, insisting 'I am not there to replace her mother and her sister. If she wants to talk about matters of the heart, she speaks to her family. It's just a working relationship – but a close one.'[5]

Elizabeth placed the same degree of trust in her longest-serving ladies-in-waiting: in 2010, she acknowledged the fiftieth anniversaries of the appointment of Mary Morrison and Susan Hussey with a reception at Buckingham Palace called 'A Century of Waiting'. Christopher Geidt, who, in 2007, replaced Robin Janvrin as her private secretary, quickly won Elizabeth's confidence. Geidt had worked for Elizabeth since 2002. By the end of his ten years as private secretary, she was ninety-one. Adroitly, Geidt addressed the delicate issue of her increasing age and the monarchy's future prospects. From 2008, he also worked with Charles. This liaison between mother and son to implement a combination of closer collaboration and greater task-sharing between monarch and heir, aimed at smoothing the transition from one reign to the next, although Elizabeth did not step back from her public duties. That Elizabeth authorized this process herself, party to its decision-making, was further proof of her practical nature. It indicated her recognition of her duty as twofold: to the nation and the Commonwealth, and to the monarchy of which she was custodian. Elizabeth's working relationship with Geidt was close: 'When Christopher speaks, you know that that's how Her Majesty thinks,' commented the cabinet secretary, Gus O'Donnell; a member of Elizabeth's staff claimed Geidt had the measure of Elizabeth, an instinctive understanding.[6] Geidt's modesty matched her own: he took pleasure, Charles's private secretary Elizabeth Buchanan claimed, chiefly in public recognition of Elizabeth's 'extraordinary' work. For her part Elizabeth appreciated his clear-sightedness, 'almost a sort of surgical capacity of cutting through the mist of details and going to what is the essence of a problem' in one assessment; his friend William Shawcross attributed his skills to 'his honesty, his modesty, his intellect, his courtesy and his persistence'.[7] Geidt had a reputation for carefully formulated answers to problems expressed in a 'very short, concise format', a style that suited Elizabeth's own business-like approach.[8] His persistence was necessary in strengthening links between Buckingham Palace and Charles's office at Clarence House. Like that of Elizabeth and her son, the relationship between the two royal offices was not always cosy.

The outcome of a general election on 6 May 2010 deprived Blair's successor, Gordon Brown, of his majority, without giving his Conservative opponents the number of seats they required to govern alone. Brown was obliged to remain in office until a workable solution could be reached. In the Cabinet Office,

Geidt advised on constitutional aspects of the dilemma. His presence in Downing Street was a reminder that any administration required Elizabeth's imprimatur, although Elizabeth's decision to remain at Windsor throughout the five-day negotiating period was a clear signal that she herself took no part in discussions and had no hand in the outcome. Brown resigned on 10 May to be replaced by a coalition of Conservatives and Liberal Democrats under David Cameron, at forty-three Elizabeth's youngest prime minister; she had first seen him as a rabbit in a prep school play. The palace greeted this resolution with relief. By eliminating any need for Elizabeth's involvement, it lessened potential controversy of the sort that had followed her 'choosing' prime ministers in 1957 and 1963.

Among early concerns of the new government were royal finances. After the expiry of Thatcher's ten-year deal in 2000, Blair had maintained the same arrangement for the next decade. By 2010, at a time of government-imposed austerity measures, the annual Civil List payment of £7.9 million fell £6 million short of running costs, with essential repairs to the fabric and structure of Buckingham Palace long overdue. The Sovereign Grant Bill of December 2011 discarded the model of royal funding introduced in 1760 at the beginning of the reign of Elizabeth's great-great-great-great-grandfather, George III. In place of Civil List funds from the Treasury, a travel costs grant from the Department of Transport and a communications grant from the Department of Culture, Media and Sport, the Bill entitled Elizabeth to a single annual payment of fifteen per cent of the profits of the Crown Estates. The new arrangement would take effect from 2013, with a review after seven years and, in a development Elizabeth's father would certainly have resented, scrutiny of the Sovereign Grant accounts by the National Audit Office. Tactfully, a Buckingham Palace statement, authorized by a monarch who knew too well the perils of financial evasiveness, described developments as 'a modern, transparent and simpler way of funding the head of state'.

∾∾

William married Catherine Middleton on 29 April 2011, days after Elizabeth's eighty-fifth birthday. The service at Westminster Abbey was watched by a global television audience estimated at 3 billion. Elizabeth conferred on her grandson the title Duke of Cambridge and colonelcy of the Irish Guards; in the sort of intervention typical of her great-great-grandmother Queen Victoria, she insisted he wore the regiment's ceremonial uniform for his wedding. In essentials, commentary on this marriage of a prince to a member of the middle classes, after a lengthy courtship, scarcely differed from that at the time of Elizabeth's own wedding despite marked differences in circumstances. 'They will carry with them the hopes of a nation,' declared *Country Life*; the same claims had been made of Princess Elizabeth and Lieutenant Philip Mountbatten in 1947, a marriage, the magazine suggested, that after sixty-four years had 'endured so firmly and for so long that, for their subjects, it has come to seem part of the unchanging foundation of the universe'.[9]

Two years earlier Philip had become the longest-serving consort in the monarchy's history, passing the record of fifty-seven years and seventy days that previously belonged to George III's wife, Charlotte of Mecklenburg-Strelitz. Days before William's wedding, his father also set a record. On 20 April, Charles's wait to succeed his mother passed that of his great-great-grandfather, Edward VII. It was not the sort of arithmetic by which Elizabeth sets store, as she demonstrated on 9 September 2015, when she herself set a similar record, becoming Britain's longest-reigning monarch. On that day, accompanied by Philip, Elizabeth opened the Scottish Borders Railway. In a short speech, she described the record as 'not one to which I have ever aspired', and she played down its significance, despite congratulatory messages from parliament, adding that 'inevitably, a long life can pass by many milestones. My own is no exception.' But she would increasingly acknowledge the discomforts and challenges, real or imagined, of Charles's position, paying public tribute to his wide-ranging charitable achievements, delegating aspects of her own workload to her son, including, after 2013, long-haul tours, and, through Christopher Geidt, facilitating his greater familiarity with the administrative business of sovereignty, government documents delivered to Charles in green boxes in place of Elizabeth's red ones. Philip's frustrations were equally difficult to assuage. At the time of his ninetieth birthday in 2011, he suggested he was ready to retire. 'I reckon I've done my bit,' he said. 'I want to enjoy myself a bit now, with less responsibility, less frantic rushing about, less preparation, less trying to think of something to say... It's better to get out before you reach your sell-by date.'[10] Fair and honest Elizabeth recognized that Philip was not, as she was, compelled by coronation oaths to lifelong service. Among her ninetieth birthday presents to her husband was a surprise final accolade: the position of Lord High Admiral, the titular head of the Royal Navy, a special compliment that she saved for their birthday lunch alone. Philip was touched by the gesture; he would not in fact retire for another six years. For her official Diamond Jubilee portrait, taken in the Centre Room at Buckingham Palace in December, Elizabeth wore Philip's wedding present, the large diamond bracelet that jeweller Philip Antrobus had made to his design using stones from Princess Andrew's tiara. A photographic portrait commissioned from Thomas Struth by the National Portrait Gallery placed husband and wife side by side on a gilded sofa, in shadowy splendour at Windsor Castle, a wintry image of stoical old age.

Struth's image was not wholly misleading in suggesting that Elizabeth was both part of, and separate from, the workaday world. As it had for Queen Victoria, Elizabeth's Diamond Jubilee became a moment of apotheosis, marked by extensive tributes. This feeling emerged before the jubilee itself, boosted by the success of William's wedding and anticipation of the Olympic Games to be hosted in London in its wake. In July 2011, the *Daily Mail* had identified public feelings for Elizabeth as reverent; affectionate veneration would characterize many Commonwealth-wide celebrations.[11] Kenneth Rose attributed her success over six decades to 'her own remarkable strength and character'; the Master of the Queen's Music, Sir Peter Maxwell Davies, described Elizabeth as 'marvellous and a true role model'; the composer claimed she had converted him from republicanism by her 'selfless dedication and example'.[12] Hagiography was not simply a response to Elizabeth's stamina and longevity, though both played their part. A state visit to the Republic of Ireland in May 2011 won near-universal praise. Extended at Elizabeth's request from an anticipated day and a half to four days, its success derived in large part from her own diplomatic skills and her clear determination that her presence consolidate Anglo-Irish amity in the wake of the 1998 Good Friday Agreement. Elizabeth toured sites of key importance to Irish nationalists. At a state banquet in Dublin Castle, wearing a dress embroidered with more than 2,000 hand-stitched shamrocks and her grandmother's Girls of Great Britain and Ireland tiara, she gave a speech that, without apologizing for British rule in Ireland, appeared to offer catharsis and healing and a compliment, too, in its opening address in Gaelic: 'President and friends'; obliquely she referred to Mountbatten's murder. A speech intended to inaugurate a new chapter in relations between Britain and her closest neighbour was received as such by the majority of her listeners. By contrast, Elizabeth's speech to the Commonwealth Heads of Government Meeting in Perth, on a ten-day tour of Australia in October, sounded valedictory notes. At eighty-five and ninety-one, both Elizabeth and Philip found their short trips to Australia and New Zealand too tiring; they would not return. At Philip's suggestion, Elizabeth quoted an Aboriginal proverb: 'We are all visitors to this time, this place. We are just passing through. Our purpose here is to observe, to learn, to grow, to love… and then we return home.' Republican prime minister Julia Gillard assured Elizabeth of the country's 'lasting affection and our very deep respect'. Since the referendum of 1999, pressure had declined for an elected head of state as Elizabeth's replacement.

In 1977, Martin Charteris had expressed concern that Elizabeth would be so tired by her jubilee travels that she would not be 'hale and hearty' for the main celebrations in the capital. In 2012, Elizabeth and Philip confined their travels to the United Kingdom. Within weeks of their return from Australia, Philip had been flown by helicopter to Papworth Hospital in Cambridgeshire for treatment for a blocked coronary artery. Formal statements issued by the palace downplayed this health-scare that nevertheless frightened Elizabeth, casting a shadow over Christmas and beyond. On their behalf, the couple's children and grandchildren toured the Commonwealth. Instead, the world came to Elizabeth and her apparently revitalized spouse in the form of a 'sovereigns' lunch at Windsor in mid-May, involving 550 horses and twice as many riders, did its best to entertain Elizabeth. The temporary renaming in her honour of each of the seventeen pubs in the small town of Otley 'The Queen Elizabeth' and sales of 30,000 cucumbers recorded by Morrisons in Bradford for cucumber sandwiches for royal-themed tea parties were also details to amuse her. Her experience of the river pageant, on a Thames spattered by the rain that dogged the whole jubilee weekend, may not have been as straightforwardly enjoyable, particularly for Philip, who was hospitalized afterwards with a bladder infection; Margaret

Rhodes said Elizabeth had dreaded the idea of it. Elizabeth was moved nevertheless by the doughtiness and size of the crowds, whom she described 'on the barges and the bridges and the banks of the river... undaunted by the rain'; at intervals her happiness was plain, in smiling exchanges with Philip.[13] Philip's subsequent absence from an outdoor concert and the service of thanksgiving at St Paul's Cathedral, to which Elizabeth was accompanied by her lady-in-waiting, Lady Farnham, focused attention on the solitariness of Elizabeth's position. But photographs taken at the Guildhall reception after the service show her happy and relaxed. Appropriately for a diamond jubilee she wore the enormous Cullinan III and IV diamond brooch she had inherited from Queen Mary, which she called 'Granny's Chips'. And with customary modesty, she was astonished by the crowds who filled the Mall, stretching as far as Admiralty Arch, for her final balcony appearance. It was William who told his grandmother, 'Those crowds are for you,' in response to her stuttering 'Oh, my goodness. How extraordinary... I didn't think it was going to be...'[14] In a broadcast of thanks issued the same evening, Elizabeth truthfully described her view of events of the jubilee as 'a humbling experience'.

'She has made her public happy and all the signs are that she is herself happy, fulfilled and at home at these encounters,' the Archbishop of Canterbury had claimed of Elizabeth's public life in the service of thanksgiving. So it would continue. Sustained by her love for her family and, recent healthscares notwithstanding, a deeply supportive marriage of sixty-five years, her own daily prayers and deep-rooted faith, attentive, affectionate staff and the pleasure she continued to draw from the knowledge of duty undertaken willingly and to the best of her ability, Elizabeth approached the future with equanimity. In a message issued on Accession Day she had dedicated herself anew to the service of kingdom and Commonwealth; responses to the jubilee strengthened her resolve. She did not rest on her laurels. Only weeks later, she again 'made her public happy' with a highly unusual appearance at the opening of the Olympic Games. It had been filmed in the spring under circumstances of some secrecy, a short James Bond sketch in which Daniel Craig visited Buckingham Palace to collect Elizabeth for a helicopter flight to the Olympic stadium. Angela Kelly acted as intermediary for film-maker Danny Boyle; Elizabeth requested she be given the line 'Good evening, Mr Bond.' A wigged stuntman parachuted from the helicopter into the opening ceremony: 'a gap in the clouds / And The Queen jumped from the sky / To the cheering crowds,' as the poet laureate, Carol Ann Duffy, remembered it. Elizabeth took her place in the royal box dressed in the clothes she had worn for filming. The brief sequence suggests she enjoyed herself. The *Daily Express* published a cartoon by Paul Thomas: Elizabeth instructs a footman with a teapot, 'One lump – shaken not stirred'. Her refusal to 'perform' for the cameras, a lifetime's habit, safeguarded her dignity; it suggested, too, as Mary Wilson had written twenty-five years before, that she is always 'the Queen'. This was how Duffy pictured Elizabeth the following summer, in a poem to commemorate the sixtieth anniversary of the coronation. In Duffy's 'The Crown', the sovereign carries with her at all times the memory of the crown's weight, actual and metaphorical: 'feel[s] it still, in private space, when it's lifted'. Monarchy, the non-royalist Duffy concluded after time spent in Elizabeth's company, resembled poetry in possessing 'the ability to transform the ordinary into the magical'.[15] Elizabeth recalled her coronation, alongside the christening of William and Catherine's first child, George, in her 2013 Christmas broadcast. She described both in terms of duty: 'my own pledge of service made in that great church on Coronation Day sixty years earlier' and the baby prince's baptism 'into a joyful faith of Christian duty and service'. It was an uncompromising vision that emerged from her most strongly held beliefs about royalty and its purpose. To the future

George VII she bequeathed the doctrine of (joyful) service to which she had devoted her life, and drew attention to the value of what, in her Diamond Jubilee address to the houses of parliament, she had called 'the regular worthy rhythm of life'.

Whatever her feelings, in the summer of her Diamond Jubilee Elizabeth could not, as she had in 1977, overtly defend the Union. Regional devolution had further politicized Celtic nationalism. At her prime minister's request, however, she made a significant if discreet intervention in the autumn of 2014. Elizabeth was at Balmoral as campaigning in a referendum on Scottish independence entered its final weeks. Polls appeared to show rising support for the nationalist cause. David Cameron panicked. In conversations between his private secretary and Elizabeth's, between Elizabeth and himself, he asked for Elizabeth's help. Later he insisted that he had not requested 'anything that would be in any way improper or unconstitutional, but just a raising of the eyebrow, even you know, a quarter of an inch, we thought would make a difference'. Elizabeth came to her prime minister's aid outside Crathie church, the Sunday before the vote. After a service that had included a prayer for safety 'from false choices', Elizabeth spoke to clusters of wellwishers. Her remarks were audible to journalists and photographers: unusually, they had been invited to observe the exchanges. To a joke about the approaching referendum, Elizabeth cautioned, 'I hope people will think very carefully about the future.' Afterwards, Cameron claimed that she had 'helped to put a slightly different perception on things' and her comment, widely reported, was interpreted as opposing Scottish separatism. It was a plausible interpretation given her opposition to Welsh and Scottish nationalism at the time of the Silver Jubilee. Those who knew her better understood her desire to preserve intact her inheritance from her father: a united kingdom, its constituent parts joined in loyalty to the crown. Elizabeth's sense of kinship with Scotland ran deep. Here she had spent almost every summer of her life, many of them in the company of her Scottish mother, her Scottish governess and her Scottish dresser, Bobo. Her husband and all her sons were educated in Scotland, where her sister was born; in Scotland, Elizabeth had said, she could 'hibernate'. Balmoral was the backdrop to so many happy memories: childhood summers with Margaret and Bowes-Lyon and Elphinstone cousins; Philip's proposal; picnics and barbecues, shooting, stalking and riding with favoured friends, her children, grandchildren and close family. David Cameron said he had 'never heard someone so happy' as Elizabeth when he told her of voters' choice to remain within the United Kingdom; she 'purred down the line'. Quite rightly, she regarded his indiscretion balefully.

∽◦∾

The 1990s criticism of royal dysfunction felt increasingly distant when William and Catherine's second child, a daughter, Charlotte Elizabeth Diana, was born on 2 May 2015. The nuclear family of the Cambridges, and intense interest in it, mirrored Elizabeth's own at the time of her accession. A month before the baby's birth, Clarence House released a tenth wedding anniversary photograph of Charles and Camilla. Edward and Sophie's marriage had proved equally successful. Bagshot's proximity to Windsor meant that Elizabeth regularly saw her Wessex grandchildren, Lady Louise Mountbatten-Windsor and James, Viscount Severn. She helped teach both to ride. Louise's decision to take up carriage riding pleased her grandfather, Philip, who continued to enjoy the esoteric sport into his nineties. Sophie shared Elizabeth's interest in British military history. She did not displace Anne in Elizabeth's affections but, given Anne's exceptionally heavy workload, was more often at hand, Elizabeth's nearest replacement for the female company of Margaret and the Queen Mother.

'Satisfaction and contentment are created by the relationships between one individual and another,' Philip had written in 1982.[16] As often, Elizabeth's thoughts mirrored her husband's. She described family and friendship as 'a constant... a source of personal comfort and reassurance'; she attributed the same sustenance to her faith.[17]

But the appearance of family tranquillity was misleading. Elizabeth's uncomfortable meeting with her favourite son Andrew, in the second week of March 2011, had lasted an hour. In the ten years since his retirement from the navy in 2001, Andrew's role as special representative for trade and investment had done 'a lot of good for the UK', claimed the foreign secretary, William Hague; it had also frequently raised questions about the costs of his extensive travel and the desirability of a number of his personal contacts. Andrew's friendship with New York financier Jeffrey Epstein ought not to have survived Epstein's 2008 conviction for procuring a child for prostitution; in December 2010, Andrew and Epstein were photographed together in Central Park in New York. Release of these photographs consolidated an impression of a prince in murky waters: his friends and associates included the son of Libyan leader Colonel Gaddafi, and the son-in-law of a Kazakhstani dictator. Mud-slinging in the press appeared to attempt to hound Andrew from his special role. For Elizabeth, who had shown her customary reluctance to involve herself earlier, her loyalties were again in conflict. Too well she understood the danger of accusations that combined extravagance with impropriety. The campaign against Andrew threatened to engulf in scandal celebration of William's wedding; it raised the spectre of the *annus horribilis*. Elizabeth's affection for her boisterous, thick-skinned second son did not blind her to scandal's potential to derail the revival of royal fortunes promised by William and his bride and worldwide fascination with the golden couple. Elizabeth understood this even without consulting Christopher Geidt. Geidt knew the extent of Andrew's expenses and was prepared to take a firm line over his activities. He was also rumoured to oppose any public role for Andrew's daughters, Beatrice and Eugenie. In the short term, government ministers rallied to Andrew's cause. The business secretary, Vince Cable, repeated companies' view of the prince as 'supportive and helpful'. But in March 2011 BBC royal correspondent Peter Hunt described as 'inevitable' Andrew's surrender of his special representative role as a result of his friendship with Epstein. This followed in July.

Elizabeth's closeness to her second son was reflected in her relationship with his daughters, which rumours of scandal did not dent. In the summer of the Diamond Jubilee, she updated the Order of Precedence at court. When William did not accompany his wife, Catherine would be required to curtsey to the blood princesses: her daughter Anne, her cousin Alexandra – and Andrew's daughters, Elizabeth's much-loved granddaughters, Beatrice and Eugenie. Like the elderly Queen Victoria, who had frequently been accompanied in public by an unmarried granddaughter, Elizabeth invited one or other of Andrew's daughters to join her at a handful of engagements, including the distribution of the Royal Maundy and royal garden parties. She entrusted to Beatrice renovation of that symbol of her own happy childhood, Y Bwthyn Bach. Later, Beatrice borrowed one of Elizabeth's dresses for her secret wedding. A mark of her favour, Elizabeth also loaned her the diamond fringe tiara that she had worn for her own wedding.

꧁꧂

It was not only Elizabeth's private secretary who acknowledged her mortality. The Diamond Jubilee had stimulated an outpouring of affection for Elizabeth that was heightened by awareness of her age. A buoyant atmosphere in royal circles was the legacy of the Golden Jubilee; after 2012, as the decade gathered pace, an autumnal quality coloured perceptions of a reign that had entered an apparently serene twilight. Assisted by her nonagenarian husband, Elizabeth maintained business as usual, albeit the pace of engagements slowed; off duty she continued to ride regularly, still without a hat, although a dependable Fell pony called Emma had replaced earlier, more spirited mounts. In 2014, the eighty-eight-year-old monarch undertook almost 400 engagements. Her diary for the following year included her fifth state visit to Germany and, in November, a state visit to Malta, a republic since 1974, to coincide with the Commonwealth Heads of Government Meeting. In Germany, excitement was considerable. Writing in the tabloid *Bild*, Franz Josef Wagner revisited the journalese of Elizabeth's youth, with a twist to reflect her advancing years: he acclaimed her as 'the mother of fairy tales' and suggested 'everyone in Germany will be enchanted. We will forget our iPhones, iPads... We will be kids again.' The Lego shop in Berlin stocked a commemorative limited-edition plastic figure of Elizabeth in a white state gown and the Garter ribbon. Elizabeth used her speech to Commonwealth heads of government in Valletta to praise her ninety-four-year-old husband, Charles and, above all, the Commonwealth itself, its sixty years of progress, growth and (relative) unity. Like her address in Perth four years before, it was in part a valediction, though Elizabeth's delivery was typically neutral. She described her six decades as head of the Commonwealth as 'a responsibility I have cherished'. An ITV reporter concluded, 'There was an inescapable feeling here that she is saying goodbye.' Her decision to restrict her travel increased the likelihood that this would be her final CHOGM. Only three years later, however, did Elizabeth herself describe a Commonwealth future without her. At the 2018 CHOGM in London, she explained her 'sincere wish... that one day the

Prince of Wales should carry on the important work started by my father in 1949'. Days later, to her considerable delight, leaders of the member states accepted her recommendation and named Charles as her successor as head of the Commonwealth. She had not only safeguarded and nurtured her inheritance through her own reign, she had made possible the inheritance of this non-hereditary role by her heir.

To the majority of her British subjects, Elizabeth's scaling-down was imperceptible, exactly as she, Geidt and palace advisers intended; Margaret Rhodes referred to her 'gradually and almost unnoticeably delegating more' while showing 'no signs of wilting in the job'. Considerable fanfare attended her ninetieth birthday, celebrated twice over. On 21 April, well-wishers gathered outside Windsor Castle as early as five o'clock in the morning: despite its short distance, Elizabeth's walkabout from the castle to the Guildhall lasted half an hour, so dense were the crowds. In an open-top Range Rover, Elizabeth and Philip were driven through the town. Described as 'terribly happy', Elizabeth opened the new Queen's Walkway. In the evening, before a private dinner in the castle's Waterloo Chamber, she lit the first of a nationwide chain of more than 1,200 beacons. In a short speech, Charles told his mother that the beacons would represent 'the love and affection in which you are held throughout this country and the Commonwealth'; by tea time, Twitter had registered more than quarter of a million tweets wishing Elizabeth a happy birthday. A trio of stylized new photographs by Annie Leibovitz marked the latest milestone: Elizabeth with her great-grandchildren and her youngest grandchildren, with her dogs and with Anne. A fourth photograph from the same sitting, of Elizabeth with Philip, was released in June in time for Elizabeth's official birthday and ahead of Philip's ninety-fifth birthday. As every year, celebrations in the summer included the birthday parade, Trooping the Colour. Many years had passed since Elizabeth rode side-saddle on Burmese; since 1987, she had attended the ceremony in a phaeton in civilian dress in place of ceremonial uniform. For her ninetieth birthday, she chose the brightest green coat, with a matching hat, designed by Stewart Parvin who, nine years earlier, had been invited to update her wardrobe. Elizabeth had never underestimated the importance of her clothes in her public life. In June 2016, her 'neon' choice electrified social media, inspiring hashtags #neonat90 and #highvishighness. It was not Elizabeth's intention; it testified to her prominence in her tenth decade.

Yet it was to be a decade marked by losses and departures. In November 2016, Margaret Rhodes died at the age of ninety-one. After the deaths of her mother and sister, the loss of Elizabeth's cousin and lifelong friend, who had lived close by in Windsor Great Park, was another unhappy break with her childhood. Elizabeth was not granted respite for grief. Days later, as planned, she hosted a reception in honour of her cousin Alexandra's eightieth birthday and the princess's work on behalf of almost a hundred charities. On 4 May 2017, Buckingham Palace announced Philip's retirement from public life. A decision the couple reached together, it represented fulfilment of the wish he had expressed six years earlier. Consequences for Elizabeth were significant. From that autumn she carried out engagements on her own or supported by other family members, including Charles, William, Harry, Alexandra, Anne and Sophie. Beginning in the year of their seventieth wedding anniversary, the couple were frequently apart, Philip at Wood Farm at Sandringham, in the care of a small staff including his pages, valet and a housekeeper; Elizabeth joined him by train whenever possible; husband and wife spoke daily on the telephone. When she was in residence in Norfolk, he joined Elizabeth in the big house, but he could not carry out long-distance the role of paterfamilias and family disciplinarian that had previously relieved Elizabeth of the burden of controlling a large, strong-minded and, in the case of some of its members, status-conscious family. Philip suffered the physical inconveniences of extreme old age. He was less mobile than Elizabeth, even after a hip replacement operation in April 2018, and his hearing had deteriorated significantly. Nothing in Elizabeth's demeanour suggested loneliness. Margaret Rhodes had identified as a characteristic of her cousin's life as monarch 'the conscious self-sacrifice of any form of private life'; habits of self-discipline were sturdily ingrained.

Yet Elizabeth would have had good reason to consider herself less well supported than previously in the autumn of 2017. Not only Philip but Christopher Geidt was no longer at her side. Geidt's departure in the summer was a decision Elizabeth had taken under pressure; among his gainsayers were Charles and Andrew. It was Geidt who announced Philip's decision to a group of 500 royal staff gathered in the ballroom of Buckingham Palace. In what newspapers called 'a rallying address', Elizabeth's private secretary asked staff across the royal palaces to work together in supporting the monarch. To this end, the following day William joined Elizabeth in welcoming to Buckingham Palace the Burmese Nobel Peace Prize winner Aung San Suu Kyi; Charles hosted the visit's formal meeting. This suggestion of concurrence, however, may have been misleading. Charles's staff resented Geidt's suggestion that Philip's departure created opportunities for all of Elizabeth's family: their preference was for an enhanced king-in-waiting role for Charles. Despite denials, Charles appeared to agree. Geidt's resignation, initiated on Elizabeth's behalf by her lord chamberlain, Earl Peel, was attributed to Charles's intervention with his mother, supported by Andrew; roots of Andrew's animosity lay in Geidt's part in his loss of his special representative role. Public statements asserted that Geidt's departure was amicable. Elizabeth may have taken the decision reluctantly; she would quickly have grounds to regret it. Newspapers reported that Geidt felt 'bruised' by her failure to support him.

For a woman living apart from the husband on whom she was accustomed to rely, with no surviving close contemporaries, ninety-one is a late age to muster the strength to resist concerted family pressure. Instinctively Elizabeth had always avoided confrontation, happier with conciliation than open disagreement, neutral in so many of her relationships as in her discharge of her royal role. Geidt had served her well and may have anticipated remaining en poste until her death. A commentator quoted by Robert Lacey blamed Charles and the staff at Clarence House for a 'shameful... shabby' decision.[18] Former deputy private secretary Edward Young took Geidt's place, genial, popular, kindly and committed to Elizabeth's best interests; his was a less commanding, less imaginative presence than Geidt's. As for Elizabeth, a book published in 2020 entitled *101 Reasons Why We Love the Queen* offered, 'she is able to weather storms, both personal and political, with quiet resilience and nerves of steel'.[19] It was not the same as an ability to devise apt, workable solutions to crises. Anne and Edward voiced their unhappiness at what had happened.

'Each day is a new beginning,' Elizabeth had offered in her 2002 Christmas broadcast. 'I know that the only way to live my life is to try to do what is right, to take the long view, to give of my best in all that the day brings, and to put my trust in God.' Elizabeth's thoughts had run on similar lines even before her parents' accession, eager as a child, a young woman and as queen 'to do what is right' and give of her best. Less than a fortnight after formal celebrations of her ninetieth birthday, a UK referendum on membership of the European Union yielded a slender majority in favour of leaving the organization that had consistently divided British opinion. It heralded a period of unusual political uncertainty and recrimination at odds with Elizabeth's preference for consensus; she would remain, as always, impartial, though some sources suggested her surprise that the government had not managed the vote more successfully, and her position above politics was challenged by constitutional wrangling, notably in the autumn of 2019, when the Supreme Court declared unlawful her prorogation of parliament on the advice of the prime minister, Boris Johnson. In a climate of flux and, for many, anxiety following the referendum, a royal romance offered distraction and the possibility of uniting the country behind the royal couple: in this case, Elizabeth's third grandson, Harry. On 27 November 2017, Harry announced his engagement to a divorced, mixed-race American actress called Meghan Markle. They were married at St George's Chapel, Windsor, on 19 May 2018, and created Duke and Duchess of Sussex. Within less than two years both husband and wife had ceased to be working members of the royal family and were living with their baby son Archie in North America, in taut emotional exile.

It was an astonishing, swift and acrimonious turnaround, in which Harry's long-term antipathy to the media, traceable to his mother's death, worsening relations with his brother William and Meghan's struggle to adapt happily or comfortably to the intense, sometimes malign scrutiny of British public life played their part. There were those who blamed Edward Young. Elizabeth's new private secretary did not evolve a strategy for Harry and Meghan: assumptions were made that they would follow a predictable royal round. A month after their wedding, Elizabeth invited Meghan to accompany her on a day of engagements in Chester, but the success of a single day was not enough to reassure the new duchess, whose life had changed so dramatically. There were tensions at court and mutual dislike between Edward Young and Meghan. In the spring of 2019, plans emerged for an overseas role for the couple, masterminded by long-term adviser Sir David Manning and Christopher Geidt, whose return to court Elizabeth had facilitated by appointing him to the ceremonial position of permanent lord-in-waiting; Geidt was chairman of the Queen's Commonwealth Trust, of which Harry was president and Meghan vice president. In the autumn, the couple did indeed visit South Africa, taking with them baby Archie; their unhappiness was clear in a television interview filmed late in the tour. By December, Harry had told Charles of their desire to step away from being senior royal figures. After some uncertainty, Elizabeth found to her surprise that the couple did not intend to spend Christmas at Sandringham.

For Elizabeth it was a disconcerting Christmas. On 20 December, Philip was flown by helicopter from Sandringham to hospital in London for 'observation and treatment of a preexisting condition', returning only on Christmas Eve.[20] Even his return could not dispel a mood lowered by the Sussexes' decision to celebrate the festivities in Canada, as well as continuing fallout from a disastrous television interview given by Andrew in November. For some time the prince had been dogged by his ill-judged friendship with Jeffrey Epstein, who had committed suicide earlier in the year, facing charges of sex offences. Makers of the *Newsnight* interview assumed Andrew would show remorse or regret; common sense seemed to dictate the manner of his response to questions about Epstein's victims, one of whom had accused him of having sex with her when she was seventeen. But Andrew, who robustly denied the allegations, was neither overtly regretful nor empathetic, with predictable results. Furious reaction to the interview forced his withdrawal from public life, described as 'temporary'. As the scandal intensified over the course of the year, Elizabeth had supported her son. In August, they were photographed together being driven to Crathie church; she continued the habit of Sunday-morning drinks at Royal Lodge, Andrew's home since the Queen Mother's death; days after the interview, they were seen riding together at Windsor. Although Elizabeth played a part in his retirement from public duties and cancelled plans for a sixtieth birthday party for Andrew in February 2020, she was criticized for her failure to prevent the interview from taking place. Twice before senior members of the royal family had resorted to television to offer the public their side of an argument. Neither Charles's interview with Jonathan Dimbleby nor Diana's with Martin Bashir ought to have encouraged Elizabeth to approve Andrew's plans.

It was Harry and Meghan, however, whose actions suggested most forcefully that Elizabeth's control over her family had faltered. On 8 January 2020, the couple announced their intention 'to step back as "senior" members of the royal family' and divide their time between Britain and North America while 'continuing to honour our duty to the Queen, the Commonwealth, and our patronages': an in/out arrangement of their own devising that offered the couple off-duty time as a family and intervals away from media intrusion. Told of the decision only minutes before the announcement was made, despite having requested that Harry not reveal any plans without discussion, Elizabeth was hurt and disappointed. She organized a meeting at Sandringham on 13 January; she allowed it to be known that she had insisted on a quick resolution. This emerged five days later. In the Sussexes' new life would be no official royal duties and no public funding; under these circumstances, they would no longer use their HRH titles. Elizabeth's official statement expressed loving finality: 'It is my whole family's hope that today's agreement allows them to start building a happy and peaceful new life.' It was an attempt to reassert control in the interests of damage limitation, and a decisive but dark beginning to a new decade. Elizabeth had never been a sentimental woman; she had acted in the only way she understood. As throughout a life in which she had consistently honoured her father's belief that 'the highest of distinctions is the service of others', she had placed the monarchy first, safeguarding its mission of service and duty that could never, she was certain, be a part-time calling. In this instance her success was short-lived. Within a year the States-based couple also had recourse to a television interview, a very public means of further airing grievances they considered unresolved.

※

Elizabeth retreated to Windsor with the imposing of national lockdown in March 2020. There, in a reduced household of Covid-safe attendants labelled 'HMS Bubble', Philip joined her from Wood Farm. At last, husband and wife enjoyed something approaching the shared leisure taken for granted by other elderly couples. Together they walked in the castle's private gardens; they dined together, spent time – as once before, on Malta – with fewer interruptions or obligations, a mostly peaceful final chapter in a marriage that had survived into its eighth decade. Only with Philip's death on 9 April 2021 did the awful bleakness of what Elizabeth described as the 'huge void' of his loss threaten to engulf her. Her family praised her characteristic concern for others in the first days of her widowhood.

Throughout a troubled year for the nation, and nations across the globe, it was Elizabeth herself who had provided light. On 11 April 2020, for the first time in a reign spanning sixty-eight years, she had issued an Easter message. She reminded listeners of the hopefulness of Easter; she ended with the conviction that 'dark as death can be... light and life are greater'. Viewers saw not Elizabeth but the symbol of a burning candle, silent witness of hope. Philip had issued a message of thanks to key workers.

※

Her Easter broadcast was one of three made by Elizabeth

during that first spring of global pandemic. During the second week of April, the image that dominated an empty Piccadilly Circus was not, as typically, an advertisement for Coca-Cola or Samsung, but Elizabeth. Snowy-haired, she wore a green dress and Queen Mary's Richmond brooch that, on account of its large size, she wore infrequently. The picture came from her coronavirus broadcast, filmed at Windsor by a single cameraman in protective clothing. Beside it, in rotation, were quotations from the broadcast, among them, 'We should take comfort that while we may still have more to endure, better days will return.' Like the Easter message that followed, Elizabeth's coronavirus broadcast offered the certainty of hope. She spoke as head of the nation to a population whose diversity was unimagined in 1952, disparate in race, religion and culture. In the *Sunday Times*, in the summer of 1977, John Grigg had written of Elizabeth, 'She looks a Queen and obviously believes in her right to be one. Her bearing is both simple and majestic – no actress could possibly match it. Wherever she may be in the world, in whatever company or climate, she never seems to lose her poise.'[21] More than forty years later, with her customary polite authority – poised, majestic and unactressy, as Grigg would have her – Elizabeth spoke to an audience of 24 million of her subjects. She thanked frontline workers and viewers self-isolating at home. She praised those whose work exposed them to risk of infection and she praised the silent majority whose compliance with emergency restrictions circumscribed their daily lives, 'the Britons of this generation... as strong as any'. To all she offered reassurance 'that if we remain united and resolute we will overcome it'. None could be surprised by her message of hope, praise for the selfless and reassurance. For seven decades they had lain at the heart of her remarkable and continuing mission.

ENDNOTES

INTRODUCTION

1   *Sunderland Daily Echo and Shipping Gazette*, 15 June 1934.
2   *Observer*, 24 December 2017.
3   *Daily Telegraph*, 13 September 2019.
4   *Reading Evening Post*, 19 February 1991.
5   *Daily Mirror*, 5 February 1982.
6   Ferrier, Neil, *The Queen Elizabeth Coronation Book* (Robinson, London, 1953), p. 37.
7   Elizabeth II, Christmas message, 1970.
8   Mary Smith to Elizabeth II, undated (April 1960), quoted in *Coventry Evening Telegraph*, 13 April 1960.
9   Philip Moore to Miss M G E Giles, Buckingham Palace, 23 November 1982, quoted in the *Guardian*, 8 February 2021.
10 *Hello*, 19 September 2018; Manser, Jose, *Hugh Casson: A Biography* (Viking, London, 2000), p. 302.

CHAPTER I

1   Duchess of York to Queen Mary, 12 April 1926, in Shawcross, William, ed., *Counting One's Blessings: The Selected Letters of Queen Elizabeth the Queen Mother* (Macmillan, London, 2012), p. 146.
2   *Scotsman*, 28 April 1926.
3   Quoted Bradford, Sarah, *George VI* (Weidenfeld & Nicolson, London, 1989), p. 113.
4   Shawcross, William, *Queen Elizabeth the Queen Mother: The Official Biography* (Macmillan, London, 2009), p. 248.
5   Duchess of York to Dr Varley, 17 December 1930, in Shawcross, *Counting One's Blessings*, p. 184.
6   Mortimer Penelope, *Queen Elizabeth: A Life of the Queen Mother* (Viking, London, 1986), p. 101.
7   Pimlott, Ben, *The Queen* (HarperCollins, London, 1996), p. 4.
8   Ziegler, Philip, *King Edward VIII: The Official Biography* (HarperCollins, London, 1991), p. 173.
9   Mortimer, op. cit., p. 86; *Coventry Evening Telegraph*, 21 April 1926.
10 Morrah, Dermot, *Princess Elizabeth* (Oldhams, London, 1947), p. 23.
11 Woolf, Virginia, 4 June 1926, in Bell, Anne Oliver, ed., *The Diary*

of Virginia Woolf, vol. 3 (Penguin, London, 1983), p. 78.

12 Shawcross, William, *Official Biography*, p. 252.

13 *Morning Post*, 21 April 1926.

14 Cathcart, Helen, *The Queen in Her Circle* (W. H. Allen, London, 1977), p. 36.

15 Bradford, op. cit., p. 116.

16 Harewood, George, *The Tongs and the Bones: The Memoirs of Lord Harewood* (Weidenfeld & Nicolson, London, 1981), p. 2.

17 Shawcross, *Official Biography*, p. 252.

18 Ibid.

19 *Spectator*, 24 April 1926.

20 Bradford, op. cit., p. 116.

21 Dennison, Matthew, *Queen Victoria: A Life of Contradictions* (William Collins, London, 2013), p. 13.

22 *Sunderland Daily Echo & Shipping Gazette*, 14 May 1926; *Brechin Advertiser*, 25 May 1926; *Belfast Telegraph*, 22 April 1926.

23 *Wells Journal*, 21 May 1926.

24 Queen Mary to Kate Rube, 24 April 1926, private collection.

25 Ziegler, op. cit., p. 172.

26 Rose, Kenneth, *George V* (Weidenfeld & Nicolson, London, 1983), p. 390.

27 *Coventry Evening Telegraph*, 22 August 1930.

28 Owens, Ed, *The Family Firm: Monarchy, Mass Media and the British Public, 1932–53* (University of London Press, 2019, published online), p. 127.

29 Nicolson, Harold, *King George V* (Constable, London, 1952), p. 420.

30 Greece, HRH Prince Christopher of, *Memoirs* (Hurst & Blackett, London, 1938), p. 161.

31 Windsor, HRH Duke of, *A King's Story* (Cassell, London, 1951), p. 183; Duff, David, *Queen Mary* (HarperCollins, London, 1985), p. 175.

32 Mortimer, op. cit., p. 164.

33 *Morning Post*, 24 April 1926.

34 Asquith, Lady Cynthia, *The Family Life of Her Majesty Queen Elizabeth* (Hutchinson, London, 1937), p. 7.

35 *Yorkshire Post*, 22 August 1930.

36 *Graphic*, 27 October 1928.

37 Airlie, Countess of (Mabell), *Thatched with Gold* (Hutchinson, London, 1962), p. 177.

38 *The Diaries of Beatrice Webb*, abr. Lynn Knight (Virago, London, 2002), p. 447.

39 Windsor, HRH Duke of, op. cit., p. 218.

40 Ring, Anne, *The Story of Princess Elizabeth* (John Murray, London, 1930), p. 13.

41 Airlie, op. cit., p. 179.

42 Ziegler, op. cit., p. 195.

43 Quoted Shawcross, *Official Biography*, p. 257.

44 See, for example, *Sketch*, 15 June 1927.

45 *Birmingham Daily Gazette*, 31 May 1926.

46 Quoted Bradford, op. cit., p. 5.

47 *Sketch*, 2 June 1926.

48 *Birmingham Daily Gazette*, 31 May 1926.

49 Ring, op. cit., pp. 11–12.

50 Shawcross, *Official Biography*, p. 258.

51 Airlie, op. cit., p. 179.

52 *The Times*, 23 April 1926.

53 Asquith, Lady Cynthia, *The King's Daughters* (Hutchinson, London, 1938), p. 10.

54 Ring, op. cit., pp. 9–10.

55 Airlie, op. cit., p. 180.

56 Speaight, Richard, *Memoirs of a Court Photographer* (Hurst & Blackett, London, 1926), p. 244.

57 *Spectator*, 15 April 1943.

58 See Duchess of York to Queen Mary, 28 October 1925, in Shawcross, *Counting One's Blessings*, p. 144.

59 *Lancashire Evening Post*, 31 August 1932.

60 Ibid.

61 Mortimer, op. cit., p. 103.

62 Quoted in Seward, Ingrid, *The Last Great Edwardian Lady* (Century, London, 1999), p. 82.

63 Mortimer, op. cit., p. 83.

64 Ring, op. cit., p. 21.

65 Shawcross, *Official Biography*, p. 263.

66 Ring, op. cit., p. 21.

67 Bradford, Sarah, *Elizabeth: A Biography of Her Majesty the Queen* (Heinemann, London, 1996), p. 216.

68 *Aberdeen Press & Journal*, 21 April 1932.

69 Asquith, *The King's Daughters*, p. 14.

70 Ibid.

71 Duchess of York to Queen Mary, 9 February 1927, in Shawcross, *Counting One's Blessings*, p. 154.

72 Ibid.

73 Ring, op. cit., p. 23.

74 *Tatler*, 13 April 1927.

75 *Sketch*, 13 April 1927.

76 Heighway, Lisa, *Marcus Adams Royal Photographer* (Royal Collection Trust, London, 2010), p. 35.

77 Shawcross, *Official Biography*, p. 274.

78 Ibid., p. 286.

79 *Westminster Gazette*, 7 February 1927.

80 Duchess of York to George V, 12 June 1927, in Shawcross, *Counting One's Blessings*, p. 161.

81 *Sketch*, 23 March 1927.

82 Asquith, *The King's Daughters*, p. 15.

83 Bradford, *George VI*, p. 132.

84 *Illustrated London News*, 2 July 1927.

85 Ibid.

86 Morrah, op. cit., p. 23.

87 Shawcross, *Official Biography*, p. 296.

88 Ibid.

89 See Royal Collection, RCIN 2108345.

90 *Tatler*, 27 July 1927.

91 Crawford, Marion, *The Little Princesses* (Orion, London, 2002), p. 9.

92 Asquith, *The Family Life of Her Majesty Queen Elizabeth*, p. 42.

93 Asquith, *The King's Daughters*, p. 16.

94 Maclean, Veronica, *Past Forgetting* (Headline, London, 2002), p. 53.

95 Asquith, *The Family Life of Her Majesty Queen Elizabeth*, p. 36

96 Asquith, Lady Cynthia, *The Duchess of York* (John Murray, London, 1926), p. 217.

97 Ibid.

98 Shawcross, *Official Biography*, p. 298.

99 Duchess of York to Queen Mary, 22 September 1927, in Shawcross, *Counting One's Blessings*, p. 162.

100 Shawcross, *Official Biography*, p. 300.

101 Airlie, op. cit., p. 180.

102 Bradford, *George VI*, p. 132.

103 *Sketch*, 14 December 1927.

104 *Aberdeen Press & Journal*, 23 April 1928.

105 *Illustrated London News*, 27 October 1928.

106 *Sketch*, 28 August 1928.

107 Asquith, *The King's Daughters*, p. 18.

108 Ibid., p. 20.

109 Ibid., p. 24.

110 Shawcross, *Official Biography*, p. 302.

111 Ibid.

112 Rose, op. cit., p. 389.

113 Ziegler, op. cit., p. 243.

114 Rose, op. cit., pp. 355–6.
115 Duchess of York to Lady (Mary) Elphinstone, 24 December 1928, in Shawcross, *Official Biography*, p. 165.
116 Quoted in Williams, Kate, *Young Elizabeth: The Making of Our Queen* (Weidenfeld & Nicolson, London, 2013), p. 46.
117 *Sheffield Daily Telegraph*, 18 March 1929.
118 *Dundee Courier*, 16 March 1929.
119 *Portsmouth Evening News*, 15 March 1929.
120 Williams, op. cit., p. 46.
121 *Portsmouth Evening News*, 27 March 1929.
122 *Sheffield Daily Telegraph*, 18 March 1929.
123 *Sketch*, 28 April 1926.
124 Shawcross, *Official Biography*, p. 307.
125 Quoted in *Hartlepool Daily Mail*, 28 August 1931.
126 *Portsmouth Evening News*, 7 June 1929.
127 Quoted in Heald, Tim, *Princess Margaret: A Life Unravelled* (Weidenfeld & Nicolson, London, 2007), p. 7.
128 Ring, op. cit., p. 100.
129 Ibid., p. 104.
130 Windsor, op. cit., p. 34.
131 *Tatler*, 11 May 1932.
132 *Hartlepool Daily Mail*, 28 August 1931.
133 *Time*, 24 April 1929.
134 *Yorkshire Post*, 3 May 1932.
135 *Lancashire Evening Post*, 17 February 1930.
136 Asquith, *The King's Daughters*, p. 19.
137 Asquith, *The Family Life of Her Majesty Queen Elizabeth*, p. 49.
138 *Yorkshire Post*, 19 May 1930.
139 *Forfar Herald*, 18 July 1930.
140 *Nottingham Journal*, 19 July 1930.
141 *Yorkshire Post*, February 1931.
142 Shawcross, *Official Biography*, p. 307.
143 *Aberdeen Press & Journal*, 21 April, 1932.
144 Ring, op. cit., pp. 97–8.
145 Shawcross, *Official Biography*, p. 311.
146 Ibid., p. 317.
147 Asquith, *The King's Daughters*, p. 51.
148 *Daily Mirror*, 11 August 1930.
149 *Western Gazette*, 8 August 1930.

CHAPTER II

1 *Western Morning News*, 22 August 1930.
2 Shawcross, *Official Biography*, p. 314.
3 Ibid., p. 317.
4 Ibid., p. 308.
5 *Morning Post*, 22 August 1930.
6 *Lancashire Evening Post*, 22 August 1930.
7 *Sheffield Daily Telegraph*, 9 September 1930.
8 Shawcross, *Official Biography*, p. 316; *Sheffield Daily Telegraph*, 4 March 1931.
9 *Sheffield Daily Telegraph*, 18 September 1930.
10 Asquith, *The King's Daughters*, p. 24.
11 Shawcross, *Official Biography*, p. 316.
12 Ibid., p. 318.
13 Ibid., p. 319.
14 *Lincolnshire Echo*, 23 September 1930.
15 Dismore, Jane, *Princess: The Early Life of Queen Elizabeth II* (The Lyons Press, Guilford, Conn., 2018), p. 72.
16 *Forfar Herald*, 21 October 1932.

17 *Sheffield Daily Telegraph*, 18 September 1930.

18 See Royal Collection RCIN2943711.

19 Duchess of York to Lady Helen Grahame, 1 October 1930, in Shawcross, *Official Biography*, p. 183.

20 Duchess of York to Duke of York, undated memo (1930–6), in ibid., p. 200.

21 Duchess of York to Duke of York, 9 September 1930, in ibid, p. 181.

22 Quoted in Thompson, Laura, *Take Six Girls* (Head of Zeus, London, 2018), p. 117.

23 *Rugby Advertiser*, 27 February 1931.

24 *Sheffield Daily Telegraph*, 13 March 1931.

25 *Lancashire Evening Post*, 13 March 1931.

26 Ibid.

27 Ibid.

28 Ibid.

29 Dismore, op. cit., p. 71.

30 *Sheffield Daily Telegraph*, 13 March 1931.

31 Crawford, op. cit., pp. 31, 87.

32 *Dundee Courier*, 25 July 1932.

33 Asquith, *The Family Life of Her Majesty Queen Elizabeth*, p. 54.

34 Ring, op. cit., p. 124.

35 See photograph published in *Western Morning News*, 21 April 1933.

36 Ring, op. cit., p. 124.

37 *Burnley News*, 21 February 1931.

38 *Western Mail*, 17 March 1932.

39 Asquith, *The Family Life of Her Majesty Queen Elizabeth*, p. 66.

40 *Western Mail*, 17 March 1932.

41 *Illustrated London News*, 16 April 1932.

42 *Falkirk Herald*, 7 March 1931.

43 *Western Mail*, 3 June 1932; *Sheffield Daily Telegraph*, 17 February 1931.

44 *Sheffield Daily Telegraph*, 4 May 1932.

45 *Portsmouth Evening News*, 20 April 1932.

46 Ibid.

47 *Yorkshire Post*, 18 April 1932.

48 Spencer Shew, Betty, *Royal Wedding* (Macdonald & Company, London, 1947), p. 32.

49 Dismore, op. cit., p. 70.

50 *Dundee Courier*, 21 April 1934.

51 Dismore, op. cit., p. 70.

52 *Dundee Courier*, 25 March 1932.

53 Windsor, Duke of, *A King's Story*, p. 278.

54 Ziegler, Philip, *Mountbatten: The Official Biography* (HarperCollins, London, 1985), p. 108.

55 *Sheffield Daily Telegraph*, 4 May 1932.

56 Bradford, *George VI*, p. 133.

57 Crawford, op. cit., p. 18; Pimlott, op. cit., p. 25.

58 Asquith, *The Family Life of Her Majesty Queen Elizabeth*, p. 51.

59 *Belfast News Letter*, 4 June 1932.

60 *Dundee Courier*, 26 July 1932.

61 *Belfast Newsletter*, 4 June 1932.

62 *Morecombe Guardian*, 27 May 1932.

63 Fitzalan Howard, Alathea, *The Windsor Diaries* (Hodder & Stoughton, London, 2020), p. 18.

64 *Sheffield Daily Telegraph*, 15 July 1932.

65 *Scotsman*, 11 July 1932.

66 Asquith, *The King's Daughters*, p. 55.

67 Asquith, *The Family Life of Her Majesty Queen Elizabeth*, p. 50.

68 *Nottingham Journal*, 6 April 1932.

69 *Thanet Advertiser*, 17 June 1932.

70 *Gloucester Echo*, 18 July 1932.

71 Shawcross, *Official Biography*, pp. 326–7.

72 Ibid., p. 327.

73 *Lincolnshire Echo*, 14 December 1933.

74 Strong, Roy, *Scenes and Apparitions: The Roy Strong Diaries 1988–2003*

(Weidenfeld & Nicolson, London, 2016), p. 35.

75 *Gloucester Citizen*, 10 January 1933.

76 *Dundee Courier*, 1 September 1932.

77 Asquith, *The King's Daughters*, p. 52.

78 *Belfast Newsletter*, 29 September 1933.

79 Crawford, op. cit., p. 3.

80 Quoted in Bradford, *Elizabeth*, p. 41.

81 *Daily Mail*, 12 September 1932.

82 Ibid.

83 Crawford, op. cit., pp. 11–12.

84 Ibid., p. 20.

85 Asquith, *The King's Daughters*, p. 53.

86 Hart-Davis, Duff, *Philip de László: His Life and Art* (Yale University Press, London, 2010), p. 245.

87 *Brechin Advertiser*, 5 December 1933.

88 *Dundee Courier*, 21 April 1934; Betty Vacani, *Happy Birthday, Dear Ma'am*, BBC television, 1986.

89 *Portsmouth Evening News*, 6 March 1935.

90 *Dundee Courier*, 21 April 1934.

91 Crawford, op. cit., pp. 25, 24.

92 *Shepton Mallet Journal*, 15 February 1935.

93 Crawford, op. cit., p. 28.

94 *Daily Telegraph*, 8 November 1934.

95 *Hull Daily Mail*, 12 September 32; *Brechin Advertiser*, 5 December 1933.

96 Crawford, op. cit., p. 19.

97 Ibid., p. 23.

98 Airlie, op. cit., p. 205.

99 Ibid., p. 206.

100 Ibid., p. 205.

101 Crawford, op. cit., p. 19.

102 Cathcart, op. cit., pp. 53-4.

103 Crawford, op. cit., p. 43.

104 Princess Elizabeth to Queen Mary, 16 February 1934, Royal Archives.

105 Crawford, op. cit., p. 23.

106 Asquith, *The King's Daughters*, p. 46.

107 *Scotsman*, 27 January 1933.

108 Sitwell, Osbert, *Queen Mary and Others* (Michael Joseph, London, 1974), p. 38.

109 *Hull Daily Mail*, 21 April 1933.

110 *Dundee Evening Telegraph*, 20 April 1933.

CHAPTER III

1 *Gloucester Citizen*, 17 September 1934.

2 Ziegler, *Edward VIII*, p. 175.

3 Ibid., p. 202.

4 Ibid., p. 229; Chips Channon, *The Diaries of Chips Channon* (Weidenfeld & Nicolson, London, 1967), pp. 29–30.

5 *Illustrated London News*, 22 October 1932.

6 *Western Mail*, 30 November 1934.

7 *Nottingham Evening Post*, 29 November 1934.

8 Pick, Michael, *Norman Hartnell: The Biography* (Zuleika, London, 2019), p. 169.

9 *Essex Newsman*, 26 January 1935.

10 Pimlott, op. cit., p. 30; Moran, *Aprons and Silver Spoons* (Penguin, London, 2013).

11 George V, Christmas broadcast 1935.

12 *Western Mail*, 16 January 1935.

13 *Gloucester Citizen*, 9 February 1935.

14 *Dundee Evening Telegraph*, 1 March 1935.

15 Ibid.

16 *Belfast Newsletter*, 7 May 1935; Channon, op. cit., p. 32.

17 Ibid.

18 *Scotsman*, 13 May 1935.

19 *Leeds Mercury*, 29 January 1936.

20 Nicolson, op. cit., p. 516.

21 Airlie, op. cit., p. 197.

22 *Aberdeen Press & Journal*, 25 September 1935.

23 Crawford, op. cit., p. 39.

24 Duchess of York to Princess Elizabeth, 29 December 1935, in Shawcross, *Counting One's Blessings*, p. 210.

25 Pimlott, op. cit., p. 32.

26 Airlie, op. cit., p. 197.

27 Lacey, Robert, *Royal: Her Majesty Queen Elizabeth II* (Little, Brown, London, 2002), p. 91.

28 *Western Mail*, 20 January 1936.

29 Ibid.

30 Hon. Lettice Bowlby to Kinara Kestyn, undated (February 1936), quoted in *Derby Daily Telegraph*, 12 February 1936.

31 Duchess of York to Queen Mary, 18 January 1936, in Shawcross, *Counting One's Blessings*, p. 215.

32 *Aberdeen Press & Journal*, 19 September 1932.

33 Asquith, *The King's Daughters*, p. 95.

34 Crawford, op. cit., p. 49.

35 Ibid.

36 Ibid.

37 *Yorkshire Post*, 28 January 1936.

38 Crawford, op. cit., p. 50.

39 Ibid., p. 51.

40 *Tatler*, 29 January 1936.

41 *Sphere*, 22 February 1936.

42 *Dundee Courier*, 17 February 1936.

43 *Leeds Mercury*, 27 March 1936.

44 *Dundee Evening Telegraph*, 10 February 1936.

45 *Eastbourne Gazette*, 11 March 1936.

46 Duchess of York to Queen Mary, 11 March 1936, in Shawcross, *Counting One's Blessings* , p. 216.

47 *Eastbourne Gazette*, 11 March 1936.

48 Moran, op. cit.

49 Grenfell, Joyce, *Darling Ma: Letters to Her Mother 1932–44* (Coronet, London, 1989), pp. 47–8.

50 Duchess of York to Queen Mary, 11 March 1936, in Shawcross, *Counting One's Blessings*, p. 216.

51 Vickers, Hugo, *Elizabeth the Queen Mother* (Hutchinson, London, 2005), p. 136.

52 *Western Morning News*, 26 May 1936.

53 *Sheffield Independent*, 26 May 1936.

54 Crawford, op. cit., p. 52.

55 See *Antiques Trade Gazette*, 19 April 2005.

56 Quoted in van der Kiste, John, *George V's Children* (Alan Sutton, Stroud, 1991), p. 83.

57 Owens, Edward, op. cit., p. 128.

58 Woolf, Virginia, in Bell, Anne Oliver, ed., *The Diary of Virginia Woolf*, vol. 5: *1936–41* (Penguin, London, 1985), p. 41.

59 Beaken, Robert, *Cosmo Lang: Archbishop in War and Crisis* (I. B. Tauris, London, 2012), p. 244.

60 Woolf, op. cit., vol. 5, p. 38.

61 Sitwell, op. cit., p. 22.

62 *Yorkshire Evening Post*, 15 February 1936.

63 Duchess of York to Queen Mary, 19 September 1936, in Shawcross, *Counting One's Blessings*, p. 220.

64 Bradford, *George VI*, p. 152.

65 Crawford, op. cit., p. 58.

66 Warwick, Christopher, *Princess Margaret* (Weidenfeld & Nicolson, London, 1983), p. 18.

67 Quoted in Williams, op. cit., p. 90.

68 Channon, op. cit., p. 60.

69 Crawford, op. cit., p. 61.

70 Pimlott, op. cit., p. 33.

71 Channon, op. cit., p. 100.

72 Crawford, op. cit., pp. 26, 22.

73 *Aberdeen Press & Journal*, 8 May 1936.

74 Asquith, *The King's Daughters*, p. 91.

75 Rhodes, Margaret, *The Final Curtsey: A Royal Memoir by the Queen's Cousin* (Birlinn, Edinburgh, 2012), p. 46.

76 Ibid., p. 176.

77 *Western Morning News*, 5 November 1936.

78 Pimlott, op. cit., p. 35.

79 Duchess of York to Queen Mary, 20 November 1936, in Shawcross, *Counting One's Blessings*, p. 225.

80 Crawford, op. cit., pp. 58–61.

81 Longford, Elizabeth, *Elizabeth R* (Weidenfeld & Nicolson, London, 1983), p. 68.

82 Campbell-Preston, Frances, *The Rich Spoils of Time* (The Dovecote Press, Wimborne Minster, 2006), p. 62.

83 *Shepton Mallet Journal*, 27 November 1936.

84 Crawford, op. cit., p. 59.

85 Longford, op. cit., p. 66.

CHAPTER IV

1 *Gloucester Citizen*, 10 December 1936.

2 Bradford, *Elizabeth*, p. 57.

3 Shawcross, *Official Biography*, p. 445.

4 *Daily Mirror*, 11 December 1936.

5 Duchess of York to Queen Mary, 21 October 1936, in Shawcross, *Counting One's Blessings*, p. 222.

6 Ziegler, *Mountbatten*, p. 95.

7 Owens, op. cit., p. 100.

8 *Aberdeen Press & Journal*, 16 January 1937.

9 Ring, op. cit., pp. 58, 125.

10 Owens, op. cit., p. 143.

11 *Sunderland Daily Echo*, 30 January 1937.

12 Ibid.

13 *Dundee Courier*, 13 January 1937.

14 Woolf, op. cit., vol. 5, p. 39.

15 *Birmingham Daily Gazette*, 11 December 1936.

16 Crawford, op. cit., p. 62.

17 Airlie, op. cit., p. 205.

18 Margaret Rhodes, quoted in Dismore, op. cit., p. 105.

19 See Owens, op. cit., p. 140.

20 Shawcross, *Official Biography*, p. 389.

21 *Dundee Courier*, 27 February 1937.

22 Cathcart, op. cit., p. 49.

23 Shawcross, *Official Biography*, p. 389.

24 *Scotsman*, 17 March 1937.

25 Windsor, op. cit., p. 279.

26 Mortimer, op. cit., p. 153.

27 Owens, op. cit., p. 131.

28 Bradford, *George VI*, p. 260.

29 Beckles, Gordon, *Coronation Souvenir Book* (Daily Express Books, London, 1937), p. 22.

30 Shawcross, *Official Biography*, p. 397.

31 *Western Mail*, 11 May 1937.

32 Crawford, op. cit., p. 65.

33 Ibid.

34 Shawcross, *Official Biography*, p. 396.

35 Crawford, op. cit., p. 67; Airlie, op. cit., p. 203.

36 Asquith, *The Family Life of Her Majesty Queen Elizabeth*, p. 96.

37 *Yorkshire Post*, 12 March 1937.

38 Ibid.

39 Hassall, Christopher, *Devil's Dyke* (Heinemann, London, 1936).

40 Fitzalan Howard, op. cit., p. 83.

41 *Buckinghamshire Examiner*, 30 April 1937.

42 Crawford, op. cit., p. 70.

43 Lacey, op. cit., p. 105.

44 *Aberdeen Press & Journal*, 7 April 1937.

45 *Derby Daily Telegraph*, 21 April 1937.

46 *Western Mail*, 11 May 1937.

47 Grenfell, op. cit., p. 47.

48 'The Coronation, 12 May 1937, To Mummy and Papa, In Memory of Their Coronation, From Lillibet, By Herself', Royal Archives RA QEII/PRIV/PERS.

49 Channon, op. cit., p. 124.

50 *The Times*, 12 May 1937.

51 *Western Mail*, 10 July 1947.

52 Bradley, Ian, *God Save the Queen: The Spiritual Dimension of Monarchy* (Dartman, Longman & Todd, 2002), p. 132.

53 Lacey, op. cit., p. 107.

54 Cathcart, op. cit., p. 71.

55 Bradford, *Elizabeth*, p. 75.

56 Cathcart, op. cit., p. 71.

57 Duchess of York to Queen Mary, 26 October 1937, in Shawcross, *Counting One's Blessings*, p. 249.

58 Longford, op. cit., p. 75.

59 See Kavanagh, Julie, *Secret Muses: The Life of Frederick Ashton* (Faber & Faber, London, 1998), p. 595.

60 *Dundee Evening Telegraph*, 29 March 1938.

61 Crawford, op. cit., p. 91.

62 Ibid., p. 74.

63 Williams, op. cit., p. 57.

64 Quoted in Bradford, *Elizabeth*, p. 62.

65 Crawford, op. cit., p. 89.

66 Duchess of York to Princess Elizabeth, 27 May 1939, in Shawcross, *Counting One's Blessings*, p. 268.

67 *Worthing Gazette*, 18 December 1940.

68 Turner, Graham, *Elizabeth: The Woman and the Queen* (Macmillan, London, 2002), p. 2.

69 See, for example, *Belfast Telegraph*, 23 March 1937.

70 Ibid.

71 Alan Lascelles to Geoffrey Dawson, 13 December 1936, quoted in Owens, op. cit., p. 146.

72 Hon. Mary Macdonald, quoted in *Western Mail*, 17 December 1937.

73 *Daily Telegraph*, 22 December 1937.

74 *Dundee Courier*, 25 September 1937.

75 *West Sussex Gazette*, 6 January 1938.

76 Duchess of York to Princess Elizabeth, 27 May 1939, in Shawcross, *Counting One's Blessings*, p. 267.

77 Crawford, op. cit., p. 82.

78 Bradford, *Elizabeth*, p. 63.

79 Crawford, op. cit., p. 117.

80 *Tatler*, 27 October 1937.

81 Bradford, *Elizabeth*, p. 64.

82 Channon, op. cit., p. 162.

83 Duchess of York to Osbert Sitwell, 11 October 1938, in Shawcross, *Counting One's Blessings*, p. 258.

84 *Northern Whig*, 28 September 1938.

85 *Yorkshire Post*, 20 June 1938.

86 *Western Mail*, 9 December 1938.

87 *Daily Mirror*, 15 November 1938.

88 Princess Elizabeth to Queen Mary, 15 November 1938, Royal Archives.

CHAPTER V

1 *Belfast Telegraph*, 10 March 1939.

2 Grenfell, op. cit., p. 47.

3 Duchess of York to Princess Elizabeth, 23 May 1939, in Shawcross, *Counting One's Blessings*, p. 266; Duchess of York to Princess Elizabeth, 27 May 1939, in ibid, p. 267.

4   Duchess of York to Princess Elizabeth, 27 May 1939, in ibid, p. 267.

5   Duchess of York to Princess Elizabeth, 5 June 1939, in ibid, p. 270.

6   Pimlott, op. cit., p. 53.

7   See Hurd, Douglas, *Elizabeth II: The Steadfast* (Allen Lane, London, 2015), p. 12; *Daily Express*, 25 November 1932; Bousfield, Arthur, *Fifty Years the Queen: A Tribute to Elizabeth II on Her Golden Jubilee* (Dundurn, Toronto, 2001), p. 35.

8   Antoinette de Bellaigue, quoted in Longford, op. cit., p. 94.

9   Duchess of York to Princess Elizabeth, 23 May 1939, in Shawcross, *Counting One's Blessings*, p. 265.

10 Crawford, op. cit., pp. 96–7.

11 Vickers, op. cit., p. 191.

12 Duchess of York to Princess Elizabeth, 13 May 1939, in Shawcross, *Counting One's Blessings*, p. 264; *Birmingham Daily Post*, 23 June 1939.

13 *Coventry Evening Telegraph*, 20 April 1939.

14 Marr, Andrew, *The Diamond Queen: Elizabeth II and Her People* (Macmillan, London, 2011), p. 56.

15 Duchess of York to Lady Tweedsmuir, 28 June 1939, in Shawcross, *Counting One's Blessings*, p. 274.

16 Crawford, op. cit., p. 101.

17 *Northern Whig*, 30 November 1934.

18 Quoted in Seward, Ingrid, *My Husband and I* (Simon & Schuster, London, 2017), p. 57.

19 Alexandra, Queen of Yugoslavia, *Prince Philip: A Family Portrait* (Hodder & Stoughton, London, 1960), p. 73.

20 Crawford, op. cit., p. 101.

21 Ibid.

22 Ibid., p. 102.

23 Eade, Philip, *Young Prince Philip* (HarperPress, London, 2012), p. 153.

24 *Torbay Express and South Devon Echo*, 24 July 1939.

25 Quoted in *West Middlesex Gazette*, 26 March 1932.

26 Channon, op. cit., p. 287.

27 Seward, *My Husband and I*, p. 61.

28 Lacey, op. cit., p. 126.

29 Rhodes, op. cit., p. 87.

30 Ziegler, *Mountbatten*, p. 687.

31 Eade, op. cit., p. 189.

32 Ziegler, *Mountbatten*, p. 102.

33 Crawford, op. cit.

34 Marie Louise, Her Highness Princess, *My Memories of Six Reigns* (Evans Brothers, London, 1957), p. 314.

35 Bedell Smith, Sally, *Elizabeth the Queen* (Penguin, London, 2012), p. 25.

36 Pimlott, op. cit., p. 586, note 19.

37 Parker, John, *Prince Philip: A Critical Biography* (Sidgwick & Jackson, London, 1990), p. 38.

38 Queen Elizabeth to the Duke of Edinburgh, 1 December 1947, in Shawcross, *Counting One's Blessings*, p. 406.

CHAPTER VI

1　*Aberdeen Weekly Journal*, 9 November 1939.

2　Quoted in Noel, Gerald, *Ena, Spain's English Queen* (Constable, London, 1999), p. 256.

3　Rhodes, op. cit., pp. 50–51.

4　Ibid., p. 50.

5　Crawford, op. cit., p. 107.

6　Lady Granville to Queen Elizabeth, 6 September 1939, in Shawcross, *Counting One's Blessings*, p. 277.

7　Crawford, op. cit., pp. 108–9, 111.

8　Shawcross, *Official Biography*, p. 495.

9　Queen Elizabeth to Prince Paul of Yugoslavia, 2 October 1939, in Shawcross, *Counting One's Blessings*, p. 279.

10　Crawford, op. cit., p. 106.

11　*Bristol Evening Post*, 23 September 1939.

12　Airlie, op. cit., p. 227.

13　*Liverpool Daily Post*, 24 February 1940.

14　*Coventry Evening Telegraph*, 8 January 1940.

15　*Dundee Evening Telegraph*, 28 March 1940.

16　Shawcross, *Official Biography*, p. 503.

17　Ibid.

18　Crawford, op. cit., p. 115.

19　*Sunday Mirror*, 30 April 1940.

20　Quoted in Williams, op. cit., p. 161.

21　*Yorkshire Post*, 1 January 1940; *Evening Despatch*, 6 April 1940; *Express and Echo*, 14 June 1940.

22　*Hull Daily Mail*, 18 July 1940; *Derby Daily Telegraph*, 18 July 1940.

23　*Sunday Mirror*, 30 April 1940.

24　Crawford, op. cit., p. 133.

25　Ibid.

26　*The Times*, 12 July 1940.

27　See Lacey, op. cit., p. 133.

28　Brown, Susannah, *Queen Elizabeth II: Portraits by Cecil Beaton* (V&A Publishing, London, 2011), p. 31.

29　Fitzalan Howard, op. cit., p. 83.

30　*Sunday Mirror*, 30 June 1940.

31　*Aberdeen Press & Journal*, 7 November 1940.

32　*Dundee Evening Telegraph*, 23 April 1940.

33　*Yorkshire Post*, 18 November 1940.

34　*Sunday Mirror*, 30 April 1940.

35　Bradford, *Elizabeth*, p. 91.

36　*Belfast Newsletter*, 27 August 1942.

37　Rhodes, op. cit., p. 68.

38　Quoted in Pimlott, op. cit., p. 57.

39　*Nottingham Evening Post*, 7 September 1940.

40　Shawcross, *Official Biography*, p. 527.

41　Crawford, op. cit., p. 145.

42　Ibid., p. 117.

43　*Daily Mirror*, 8 July 1940.

44　*Daily Herald*, 27 December 1940.

45　Grenfell, op. cit., p. 231.

46　Morrah, op. cit., p. 82.

47　*International Women's Suffrage News*, 1 November 1940.

48　Grenfell, op. cit., p. 231.

49　Queen Elizabeth to Lady Violet Bonham Carter, 7 March 1944, in Shawcross, *Counting One's Blessings*, p. 360.

50　Grenfell, op. cit., p. 210.

51　*Daily Mirror*, 26 June 1941.

52　*Tatler*, 22 April 1942.

53　Ibid., 26 August 1942.

54　*Daily Record*, 20 April 1940.

55　*Sketch*, 5 February 1941.

56　Bradford, *Elizabeth*, p. 101.

57　Airlie, op. cit., pp. 219–20.

58　*Scotsman*, 22 April 1942.

59　*Daily Mail*, 21 April 1942.

60 Bradford, *Elizabeth*, p. 99.

61 *Sunday Post*, 17 February 1946.

62 Strong, Roy, *Cecil Beaton: The Royal Portraits* (Thames & Hudson, London, 1988), p. 88.

63 *Evening Despatch*, March 1942.

64 *Tatler*, 4 November 1942.

65 *Yorkshire Evening Post*, 26 October 1942.

66 Bradford, *Elizabeth*, p. 98.

67 Shawcross, *Official Biography*, p. 576.

68 Queen Elizabeth to Queen Mary, 7 January 1941, in Shawcross, *Counting One's Blessings*, p. 302.

69 Crawford, op. cit., p. 135.

70 Queen Elizabeth to Eleanor Roosevelt, 11 June 1940, in Shawcross, *Counting One's Blessings*, p. 291.

71 Queen Elizabeth to Queen Mary, 31 October 1940, in ibid., p. 291.

72 See Pimlott, op. cit., p. 65; Bedell Smith, op. cit., p. 18.

73 Middleboe, Penelope, ed., *Edith Olivier: From Her Journals, 1924–48* (Weidenfeld & Nicolson, London, 1989), p. 272.

74 Pimlott, op. cit., p. 68.

75 Shawcross, *Official Biography*, p. 578.

76 *Portsmouth Evening News*, 4 February 1942.

77 Fitzalan Howard, op. cit., p. 71.

78 Bradford, *Elizabeth*, p. 101.

79 Crawford, op. cit., p. 140.

80 Ibid., p. 160.

81 Sheridan, Lisa, *From Cabbages to Kings* (Odhams, London, 1955), p. 115.

82 Shawcross, *Official Biography*, p. 578.

83 Ibid.

84 Eade, op. cit., p. 155.

85 Edward Ford quoted in Lloyd, Ian, *The Duke* (The History Press, Cheltenham, 2021), p. 80.

86 Airlie, op. cit., p. 227.

87 Middleboe, op. cit., p. 272.

88 Shawcross, *Official Biography*, p. 577; Shawcross, *Counting One's Blessings*, note, p. 359.

89 Glendinning, Victoria, *Rebecca West* (Weidenfeld & Nicolson, London, 1987), p. 170.

90 Shawcross, *Official Biography*, p. 579.

91 *Aberdeen Press & Journal*, 13 January 1944.

92 Morrah, op. cit., pp. 73–4.

93 Longford, op. cit., p. 93.

94 Pimlott, op. cit., p. 68.

95 *Aberdeen Press & Journal*, 13 January 1944.

96 Manser, op. cit., p. 307.

97 Printed in *Lichfield Mercury*, 7 April 1944.

98 *Tatler*, 17 May 1944.

99 Shawcross, *Official Biography*, p. 581.

100 Queen Elizabeth to Queen Mary, 11 April 1944, in Shawcross, *Counting One's Blessings*, p. 361.

101 *Sketch*, 31 May 1944.

102 For example, see Mary Gibb, 'The Girl Who Was Born to Be Queen', *Aberdeen Press & Journal*, 13 January 1944.

103 Queen Elizabeth to Princess Elizabeth, 27 June 1944, in Shawcross, *Counting One's Blessings*, p. 365.

104 Queen Elizabeth to Queen Mary, 17 July 1944, in ibid., p. 367.

105 McDowell, Colin, *A Hundred Years of Royal Style* (Hutchinson, London, 1986), p. 23.

106 See Garfield, Simon, ed., *Our Hidden Lives: The Remarkable Diaries of Postwar Britain* (Ebury Press, London, 2005), p. 237.

107 *Perthshire Advertiser*, 18 October 1944.

108 Pimlott, op. cit., p. 110.
109 Crawford, op. cit., pp. 157–8.
110 Ibid., p. 156.
111 Williams, op. cit., p. 189.
112 Elizabeth II, 6 May 1995, reply to address of Houses of Parliament (fiftieth anniversary VE Day).
113 Lacey, op. cit., p. 137.
114 Ibid.
115 *Yorkshire Post*, 4 March 1950.
116 Clara 'Alah' Knight to Ethel Taylor, undated, quoted *Daily Express*, 21 September 2017.
117 Bradford, *Elizabeth*, p. 108.

118 Queen Elizabeth to Queen Mary, 10 April 1945, in Shawcross, *Counting One's Blessings*, p. 381.
119 Crawford, op. cit., p. 157.
120 Pimlott, op. cit., p. 79; Morrow, Ann, *The Queen* (HarperCollins, London, 1983), p. 93.
121 Rhodes, op. cit., p. 84.
122 Ibid., p. 86.
123 Quoted Pimlott, op. cit., p. 81.
124 Rhodes, op. cit., pp. 84–5.
125 Crawford, op. cit., p. 179.
126 Clara 'Alah' Knight to Ethel Taylor, undated (see n. 116 above).

CHAPTER VII

1 Alexandra, Queen of Yugoslavia, op. cit., p. 102.
2 Eade, op. cit., p. 178.
3 Garfield, op. cit., p. 320.
4 Ibid., p. 237.
5 Quoted in Vickers, op. cit., p. 251.
6 Quoted in Williams, op. cit., p. 198.
7 Quoted in Roger, Malcolm, *Elizabeth II: Portraits of Sixty Years* (National Portrait Gallery Publications, London, 1986), p. 50.
8 *Shields Daily News*, 30 April 1946.
9 Pottle, Mark, ed., *Daring to Hope: The Diaries and Letters of Violet Bonham Carter, 1946–69* (Orion, London, 2000), p. 16.
10 Morrah, op. cit., p. 100.
11 Parker, op. cit., p. 114.
12 Bradford, *Elizabeth*, p. 116.
13 Lacey, op. cit., p. 136.
14 Bradford, *Elizabeth*, p. 116.
15 Quoted in ibid, p. 418.
16 Quoted in Bradford, *George VI*, p. 18.
17 Jebb, Miles, ed., *The Diaries of Cynthia Gladwyn* (Constable, London, 1995), p. 92.

18 Viney Graham, *The Last Hurrah* (Robinson, London, 2019), p. 276.
19 Turner, op. cit., p. 21.
20 Queen Elizabeth to Alan Lascelles, in Shawcross, *Official Biography*, p. 626; Bradford, *Elizabeth*, p. 121.
21 Airlie, op. cit., p. 224.
22 Parker, op. cit., p. 110.
23 Shawcross, *Official Biography*, p. 630.
24 Viney, op. cit., p. 25.
25 Ibid., p. 154.
26 *Hull Daily Mail*, 6 February 1947; *Dundee Courier*, 14 February 1947.
27 *Coventry Evening Telegraph*, 26 February 1947.
28 Viney, op. cit., p. 101.
29 Garfield, op. cit., p. 357.
30 Bedell Smith, op. cit., p. 35.
31 *Leicester Chronicle*, 1 February 1947.
32 Roberts, Hugh, *The Queen's Diamonds* (Royal Collection Trust, London, 2012), p. 272.
33 Ibid.
34 Quoted in Viney, op. cit., p. 285.
35 Quoted in Longford, op. cit., pp. 103–4.
36 Spencer Shew, op. cit., p. 65.

37 Nicolson, Nigel, ed., *Vita and Harold: The Letters of Vita Sackville-West and Harold Nicolson, 1919–62* (Weidenfeld & Nicolson, London, 2007), p. 372.

38 Quoted in Bradford, *Elizabeth*, p. 109; Pimlott, op. cit., p. 110; Strong, *Cecil Beaton: The Royal Portraits*, p. 123.

39 Campbell-Preston, op. cit., p. 217.

40 Spencer Shew, op. cit., p. 71.

41 Viney, op. cit., p. 265.

42 Alan Lascelles to Dermot Morrah, 10 March 1947.

43 Viney, op. cit., p. 275.

44 *Belfast Telegraph*, 22 April 1947.

45 Hardman, Robert, *Queen of the World* (Pegasus, London, 2019), p. 119.

46 Ibid., p. 120.

47 Ibid.

48 Airlie, op. cit., p. 228; Glendinning, op. cit., p. 170.

49 Wellesley, Lady Jane, *Wellington: A Journey Through My Family* (Orion, London, 2008).

50 Shawcross, *Official Biography*, p. 626.

51 Nicholson, Virginia, *Millions Like Us: Women's Lives During the Second World War* (Penguin, London, 2012), p. 412.

52 *Spectator*, 10 July 1947.

53 Quoted in *Gloucestershire Echo*, 31 October 1947.

54 Garfield, op. cit., p. 408.

55 Princess Elizabeth to Betty Spencer Shew, undated (1947), Balmoral.

56 See Longford, op. cit., p. 114.

57 *Scotsman*, 10 July 1947.

58 *Coventry Evening Telegraph*, 10 July 1947.

59 Dismore, op. cit., p. 263.

60 *Belfast Telegraph*, 20 November 1947.

61 Garfield, op. cit., p. 424.

62 Shawcross, *Official Biography*, p. 628.

63 *Manchester Evening News*, 30 October 1947.

64 Morrah, op. cit., p. 126.

65 Pottle, op. cit., p. 31.

66 *Daily Mail*, 22 July 1947.

67 *Cheltenham Chronicle*, 18 October 1947.

68 *Yorkshire Post*, 29 October 1947; *Scotsman*, 30 October 1947.

69 *Liverpool Echo*, 17 October 1947; *Illustrated London News*, 1 April 1950.

70 See *Gloucestershire Echo*, 31 October 1947.

71 Lees-Milne, James, diary, 18 November 1947, in Lees-Milne, James, *Caves of Ice and Midway on the Waves* (John Murray, London, 1996), p. 204.

72 Pimlott, op. cit., p. 135.

73 Nancy Mitford to Humphrey Hare, 23 November 1947, in Mosley, Charlotte, ed., *Love from Nancy: The Letters of Nancy Mitford* (Hodder & Stoughton, London, 1993), p. 193.

74 Payn, Graham, and Morley, Sheridan, eds., *The Noël Coward Diaries* (Weidenfeld & Nicolson, London, 1982), p. 96.

75 Bedell Smith, op. cit., p. 39.

76 See Roberts, Margery, *A Time Remembered* (Royal Pavilion Libraries and Museum, Brighton, 1998).

77 *Yorkshire Evening Post*, 20 November 1947.

78 Crawford, op. cit., p. 204.

79 Queen Elizabeth to Princess Elizabeth, 24 November 1947, in Shawcross, *Counting One's Blessings*, p. 404.

80 Morrow, op. cit., p. 36.

81 *Belfast Telegraph*, 20 November 1947.
82 Payn and Morley, op. cit., p. 96.
83 Queen Elizabeth to Princess Elizabeth, 30 November 1947, in Shawcross, *Counting One's Blessings*, p. 405.
84 Bradford, *Elizabeth*, p. 130.
85 *Shields Daily News*, 20 November 1947.
86 Marie Louise, Her Highness Princess, op. cit., p. 313.
87 Queen Elizabeth to Princess Elizabeth, 24 November 1947, in Shawcross, *Counting One's Blessings*, p. 404.
88 Longford, op. cit., p. 121.
89 Shawcross, *Counting One's Blessings*, p. 629.
90 Ibid., p. 630.
91 *Yorkshire Post*, 28 May 1948.
92 Garfield, op. cit., p. 467.
93 For example, see *Nottingham Evening Post*, 28 February 1948.
94 Shawcross, *Official Biography*, p. 630.
95 Crawford, op. cit., p. 207.
96 Queen Elizabeth to Princess Elizabeth, 24 November 1947, in Shawcross, *Counting One's Blessings*, pp. 403–4.
97 *Nottingham Journal*, 27 November 1947.
98 *Manchester Evening News*, 23 October 1947.

CHAPTER VIII

1 *Coventry Evening Standard*, 29 May 1948.
2 Jebb, op. cit., p. 92.
3 *Coventry Evening Standard*, 29 May 1948.
4 Letter from K. E. Pratt, London NW2, undated, to *Sunday Mirror*, 7 March 1948.
5 Duke of Edinburgh to Queen Elizabeth, undated (November 1947), quoted in Shawcross, *Counting One's Blessings*, p. 403.
6 Bradford, *Elizabeth*, p. 140.
7 Pimlott, op. cit., p. 121.
8 Morrah, Dermot, *The Royal Family* (Odhams, London, 1950), p. 86.
9 *Western Daily Press*, 24 January 1948.
10 See, for example, *Aberdeen Press & Journal*, 24 January 1948.
11 *Liverpool Echo*, 17 February 1948.
12 *Spectator*, 26 December 1947.
13 Ibid., 21 November 1947.
14 Pimlott, op. cit., p. 150.
15 *Western Mail*, 15 May 1948.
16 Edwards, Anne, *Royal Sisters* (William Morrow & Co., New York 1990), p. 211.
17 Quoted in Hardman, op. cit., p. 276.
18 Shawcross, *Official Biography*, p. 631.
19 Channon, op. cit., 30 May 1948, p. 425.
20 *Scotsman*, 7 January 1948.
21 *Western Morning News*, 1 March 1949.
22 Turner, op. cit., p. 34.
23 Crawford, op. cit., p. 221.
24 Shawcross, *Official Biography*, pp. 630–1.
25 George VI, undated (1947), 'To the bishops and clergy of the province of Canterbury in convocation assembled' (on the occasion of Princess Elizabeth's engagement).
26 Eade, op. cit., p. 201.
27 Jebb, op. cit., p. 92.
28 *Wells Journal*, 17 September 1948.

ENDNOTES

29 Queen Louise of Sweden to Mountbatten, 14 December 1948, quoted in Vickers, Hugo, *Alice: Princess Andrew of Greece* (Penguin, London, 2001), p. 332.

30 Eade, op. cit., p. 224.

31 Bedell Smith, op. cit., p. 49.

32 Eade, op. cit., p. 224.

33 Crawford, op. cit., p. 228.

34 Dimbleby, Jonathan, *The Prince of Wales* (Little, Brown, London, 1994), p. 6.

35 *The Times*, 15 November 1948.

36 Vickers, *Alice*, p. 332.

37 *Illustrated London News*, 8 January 1949.

38 Dismore, op. cit., p. 250.

39 Ibid.

40 Queen Elizabeth to Winston Churchill, 27 December 1948, in Shawcross, *Counting One's Blessings*, p. 412.

41 Morrah, *Royal Family*, p. 95.

42 Williams, op. cit., p. 240.

43 Princess Elizabeth to Lady Olivier, Buckingham Palace, 22 April 1949.

44 *Scotsman*, 22 December 1949.

45 Ibid.

46 Vickers, *Elizabeth the Queen Mother*, p. 309.

47 Jebb, op. cit., p. 88.

48 Nicolson, Nigel, *Long Life: Memoirs* (Weidenfeld & Nicolson, London, 1997), p. 280.

49 Jebb, op. cit., p. 94.

50 Dimbleby, op. cit., note, p. 16.

51 Princess Elizabeth to 'Mary', 24 April 1945.

52 Dismore, op. cit., p. 251.

53 *Banbury Gazette*, 28 April 1949.

54 Channon, op. cit., pp. 438–9.

55 Brown, op. cit., p. 33.

56 Knight, Laura, *The Magic of a Line: The Autobiography of Laura Knight* (William Kimber, London, 1965).

57 Morrah, *Royal Family*, p. 92.

58 *Western Morning News*, 31 October 1949.

59 Bradford, *Elizabeth*, p. 151.

60 Dismore, op. cit., p. 256.

61 *Illustrated London News*, 3 December 1949.

62 Ziegler, *Mountbatten*, p. 492.

63 Ibid.

64 Queen Elizabeth to Prince Paul of Yugoslavia, 5 January 1949, in Shawcross, *Counting One's Blessings*, p. 413; Queen Elizabeth to Princess Elizabeth, 21 December 1949, in ibid, p. 420.

65 Quoted in Eade, op. cit., p. 236.

66 Cathcart, op. cit., p. 125.

67 Quoted in Eade, op. cit., p. 235.

68 Quoted in Pimlott, op. cit., p. 162.

69 *Illustrated London News*, 11 October 1947.

70 Dismore, op. cit., p. 260.

71 Vickers, *Elizabeth the Queen Mother*, p. 283.

72 Ibid., p. 286.

73 *Nottingham Evening Post*, 10 March 1950.

74 *Scotsman*, 16 August 1950.

75 Bradford, *Elizabeth*, p. 159; Dismore, op. cit., p. 260.

76 Bradford, *Elizabeth*, p. 159.

77 Dismore, op. cit., p. 260.

78 *Nottingham Evening Post*, 6 December 1950.

79 Turner, op. cit., p. 37.

80 Queen Elizabeth to Princess Elizabeth, 29 December 1950, in Shawcross, *Counting One's Blessings*, p. 435.

81 *Sunday Mirror*, 4 February 1951.

82 Cathcart, op. cit., p. 126.

83 Pathé Films, 'God Save the Queen', broadcast 11 February 1952.

84 *Western Mail*, 8 October 1951.

85 *Belfast Telegraph*, 29 October 1951.

86 *Aberdeen Evening Express*, 12 October 1951.

87 Pimlott, op. cit., p. 368.

88 Eader, op. cit., p. 246; *Aberdeen Evening Express*, 12 October 1951.

89 Queen Elizabeth to Princess Elizabeth, 15 October 1951, in Shawcross, *Counting One's Blessings*, p. 441.

90 *Belfast Telegraph*, 2 November 1951.

91 Pimlott, op. cit., p. 172.

92 *Rugby Advertiser*, 23 November 1951.

93 Pimlott, op. cit., p. 170.

94 *Illustrated London News*, 2 February 1952.

95 Seward, *My Husband and I*, p. 85.

96 Martin Charteris, quoted in Bradford, *George VI*, p. 460.

97 Lacey, op. cit., p. 166.

98 *Daily Telegraph*, 2 June 2003.

99 Ferrier, op. cit., p. 133; Shawcross, *Official Biography*, p. 666; *Daily Telegraph*, 2 June 2003.

100 Brendon, Piers, and Whitehead, Phillip, *The Windsors* (Pimlico, London, 2000), p. 130.

101 Bradford, *George VI*, p. 461.

102 Longford, op. cit., p. 236.

CHAPTER IX

1 Campbell-Preston, op. cit., p. 219.

2 *Northern Whig*, 18 February 1952.

3 Elizabeth II to Ethel Taylor, 5 April 1952; Elizabeth II to Mrs Tanner, 23 March 1952.

4 Pathé Films, 'God Save the Queen', broadcast 11 February 1952.

5 Masefield, John, 'Our Glorious Sovereign'.

6 Cathcart, op. cit., p. 131.

7 Shawcross, William, *Queen and Country* (BBC Books, London, 2002), p. 16; Shawcross, *Official Biography*, p. 665; Pimlott, op. cit., pp. 187, 175.

8 *Northern Whig*, 18 February 1952.

9 Bedell Smith, op. cit., p. 124.

10 Ibid., p. 67.

11 *Daily Telegraph*, 5 March 1952.

12 *Birmingham Daily Gazette*, 11 March 1952.

13 Ibid., 3 April 1952.

14 Manser, op. cit., p. 294.

15 Elizabeth II, in the documentary *Elizabeth R* (1992).

16 Marie Louise, Her Highness Princess, op. cit., p. 313.

17 Manser, op. cit., p. 293.

18 Quoted in *Portsmouth Evening News*, 11 October 1950.

19 Fry, Christopher, *A Queen is Crowned*, The Rank Organisation, 1953.

20 Longford, op. cit., p. 147.

21 Warwick, op. cit., p. 57.

22 Williams, op. cit., p. 268.

23 Seward, *My Husband and I*, p. 89.

24 Vickers, *Alice*, p. 344.

25 Alexandra, Queen of Yugoslavia, op. cit., p. 167.

26 Rhodes, op. cit., p. 151.

27 Shawcross, *Official Biography*, p. 671.

28 Queen Elizabeth the Queen Mother to Elizabeth II, 14 December 1953, in Shawcross, *Counting One's Blessings*, p. 476.

29 Seward, *My Husband and I*, p. 90.

30 Brandreth, Gyles, *Philip and Elizabeth: Portrait of a Marriage* (Century, London, 2004), p. 258.

31 Quoted in Longford, Elizabeth, *Royal Throne* (Hodder & Stoughton, London, 1993), p. 155.

32 Countess Mountbatten of Burma: see Seward, *My Husband and I*, p. 90.

33 Pimlott, op. cit., p. 184.

34 Eade, op. cit., p. 262.

35 Bradford, *Elizabeth*, p. 285.

36 Quoted in *Newcastle Journal*, 12 April 1952.

37 *Lancet*, May 1952.

38 Boothroyd, Basil, *Philip: An Informal Biography of HRH the Duke of Edinburgh* (Longmans, London, 1971), p. 49.

39 *Lancet*, May 1952.

40 Longford, *Elizabeth R*, p. 157.

41 Forster, Margaret, *Daphne du Maurier* (Chatto & Windus, London, 1993), p. 230.

42 Brandreth, Gyles, *Something Sensational to Read in the Train: The Diary of a Lifetime* (John Murray, London, 2009), p. 217.

43 Marie Louise, Her Highness Princess, op. cit., p. 315.

44 Turner, op. cit., p. 46.

45 Pimlott, op. cit., p. 181.

46 Nicolson, Nigel, ed., *Harold Nicolson Diaries and Letters 1945–62* (Collins, London, 1968), p. 220.

47 Turner, op. cit., p. 46.

48 Dismore, op. cit., p. 264.

49 *Dundee Courier*, 5 November 1952.

50 *Birmingham Daily Gazette*, 5 November 1952.

51 Anonymous, 'The Queen, God Bless Her', *Hastings & St Leonards Observer*, 30 May 1953.

52 Queen Mary to Duke of Baena, 18 March 1953, quoted in Pope-Hennessy, James, *Queen Mary* (George Allen and Unwin, London, 1959), p. 621.

53 Bloch, Michael, ed., *James Lees-Milne Diaries 1942–1954* (John Murray, London, 2006), p. 448.

54 Vickers, Hugo, ed., *The Quest for Queen Mary* (Hodder & Stoughton, London, 2018), p. 21.

55 See, for example, *Falkirk Herald*, 30 May 1953.

56 *Daily Express*, quoted in Feingold, Ruth P., 'Marketing the Modern Empire: Elizabeth II and the 1953–1954 World Tour', *Antipodes*, vol. 23, no. 2 (December 2009), pp. 147–54.

57 Lloyd, Christopher, *Ceremony and Celebration: Coronation Day 1953* (Royal Collection Enterprises, London, 2003), p. 29; Eade, op. cit., p. 265.

58 *Yorkshire Post*, 9 February 1952.

59 Alice, HRH Princess, *For My Grandchildren* (Evans, London, 1967), p. 287.

60 Eade, op. cit., p. 278.

61 The Order of Divine Service for Trinity Sunday, 31 May 1953, p. 13.

62 Quoted in Marr, op. cit., p. 159.

63 Channon, op. cit., p. 477.

64 *Western Mail*, 11 November 1952.

65 Martin Longman of the Worshipful Company of Gardeners, quoted in *Coventry Evening Telegraph*, 18 April 1953.

66 In fact the final bouquet included flowers garnered from the four countries of the Union: England, Scotland, Wales and Northern Ireland.

67 Elizabeth Taylor to 'Dear Robert', 10 June 1953, quoted in Spurling, Hilary, *Ivy: The Life of Ivy Compton-*

Burnett (Knopf, New York, 1984), p. 474.

68 Quoted in Williams, op. cit., p. 283.

69 *West Sussex County Times*, 5 June 1953.

70 Paul Gallico, quoted in *Western Mail*, 2 June 1953.

71 Nicolson, *Vita and Harold*, p. 405.

72 *Nottingham Journal*, 22 May 1953; *Coventry Evening Telegraph*, 26 May 1953.

73 *Coventry Evening Telegraph*, 26 May 1953.

74 Parker, Eileen, *Step Aside for Royalty* (Bachman & Turner, London, 1983), p. 130.

75 Quoted in Strong, Roy, *Coronation: A History of Kingship. and the British Monarchy* (HarperCollins, London, 2005), p. 486.

76 Parker, Eileen, op. cit., p. 162.

77 Pottle, op. cit., p. 123.

78 Payn and Morley, op. cit., p. 214.

79 Bloch, op. cit. p. 454.

80 Pick, op. cit., p. 345.

81 Parker, op. cit., p. 129.

82 Healey, Edna, *The Queen's House: A Social History of Buckingham Palace* (Pegasus, London, 2012), p. 342; Lady Raine, quoted in Brown, op. cit., p. 92; Duffy, Carol Ann, 'The Crown'.

83 Alice, HRH Princess, op. cit., p. 287; Campbell-Preston, op. cit., p. 219.

84 Bloch, op. cit., p. 453.

85 Longford, *Royal Throne*, p. 22.

86 Frances Woodsford to Paul Bigelow, 6 June 1953, in Woodsford, Frances, *Dear Mr Bigelow* (Chatto & Windus, London, 2009), pp. 136–7.

87 Parker, op. cit., p. 127.

88 Nicolson, Nigel, *The Queen and Us: The Second Elizabethan Age* (Weidenfeld & Nicolson, London, 2003), p. 31.

89 *Daily Telegraph*, 2 June 2003.

90 Shawcross, *Queen and Country*, p. 54.

CHAPTER X

1 Shawcross, *Official Biography*, p. 686.

2 Cynthia Gladwyn, quoted in Heald, op. cit., p. 155.

3 Princess Margaret to Mrs Douglas, 30 October 1950.

4 Lady Anne Glenconner, quoted in Bedell Smith, op. cit., p. 87.

5 Glendinning, op. cit., p. 170.

6 Queen Elizabeth the Queen Mother to Alan Lascelles, 12 June 1953, in Shawcross, *Counting One's Blessings*, p. 470; Bradford, *Elizabeth*, p. 205.

7 Queen Elizabeth the Queen Mother to Elizabeth II, 10

January 1954, in Shawcross, *Counting One's Blessings*, p. 480.

8 Quoted in Warwick, op. cit., p. 61.

9 Bradford, *Elizabeth*, p. 204.

10 Payn and Morley, op. cit., p. 215.

11 Masefield, John, 'On Our Queen's Going to Her Peoples', *The Times*, 23 November 1953.

12 *Portsmouth Evening News*, 23 November 1953.

13 *Dundee Courier*, 20 November 1953.

14 Queen Elizabeth the Queen Mother to Elizabeth II, 23 November 1953, in Shawcross, *Counting One's Blessings*, p. 474.

15 Shawcross, *Official Biography*, p. 691.

16 Queen Elizabeth the Queen Mother to Princess Margaret, 25 February 1979, in Shawcross, *Counting One's Blessings*, p. 573.

17 Dimbleby, op. cit., p. 23.

18 *Londonderry Sentinel*, 9 January 1954.

19 *Shields Daily News*, 2 March 1954.

20 Shawcross, *Official Biography*, p. 691.

21 Cathcart, op. cit., p. 143.

22 Quoted in Tomlinson, Richard, *Divine Right: The Inglorious Survival of British Royalty* (Little, Brown, London, 1994), p. 224.

23 Longford, *Elizabeth R*, p. 166.

24 Bradford, *Elizabeth*, p. 216.

25 Feingold, op. cit.

26 Bedell Smith, op. cit., p. 102.

27 Shawcross, *Queen and Country*, p. 57.

28 *Sydney Morning Herald*, 18 February 1954.

29 Quoted in Bedell Smith, op. cit., p. 103.

30 Pimlott, op. cit., p. 225.

31 *Belfast Newsletter*, 13 January 1954; Longford, *Elizabeth R*, p. 168.

32 Queen Elizabeth the Queen Mother to Elizabeth II, 10 March 1954, in Shawcross, *Counting One's Blessings*, p. 481.

33 Quoted in Nicolson, *The Queen and Us*, p. 36.

34 Seward, Ingrid, *The Queen's Speech* (Simon & Schuster, London, 2016), p. 59.

35 *Coventry Evening Telegraph*, 11 December 1953.

36 *Birmingham Daily Post*, 1 January 1954.

37 Quoted in Edwards, op. cit., p. 282.

38 Shawcross, *Official Biography*, p. 692.

39 Quoted in Bedell Smith, op. cit., p. 107.

40 Mann, A. C., 'The Queen's Jewels', in *The Queen*, 17 November 1954.

41 Shawcross, *Queen and Country*, p. 63.

42 *Yorkshire Post*, 30 April 1955; *Tatler*, 11 November 1955.

43 Pottle, op. cit., p. 147.

44 Shawcross, *Queen and Country*, p. 70.

45 Pimlott, op. cit., p. 244.

46 Shawcross, *Queen and Country*, p. 71; Bradford, *Elizabeth*, p. 228.

47 Shawcross, *Official Biography*, p. 697.

48 The Prince of Wales, quoted in Dimbleby, op. cit., p. 138.

49 Warwick, op. cit., p. 76.

50 Quoted in Pimlott, op. cit., p. 235.

51 Shawcross, *Official Biography*, p. 700.

52 *Daily Mirror*, 28 October 1955.

53 Shawcross, *Official Biography*, p. 726.

54 Bradford, *Elizabeth*, p. 287.

55 *Coventry Evening Telegraph*, 3 November 1955.

56 *Illustrated London News*, 28 April 1956.

57 Strong, *Cecil Beaton: The Royal Portraits*, p. 124.

58 *Birmingham Daily Post*, 26 January 1956.

59 Longford, *Elizabeth R*, p. 254.

60 Seward, *My Husband and I*, p. 93.

CHAPTER XI

1 *Tatler*, 14 November 1956.

2 *Northern Whig*, 17 October 1956.

3 Parker, op. cit., p. 174.

4 Ibid., p. 181.

5 Bradford, *Elizabeth*, p. 268.

6 Ibid., p. 230.

7 Payn and Morley, op. cit., p. 337.

8 Bradford, *Elizabeth*, p. 234.

9 Ibid., p. 255.

10 Ibid., p. 235.

11 Jebb, op. cit., p. 207.

12 Ibid.

13 Ibid.

14 Brendon and Whitehead, op. cit., p. 152.

15 Bedell Smith, op. cit., p. 130.

16 *Daily Mirror*, 26 September 1956.

17 Ibid.

18 Manser, op. cit., p. 319.

19 Brendon and Whitehead, op. cit., p. 153.

20 Jebb, op. cit., p. 207.

21 *Daily Mirror*, 28 September 1956.

22 Harewood, op. cit., p. 138.

23 Jebb, op. cit., p. 207.

24 *The Times*, 11 January 1957.

25 *Daily Herald*, 12 January 1957.

26 *The Times*, 11 January 1957.

27 Pathé, 'The Queen Leaves for Portugal', 1957.

28 *Lancashire Evening Post*, 18 February 1957.

29 Vickers, *Elizabeth the Queen Mother*, p. 368.

30 *Daily Mirror*, 22 February 1957.

31 Quoted in Bedell Smith, op. cit., p. 114.

32 Princess Elizabeth to Frederick 'Boy' Browning, 26 April 1955.

33 Healey, op. cit., p. 343.

34 Bradford, *Elizabeth*, p. 284.

35 *Daily Mirror*, 6 December 1962.

36 *Liverpool Echo*, 8 August 1957.

37 *Birmingham Daily Post*, 2 November 1957.

38 Vickers, *Quest for Queen Mary*, p. 224.

39 Quoted in *Daily Herald*, 7 August 1957.

40 Quoted in *Coventry Evening Telegraph*, 7 August 1957.

41 Bradford, *Elizabeth*, p. 246.

42 Alistair, 9th Marquess of Londonderry, *New Statesman*, 15 August 1957.

43 Pathé, 'Peer Raises a Storm', 1957.

44 Quoted in *Lancashire Evening Post*, 31 August 1957.

45 Vickers, *Quest for Queen Mary*, p. 222.

46 Pottle, op. cit., p. 167.

47 MacCarthy, Fiona, *The Last Curtsey: The End of the Debutantes* (Faber & Faber, London, 2006), p. 17.

48 Bradford, *Elizabeth*, p. 243.

49 Dennison, *Queen Victoria*, p. 115; Bedell Smith, op. cit., p. 161.

50 Whitehead & Brendon, *The Windsors*, p. 154.

51 Quoted in Bradford, *Elizabeth*, p. 280.

52 Bedell Smith, op. cit. p. 133.

53 Vickers, *Quest for Queen Mary*, p. 222.

54 Seward, *The Queen's Speech*, p. 67.

55 Vickers, *Quest for Queen Mary*, p. 224.

56 *New York Herald Tribune*, 26 December 1957.

57 *People*, 23 March 1958.

58 Queen Elizabeth the Queen Mother to Elizabeth II, 18 February 1958, in Shawcross, *Counting One's Blessings*, p. 499.

59 *Sphere*, 22 November 1958; Pimlott, op. cit., p. 310.

60 Jebb, op. cit., p. 207.

61 Frances Woodsford to Paul Bigelow, 13 April 1957, in Woodsford, op. cit., p. 245.

62 Bradford, *Elizabeth*, p. 243.

63 Quoted in Pimlott, op. cit., p. 302.

64 Bedell Smith, op. cit., p. 163.

65 Queen Elizabeth the Queen Mother to Elizabeth II, 12 April 1956, in Shawcross, *Counting One's Blessings*, p. 494.

66 Shawcross, *Queen and Country*, p. 83.

67 Murphy, Philip, *Monarchy and the End of Empire: The House of Windsor, the British Government and the Postwar Commonwealth* (Oxford University Press, Oxford, 2013), p. 70.
68 Ibid., p. 71.
69 Ibid., p. 74.
70 *Newcastle Evening Chronicle*, 10 February 1960.
71 Macmillan, see Bedell Smith, op. cit., p. 146.
72 Ibid.
73 Vickers, *Quest for Queen Mary*, p. 225.
74 Parker, John, op. cit., p. 202.

75 *Coventry Evening Telegraph*, 27 February 1960.
76 Victoria & Albert Museum, PH.1708-1987.
77 Strong, *Cecil Beaton: The Royal Portraits*, pp. 166–7.
78 Queen Elizabeth the Queen Mother to the Marquess of Salisbury, 23 March 1960, in Shawcross, *Counting One's Blessings*, p. 509.
79 Princess Margaret to Queen Elizabeth the Queen Mother, 16 May 1960, in Shawcross, *Counting One's Blessings*, note p. 510.
80 *Coventry Evening Telegraph*, 5 April 1960.

CHAPTER XII

1 Murphy, op. cit., p. 77.
2 Queen Elizabeth the Queen Mother to Elizabeth II, 10 November 1961, in Shawcross, *Counting One's Blessings*, p. 520.
3 Bradford, *Elizabeth*, p. 298.
4 *Guardian*, 26 November 1961.
5 Pimlott, op. cit., p. 308.
6 Turner, op. cit., p. 115.
7 Queen Elizabeth the Queen Mother to Elizabeth II, 18 October 1982, in Shawcross, *Counting One's Blessings*, p. 580.
8 Turner, op. cit., p. 115.
9 Quoted in Bedell Smith, op. cit., p. 210.
10 Cathcart, Helen, *The Queen Herself* (Star, London, 1983), p. 179.
11 Harewood, op. cit., p. 27.
12 Hibbert, Christopher, *The Court at Windsor: A Domestic History* (Longmans, London, 1964), p. 140.

13 Peacock, Lady, *Their Royal Highnesses Prince Charles and Princess Anne* (Hutchinson, London, 1955), pp. 15–20.
14 Elizabeth II, Christmas broadcast, 1979.
15 Turner, op. cit., p. 115; Elizabeth II to Lady Fermoy, 26 December 1952.
16 *People*, 29 October 1961.
17 Turner, op. cit., p. 117.
18 Queen Elizabeth the Queen Mother to Elizabeth II, 17 February 1961, in Shawcross, *Counting One's Blessings*, p. 513.
19 Elizabeth II, Christmas broadcast 2011.
20 Manser, op. cit., pp. 294, 308.
21 Turner, op. cit., p. 114.
22 Crawford, Marion, *Our Queen Visits Australia and New Zealand* (Dymock's, Sydney, 1954), p. 55.
23 Bradford, *Elizabeth*, p. 327.

24 *People*, 29 October 1961.

25 Frances Woodsford to Paul Bigelow, 17 November 1952, in Woodsford, op. cit., p. 102.

26 Ibid.

27 Quoted in Bedell Smith, Sally, *Charles: The Misunderstood Prince* (Penguin, London, 2017), p. 13.

28 Dimbleby, op. cit., p. 36.

29 Strong, *Cecil Beaton: The Royal Portraits*, p. 167.

30 *Sunday Mirror*, 6 July 1961.

31 Queen Elizabeth to Princess Elizabeth, 12 December 1950, in Shawcross, *Counting One's Blessings*, p. 433.

32 Queen Elizabeth the Queen Mother to Elizabeth II, 23 May 1961, in ibid, p. 516.

33 *Daily Herald*, 31 July 1961.

34 See Turner, op. cit., p. 120.

35 Beaton, Cecil, *Beaton in the Sixties: More Unexpurgated Diaries* (Weidenfeld & Nicolson, London, 2003), p. 231.

36 Sheridan, Lisa, *A Day with Prince Andrew* (Hodder & Stoughton, London, 1962), p. 1.

37 Whittle, Peter, *Monarchy Matters* (Social Affairs Unit, London 2011), p. 19.

38 *Sunday Express*, 22 October 1961.

39 Quoted in Pimlott, op. cit., p. 282; Dimbleby, op. cit., p. 101.

40 Beaton, op. cit., p. 146.

41 Prochaska, Frank, *Royal Bounty: The Making of a Welfare Monarchy* (Yale University Press, London, 1995), p. 254.

42 Williams, Marcia, *Inside Number 10* (Weidenfeld & Nicolson, London, 1972), p. 17.

43 Queen Elizabeth the Queen Mother to Cecil Beaton, 20 February 1964, in Shawcross, *Counting One's Blessings*, p. 527.

44 Dimbleby, op. cit., p. 494.

45 Ted Hughes to Frieda Hughes, 23 November 1974, in Reid, Christopher, ed., *Letters of Ted Hughes* (Faber & Faber, London, 2009), p. 357.

46 Pimlott, op. cit., p. 317.

47 Pathé, 'Royal Decade', 1962.

48 Quoted in *Birmingham Daily Post*, 4 March 1963.

49 Partridge, Frances, *Hanging On: Diaries 1960–1963* (William Collins, London, 1990), p. 171.

50 Bedell Smith, *Elizabeth*, p. 162; *Daily Mirror*, 10 June 1963.

51 *Daily Mirror*, 10 June 1963.

52 Ibid., 24 June 1963.

53 Vickers, Hugo, *The Crown: Truth and Fiction* (Zuleika, London, 2017), p. 49.

54 *Daily Mirror*, 14 October 1963.

55 Longford, *Elizabeth R*, p. 240.

56 Turner, op. cit., p. 89.

57 *Coventry Evening Telegraph*, 18 October 1963.

58 *Daily Mirror*, 14 October 1963.

59 Bradford, *Elizabeth*, p. 324.

60 Elizabeth II to Helen Rowe, 5 August 1964.

61 Mayer, Catherine, *Charles: The Heart of a King* (W. H. Allen, London, 2015), p. 98.

62 Reynelle, Margaret, *The 1973 Royal Family Yearbook* (Clipper Press, 1973), p. 9.

CHAPTER XIII

1   Beaton, op. cit., p. 270.

2   *Sunday Telegraph*, 22 January 1967.

3   *Illustrated London News*, 10 June 1967; Partridge, Frances, *Good Company: Diaries 1967–70* (HarperCollins, London, 1994), p. 2.

4   Seward, *My Husband and I*, p. 154.

5   Pearson, John, *The Ultimate Family: The Making of the Royal House of Windsor* (Michael Joseph, London, 1986), p. 167.

6   Roy Hattersley, quoted in Shawcross, *Queen and Country*, p. 113.

7   Winstone, Ruth, ed., *The Benn Diaries* (Hutchinson, London, 1995), p. 181.

8   *Liverpool Echo*, 8 September 1966.

9   *Daily Express*, 19 May 1965.

10 *Guardian* , 2 February 1965.

11 *Daily Mirror*, 28 October 1966.

12 *People*, 30 October 1966.

13 Ibid.

14 *Daily Mirror*, 20 June 1969.

15 Beaton, op. cit., p. 343.

16 Pimlott, op. cit., p. 379.

17 Beaton, op cit., p. 146.

18 *Daily Mirror*, 20 June 1969.

19 Beaton, op. cit., p. 342.

20 Payn and Morley, op. cit., p. 634.

21 Whittle, op. cit., p. 18.

22 Tomlinson, op. cit., p. 218.

23 *Daily Mirror*, 3 January 1967.

24 Pottle, op. cit., pp. 341–2.

25 *Birmingham Daily Post*, 2 July 1969.

26 Pick, op. cit., p. 435; Jebb, op. cit., p. 346.

27 Payn and Morley, op. cit., p. 678.

28 Jebb, op. cit., p. 346.

29 Clark, Brigadier Stanley, *Palace Diary* (George G. Harrap & Co., London, 1958), p. 202.

30 Pearson, op. cit., p. 197.

31 Garfield, op. cit., p. 364.

32 Pearson, op. cit., p. 199.

33 Winstone, op. cit., pp. 211–12.

34 Shawcross, *Crown and Country*, p. 113.

35 Clark, op. cit., p. 5.

36 Grenfell, Joyce, *In Pleasant Places* (Macmillan, London, 1979), p. 275.

37 Clark, op. cit., p. 174.

38 Partridge, Frances, *Other People: Diaries 1963–66* (HarperCollins, London, 1993), p. 100.

39 Hibbert, Christopher, *The Court at Windsor* (Prentice Hall Press, London 1972), p. 149.

40 Bedell Smith, *Elizabeth*, p. 175.

41 Healey, op. cit., p. 357.

42 Quoted in Pearson, op. cit., p. 186.

43 Quoted in Pimlott, op. cit., p. 344.

44 Bradford, *Elizabeth*, p. 321.

45 Quoted in Pimlott, op. cit., p. 358.

46 Quoted in Bradford, *Elizabeth*, p. 322.

47 Monica Davies, *Illustrated London News*, 2 March 1968.

48 David Gentleman to Antony Wedgwood Benn, undated (January 1965).

49 Winstone, op. cit., p. 126.

50 Ibid., p. 127.

51 Wilson, A. N., *The Queen* (Atlantic, London, 2016), p. 144.

52 Winstone, op. cit., p. 142.

53 Ibid., p. 140.

54 Quoted in *Liverpool Echo*, 6 March 1967.

55 Elizabeth II, Christmas broadcast, 1969.

56 Quoted in Bradford, *Elizabeth*, p. 409.

57 Fitzalan Howard, *The Windsor Diaries*, p. 108.

58 See *Antiques Trade Gazette*, 19 March 2019.

59 See Carpenter, Humphrey, *Benjamin Britten: A Biography* (Faber & Faber, London, 1992), p. 464.

60 Brandreth, op. cit., p. 161.

61 Heald, op. cit., p. 195.

62 *Aberdeen Press & Journal*, 2 October 1967.

63 Quoted in Strong, Roy, *The Roy Strong Diaries 1967–87* (Weidenfeld & Nicolson, London, 1997), p. 179.

64 See *Design* (November 1960), published by the Council of Industrial Design.

65 Cathcart, *The Queen Herself*, p. 196.

66 *Inside Page* magazine, quoted in *Daily Mirror*, 29 September 1969; quoted in Pimlott, op. cit., p. 251.

67 Pearson, op. cit., p. 190.

68 Shawcross, *Crown and Country*, p. 230.

69 *Daily Mirror*, 29 September 1969.

70 Ibid., 2 March 1970.

71 Grenfell, *In Pleasant Places*, p. 213.

72 Winstone, op. cit., p. 423.

CHAPTER XIV

1 Shawcross, *Crown and Country*, p. 117.

2 Whittle, op. cit., p. 49.

3 British Movietone, 1972.

4 *Daily Telegraph*, 21 October 1969.

5 Quoted in Heald, op. cit., p. 174.

6 Murphy, op. cit., pp. 107–8.

7 Pimlott, op. cit., p. 425.

8 Quoted in Hardman, op. cit., p. 146.

9 Heath, Edward, *The Course of My Life* (Hodder & Stoughton, London, 1998), p. 391.

10 *Guardian*, 13 October 1972.

11 Beaton, *The Unexpurgated Beaton* (Weidenfeld & Nicolson, London, 2002), p. 244; Brandreth, op. cit., p. 236.

12 Beaton, *The Unexpurgated Beaton*, p. 335.

13 Grenfell, *In Pleasant Places*, p. 277.

14 Ibid.

15 Ted Hughes to Frieda Hughes, 23 November 1974, in Reid, op. cit., p. 356.

16 Grenfell, *In Pleasant Places*, p. 279.

17 *Daily Mirror*, 31 July 1975.

18 Ibid.

19 Pimlott, op. cit., p. 454.

20 Quoted in Bedell Smith, *Elizabeth*, p. 259.

21 *Daily Mirror*, 8 February 1977.

22 Hamilton, Willie, *My Queen and I* (Quartet Books, London, 1975), p. 182.

23 Elizabeth II to Hardy Amies, quoted in Pimlott, op. cit., p. 423.

24 Bedell Smith, *Elizabeth*, p. 258.

25 *Liverpool Echo*, 6 December 1976.

26 Seward, *The Queen's Speech*, p. 107.

27 Amies, Hardy, *Still Here: An Autobiography* (Weidenfeld & Nicolson, London, 1984), p. 109.

28 Pimlott, op. cit., p. 450; Ziegler, Philip, *Crown and People* (HarperCollins, London, 1978), p. 183.

29 John Masefield, 'On the Coming Marriage of the Princess Elizabeth', 1947.

30 Lacey, op. cit., p. 246.

31 *Daily Mail*, 8 June 1977.

32 Strong, *The Roy Strong Diaries 1967–87*, p. 194.

33 Ibid.

34 Ibid., p. 193.

35   Quoted in Bedell Smith, *Elizabeth*, p. 245.
36   Manser, op. cit., p. 315.
37   John Grigg, *Sunday Times*, quoted in Pimlott, op. cit., p. 452.
38   Ibid.
39   Larkin, Philip, *Selected Poems* (Faber & Faber, London, 2001), p. 210.
40   *Daily Mirror*, 5 February 1982.
41   Longford, *Elizabeth R*, p. 279.
42   Shawcross, *Official Biography*, p. 805.
43   Seward, *My Husband and I*, p. 254.
44   William Heseltine, 17 March 1978, quoted in *Reading Evening Post*, 2 May 1978.
45   Quoted in Heald, op. cit., p. 197.
46   Queen Elizabeth the Queen Mother to Elizabeth II, 25 April 1976, in Shawcross, *Counting One's Blessings*, p. 563.

47   Strong, *The Roy Strong Diaries 1967–87*, p. 283.
48   Galli Pahlavi, Anna, ed., *The Diaries of Auberon Waugh: A Turbulent Decade 1976–85* (Private Eye/Andre Deutsch, London, 1985), p. 49.
49   For example, see *Birmingham Daily Post*, 10 November 1977.
50   Bedell Smith, *Charles*, p. 116.
51   Ibid., p. 111.
52   Ziegler, *Mountbatten*, p. 686.
53   Shawcross, *Crown and Country*, p. 130.
54   Dimbleby, op. cit., p. 261.
55   *Leicester Chronicle*, 21 October 1977.
56   Ziegler, *Mountbatten*, p. 699.
57   Bedell Smith, *Charles*, p. 119.
58   Marr, op. cit., pp. 277–8.
59   Elizabeth II to Mrs Tanner, 26 April 1972.

CHAPTER XV

1   *Zambia Daily Mail*, 1 August 1979, quoted in Brendon and Whitehead, op. cit., p. 195.
2   Winstone, op. cit., p. 439.
3   Ibid., p. 473.
4   Michael Gill, quoted in Plumb, J. H., and Weldon, Huw, *Royal Heritage* (BBC Books, London, 1977), p. 331.
5   *Daily Mirror*, 14 September 1982.
6   Quoted in Hoey, Brian, *Her Majesty: 60 Regal Years* (Robson Press, London, 2012), p. 20.
7   Elizabeth II, *Elizabeth R*, 1992.
8   Thorpe, Richard, ed., *Who Loses, Who Wins: The Journals of Kenneth Rose Volume Two 1979–2014* (Weidenfeld & Nicolson, London, 2019), p. 124.
9   Turner, op. cit., p. 179.

10   Lees-Milne, James, *Deep Romantic Chasm, Diaries 1979–81* (John Murray, London, 2000), p. 74.
11   *Daily Mirror*, 7 July 1979.
12   *Newcastle Journal*, 30 July 1986.
13   *Birmingham Daily Post*, 3 August 1979.
14   *The Queen and Commonwealth*, Thames Television, 1986.
15   Elizabeth II, Christmas broadcast, 1980.
16   Morrow, op. cit., p. 149.
17   *Newcastle Journal*, 30 July 1986.
18   Queen Elizabeth the Queen Mother to the Prince of Wales, 6 August 1984, in Shawcross, *Counting One's Blessings*, p. 587; Ted Hughes to Frieda Hughes, 23 November 1974, in Reid, op. cit., p. 357.
19   Hardman, op. cit., p. 336.

20 Strong, *The Roy Strong Diaries 1967–87*, p. 264.

21 Queen Elizabeth the Queen Mother to Princess Margaret, 5 August 1980, in Shawcross, *Counting One's Blessings*, pp. 575–6.

22 Shawcross, *Official Biography*, p. 862.

23 Barratt, John, *With the Greatest Respect: The Private Lives of Earl Mountbatten and Prince and Princess Michael of Kent* (Sidgwick & Jackson, London, 1979), p. 79.

24 Quoted in Mayer, op. cit., p. 97; Queen Elizabeth the Queen Mother to the Prince of Wales, 19 April 1983, in Shawcross, *Counting One's Blessings*, p. 584.

25 *Daily Mirror*, 18 November 1980.

26 Seward, *My Husband and I*, p. 165.

27 Vickers, *Elizabeth the Queen Mother*, p. 424.

28 Ibid.

29 Thorpe, op. cit., 24 February 1981, p. 34.

30 Quoted in *Newcastle Journal*, 26 March 1981.

31 Seward, Ingrid, *The Queen and Di* (HarperCollins, London, 2000), p. 48.

32 Bennett, Alan, *Writing Home: Diaries* (Faber & Faber, London, 1994), p. 310.

33 Amies, op. cit., p. 112.

34 Ibid., p. 159.

35 *Daily Mirror*, 15 June 1981.

36 *Sunday Mirror*, 14 June 1981.

37 *Elizabeth at 90: A Family Tribute*, BBC, 2016.

38 For example, see *Liverpool Echo*, 16 June 1981.

39 *Reading Evening Post*, 16 June 1981.

40 Ruth, Lady Fermoy, quoted in Strong, *The Roy Strong Diaries 1967–87*, p. 317.

41 Ibid., p. 315.

42 Harold Wilson quoted in *Reading Evening Post*, 4 February 1982.

43 Winstone, op. cit., p. 532.

44 Elizabeth II, Christmas broadcast, 1982.

45 Quoted in Brendon and Whitehead, op. cit., p. 203.

46 Ibid., p. 204.

47 Harold Wilson quoted in *Reading Evening Post*, 4 February 1982.

48 *Illustrated London News*, 1 August 1982.

49 Pimlott, op. cit., p. 488.

50 For example, see *Daily Mirror*, 21 September 1982.

51 *Aberdeen Evening Express*, 22 November 1982.

52 Andrew Morton, quoted in Mayer, op. cit., p. 116.

53 *Liverpool Echo*, 4 October 1982.

54 Adie, Kate, *The Autobiography: The Kindness of Strangers* (Headline, London, 2003), p. 221.

55 Ibid.

56 *Maclean's* magazine, 21 March 1983.

57 Powell, Antony, *Journals 1982–6* (Heinemann, London, 1995), p. 210.

58 *Illustrated London News*, 1 April 1986.

59 Letter, Elizabeth II, undated (April 1986).

60 Kavanagh, op. cit., p. 587.

61 Lees-Milne, James, *Holy Dread Diaries 1982–4* (John Murray, London, 2001), p. 16.

62 Ibid.

63 Queen Elizabeth the Queen Mother to Elizabeth II, 10 April 1986, in Shawcross, *Counting One's Blessings*, p. 589.

64 Strong, *The Roy Strong Diaries 1967–87*, pp. 361–2.

65 *New York Times*, 5 October 1984.

66 Ibid.
67 Elizabeth II, Christmas broadcast, 1986.
68 Powell, op. cit., p. 254.
69 *Sunday Tribune*, 27 July 1986.
70 *Sunday Times*, 20 July 1986.
71 Turner, op. cit., p. 182.
72 *Spectator*, 3 December 1937.
73 *Newcastle Journal*, 15 June 1987.
74 *Liverpool Echo*, 19 June 1987.
75 Barnes, Julian, *Letters from London 1990–1995* (Jonathan Cape, London, 1998), p. 159.

76 Hardman, Robert, *Our Queen* (Random House, London, 2011), p. 83.
77 Pearson, op. cit., p. 295.
78 Seward, Ingrid, *Prince Philip Revealed* (Simon & Schuster, London, 2020), p. 186.
79 Quoted in ibid, p. 243.
80 *Daily Mirror*, 13 June 1987.
81 Lady Selina Hastings, quoted in Heald, op. cit., p. 245.

CHAPTER XVI

1 Strong, *The Roy Strong Diaries 1967–87*, p. 430.
2 Lacey, op. cit., p. 299.
3 Hardman, *Our Queen*, p. 79.
4 Ibid., p. 81.
5 *Irish Independent*, 6 January 1989.
6 Bennett, op. cit., p. 233.
7 *Guardian*, 23 February 1991.
8 Seward, *Prince Philip Revealed*, p. 333.
9 *Liverpool Echo*, 12 February 1991.
10 *The Times*, 26 February 1991.
11 Shawcross, *Crown and Country*, p. 186.
12 Lees-Milne, James, *Milk of Paradise: Diaries 1993–7* (John Murray, London, 2005), p. 47.
13 Vickers, *Quest for Queen Mary*, p. 224.
14 Lees-Milne, James, *Ceaseless Turmoil: Diaries 1988–92* (John Murray, London, 2004), p. 288.
15 See Wilson, Mary, *New Poems* (Hutchinson, London, 1979).
16 Edward Mirzoeff interview in *Christian Science Monitor*, 10 September 1992.
17 Queen Elizabeth the Queen Mother to Elizabeth II, 3 February 1993, in Shawcross, *Counting One's Blessings*, p. 605.
18 Queen Elizabeth the Queen Mother to Elizabeth II, 5 February 1992, in ibid, p. 603.
19 Hughes, Ted, *Rain Charm for the Duchy* (Faber & Faber, London, 1992), p. 61.
20 *Independent*, 13 December 1992.
21 Hoey, op. cit., p. 139.
22 Quoted in Wilson, *The Queen*, p. 53.
23 Wilson, A. N., *Our Times: The Age of Elizabeth II* (Hutchinson, London, 2008), p. 321.
24 Turner, Graham, op cit., p. 5.
25 Lees-Milne, *Ceaseless Turmoil*, p. 296.
26 Elizabeth II to Cyril and Iris Woods, undated (19 December 1992).
27 Thorpe, op. cit., p. 322.
28 *Daily Telegraph*, 25 November 1992.
29 *The Times*, 26 November 1992.
30 Brandreth, op. cit., p. 543.
31 Queen Elizabeth the Queen Mother to Elizabeth II, 3 February 1993, in Shawcross, *Counting One's Blessings*, p. 605.

32 Tony Banks MP, quoted in *Washington Post*, 10 December 1992.

33 Brendon and Whitehead, op. cit., p. 240.

34 Vickers, *Elizabeth the Queen Mother*, p. 475.

35 Shawcross, *Official Biography*, pp. 898–9.

36 Hoey, op. cit., p. 139.

37 Shawcross, *Official Biography*, p. 896.

38 Seward, *Prince Philip Revealed*, pp. 294–5.

39 Prince of Wales to Marjorie Dawson, 25 July 1994.

40 For example, see Dimbleby, op. cit., p. 49.

41 Lloyd, op. cit., p. 108.

42 *Washington Post*, 18 October 1994.

43 *Daily Mirror*, 9 March 1995.

44 *Sunday Tribune*, 12 March 1995.

45 Hardman, *Queen of the World*, p. 409.

46 Sampson, Anthony, *Mandela: The Authorised Biography* (HarperCollins, London, 1999), p. xxiii.

47 Sir Antony Reeve to Douglas Hurd, 5 April 1995.

48 Thorpe, op. cit., p. 272.

49 Ibid., p. 271.

50 Ibid., p. 283.

51 Pimlott, op. cit., p. 575.

52 *Kilroy*, BBC1, 21 November 1997.

53 Winstone, Ruth, ed., *Free at Last: Tony Benn Diaries 1991–2001* (Hutchinson, London, 2002), p. 341.

54 Quoted in Bedell Smith, *Elizabeth*, p. 386.

55 *Herald*, 18 March 1996.

56 *Daily Telegraph*, 'Elizabeth: A Life in Pictures' (April 1996).

57 Whittle, op. cit., p. 21.

58 *Witness History*, BBC World Service.

59 *Liverpool Echo*, 12 February 1991.

60 Lees-Milne, *The Milk of Paradise*, p. 288.

61 Lacey, Robert, *Battle of Brothers* (Williams Collins, London, 2020), p. 19.

62 Brandreth, op. cit., p. 629.

63 Quoted in Bedell Smith, *Elizabeth*, p. 401.

64 Lacey, *Majesty*, p. 379.

65 Elizabeth II to Henriette Abel Smith, 12 September 1997.

66 Quoted in Shawcross, *Official Biography*, p. 911.

67 Sir Kenneth Scott to Richard Williams, 5 May 1995.

CHAPTER XVII

1 Seward, *My Husband and I*, p. 283.

2 Strong, *Scenes and Apparitions*, p. 249.

3 Ted Hughes to Hilda Farrar, 19 October 1998, in Reid, op. cit., p. 738.

4 Bedell Smith, *Charles*, p. 327.

5 The Gloucestershire estate, near Tetbury, was purchased by the Duchy of Cornwall in 1980.

6 Turner, op. cit., p. 166.

7 *Sunday Tribune*, 10 January 1999.

8 *Illustrated London News*, 1 June 1999.

9 Another eighteenth-century house in southern Gloucestershire, six miles from Highgrove.

10 Strong, *Scenes and Apparitions*, p. 300.

11 Marr, op. cit., p. 348.

12 Seward, *The Queen's Speech*, p. 172.

13 Glenconner, Anne, *Lady in Waiting* (Hodder & Stoughton, London, 2019), pp. 281–2.

14 Thorpe, op. cit., p. 377.

15 *Tablet*, 21 October 2000.

16 Strong, *Scenes and Apparitions*, p. 377.

17 Shawcross, *Official Biography*, p. 935.

18 *Daily Mail*, 1 June 2002.

19 *Memoirs of HRH Prince Christopher of Greece* (Hurst & Blackett, London, 1938), p. 161.

20 Seward, *Prince Philip Revealed*, p. 180.

21 See Bedell Smith, Sally, op. cit. *Charles*, p. 385.

22 Strong, *Scenes and Apparitions*, p. 418.

23 *Daily Telegraph*, 1 June 2003.

24 Turner, op. cit., p. 163; Bedell Smith, *Charles*, p. 360.

25 See *Daily Telegraph*, 16 August 2001.

26 Quoted in Daily *Telegraph*, 27 October 2002.

27 Thorpe, op. cit., p. 386.

28 Lady Susan Hussey to Marjorie Dawson, 14 May 2003.

29 *Daily Telegraph*, 20 April 2006.

30 Winstone, Ruth, ed., *More Time for Politics: Tony Benn Diaries 2001–2007* (Hutchinson, London, 2007), p. 336.

31 Prince Philip, Duke of Edinburgh to Daphne du Maurier, 26 May 1977.

32 *Daily Telegraph*, 4 February 2007.

33 Ibid.

CHAPTER XVIII

1 *Daily Telegraph*, 6 October 2010.

2 *Monarchy: The Royal Family at Work*, BBC, 2007.

3 Quoted in Bedell Smith, *Elizabeth*, p. 497.

4 *Daily Telegraph*, 17 January 2010.

5 *Daily Express*, 12 October 2012.

6 'Profile' (Christopher Geidt), 10 May 2015, Radio 4; *Guardian*, 23 November 2019.

7 'Profile' (Christopher Geidt).

8 Ibid., Dr Jonathan Eyal.

9 *Country Life*, 20 April 2011.

10 Seward, *Prince Philip Revealed*, p. 325.

11 Bedell Smith, *Elizabeth*, p. 465.

12 Thorpe, op. cit., p. 430; *Daily Telegraph*, 22 November 2013.

13 Elizabeth II, Christmas broadcast, 2012.

14 *Daily Telegraph*, 6 June 2012.

15 Carol Ann Duffy quoted in *Irish Times*, 2 May 2009.

16 Philip, HRH Prince, Duke of Edinburgh, *A Question of Balance* (Michael Russell, London, 1982), see chapter entitled 'Satisfaction and Contentment'.

17 Elizabeth II, Christmas broadcast, 2018.

18 Lacey, *Battle of Brothers*, p. 270.

19 Dunne, E., and Sutcliffe, H., *101 Reasons Why We Love the Queen* (Short Books, London, 2020), p. 93.

20 *Daily Telegraph*, 24 December 2019.

21 Quoted in Bradford, Sarah, *Queen Elizabeth II: Her Life in Our Times* (Viking, London, 2011).

BIBLIOGRAPHY

Among those I interviewed during research for this book were some who asked to remain unidentified; I have extended this confidentiality to all the interviewees whose information and opinions shaped this account and whose views are embedded within the text. Listed below are the principal secondary sources consulted during my research; several, written over the long span of the Queen's reign, have themselves become primary sources. These published accounts were an aspect of my research, alongside unpublished written sources in public and private collections, the archives of national and regional newspapers and magazines, newsreel and television footage.

Adie, Kate, *The Kindness of Strangers: An Autobiography* (Headline, London, 2002)

Alexandra, Queen of Yugoslavia, *Prince Philip: A Family Portrait* (Bobbs-Merrill, New York, 1959)

Alice, Princess, Countess of Athlone, *For My Grandchildren* (Evans Brothers, London, 1966)

Alice, Princess, Duchess of Gloucester, *The Memoirs of Princess Alice, Duchess of Gloucester* (Collins, London, 1983)

Amies, Hardy, *Still Here: An Autobiography* (Weidenfeld & Nicolson, London, 1984)

Asquith, Lady Cynthia, *The Duchess of York* (Hutchinson & Co, London, 1926)

——, *The King's Daughters* (Hutchinson & Co, London, 1937)

——, *The Family Life of Queen Elizabeth* (Hutchinson & Co, London, 1937)

Barratt, John, *With the Greatest Respect: The Private Lives of Earl Mountbatten and Prince & Princess Michael of Kent* (Sidgwick & Jackson, London, 1991)

Basford, Elizabeth, *Princess Mary* (The History Press, Stroud, 2020)

Bath and Wells, Bishop of, et al, *The Coronation Book of Queen Elizabeth II* (Odhams, London, 1953)

Beckles, Gordon, *Coronation Souvenir Book 1937* (Daily Express Publications, London, 1937)

Bedell Smith, Sally, *Elizabeth the Queen* (Penguin, London, 2012)

——, *Charles: The Misunderstood Prince* (Penguin, London, 2017)

Bennett, Alan, *Writing Home* (Faber & Faber, London, 1995)

Blair, Tony, *A Journey* (Hutchinson, London, 2010)

Bogdanor, Vernon, *The Monarchy and the Constitution* (OUP, Oxford, 1995)

Boothroyd, Basil, *Philip: An Informal Biography* (Longman, London, 1971)

Bradford, Sarah, *George VI* (Weidenfeld & Nicolson, London, 1989)

——, *Elizabeth* (William Heinemann, London, 1996)

——, *Queen Elizabeth II: Her Life in Our Times* (Viking, London, 2011)

Bradley, Ian, *God Save the Queen: The Spiritual Dimension of Monarchy* (Darton, Longman & Todd, London, 2002)

Brandreth, Gyles, *Philip and Elizabeth: Portrait of a Marriage* (Century, London, 2004)

——, *Something Sensational to Read in the Train: The Diary of a Lifetime* (John Murray, London, 2009)

Brendon, Piers, & Whitehead, Phillip, *The Windsors: A Dynasty Revealed 1917–2000* (Pimlico, London, 2000)

Brooke-Little, John, *Royal Ceremonies of State* (Country Life Books, London, 1980)

Brown, Craig, *Ma'am Darling: 99 Glimpses of Princess Margaret* (Fourth Estate, London, 2018

Brown, Susanna, *Queen Elizabeth II: Portraits by Cecil Beaton* (V&A Publishing, London, 2011)

Burnet, Alistair, *In Private – In Public: The Prince and Princess of Wales* (ITN books, London, 1986)

Campbell-Preston, Frances, & Vickers, Hugo, ed., *The Rich Spoils of Time* (The Dovecote Press, Wimborne Minster, 2006)

Cannadine, David, *Margaret Thatcher: A Life & Legacy* (OUP, Oxford, 2017)

Carpenter, Humphrey, *Benjamin Britten: A Biography* (Faber & Faber, London, 1993)

Cathcart, Helen, *The Queen in her Circle* (W. H. Allen, London, 1977)

——, *The Queen Herself* (Star, London, 1983)

Clark, Brigadier Stanley, *Palace Diary* (George G. Harrap & Co., London, 1958)

Colville, John, *The Fringes of Power: Downing Street Diaries 1939–1955* (Hodder & Stoughton, London, 1989)

Cornforth, John, *Queen Elizabeth the Queen Mother at Clarence House* (Michael Joseph, London, 1996)

Cumming, Valerie, *Royal Dress* (B. T. Batsford, London, 1989)

d'Abo, Lady Ursula, *The Girl with the Widow's Peak: The Memoirs* (d'Abo Publications, London, 2014)

de Courcy, Anne, *Snowdon* (Weidenfeld & Nicolson, London, 2008)

Dimbleby, Jonathan, *The Prince of Wales: A Biography* (Little, Brown & Company, London, 1994)

Dismore, Jane, *Princess: The Early Life of Queen Elizabeth II* (LP, Guilford, Connecticut, 2018)

Donaldson, Frances, *King George VI and Queen Elizabeth* (Weidenfeld & Nicolson, London, 1977)

Duff, David, *Queen Mary* (William Collins, London, 1985)

——, *George & Elizabeth* (William Collins, London, 1983)

Duncan, Andrew, *The Reality of Monarchy* (William Heinemann, London, 1970)

Dunne, E., & Sutcliffe, H., *101 Reasons Why We Love the Queen* (Short Books, London, 2020)

Eastoe, Jane, *Elizabeth Reigning in Style* (Pavilion, London, 2012)

Edwards, Anne, *Matriarch Queen Mary & the House of Windsor* (Hodder & Stoughton, London, 1984)

——, *The Queen's Clothes* (Elm Tree Books, London, 1977)

——, *Royal Sisters* (William Morrow & Company, New York, 1990)

Elborn, Geoffrey, *Princess Alexandra* (Sheldon Press, London, 1982)

Ellis, Jennifer, ed., *Thatched with Gold: The Memoirs of Mabell, Countess of Airlie* (Hutchinson, London, 1962)

Ferrier, Neil, *The Queen Elizabeth Coronation Book* (L. T. A. Robinson, London, 1953)

Field, Leslie, *The Queen's Jewels* (Weidenfeld & Nicolson, London, 1987)

Ford, Colin, ed., *Happy and Glorious: 130 Years of Royal Photographs* (National Portrait Gallery, London, 1977)

Galli-Pahlavi, Anna, ed., *A Turbulent Decade: The Diaries of Auberon Waugh 1976–1985* (Private Eye/Andre Deutsch, London, 1985)

Garrett, Richard, *Royal Travel* (Blandford Press, Poole, 1982)

Glenconner, Anne, *Lady in Waiting: My Extraordinary Life in the Shadow of the Crown* (Hodder & Stoughton, London, 2019)

Girouard, Mark, *Windsor: The Most Romantic Castle* (Hodder & Stoughton, London, 1993)

Gordon, Sophie, *Noble Hounds and Dear Companions* (Royal Collection, London, 2007)

Graham, Tim, *The Royal Year 1994* (Michael O Mara Books, London, 1994)

Greig, Geordie, *Louis and the Prince* (Hodder & Stoughton, London, 1999)

Grenfell, Joyce, *In Pleasant Places* (Macmillan, London, 1979)

Hall, Phillip, *Royal Fortune: Tax, Money & the Monarchy* (Bloomsbury, London, 1992)

Hardman, Robert, *Our Queen* (Hutchinson, London, 2011)

——, *Queen of the World* (Century, London, 2018)

Harewood, Lord, *The Tongs and the Bones* (Weidenfeld & Nicolson, London, 1981)

Harris, Kenneth, *The Queen* (Weidenfeld & Nicolson, London, 1994)

Hartnell, Norman, *Silver and Gold* (Evans Brothers, London, 1955)

Heald, Tim, *The Duke: A Portrait of Prince Philip* (Hodder & Stoughton, London, 1991)

——, *Princess Margaret: A Life Unravelled* (Weidenfeld & Nicolson, London, 2007)

Healey, Edna, *The Queen's House* (Pegasus, New York, 1998)

Heighway, Lisa, *Marcus Adams: Royal Photographer* (Royal Collection Publications, London, 2010)

Hibbert, Christopher, *The Court of St James's* (Weidenfeld & Nicolson, London, 1979)

Hoey, Brian, *At Home with the Queen* (HarperCollins, London, 2002)

——, *Her Majesty: 60 Regal Years* (The Robson Press, London, 2012)

Howard, Anthony, ed., *The Crossman Diaries Selections from the Diaries of a Cabinet Minister 1964–70* (Hamish Hamilton, London, 1979)

Hussey, Christopher, *Clarence House* (Country Life Books, London, 1949)

Jay, Anthony, *Elizabeth R: The Role of the Monarchy Today* (BBC Books, London, 1992)

——, *Confessions of a Reformed BBC Producer* (Centre for Policy Studies, London, 2007)

Jebb, Miles, ed., *The Diaries of Cynthia Gladwyn* (Constable, London, 1995)

Judd, Denis, *Prince Philip: A Biography* (Michael Joseph, London, 1980)

Junor, Penny, *The Firm: The Troubled Life of the House of Windsor* (HarperCollins, London, 2006)

Kelleway, Philip, *Highly Desirable: The Zinkeisen Sisters & their Legacy* (Leiston Press, 2016)

Kelly, Angela, *The Other Side of the Coin: The Queen, the Dresser and the Wardrobe* (HarperCollins, London, 2019)

Lacey, Robert, *God Bless Her! Queen Elizabeth the Queen Mother* (Century, London, 1987)

——, *Royal* (Little, Brown, London, 2002)

——, *Battle of Brothers* (William Collins, London, 2020)

Laredo, Rodney, *Informally Royal: Studio Lisa and the Royal Family 1936–66* (The History Press, Stroud, 2019)

Laird, Dorothy, *Queen Elizabeth the Queen Mother* (Hodder & Stoughton, London, 1966)

Lees-Milne, James, *Caves of Ice & Midway on the Waves: Diaries 1946–49* (John Murray repr., London, 1996)

——, *Diaries 1942–54* (John Murray, London, 2006)

——, *Deep Romantic Chasm: Diaries 1979–81* (John Murray, London, 2000)

——, *Holy Dread: Diaries 1982–84* (John Murray, London, 2001)

——, *Beneath a Waning Moon: Diaries 1985–87* (John Murray, London, 2003)

——, *Ceaseless Turmoil Diaries 1988–92* (John Murray, London, 2004)

——, *The Milk of Paradise: Diaries 1993–97* (John Murray, London, 2005)

Le Hardy, William, *The Coronation Book 1953* (Staples, Rochester, 1953)

Lloyd, Christopher, *Ceremony & Celebration: Coronation Day 1953* (Royal Collection, London, 2003)

Lloyd, Ian, *The Duke* (The History Press, Cheltenham, 2021)

Longford, Elizabeth, *The Queen Mother: A Biography* (Weidenfeld & Nicolson, London, 1981)

——, *Elizabeth R* (Weidenfeld & Nicolson, London, 1983)

——, *Royal Throne: The Future of the Monarchy* (Hodder & Stoughton, London, 1993)

MacCarthy, Fiona, *Last Curtsey: The End of the English Debutante* (Faber & Faber, London, 2006)

Machin, Arnold, *Artist of an Icon* (Frontier Publishing, Kirstead, 2002)

Maclean, Veronica, *Past Forgetting* (Headline Review, London, 2002)

Marie Louise, Princess, *My Memories of Six Reigns* (Evans Brothers, London, 1956)

Marr, Andrew, *The Diamond Queen* (Macmillan, London, 2011)

Matson, John, *Sandringham Days: The Domestic Life of the Royal Family in Norfolk 1862–1952* (History Press, Stroud, 2013)

Mayer, Catherine, *Charles: The Heart of a King* (W. H. Allen, London, 2015)

McDowell, Colin, *A Hundred Years of Royal Style* (Muller, Blond & White, London, 1985)

Menkes, Suzy, *The Royal Jewels* (Grafton, London, 1985)

Middleboe, Penelope, ed., *Edith Olivier: From her Journals 1924–48* (Weidenfeld & Nicolson, London, 1989)

Moore, Charles, *Margaret Thatcher: The Authorised Biography, Volume One: Not For Turning* (Allen Lane, London, 2013)

——, *Margaret Thatcher: The Authorised Biography, Volume Two: Everything She Wants* (Allen Lane, London, 2015)

Moorhouse, Paul, *The Queen: Art & Image* (National Portrait Gallery, London, 2012)

Morrah, Dermot, *Princess Elizabeth* (Odhams, London, 1947)

——, *The Royal Family* (Odhams, London, 1950)

——, *To Be a King* (Hutchinson, London, 1968)

Morrow, Ann, *The Queen* (Granada Publishing, London, 1983)

Mortimer, Penelope, *Queen Elizabeth: A Life of the Queen Mother* (Viking, London, 1986)

Mosley, Charlotte, ed., *The Letters of Nancy Mitford* (Hodder & Stoughton, London, 1993)

——, *The Mitfords: Letters Between Six Sisters* (Fourth Estate, London, 2007)

Mountbatten, Pamela, *India Remembered* (Pavilion, London, 2007)

Nairn, Tom, *The Enchanted Glass: Britain and its Monarchy* (Radius, London, 1988)

Nicolson, Harold, *King George V: His Life & Reign* (Constable, London, 1952)

Nicolson, Nigel, *Long Life Memoirs* (Weidenfeld & Nicolson, London, 1997)

——, *The Queen & Us* (Weidenfeld & Nicolson, London, 2003)

——, *Harold Nicolson: Diaries and Letters, 1939–1945* (Collins, London, 1967)

——, *Vita & Harold: The Letters of Vita Sackville-West & Harold Nicolson 1910–62* (Phoenix, London, 1993)

——, *Harold Nicolson: The Later Years, 1945–1962* (Athenaeum, New York, 1968)

Owens, Susan, *Watercolours and Drawings from the Collection of Queen Elizabeth the Queen Mother* (Royal Collection Publications, London, 2005)

Parker, Eileen, *Step Aside for Royalty* (Bachman & Turner, Maidstone, 1982)

Parker, John, *Prince Philip: A Critical Biography* (Sidgwick & Jackson, London, 1990)

Paxman, Jeremy, *On Royalty* (Viking, London, 2006)

Payn, Graham, & Morley, Sheridan, eds., *The Noel Coward Diaries* (Macmillan, London, 1982)

Peacock, Lady, *TRH Prince Charles & Princess Anne* (Hutchinson, London, 1955)

Pearson, John, *The Ultimate Family: The Making of the House of Windsor* (Michael Joseph, London, 1986)

Pick, Michael, *Norman Hartnell: The Biography* (Zuleika, London, 2019)

Pimlott, Ben, *The Queen* (HarperCollins, London, 1996)

Pope-Hennessy, James, *Queen Mary* (George Allen & Unwin, London, 1959)

——, & Vickers, Hugo, ed., *The Quest for Queen Mary* (Zuleika, London, 2018)

Pottle, Mark, ed., *Daring to Hope: The Diaries and Letters of Violet Bonham Carter 1946–69* (Weidenfeld & Nicolson, London, 2000)

Powell, Anthony, *Journals 1982–86* (Heinemann, London, 1995)

Prochaska, Frank, *Royal Bounty: The Making of a Welfare Monarchy* (Yale University Press, New Haven & London, 1995)

Quennell, Peter, ed., *A Lonely Business: A Self-Portrait of James Pope-Hennessy* (Weidenfeld & Nicolson, London, 1981)

Reed, Freddie, *Freddie Reed's Royal Tours: 50 Years of Royal Photographs* (David & Charles, Newton Abbot, 1989)

Reynelle, Margaret, *The 1973 Royal Family Year Book* (Clipper Press, Farnham, 1973)

Rhodes James, Robert, ed., *Chips: The Diaries of Sir Henry Channon* (Weidenfeld & Nicolson, London, 1967)

Ring, Anne, *The Story of Princess Elizabeth Brought up to date and including some Stories of Princess Margaret* (John Murray, London, 1932)

Rhodes, Margaret, *The Final Curtsey* (Umbria Press/Berlinn, London, 2012)

Robinson, John Martin, *Royal Palaces: Windsor Castle* (Michael Joseph, London, 1996)

Roberts, Hugh, *The Queen's Diamonds* (Royal Collection Publications, London, 2012)

Rogers, Malcolm, *Elizabeth II: Portraits of Sixty Years* (National Portrait Gallery, London, 1986)

Roosevelt, Eleanor, *This I Remember* (Hutchinson, London, 1950)

Rose, Kenneth, *King George V* (Weidenfeld & Nicolson, London, 1983)

Salisbury, F. G. H., *George V and Edward VIII* (Daily Express Publications, London, 1936)

Sebba, Anne, *That Woman: The Life of Wallis Simpson Duchess of Windsor* (Weidenfeld & Nicolson, London, 2011)

Seward, Ingrid, *The Last Great Edwardian Lady* (Century, London, 1999)

——, *The Queen & Di* (HarperCollins, London, 2000)

——, *The Queen's Speech* (Simon & Schuster, London, 2016)

——, *My Husband & I* (Simon & Schuster, London, 2017)

——, *Prince Philip Revealed: A Man of His Century* (Simon & Schuster, London, 2020)

Shawcross, William, *Queen Elizabeth the Queen Mother: The Official Biography* (Macmillan, London, 2009)

——, *Queen and Country* (BBC Books, London, 2002)

Shawcross, William, ed., *Counting One's Blessings: The Selected Letters of Queen Elizabeth the Queen Mother* (Macmillan, London, 2012)

Sheridan, Lisa, *Our Princesses at Home* (John Murray, London, 1940)

——, *Our Princesses in 1942* (John Murray, London, 1942)

——, *From Cabbages to Kings* (Odhams, London, 1955)

——, *A Day with Prince Andrew* (Hodder & Stoughton, London, 1962)

Sitwell, Osbert, *Queen Mary and Others* (Michael Joseph, London, 1974)

Smith, Horace, *A Horseman Through Six Reigns* (Odhams, London, 1955)

Speaight, Richard N., *Memoirs of a Court Photographer* (Hurst & Blackett, London, 1926)

Strong, Roy, *Cecil Beaton: The Royal Portraits* (Thames & Hudson, London, 1988)

——, *Coronation* (HarperCollins, London, 2005)

——, *The Roy Strong Diaries, 1967–1987* (Weidenfeld & Nicolson, London, 1997)

——, *Scenes and Apparitions: The Roy Strong Diaries 1988–2003* (Weidenfeld & Nicolson, London, 2016)

Sykes, Eric, *If I Don't Write It, Nobody Else Will* (Harper Perennial, London, 2006)

Tennant, Emma, *The Autobiography of the Queen* (Arcadia, London, 2007)

——, *Waiting for Princess Margaret* (Quartet Books, London, 2009)

Thatcher, Margaret, *The Downing Street Years* (HarperCollins, London, 1993)

Thomson, Malcolm, et al, *The Life and Times of King George VI* (Odhams, London, 1952)

Thorpe, D. R., ed., *Who Loses Who Wins: The Journals of Kenneth Rose, Volume Two 1979–2014* (Weidenfeld & Nicolson, London, 2019)

Tomlinson, Richard, *Divine Right: The Inglorious Survival of British Royalty* (Little, Brown & Company, London, 1994)

Turner, Graham, *Elizabeth: The Woman and the Queen* (Macmillan, London, 2002)

Van der Kiste, John, *George V's Children* (Alan Sutton, Stroud, 1991)

Vickers, Hugo, intro., *The Unexpurgated Beaton: The Cecil Beaton Diaries as he wrote them* (Weidenfeld & Nicolson, London, 2002)

——, *Beaton in the Sixties: More Unexpurgated Diaries* (Weidenfeld & Nicolson, London, 2003)

Vickers, Hugo, *Alice, Princess Andrew of Greece* (Penguin, London, 2001)

——, *Elizabeth, the Queen Mother* (Hutchinson, London, 2005)

——, *The Crown: Truth & Fiction* (Zuleika, London, 2017)

——, *The Crown Dissected: Seasons 1, 2 and 3* (Zuleika, London, 2019)

Viney, Graham, *The Last Hurrah* (Robinson, London, 2018)

Warwick, Christopher, *Princess Margaret* (Weidenfeld & Nicolson, London, 1983)

——, *George and Marina: The Duke and Duchess of Kent* (Weidenfeld & Nicolson, London, 1988)

——, *Her Majesty* (Taschen, London, 2013)

Warwick, Christopher, ed., *Queen Mary's Photograph Albums* (Sidgwick & Jackson, London, 1989)

Wheeler Bennett, John, *King George VI: His Life & Reign* (Macmillan, London, 1958)

Whitelaw, William, *The Whitelaw Memoirs* (Aurum Press, London, 1989)

Williams, Kate, *Young Elizabeth: The Making of Our Queen* (Weidenfeld & Nicolson, London, 2013)

Williams, Marcia, *Inside Number 10* (Weidenfeld & Nicolson, London, 1972)

Wilson, A. N., *The Rise & Fall of the House of Windsor* (Sinclair Stevenson, London, 1993)

——, *The Queen* (Atlantic, London, 2016)

——, *Our Times: The Age of Elizabeth II* (Hutchinson, London, 2008)

Wilson, Mary, *New Poems* (Hutchinson, London, 1979)

Windsor, HRH The Duke of, *A King's Story* (Cassell & Company, London, 1951)

Winstone, Ruth, ed., *The Benn Diaries* (Hutchinson, London, 1995)

——, *Tony Benn: Free at Last! Diaries 1991–2001* (Hutchinson, London, 2002)

——, *Tony Benn: More Time for Politics, Diaries 2001–2007* (Hutchinson, London, 2007)

Ziegler, Philip, *Crown and People* (HarperCollins, London, 1978)

——, *Mountbatten: The Official Biography* (William Collins, London, 1985)

——, *King Edward VIII: The Official Biography* (Fontana, London, 1990)

——, *Wilson: The Authorised Life* (Weidenfeld & Nicolson, London, 1993)

——, *Between the Wars* (Quercus, London, 2017)

PICTURE CREDITS

Every effort has been made to trace copyright holders and gain permission to reproduce images. We apologize if there are any errors or omissions and would be happy to make any amendments in future editions.

Section 1: p. 1 The Life Picture Collection / Getty Images; Popperfoto / Getty Images; Photograph by Marcus Adams / The Royal Collection, Camera Press London; p. 2 Sueddeutsche Zeitung Photo / Alamy Stock Photo; Getty Images; p. 3 Magite Historic / Alamy Stock Photo; PA Images / Alamy Stock Photo; p. 4 PA / TopFoto; Hulton Archive / Getty Images; Hulton Archive / Getty Images; p. 5 Photograph by Marcus Adams / Camera Press London; p. 6 © Cecil Beaton / Victoria and Albert Museum, London; Granger, NYC / TopFoto; Popperfoto / Getty Images; p. 7 Topical Press Agency / Getty Images; Popperfoto / Getty Images; p. 8 ANL / Shutterstock; PA Images / Alamy Stock Photo.

Section 2: p. 1 Hulton Archive / Getty Images; © Cecil Beaton / Victoria and Albert Museum, London; p. 2 Annigoni Portrait / Camera Press London; p. 3 Hulton Archive / Getty Images; TopFoto; p. 4 Mirrorpix / Getty Images; PA Images / Alamy Stock Photo; p. 5 PA Images / Alamy Stock Photo; Wikimedia Commons; p. 6 © Estate of Kenneth Hughes / National Portrait Gallery, London; on loan from American Friends of the National Portrait Gallery Foundation, Inc.; Gift of Mr Ford Hill; p. 7 PA Images / Alamy Stock Photo; Ray Bellisario / Popperfoto / Getty Images; p. 8 Popperfoto / Getty Images; Lynn Pelham / The Life Picture Collection / Getty Images.

Section 3: p. 1 Hulton Archive / Getty Images; Lichfield Archive / Getty Images; p. 2 Anwar Hussein / Getty Images; Lichfield Archive / Getty Images; p. 3 Tim Graham / Getty Images; Trinity Mirror / Mirrorpix / Alamy Stock Photo; p. 4 Serge Lemoine / Getty Images; Mirrorpix / Getty Images; p. 5 © Norman Parkinson Archive / Iconic Images; Tim Graham / Getty Images; p. 6 Tim Graham / Getty Images; PA Photos / TopFoto; p. 7 Hulton Archive / Getty Images; Dan Kitwood / Getty Images; p. 8 Tim Graham / Getty Images; Kensington Palace / Getty Images.

INDEX

INDEX